SHARON WELCHER
62-27 108TH STREET
FOREST HILLS, NEW YORK 11375
Phone / Fax: (718) 271-7466/(877) 600-7466 (Toll Free)

September 2007

To the Assistant Principal and All Physics and Chemistry Teachers:

Also by Sharon H. Welcher: High Marks: Regents Chemistry Made Easy, The Physical Setting, helps students pass the Chemistry Regents and get high marks

High Marks: Regents Physics Made Easy, The Physical Setting, by **Sharon H. Welcher,** helps students pass the Physics Regents and get high marks. Your school can have an increased percentage of students passing this important exam.

Why Should You Buy This Book?

1. High Marks: Regents Physics Made Easy, The Physical Setting contains **all the topics you need to know** for the **New York State Physics Regents** –The Physical Setting.

2. This **book** is in **clearer and easier language** than other books, teaching the student how to solve Regents-type problems.

3. This book **teaches** the **student** how to look at a problem, **figure out** what **equation** to use, and then **use** a **step by step approach** to **solve** the **problem**. This step by step approach in solving problems is used throughout the book, making it possible for students to answer more questions correctly on the Physics Regents.

4. **Hundreds of Regents-type questions** with **worked out solutions enable** the **students to do** the **homework questions.** There are over 700 Regents-type homework questions, including multiple choice and free response. The book contains the last five Regents exams, including June 2007.

5. The **Reference Tables** are included in the book; these tables are needed to answer Regents questions. Each chapter of the **book explains which tables to use** for that chapter and **how to use them**. For emphasis, the name of the **table** is on the side of those pages on which it is taught. The **Reference Table Section**, with explanations, at the end of the book, **lists** the **pages** on which it was originally **learned**, so that students can review it.

6. **Bold** words emphasize important points.

As you can see, *High Marks: Regents Physics Made Easy* can easily help **your** school achieve a higher percentage of students passing and earning excellent marks on the Physics Regents.

Sincerely,

Sharon Welcher

Sharon Welcher
***Adjunct Instructor**, Chemistry and Physics, CUNY*
***Chairperson**, Machon Academy High School*

Schools may purchase **High Marks: Regents Physics Made Easy, Physical Setting** at a reduced price of **$8.45** per copy (plus $0.30 postage and handling), a savings of more than four dollars below the retail price. An answer key is available for students at the teacher's request. To order, please contact Sharon Welcher directly at: **(877) 600-7466** or **(718) 271-7466**. Purchase orders should be sent or faxed to the address above or e-mailed to chemistry@highmarksinschool.com.

High Marks:
REGENTS PHYSICS MADE EASY
The Physical Setting

SHARON WELCHER

ADJUNCT INSTRUCTOR
Chemistry and Physics
City University of New York

CHAIRPERSON
Machon Academy High School

Teacher of High School Chemistry,
Physics, Biology,
Earth Science,
REGENTS REVIEW COURSES

See our Website:
http://www.HighMarksinSchool.com

High Marks Made Easy
Forest Hills, NY   *(877) 600-7466*

DEDICATION

*I dedicate this book to
my father, Rav Jacob Joseph Mazo, ז"ל,
my mother, Claire Mazo,
my husband, Dr. Marvin Welcher,
and my children*

ISBN:0-9714662-1-1

First Printing: High Marks Made Easy, February 2006
Second Printing: High Marks Made Easy, September 2006
Third Printing: High Marks Made Easy, August, 2007.
10 9 8 7 6 5 4 3 2 1

All sales through
(718) 271-7466 / (877) 600-7466

INTRODUCTION

WHY IS THIS BOOK SO GOOD AND SO NECESSARY?

1 This book follows the **New York State Physical Setting: Physics Core Curriculum** and covers all the topics on the New York State Physics Regents.

2 This book is in **simple, clear, easy language**, explaining step by step how to solve physics problems. Physics is a very difficult subject, and **this book makes Physics easier.**

3 If you **don't understand** a topic in physics, **read** the same topic in this **book**, and it will **help** you **understand** it. This book is your **private tutor.**

4 All questions are **Regents** and **Regents-type questions** to give you practice for the examination. Included in the book are **constructed response questions**, a type of question that is in the revised Physics Regents.

5 This book **emphasizes** how to use the **Reference Tables**. Questions on the **Regents** will **involve** these **tables**. These are very **easy points** to get and require little studying. Each chapter of the book explains, in simple, clear language, **which tables** to use for that chapter and **how to use them.** For emphasis, the **name** of the **Table** is indicated on the **side** of the **pages** where it is taught.

In addition, all the Reference Tables are put together in the **Reference Table section** at the end of the book, with a short **description** under each **Reference Table**. If you need more explanation of how to use a specific Table, go back to the original page in the book where it was taught.

6 At the beginning of the Exam section is a detailed description of the Physics Regents and **test-taking strategies** to get higher marks.

7 The exam section contains **June** and **January Regents**.

8 If you don't understand a physics term, go to the Glossary, which has definitions in simple, easy language.

9 At the end of the book is an **index**, which makes it easier for you to find what you are looking for.

10 **Answer keys** to homework questions and Regents are available to the **students** at the **teacher's request.**

With this clear and simple book, Physics is made **EASY**, and you can get **High Marks** on the **Physics Regents** and all Physics exams.

Good Luck!

FOREWORD

This is the first edition of **High Marks: Regents Physics Made Easy**. This book is based on the New York State Physical Setting: Physics core curriculum. Teachers should consult the State Education website, www.NYSED.gov, for updates.

My students are the ones who gave me the idea to write a book. They realized that my review sheets were in simple, clear, easy language, while the other books were difficult for many of them to understand.

I wrote High Marks: Regents Chemistry Made Easy, which was very successful. Over 100,000 books were sold. Numerous chairmen, teachers, parents, and students informed me that the book High Marks: Regents Chemistry Made Easy was a tremendous help and benefit to the students. **People** called and thanked me for writing the book and **asked** if there were **other books** in other subjects, such as **physics**, biology, and math.

Because physics is such a difficult subject, I decided to take on the challenge and write a physics review book to help students get high marks on the Regents, other state exams, tests, and quizzes. I have taken all my strategies of teaching over the years and incorporated them into books to help all students, and not only my own.

ACKNOWLEDGEMENTS

I thank my brilliant father, Rav Jacob Joseph Mazo, ז״צל, for teaching me how to be an excellent teacher and how to help students get high marks on exams. I thank my dear mother, Claire Mazo, for encouraging me to write a book. I also thank my thoughtful husband, Dr. Marvin Welcher, for typing the book and helping to proofread the book, and my children for being considerate and good.

I express my gratitude to S. Malkah Cohen for a professional job in typesetting three books, some typing and some electricity graphics. S. Malkah Cohen helped to bring this book to publication. I thank Devorah Moskowitz for an excellent job on the computer graphics in this physics book.

I thank my students for giving me the idea to write a book. They knew my book would be in simple, clear, easy language and would help students get high marks on the Regents and exams.

Sharon Welcher

TABLE OF CONTENTS

Chapter 4: Waves

Chapter 5: Modern Physics

ABOUT THE AUTHOR:
SHARON WELCHER

Sharon Welcher is an adjunct instructor of **chemistry** and **physics** at **City University of New York**, Science **Chairperson** of Machon Academy High School, and a proven **master teacher**, teaching **chemistry, physics, biology** and **earth science** in both **public** and **private** high schools in New York City.

Sharon Welcher wrote High Marks: Regents Chemistry Made Easy, which was very successful. Over 100,000 books were sold. Numerous chairmen, teachers, parents, and students informed her that the book **High Marks: Regents Chemistry Made Easy** was a tremendous help and benefit to the students.

Almost all her students **pass** the **Regents** every year, because she explains the subjects in a simple, clear, **easy to understand** manner and **concentrates** on what the New York State **Regents emphasizes**. Her ability to focus on what is important for the Regents and make it easy to understand has helped innumerable students get **excellent marks** on the **Regents** and exams.

Because physics is such a difficult subject, Sharon Welcher decided to take on the challenge and write a physics review book to help students get high marks on the Regents, other state exams, tests, and quizzes. She took all her strategies of teaching over the years and incorporated them into books to help all students, and not only her own.

CHAPTER 1: MECHANICS

Section *1*:

Mechanics is the study of the motion (movement) of an object or objects.

Kinematics is the branch of mechanics dealing with **motion** (movement) of an object or objects, without discussing force and mass.

Most of the equations used in this chapter are found on Reference Table: Mechanics on pages reference tables 22-23.

SPEED

Speed– how fast it is moving. Example: a car travels at 30 meters per second (m/s).

$$\text{Speed} = \frac{distance}{time} \quad \text{Example: Speed} = \frac{30m}{s}$$

Speed is the rate at which distance is covered, distance divided by time (distance covered per unit of time).

1. Instantaneous speed:
A bus travels at 30 meters per second (m/s), then stops to pick up passengers at 0 meters per second, and then rides in heavy traffic at 10 meters per second. The instantaneous speed is the speed at that instant or that second:

The instantaneous speed at the beginning is 30 meters per second.

The instantaneous speed when the bus picked up passengers is 0 meters per second.

The instantaneous speed in heavy traffic is 10 meters per second.

2. Average speed:

$$\text{Average speed or average velocity} = \frac{total\ distance}{(total)\ time\ or\ time\ interval}$$

$$\bar{v} = \frac{d}{t}$$

(Note: Velocity means speed and direction, which you will learn more about on the next page.)

Example: A car rode 120 meters in 3 seconds. What is the average speed?
Use the equation:

$$\bar{v} = \frac{d}{t}$$

Substitute in the equation above 120 m for d (distance). **Substitute 3 seconds** for t (time).

$$\bar{v} = \frac{120 \ meters}{3 \ seconds} = 40 \ m/s \quad \text{Average speed } (\bar{v}) = 40 \ m/s$$

VELOCITY

40 m/s is speed.
40 m/s south is **velocity**.
Velocity is **speed** (example 40 m/s) **and direction** (south).

You learned speed is **how fast** it moves.
Velocity is **how fast** it moves **and** in what **direction**.

Speed is a **scalar** quantity because it only has magnitude (a number: example: 40 m/s).
Velocity is a **vector** quantity because it has **both magnitude** (a number: example: 40 m/s) and **direction** (example: south)
40 m/s south is a vector quantity because it has both magnitude (a number) and direction.

1. **Constant velocity** means **both constant speed** (speed does not change) **AND constant direction** (which means it moves in a straight line–direction does not change, and it does not curve).

   Example: A car travels at a constant velocity of 40 meters/second north. The speed is always 40 meters per second and it always goes in a straight line to the north.

2. **Changing velocity**: The velocity is changing which means either:
   a. The speed is changing and direction is constant.
   or   b. The speed is constant and the direction is changing.
   or   c. The speed and direction both change.

3. **Average velocity** $(\bar{v})$:

   a. You learned, to find average speed or average velocity, use the equation

---

$$\bar{v} = \frac{d}{t}$$

$$\frac{\text{average velocity}}{\text{or average speed}} = \frac{(total) \ distance}{(total) \ time}$$

Look at the equation given below, or on Reference Table: Mechanics on pages Reference Tables 22-23 . Use equations given on the reference table to help you solve problems. (The box on the side of the page shows that the equation is given on Reference Table: Mechanics.)

$$\bar{v} = \frac{d}{t}$$

d = displacement/distance

t = time interval

$\bar{v}$ = average velocity/average speed

    b. Another way to find the average velocity: add the initial velocity (the starting velocity v_i) and the final velocity (the velocity at the end v_f) and divide them by 2. The equation is:

$$\bar{v} = \frac{v_i + v_f}{2}.$$

Average velocity = $\dfrac{initial \ velocity \ + \ final \ velocity}{2}$

Memorize the equation; it is not given on the reference table.

Question: A car begins to ride at 20 m/s north and finishes at 30 m/s north. What is the average velocity?

Solution: Write down what is given and what you need to find. Given: Beginning velocity (initial velocity)(v_i) = 20 m/s north. Velocity at the end, final velocity (v_f) = 30 m/s north.

Find: Average velocity $\bar{v}$.

Use the equation:

$$\bar{v} = \frac{v_i + v_f}{2}$$

Then substitute for v_i (initial velocity) 20 m/s north and **substitute for** v_f (final velocity) 30 m/s north.

$$\bar{v} = \frac{20 \ m/s \ north \ + \ 30 \ m/s \ north}{2} = 25 \text{ m/s north}$$

Question: A car having an initial speed of 16 meters per second is uniformly brought to rest in 4.0 seconds. How far does the car travel during this 4.0 second interval?

(1) 32 meters   (2) 82 meters   (3) 96 meters   (4) 4.0 meters

Solution: Write down what is given and what you need to find.
Given: initial speed = 16 meters per second (m/s)
        final speed = brought to rest (which means final speed is zero)
        time = 4 seconds
Find: How far does the car travel during this 4.0 second interval. How far means find distance (d).
Since speed (v) and time (t) are given, and the question asks you to find how far, which means distance (d), *look for an equation* below or on Reference Table: Mechanics, on pages reference tables 22-23, that has v (speed), t (time), and d (distance).
Use the equation

$$\bar{v} = \frac{d}{t}$$

d = displacement/distance

t = time interval

$\bar{v}$ = average velocity/average speed

$\bar{v}$ is **average speed** or average velocity. The line over the v means average.

In the question, you were given initial speed (16 m/s) and final speed (at rest, which means 0 m/s) but not average speed ($\bar{v}$) . In this

equation $\bar{v} = \frac{d}{t}$, you don't know both $\bar{v}$ (average speed) and d

(distance), (two unknowns); therefore, *first find $\bar{v}$* and then substitute

$\bar{v}$ in the equation $\bar{v} = \frac{d}{t}$ to find d (distance).

First find $\bar{v}$ (average speed). *Use the equation* $\bar{v} = \dfrac{v_i + v_f}{2}$ *to find* $\bar{v}$.

Memorize this equation; it is not given on the reference table.
Substitute 16 m/s (meters per second) given *for v_i* (initial or starting speed). **Substitute 0 m/s for v_f** (final speed or speed at the end). An object at rest or brought to rest (example: car brought to rest) has zero speed or zero velocity (object is not moving). **Substitute 4.0 s (seconds) for t** (time).

$$\bar{v} = \frac{v_i + v_f}{2}$$

$$\bar{v} = \frac{16 \ m/s \ + \ 0 \ m/s}{2} = 8 \ m/s$$

In the equation $\bar{v} = \frac{d}{t}$, *then substitute for* $\bar{v}$ 8 m/s (from above).

Substitute for t 4.0 s

$8 \ m/s = \dfrac{d}{4.0 \ s}$	Or, rearrange the equation
Cross multiply	$d = \bar{v} \ t$
8 m/s x 4.0 s = d	d = 8 m/s x 4.0 s
d = 32 m	d = 32 m
d (distance, how far) = 32 m	d (distance, how far) = 32 m
Answer *1*	Answer *1*

Note: You will learn later that you can also use the equation $d = v_i t + 1/2at^2$ to find distance.

$\bar{v} = \frac{d}{t}$ **CAN ALSO BE USED TO FIND DISTANCE AND TIME.**

You can find time (t) if velocity/speed (v) and distance (d) are given.
You can find distance (d) if velocity/speed (v) and time (t) are given.

Question: A baseball pitcher throws a fastball at 42 meters per second. If the batter is 18 meters from the pitcher, approximately how much time does it take for the ball to reach the batter?
Show all work, including the equation and substitution with units.

Solution: Write down what is given and what you need to find.

Given: pitcher throws a fastball 42 meters per second (it means v (speed) = 42 m/s (meters per second)).

batter is 18 meters from pitcher (it means distance (d) is 18 m (meters))

Find: time (t)

Since speed (v) and distance (d) are given, and the question asks you to find time (t), *look for an equation* below or on Reference Table: Mechanics, on pages reference tables 22-23, that has v (speed), t (time), and d (distance).

Use the equation

$$\bar{v} = \frac{d}{t}$$

d = displacement/distance

t = time interval

$\bar{v}$ = average velocity/average speed

In the equation $\bar{v} = \frac{d}{t}$, *then substitute for* $\bar{v}$ 42 m/s (given).

Substitute for d 18 m (meters) (given).

$$42\ m/s = \frac{18\ m}{t}$$

Cross multiply
42 m/s t = 18 m
t = 0.43 s

Or, rearrange the equation

$$t = \frac{d}{v}$$

$$t = \frac{18\ m}{42\ m/s}$$

t = 0.43 s

Rule: When a question asks for substitution with units, include units when substituting in the equation and also in the final answer (see question above). Example: $t = \frac{d}{v}$, $t = \frac{18\ m}{42\ m/s}$, t = 0.43 s

Now do Homework Questions #1-7, page 135
(Look for page Chap. 1:135, meaning Chapter 1, page 135)

ACCELERATION

Acceleration (a) is how fast the velocity is changing or rate at which velocity is changing. Acceleration is a vector quantity.
Look at Reference Table: Mechanics below or on pages reference tables 22-23.

Table: Mechanics

$$a = \frac{\Delta v}{t}$$

a = acceleration

t = time interval
v= velocity/speed
Δ = change

$$\text{Acceleration} = \frac{\textit{change of velocity}}{\textit{time}}$$

which means $\frac{\textit{change of speed or direction or both}}{\textit{time}}$

Acceleration can be a change in speed–increase in speed or a decrease in speed (brakes of a car decrease the speed). Decrease in speed is deceleration (negative acceleration).
Acceleration can also be a change in direction-a car going around a curve in the road.
Acceleration is a vector quantity.

Question: A car had a velocity of 25 meters per second (m/s) and then increased its velocity to 35 m/s in 5 seconds. What is the acceleration?
Solution: Write down what is given and what you need to find.
Given: Initial velocity or starting velocity (v_i) = 25 meters per second (m/s). Final velocity (v_f) = 35 m/s. Time (t) = 5 seconds (s)
Find: Acceleration (a)

You know initial velocity (v_i), final velocity (v_f), and time (t). There is one unknown, acceleration (a). *Look for an equation* on reference table mechanics below or on pages reference tables 22-23 that has v (velocity), t (time) and a (acceleration).
Use the equation

$$a = \frac{\Delta v}{t}$$

a = acceleration

t = time interval
v = velocity/speed
Δ = change

Δv (change in velocity) means final velocity (v_f) −initial or starting velocity (v_i).
Substitute for Δv (change in velocity) 35 m/s (final velocity) - 25 m/s (starting velocity or initial velocity) = 10 m/s.
Substitute for t 5 s (seconds).

$$a = \frac{10 \ m/s}{5 \ s} = \frac{2 \ m}{s^2}$$

Realize, you knew in this question to use the equation $a = \frac{\Delta v}{t}$ because

t and v_f and v_i were **given. You know** Δv (change in velocity) because v_f (final velocity) and v_i (initial velocity) were given; $\Delta v = v_f - v_i$. You have only one unknown, acceleration (a).
You will learn later that you can also use the equation $v_f = v_i + at$ to find acceleration (a), because you know v_f, v_i, and t and you have only one unknown, a (acceleration). (This is another form of

$a = \frac{\Delta v}{t}$).

Question: During a 5.0 second interval, an object's velocity changes from 25 meters per second east to 15 meters per second east. Determine the magnitude and direction of the object's acceleration.
Solution: Write down what is given and what you need to find.
Given: 5.0 second interval
Initial velocity or starting velocity (v_i) = 25 meters per second east. Final velocity (v_f) = 15 meters per second east. Time (t) = 5.0 seconds.
Find: magnitude (number) and direction of the object's acceleration (a).
You know initial velocity (v_i), final velocity (v_f), and time (t). There is one unknown, acceleration (a). *Look for an equation* on Reference Table: Mechanics below or on pages reference tables 22-23 that has v (velocity), t (time) and a (acceleration).
Use the equation $a = \frac{\Delta v}{t}$
Substitute for Δv (change in velocity) 15 m/s east (final velocity) - 25 m/s east (starting velocity or initial velocity) = −10. m/s.

Substitute for *t* 5.0 seconds.

$$a = \frac{-10.\ m/s}{5.0\ s}\ east$$

$$a = \frac{-2.0\ m}{s^2}\ east \qquad \text{Answer } a = -2.0\ m/s^2\ east$$

Realize, you knew in this question to use the equation $a = \dfrac{\Delta v}{t}$ because

t and v_f and v_i were **given. You know** Δv (change in velocity) because v_f (final velocity) and v_i (initial velocity) were given; $\Delta v = v_f - v_i$. You have only one unknown, acceleration (a).

You will learn later that you can also use the equation $v_f = v_i + at$ to find acceleration (a), because you know v_f, v_i, and t and you have only one unknown, a (acceleration). (This is another form of

$a = \dfrac{\Delta v}{t}$). Note: The answer to the question is a $= -2.0\ m/s^2$ east, or

the answer can also be written as a $= +2.0\ m/s^2$ west. When velocity decreases, (object slows down from 25 m/s east to 15 m/s east), acceleration can also be written (with the opposite sign) in the opposite direction (example: acceleration equals $-2.0\ m/s^2$ east or $+2.0\ m/s^2$ west).

Now Do Homework Questions #8-13, pages 135-136,
(Look for page Chap. 1:135, meaning Chapter 1, page 135)

DISTANCE AND DISPLACEMENT

Distance: Distance is **how far** you or an object (example: car) travels, the total path the person or object moves on, the number of meters that is traveled or the total length of the path.
Examples: A car travels 100 meters. The distance is **100 meters**.
   A ball falls 100 meters from the top of a cliff. The distance = 100 meters.
The meter is the metric unit of length. Distance is usually measured in meters, cm, or km.
Distance is **scalar** because it has only magnitude (a **number** such as 100 meters) and **no direction** (north, south, east or west).

Displacement: Displacement is both **distance** (example: 100 meters) and **direction** (north, south, etc.). Examples of displacement are **100 meters north,** 70 meters south.
Displacement is a **vector quantity** because it has both magnitude (a number such as 100 meters) and direction (north, southeast, etc.).
As you learned, examples of displacement are 100 meters north or 70 meters southeast, or 15 meters (distance) at 34° north of east (direction).

Example: Look at the figure. A girl walks 30 meters (m) north to school; displacement is 30 meters (m) north. Then the girl walks 40 meters (m) east to the library; displacement is 40 meters (m) east.

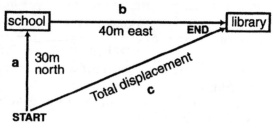

Total displacement (also called resultant displacement) is **from start to end** (see figure above).

Use the Pythagorean Theorem for right triangles to find the total displacement (which is from start to end).

$c^2 = a^2 + b^2$ given on Reference Table: Geometry and Trigonometry.

Substitute 30 m for a and 40 m for b.

$c^2 = (30 \text{ m})^2 + (40 \text{ m})^2$

$c^2 = 900 \text{ m}^2 + 1600 \text{ m}^2 = 2500 \text{ m}^2$

$c = 50 \text{ m}$

Total displacement (resultant displacement) is **50 meters northeast**.

Distance: The distance the girl actually walks is different from the total (resultant) displacement. The distance she walks is 30 meters to school and 40 meters to the library = 70 meters.

Distance = 70 meters

Question: What is the total displacement of a student who walks 3 blocks east, 2 blocks north, 1 block west, and then 2 blocks south?

  (1) 0   (2) 2 blocks east

  (3) 2 blocks wes   (4) 8 blocks

Solution: Look at the figure. A student walks 3 blocks east, 2 blocks north, 1 block west, and then 2 blocks south. Total **displacement** is from **start to end** (finish), therefore 2 blocks east.

Answer 2

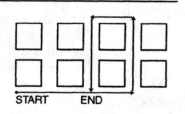

GRAPHS OF DISTANCE VS. TIME

On a distance or displacement vs. time graph, time is on the x-axis and distance or displacement is on the y-axis. The line on a

distance vs. time graph shows speed; $\dfrac{distance}{time}$ = speed. The line

on a displacement (distance and direction) vs. time graph shows velocity (speed and direction).

On a distance vs. time graph,

$$\text{slope of the line} = \frac{\text{change in } y \ (\text{change in distance})}{\text{change in } x \ (\text{change in time})} = \text{speed.}$$

A straight line shows constant speed; a curved line shows that speed is changing.

Note: On a displacement vs. time graph, the slope equals velocity (speed and direction).

DISTANCE VS. TIME GRAPHS

A **straight line** shows **constant speed.** When time increases, distance increases.	A **straight line** shows **constant speed.** When time increases, distance decreases.
As time increases, distance stays the same. The object is **at rest** (standing still/not moving).	**First part:** **constant speed.** **Second part**: the object is at rest (standing still/not moving).
(Beginning of the graph is when time is zero or close to zero.) When the **line at the end** of the distance/time graph becomes **steeper,** it shows there is a bigger change in distance/time (bigger slope, **more distance/time**) than in the beginning of the graph, therefore **speed increases. End** of **graph steeper, shows speed increases.** A curved line shows a change in speed.	When the **line at the end** of the distance/time graph becomes **less steep (flatter)**, it shows there is less change in distance/time (smaller slope, **less distance/time**) than in the beginning of the graph, therefore **speed decreases. End** of **graph less steep (flatter), speed decreases.** A curved line shows a change in speed.

Study the graphs.

Question: Which graph best represents the motion of a block accelerating uniformly down an inclined plane?

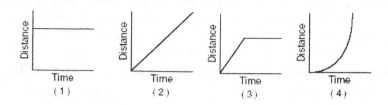

(1)   (2)   (3)   (4)

Solution: Answer *4* The block is **accelerating** down an inclined plane, which means the block is increasing in speed. When you look at the curved line graph, more distance is covered in the same time than at constant speed (a straight line graph). Wrong choices: (1) at rest   (2) constant speed   (3) constant speed, then at rest.

Question: What is the physical significance of the slope of this graph?

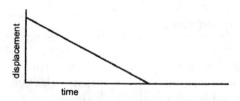

Solution: Slope means the change in y (Δy) over the change in x (Δx). In this graph, slope is the change in y (displacement) over the change in x (time). $\dfrac{displacement}{time}$ = **velocity.** Slope of the graph is
velocity.

GRAPHS OF SPEED VS TIME

On a speed/velocity vs. time graph, time is on the x-axis and speed/velocity is on the y-axis. The line on a speed/velocity vs. time graph shows acceleration; $\dfrac{change\ in\ speed/velocity}{time}$ = acceleration.

On a speed vs. time graph,

$$\text{slope of the line} = \frac{\textit{change in y (change in speed)}}{\textit{change in x (change in time)}} = \text{acceleration.}$$

When the slope equals a positive number, it is positive acceleration; when the slope equals a negative number, it is negative acceleration. When the slope is a small number, it is a small acceleration. When the slope is a large number, it is a large acceleration.

A straight line shows constant acceleration; a curved line shows that acceleration is changing.

SPEED VS. TIME GRAPHS

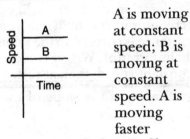

A is moving at constant speed; B is moving at constant speed. A is moving faster (higher speed) than B. Slope

$$\left(\frac{\textit{change in speed/velocity}}{\textit{time}}\right) \text{ of}$$

lines A and B is zero (lines are horizontal), which means change of speed is zero and therefore acceleration

$$\left(\frac{\textit{change in speed}}{\textit{time}}\right) \text{ is zero.}$$

A is moving at constant speed; B is moving at constant speed. You can see A and B are moving in opposite directions because A has positive speed (above the x axis) and B has negative speed (below the x axis). B is moving faster (larger speed) than A. Slope

$$\left(\frac{\textit{change in speed/velocity}}{\textit{time}}\right)$$

of lines A and B is zero (lines are horizontal), which means change of speed is zero and therefore acceleration is zero (see equation above).

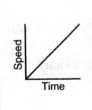

A **straight line** shows **constant acceleration.** When time increases, speed increases.

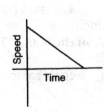

A **straight line** shows **constant acceleration.** When time increases, speed decreases.

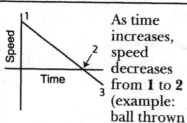

As time increases, speed decreases from **1** to **2** (example: ball thrown up in the air slows down and reaches its highest point at **2**). At **2**, the object has zero speed. From **2** to **3**, as time increases, speed increases (example: from 10 m/s to 20 m/s to 30 m/s, but we write −10 to −20 to −30 to show the ball is going in the opposite direction (downward)).

$$\text{Slope} = \frac{change\ in\ speed}{change\ in\ time} = $$ acceleration.

$$\text{Slope} \left(\frac{change\ in\ speed}{change\ in\ time}\right) \text{ of}$$ this graph is a negative number, which means negative acceleration.

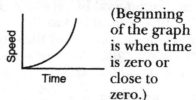

(Beginning of the graph is when time is zero or close to zero.)

When the **line at the end** of the speed/time graph becomes **steeper,** it shows there is a bigger change in speed/time (bigger slope, **more speed/time**) than in the beginning of the graph, therefore acceleration **increases. End of graph steeper, shows acceleration increases.**

A curved line shows a change in acceleration.

Study these graphs.

Question: Base your answer on the speed-time graph below, which represents the linear motion of a cart. Calculate the distance traveled by the cart during interval BC. [Show all calculations, including the equation and substitution with units.]

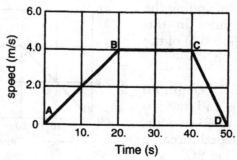

Solution:
Method 1:
Given: For interval BC, speed = 4.0 m/s
time is from 20 s to 40 s
Find: Distance traveled by the cart during interval BC.
Look for an equation on Reference Table: Mechanics that has distance (d), time (t), and speed (v).

Use the equation $\bar{v} = \dfrac{d}{t}$.

Look at the graph in the question. In the interval BC, the cart traveled at a speed (v) of 4.0 m/s for a time (t) of 20 s (interval BC is from 20 seconds to 40 seconds).

In the equation $\bar{v} = \dfrac{d}{t}$, *then substitute for $\bar{v}$* 4.0 m/s. *Substitute for t* 20 s.

$\bar{v} = \dfrac{d}{t}$.	Or, rearrange the equation:
$4.0 \text{ m/s} = \dfrac{d}{20 \ s}$	$d = \bar{v}t$
$(4.0 \text{ m/s})(20 \text{ s}) = d$	$d = (4.0 \text{ m/s})(20 \text{ s})$
$d = 80.0 \text{ m}$	$d = 80.0 \text{ m}$

Note: If the question asked the distance traveled from A to B, similarly, you would use the equation $\bar{v} = \dfrac{d}{t}$ or rearranged equation $d = \bar{v}t$.

You learned $\bar{v} = \dfrac{v_i + v_f}{2}$. From the graph, $v_1 = 0$ m/s and $v_2 = 4.0$ m/s.

$\bar{v} = \dfrac{0 \ m/s + 4.0 \ m/s}{2} = 2.0$ m/s. In the equation $d = \bar{v}t$, substitute for $\bar{v}$ 2.0 m/s. Substitute for t 20 s (seconds). $d = \bar{v}t = (2.0 \text{ m/s})(20$ s$) = 40$ m.

Method 2: The question asks to find the distance during interval BC (see graph). You can find distance traveled by finding the area under the line (in this example, under line BC) of the speed vs. time graph.

During interval BC (see graph) speed = 4.0 m/s and time is from 20 seconds to 40 seconds, which is the shaded area, a rectangle, under line BC.

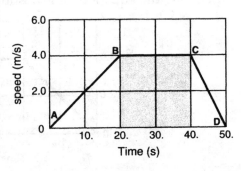

time is from 20 seconds to 40 seconds, which is the shaded area, a rectangle, under line BC.

Look at Reference Table: Geometry and Trigonometry on page reference tables 21 for an equation for the area of a rectangle. A =bh (area = base x height). Substitute for b 20 s (the time from 20 s to 40 s).Substitute for h 4.0 m/s. A = bh = 20 s x 4.0 m/s=80m. Area of rectangle under line BC = 80 m.

Note: If the question asked the distance traveled from A to B, the area under line AB is a triangle, and you would look at Reference Table: Geometry and Trigonometry for the area of a triangle:

$A = \dfrac{1}{2} bh$ (area $= \dfrac{1}{2}$ base x height). Substitute for b 20 s. Substitute for h 4.0 m/s. Area of triangle under line $AB = \dfrac{1}{2} bh = \dfrac{1}{2}$ x 20 s x 4.0 m/s $= 40$ m.

Now Do Homework Questions #14-30, pages 136-137.

GRAPHING EXPERIMENTAL DATA

Let's see how we can draw graphs based on experimental data.

Problem:

A car is traveling due north at 24.0 meters per second (m/s) when the driver sees an obstruction on the highway. The data table below shows the velocity of the car at 1.0-second intervals as it is brought to rest on the straight, level highway.

Time (s)	Velocity (m/s)
0.0	24.0
1.0	19.0
2.0	14.0
3.0	10.0
4.0	4.0

How to draw the graph:

1. On the x axis, put "Time, (s)". The **thing you change** (in this case time) is always put on the **x axis**. What you change is called the independent variable. Space the lines along the axis equally; there must be an equal number of seconds between each two lines.

2. On the y axis, put "Velocity, m/s". The **result** you get (velocity) because you changed the time is always put on the **y axis**. It is called the dependent variable. Space the lines

along the axis equally; there must be an equal number of m/s between each two lines.

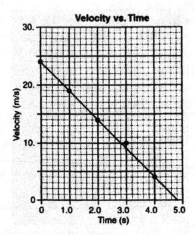

3.   Plot the data points for velocity vs. time on the graph. You can draw a circle around each point. Connect the points with the best fit line. (A best fit line is a straight line or curve that is closest to all the points.) Do not continue the line past the last point.

4.   Put a title on the graph which shows what the graph is about. Example: "Velocity vs. Time".

Question: Which graph best illustrates the motion of an object that is *not* in equilibrium as it travels along a straight line?

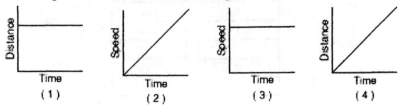

Solution: Answer 2. An object is in equilibrium when the object is at rest or moving with a constant velocity. The question asks for an object **not** in equilibrium. In choice 2, as time increases, speed also increases; speed is not constant, therefore it is not in equilibrium. Wrong choices:
Choice *1*: The graph shows, as time increases, distance is constant. The object is not moving; the object is at rest. It is in equilibrium.
Choice *3*: As time increases, speed is constant. The object is in equilibrium.

SI UNITS OF MEASUREMENT

Scientists use the **SI** (Systeme International) **units of measurement**, which are used all over the world. **Remember,** in **solving problems**, **use SI units** listed below, **meters (m)** for length, **kilograms (kg)** for mass, **seconds (s)** for time, **Newtons (N)** for force, **watts (W)** for power, etc.

Look at Reference Table: Prefixes for Powers of Ten with explanations on page reference tables 4. It explains how to convert centimeters (cm) to meters (m) or grams to kilograms, etc. Study and know how to use this table.

Table: Prefixes-Powers of Ten

Question: Find the length of a dollar bill in meters.

Solution: Measure a dollar bill with a centimeter ruler; the dollar bill is 15 cm long. 1 cm = 10^{-2} m, given on **Reference Table: Prefixes for Powers of Ten.** Therefore, a dollar bill of 15 cm = 15×10^{-2} m or 1.5×10^{-1} m.

You know 1 meter (m) = 39.37 inches.
You know 1 kilogram (kg) = 2.2 pounds. A man has a mass of 70 kg (about 155 pounds); a small car has a mass of 1000 kg or 10^3 kg (about 2200 pounds).

FUNDAMENTAL SI UNITS

Measurement	SI Unit
length	meter
mass	kilogram
time	second
current	ampere
temperature	kelvin

You will also learn later in the book about derived SI units that are combinations of fundamental SI units. Example: force is measured in newtons. A newton is a kilogram•meter/second^2.

DERIVED SI UNITS

Measurement	SI Unit
force	newton
power	watt
energy/work	joule
amount of electric charge	coulomb
potential difference	volts
resistance	ohm
magnetic flux	weber
frequency	hertz

Now Do Homework Questions #31-44, page 137-139.
(Look for page Chap. 1:137, meaning Chapter 1, page 137)

Section 2:
FREE FALL

A rock falls from the top of a cliff. Free fall: when a rock (or another object) falls down on its own (not thrown down) or is dropped; the speed of the rock increases (goes faster) as it falls down (due to the force of gravity).

In free fall, the initial velocity v_1, **the starting velocity** (example: of the rock or ball) at the **top of** the **cliff** (or **top of** a **building** or **top of anything**) is **zero meters/second**. The force of gravity causes the rock to accelerate (increase in speed) as it falls to the ground.

Top of cliff

0 s	v = 0 m/s
1 s	v = 9.81 m/s
2 s	v = 19.6 m/s
3 s	v = 29.4 m/s

At the end of the first second, the velocity of the rock (or ball or stone, etc.)is 9.81 m/s (meters/second); at the end of the second second, the velocity of the rock (or ball, etc.) is 19.6 m/s (meters/second), and at the end of the third second, the velocity is 29.4 m/s. The acceleration (a) due to the force of gravity is constant (always the same), 9.81 m/s². Every second that the rock falls to the ground, the speed increases by 9.81 m/s.

IMPORTANT: In **equations** used to solve **free fall problems** (problems with objects falling to the ground), *substitute for a* (acceleration) **9.81 m/s²** and for v_i (initial velocity) **zero**.

Question: What is the distance the rock traveled in 1 second after being released from the top of a cliff ?

Solution:

Look for an equation on Reference Table: Mechanics below or on page 22-23 that has distance and time. You can *use the equation*

$$\bar{v} = \frac{d}{t},$$

d = displacement/distance

t = time interval

$\bar{v}$ = average velocity/average speed

You need to find distance, therefore *first find* $\bar{v}$ (average velocity

for one second) and *then substitute* $\bar{v}$ (for one second) in the

equation $\bar{v} = \frac{d}{t}$

First find $\bar{v}$ for 1 second: Use the equation

$$\dot{v} = \frac{v_i + v_f}{2}$$

Average velocity = $\dfrac{\textit{initial (starting) velocity} + \textit{final velocity}}{2}$

Substitute for v_i (at the top of the cliff) 0. **Velocity** (example: of a rock or ball) **at the top** of a cliff (or mountain, building , etc.) **equals zero.** *Substitute for* v_f (after 1 second) 9.81 m/s. (You learned at the end of the first second the velocity of a rock or ball falling from the top of a cliff is 9.81 m/s.)

$$\bar{v} = \frac{0 \ m/s + 9.81 \ m/s}{2}$$

$$\bar{v} \quad = 4.9 \text{ m/s downward (going down)}$$

Then *substitute for* $\bar{v}$ 4.9 m/s in the equation $\bar{v} = \dfrac{d}{t}$ (or, cross

multiply, d = $\bar{v}$t),

$\bar{v} = \dfrac{d}{t}$	Or, rearrange the equation:
	d = $\bar{v}$t
$4.9 \text{ m/s} = \dfrac{d}{1 \ s}$	d = (4.9 m/s) (1s)
	d = 4.9 m
(4.9 m/s) (1s) = d	
d = 4.9 m	

You will learn later that you can also use the equation d = v_it + 1/2at^2 to find distance, because you know v_i, t, and a and you have only one unknown, (d) distance.

Similarly, if you calculated the distance the rock travels in two seconds, three seconds, and four seconds after the rock is dropped, you would get the following results:

Time	0 sec	1 sec	2 sec	3 sec	4 sec
Speed	0 m/s	9.81 m/s	19.6 m/s	29.4 m/s	39.2 m/s
Distance	0 m	4.9 m	19.6 m	44.1 m	78.5 m

Time	Distance Rock Fell	Velocity
0 s	Top of Cliff	v = 0
1 s	distance = 4.9 m	v = 9.81 m/s
2 s	distance = 19.6 m	v = 19.6 m
3 s	distance = 44.1 m	v = 29.4 m/s
4 s	distance = 78.5 m	v = 39.2 m/s

As you can see from the figure on the previous page, in 1 second the rock fell a distance of 4.9 m; in 2 seconds the distance the rock fell more than doubled (19.6 m).

Look again at the figure. In free fall, the rock accelerated at 9.81 m/s² and the velocity at 2 seconds (19.6 m/s) is more than the velocity at 1 second (9.81 m/s), therefore, the distance covered in 2 seconds is more than double (four times) the distance at 1 second (only 4.9 m).

Now Do Homework Questions #45-48, pages 139-140.

Ball Thrown Up Into the Air, Then Ball Falls Down (Free Fall)

A boy throws a ball straight up at a velocity of 40 m/s. In 1 second, the ball decelerates (slows down) to about 30 m/s. In 2 seconds, it slows down to about 20 m/s, in 3 seconds to 10 m/s, and after 4 seconds, to 0 m/s. See figure below.

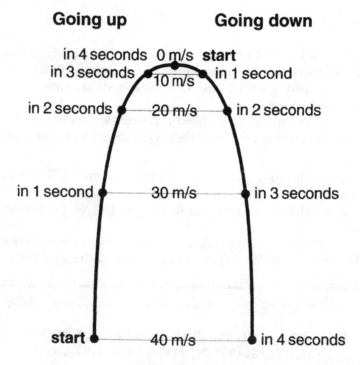

As you see, the ball goes up to the highest point in 4 seconds. Now the **ball** will **go down (free fall)** in the next 4 seconds. The total time that the ball is in the air (up and down) is 8 seconds. See figure above.
As you learned, when the ball falls down (free fall), it increases in speed and accelerates at 9.81 m/s²: When the ball goes down, in 1 second, speed is 9.81 m/s, about 10 m/s. In 2 seconds, the speed is 19.6 m/s, about 20 m/s, in 3 seconds 29.4 m/s, about 30 m/s, and in 4 seconds 39.2 m/s, about 40 m/s.

Question: Which two graphs best represent the motion of an object falling freely from rest near Earth's surface?

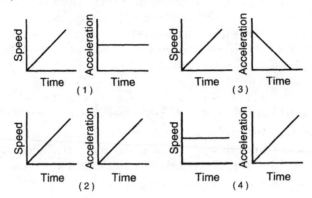

Solution: You learned when an object (example: ball) **falls freely** (free fall) **speed increases** and **acceleration** is **constant** (9.81 m/s²). Each choice has two graphs; the first is speed vs. time, the second acceleration vs. time.

Choice *1*: in the first graph, speed increases with time. In the second graph, acceleration is constant (always the same) with time. Answer *1*

Wrong choices:
Choice *2*: acceleration increases with time. In free fall acceleration is constant.
Choice *3*: acceleration decreases with time. In free fall acceleration is constant.
Choice *4*: speed is constant with time and acceleration increases with time. In free fall velocity increases with time and acceleration is constant (9.81 m/s²).

Now Do Homework Questions #49-52, page 140.

CALCULATING INITIAL AND FINAL VELOCITY, ACCELERATION, TIME AND DISTANCE

You learned how to use the equations

Table: Mechanics

1. $\bar{v} = \dfrac{d}{t}$

d = displacement/distance

t = time interval

$\bar{v}$ = average velocity/average speed

which can be used to find v (velocity or speed), d (distance or displacement) or t (time).

2. $a = \dfrac{\Delta v}{t}$

a = acceleration

t = time interval
v = velocity/speed
Δ= change

which can be used to find a (acceleration), t (time), Δv (change in velocity) and also v_i (when v_f is known) or v_f (when v_i is known).

We will learn three more equations for distance, velocity, acceleration, and time, equations **3** and **4** now and equation **5** a few pages later. These equations are given on Reference Table: Mechanics.

Look at Reference Table: Mechanics below or on page reference tables 22-23

Look at Reference Table: Mechanics below or on page reference tables 22-23

3. $v_f = v_i + at$

a = acceleration
t = time interval
v = velocity/speed

v_f = v_i +   a   t
Final velocity   = initial velocity + acceleration x time
(velocity at end) = (starting velocity)

Question: A car starts at rest. It accelerates at a rate of 2 m/s² for 3 seconds. What is the final velocity of the car?

Solution:
Given: car starts at rest (which means $v_i = 0$ m/s)
       acceleration (a)= 2 m/s²
       time (t) = 3 seconds (s).
Find: final velocity of car
Look for an equation on Reference Table: Mechanics that has v_i (initial velocity), a (acceleration), t (time), and v_f (final velocity).
Use the equation
$v_f = v_i + at$
In the equation above, **substitute for v_i** 0 m/s. **Substitute for a** 2 m/s².
Substitute for t 3 s (seconds).
$v_f = 0 + (2$ m/s²$)(3$ s$)$
$v_f = 6$ m/s   Final velocity = 6 m/s

---

4. $d = v_i t + \dfrac{1}{2}at^2$

a = acceleration

d = displacement/distance
t = time interval
v = velocity/speed

$$d \quad = \quad v_i \quad \times \ t \ + \ \frac{1}{2} \quad a \quad \times \ t^2$$

distance = initial velocity   x time $+ \ \frac{1}{2}$ acceleration x time^2
(starting velocity)

This equation $d = v_i t + \frac{1}{2}at^2$ is **used** to **find distance in free fall**

examples. Also, this equation can be used to **find d** (example, distance a car travels) **when v_i, t, and a** are **given**.

Question: How far will a brick starting from rest fall freely in 3.0 seconds?

Solution: How far means to **find** the **distance.**
Write down what is given and what you need to find.
Given: $v_i = 0$ When the question says **(starts) at rest** or **(starts) from rest,** that **means (starting velocity)** $v_i = 0$.
        t (time) = **3 seconds**
This question says **falls freely**, which **means free fall.**
        a (acceleration in free fall) = **9.81 m/s^2**

Find: Distance (d)
In short, you know $v_i = 0$, t =3 seconds, a= 9.81 m/s^2.

You know v_i, t, and a. You have three knowns and only one unknown (d). *Look for an equation* on Reference Table: Mechanics that has v_i, t, a, and d.

Use the equation

$$d \ = \ v_i t \ + \ \frac{1}{2}at^2$$

Substitute for v_i 0 m/s (meters/second). *Substitute for t* 3 s (seconds). *Substitute for a* (acceleration) 9.81 m/s^2 .

$$d \ = \ (0m/s)(3s) + \ \frac{1}{2}(9.81 \ m/s^2)(3s)^2 \ = 44 \ m$$

You used the equation $d \ = \ v_i t \ + \ \frac{1}{2}a \ t^2$

because you have three knowns, v_i, t, and a, and only one unknown, d (distance).
Note: In the equation above, since the ball falls freely (moves only vertically), you can use d or d_y for the distance the ball falls.

In free fall examples, in the equation $d = v_i t + \frac{1}{2}at^2$, $v_i = 0$, then $v_i t =$

0 (see equation above), therefore $d = \frac{1}{2}at^2$. In this example,

$$d = \frac{1}{2}(9.81\,\text{m/s}^2)(3\text{s})^2 = 44 \text{ m}.$$

Question: A basketball player jumped straight up to grab a rebound. If she was in the air for 0.80 second, how high did she jump?
     (1) 0.50 m   (2) 0.78 m   (3) 1.2 m   (4) 3.1 m

Solution: Write down what is given and what you need to find.
Given: A basketball player jumped up to grab the ball. She was in the air 0.80 seconds.
Find: How high she jumped.
She was in the air for 0.80 seconds from the time she jumped up until her feet landed on the ground (came down). It took her 0.40 seconds to jump up and 0.40 seconds to return to the ground; the distance she jumped up equals the distance she came down to the ground. Find the distance she came down because it is equal to the distance she jumped up (how high she jumped).

In jumping down, you know v_i (initial or starting velocity) = **0** (at top of jump, $v_i = 0$ m/s). You also know **a = 9.81 m/s²** (free fall) and **t = 0.40 s.** In short, you know $v_i = 0$, a = 9.81 m/s² and t = 0.40 second. You know three things, v_i, a, and t, and there is only one unknown, d (distance). *Look for an equation* on Reference Table: Mechanics that has v_i, a, t, and d.

Use the equation $d = v_i t + \frac{1}{2}at^2$
Note: You cannot solve the problem jumping up, because you do not know v_i and d, two unknowns, but in jumping down, you know v_i (at the top = 0) and you have only one unknown, d.

In the equation above, **substitute for v_i** 0 m/s. **Substitute for a** 9.81 m/s². **Substitute for t** 0.40 s (seconds) (given).
        $d = v_i t + \frac{1}{2}at^2$
        $d = 0 \text{ m/s t} + \frac{1}{2}(9.81 \text{ m/s}^2)(0.40 \text{ s})^2$
        $d = \qquad \frac{1}{2}(9.81 \text{ m/s}^2)(0.16\text{s}^2)$
        $d = 0.78 \text{ m}$
Distance jumped down = 0.78 m, which is equal to how high she jumped up = 0.78 m.   Answer 2

Question: A child kicks a ball with an initial velocity of 8.5 meters per second at an angle of 35° with the horizontal, as shown. The ball has an initial vertical velocity of 4.9 meters per second and a total time of flight of 1.0 second. [Neglect air resistance.] The maximum height reached by the ball is approximately

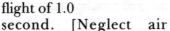

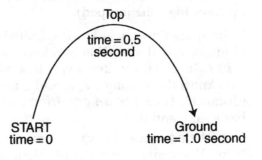

(1) 1.2 m   (2) 2.5 m   (3) 4.9 m   (4) 8.5 m

Solution:

Given: Ball has an initial vertical velocity = 4.9 m/s

Total time of flight = 1.0 second.

Find: **Maximum height** reached by the ball (**vertical distance** between ball on ground and the top-maximum height).

v_i means initial velocity or starting velocity.

v_{iy} shows the amount of the initial velocity that is in the vertical direction (initial vertical velocity).

Since the question asks to find height (distance in the vertical direction), use velocity, time, etc., also in the vertical direction. Initial vertical velocity = **4.9 m/s** (given). Since the ball was in the air for 1.0 second, you know it took the ball **0.5 second (s)** to go up and **reach the top** (maximum height-see figure) and it took 0.5 second for the ball to go from the top (maximum height) to the ground. Time **(t)** to reach the top = **0.5 second (s)**. Acceleration **(a)** = **−9.81 m/s²** and is constant. (Note: Acceleration is negative when a ball is thrown upward.) You need to find the maximum height reached by the ball (distance between ball on ground and top, maximum height).

In short, you know initial vertical velocity = 4.9 m/s (given), time = 0.5 seconds, and acceleration = −9.81 m/s². You know three things, v_i, t, and a, and there is one unknown, height (vertical distance) d, therefore, *look for an equation* on Reference Table: Mechanics that has d, v_i, t and a.

Use the equation $d = v_i t + \frac{1}{2}at^2$.

Since the question asks to find height (distance in the vertical direction), obviously the rest of the equation v, t, and a must also be in the vertical direction.

Then substitute 4.9 m/s (initial vertical velocity) for v_i (given). *Substitute 0.5 s* for t (time to reach maximum height) (calculated above).

Substitute −9.81 m/s² (as explained below) for a.

$a = -9.81$ m/s². In going up (ball went from ground to maximum height), acceleration is -9.81 m/s² (negative acceleration or deceleration). Note: Acceleration is negative because a $= \dfrac{\Delta v}{t}$ and velocity decreases (Δv is negative) as you go up.

$$d = v_i t + \frac{1}{2}at^2$$
$$d = 4.9 \text{ m/s}(0.5 \text{ s}) + \frac{1}{2}(-9.81 \text{ m/s}^2)(0.5 \text{ s})^2$$
$$d = 2.45 \text{ m} + (-4.9 \text{ m/s}^2)(.25 \text{ s}^2)$$
$$d = 2.45 \text{ m} + (-1.23 \text{ m}) = 1.2 \text{ m}$$

The maximum height is 1.2 m

Answer 1

Throwing a Ball Horizontally

When a boy throws a ball horizontally, it goes (at the same time) both horizontally away from the boy and vertically down to the ground.

When the ball goes horizontally, it goes at constant speed, but when the ball goes down, it accelerates at 9.81 m/s² just like free fall. To find the time it took the ball to hit the ground vertically, just like in free fall, use the equation $d_y = v_i t + \frac{1}{2}at^2$, where $v_i = 0$, and $a = 9.81$ m/s².

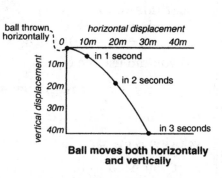

Ball moves both horizontally and vertically

Question: The diagram shows a student throwing a baseball horizontally at 25 meters per second from a cliff 45 meters above the level ground.

Approximately how far from the base of the cliff does the ball hit the ground?[Neglect air resistance.]

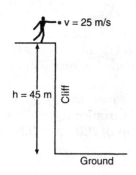

(1) 45 m   (2) 75 m
(3) 140 m   (4) 230 m

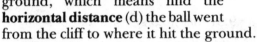
• v = 25 m/s

h = 45 m   Cliff

horizontal distance

Solution:

Given: A student throws a baseball horizontally at 25 meters per second (m/s). The cliff is 45 meters (m) above ground.

Find: How far from the base of the cliff does the ball hit the ground?

Ball began at the cliff. The question is how far from the base (bottom) of the cliff does the ball hit the ground, which means find the **horizontal distance** (d) the ball went from the cliff to where it hit the ground.

Look at Reference Table: Mechanics for equations with distance.

Use the equation

$d = v_i t + \frac{1}{2}at^2$

Since you are looking for horizontal distance, you can also write

$d_x = v_i t + \frac{1}{2}at^2$

When the ball goes horizontally, there is zero acceleration (a), therefore **substitute 0 for a.**

$$d_x = v_i t + \frac{1}{2}at^2$$
$$d_x = v_i t + \frac{1}{2}0t^2 \qquad d_x = v_i t$$

Or, you can use the equation

$$\bar{v} = \frac{d}{t} \quad \text{or rearrange the equation to} \quad d = \bar{v}t.$$

In the horizontal direction, velocity is constant, therefore v_i (initial velocity) is the same as $\bar{v}$ (average velocity).

First you need to find the time (t) the ball went horizontally (until it reached the ground), then put it into the equation $d = vt$ to find horizontal distance. The time the ball went horizontally until it hit the ground equals the time the ball went vertically down and hit the ground. Therefore, find the time (t) it took the ball to go vertically down and hit the ground.

Note: You do not have enough information to find the time that it went horizontally because you do not have the horizontal distance and time.

Use the equation $d = v_i t + \frac{1}{2}at^2$ or you can also write $d_y = v_i t + \frac{1}{2}at^2$.
Vertical distance $d_y = 45$ m (cliff is 45 meters above ground-given).
$v_i = 0$ top of cliff $a = 9.81$ m/s^2

Substitute 45 m for d. and *substitute 9.81 m/s² for a.*

$d_y = v_it + \frac{1}{2}at^2$

$45 \text{ m} = 0 + \frac{1}{2}(9.81\text{m/s}^2)t^2$

$45 \text{ m} = \qquad 4.9\text{m/s}^2t^2$

$\dfrac{45}{4.9} = t^2, t^2 = 9$

$t = 3$ s   t (time) to hit the ground vertically equals 3 seconds

Since the time (t) vertically to hit the ground = time (t) horizontally to hit the ground, **substitute 3 seconds** for t in the equation for horizontal distance, $d_x = vt$.

$d_x = vt$

$d_x = (25\text{m/s})(3\text{s}) = 75$ meters

Horizontal distance (how far from the cliff the ball hits the ground) = 75 meters

Answer 2

Summary (how to solve the question): how far means distance. When a question asks how far from the base of a cliff, mountain, building, etc. it means horizontal distance. Look at Reference Table: Mechanics to find the distance equations:

$d = v_it + \frac{1}{2} at^2, \quad v = \dfrac{d}{t}$.

As you can see in the equations above, you do not know distance and time, therefore, *first find time* it took the ball to hit the ground **vertically**, by using the equation $d_y = \quad v_it + \frac{1}{2}at^2$. **Next, put time (t) into** the **equation** for horizontal distance $d_x = v_it + \frac{1}{2} at^2$, or $v = \dfrac{d}{t}$, (or rearranged, $d = vt$).

Remember, in horizontal distance, a = 0.

(Note: You cannot use $v_f^2 = v_i^2 + 2ad$ to find d (distance) for any object thrown horizontally, because velocity is constant and therefore there is zero acceleration a; **2ad = 0** and you cannot solve for d.)

Table: Mechanics

Question: A skier starting from rest skis straight down a slope 50. meters long in 5.0 seconds. What is the magnitude of the acceleration of the skier?

(1) 20 meters/sec²	(2) 9.8 meters/sec²
(3) 5.0 meters/sec²	(4) 4.0 meters/sec²

Solution: Write down what is given and what you need to find.

Given: skier starting from rest, distance (d) = 50. meters (m), time (t) = 5.0 seconds (s).

Find: acceleration (a)

When the problem says **(starts) at rest**, that **means** v_i (starting velocity) **= 0.**

Note: You learned that when an object is at the **top** of a cliff or **top** of a building, etc., $v_i = 0$.

When a **skier goes down** a **slope** (example: side of a mountain), it is **not free fall** (he is not going vertically down), and **acceleration** is **not equal** to **9.81 m/s²**.

In short, you know $v_i = 0$ m/s, d = 50. m, and t = 5.0 s.

You know three things, v_i, d and t and there is only one unknown, a, therefore *look for an equation* on Reference Table: Mechanics that has v_i, d, t and a.

Table: Mechanics

Use the equation $d = v_i t + \frac{1}{2}at^2$

Substitute for d 50. m (meters) (given). *Substitute for* v_i 0 m/s.
Substitute for t 5.0 s (seconds) (given).

$$50. \text{ m} = 0\text{m/s} \times 5\text{s} + \frac{1}{2}a5^2s^2$$

$$50. \text{ m} = 0 + \frac{1}{2}a(25\ s^2)$$

$$\frac{50\ m}{12\frac{1}{2}\ s^2} = 0 + \frac{12\frac{1}{2}\ as^2}{12\frac{1}{2}\ s^2}$$

$$4 \text{ m/s}^2 = a$$

$$\text{Acceleration} = 4 \text{ m/s}^2$$

In this example, you used the equation $d = v_i t + \frac{1}{2}at^2$ because you have three knowns, v_i, t, and a, and only one unknown, d (distance).

As you can see above, $d = v_i t + \frac{1}{2}at^2$ is used to find acceleration when you know d (50. m), v_i (0 m/s), and t (5.0 s).

Questions 1 & 2: Base your answers to questions 1 and 2 on the information below. A physics class is to design an experiment to determine the acceleration of a student on in-line skates coasting straight down a gentle incline. The incline has a constant slope. The students have tape measures, traffic cones, and stopwatches.

Question 1: Describe a procedure to obtain the measurements necessary for this experiment.

Question 2: Indicate which equation(s) they should use to determine the student's acceleration.

Solution 1:
Given: Student on in-line skates coasting straight down a gentle slope (means going down a hill). Incline has a constant slope. Students have tape measures, traffic cones, and stopwatches.

Find: Describe a procedure to obtain measurements needed to find acceleration of a student on in-line skates going down a gentle slope.

Using a tape measure, set up a measured distance on the slope. Mark the ends of the measured distance with traffic cones. With the student starting at rest, use a stopwatch to time how long it takes the student to go from the top to the bottom of the measured slope.

Solution 2:

Given: Student on in-line skates coasting straight down a gentle slope. Incline has a constant slope. Students have tape measures, traffic cones, and stopwatches.

Find: Which equation they should use to find the student's acceleration.

You need to find acceleration (a).

You found d (by measuring the length of the slope); you found t (by using a stopwatch). The student started from at rest, therefore $v_i = 0$.

You know three things, d, t and v_i, and there is one unknown, a, therefore *look for an equation* on Reference Table: Mechanics that has d, t , v_i, and a.

Use the equation $d = v_i t + \frac{1}{2}at^2$

Answer: $d = v_i t + \frac{1}{2}at^2$

Now Do Homework Questions #53-64, pages 140-142.

Look below or on Reference Table: Mechanics, on pages reference tables 22-23.

5. $\quad v_f^2 = v_i^2 + 2ad \qquad$ a = acceleration
$\qquad\qquad\qquad\qquad\qquad$ d = displacement/distance
$\qquad\qquad\qquad\quad$ v = velocity/speed

$$v_f^2 \quad = \quad v_i^2 \quad + 2 \quad a \qquad d$$

final velocity² = initial velocity² + 2 x acceleration x distance
(velocity at the   (velocity at the
 end)²   beginning)²

Question: An object falls freely from rest near the surface of Earth. What is the speed of the object after having fallen a distance of 4.90 meters?

Solution: When the question asks the **speed after falling 4.90 meters**, it **means** to find the **final velocity**, v_f.

Given: object falls freely from rest
$\qquad\qquad$ distance (d) = 4.90 meters (m)

Find: final velocity (v_f)

From rest means initial velocity (v_i) = 0.

Acceleration (a) in free fall (falls freely) = 9.81 m/s² which is due to (caused by) gravity. Reference Table: List of Physical Constants, on page reference tables 2-3, lists the acceleration due to gravity as g = 9.81 m/s².

In short, you know v_i = 0 m/s, d = 4.90 m, and a = 9.81 m/s².
You know three things, v_i, d and a and there is one unknown, v_f, therefore *look for an equation* on Reference Table: Mechanics that has v_i, d, a and v_f.

Use the equation $\quad v_f^2 = v_i^2 + 2ad$
Substitute for v_i 0. *Substitute for a*(acceleration) 9.81 m/s².
Substitute for d 4.90 meters.

$$v_f^2 = 0\,m/s + 2(9.81 m/s^2)4.90m$$
$$v_f^2 = 0m/s + 96.14 m^2/s^2$$
$$v_f = 9.80 m/s$$

You used the equation $\qquad v_f^2 = v_i^2 + 2ad$
because you have three knowns, v_i, a, and d, and only one unknown, v_f (final velocity).

Note: When a ball or any object falls off a table or (lab) counter, or a student jumps off a table or (lab) counter, v_i = 0.

Summary: Use the five equations on Reference Table: Mechanics to solve questions with distance, time, acceleration, average velocity, initial velocity, and final velocity.

1. $\bar{v} = \dfrac{d}{t}$ $\qquad$ 2. $a = \dfrac{\Delta v}{t}$ $\qquad$ 3. $v_f = v_i + at$

4. $d = v_i t + \dfrac{1}{2}at^2$ $\quad$ 5. $v_f^2 = v_i^2 + 2ad$

Now Do Homework Questions #65-69, page 142.

Section 3:
SCALAR AND VECTOR QUANTITIES

Scalar- A scalar quantity only has magnitude (a **number** and **units**) but **no direction**.

Examples:	Speed	40 meters per second
	Distance	40 meters

Vector- A vector quantity has **both** magnitude (a **number** and **units**) **and direction**.

Examples:	Velocity	40 meters per second west
	Displacement	40 meters south

VECTOR AND SCALAR QUANTITIES

SCALARS	VECTORS
magnitude (number & units)	**magnitude (number & units) and direction**
Speed (example: 40 meters/second)	Velocity (example: 40 meters/second west)
Distance (example: 40 meters)	Displacement (example: 40 meters north)
Energy (example: 40 joules)	Acceleration (example: 40 m/s² south)
Time (example: 4 seconds)	Force (example: 40 newtons down)
Mass	
Power	Momentum
Charge	Torque

VECTORS

Force is a push or a pull and is a vector quantity. Force is measured in newtons (N). **Velocity, acceleration, displacement** and **force** are **vector quantities** because they have both magnitude (number) and direction; they can be shown by vectors (see below).

A line with an arrowhead —➤ **is a vector**. The arrowhead is the head of the vector; the end of the vector is called the tail of the vector.

Tail —➤ Head

vector

If one cm on the line represents 10 meters and the line is 5 cm long, it represents 50 meters.

————————————➤

5 cm = 50 meters.

If the arrowhead is pointing east, it shows the direction is east. The vector ————————————➤ represents 50 meters east.

As you can see, a vector is a line with an arrowhead which shows magnitude (a number, example 50 meters) and direction (example, east). When you **draw** a **vector**, the vector must always have a **line with** an **arrowhead**.

Combining vectors (adding vectors, subtracting vectors, etc.):
1. Adding forces:

A. When you have a force of 10 newtons (N) and a force of 7 newtons (N), both pulling east (same direction, on the same point), add the forces together to get the resultant (combined force).

10 N
———➤   Add the forces (N)

7 N
——➤

10 N   7 N
———➤ ——➤
equals 17 N
————————➤

Resultant (combined force) = 17 N

Both forces are pulling on the same point and the combined force (resultant, also called net force) is 17 N east.

B. When you have a force of 15 newtons (N) and a force of 7 newtons (N) both pulling north (same direction, on the same point), add the forces together to get the resultant (combined force, net force).

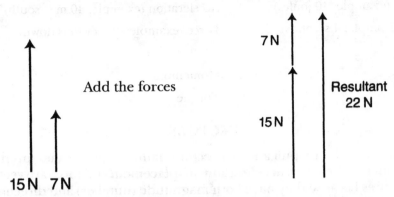

The forces acting on the same point (example: 15 N and 7 N) are called concurrent forces. The combined force (example: 22N north) is called the resultant.

2. Subtracting forces: When you have a force of 10 N and a force of 7 N both pulling in **opposite directions,** you **subtract** the forces.

$$7 \text{ N} \qquad 10 \text{ N}$$
$$\longleftarrow \quad \bullet \quad \longrightarrow \quad 10 \text{ N} - 7 \text{ N} = 3 \text{ N}$$
$$\bullet \rightarrow \text{ Resultant 3 N}$$

The concurrent forces, the forces pulling on the point, are 7 N west and 10 N east, and the resultant or combined force is 3 N east.

RULE: **Vectors** in the **same direction** have **0°** between them. You add the forces, 10 N + 7 N = 17 N and you get the **largest resultant** (combined force) (see 1. Adding forces, above).

Vectors in **opposite directions** have a **180° angle** between them. You subtract the forces (or velocity, etc.) and you get the **smallest resultant,** 10 N − 7 N = 3N (see 2. Subtracting forces, above).

Vectors between 0° and 180° have a **resultant** force **between** the **smallest** (minimum) **resultant** (3 N) (see 2. Subtracting forces, above), produced by two vectors in opposite directions (180° angle between the vectors), **and** the **largest** (maximum) **resultant** (17 N) (see 1. Adding forces, above), produced by two vectors in the same direction (0° angle between the vectors).

Example: Given two vectors, 5 N and 12 N:
When the angle between the two vectors is 0°, resultant = 17 N.
When the angle between the vectors is 90°, resultant = 13 N
When the angle between the two vectors is 180°, resultant = 7 N.
As you can see from the example above, the
smaller the **angle** between two vectors, the **bigger**
is the **resultant**. The **bigger** the **angle** between two
vectors, the **smaller** is the **resultant**.

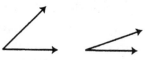

Question: Two concurrent forces have a maximum resultant of 45 newtons and a minimum resultant of 5 newtons. What is the magnitude of each of these forces?

    (1) 0 N and 45 N   (2) 5 N and 9 N
    (3) 20 N and 25 N   (4) 0 N and 50 N

Solution:

Maximum resultant: To have a maximum resultant of 45 N (newtons), the two forces must add to 45N (newtons).

Same direction: 20 N (newton) force and 25 N (newton) force.

20 N
⟶
          = 45 N (maximum resultant)
    ⟶
25 N

When the **forces** are in the **same direction**, (example 20 N and 25 N) **add** the **forces** together, and you get the **maximum resultant** (45 N).

Minimum resultant: To have a minimum resultant of 5 N (newtons), when you subtract the two forces, they must equal 5 N (newtons).

Opposite directions: 20 N (newton) force and 25 N (newton) force.

⟵   ⟶
20 N   25 N   25 N - 20 N = 5 N (minimum resultant)

When the **forces** are in **opposite directions**, (example 20 N and 25 N) **subtract** the two **forces** and you get the **minimum resultant** (5 N).

These two forces, 25 N and 20 N, have a maximum resultant of 45 N and a minimum resultant of 5 N.   Answer 3

Question: Which pair of concurrent forces could produce a resultant force having a magnitude of 10. newtons?

    (1) 10. N, 10. N   (2) 10. N, 30. N
    (3) 4.7 N, 4.7 N   (4) 4.7 N, 5.0 N

Solution: Choice *1*

Same direction: You learned when vectors (example, force vectors) are in the same direction, 0° angle between them, you **add** the **vectors**.
For example, **10 N** force **+10 N** force in the same direction = **20 N** which is the largest resultant (largest combined force).

Opposite directions: You learned when vectors are in the opposite direction, 180° angle between them, you **subtract** the **vectors**.
For example, 10 N force and 10 N force in opposite directions
    10 N −10 N = 0 N, which is the smallest resultant (smallest combined force).

Other directions: When vectors are not in the same direction and not in opposite directions, (angle between the vectors is between 0° and 180°) the resultant must be between the maximum resultant (example, force resultant of 20 N) and the minimum resultant (example, force of zero N). **Choice 1** is the **answer** because a resultant of **10 N** is **between** the **20 N** maximum resultant **and** the **0 N** minimum resultant.

Wrong choices:
Choice 2: 10 N and 30 N forces. If the forces act in the same direction, add the forces: 10 N + 30 N = **40 N force** (maximum resultant).
If the forces are in opposite directions, subtract the forces: 30 N − 10 N = **20 N** (minimum resultant). Other resultants can be between 20 N and 40 N. Therefore, the resultant can be 20 N, between 20 N and 40 N, or 40 N. These two forces cannot produce a 10 N resultant force.
Choice 3: 4.7 N + 4.7 N = 9.4 N(maximum resultant).
    4.7 N − 4.7 N = 0 N (minimum resultant).
The resultant can be 0 N, between 0 N and 9.4 N, or 9.4 N. These two forces cannot produce a 10 N force.
Choice 4: 4.7 N + 5.0 N = 9.7 N(maximum resultant).
    5.0 N − 4.7 N = 0.3 N (minimum resultant).
The resultant can be 0.3 N, between 0.3 N and 9.7 N, or 9.7 N. These two forces cannot produce a resultant force of 10 N.

Now Do Homework Questions #70-77, pages 142-143.

FINDING A RESULTANT GRAPHICALLY

Let's learn how to measure the resultant of two vectors (example, force vectors) graphically.

Question: Two forces are pulling on one point.
There is a 40° angle between the 30 newton and 40 newton vectors.
What is the resultant of the two vectors?

Solution:

Given: 30 newton force. 40 newton force. 40° angle between the forces.
Find: Resultant (resultant has magnitude, which is a number, and direction, such as north or south).

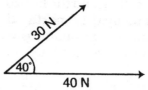

Let 1 cm represent a 10 N (newton) force; therefore, 3 cm represents a 30 N (newton) force and 4 cm represents a 40 N (newton) force.

Method 1–Parallelogram method: Make a parallelogram–use a ruler and a protractor to measure the resultant.

1. Draw two vectors from one point with tails touching each other. How to draw it: In this example, let 1 cm represent a 10 N force.

Use a ruler to measure a 4 cm vector to represent a 40 N force. Use a protractor to measure a 40° angle between the two vectors (see figure at right). Put the line which is on the bottom of the protractor (the line connecting 0° and 180°) along (on top of) the horizontal 4 cm vector. Put the reference point (hole or marker) on the bottom of the protractor at the start of

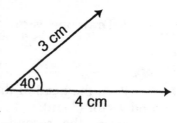

the 4 cm vector. Measure a 40° angle from the horizontal 4 cm vector and draw the 3 cm vector (see figure above).

The figure above shows two vectors from one point with tails touching each other.

2. Make a parallelogram.

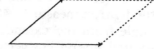

3. Draw a diagonal from where the tails are touching each other.
The diagonal you drew is the resultant.

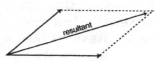

4. Measure the resultant: Use a ruler to measure the length of the resultant in cm. Use a protractor to find the angle between the resultant and the horizontal vector. In this example, the resultant is 6.4 cm, which represents 64 N (newtons). The angle between the

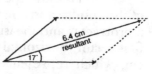

resultant and the horizontal vector is 17°, which means the resultant is pointed 17° north (direction) of the horizontal east line.
Answer: Resultant is 64 N, pointed 17° north (direction) of the horizontal east line.

Method 2–Triangle Method: Same problem as in method 1. Two forces are pulling on a point . There is a 40° angle between the 30 newton and 40 newton vectors. What is the resultant of the two vectors? Draw a diagram of what is given.

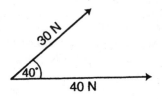

Now let 1 cm represent 10 N (newtons), therefore, 3 cm represents 30 N (newtons) and 4 cm represents 40 N (newtons). Draw the two forces at a 40° angle to each other (see below). Make a triangle. Use a ruler to measure the length of the resultant in cm; use a protractor to measure the angle between the resultant and the horizontal vector.

1. Draw one vector (4 cm). A vector has a head and a tail:

       Tail   ——▶   Head

          vector

2. At the **head** of the first vector (4 cm) put the tail of the second vector (3 cm).

Draw the second vector with the same length and same angle (40°) as in the original question. Extend the 4 cm vector (see dotted line in the figure); measure a 40° angle from the extended (dotted line) 4 cm vector and draw the 3 cm vector.

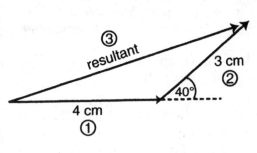

Remember: Always put the **HEAD** of the first vector (or previous vector) **TO** the **TAIL** of the next vector, **HEAD TO TAIL**.

3. Draw the resultant from the beginning point (tail of the first vector) to the end (which is the head of the last vector).

4. Measure the resultant: Use a ruler to measure the length of the resultant in cm. (1 cm is being used to represent 10 N). Use a protractor and measure the angle between the resultant and the first vector (horizontal vector). In this example, the resultant is 6.4 cm, which represents 64 N (newtons). The angle between the resultant and the horizontal vector is 17°, which means the resultant is pointed 17° north (direction) of the horizontal east line.

Answer: Resultant is 64 N, pointed 17° north (direction) of the horizontal east line.

Questions 1-4: Base your answers to questions 1 through 4 on the information below. A force of 6.0 x 10⁻¹⁵ newton due south and a force of 8.0 x 10⁻¹⁵ newton due east act concurrently on an electron, e^-.

Question 1: Copy the diagram on a separate sheet of paper. On your diagram, draw a force diagram to represent the

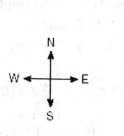

two forces acting on the electron. (The electron is represented by a dot.) Use a metric ruler and the scale of 1.0 centimeter = 1.0 x 10⁻¹⁵ newton. Begin each vector at the dot representing the electron and label its magnitude in newtons.

Question 2: On the diagram, determine the resultant force on the electron, *graphically*. Label the resultant vector R.

Question 3: Determine the magnitude of the resultant vector R.

Question 4: Determine the angle between the resultant and the 6.0 x 10⁻¹⁵ newton vector.

Solutions 1-4:

Given: A force of 6.0 x 10⁻¹⁵ newton (N) due south and a force of 8.0 x 10⁻¹⁵ newton (N) due east act concurrently on an electron, e^-.

Solution 1: Copy the dot representing the electron onto your paper. On the paper, draw a force diagram to represent the two forces acting on the electron (electron is represented by a dot.) Use a metric ruler and a scale of 1.0 centimeter = 1 x 10⁻¹⁵ N (newton). Look at the figure. Begin each vector at the dot. Draw a 6.0 centimeter (cm)

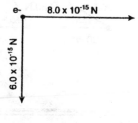

vector due (pointing) south, representing the 6.0 x 10⁻¹⁵ N (newton) force pointing south. From the dot, draw an 8.0 centimeter (cm) vector due (pointing) east, representing the 8.0 x 10⁻¹⁵ N force pointing east. Label each vector with its magnitude (number of newtons).

Solution 2: On the diagram, draw a parallelogram (rectangle). Draw the resultant

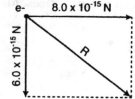

(diagonal) from point e^- to x, where the two dashed lines meet. Label the resultant vector R.

Solution 3: Measure the resultant using a metric ruler. The resultant is 10.0 cm long. 1.0 cm represents 1.0×10^{-15} N, therefore resultant of 10.0 cm = 10.0 $\times$ (1.0 $\times$ 10^{-15} N) = 10.0 $\times$ 10^{-15} N (newtons).

Or, you can set up a proportion to find the resultant. Let x = number of N (newtons) in the 10.0 cm resultant.

$$\frac{1.0 \ cm}{1.0 \ x \ 10^{-15} \ N} = \frac{10.0 \ cm}{x}$$

Cross multiply

$$\frac{(1.0 \ cm)(x)}{1.0 \ cm} = \frac{(1.0 \ x \ 10^{-15} \ N)(10.0 \ cm)}{1.0 \ cm}$$

$$x \quad = \quad 10.0 \ x \ 10^{-15} \ N$$
$$\text{Resultant} = \quad 10.0 \ x \ 10^{-15} \ N$$

Solution 4: Use a protractor. Put the line on the bottom of the protractor (the line connecting 0° and 180°) along (on top of) the 6.0 $\times$ 10^{-15} N vector. Put the reference point (hole or marker) on the bottom of the protractor on the dot representing the e. Measure the angle between the resultant and the 6.0 $\times$ 10^{-15} N vector. The angle = 53°.

If a question asks which choice will give a resultant of 30 newtons (see diagram) or a resultant of 20 m/s, draw the resultant for all the choices, using the parallelogram method, and see which resultant is 30 N (newtons). 30 N resultant must be the same length as each 30 N vector.

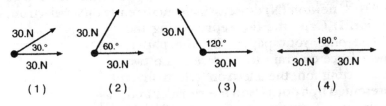

(1)   (2)   (3)   (4)

Answer 3

Question: A force vector was resolved into two perpendicular components, F_1 and F_2, as shown in the diagram.
Which vector represents the original force?

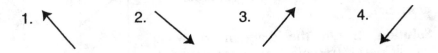

Solution:
Method 1-Parallelogram Method:
1. Draw the vectors from one point with the tails touching each other. 2. Make a parallelogram. 3. Draw the resultant (diagonal line) from where the tails are touching each other.
As you can see , choice 4 is the resultant which is the original force.

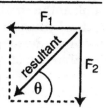

Answer 4

Method 2-Triangle Method:
1. Draw vector F_1. 2. At the head of vector F_1, put the tail of vector F_2. Draw F_2 with the same length and same angle as in the original question. 3. Draw the resultant from the beginning (tail of vector # 1) to the end (head of vector # 2).
As you can see, choice 4 is the resultant, which is the original force

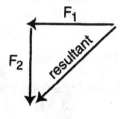

Answer 4

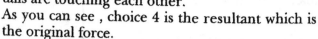

Now Do Homework Questions #78-81, pages 143-144.

FINDING A RESULTANT ALGEBRAICALLY

Two forces are pulling on one point.
There is a force of 3 N north and 4 N east. What is the resultant?

Let's use algebra also to find a resultant when the vectors are at right angles to each other.
Method 1–Parallelogram method. Make a parallelogram, just like you did before in steps 1,2, and 3 in "Method 1-Parallelogram Method" of "Finding a Resultant Graphically", and then use algebra to find the resultant.

    1. Draw two vectors from one point, with tails touching each other.

    2. Make a parallelogram.

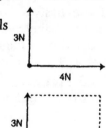

    3. Draw a resultant (diagonal) from where the tails touch each other.
Opposite sides of a rectangle are equal, therefore the dotted side opposite 3 N also equals 3 N.

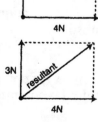

4. Look at the shaded area of the parallelogram.
Use the Pythagorean Theorem for right triangles, given
below or on Reference Table: Geometry and Trigonometry on
page reference tables 21, to find the resultant:

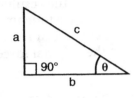

On the reference table:
  Right Triangle:

$$c^2 = a^2 + b^2$$
$$\text{hypotenuse}^2 = (\text{one side})^2 + (\text{other side})^2$$

Hypotenuse is the longest side, opposite 90° angle.
Hypotenuse is the resultant.

Use the equation $c^2 = a^2 + b^2$ to find the resultant.
$$c^2 = a^2 + b^2$$
Substitute for a (one side) 3N. Substitute for b (other side) 4N.
$$c^2 = (3\text{ N})^2 + (4\text{ N})^2$$
$$c^2 = 9\text{ N}^2 + 16\text{ N}^2 = 25\text{ N}^2$$
$$c = 5\text{ N} \quad \text{Resultant} = 5\text{ N.}$$

Method 2–Triangle Method. Make a triangle, in steps
1, 2, and 3, just like in the triangle method on page 38,
and then use algebra to find the resultant. See figure
at right.

1. Draw the 4 N vector.
2. At the **head** of the first vector (4 N) put the tail of
the second vector (3 N). Draw the second vector (3
N) with the same length and same angle as in the
figure above. Remember: Always put the **HEAD** of
the first vector (or previous vector) **TO** the **TAIL** of
the next vector, **HEAD TO TAIL.**
3. Draw the resultant from the beginning point (tail
of the first vector) to the end (head of the last
vector). Label vectors and resultant.

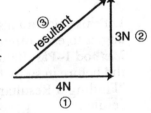

4. Use the Pythagorean Theorem for right triangles,
$c^2 = a^2 + b^2$, to find the resultant:

On the reference table:
  Right Triangle:

$$c^2 = a^2 + b^2$$
$$\text{hypotenuse}^2 = (\text{one side})^2 + (\text{other side})^2$$

In the equation above, substitute for a   3N.
Substitute for b 4N.
$$c^2 = (3\text{ N})^2 + (4\text{ N})^2$$
$$c^2 = 9\text{ N}^2 + 16\text{ N}^2 = 25\text{ N}^2$$
$$c \text{ (hypotenuse, which is the resultant)} = 5\text{N} \qquad \text{Resultant} = 5\text{ N}$$
Note: Hypotenuse (c) is the longest side, opposite the 90° angle.

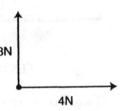

Question: Two students push on a sled. One pushes with a force of 30. newtons east and the other exerts a force of 40. newtons south, as shown in the top view diagram below.

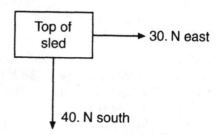

Which vector best represents the resultant of these two forces?

1. 70. N   2. 70. N   3. 50. N   4. 50. N

Solution: You can find a resultant graphically or algebraically. Let's find the resultant algebraically.

Method 1: Parallelogram method. Make a parallelogram and then use algebra to find the resultant (see figure below).

1. Draw the vectors from one point with the tails touching each other.

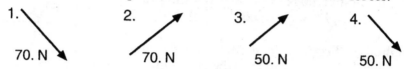

2. Make a parallelogram.

3. Draw the resultant (diagonal) from where the two tails are touching each other. Opposite sides of a rectangle are equal, therefore the dotted side opposite 30 N also equals 30 N. You see in the figure, the **resultant** vector **points down** and to **the right**.

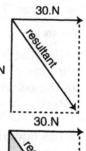

4. Look at the shaded area of the parallelogram. Use the Pythagorean Theorem for right triangles, $c = a^2 + b^2$, to find the magnitude (number) of the resultant:

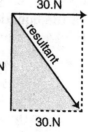

On the reference table:
Right triangle:
$$c^2 = a^2 + b^2$$
$$\text{hypotenuse}^2 = (\text{one side})^2 + (\text{other side})^2$$

Use the equation $c^2 = a^2 + b^2$ to find the resultant.
$$c^2 = a^2 + b^2$$
Substitute for a (height) 40 N; substitute for b (base) 30 N.
$$c^2 = (40 \text{ N})^2 + (30 \text{ N})^2$$
$$c^2 = 1600 \text{ N}^2 + 900 \text{ N}^2$$
$$c^2 = 2500 \text{ N}^2$$
c (hypotenuse, which is the resultant) = 50 N

The **resultant** is **50 N** (newtons)
The resultant is 50 N (newtons), pointing down
and to the right (see previous page).

Method 2: Triangle method. Make a triangle
and then use algebra to find the resultant.

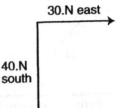

1. Draw the 30 N vector.
2. At the **head** of the first vector (30 N) put
the tail of the second vector (40 N). Draw
the second vector (40 N) with the same
length and same angle as in the original
question. Remember: Always put the **HEAD**
of the first vector (or previous vector) **TO**
the **TAIL** of the next vector, **HEAD TO TAIL**.
3. Draw the resultant from the beginning
(tail of the first vector) to the end (head of
last vector). You see in the figure, the **resultant** vector **points down**

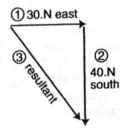

and **to the right.**

4. Use the Pythagorean Theorem for right
triangles, $c^2 = a^2 + b^2$, to find the resultant:
On the reference table:
Right triangle:
$$c^2 = a^2 + b^2$$
In the equation above, substitute for a (one
side) 40 N; substitute for b (other side) 30 N.
$$c^2 = a^2 + b^2$$
$$c^2 = (40 \text{ N})^2 + (30 \text{ N})^2$$
$$c^2 = 1600 \text{ N}_2 + 900 \text{ N}^2$$
$$c^2 = 2500 \text{ N}^2$$
c (hypotenuse, which is the resultant) = 50 N

The **resultant** is **50 N (newtons)**.

The resultant is 50 N (newtons), pointing down and to the right (see above).

Answer 4.

Now Do Homework Questions #82-94, pages 144-146.

HOW TO DO THE REVERSE: RESULTANT GIVEN, FIND THE HORIZONTAL AND VERTICAL COMPONENTS

You have the resultant and want to find the horizontal and vertical components.

As you can see from the diagram, the resultant and the horizontal and vertical components are all vectors.

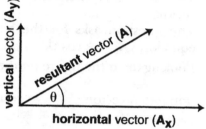

To find the horizontal and vertical components, use the equations given below or on Reference Table: Mechanics on pages reference tables 22-23:

$A_y = A \sin \theta$ A = any vector quantity
$A_x = A \cos \theta$ θ = angle

Realize: A = any vector quantity, which can be force, displacement, velocity, etc.

A_x means horizontal component (vector). See figure above.
A_y means vertical component (vector). See figure above.
θ is the angle between the resultant and the horizontal component (vector).

HORIZONTAL COMPONENT

Question: The resultant is a 10 N force. There is a 30° angle between the resultant and the horizontal. Find the horizontal force.

Solution:

Given: 10 N resultant force.
    30° angle between resultant and horizontal
Find: Horizontal force

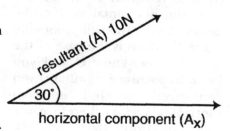

The 10 N resultant can be

broken down into two parts, the horizontal component (horizontal force or horizontal vector) and the vertical component (vertical force or vertical vector). This question asks to find the horizontal force, which means horizontal vector (see figure on previous page).

Look for an equation on Reference Table: Mechanics that has horizontal vector. The reference table says A = vector. There are two equations on **Reference Table: Mechanics** with the letter A.

$$A_y = A \sin \theta$$
$$A_x = A \cos \theta$$

You can see A_x means horizontal vector and A_y means vertical vector.

The question asks for the horizontal vector, therefore use the equation $A_x = A \cos \theta$.

Look again at the figure on the previous page and the equation.

A_x		=	A		$\cos \theta$

horizontal vector = resultant x cos of angle between resultant and horizontal.

$$A_x = A \cos \theta.$$

Substitute for A (resultant) 10 N. *Substitute for θ 30°*

$A_x = (10 \text{ N}) (\cos 30°)$ Cos 30° = 0.866 (use calculator: press 30, then press cos)

$A_x = (10 \text{ N}) (0.866) = 8.66 \text{ N}$
A_x = horizontal component (horizontal vector) = 8.66 N.

OR

Look at Figure 1 and draw a line from the resultant, perpendicular to the horizontal line, to complete a right triangle. See figure 2.

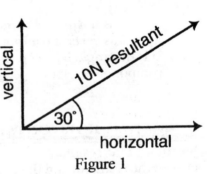

Figure 1

You know θ (angle) equals 30° (given). You know hypotenuse (resultant) equals 10 N (given). Find the **horizontal vector**, the **adjacent** side, the side touching angle θ, which is the base of the triangle. You know θ and you know **hypotenuse** (resultant) and you need to find **adjacent** (horizontal vector), therefore, use the equation that has θ,

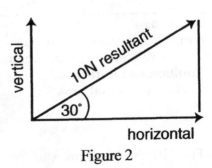

Figure 2

hypotenuse, and adjacent. Use the equation $\cos \theta = $ adjacent/hypotenuse. which is given on Reference Table: Geometry and Trigonometry.

$$\cos \theta = \frac{adjacent}{hypotenuse}$$

Substitute 30° for θ. Substitute 10 N for hypotenuse.

$$\cos 30° = \frac{adjacent}{10\ N}$$ Cos 30° = 0.866 (use calculator:
press 30, then press cos)

$$0.866 = \frac{adjacent}{10\ N}$$

Cross multiply
(0.866)(10 N) = adjacent
Adjacent = 8.66 N
Horizontal component or horizontal vector (adjacent) = 8.66 N

Rule: To find the horizontal vector, use the equation
   $$A_x = A \cos \theta$$

or   cosine $\theta = \frac{adjacent}{hypotenuse}$. Adjacent side is the horizontal vector.

Question: A child kicks a ball with an initial velocity of 8.5 meters per second at an angle of 35° with the horizontal, as shown. The ball has an initial vertical velocity of 4.9 meters per second and a total time of flight of 1.0 second. [Neglect air resistance.] The horizontal component of the ball's velocity is approximately

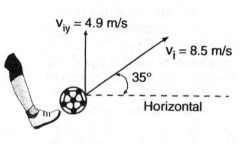

   (1) 3.6 m/s   (2) 4.9 m/s   (3) 7.0 m/s   (4) 13 m/s

Solution:
Given: v_i = 8.5 m/s
   $\theta = 35°$
Find: The horizontal component (A_x).
The resultant, 8.5 m/s, is broken down into the horizontal component (vector) and the vertical component (vector).

Look for an equation on Reference Table: Mechanics that has horizontal vector. The reference table says **A** = any **vector** quantity. A_x means **horizontal vector**.

Use the equation on Reference Table: Mechanics that begins with A_x.

$$A_x = A \quad \cos \theta$$

horizontal component = resultant x cos of angle between resultant and horizontal.

A refers to the resultant (8.5 m/s).
$\theta = 35°$

$A_x = A \quad \cos \theta$
Substitute for A (resultant)
8.5 m/s. **Substitute for** θ
35°.

$A_x = (8.5 \text{ m/s})(\cos 35°)$
$\cos 35° = .819$
$A_x = (8.5 \text{ m/s})(.819) =$
6.95 Since the number after
the 9 in 6.95 is 5 or more,
increase the previous digit
(the 9) by 1. A_x (horizontal component) rounded to the nearest
tenth = 7.0 m/s.

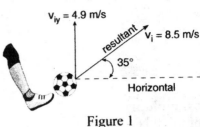

$V_{iy} = 4.9$ m/s

resultant

$V_i = 8.5$ m/s

35°

Horizontal

Figure 1

Answer 3

OR

Look at Figure 1 at right and
draw a line from the resultant,
perpendicular to the horizontal
line, to complete a right
triangle. See figure 2.
You know θ (angle) equals 35°
(given). You know hypotenuse
equals 8.5 m/s (given). Find the
horizontal vector, the **adjacent**
side, the side touching angle
θ, which is the base of the
triangle. You know θ and you
know **hypotenuse** and you
need to find **adjacent**
(horizontal vector), therefore,
use the equation that has θ,
hypotenuse, and adjacent. Use
the equation $\cos \theta =$
adjacent/hypotenuse. which is
given on Reference Table:
Geometry and Trigonometry.

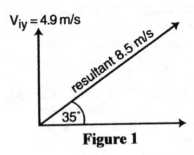

$V_{iy} = 4.9$ m/s

resultant 8.5 m/s

35°

Figure 1

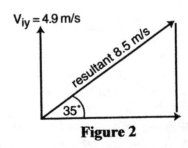

$V_{iy} = 4.9$ m/s

resultant 8.5 m/s

35°

Figure 2

$$\text{Cos } \theta = \frac{adjacent}{hypotenuse}$$

Substitute 35° for θ. Substitute 8.5 m/s for hypotenuse.

$$\text{Cos } 35° = \frac{adjacent}{8.5 \ m/s}$$ Cos 35° = 0.819 (use calculator:

press 35, then press cos)

$$0.819 = \frac{adjacent}{8.5 \ m/s}$$

Cross multiply
(0.819)(8.5 m/s) = adjacent
Adjacent = 6.95 m/s
Horizontal vector (adjacent) = 6.95 m/s

Horizontal component = 6.95 m/s.   Since the number after the 9
in 6.95 is 5 or more, increase the previous digit (the 9) by 1. A_x
(horizontal component) rounded to the nearest tenth = 7.0 m/s

Answer 3

Rule: To find the horizontal vector, use the equation
$$A_x = A \cos \theta$$

or   cosine $\theta = \frac{adjacent}{hypotenuse}$. Adjacent side is the horizontal vector.

Question: The diagram below shows a force of magnitude F applied
to a mass at angle θ relative to a horizontal frictionless surface.

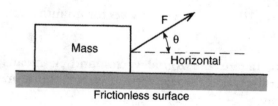

Frictionless surface

As angle θ is increased, the horizontal acceleration of the mass
   (1) decreases   (2) increases   (3) remains the same
Solution: As angle θ increases, more force goes into the vertical
component and less goes into the horizontal. Since F = ma, when
mass is constant, if more F (force) goes into the vertical, more
a (acceleration} would go into the vertical. The vertical component
increases and the horizontal component decreases.   *Answer 1*

Question: The resultant is a 10 N force. There is a 30° angle between the resultant and the horizontal. Find the vertical force.

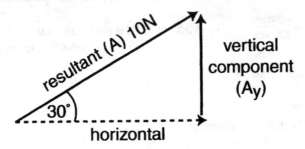

resultant (A) 10N

vertical component (A$_y$)

30°

horizontal

Solution:
Given: 10 N resultant force
       30° angle between resultant and horizontal
Find: Vertical force
The 10 N resultant can be broken down into two parts, the horizontal component (horizontal force or horizontal vector) and the vertical component (vertical force or vertical vector). This question asks to find the vertical force, which means vertical vector (see figure above).

Look for an equation on Reference Table: Mechanics that has vertical vector. The reference table says A = any vector quantity. There are two equations on Reference Table: Mechanics with the letter A.

$$A_y = A \sin \theta \qquad A = \text{any vector quantity}$$
$$A_x = A \cos \theta \qquad \theta = \text{angle}$$

You can see A$_x$ means horizontal vector and A$_y$ means vertical vector. The question asks for the vertical vector, therefore use the equation
$$A_y = A \sin \theta.$$
Look above at the figure and the equation.

A_y	=	A	$\sin \theta$
vertical vector	=	resultant x	sin of angle between
			resultant and horizontal

$$A_y = A \ \sin \theta.$$
Substitute for A (resultant) 10 N. *Substitute for* θ (angle between resultant and horizontal) 30°.

$A_y = (10 \text{ N}) (\sin 30)$ Sin 30 = 0.500 (use calculator: press 30, then press sin)

$A_y = (10 \text{ N}) (0.500) = 5.00 \text{ N}$
$A_y = $ vertical component (vertical vector) = 5.00 N(newtons).

Table: Mechanics

OR

Look at the figure below.

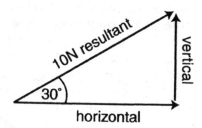

You know θ (angle) equals 30° (given). You know hypotenuse equals 10 N (given). Find the **vertical vector**, the side **opposite** angle θ, which is the height of the triangle. You know θ and you know **hypotenuse** and you need to find **opposite** (vertical vector), therefore, use the equation that has θ, hypotenuse, and opposite. Use the equation

$\sin θ = \frac{opposite}{hypotenuse}$, which is given on Reference Table: Geometry and Trigonometry.

Substitute 30° for θ. Substitute 10 N for hypotenuse.

$Sin\ 30° = \frac{opposite}{10\ N}$ 　　　　　Sin 30° = 0.500 (use calculator: press 30, then press sin)

$0.500 = \frac{opposite}{10\ N}$

Cross multiply
(0.500)(10 N) = opposite
Opposite = 5.00 N
Vertical component or vertical vector (opposite) = 5.00 N

Rule: To find the vertical vector, use the equation
　　　$A_y = A \sin θ$

or　　$\sin θ = \frac{opposite}{hypotenuse}$. Opposite side is the vertical vector.

Question: A cannon elevated at an angle of 35° to the horizontal fires a cannonball, which follows the path shown in the diagram.

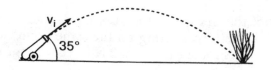

[Neglect air resistance and assume the ball lands at the same height above the ground from which it was launched.]

If the angle of elevation of the cannon is decreased from 35° to 30°, the vertical component of the ball's initial velocity will

   (1) decrease and its horizontal component will decrease
   (2) decrease and its horizontal component will increase
   (3) increase and its horizontal component will decrease
   (4) increase and its horizontal component will increase

Solution: As the angle of elevation decreases, more velocity or more force goes into the horizontal component and less goes into the vertical. The horizontal component increases and the vertical component decreases.

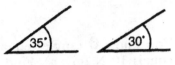

   Answer 2

Question: A vector makes an angle, θ, with the horizontal. The horizontal and vertical components of the vector will be equal in magnitude if angle θ is

   (1) 30°   (2) 45°   (3) 60°   (4) 90°

Solution:

Given: Vector makes angle θ with the horizontal. Horizontal and vertical components of the vector are equal in magnitude

Find: angle θ.

The horizontal and vertical components of a vector are always at right angles to each other (90° angle). Therefore, this is a right triangle (one angle is 90°).

Since the horizontal and vertical components are equal (given), it is an isosceles right triangle, and the two other angles are equal.

As you know, in a triangle, the sum of the angles is 180°. 90° is the right angle; the remaining 90° is divided equally between the two other angles. Each angle equals 45°.

Angle θ = 45°.   Answer 2

Now Do Homework Questions #95-101, pages 147-148.

Section 4:

EQUILIBRIUM

At **equilibrium**, the **net** force (the sum of all concurrent forces, which means all the forces acting on the same point) must **equal zero** (example: a 2 N force east and a 2 N force west means the net

---

force = 0) ; there is **no unbalanced** force (**no extra force**, example: 2N force or 3N force more, in any direction). The object is at **equilibrium**, which means the object is **at rest** or moving at **constant** velocity.

Question: If the sum of all the forces acting on a moving object is zero, the object will
(1) slow down and stop
(2) change the direction of its motion
(3) accelerate uniformly
(4) continue moving with constant velocity

Solution: If **all the forces** balance each other, the net force (total force) **= 0,** and the **object** is **at equilibrium**; the object is either at rest or keeps **moving at constant velocity.**   Answer 4

Question: What is an essential characteristic of an object in equilibrium?
(1) zero velocity
(2) zero acceleration
(3) zero potential energy
(4) zero kinetic energy

Solution: At equilibrium, an object is at rest or moves at constant velocity (velocity does not change, no change or zero change in velocity).
Acceleration is **change** in **velocity** or speed over time:

$$a = \frac{\Delta v}{t}$$

At **equilibrium,** there is **NO change** in **velocity**, which means **NO** or **zero acceleration.**   Answer 2

Question: An airplane is moving with a constant velocity in level flight. Compare the magnitude of the forward force provided by the engines to the magnitude of the backward frictional drag force.
Solution: At **constant velocity**, there is no unbalanced force (no extra force), which means the forward force (provided by the engines) equals the backward force (caused by friction).

Question: In the diagram below, a box is on a frictionless horizontal surface with forces F_1 and F_2 acting as shown.

F_2 ◄——— box ——►F_1

_____
Frictionless surface
If the magnitude of F_1 is greater than the magnitude of F_2, then the box is
(1) moving at constant speed in the direction of F_1
(2) moving at constant speed in the direction of F_2
(3) accelerating in the direction of F_1
(4) accelerating in the direction of F_2

Solution: F_1 is greater than F_2; therefore, the forces are not equal to zero. There is an extra (concurrent) force and the box accelerates in the direction of F_1 (bigger force).   Answer 3

Question: Which graph best represents the motion of an object that is *not* in equilibrium as it travels along a straight line?

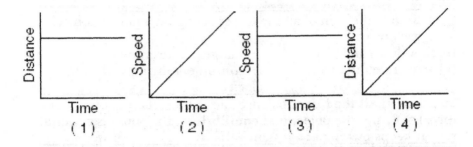

(1)   (2)   (3)   (4)

Solution: Review the graphs in this chapter, pages 10 and 12, and look at the graphs above. When the object is at rest or moves at constant velocity (speed does not change and direction does not change), it is in equilibrium. The **question** asks **which graph** shows an object **not in equilibrium.**

Choice *2* is the correct answer. The graph shows as time increases, speed increases. **Equilibrium** is when **speed**/velocity (of an object) **is constant** or the object is at rest. In **choice *2*, speed** increases (**not constant**) as time increases, therefore, the object is **not in equilibrium.**

Answer 2

Wrong Choices:
Choice *1* As time increases, the distance remains the same. The object is **at rest** or **standing still**; the object is **in equilibrium**.
Choice *3* As time increases, speed is constant. It is in equilibrium.

Choice *4* You learned $\bar{v} = \dfrac{d}{t}$. The graph shows as time increases,

distance increases proportionately. On a distance vs. time graph, a straight line shows constant speed. It has constant speed, therefore it is in equilibrium.

Question: Which combination of three concurrent forces acting on a body could *not* produce equilibrium?
    (1) 1 N, 3 N, 5 N   (2) 2 N, 2 N, 2 N
    (3) 3 N, 4 N, 5 N   (4) 4 N, 4 N, 5N

Solution:
When two forces are in the same direction (0° apart ➤ ➤), they have the largest resultant; add the forces together to get the total force (example: 10 N + 7 N = 17 N).
When two forces are in opposite directions (180° apart ➤ ◄), they have the smallest resultant; subtract the forces to get the total force (example: 10 N − 7 N = 3 N).

When two forces(example: 10 N and 7 N) are between 0° and 180° apart, the resultant is between the largest resultant (17 N) and smallest resultant (3 N).

Choice 1: If there is a 1 N force and a 3 N force on one point in the same direction (0° apart), they have the largest resultant; add the forces together to get the total net force: 1 N + 3 N = 4 N.

If there is a 1 N force and a 3 N force on one point in opposite directions (180° apart), they have the smallest resultant ; subtract the forces to get the total net force: 3 N − 1 N = 2 N.

If the two forces are between 0° and 180° apart, the resultant (total force) of the two forces on one point is between 2 N and 4 N.

The **resultant** (in this example, total force) of the two forces can be **2 N, 2 N to 4 N, or 4 N.** The question asks which choice cannot produce equilibrium. At **equilibrium,** all the forces are balanced; there is **no extra force in any direction** and all the forces together equal zero. Therefore, at equilibrium, the **third force** must be the same amount or equal to the resultant (total net force) of the other two forces (**2 N, 2 N to 4 N, or 4 N** - see above) but pulling in the **opposite direction**.

In choice 1, the third force given is 5 N. At equilibrium, the third force must be 2 N, 2 N to 4 N, or 4 N, therefore, 5 N cannot produce equilibrium.   Answer 1

Example of wrong choice: Choice 2: Forces are 2 N, 2N, and 2 N.

$$2 N + 2N = 4N \text{ maximum (largest) resultant}$$
$$2 N - 2 N = 0 N \text{ minimum (smallest) resultant}$$

The resultant of the two forces can be 0 N, 0 N to 4 N, or 4 N. The third force, 2 N, can equal the resultant, but pull in the opposite direction, so that all three forces (resultant of the two forces plus the third force pulling in the opposite direction) can equal zero; choice 2 can produce equilibrium.

Now Do Homework Questions #102-105, pages 148-149

NEWTON'S THREE LAWS OF MOTION

Newton's First Law:

An **object at rest remains at rest** or an **object that moves will continue to move at constant velocity** unless (until) an unbalanced force (an extra force) acts on it. If there is no unbalanced force (no extra force in any direction-all the forces balance each other) and the **net force = zero,** the object then either remains **at rest** or keeps moving at **constant velocity.** The object is in equilibrium.

When the **object** is at **rest,** it is at **static equilibrium.** When the **object moves** with **constant velocity** (constant speed in a straight line) it is called **dynamic equilibrium.**

Question: A ball rolls through a hollow semi-circular tube lying flat on a horizontal tabletop. Which diagram best shows the path of the ball after emerging from the tube, as viewed from above?

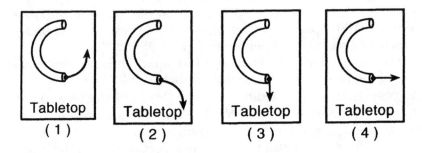

Solution: You learned that an object continues to move at constant velocity (same speed and same direction) unless an unbalanced force acts on it. When the ball comes out of the tube there is no outside force acting on it, therefore the ball continues to move at the same velocity (same direction, same speed) as when it left the tube.   Answer *4*

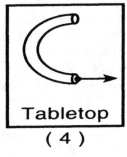

Inertia is how much an object **resists change in motion**. The **more mass**, the **more inertia**, the **more** it will **not change** (its velocity or its position-where it is) or it will **change less**.

Question: Which object has the most inertia?
     (1) a 0.001-kilogram bumblebee traveling at 2 meters per second
     (2) a 0.1-kilogram baseball traveling at 20 meters per second
     (3) a 5-kilogram bowling ball traveling at 3 meters per second
     (4) a 10-kilogram sled at rest

Solution: The object with the **most mass** has the **most inertia**. You can see on Reference Table: List of Physical Constants that **kilograms** (kg) are a unit of **mass** (example given on the reference table: **Mass of Earth = 5.98×10^{24} kg**).
Choice 4 has the **most mass** (10 kg), therefore it has the most inertia.
Note: Grams(g), milligrams (mg), etc. are also (units of) mass.
                                           Answer *4*

Question: Compared to the inertia of a 0.10-kilogram steel ball, the inertia of a 0.20-kilogram Styrofoam ball is
    (1) one-half as great   (2) twice as great
    (3) the same   (4) four times as great

Solution: Inertia is directly proportional to mass; the more mass, the more inertia. Kilogram (kg) is a unit of mass. A 0.20-kilogram (Styrofoam) ball has **twice the mass** of a 0.10-kilogram (steel) ball, therefore, the 0.20-kilogram ball has **twice the inertia**.

Now do Homework Questions #106-112, pages 149-150.

Newton's Second Law:

$$F_{net} = m\ a \qquad OR \qquad a = \frac{F_{net}}{m}$$

Net force = mass x acceleration $acceleration = \frac{net\ force}{mass}$

$$a = \frac{F_{net}}{m}$$

a= acceleration

f_{net} = net force
m = mass

From the equation $a = \dfrac{F_{net}}{m}$, **when m (mass) is constant,** you can see

a (acceleration) is directly proportional to the F$_{net}$ (net force or total force). Some of the forces balance out (when two forces go in opposite directions, example: +5 N and −5 N), therefore the acceleration is directly proportional to the extra unbalanced force and inversely proportional to mass.

F (force) is in newtons, m (mass) is in kilograms and a (acceleration) is in meters per second^2 (m/s^2) .

$$F_{net} = m\ a$$

1 newton = 1 kg   m/s^2

Question: The diagram below shows a horizontal 8.0 newton force applied to a 4.0 kilogram block on a frictionless table.

What is the magnitude of the block's acceleration?

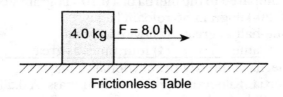

Frictionless Table

(1) 0.50 m/s²   (2) 2.0 m/s²   (3) 9.8 m/s²   (4) 32 m/s²

Solution:
Given: Force = 8.0 newtons (N)
         4.0 kilogram (kg) block on a frictionless table
Find: acceleration (a).
A kilogram (kg) is a unit of mass (see example given on **Reference Table**: List of Physical Constants: Mass of Earth = 5.98 x 10²⁴ kg).
4.0 kg block means mass (of the block) is 4.0 kg.
In short, you know F (force) = 8.0 N (given), m (mass) = 4.0 kg.

You know two things, F and m, and there is one unknown, a, therefore *look for an equation* on Reference Table: Mechanics that has F, m and a.

Use the equation

$$a = \frac{F_{net}}{m}$$ a = acceleration

                        F_{net} = net force
                        m = mass

Substitute for F (force) 8.0 N (newtons). *Substitute for m* (mass) 4.0 kg (kilograms).

$$a = \frac{8.0\ N\ or\ 8.0\ kg{\cdot}m/s^2}{4.0\ kg} = 2.0\ m/s^2 \quad \text{Answer 2}$$

Question: Which unit is equivalent to a newton per kilogram?

(1) $\dfrac{m}{s^2}$ (2) $\dfrac{W}{m}$ (3) J•s   (4) $\dfrac{kg{\cdot}m}{s}$

Solution:
Given: newton per kilogram

Find: equivalent for newton per kilogram ($\dfrac{N}{kg}$).

Force (F) is given in newtons (N). $a = \dfrac{F}{m}$ or F = ma

$$\begin{array}{llll} \text{Force} & = \text{mass} & \text{x} & \text{acceleration} \\ \text{in \textbf{newtons}} & \text{in \textbf{kg}} & & \text{in \textbf{m/s}}^2 \end{array}$$

The question asks which is equivalent to newtons per kilogram ($\frac{N}{kg}$). From the equation above showing force in newtons, you see newton = $kg \bullet m/s^2$. *Substitute for newton* $kg \bullet m/s^2$.

$$\frac{newtons\ (N)}{kilograms\ (kg)} = \frac{kg \bullet m/s^2}{kg} = \frac{m}{s^2} \qquad \text{Answer 1}$$

Or

You can see $\dfrac{newtons}{kilograms}$ means $\dfrac{F\ (force)}{m\ (mass)}$ which equals a (acceleration).

$$a = \frac{F}{m}$$ a (acceleration) is in m/s², therefore $\dfrac{F}{m}$ (which equals a) is in m/s². $\qquad$ Answer 1

Question: A 40-kilogram mass is moving across a horizontal surface at 5.0 meters per second. What is the magnitude of the net force required to bring the mass to a stop in 8.0 seconds?

(1) 1.0 N (2) 5.0 N (3) 25 N (4) 40. N

Solution:

Given: Mass = 40 kilogram (kg).

Mass moves across a surface at 5.0 meters per second.

Mass comes to a stop in 8.0 seconds.

Mass comes to a stop, which means final velocity equals zero.

Find: **Net force** required to bring mass to a stop in 8.0 seconds.

The question asked for net force (F_{net}). *Look for an equation* on Reference Table: Mechanics that has F_{net}.

Use the equation

$$a = \frac{F_{net}}{m}$$ a = acceleration

F_{net} = net force
m = mass

You need to find F_{net} (you don't know F_{net}) and you don't know acceleration (a). You have 2 unknowns, F_{net} (net force) and a (acceleration), therefore, *first find a (acceleration)* and *then substitute a* in the equation, $a = \dfrac{F_{net}}{m}$ to find F_{net} (net force).

First find acceleration.

Table: Mechanics

You know v, velocity (v_f, which means final velocity and v_i, which means initial or starting velocity), and t (time).
Look for an equation with acceleration (a), velocity (v), and time (t).

Use either equation:

$$a = \frac{\Delta v}{t} \qquad \text{Or} \qquad v_f = v_i + at$$

Method 1: to **find acceleration (a)** you can use this equation.

$$a = \frac{\Delta v}{t}$$

a = acceleration

t = time interval
v = velocity/speed
Δ = change

$$a = \frac{\Delta v \ (change \ in \ velocity)}{t \ (time)} = \frac{v_f - v_i}{t}.$$

v_i (starting or initial velocity of the moving mass) = 5.0 m/s (meters/second) (given).
v_f (final velocity, when mass **stops**) = 0 m/s.
Remember: When an object (example: mass or car) comes to a stop or an object is at rest, velocity = 0 m/s.
t (time) = 8.0 s (seconds).

In the equation $a = \dfrac{\Delta v}{t} = \dfrac{v_f - v_i}{t}$, *substitute for v_f* 0 m/s.

Substitute for v_i 5.0 m/s. *Substitute for t* 8.0 s (seconds) .

$$a = \frac{0 \ m/s - 5.0 \ m/s}{8.0 \ s} = \frac{-5.0}{8.0} \ m/s^2$$

Method 2: Or, to **find acceleration** you can use the equation $v_f = v_i + at$.
Substitute for v_f 0 m/s. *Substitute for v_i* 5.0 m/s. *Substitute for t* 8.0 s.

$v_f = v_i + at.$

0 m/s = 5.0 m/s + a (8.0 s)

-5.0 m/s = a (8.0 s)

a (acceleration) $= -\dfrac{5.0 \ m/s}{8.0 \ s}$

$= -\dfrac{5.0}{8.0} \ m/s^2$

Or, rearrange the equation

$a = \dfrac{v_f - v_i}{t}$

$a = \dfrac{0 \ m/s - 5.0 \ m/s}{8.0 \ s}$

$a = -\dfrac{5.0}{8.0} \ m/s^2$

You found acceleration (a) $= -\dfrac{5.0}{8.0} \ m/s^2$ (using either method 1 or method 2).

Then, in the equation a $= \dfrac{F_{net}}{m}$, *substitute for a* (acceleration) $-\dfrac{5.0}{8.0} \ m/s^2$ (calculated above). **Substitute for m** (mass) 40 kg (given).

a $= \dfrac{F_{net}}{m}$

$-\dfrac{5.0}{8.0} \ m/s^2 = \dfrac{F_{net}}{40 \ kg}$

Cross multiply
-200 kg•m/s^2 = 8.0 F_{net}
-25 kg•m/s^2 = F_{net}
$F_{net} = -25$ kg•m/s^2 = -25 N
Force is negative because the force brings it to a stop (opposite direction).

Or, rearrange the equation.
$F_{net} = m \quad a$

$F_{net} = 40$ kg $(-\dfrac{5.0}{8.0} \ m/s^2)$

$F_{net} = -\dfrac{200 \ kg \cdot m/s^2}{8.0}$

$F_{net} = -25$ kg•m/s^2 = -25 N
Force is negative because the force brings it to a stop (opposite direction).

Question: A net force of 10. newtons accelerates an object at 5.0 meters per second^2. What net force would be required to accelerate the same object at 1.0 meter/second^2?

    (1) 1.0 newton   (2) 2.0 newton
    (3) 5.0 newton   (4) 50. newton

Solution:
Given: Net force of 10. newtons (N).
        Acceleration = 5.0 meters per second^2.
Find: Net force to accelerate the same object at 1.0 meter/second^2.

Look for an equation on Reference Table: Mechanics that has net force (F_{net}).

Use the equation $a = \dfrac{F_{net}}{m}$

Acceleration (a) = 5.0 m/s²:

$$a = \frac{F_{net}}{m}$$

Acceleration (a) = 1.0 m/s²:

$$a = \frac{F_{net}}{m}$$

Since the object is the same (**mass** is the **same**) at 5.0 m/s² and 1.0 m/s², first rearrange the equations to m (mass) = $\dfrac{F_{net}}{a}$, then set both equations equal to each other and solve for force (F) required at 1.0 m/s².

At 5.0 m/s²:

First, $m = \dfrac{F_{net}}{a}$

$$m = \frac{10.\ N}{5.0\ m/s^2}$$

At 1.0 m/s²

$$m = \frac{F_{net}}{a}$$

Let x = force required at 1.0 m/s²

$$m = \frac{x\ N}{1.0\ m/s^2}$$

Then, since both fractions ($\dfrac{10.}{5.0}$ and $\dfrac{x}{1.0}$) are equal to the same mass (m), you can make the two fractions equal to each other.

$$\frac{10.}{5.0} = \frac{x}{1.0}$$

Cross multiply

5.0 x = 10.

x = 2.0 N   Net force required at 1.0 m/s² = 2.0 N   Answer 2

Question: A constant unbalanced force is applied to an object for a period of time. The graph should represent the acceleration of the object as a function of time.

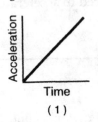

Time

(1)

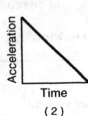

Time

(2)

Time

(3)

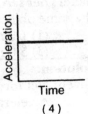

Time

(4)

Solution:

Look for an equation on Reference Table: Mechanics with force and acceleration.

Use the equation $a = \dfrac{F_{net}}{m}$ or rearrange the equation, $F_{net} = ma$.

Force (F) is constant (given), and, obviously, mass (m) of the object is constant.

Look at the equation $F_{net} = ma$. If F_{net} is constant (a specific number) and m is constant (a specific number), then obviously a (acceleration) is constant (a specific number).

$$
\begin{array}{ccccc}
F_{net} & = & m & & a \\
\text{constant} & & \text{constant} & then & \text{constant}
\end{array}
$$

In the graph in choice 4, the line for acceleration is straight across, which means acceleration is constant (a specific number). Answer *4*

Now do Homework Questions #113-125, pages 150-152.

Newton's Third Law:
For **every action**, there is an **equal and opposite reaction.**

Examples:
1. Rocket

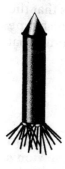

Action: gases go out↓ =
Reaction: rocket goes up↑.

2. Balloon **Action**: air goes out. **Reaction**: balloon moves horizontally.

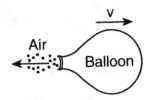

3. Soccer ball hits a student's foot: **Action**: soccer ball exerts a force on student's foot.
Reaction: student's foot exerts an equal force on the soccer ball, but in the opposite direction.

Question: The magnitude of the force that a baseball bat exerts on a ball is 50. newtons. The magnitude of the force that the ball exerts on the bat is

    (1) 5.0 N   (2) 10. N   (3) 50. N   (4) 250 N

Solution: Newton's Third Law: For every action (example: **bat exerts a 50. N force on** the **ball**-given) there is an equal and opposite reaction (equal: ball exerts a 50. N force on the bat, and opposite reaction: ball exerts force on the bat in the opposite direction.)
                                       Answer *3*

Question: A man standing on a scale in an elevator notices that the scale reads 30 newtons greater than his normal weight. Which type of movement of the elevator would cause this greater-than-normal reading?

    (1) accelerating upward
    (2) accelerating downward
    (3) moving upward at constant speed
    (4) moving downward at constant speed

Solution: The **elevator** is **accelerating upward** under the man and exerting a force upward under him. Then, according to **Newton's Third Law** (for every action, there is an equal and opposite reaction), the **man exerts** a **downward force** on the elevator, **causing** the **scale** to **read more.**   Answer *1*

Note: If, however, the elevator was accelerating downward instead of upward, the result would be opposite. The elevator is moving away from the man and there is less force pushing upward under the man. Therefore, the man exerts less force on the floor of the elevator and on the scale. The scale would read less than his actual weight.

Now Do Homework Questions #126-134, pages 152-153.

Section 5:

TWO-DIMENSIONAL MOTION

Two-Dimensional Motion: When an **object** is **moving** both **horizontally** (left to right or right to left) **and vertically** (going up or going down) **at the same time,** (example: a ball thrown- the ball goes horizontally and vertically down to the ground at the same time) we separate its motion (how it moves) into horizontal and vertical (components of) displacement, velocity, and acceleration.

I. PROJECTILE (OBJECT) FIRED HORIZONTALLY

Bullet fired (or rock thrown) horizontally from top of cliff

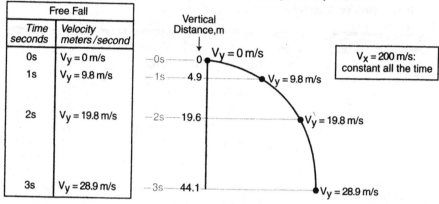

Free Fall		Vertical Distance, m
Time seconds	Velocity meters/second	
0s	$V_y = 0$ m/s	
1s	$V_y = 9.8$ m/s	
2s	$V_y = 19.8$ m/s	
3s	$V_y = 28.9$ m/s	

$V_x = 200$ m/s: constant all the time

An object **fired or thrown horizontally**, such as a **bullet fired horizontally** from a rifle at 200 meters/second or a **ball thrown horizontally** out a window, **moves both horizontally and vertically** (falls to the ground).

A bullet was fired horizontally at 200 meters/second (m/s):

1. **Initial horizontal velocity,** v_{ix} = 200 meters/second (v_i is initial velocity, starting velocity, x is horizontal). **Horizontal velocity remains constant. V_x = 200 meters/second** always in this example. Any v_x (horizontal velocity) remains constant. (See figure above.)

2. **Initial vertical velocity** v_{iy} = 0, **just like free fall.** (v_i is initial velocity, meaning starting velocity, y is vertical).

A bullet is fired (or rock thrown) horizontally; when the bullet (or rock) is falling down to the ground, treat the vertical velocity v_y like free fall, a rock dropping off a cliff. Therefore, v_{iy}, **initial vertical velocity =** **zero.** (See figure above.)

You learned free fall acceleration = 9.81 m/s². (Every second that the rock falls to the ground, the speed increases by 9.81 m/s.) When an **object** is **thrown horizontally,** the **object** also **falls down** to the ground with an **acceleration = 9.81 m/s² (just like in free fall).** (Every second the object which is thrown horizontally falls to the ground, its speed increases by 9.81 m/s.) See figure above.

In 1 second, just like in free fall, V_y (vertical velocity)= 9.81 meters/second, or, rounded, 10 meters/second.

In 2 seconds, V_y (vertical velocity) = 19.6 meters/second, or, rounded, 20 meters/second.(See figure on previous page.)

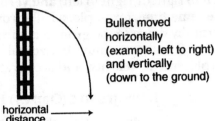

Bullet fired (or ball thrown) horizontally away from cliff or building

Bullet moved horizontally (example, left to right) and vertically (down to the ground)

As you can see, when a projectile (an object, example ball, bullet, etc.) is **thrown horizontally** off a cliff or building, etc.,the object **moves both horizontally** (example: away from cliff or building) **and vertically**(down to the ground).

horizontal distance

Question: A ball is projected horizontally to the right from a height of 50 meters, as shown in the diagram below.

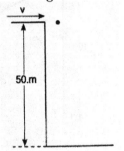

50.m

Which diagram best represents the position of the ball at 1.0-second intervals? [Neglect air resistance.]

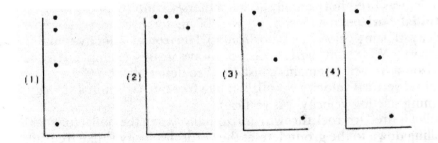

(1)   (2)   (3)   (4)

Solution: When the ball is thrown horizontally, it moves both horizontally (at constant velocity) and vertically (down to the ground, with acceleration = 9.81m/s^2.)

Choice 4 shows the ball moves horizontally at constant velocity and, vertically, the ball is accelerating. The horizontal distance increases by the same amount each second (from 1 second to 2 seconds, from 2 seconds to 3 seconds, or from 3 seconds to 4 seconds). Horizontal velocity is constant.

The vertical distance that the ball goes down each second increases. From the first to the second second (from the first dot to the second dot on the graph), the ball goes vertically down a certain distance. From the second second to the third second (from the second dot to the third dot on the graph), the ball goes vertically down even a bigger distance than in the previous second. From the third to the fourth second (from the third to the fourth dot on the graph), the vertical distance is even more, because the ball is accelerating.

Answer 4

Wrong choices:

Choice 1: It has no horizontal velocity, only vertical acceleration.

Choice 2: For the first three seconds, there is constant horizontal velocity (the horizontal distance moved each second is the same) but no vertical acceleration.

Choice 3: Horizontal velocity increases (not constant velocity). (The horizontal distance the ball moves each second keeps increasing.)

Questions 1, 2 and 3: Projectile A is launched horizontally at a velocity of 20. meters per second from the top of a cliff and strikes a level surface below, 3.0 seconds later. Projectile B is launched horizontally from the same location at a speed of 30 meters per second.

Question 1: What is the horizontal velocity of Projectile A just before it reaches the ground? [Neglect air resistance.]

    (1) 10. m/s   (2) 20. m/s   (3) 9.8 m/s   (4) 30. m/s

Question 2: The time it takes projectile B to reach the level surface is

    (1) 4.5 s   (2) 2.0 s   (3) 3.0 s   (4) 10. s

Question 3: Approximately how high is the cliff?

    (1) 29 m   (2) 44 m   (3) 60. m   (4) 104 m

Solution 1: Projectile A is launched horizontally at a velocity of 20. meters per second (m/s) from the top of a cliff (given). Horizontal velocity remains constant (stays the same) all the time, therefore the horizontal velocity of Projectile A just before it reaches the ground is also 20. meters per second (m/s).

Answer 2

Solution 2: In free fall or when an object is thrown horizontally, when **two objects** are thrown from the **same height** (example: projectile A and projectile B), they take the **same time** (because they have the same vertical velocity) to reach the ground. Therefore projectile B (just like projectile A) will take 3.0 seconds to reach the ground.

Answer 3.

Solution 3: When the question asks **height**, it means the **vertical distance d_y.**

Given: ball is thrown horizontally

Information **you know** in the **vertical direction**:

d_y shows height or distance in the vertical direction

v_{iy} means initial vertical velocity

$v_{iy} = 0$ This is true for any object dropped from the top of a cliff (free fall) or thrown horizontally.

(a) acceleration $= 9.81$ m/s^2

(t) time for projectile A to go from top of cliff to ground $=$ **3.0 seconds** (given); or **(t) time** for projectile B to go from top of cliff to ground $=$ **3.0 seconds** (from solution 2).

Find: vertical distance d_y.

You know three things, v_{iy}, a and t. There is one unknown, d_y (height), therefore *look for an equation* on Reference Table: Mechanics that has v_i, a and t.

Use the equation:

$$d = v_i t + \tfrac{1}{2}at^2.$$

To find height (vertical distance), write $d_y = v_{iy}t + \tfrac{1}{2}at^2.$

Use the equation

$$d_y = v_{iy}t + \tfrac{1}{2}at^2.$$

Substitute for v_{iy} 0. *Substitute for t* 3 seconds (given or from solution 2 on the previous page).

$$d_y = 0(3 \text{ s}) + \tfrac{1}{2}(9.81 \text{ m/s}^2)(3s)^2$$

$d_y = 0 \qquad + (4.9 \text{ m/s}^2)(9 \text{ s}^2)$

d_y (vertical distance) $= 44.1$ m

Distance $= 44.1$ m   Height of cliff $= 44.1$ m   Answer 2

Question: The diagram below shows the muzzle of a cannon located 50. meters above the ground. When the cannon is fired, a ball leaves the muzzle with an initial horizontal speed of 250. meters per second. [Neglect air resistance.]

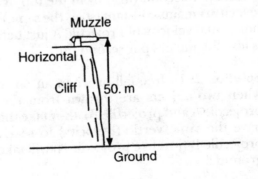

Which action would most likely increase the time of flight of a ball fired by the cannon?

    (1) pointing the muzzle of the cannon toward the ground
    (2) moving the cannon closer to the edge of the cliff
    (3) positioning the cannon higher above the ground
    (4) Giving the ball a greater initial horizontal velocity

Solution: You learned in free fall or when an object is thrown horizontally, when two objects are thrown from the same height, they take the same time to reach the ground.

But, **when** an **object is higher up**, it **takes more time** for the object **to reach** the **ground**; when an object is lower down, it takes less time for the object to reach the ground.   Answer 3

Question: The diagram shows a student throwing a baseball horizontally at 25 meters per second from a cliff 45 meters above the level ground. Approximately how far from the base of the cliff does the ball hit the ground?

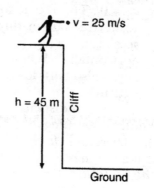

    (1) 45 meters
    (2) 75 meters
    (3) 145 meters
    (4) 230 meter

Solution:

Given: ball thrown horizontally
    horizontal velocity = 25 m/s

    height of cliff 45 m (meters) (given), means d_y (vertical distance) = 45 m (meters)

Find: how far from base of cliff does ball hit ground, which means **find** the **horizontal distance (d_x)** from base of cliff to where ball hits ground.

Look for an equation on Reference Table: Mechanics that has distance (d) and velocity (v).

Use the equation $\bar{v} = \dfrac{d}{t}$ or $d = v_i t + \frac{1}{2} a t^2$ to find horizontal distance.

Note: You cannot use $v_f^2 = v_i^2 + 2ad$. You know, in the horizontal direction, velocity is constant, which means there is zero acceleration, and therefore, in the equation above, $2ad = 0$ and you cannot solve for d.

Table: Mechanics

First find time (t) and then substitute t in the equation $v = \dfrac{d}{t}$ or d

$= v_i t + \frac{1}{2} at^2$ to find horizontal distance.

First find time. We cannot find the time the ball went horizontally, therefore we must find the time the ball went vertically. The **time** it takes the **ball** to **reach** the **ground** (time in the vertical direction) is **equal** to the **time** the ball **moves horizontally**.
Find the **TIME** it takes the ball to **HIT** the **GROUND VERTICALLY** because it **EQUALS** the **TIME** the ball traveled **HORIZONTALLY**.

Information **you know** in the **vertical direction**:

v_{iy} means initial vertical velocity.
$v_{iy} = 0$. This is true for any object dropped from the top of a cliff (free fall) or thrown horizontally.
acceleration (a) = 9.81 m/s² (in free fall or thrown horizontally). When an object is thrown horizontally, the object also falls down to the ground with an acceleration = 9.81 m/s².
d_y (vertical distance) = 45 m (given).

You know three things, v_i, d, and a and there is one unknown, t (time), therefore *look for an equation* on Reference Table: Mechanics that has v_i, a, t and d.
Use the equation $d = v_i t + \frac{1}{2} at^2$
Substitute for d_y (vertical distance) 45 m. *Substitute for* v_{iy} 0.
Substitute for a (acceleration) 9.81 m/s².

$$d = v_i t + \frac{1}{2} \; a \quad t^2 \quad \text{note: t (time) is in seconds (s)}$$

$$45 \text{ m} = 0t + \frac{1}{2}(9.81 \text{m/s}^2)t^2 \text{ (s)}^2 \quad \text{note: } t^2 \text{ is in seconds}^2 \text{ (s}^2\text{)}$$

$$45 \text{ m} = 0 + 4.9 \text{ mt}^2$$

$$\frac{45 \; m}{4.9 \; m} = \frac{4.9 \; mt^2}{4.9 \; m}$$

$$9 = t^2$$
$$3 = t$$
$$t = 3 \text{ s}$$

Time (t) for the ball to hit the ground **vertically** = **time (t)** the ball went **horizontally** = **3 s (seconds)**.

The **QUESTION** asks to find **HORIZONTAL DISTANCE**. You know the velocity in the horizontal direction is constant, 25 m/s (given). You know the time the ball went horizontally = 3 s (seconds) (from previous part of solution).
Substitute these numbers in the equations below:
As you saw in the beginning of the problem, use the equations

$$\overline{v} = \frac{d}{t}$$

or, rearrange the equation:

$$d = \overline{v}t \text{ or } d_x = \overline{v}_x t.$$

d_x means horizontal distance (how far from the base of the cliff).

Since horizontal velocity is

constant, $\overline{v}$ equals 25 m/s. Then,

substitute for $\overline{v}$ 25 m/s (given).

Substitute for t 3 s (from previous part of solution).

$$d = \overline{v} \quad t$$

$$d = (25 \text{ m/s})(3 \text{ s}) = 75 \text{ m}$$

OR $d = v_i t + \frac{1}{2}at^2$.

Horizontal has no acceleration (zero acceleration), therefore $\frac{1}{2}at^2 = 0$.

Since horizontal velocity is constant, v_i equals 25 m/s. *Then, substitute for v_i* 25 m/s (given). *Substitute for t* 3 s (from previous part of solution). *Substitute for* $\frac{1}{2}at^2$ 0.

$$d_x = v_i t + \frac{1}{2}at^2$$
$$d_x = 25\text{m/s}(3\text{s}) + 0 = 75\text{m}$$

Distance from base of cliff to where ball hits the ground (horizontal distance) is 75 meters (m).   Answer 2

Now do Homework Questions #135-153, pages 153-156.

II. PROJECTILE FIRED AT AN ANGLE

A boy throws a baseball at an angle of 30° above the horizontal. The ball goes up in the air and then comes down. The path the ball travels is a parabola.

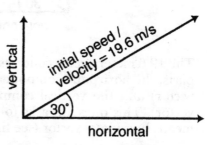

Path of Ball

When the ball goes up in the air or comes down, the horizontal velocity v_x is constant. As the ball goes up in the air, the **vertical velocity** gradually **decreases** to **zero** at the **highest point.** Vertical velocity **increases** as the ball **goes down,** because the force of gravity is pulling it down.

You learned, on pages 1:45-1:51, when you are given the resultant, you can find the horizontal and vertical components (example, horizontal and vertical velocity).

A boy throws a baseball with an initial speed of 19.6 meters per second at an angle of 30° above the

initial speed / velocity = 19.6 m/s

vertical

30°

horizontal

horizontal. Initial speed of 19.6 m/s is the resultant. You can **resolve** (separate) the initial velocity (example: 19.6 m/s) into its horizontal and vertical components (horizontal and vertical velocities) (see figure on the previous page).

To find the horizontal and vertical components (horizontal and vertical velocities), use the equations given below or on Reference Table: Mechanics:

$A_y = A \sin \theta$ $A =$ any vector quantity
$A_x = A \cos \theta$ $\theta =$ angle

Realize: $A =$ any vector quantity, which can be velocity, force, displacement, etc. (Example: A is the resultant, velocity of 19.6 m/s). Look at the figure on the previous page.
A_x means horizontal component (vector).
A_y means vertical component (vector)
θ is the angle between the resultant and the horizontal component (vector), which is 30°.

FINDING HORIZONTAL COMPONENT

Question: An outfielder throws a baseball to the first baseman at a speed of 19.6 meters per second and an angle of 30° above the horizontal. What is the initial horizontal velocity (v_x) of the baseball?

(1) $v_x = 17.0$ m/s   (2) $v_x = 9.80$ m/s
(3) $v_x = 19.4$ m/s   (4) $v_x = 19.6$ m/s

Solution:
Given: Baseball is thrown at a speed of 19.6 m/s.
         Angle is 30° above horizontal
Find: Initial horizontal velocity.

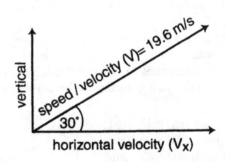

The 19.6 meters per second resultant can be broken down into two parts, the horizontal component (horizontal velocity or horizontal vector) and the vertical component (vertical velocity or vertical vector). This question asks to find the horizontal velocity, which means horizontal vector (see figure above).

Look for an equation on Reference Table: Mechanics that has horizontal vector. The reference table says A = vector. There are two equations on Reference Table: Mechanics with the letter A.

$A_y = A \sin \theta$

$A_x = A \cos \theta$

You can see A_x means horizontal vector and A_y means vertical vector. The question asks for the horizontal vector, therefore use the equation

$A_x = A \cos \theta$.

Look at the figure on the previous page and the equation.

A_x = A $\cos \theta$

horizontal component = resultant x cos of angle between resultant and horizontal.

$A_x = A \cos \theta$.

Substitute for A (resultant) 19.6 m/s. *Substitute for* θ (angle between resultant and horizontal) 30°.

$A_x = (19.6 \text{ m/s}) (\cos 30)$ Cos 30 = 0.866

$A_x = (19.6) (0.866) = 17.0 \text{ m/s}$

A_x = horizontal component (horizontal vector) = 17.0 m/s.

Answer 1

Reference table mechanics gives a generalized formula $A_x = A \cos \theta$ to find the horizontal component of any vector quantity [example: force (f), acceleration (a), velocity (v), displacement (d) etc.]. A = any vector quantity . You can see

Let v_x = initial horizontal velocity, then $v_x = v \cos \theta$

$v_x = (19.6 \text{ m/s})(\cos 30)$

or   Let v_{ix} = initial horizontal velocity then $v_{ix} = v_i \cos \theta$

$v_{ix} = (19.6 \text{ m/s})(\cos 30)$

Let F_x = horizontal force

$F_x = F \cos \theta$

$F_x = (10N)(\cos 30)$

or $F_{ix} = F_i \cos \theta$

$F_{ix} = (10N)(\cos 30)$

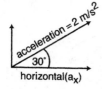

Let a_x = horizontal acceleration

$a_x = a \cos \theta$

$a_x = (2 \text{ m/s}^2)(\cos 30)$

or $a_{ix} = a_i \cos \theta$

$a_{ix} = (2 \text{ m/s}^2)(\cos 30)$

Method 2: To find horizontal velocity;
Look at Figure 1. Draw a line from the resultant (hypotenuse), perpendicular to the horizontal line, to complete a right triangle. See Figure 2.

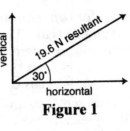

horizontal

Figure 1

You know θ (angle) equals 30° (given). You know hypotenuse (resultant) equals 10 N (given). Find the **horizontal vector**, the **adjacent** side, the side touching angle θ, which is the base of the triangle. You know θ and you know **hypotenuse** (resultant) and you need to find **adjacent** (horizontal vector), therefore, use the equation that has θ, hypotenuse, and adjacent.
Use the equation

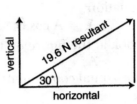

horizontal

Figure 2

$$\cos\ \theta = \frac{adjacent}{hypotenuse}$$ See Reference Table

Geometry and Trigonometry.
Substitute for hypotenuse 19.6 m. Substitute for θ 30°.

$$\cos 30° = \frac{adjacent\ (horizontal)}{19.6}$$ Cos 30° = 0.866.

$$0.866 = \frac{horizontal}{19.6}$$

Cross-multiply:
0.866 x 19.6= horizontal = 17.0 m/s
Horizontal component or horizontal vector = 17.0 m/s   Answer 1

Note: $\cos\ \theta = \dfrac{adjacent\ (horizontal)}{hypotenuse}$ can be used to find the horizontal component of any vector quantity (velocity, force, acceleration, etc.).

Question: A projectile is launched at an angle of 60° above the horizontal at an initial speed of 40. meters per second, as shown in the diagram below. The projectile reaches its highest altitude at point P and strikes a target at point T. [Neglect air resistance.]

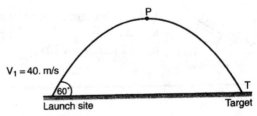

Which graph best represents the horizontal speed of the projectile as a function of time? [Neglect air resistance.]

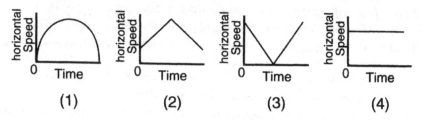

(1)   (2)   (3)   (4)

Solution: When a projectile (object) is thrown at an angle (or thrown horizontally), the horizontal speed is constant. Constant speed is shown in Choice 4.   Answer Choice 4

FINDING VERTICAL COMPONENT

Question 1: An outfielder throws a baseball to the first baseman at a speed of 19.6 meters per second and an angle of 30° above the horizontal. What is the initial vertical velocity (v_y) of the baseball?

    (1) $v_y = 9.80$ m/s   (2) $v_y = 17.0$ m/s
    (3) $v_y = 5.90$ m/s   (4) $v_y = 19.6$ m/s

Solution:
Given: Baseball is thrown at a speed of 19.6 m/s.
       Angle is 30° above horizontal
Find: Initial vertical velocity.

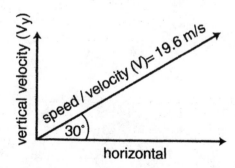

The 19.6 m/s resultant can be broken down into two parts, the horizontal component (horizontal velocity or horizontal vector) and the vertical component (vertical velocity or vertical vector). This

question asks to find the vertical velocity, which means vertical vector (see figure on the previous page).

Look for an equation on Reference Table: Mechanics that has vertical vector. The reference table has A = any vector quantity. There are two equations on Reference Table: Mechanics with the letter A.

$$A_y = A \sin \theta \qquad\qquad A = \text{any vector quantity}$$
$$A_x = A \cos \theta \qquad\qquad \theta = \text{angle}$$

You can see A_x means horizontal vector and A_y means vertical vector. The question asks for the vertical vector, therefore use the equation

$$A_y = A \sin \theta.$$

Look at the figure on the previous page and the equation.

A_y	=	A	$\sin \theta$
vertical vector	=	resultant x	sin of angle between resultant and horizontal

$$A_y = A \quad \sin \theta.$$

Substitute for A (resultant) 19.6 m/s. *Substitute for* θ (angle between resultant and horizontal) 30°

$$A_y = (19.6 \text{ m/s}) (\sin 30°) \qquad \text{Sin } 30° = 0.500$$

$$A_y = (19.6 \text{ m/s}) (0.500) = 9.80 \text{ m/s}$$
$$A_y = \text{vertical component (vertical vector)} = 9.80 \text{ m/s}$$

Answer 1

Reference table mechanics gives a generalized formula $A_y = A \sin \theta$ to find the vertical component of any vector quantity (examples: velocity-v, force-f, acceleration-a, etc.). A = any vector quantity. You can see

Let v_y = initial vertical velocity, then $v_y = v \sin \theta$
$v_y = (19.6)(\sin 30°)$

or Let v_{iy} = initial vertical velocity, then
$v_{iy} = v_i \sin \theta$
$v_{iy} = (19.6)(\sin 30°)$

Let F_y = vertical force
$F_y = F \sin \theta$
$F_y = (10\ N)(\sin 30°)$

or $F_{iy} = F_i \sin \theta$
$F_{iy} = (10N)(\sin 30°)$

Let a_y = vertical acceleration
$a_y = a \sin \theta$
$a_y = (2\ m/s^2)(\sin 30°)$

or $a_{iy} = a_i \sin \theta$
$a_{iy} = (2\ m/s^2)(\sin 30°)$

Answer 1

OR

Look at the figure below.
You know θ (angle) equals 30° (given). You know hypotenuse equals 19.6 m/s (given). Find the **vertical vector**, the side **opposite** angle θ, which is the height of the triangle. You know θ and you know **hypotenuse** and you need to find **opposite** (vertical vector), therefore, use the equation that has θ, hypotenuse, and opposite.

Use the equation

$\sin \theta = \dfrac{opposite}{hypotenuse}$, which is given on

Reference Table: Geometry and Trigonometry.
Substitute 30° for θ. Substitute 19.6 m/s for hypotenuse.

$\text{Sin } 30° = \dfrac{opposite}{19.6\ m/s}$ $\text{Sin } 30° = 0.500$

$$0.500 = \frac{opposite}{19.6 \ m/s}$$

Cross multiply
(0.500)(19.6 m/s) = opposite
Opposite = 9.80 m/s
Vertical component or vertical vector (opposite) = 9.80 m/s

Answer 1

Note: $\sin \theta = \dfrac{opposite \ (vertical)}{hypotenuse}$ can be used to find any vertical component of any vector quantity (velocity, force, acceleration, displacement, etc.).

Question 2: An outfielder threw a ball to the first baseman at a speed of 19.6 m/s and an angle of 30° above the horizontal. If the ball is caught at the same height from which it was thrown, calculate the amount of time the ball was in the air. [Show all work, including the equation and substitution with units.]

Solution:
Given: Outfielder threw a ball at a speed of 19.6 m/s at an angle of 30° above the horizontal. The ball is caught at the same height from which it is thrown. Find: The time (t) the ball was in the air.

The time it takes the ball to go vertically up to the highest point and the time it takes the ball to go vertically down is the time the ball was in the air. The time the ball went up equals the time the ball went down.

First: find the **time** it took the ball that was thrown (I) to **go** to the **highest point** on the arc (II); **then find** the **total time** the ball was in the air.

When you need to find the **time** it takes to go to the **highest point**, you need the **vertical velocity**. You found in question 1 the initial vertical velocity = 9.80 m/s. The time it takes obviously depends on velocity (speed and direction).

Initial vertical velocity v_i (or v_{iy}) of the ball = 9.80 m/s (answer in Question 1).
The speed of the ball at the highest point (the top), the final vertical velocity v_f (or v_{fy}), = 0.
v_y **(vertical velocity)** is always **zero at** the **top when** an **object is thrown** at an **angle.**

Note: also, v_y = **zero** at the **top** in **free fall** examples **and** when an **object** is **thrown horizontally**. If a ball is thrown vertically up in the air, the vertical velocity at the top is also zero.

You know, when the ball was thrown up, acceleration (a) = -9.81 m/s² (deceleration).

In short, you know v_i (initial velocity) = 9.8 m/s, v_f (final velocity) = 0, a (acceleration) = -9.81 m/s²

You know three things, v_f, v_i, and a and there is one unknown, t (time) to go to the highest point, therefore *look for an equation* on Reference Table: Mechanics that has v_i, v_f, a and t.

Use the equation $v_f = v_i + at$

Substitute for v_{fy} 0. Substitute for v_{iy} 9.8 m/s. Substitute for a -9.81 m/s².

$$v_{fy} = v_{iy} + at$$
$$0 = 9.8 + (-9.81t)$$
$$\underline{-9.8 = -9.8}$$
$$-9.8 = \qquad -9.8t$$

divide by -9.8:

$$\frac{-\ 9.8}{-\ 9.8} = \frac{-\ 9.8\ t}{-\ 9.8}$$

1.0 = t   (Note: when you divide (or multiply) two negative numbers, you get a positive number.

t = 1.0 second (time to go to the highest point = 1 second.)

Then, find total time the ball was in the air. It took 1.0 second for the ball to reach II (the top). It takes another 1.0 second for the ball to go from II (the top) to III; therefore, the ball was in the air for 2.0 seconds.

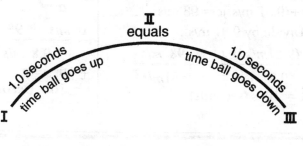

II equals

1.0 seconds time ball goes up

1.0 seconds time ball goes down

I

III

Answer: 2.0 seconds

Now do Homework Questions #154-155, page 155.

Question: A projectile is fired from a gun near the surface of Earth. The initial velocity of the projectile has a vertical component of 98 meters per second and a horizontal component of 49 meters per

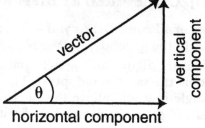

vector

θ

horizontal component

vertical component

Table: Mechanics

second. How long will it take the projectile to reach the highest point in its path?

    (1) 5.0 seconds   (2) 10. seconds
    (3) 20. seconds   (4) 100. seconds

Solution:
Given: Initial vertical velocity of the projectile is 98 meters per second.
Find: Time needed for the projectile to reach the highest point.

Initial vertical velocity of the projectile v_i (or v_{iy}) = 98 meters/second.

At the **highest point**, final **vertical velocity** v_f (or v_{fy}) = **zero**.

You know, when the **projectile** was **fired toward** the **highest point**, a (acceleration) = -9.81 meters/second². **Acceleration** is **negative**, **−9.81 m/s²**, because velocity decreases from v_i 98 m/s, to v_f 0 m/s.

In short, you know v_i (initial velocity) = 98 m/s, v_f (final velocity) = 0, a (acceleration) = −9.81 m/s². You know three things v_f, v_i, a, and there is one unknown, t (time). *Look for an equation* on Reference Table: Mechanics that has v_f, v_i, a, and t.

Use the equation $v_f = v_i + at$.
Substitute for v_f 0 m/s. *Substitute for* v_i 98 m/s. *Substitute for a* −9.81 m/s².

$v_f = v_i + at$. 0 m/s = 98 m/s + (-9.81 m/s²)t Solve for t: +(9.81 m/s²)t = 98 m/s Divide by 9.81 m/s²: $\dfrac{(9.81 m/s^2)\ t}{9.81 m/s^2} = \dfrac{98\ m/s}{9.81 m/s^2}$ t = 10. s (seconds)	Or, rearrange the equation: $\dfrac{v_f - v_i}{a} = t$ $\dfrac{0\ m/s\ -\ 98\ m/s}{-\ 9.8\ m/s^2} = t$ + 10. s = t t = 10. s (seconds)

Table: Mechanics

Now Do Homework Questions #156-165, pages 155-156.

RANGE, ALTITUDE (HEIGHT) AND TIME IN THE AIR OF A PROJECTILE FIRED AT DIFFERENT ANGLES TO THE GROUND

Range of a Projectile: As you learned, projectiles can be fired at different angles to the ground.

Look at the figure on the next page. Projectiles are fired from different angles at the same initial speed. The highest point on the graph of Range vs. Angle is at 45° above the horizontal axis, which corresponds to a 20 meter range (range means how far it travels along the ground).

As you can see in the graph at right, at 45° the range (how far the projectile travels until it hits the ground) is biggest, 20 meters.

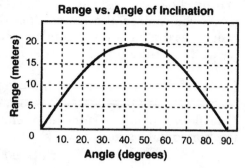

Range vs. Angle of Inclination

Look at the graph again. At 30° (which is 15° less than 45°) or 60° (which is 15°more than 45°) the range (how far the projectile travels until it hits the ground) is the same for both 30° and 60°, about 18 meters (which is less than 20 meters).

Look at the graph again. At 10° (which is 35° less than 45°) or at 80° (which is 35° more than 45°) the range (how far the projectile travels until it hits the ground) is the same for both 10° and 80°, about 7 meters (which is less than 20 meters and less than 18 meters).

At 0° (which is 45° less than 45°) or at 90° (which is 45° more than 45°) the range (how far the projectile travels until it hits the ground) is the same for both 0° and 90°, zero meters. (At 0°, the projectile hits the ground right away, because the projectile is on the ground; therefore range is zero meters.)

In short, at 45° (when a projectile is fired at an angle of 45°) the range is the largest (example: 20 meters).

At 30° or 60° the range is less; at 10° or 80° the range is even less, and at 0° or 90° the range is the least (zero meters).

Question: Projectiles are fired from different angles with the same initial speed of 14 meters per second. The graph below shows the range of the projectiles as a function of the original angle of inclination to the ground, neglecting air resistance.

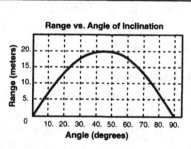

Range vs. Angle of Inclination

The graph shows that the range of the projectiles is

       (1) the same for all angles
       (2) the same for angles of 20° and 80°
       (3) greatest for an angle of 45°
       (4) greatest for an angle of 90°

Solution: The highest point on the curve of the graph is at 45° above the horizontal axis, which corresponds to 20 meters on the y axis.

As you can see in the graph above, at 45° the range (how far the projectile travels along the ground) is biggest, 20 meters.

                                          Answer *3*

Wrong choices:
(1) As you can see, the range is not the same for all angles. If the range was the same for all angles, it would be a horizontal line.
(2) at 20°, range (on the y axis) is 13 meters. At 80°, range is 7 meters.
(4) At 90° there is zero range (no range, no distance).

Question: A machine launches a tennis ball at an angle of 45° with the horizontal, as shown.

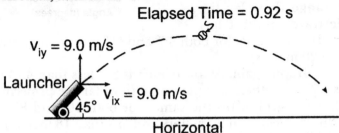

The speed at which the launcher fires tennis balls is constant, but the angle between the launcher and the horizontal can be varied. As the angle is decreased from 45° to 30°, the range of the tennis balls
     (1) decreases   (2) increases   (3) remains the same

Solution: At an angle of 45°, the range is the biggest. As the angle moves away from 45° (example: to 30° or to 60°, etc.), the range decreases.   **Answer** *1*

===

Altitude (Height) and Time in the Air:

1. Two balls (or projectiles) are thrown at the same initial speed. When a **ball** (or **projectile**) is **thrown** at a **bigger angle** (75° angle instead of 30° angle above the ground) more of the velocity is in the vertical direction (less horizontal velocity), therefore the **ball** (or **projectile**) **goes higher up** and it takes **more time for** the **ball** (thrown at 75°) to **reach** the **ground** (the ball has **more time in** the **air**).

2. Two balls are thrown with two different initial speeds at the same angle. The ball thrown at a **higher initial speed goes higher up** and the ball has more time in the air.

Section 6:

UNIFORM CIRCULAR MOTION

Newton's First Law of Motion states that an object at rest continues at rest and an object that moves continues to move at the same velocity (uniform motion), until an unbalanced force (extra force in any direction) acts on it.

Uniform Circular Motion: motion (movement) of an object at **constant speed in** a **circular path**.

Look at the figure. A cart keeps going in the same direction at constant velocity when no force acts on it. The velocity is tangent to the circle. Centripetal force (F_c) is perpendicular to the velocity (v) and also perpendicular to the circle. **Centripetal force** is directed **toward** the **center of** the **circle**, **pulls** the **cart** and makes the cart accelerate **inward toward** the **center of** the **circle**; therefore, the **cart moves in** a **circle**. This is called **uniform circular motion**.

In **uniform circular motion**, the speed of the object (example: cart) is constant and the **direction** keeps **changing** (direction is not in a straight line but in a circle). When direction changes, it means velocity changes. Velocity equals direction and speed. If direction (or speed) changes, **velocity changes**.

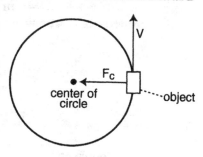

F_c = centripetal force
v = velocity

Centripetal acceleration (a_c) – acceleration (just like centripetal force (F_c)) is toward the center of the circle (see figure below).

The equation is $a_c = \dfrac{v^2}{r}$

a_c = centripetal acceleration

r = radius/ distance between centers
v = velocity/speed

Centripetal acceleration $= \dfrac{speed\ or\ velocity\ squared}{radius}$

Centripetal acceleration is directly proportional to the square of the speed and inversely proportional to the radius.

The speed or velocity (v) of the object is in meters/second (m/s), the radius (r) of the circle is in meters, and centripetal acceleration (a_c) is in meters per second^2 (m/s^2).

Mass has no effect on centripetal acceleration.

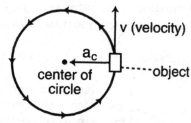

a_c = centripetal acceleration
v = velocity

Centripetal force and centripetal acceleration both are vector quantities (both have a number and direction, example, centripetal force of 20 newtons east).

You had the equation $a = \dfrac{F_{net}}{m}$, given on Reference Table: Mechanics.

Or, you can rearrange the equation and say

$$F \quad = \quad m \quad\quad\quad a$$
Force $\quad$ = mass x $\quad$ acceleration

The equation for **centripetal force** (F_c) is

$$F_c \quad\quad = \quad m \ x \quad\quad a_c.$$
centripetal force = mass x centripetal acceleration.

$F_c = ma_c$ $\qquad\qquad$ F_c = centripetal force

$\qquad\qquad\qquad\qquad\qquad$ m = mass

$\qquad\qquad\qquad\qquad\qquad$ a_c = centripetal acceleration

You learned that $a_c \ = \ \dfrac{v^2}{r}$

$\qquad\qquad$ Centripetal
$\qquad\qquad$ acceleration

In the equation $F_c = ma_c$, you can **substitute** $\dfrac{v^2}{r}$ for a_c.

$$F_c = ma_c = m\,\frac{v^2}{r}.$$

From the equation $F_c = ma_c$, you know that centripetal force (F_c) is directly proportional to the product of mass (m) times centripetal acceleration (a_c). The bigger the mass (m), the bigger is the centripetal force (F_c) (when a_c is constant).

Questions 1 and 2: Base your answer to questions 1 and 2 on the information below. A 2.0×10^3-kilogram car travels at a constant speed of 12 meters per second around a circular curve of radius 30. meters.

Question 1: What is the magnitude of the centripetal acceleration of the car as it goes around the curve?

$\quad$ (1) 0.40 m/s^2 $\quad$ (2) 4.8 m/s^2 $\quad$ (3) 800 m/s^2 $\quad$ (4) 9600 m/s^2

Question 2: As the car goes around the curve, the centripetal force is directed

$\quad$ (1) toward the center of the circular curve

$\quad$ (2) away from the center of the circular curve

$\quad$ (3) tangent to the curve in the direction of motion

$\quad$ (4) tangent to the curve opposite the direction of motion

Solution 1: First write down what is given and what is to find.

Given: speed = 12 meters per second (m/s)

$\qquad\quad$ radius = 30 meters (m)

Find: centripetal acceleration (a_c)

You know two things, speed (v) and radius (r), and there is one unknown, centripetal acceleration (a_c), therefore *look for an equation on Reference Table: Mechanics that has v, r, and a_c.*

Use the equation

$$a_c = \frac{v^2}{r} \qquad a_c = \text{centripetal acceleration}$$

$$r = \text{radius/ distance between centers}$$
$$v = \text{velocity/speed}$$

Substitute for v (speed) 12 m/s. *Substitute for r* (radius) 30. m (meters).

$$a_c = \frac{(12 \ m/s)^2}{30. \ m} = \frac{144 \ m^2/s^2}{30. \ m} = 4.8 \ m/s^2$$

Centripetal acceleration (a_c) = 4.8 m/s²   Answer 2

Solution 2: Centripetal force is directed toward the center of the circular curve (circle).   Answer 1.

Question: An athlete in a hammer-throw event swings a 7.0 kilogram hammer in a horizontal circle at a constant speed of 12 meters per second. The radius of the hammer's path is 2.0 meters. If the hammer is released at the point shown, it will travel toward point

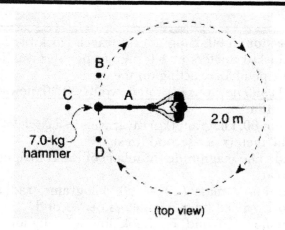

(top view)

   (1) A   (2) B   (3) C   (4) D

Solution: Before the hammer is released, the man (shown in the figure above in the center of the circle) is swinging the hammer in the direction shown by the arrows. Centripetal force causes the hammer to go in a circular path (circle).

With no centripetal force, the velocity of the hammer would be a straight line, tangent to the circle. When the hammer is released, there is no centripetal force making the hammer go in a circle, and the hammer moves in a straight line, tangent to the circle, and travels toward B.   Answer 2

Question: A 1.50 kilogram cart travels in a horizontal circle of radius 2.40 meters at a constant speed of 4.00 meters per second. Copy the diagram on a sheet of paper. Draw an arrow on the diagram to represent the direction of the acceleration of the cart in the position shown.

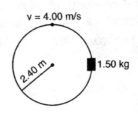

Solution: The direction of acceleration is toward the center of the circle. Draw the arrow toward the center of the circle. See figure.

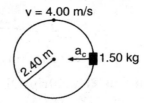

Question: A 60.-kilogram car travels clockwise in a horizontal circle of radius 10. meters at 5.0 meters per second. The magnitude of the centripetal force acting on the car is

(1) 590 newtons (2) 150 newtons (3) 30. newtons (4) 2.5 newtons

Solution:
Given: 60. kilogram (kg) car travels in a circle of radius 10. meters (m) at 5.0 meters per second (m/s).
Find: The magnitude (number) of the centripetal force (F_c) acting on the car.
You know mass (m) = 60. kilograms, radius (r) = 10. meters, velocity/speed (v) = 5.0 meters per second.
You need to find F_c. Look for an equation on Reference Table: Mechanics that has F_c (centripetal force). The only equation for F_c is $F_c = ma_c$. You are not given a_c (centripetal acceleration), but are given v and r, therefore, **use both centripetal equations** below, which are given on Reference Table: Mechanics on page reference tables 22-23.
Note: Subscript c next to F means centripetal force (F_c) ; subscript c next to a means centripetal acceleration (a_c).

$$F_c = ma_c \qquad a_c = \text{centripetal acceleration}$$

$$a_c = \frac{v^2}{r} \qquad F_c = \text{centripetal force}$$

m = mass
r = radius/distance between centers
v = velocity/speed

You learned $a_c = \dfrac{v^2}{r}$

In the equation $F_c = ma_c$, substitute for a_c $\dfrac{v^2}{r}$.

$$F_c = \frac{mv^2}{r}$$

Substitute for m (mass) 60 kg (kilograms). *Substitute for* r (radius) 10 m (meters). *Substitute for* v (speed) 5 m/s (meters/ second).

$$F_c = \frac{mv^2}{r}$$

$$F_c = \frac{(60.\ kg)(5.0\ m/s)^2}{10.\ m}$$

$$F_c = \frac{(60.\ kg)(25 m^2/s^2)}{10.\ m} = 150\ kg{\cdot}m/s^2 = 150\ N\ (newtons)$$

Answer 2

Or

Method 2:
Given: 60. kilogram (kg) car travels in a circle of radius 10. meters (m) at 5.0 meters per second (m/s).
Find: The magnitude (number) of the centripetal force (F_c) acting on the car.
You know mass (m) = 60. kilograms, radius (r) = 10. meters, velocity/speed (v) = 5.0 meters per second.
You need to find F_c. *Look for an equation* on Reference Table: Mechanics that has F_c (centripetal force). The only equation for F_c is F_c = ma_c. You have two unknowns, F_c and a_c. First find a_c and then substitute a_c in the equation $F_c = ma_c$ (see below).

First find a_c.. *Look for an equation* on Reference Table: Mechanics for a_c.
Use the equation

$a_c = \dfrac{v^2}{r}$. Substitute for v 5.0m/s (given), substitute for r 10. m (given).

$$a_c = \frac{(5.0\ m/s)^2}{10.\ m} = \frac{25\ m^2/s^2}{10.\ m} = 2.5\ m/s^2$$

In the equation $F_c = ma_c$, *then substitute for* a_c 2.5 m/s². *Substitute for* m (mass) 60. kg.
F_c = 60. kg (2.5 m/s²) = 150 kg${\cdot}$m/s² = 150 N (newtons).   Answer 2

Question: A child is riding on a merry-go-round. As the speed of the merry-go-round is doubled, the magnitude of the centripetal force acting on the child

(1) remains the same   (2) is doubled

(3) is halved   (4) is quadrupled

Solution:

Given: Child is riding on a merry-go-round. Speed of the merry-go-round is doubled.

Find: magnitude of the centripetal force acting on the child when the speed is doubled (look at the choices in the question).

Look for an equation for centripetal force (F_c) on Reference Table: Mechanics.

Use the equation

$$F_c = m \times a_c$$

centripetal force = mass x centripetal acceleration

Since centripetal force = mass x centripetal acceleration, look also for an equation on Reference Table: Mechanics for centripetal acceleration (a_c). In general, when a question asks for centripetal force (F_c) look at both centripetal equations ($F_c = ma_c$ and $a_c = \dfrac{v^2}{r}$).

$$F_c = ma_c \qquad a_c = \text{centripetal acceleration}$$

$$a_c = \dfrac{v^2}{r} \qquad F_c = \text{centripetal force}$$

$$m = \text{mass}$$
$$r = \text{radius/distance between centers}$$
$$v = \text{velocity/speed}$$

Look at the equations above. Since the question asked about centripetal force (F_c), *use the equation* $F_c = ma_c$. Since the question is about speed (v), *substitute for* a_c $\dfrac{v^2}{r}$ in the equation $F_c = ma_c$.

$$F_c = ma_c = m\,\dfrac{v^2}{r}.$$

Table: Mechanics

OLD	NEW

$$F_c = \frac{mv^2}{r}$$

Note: no number in front of m means 1; you can write

$$F_c = \frac{1mv^2}{r} \quad \text{or} \quad \frac{(1)mv^2}{r}$$

Speed (v) is doubled
New speed = 2v

In $F_c = \dfrac{mv^2}{r}$, *substitute 2v* for v

$$\text{New } F_c = \frac{m(2v)^2}{r} = \frac{m(2v)(2v)}{r}$$

$$= \frac{4mv^2}{r}$$

Old $F_c = \dfrac{(1)mv^2}{r}$

Old centripetal force

New $F_c = \dfrac{4mv^2}{r}$

New centripetal force

Look at the new F_c and the old F_c. New F_c = 4 times the old F_c, which means the new F_c is quadrupled.   Answer *4*

Question: The combined mass of a race car and its driver is 600. kilograms. Traveling at constant speed, the car completes one lap around a circular track of radius 160 meters in 36 seconds. Calculate the speed of the car. [Show all work, including the equation and substitution with units.]

Solution:

Given: A car completes one lap around a circular track, traveling at constant speed. Radius of the circular track is 160 meters (m). Time to complete one lap around a circular track is 36 seconds (s).

Find: speed (v) of the car.

The car travels at constant speed.

Look for an equation that has speed v and time t.

Use the equation

$$\bar{v} = \frac{d}{t}$$

     d = displacement/distance

     t = time interval

     $\bar{v}$ = average velocity/average speed

First you need to find distance (d) around a circular path. Look at Reference Table: Geometry and Trigonometry.

Circle

    $C = 2\pi r$ C= circumference

The equation for the **distance (d)** around a circle (circumference of a circle) = **2πr.**

In the equation $\bar{v} = \dfrac{d}{t}$, *substitute for d* 2πr.

$$\bar{v} = \dfrac{2\pi r}{t}$$

Then, in the equation $\bar{v} = \dfrac{2\pi r}{t}$ (see above), *substitute for π 3.14.*

Substitute for r (radius) 160 m (meters) (given). *Substitute for t* (time) 36 s (seconds) (given).

$$\bar{v} = \dfrac{2\pi r}{t}$$

$$\bar{v} = \dfrac{2(3.14) \; x \; 160m}{36 \; s}$$

Answer $\bar{v}$ = 28 m/s (also acceptable, 27.9 m/s)

Remember: When a question deals with a circular path, use 2πr (circumference of a circle) for distance.

Question: On the diagram, draw an arrow to represent the direction of the net force acting on the car when it is in position A.

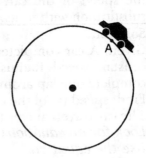

Solution: In a circle, the net force is the centripetal force. The net force (centripetal force) is directed toward the center of the circle.

Question: A 1.50-kilogram cart travels in a horizontal circle of radius 2.40 meters at a constant speed of 4.00 meters per second. Describe a change that would quadruple the magnitude of the centripetal force.

v = 4.00 m/s

2.40 m

1.50 kg

Solution:
Given: Cart is 1.50 kilograms (kg). Radius of circle is 2.40 meters (m). Speed is constant. Speed is 4.00 meters per second (m/s).
Find: a change that would quadruple the centripetal force (F_c).

Look for an equation for centripetal force (F_c) on Reference Table: Mechanics.

$F_c = ma_c$ a_c = centripetal acceleration
               F_c = centripetal force
               m = mass

Find a change that would quadruple the centripetal force (F_c).

1. Look at the equation above. If the **mass (m)** is **quadrupled**, four times as much (4m), **then** the F_c (centripetal force) would also be **quadrupled**, four times as much ($4F_c$).
$$F_c = ma_c$$
$$4F_c = 4ma_c$$
As you can see, F_c (centripetal force) is directly proportional to m (mass) when a_c is constant.

Other changes that would **quadruple centripetal force (F_c):**
The two centripetal equations on Reference Table: Mechanics show other changes that would quadruple centripetal force (F_c). See below and on the next page.

$F_c = ma_c$ a_c = centripetal acceleration

$a_c = \dfrac{v^2}{r}$ F_c = centripetal force

               m = mass
               r = radius/distance between centers
               v = velocity/speed

In the equation $F_c = ma_c$, *substitute for a_c* $\dfrac{v^2}{r}$.

$$F_c = \frac{mv^2}{r}$$

By looking at this equation, you see that velocity (v) and radius (r) both also affect centripetal force (F_c).

2. Look at the equation $F_c = \dfrac{mv^2}{r}$. If **velocity (v) is doubled**, 2 times as much, (2v) example: from 4.00 m/s to 8.00 m/s, the centripetal force (F_c) is quadrupled, four times as much (see below).

OLD	NEW
$F_c = \dfrac{mv^2}{r}$	Speed (v) is doubled New speed = 2v
Note: no number in front of m means 1; you can write	Substitute 2v for v in $F_c = \dfrac{mv^2}{r}$
$F_c = \dfrac{1mv^2}{r}$ or $\dfrac{(1)mv^2}{r}$	New $F_c = \dfrac{m(2v)^2}{r} = \dfrac{m(2v)(2v)}{r}$ $= \dfrac{4mv^2}{r}$
Old $F_c = \dfrac{(1)mv^2}{r}$ Old centripetal force	New $F_c = \dfrac{4mv^2}{r}$ New centripetal force

Look at the new F_c and the old F_c. New F_c = 4 times the old F_c, which means the new F_c is quadrupled.

3. Look again at the equation $F_c = \dfrac{mv^2}{r}$. If **radius (r) is quartered**,

¼ as much, $\dfrac{1}{4}r$, (example: from 2.40 meters to 0.60 m), centripetal force (F_c) is quadrupled, four times as much (see below).

OLD	NEW
$F_c = \dfrac{mv^2}{r}$	Radius (r) is quartered. New radius = $\dfrac{1}{4}r$ Substitute $\dfrac{1}{4}r$ for r in $F_c = \dfrac{mv^2}{r}$ New $F_c = \dfrac{mv^2}{\frac{1}{4}r}$ or $\dfrac{mv^2}{\frac{(1)r}{4}} = \dfrac{4mv^2}{r}$

| Old $F_c = \dfrac{mv^2}{r}$ | New $F_c = \dfrac{4mv^2}{r}$ |

Look at the new F_c and the old F_c. New F_c = 4 times the old F_c, which means the new F_c is quadrupled.

Now do Homework Questions #166-196, pages 155-161.

NEWTON'S UNIVERSAL LAW OF GRAVITATION

The **gravitational force** (or force due to gravity) **(F_g) is** the attractive force **(force of attraction) between** two **objects** in newtons.

$$F_g = \frac{Gm_1m_2}{r^2}$$

F_g = weight/force due to gravity
G = universal gravitational constant
m = mass
r = radius/distance between centers

G = universal gravitational constant = 6.67×10^{-11} N•m^2/Kg^2 , given on the Reference Table: List of Physical Constants.
m_1 = mass of one object in kilograms (kg).
m_2 = mass of the other object in kilograms (kg).
r = distance between the centers of the two objects in meters (m).

FINDING GRAVITATIONAL FORCE: To find gravitational force, also called force due to gravity, (F_g) , use the equation $F_g = \dfrac{Gm_1m_2}{r^2}$

A. Multiply G, which is 6.67×10^{-11} N•m^2/kg^2 times mass of one object (m_1) times mass of the other object (m_2).
B Divide (the answer in Part A) by the distance between the two objects (r) squared (square the distance between the two objects).

As you see from the equation, the bigger the masses (m), the bigger is F_g (gravitational force or force due to gravity). The bigger the distance between the (centers of the) two objects, the smaller is F_g.

Look at the equation $F_g = \dfrac{Gm_1m_2}{r^2}$. If m_1 (mass of one object) is doubled, F_g is doubled.

If m_1 is doubled (two times as much) and m_2 is doubled (two times as much), then F_g is quadrupled (4 times as much).

$$m_1 \qquad\qquad m_2$$

$$2 \quad \text{x} \quad 2 \quad = \quad 4$$

Table: Mechanics

Look again at the equation $F_g = \dfrac{Gm_1m_2}{r^2}$ and see what happens if radius is doubled. If radius (r) is doubled (two times as much), then r^2 is 2 x 2 = 4 times as much. Since r^2 (4 times as much) is in the denominator (the bottom part), F_g is ¼ as much.

NEWTON'S UNIVERSAL LAW OF GRAVITATION $F_G = \dfrac{Gm_1m_2}{r^2}$: Two bodies

(objects) attract each other with a force that is directly proportional to the product of the masses and inversely proportional to the square of the distance between the objects.

Look at the equation $F_g = \dfrac{Gm_1m_2}{r^2}$. The Earth (mass 1) and the Moon (mass 2) have an attractive force (F_g) between them; therefore, the Moon and the Earth do not move apart (do not separate). The gravitational force of attraction of the Earth on the Moon is equal to the (gravitational) force of attraction of the Moon on the Earth, but in the opposite direction.

Force of Gravity (Fg)
of Earth attracts (pulls on) Moon

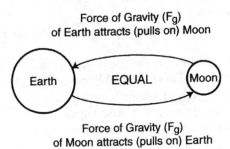

Force of Gravity (Fg)
of Moon attracts (pulls on) Earth

Gravitational force of m_1 (example: Earth) on m_2 (example: Moon) equals gravitational force of m_2 (example: Moon) on m_1 (example: Earth) but in the opposite direction.

Question: If the magnitude of the gravitational force of Earth on the Moon is F, the magnitude of the gravitational force of the Moon on Earth is
    (1) smaller than F   (2) larger than F   (3) equal to F

Solution: The gravitational force (attractive force) of the Earth on the Moon is equal to the gravitational force (attractive force) of the Moon on the Earth, but in the opposite direction. The gravitational force of the Earth on the Moon is F; therefore, the gravitational force of the Moon on the Earth is also equal to F.   Answer 3

WEIGHT OF AN OBJECT: Weight = F_g (force of gravity or force due to gravity).
Example: An object **weighs 100 newtons**; it means F_g = 100 newtons.
A "**60-newton object**" (example box) means **object weighs 60 newtons, F_g = 60 newtons (N)**.

F_g = weight/force due to gravity, given on Reference Table: Mechanics.

Question: The magnitude of the gravitational force of attraction between Earth and the Moon is approximately
(1) 2.0×10^{20} N   (2) 6.0×10^{24} N   (3) 6.7×10^{-11} N   (4) 7.8×10^{28} N

Solution:

Given: There is a gravitational force of attraction between Earth and the Moon.

Find: Magnitude (number) of gravitational force of attraction between Earth and Moon.

The question asks for the gravitational force of attraction between the Earth and the Moon. On Reference Table: Mechanics there are two equations for gravitational force (F_g). One equation has one mass (m) (example, one object such as the Moon) and the other equation has two masses (m_1, m_2)(example, two objects such as the Earth and the Moon). Since you need to find the gravitational force of attraction between the Earth and the Moon (two masses), look for an equation with gravitational force and two masses.

Use the equation

$$F_g = \frac{G m_1 m_2}{r^2}$$

F_g = weight/force due to gravity

G = universal gravitational constant
m = mass
r = radius/distance between centers

Note: You also know to use this equation because the question asks for the gravitational attraction **between** the **Earth** and the **Moon**, which means look for an equation with gravitational force (F_g) and **distance** (r) between Earth and Moon.

First find the values of G, m_1, m_2, and r, given on Reference Table: List of Physical Constants; then substitute these values in the equation $F_g = \frac{G m_1 m_2}{r^2}$ to find F_g (gravitational force).

First find G, m_1, m_2, and r by looking at Reference Table: List of Physical Constants below or on page Reference Tables 2:

List of Physical Constants		
Name	**Symbol**	**Value**
Universal gravitational constant	G	6.67×10^{-11} N•m²/kg²
Acceleration due to gravity	g	9.81 m/s²
Speed of light in a vacuum	c	3.00×10^8 m/s
Mass of Earth		5.98×10^{24} kg
Mass of the Moon		7.35×10^{22} kg
Mean radius of Earth		6.37×10^6 meters
Mean distance-Earth to the Moon		3.84×10^8 m

In the equation $F_g = \dfrac{Gm_1m_2}{r^2}$, *substitute for G* 6.67×10^{-11}
$N \bullet m^2/kg^2$.

Substitute for m_1 (mass of Earth) 5.98×10^{24} kg.
Substitute for m_2 (mass of Moon) 7.35×10^{22} kg.
Substitute for r (mean distance Earth to the Moon) 3.84×10^8 m.

$$F_g = \dfrac{Gm_1m_2}{r^2}$$

$$F_g = \dfrac{(6.67 \times 10^{-11}\ N\bullet m^2/kg^2)(5.98 \times 10^{24}\ kg)(7.35 \times 10^{22}\ kg)}{(3.84 \times 10^8\ m)^2}$$

$F_g = 1.99 \times 10^{20}$ N (newtons)   **Answer 1** 2.0×10^{20} N

Question: Which is a vector quantity?
          (1) distance   (2) speed   (3) power   (4) force

Solution: Force is a vector quantity because it has both magnitude
(a number) and direction. Example: force, 20 newtons south.
                                                                    Answer 4.

Question: When a satellite is a distance R from the center of Earth,
the force due to gravity on the satellite is **F**. What is the force due
to gravity on the satellite when its distance from the center of Earth
is 3R?

          (1) $\dfrac{F}{9}$ (2) $\dfrac{F}{3}$ (3) F   (4) 9F

Solution: *Look for an equation* on Reference Table: Mechanics that
has force due to gravity and distance.
Use the equation:

$$F_g = \dfrac{Gm_1m_2}{r^2}$$

F_g = weight/force due to gravity

G = universal gravitational constant
m = mass
r = radius/distance between centers

Table: Mechanics

OLD	NEW
Old $F_g = \dfrac{1Gm_1m_2}{r^2}$	Distance R is tripled. Let new r = 3R (or 3r). $F_g = \dfrac{1Gm_1m_2}{(3r)^2} = \dfrac{1Gm_1m_2}{9r^2}$
Old $F_g = \dfrac{(1)Gm_1m_2}{r^2}$ or $\dfrac{1Gm_1m_2}{r^2}$ Old	$F_g = \dfrac{1Gm_1m_2}{9r^2}$ or $\dfrac{1}{9}\dfrac{Gm_1m_2}{r^2}$ New

Look at the new force and the old force, F (F_g).

New force = 1/9 old force = 1/9 F (or $\dfrac{F}{9}$).   **Answer 1**

Question: Gravitational force F exists between point objects A and B separated by distance R. If the mass of A is doubled and distance R is tripled, what is the new gravitational force between A and B?

    (1) 2/9 F   (2) 2/3 F   (3) 3/2 f   (4) 9/2 F

Solution:
Look for an equation on Reference Table: Mechanics that has force due to gravity (gravitational force), mass, and distance.
Use the equation:

$$F_g = \frac{Gm_1 m_2}{r^2}$$

F_g = weight/force due to gravity

G = universal gravitational constant

m = mass

r = radius/distance between centers

OLD	**NEW**
Old $F_g = \dfrac{Gm_1 m_2}{r^2}$	Mass is doubled. Let new mass equal $2m_1$. Distance R is tripled. Let new r equal 3R (or 3r). New $F_g = \dfrac{G(2m_1)m_2}{(3r)^2} = \dfrac{2Gm_1 m_2}{9r^2}$
Old $F_g = \dfrac{Gm_1 m_2}{r^2}$ Old Gravitational Force	New $F_g = \dfrac{2Gm_1 m_2}{9r^2}$ New Gravitational Force when mass is doubled and radius is tripled

Look at the new force and the old force, F (F_g).
New force = 2/9 old force = 2/9 F.   Answer *1.*

Question: An object weighs 100. newtons on Earth's surface. When it is moved to a point one Earth radius above Earth's surface, it will weigh

    (1) 25.0 N   (2) 50.0 N   (3) 100. N   (4) 400. N

Solution: *Look for an equation* on Reference Table: Mechanics that has weight (F_g) and radius (r).
Use the equation:

$$F_g = \frac{Gm_1 m_2}{r^2}$$

OLD	NEW
Old $F_g = \dfrac{1Gm_1m_2}{r^2}$	At one radius above surface, new radius = 2r. (One r is from center of Earth to surface; second r is above surface.) New $F_g = \dfrac{1Gm_1m_2}{(2r)^2} = \dfrac{1Gm_1m_2}{4r^2}$ New Weight
Old $F_g = \dfrac{(1)Gm_1m_2}{r^2}$ or $\dfrac{1Gm_1m_2}{r^2}$ Old Weight	New $F_g = \dfrac{1Gm_1m_2}{4r^2}$ or $\dfrac{1}{4}\dfrac{Gm_1m_2}{r^2}$ New Weight

Old $F_g = 100.$ newtons (given)
Old Weight

Look at the new F_g and the old F_g.

New $F_g = \dfrac{1}{4}$ (old F_g) $= \dfrac{1}{4}$ (100. newtons) = 25.0 newtons

New Weight   Answer 1

Now Do Homework Questions #197-201, page 162.

GRAVITATIONAL FIELD STRENGTH (g)

A gravitational field is a **region** or **area** such as the Earth or Moon which is **surrounded** by a **gravitational force**. In the diagram at right, the Earth is surrounded by gravitational lines of force (gravitational field lines). Gravitational field lines (gravitational lines of force) are perpendicular to the Earth (or any other object). **Gravitational field strength (g)** (**acceleration due to gravity**) is **how strong** the **gravitational field** is. Gravitational field strength (g) is $g = \dfrac{F_g}{m}$, given on Reference Table: Mechanics.

$$g = \frac{F_g}{m}$$

g = acceleration due to gravity
or gravitational field strength
F_g = weight/force due to gravity
m = mass

To explain: F_g = weight of the object (example: man standing on Earth or rock on Earth) or force of gravity on the object (example: man or rock).

$g = \dfrac{F_g}{m}$. Cross multiply: $F_g = mg$. As you can see from the equation

$F_g = mg$, since m (mass), example: mass of man, is constant, the bigger

F_g (force due to gravity) is, the bigger is g (acceleration due to gravity or gravitational field strength). g is the acceleration caused by the force of gravity (F_g) on the mass (m).

From the first and second equations, $F_g = \dfrac{Gm_1m_2}{r^2}$, and $g = \dfrac{F_g}{m}$, you see: smaller r (distance between the two objects) means bigger F_g (force of gravity) and, shown in the second equation, bigger F_g means bigger g (gravitational field strength or acceleration due to gravity).

g (acceleration due to gravity) is in newtons per kilogram or m/s² as explained below. F_g is in newtons, and m is in kilograms.

$g = \dfrac{F_g}{m}$ $\dfrac{\text{(gravitational force) in newtons}}{\text{(mass) in kilograms}}$, therefore g is in $\dfrac{newtons}{kilogram}$.

g is also measured in m/s²:

g (acceleration due to gravity) $= \dfrac{F_g}{m}$

a (acceleration) $= \dfrac{F_{net}}{m}$, given on Reference Table: Mechanics.

Cross multiply: F = ma

Since ma = F, **substitute ma for F_g** in the equation $g = \dfrac{F_g}{m}$.

$g = \dfrac{ma}{m}$ in $\dfrac{kg \cdot m/s^2}{kg}$ $= \dfrac{m}{s^2}$. Therefore, g is in m/s². As you can see, g is in newtons/kilogram or meters/second².

$$g \qquad = \qquad \dfrac{F_g}{m}$$

Acceleration due to gravity $= \dfrac{weight\ of\ an\ object\ or\ force\ of\ gravity}{mass}$

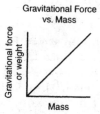

Gravitational Force
vs. Mass

Gravitational force or weight

Mass

Slope of Line Equals Acceleration

For objects near the surface of the Earth (short distances) g (acceleration due to gravity or gravitational field strength) = 9.81 m/s² or 9.81 N/kg.

Look for g (acceleration due to gravity or gravitational field strength) on Reference Table: List of Physical Constants on page reference tables 2-3.

Acceleration due to gravity	g	9.81 m/s²

Question: The graph below represents the relationship between gravitational force and mass for objects near the surface of Earth. The slope of the graph represents the
(1) acceleration due to gravity
(2) universal gravitational constant
(3) momentum of objects
(4) weight of objects

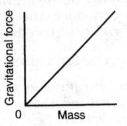

Solution: The slope $\left(\frac{\Delta y}{\Delta x}\right)$ of the graph is $\dfrac{gravitational\ force\ (F_g)}{mass\ (m)}$. Look on Reference Table: Mechanics for an equation with $\dfrac{F_g}{m}$. $\dfrac{F_g}{m} = g$. Slope of the graph is g (acceleration due to gravity).

$$\underset{\substack{\text{acceleration due}\\\text{to gravity}}}{g} = \underset{mass}{\dfrac{F_g}{m}} \, gravitational\ force$$

Acceleration is a vector quantity (has both a number and direction), example 9.81 m/s² downward.

Force is a vector quantity; F_g (force of gravity or weight) is a vector quantity in newtons (N). One newton equals about 0.22 pounds, less than ¼ of a pound.

Mass is a scalar quantity in kilograms.

g (acceleration due to gravity) near the surface of the Earth is 9.81 m/s².
g (acceleration due to gravity) near the moon is 1/6 (9.81 m/s²), which is 1.6 m/s².

$g = \dfrac{F_g\ (weight)}{m}$ or cross multiply m x g = F_g.

Look at the equation F_g = mg.
If g (acceleration) on the moon is 1/6 that of Earth, then F_g (force of gravity or weight on the moon) is 1/6 that on Earth. If a person weighs 120 pounds on Earth, the person on the moon would weigh 1/6 of the weight; 1/6 x 120 = 20 pounds.

Question: A 70-kilogram astronaut has a weight of 560 newtons on the surface of planet Alpha. What is the acceleration due to gravity on planet Alpha?
(1) 0.0 m/s²   (2) 8.0 m/s²   (3) 9.8 m/s²   80. m/s²

Solution:
Given: weight = 560 newtons (N)
           70 kilogram astronaut

Find: acceleration due to gravity (g)

A 70-kilogram astronaut means a mass of 70 kilograms. On Reference Table: List of Physical Constants **mass** of Earth equals 5.98×10^{24} **kilograms,** therefore you know **kilograms** is **mass.**

Look for an equation on Reference Table: Mechanics that has weight (F_g), mass (m) and acceleration due to gravity (g).

Use the equation

$$g = \frac{F_g}{m}.$$

g = acceleration due to gravity.

F_g = weight/ force due to gravity.

m = mass

Weight of 560 newtons means F_g = 560 newtons (N). 70-kilogram astronaut means mass (m) = 70 kilograms (kg).

In the equation $g = \frac{F_g}{m}$, *substitute for F_g* 560 N. *Substitute for m* 70 kg.

$$g = \frac{F_g}{m} = \frac{560 \text{ newtons}}{70 \text{ kilograms}} = \frac{560 \text{ N}}{70 \text{ kg}} = \frac{8 \text{ N}}{kg} \text{ or } \frac{8 \text{ m}}{s^2}$$

Note: $\dfrac{newtons}{kilograms} = \dfrac{meters \ (m)}{seconds^2 \ (s)^2}$

Answer 2

Question: Which graph best represents the relationship between acceleration due to gravity and mass for objects near the surface of Earth?[Neglect air resistance.]

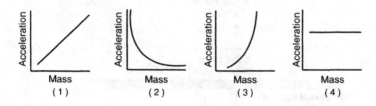

Solution: Acceleration due to gravity is 9.81 m/s² near the surface of the Earth. Acceleration is constant. Mass has no effect on acceleration.

Answer 4

FINDING SLOPE OF A GRAPH

The slope of a graph is $\dfrac{\Delta y}{\Delta x} \dfrac{(change \ in \ y)}{(change \ in \ x)}$. Choose any two points on the line. (See the graph on the next page.)

Examples:

1. (25,150) and (50, 300).

$$\text{Slope} = \frac{\Delta y}{\Delta x} = \frac{(300 \text{ N} - 150 \text{ N})}{(50 \text{ kg} - 25 \text{ kg})} = \frac{150 \text{ N}}{25 \text{ kg}} = 6.0 \frac{N}{kg} = 6.0 \frac{m}{s^2}$$

2. $(0, 0)$ and $(50, 300)$

Slope $= \dfrac{\Delta y}{\Delta x} = \dfrac{(300\ N - 0\ N)}{(50\ kg - 0\ kg)} = \dfrac{300\ N}{50\ kg} = 6.0\ \dfrac{N}{kg} = 6.0\ \dfrac{m}{s^2}$

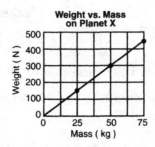

**Weight vs. Mass
on Planet X**

Now do Homework Questions #202-211, pages 161-163.

Section 7:

FORCES

FORCE OF GRAVITY, NORMAL FORCE, WEIGHT

Look at the figure below. There is a steel block on a **horizontal** steel **surface.** The steel block is on the table. The $\mathbf{F_g}$ (force of gravity) **pulls** the block **down** with a force of **20 N.** The **upward force,** which is

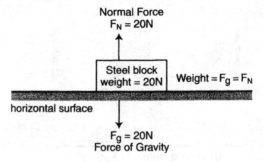

Normal Force
$F_N = 20N$

Steel block
weight = 20N Weight = F_g = F_N

horizontal surface

$F_g = 20N$
Force of Gravity

perpendicular to the horizontal surface, is called $\mathbf{F_N}$ (normal force). As you can see, F_g (downward force) is in the opposite direction to F_N (upward force), but F_g (example: 20 N) equals F_N (example 20 N).
On a horizontal surface, weight of steel block = 20 N (see above), which means force of gravity $(F_g) = 20$ N and also $F_N = 20$ N.
Another example: A steel pot on a horizontal table weighs 10 N. Weight of steel pot = 10 N, $F_g = 10$ N and $F_N = 10$ N. In short, **on a horizontal surface**, **weight** of any **object** $= \mathbf{F_g} = \mathbf{F_N}.$

On a horizontal surface, force of gravity (F_g) = Normal force (F_N) = weight. weight $F_g = F_N$.
On a horizontal surface, F_g is in the opposite direction to F_N.
F_g is downward ↓.
F_N is upward ↑.

FRICTIONAL FORCE (FRICTION) AND APPLIED FORCE

When two surfaces (example: steel box on steel table) are in contact with each other, there are frictional forces (friction). Friction (a vector quantity) is in the opposite direction to the object's motion (movement). Friction opposes (slows down) motion of two objects in contact with each other.

Static friction–opposes the start of motion (when object is at rest).

Kinetic friction–friction when object s in contact are moving past each other.

Look at the figures below. In order for the steel block to start moving, the static friction must be overcome with an equal force.

In order to keep it moving, the kinetic friction must be overcome with an equal force in the opposite direction.

Static friction is always more than kinetic friction.

Look again at the example of a 20 N steel box on a horizontal steel surface (see figures below). F_{fs} (static frictional force) = 14.8 N. Applied force must be 14.8 N to overcome static frictional force and in the opposite direction.

$$F_{f_s} = 14.8\,N \leftarrow \boxed{\begin{array}{c} 20\ N \\ \text{steel box} \end{array}} \rightarrow F_{applied} = 14.8\,N$$

Static frictional force   Applied force

F_{fk}(kinetic frictional force) = 11.4 N. Applied force must be 11.4 N to overcome kinetic frictional force and in the opposite direction.

$$F_{f_k} = 11.4\,N \leftarrow \boxed{\begin{array}{c} 20\ N \\ \text{steel box} \end{array}} \rightarrow F_{applied} = 11.4\,N$$

Kinetic frictional force   Applied force

In short, F_f (frictional force) = applied force in the opposite direction when the object is at rest or moving at constant velocity. (It is at equilibrium, with all the forces balanced, no extra force in any direction.) As you can see in the figures, the frictional force or friction is always parallel to the surface (example: top of table) that the box is moving on.

SUMMARY: Weight of an object **on a horizontal surface** = F_g = F_N. F_f = **applied force** in the **opposite direction** when the object is **at rest** or **at constant velocity**.

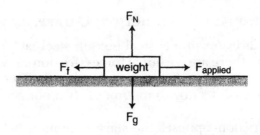

Questions 1 and 2: A 5.0-kilogram block weighing 49 newtons sits on a frictionless, horizontal surface. A horizontal force of 20. newtons toward the right is applied to the block. [Neglect air resistance.]

Question 1: Copy the diagram below onto separate paper. Draw a vector to represent each of the three forces acting on the block. Use a ruler and a scale of 1.0 centimeter = 10. newtons. Begin each vector at point C and label its magnitude in newtons.

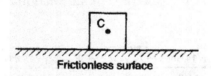

Frictionless surface

Question 2: Calculate the magnitude of the acceleration of the block. [Show all calculations, including the equation and substitution with units.]

Solution 1:
Given: 5.0-kilogram block.
    Weight = 49 newtons (N).
    Frictionless surface.
    Horizontal force of 20. newtons (N) is applied.
Find: Draw the three forces acting on the block. Let 1 cm = 10. newtons. Each vector begins at point C.
Weight = 49 newtons (given), which means F_g = 49 newtons. On a horizontal surface, weight of object = force of gravity = normal force. In this example, weight of box = 49 newtons = F_g = F_N.

Since 1 cm = 10. newtons and F_g (force of gravity) = 49 newtons, use a ruler and draw the F_g vector 4.9 cm downward.

F_N = 49 newtons, therefore draw the F_N (normal force) vector 4.9 cm upward.

Horizontal force applied (applied force) is 20. newtons (given), therefore draw the applied force vector 2.0 cm to the right.

Solution 2:

Given: 5.0-kilogram block. Weight = 49 newtons. Frictionless surface (means no friction). Horizontal force applied (applied force) is 20. newtons (N) to the right.

Find: Acceleration of the block

Look for an equation on Reference Table: Mechanics that has acceleration and force.

Use the equation

$$a = \frac{F_{net}}{m}$$

a = acceleration

F_{net} = net force
m = mass

Table: Mechanics

$$acceleration = \frac{net\ force}{mass}$$

F_N is balanced by F_g (F_N = 49 N upward, F_g = 49 N downward); the two forces cancel each other. Since the frictional force equals zero (there is no friction), given, and the applied force equals 20. newtons (given), therefore the net force (total force) = 20. newtons.

In the equation $a = \dfrac{F_{net}}{m}$, *substitute for F_{net}* 20. N (newtons).

Substitute for mass 5.0 kg (kilograms). $a = \dfrac{20.\ N}{5.0\ kg} = 4.0\ N/kg.$

Question: A horizontal force is used to pull a 5.0-kilogram cart at a constant speed of 5.0 meters per second across the floor, as shown in the diagram.

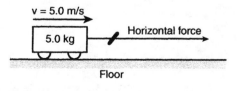

If the force of friction between the cart and the floor is 10. newtons, the magnitude of the horizontal force along the handle of the cart is

    (1) 5.0 N   (2) 10. N   (3) 25 N   (4) 50. N

Solution:

Given: Cart moves at constant speed (5.0 meters per second).

        Force of friction (frictional force) = 10. newtons (N).

        Mass of cart = 5.0 kilograms (kg).

Find: magnitude (number) of horizontal force (applied force) along the handle of the cart.

When the object is at rest or at **constant velocity**, the **applied force = force of friction**, but the applied force is in the opposite direction.

In this question, the cart is at constant speed across the floor, therefore the applied force = force of friction.

Since the force of friction (frictional force) is 10 N, the horizontal force (applied force) is the same 10 newtons (N) Answer 2 10 newtons

Question: If a 30-newton force is required to accelerate a 2-kilogram object at 10 meters per second^2, over a level floor, then the magnitude of the frictional force acting on the object is

    (1) 0 N   (2) 10 N   (3) 20 N   (4) 30 N

Solution:

Given: 30-newton force

        2-kilogram object means mass of the object is 2 kilograms

        2-kilogram object accelerates at 10 meters per second^2

        level floor

Find: frictional force

Look for an equation on Reference Table: Mechanics that has force, mass and acceleration.

Use the equation

$$a = \frac{F_{net}}{m}.$$

First find F_{net}, net force (number of newtons) required to accelerate the object if there is no friction, then compare it with the 30-newton force needed in this example when there is friction.

In the equation $a = \dfrac{F_{net}}{m}$ *substitute for* m 2 kg. *Substitute for a* 10 m/s^2.

$$a = \frac{F_{net}}{m}$$

$$10 \text{ m/s}^2 = \frac{F_{net}}{2 \text{ kg}}$$

F_{net} = 20 N (when there is no frictional force).

30 N force (given) is needed when there is frictional force (friction), but only 20 N force (F_{net}) is needed if there is no frictional force (friction). Therefore, 30 N force (needed when there is the frictional force) −20N force (needed when there is no frictional force) equals 10N force (extra force needed to overcome the frictional force); therefore, frictional force equals 10N.

Answer 2

Now Do Homework Questions #212-217, pages 163-164.

Relationship Between Weight and Friction

If an object has more weight (= F_g) (it rubs more on the surface it is in contact with) it has more friction and therefore needs more applied force to overcome the friction.

Example 1: An elephant has a **large weight** (rubs more on the ground), has **more friction**, and you need a **big force** to overcome friction and start and continue to move the elephant.

Example 2: A feather has a **little weight,** has **less friction,** and **little force** is needed to overcome friction and start and continue to move the feather.

Summary: If an object has more weight (F_g), then it has more friction and more applied force is needed to overcome the friction.

FORCE OF FRICTION

There is an equation on Reference Table: Mechanics that shows the relationship between force of friction (F_f), coefficient of friction (μ) and normal force (F_N).

$$F_f = \mu F_N$$

$$\text{force of friction} = \text{coefficient of friction} \times \text{normal force}$$

$F_f = \mu F_N$

F_f = force of friction
μ = coefficient of friction
F_N = normal force

The force of friction (F_f) is proportional to the normal force(F_N) . μ is the coefficient of friction.

$F_f = \mu F_N$. To find μ (the coefficient of friction), divide both sides by F_N.

$$\frac{F_f}{F_N} = \frac{\mu F_N}{F_N} \qquad \qquad \mu = \frac{F_f}{F_N}$$

Coefficient of friction (μ)= Force of friction (F_f) divided by the normal force (F_N).

Look at the reference table at the right for approximate coefficients of friction for different materials. Example: There is a **wooden block** on a **wooden surface**. Look at Reference Table: Approximate Coefficients of Friction, at the right or on page reference tables 5, for **wood on wood**. When the block is at rest, the static coefficient of friction $(\mu_s) = 0.42$, which is a constant (the static coefficient of friction for wood on wood is always 0.42). When the block is moving, the kinetic coefficient of friction $(\mu_k) = 0.30$, which is also a constant (the kinetic coefficient of friction for wood on wood is always 0.30).

Approximate Coefficients of Friction		
	KINETIC	STATIC
wood on wood	0.30	0.42
steel on steel	0.57	0.74
waxed ski on snow	0.05	0.14
teflon on teflon	0.04	

Question: When a 12-newton horizontal force is applied to a box on a horizontal tabletop, the box remains at rest. The force of static friction acting on the box is

(1) 0 N   (2) between 0 N and 12 N
(3) 12 N   (4) greater than 12 N

Solution: Box is at rest. At rest and also at constant velocity, applied force = force of friction (frictional force). 12 N applied force = 12 N frictional force. At rest, frictional force means the force of static friction.

Answer 3

Questions 1-5: A force of 10. newtons toward the right is exerted on a wooden crate initially moving to the right on a horizontal wooden floor. The crate weighs 25 newtons.

Question 1: Calculate the magnitude of the force of friction between the crate and the floor. [Show all work, including the equation and substitution with units.]

Question 2: On the diagram, draw and label all vertical forces acting on the crate.

Question 3: On the diagram, draw and label all horizontal forces acting on the crate.

Question 4: What is the magnitude of the net force acting on the crate?

Question 5: Is the crate accelerating? Explain your answer.

Solution 1:

Given: Wooden crate is on a horizontal wooden floor.

Crate weighs 25 newtons (N).

Force exerted (means applied force) = 10 newtons (N)

Find: Force of friction (F_f).

Look for an equation on Reference Table: Mechanics that has force of friction (F_f). There is only one equation for F_f (force of friction) on the reference table.

Use the equation

$$F_f = \mu F_N$$

F_f = force of friction
F_N = normal force
μ = coefficient of friction

In the equation above, you do not know μ (coefficient of friction) and F_N (normal force).

First, find μ by looking on Reference Table: Coefficients of Friction and also find F_N (which, on a horizontal surface, equals F_g = weight), and then substitute μ and F_N in the equation $F_f = \mu F_N$ to find F_f (force of friction).

First find coefficient of friction (μ). Look below or on Reference Table: Approximate Coefficients of Friction on page reference tables 5.

The problem states a **wooden** crate **moving** on a horizontal **wooden** floor. Since the crate is **moving**, use the **kinetic** (moving) **coefficient of friction** (μ) for wood on wood (wooden crate on wooden floor), which equals **0.30** (see table below).

Approximate Coefficients of Friction		
	Kinetic	**Static**
wood on wood	0.30	0.42
steel on steel	0.57	0.74

Find F_N (normal force). Crate is on a **horizontal** floor. Weight of crate = 25 newtons (N). Weight = F_g = F_N Therefore, F_g = 25 newtons (N) and F_N = 25 newtons (N).

In the equation $F_f = \mu F_N$, *then substitute for μ 0.30 and substitute for F_N 25 N.*

$$F_f = \mu \, F_N$$
$$F_f = 0.30(25 \text{ N}) = 7.5 \text{ N(newtons)}$$

Solutions 2 & 3:

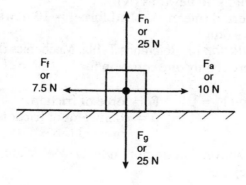

Vertical forces are F_N (normal force) and F_g (force of gravity).
Horizontal forces are F_a (applied force) and F_f (force of friction).

Solution 4: The net force is the (sum) total of **all** the forces acting on the object.

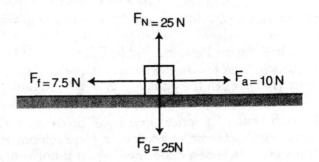

On a horizontal surface, $\uparrow F_N = F_g \downarrow$ but in opposite directions –the two forces cancel each other.

$\qquad$ $F_a = 10$ N $\quad \rightarrow$ to the right.
$\qquad$ $F_f = 7.5$N $\quad \leftarrow$ to the left.
$\qquad$ therefore, net force = 2.5 N to the right. (10 N right − 7.5 N left
$\qquad$ = 2.5 N right). $\qquad\qquad$ Answer: Net force = 2.5 N

Solution 5: Yes, because a net force acts on it.

Question: A force of 10. newtons toward the right is exerted on a steel crate initially moving to the right on a horizontal steel floor. The crate weighs 40 newtons. Calculate the magnitude of the force of friction between the crate and the floor. [Show all work, including the equation and substitution with units.]

Solution:
Given: Steel crate is on a horizontal steel floor.
$\qquad$ Crate weighs 40 newtons (N).
$\qquad$ Force exerted (means applied force) = 10 newtons (N)
Find: Force of friction F_f.

Look for an equation on Reference Table: Mechanics that has force of friction (F_f). There is only one equation for F_f (force of friction) on the reference table.

Use the equation $F_f = \mu F_N$ $\quad$ F_f = force of friction
$\qquad\qquad\qquad\qquad\qquad$ μ = coefficient of friction
$\qquad\qquad\qquad\qquad\qquad$ F_N = normal force

In the equation above, you do not know μ (coefficient of friction) and F_N (normal force).

First, find μ by looking on Reference Table: Coefficients of Friction and also find F_N (which, on a horizontal surface, equals F_g = weight), and then substitute μ and F_N in the equation $F_f = \mu F_N$ to find F_f (force of friction).

First find coefficient of friction (μ). Look below or on Reference Table: Approximate Coefficients of Friction on page reference tables 5. The problem states a **steel** crate **moving** on a horizontal **steel** floor. Since the crate is **moving**, use the **kinetic** (moving) **coefficient of friction** (μ) for steel on steel (steel crate on steel floor), which equals **0.57** (see table below).

Approximate Coefficients of Friction		
	Kinetic	Static
wood on wood	0.30	0.42
steel on steel	0.57	0.74
copper on steel	0.36	0.53

Find F_N (normal force). Crate is on a **horizontal** floor. Weight of crate = 40 newtons (N). Weight = $F_g = F_N$ Therefore, F_g = 40 newtons (N) and F_N = 40 newtons (N).

In the equation $F_f = \mu F_N$, *then substitute for* μ **0.57** and *substitute for F_N* 40 N.

$$F_f = \mu \; F_N$$
$$F_f = 0.57(40 \text{ N}) = 22.8 \text{ N(newtons)}$$

Note: If the question was a copper crate on a steel surface at rest, look again at Reference Table: Coefficient of Friction above for copper on steel. Use 0.53 (static - at rest) for coefficient of friction (μ). *Substitute 0.53 for μ in the equation $F_f = {}_\mu F_N$.*

Question: The diagram below shows a student applying a 10.-newton force to slide a piece of wood at constant speed across a horizontal surface. After the wood is cut in half, one piece is placed on top of the other, as shown.

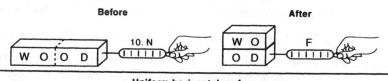

Before   After

Uniform horizontal surface

What is the magnitude of the force, F, required to slide the stacked wood at constant speed across the surface?

    (1) 40. N   (2) 20. N   (3) 10. N   (4) 5.0 N

Solution: You need the same force to slide a whole piece of wood or a cut up piece of wood. The force needed does not depend on the surface area of the wood (whether it is whole or cut and stacked). You learned, when an object is at rest or moving at constant velocity, the applied force, force needed to slide the wood (to overcome friction) equals the frictional force (force of friction).

Force of friction = coefficient of friction x normal force

$$F_f \qquad = \qquad \mu \qquad\qquad F_N$$

Look at the equation above. For the whole and cut up pieces of wood, μ (coefficient of friction) is the same because the student is sliding wood on the same horizontal surface. F_N (normal force) is the same, because $F_N = F_g$ = weight, and the weight of the whole piece of wood and the cut up pieces of wood are the same. By looking at the equation $F_f = \mu F_N$, since μ and F_N are the same for the whole and cut up pieces, F_f (force of friction) is the same, and therefore, the same applied force is needed. Since a 10 N force is needed to slide the whole piece of wood, the same 10 N force is needed to slide the cut up and stacked piece of wood.

Answer *3* 10 newtons

Question: Explain how to find the coefficient of kinetic friction between a wooden block of unknown mass and a tabletop in the laboratory. Include the following in your explanation: measurements required; equipment needed; procedure; equation(s) needed to calculate the coefficient of friction.

Solution: *Look for an equation* on Reference Table: Mechanics that has coefficient of friction (μ). There is only one equation for μ (coefficient of friction) on the reference table. *Use the equation* $F_f = \mu F_N$. To find the coefficient of friction (μ), you need to find F_N (the normal force) and F_f, (the force of friction).

In the equation $F_f = \mu F_N$, you have three things you do not know, μ, F_N, and F_f. First find F_N and F_f, and then substitute F_N and F_f in the equation $F_f = \mu F_N$ to find μ.

First find F_N: You know on a horizontal surface, $F_N = F_g$. Therefore, *look for an equation* on Reference Table: Mechanics with F_N or F_g. *Use the equation* $g = \dfrac{F_g}{m}$. Cross multiply. $F_g = mg$. Measure the mass (m) of the wooden block with a triple beam balance or an electronic balance. Using the equation $F_g = mg$ or $g = \dfrac{F_g}{m}$, multiply m (mass) in kilograms (kg) times g (9.81m/s^2, given on Reference Table: List of Physical Constants) to get F_g (weight), which is equal to F_N on a horizontal surface. Now you know F_N.

Find F_f: Using a spring scale, pull the block across the tabletop (tabletop is horizontal) at constant speed. The reading on the spring scale is F_a (applied force), which equals F_f (frictional force). Now you know F_f (frictional force).

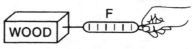

Use the equation $F_f = \mu F_N$. *Then substitute* the measurements for F_f and F_N in the equation $F_f = \mu F_N$ and solve for μ. *Or, you can substitute* the measurements for F_f and F_N in the rearranged equation $\mu = \dfrac{F_f}{F_N}$ and solve for μ.

Solution in short:
Measurements required: mass of block and applied force.

Equipment needed: triple beam balance or electronic balance, spring scale, wooden block, tabletop.

Procedure: Measure mass with triple beam balance. Using equation $g = \dfrac{F_g}{m}$ or $F_g = mg$, multiply mass times 9.81 m/s² and you get F_g, which equals F_N (normal force).

Using a spring scale, pull block at constant speed across the tabletop to find F_f (force of friction, also called frictional force).

To find μ (coefficient of friction) use the equation $F_f = \mu F_N$ and substitute values for F_N and F_f

Equations needed: $F_f = \mu F_N$. $g = \dfrac{F_g}{m}$ or $F_g = mg$.

Sand is often placed on an icy road to prevent cars from slipping. Look at the equation $F_f = \mu F_N$. With sand on the road, the coefficient of friction (μ) increases, and therefore the frictional force (friction)(F_f) increases and prevents the car from slipping.

Now do Homework Questions #218-227, pages 164-165.

FORCES ON A RAMP

You learned about the forces acting on a block on a horizontal surface.

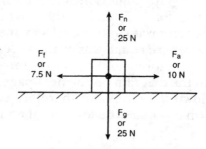

Let's learn about the forces on a block sliding down a ramp.

A is the sliding force pulling the block down the ramp.

B is the force of friction.

C is the **force of gravity (always downward,** always vertically down ↓).

D is the **upward force perpendicular** (at right angles) to the **surface** (of the **ramp**). D is the normal force (F_N) (perpendicular to the surface).

E is the **downward force perpendicular** to the **ramp.**

Note: You learned, on a horizontal surface, the weight or F_g (force of gravity) is downward, perpendicular to the horizontal surface and F_g is equal and opposite to F_N (normal force).

But on a ramp it is different. (See figure above.) The force of gravity (C) is **not** perpendicular to the ramp and therefore not equal and opposite to F_N.

The **perpendicular vector E** (perpendicular to the ramp) is **equal and opposite to F_N (D),** which is also perpendicular to the ramp.

Question: The diagram below shows a 10.0 kilogram mass held at rest on a frictionless 30.0° incline by force F. What is the approximate magnitude of force F?

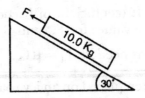

(1) 9.81 N	(2) 49.1 N	(3) 85.0 N	(4) 98.1 N

Solution:

Given: mass = 10.0 kilograms (kg), held at rest
　　　 Angle = 30.0°
　　　 frictionless incline (ramp)

Find: force (F) pulling the mass up the ramp (see diagram).

At rest or at constant velocity means the object is at equilibrium - forces are equal (this example is at rest.).

　　　 force up the ramp = force down the ramp.

In the diagram on the next page, vector #3 is parallel to the force down the ramp and therefore equal to the force down the ramp (which equals the force up the ramp). **Find #3.**

Step 1: Draw vectors.

Draw: F_g, (vertically straight down), #1
Draw vector perpendicular to ramp, #2
Draw vector parallel to the ramp, #3

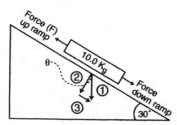

First, in step 2, find F_g (vector #1) and then, in step 3, find θ and use the equation $\sin \theta = \dfrac{opposite}{hypotenuse}$ or $A_y = A \sin \theta$ to find vector #3 (force down the ramp), which equals the force up the ramp.

Step 2: Calculate F_g (vector #1)
Look for an equation on Reference Table: Mechanics with F_g (force of gravity) and m (mass)

Use the equation $\qquad g = \dfrac{F_g}{m}$

acceleration due to gravity= $= \dfrac{Force\ of\ gravity}{mass}$

mass (m) = 10.0 kg (given)
g (acceleration due to gravity) = 9.81 m/sec², given on Reference Table: List of Physical Constants

In the equation $g = \dfrac{F_g}{m}$ *substitute 9.81 m/s² for g and* 10.0 kg for m (mass)

$9.81\ m/s^2 = \dfrac{F_g}{10.0\ kg}$

Cross multiply:
$F_g = 9.81$ m/s² x 10.0 kg = 98.1 kg•m/s² = 98.1 N
F_g (vector #1) = 98.1 N

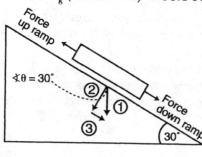

Step 3: You took F_g (98.1 N, vector #1) and broke it up into perpendicular vector #2 (perpendicular to the ramp) and parallel vector #3 (parallel to the ramp).

Angle θ (the angle between F_g (vector #1) and the vector perpendicular to the ramp (#2))= **30° because** the **angle** of the **incline** is **30°** (angle between horizontal and ramp).

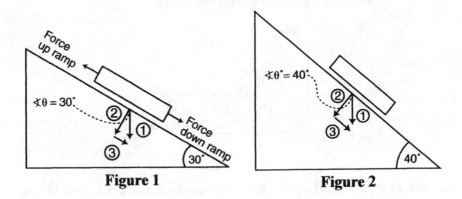

Figure 1   **Figure 2**

Rule: Like θ in this example, the angle between F_g (resultant #1) and the perpendicular vector #2 is always **equal to** the **angle of** the **incline** (angle between horizontal and ramp). See figure 1.

Note: In a different example, if angle of incline = 40°, then θ would be 40° (see figure 2).

Now let's find parallel vector #3, because it is equal and opposite (direction) to the force up the ramp. In a ramp problem, F_g (vector #1) is the **resultant** or **hypotenuse**. Look at the figure above. Let **y = parallel vector (#3)**.

$$Sin\ \theta = \frac{opposite}{hypotenuse}$$, given on Reference Table: Geometry and Trigonometry.

$$Sin\ 30 = \frac{y\ (vector\ \#3)}{98.1\ N\ (vector\ \#1)(answer\ from\ step\ 2)}$$

$\sin 30 = 0.500$

Substitute 0.500 for sin 30°

$$0.500 = \frac{y}{98.1\ N}$$

Cross multiply:

y = 98.1 N (0.500) = 49.1 N (newtons)

y (vector #3) = 49.1 N (newtons), which is equal and opposite to force F up the ramp, therefore Force F equals 49.1 N (newtons)   Answer 2

Or

Alternate method to find the parallel vector (#3). You can use the equation:

$$A_y = A \sin \theta \qquad A = \text{any vector quantity}$$

$$\theta = \text{angle}$$

Let A_y = vector #3 (opposite angle θ) parallel to the ramp.
Let A = vector #1(F_g) resultant = 98.1 N (answer from step 2)
Substitute for A 98.1 N and **substitute for** θ 30°.
$A_y = A \sin \theta$
$A_y = 98.1$ N sin 30
Sin 30° = 0.500
Substitute 0.500 for sin 30°
$A_y = 98.1$ N (0.500) = 49.1 N
A_y (vector #3) = 49.1 N (newtons), which is equal and opposite to Force F up the ramp, therefore Force F equals 49.1 N (newtons).

The ramp can be drawn this way (see diagram at right) which is the opposite (reverse) to the ramps previously drawn (see diagram at left) with the same results.

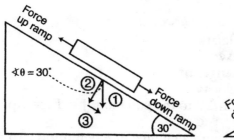

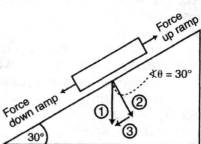

Now do Homework Questions #228-236, pages 165-167

Section 8:

MOMENTUM

Momentum (p) is **mass** (m) **times velocity** (v) and is a vector quantity.

p	=	m		v
momentum	=	mass	x	velocity

$$p = mv$$

m = mass
p = momentum
v = velocity/speed

Mass (m) is in kilograms (kg).
Velocity (v) is in meters per second (m/s).
Momentum (p) is in kilogram•meters/second (kg•m/s).
Momentum (p) is in the same direction as velocity.

Impulse (J) is a **force** over a period of time and causes a change in momentum (p).

$$J = F \quad t = \Delta p$$

impulse = force x time = change in momentum

$$J = Ft = \Delta p$$

F = force
J = impulse
p = momentum
t = time interval

Force (F) is in newtons, time (t) is in seconds and impulse (J) is in newton•seconds.

You learned p = m v
momentum = mass x velocity

Therefore, Δp = m Δv
change in =mass x **change in**
momentum   velocity

Since $\Delta p = m\Delta v$, you can add $m\Delta V$ to the equation, $J = Ft = \Delta p$.
$J = Ft = \Delta p = m\Delta v$.
Force causes a **change in velocity** and a **change** in **momentum** ($\Delta p = m\Delta v$).

Question: A student drops two eggs of equal mass simultaneously from the same height. Egg A lands on the tile floor and breaks. Egg B lands intact, without bouncing, on a foam pad lying on the floor. Compared to the magnitude of the impulse on egg A as it lands, the magnitude of the impulse on egg B as it lands is
      (1) less   (2) greater   (3) the same

Solution:
Given: Student drops two eggs of equal mass simultaneously from the same height.
Find: Is the magnitude of impulse on egg B as it lands less, greater, or the same as the impulse on egg A.
Look for an equation on Reference Table: Mechanics that has impulse (J).

Use the equation
$$J = Ft = \Delta p.$$

F = force
J = impulse
p = momentum
t = time interval

You know mass (m) is the same for both eggs (given). You know, when two objects fall from the same height (free fall), the time the objects hit the ground is the same, because the velocity (starting velocity, final velocity, and change in velocity Δv) is the same for both eggs.

Look for an equation on Reference Table: Mechanics that has mass and velocity. **Use the equation**

$$p \quad = \quad m \qquad v$$
momentum = mass x velocity

Therefore, $\Delta p \quad = \quad m \qquad \Delta v$
change in =mass x **change in**
momentum velocity

Since $\Delta p = m\Delta v$, you can add $m\Delta v$ to the equation $J = Ft = \Delta p$.
$J = Ft = \Delta p = m\Delta v$.

As explained above, m (mass) and Δv (change in velocity) is the same for both eggs, therefore J (impulse) is also the same.

Answer 3

Note: Look at the equation $J = Ft$. Since J is the same for both eggs, Force (F) x time (t), (which equals J), is the same for both eggs. The egg that hits the soft floor takes more time (t) to stop than the egg that hits the tile floor and therefore has less F (force) so the egg does not break.

Question: A 0.10 kg model rocket's engine is designed to deliver an impulse of 6.0 newton•seconds. If the rocket engine burns for 0.75 seconds, what average force does it produce?

(1) 4.5 N   (2) 8.0 N   (3) 45 N   (4) 80 N

Solution:
Given: Impulse = 6.0 newton•seconds (N•s).
        Time = 0.75 seconds (s).
Find: Average force
Look for an equation on Reference Table: Mechanics that has impulse (J), time (t) and force (F). There is only one equation on Reference Table: Mechanics that has impulse (J).

$$J \quad = \quad Ft = \Delta p$$

F = force
J = impulse
p = momentum
t = time interval
Δ = change

The question has impulse (J), time (t), and force (F).

Use the equation
$$J = Ft$$
In the equation $J = Ft$, *substitute for J* 6.0 N•s (given).
Substitute for t 0.75 s (given).

$J = Ft$	Or, rearrange the
6.0 N•s= F (0.75 s)	equation:
Divide both sides by 0.75s:	$F = \dfrac{J}{t}$
$\dfrac{6.0 \ N•s}{0.75 \ s} = \dfrac{F(0.75 \ s)}{0.75 \ s}$	
$\dfrac{6.0 \ N}{0.75} = F$	$F = \dfrac{6.0 \ N•s}{0.75 \ s}$
$8.0 \ N = F$	Force (F) = 8.0 N
Force (F) = 8.0 N Answer 2	Answer 2

Question: A 1200-kilogram car traveling at 10. meters per second hits a tree and is brought to rest in 0.10 second. What is the magnitude of the average force acting on the car to bring it to rest?
(1) 1.2×10^2 N   (2) 1.2×10^3 N   (3) 1.2×10^4 N   (4) 1.2×10^5 N

Solution:
Given: m = 1200 kilogram (kg) car means mass (m) = 1200 kg.
   v_i (initial velocity, meaning starting velocity) = 10. meters per second (m/s).
   v_f (final velocity, meaning velocity at the end) = zero meters per second. At rest means velocity = 0 m/s.
   t = 0.10 second (s).
Find: average force (F).
Look for an equation on Reference Table: Mechanics that has mass, velocity, time, and force.
Look at the equations

$$J = Ft = \Delta p$$
$$p = m v$$

F = force
J = impulse
m = mass
p = momentum
t = time interval
v = velocity/speed
Δ = change

You learned p = mv, therefore $\Delta p = m\Delta v$. Since $\Delta p = m\Delta v$, you can add $m\Delta v$ to the equation $J = Ft = \Delta p$. $J = Ft = \Delta p = m\Delta v$.
$$J = Ft = \Delta p = m\Delta v$$

Use the equation **Ft = mΔv** because three of the four things (variables) are given, time (t), mass (m), and velocity (v); you need to find only one thing, force (F).
Remember: In questions similar to this, **use the equation Ft = mΔv** when the question deals with mass (m), velocity (v), time (t), and force (F).
In the equation Ft = mΔv, substitute for m (mass) 1200 kg (given).

Substitute for t (time) 0.10 s (seconds).
You need to substitute a number for Δv. Δv (change in velocity) means final velocity (v_f) − initial velocity (v_i). $\Delta v = v_f - v_i = 0$ m/s − 10 m/s = **-10 m/s.** Substitute for Δv − 10 m/s.

F t = m Δv	Or. Rearrange the equation:
F (0.10 s) = 1200 kg (− 10 m/s)	$\dfrac{Ft}{t} = \dfrac{m\Delta v}{t}$
F (0.10 s) = − 12000 kg•m/s	
Divide both sides by 0.10 s:	$F = \dfrac{m\Delta v}{t}$
$\dfrac{F \; 0.10 \; s}{0.10 \; s} = \dfrac{-12000 \; kg•m/s}{0.10 \; s}$	
F = − 120000 kg•m/s²	$F = \dfrac{1200 kg(-10 \; m/s)}{0.1 \; s}$
= − 1.2 x 10⁵ kg•m/s²	F = − 120000 kg•m/s²
= − 1.2 x 10⁵ N	= − 1.2 x 10⁵ kg•m/s²
Answer 4	= − 1.2 x 10⁵ N
	Answer 4

Note: **F** (force) is in **N (newtons).**
$a = \dfrac{F}{m}$ or **F** = ma in **kg•m/s².**
Therefore, F is in N or kg•m/s²

Now Do Homework Questions #237-252, pages 167-169.

CONSERVATION OF MOMENTUM

You know p (momentum) = mv (mass times velocity).
Conservation of momentum: the total amount of momentum before (example: before cars collide) equals the total amount of momentum after (example: after cars collide). Another example: Two cars are held together by a string; when the string is cut, a spring pushes the cars apart. Total momentum before cutting the string equals total momentum after cutting the string.

$$P_{before} = P_{after.}$$
momentum before = momentum after

Question: The diagram below shows a 4.0 kg cart moving to the right and a 6.0 kg cart moving to the left on a horizontal frictionless surface.

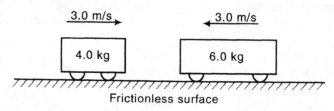

3.0 m/s   3.0 m/s

4.0 kg   6.0 kg

Frictionless surface

Table: Mechanics

When the two carts collide they lock together. The magnitude of the total momentum of the two-cart system after the collision is
(1) 0.0 kg•m/s   (2) 6.0 kg•m/s   (3) 15 kg•m/s   (4) 30. kg•m/s

Solution:
Given: One cart is 4.0 kg (means mass = 4.0 kg), moving at 3.0 m/s to the right (means velocity = 3.0 m/s).
        Other cart is 6.0 kg (means mass = 6.0 kg), and moving at 3.0 m/s to the left (which is the opposite direction). You must realize, since the **6.0 kg cart** is moving in the **opposite direction**, the **velocity** is a **negative number**, -3.0 **m/s**.
Find: Total momentum after collision.
Let's call the 4.0 kg cart Cart 1. Let's call the 6.0 kg cart Cart 2.

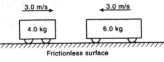

Since the question has to do with momentum after collision, look for equations on Reference Table: Mechanics that have to do with momentum and momentum after collision.

$$p \quad = \quad m \quad \quad v$$

momentum = mass x velocity

$$P_{before} \quad \quad = \quad \quad P_{after}$$
momentum before = momentum after

$p = mv$ m = mass
$P_{before} = P_{after}$ p = momentum
                  v = velocity/speed

The total amount of momentum before (example: before carts collide) equals the total amount of momentum after (example: after carts collide).

The question is to find the momentum (p) after the collision. Since you do not know the velocity (v) of the locked carts after the collision, you cannot find p (p = mv) after collision, therefore find p (momentum) before collision; $p_{before = P_{after}}$ (momentum before = momentum after) .

First: find total p (momentum) before collision (before carts collide).
You learned p = mv (momentum = mass times velocity).
p (momentum) of cart 1 = m_1v_1;   p (momentum) of cart 2 = m_2v_2.
Add p (momentum) of cart 1 and p (momentum) of cart 2) before collision.

P_{before}: m_1v_1 + m_2v_2 =
        4.0 kg(3.0 m/s)   +   6.0 kg(-3.0 m/s)   =
        12 kg•m/s   −   18 kg•m/s   = -6.0 kg•m/s
Total p (momentum) before collision   = -6.0 kg•m/s

Next: $P_{before} = P_{after}$

(Total) $p_{before} = -6.0 \text{ kg} \cdot \text{m/s}$, therefore, (total) $p_{after} = -6.0 \text{ kg} \cdot \text{m/s}$
The magnitude (number) is $6.0 \text{ kg} \cdot \text{m/s}$ Answer 2

Question: a 1.2 kg block and a 1.8 kg block are initially at rest on a frictionless horizontal surface. When a compressed spring between the blocks is released, the 1.8 kg block moves to the right at 2.0 meters per second, as shown.

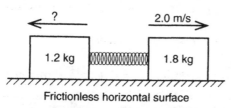

What is the speed of the 1.2 kg block after the spring is released?
       (1) 1.4 m/s   (2) 2.0 m/s   (3) 3.0 m/s   (4) 3.6 m/s

Solution:
Given:
Before (spring released): One block:1.2 kg (means mass = 1.2 kg)
                     Other block:1.8 kg (means mass = 1.8 kg)
       1.2 kg block and 1.8 kg block at rest means velocity = 0

After (spring released):   One block: 1.2 kg (means mass = 1.2 kg)
                     Other block:1.8 kg (means mass = 1.8 kg)
                     1.8 kg block has velocity = 2.0 m/s
Find: Speed of 1.2 kg block after spring is released.
Note: Velocity is speed with direction.
Let's call the 1.2 kg block Block 1.
Let's call the 1.8 kg block Block 2.
You see the question has mass and velocity (at rest) before the spring is released. The question also has mass and velocity after the spring is released. *Look for an equation* on Reference Table: Mechanics that has to do with mass (m) and velocity (v) and also before and after.
Use the equations $p = mv$ m = mass
                 $P_{before} = P_{after}$ p = momentum
                                  v = velocity/speed

The total amount of **momentum** of the **two blocks before** (the spring is released) = total amount of **momentum** of the **two blocks after** (the spring is released).
p (momentum) of block 1 = $m_1 v_1$; p (momentum) of block 2 = $m_2 v_2$.
P (momentum) before (spring is released) = $m_1 v_{1i} + m_2 v_{2i}$; i means initial (beginning) momentum before spring is released.

P (momentum) after (spring is released) = $m_1v_{1f} + m_2v_{2f}$; f means final momentum after spring is released.

$$\underset{P_{before}}{m_1v_{1i} \quad + \quad m_2v_{2i}} \quad = \quad \underset{P_{after}}{m_1v_{1f} \quad + \quad m_2v_{2f}}$$

Let x = velocity of 1.2 kg block
after (spring released)

1.2 kg(0 m/s) + 1.8 kg(0 m/s) = 1.2 kg (x m/s) + 1.8 kg(2.0 m/s)

At rest means velocity (v) = 0
and therefore mv = 0

$P_{before} = m_1v_{1i} + m_2v_{2i}$
$P_{before} = 0 \quad + \quad 0 = 0$

P_{before}		P_{after}
0 kg•m/s	=	1.2x kg•m/s + 3.6 kg•m/s
-3.6 kg•m/s	=	−3.6 kg•m/s
-3.6 kg•m/s	=	1.2x kg•m/s

Divide by 1.2 kg•m/s:

−3.0 = x, x = −3.0   speed = 3.0 m/s **Answer 3**

Question: Ball A of mass 5.0 kg moving at 20. meters per second collides with Ball B of unknown mass moving at 10. meters per second in the same direction. After the collision, Ball A moves at 10. meters per second and Ball B at 15 meters per second, both still in the same direction. What is the mass of Ball B?

(1) 6.0 kg   (2) 2.0 kg   (3) 10. kg   (4) 12 kg

Solution:
Given:
Before: Ball A mass   = 5.0 kg.
              velocity = 20. meters per second (m/s)
        Ball B mass is unknown. mass= x kg
              velocity = 10. meters per second (m/s)
After collision: Mass of Ball A and mass of Ball B obviously are the same as before the collision.
        Ball A mass = 5.0 kg.
        Ball B mass is unknown. mass = x kg
        Ball A velocity = 10. meters per second (m/s)
        Ball B velocity = 15 meters per second (m/s)
Find: mass of Ball B.
You see the question has mass and velocity before the collision. The question also has mass and velocity after the collision.
Look for an equation on Reference Table: Mechanics that has to do with mass (m) and velocity (v) and also before and after.

Use the equations

p   = mv   m = mass
$P_{before} = P_{after}$ p = momentum
                          v = velocity/speed

In this example, the equation $P_{before} = P_{after}$ means momentum (of Ball A and Ball B) before = momentum (of Ball A and Ball B) after.

p (momentum) of ball A = $m_A v_A$; p (momentum) of ball B = $m_B v_B$.
p (momentum) before collision = $m_A v_{Ai}$ + $m_B v_{Bi}$; *i* means initial (beginning) momentum before collision.
p (momentum) after collision = $m_A v_{Af}$ + $m_B v_{Bf}$; *f* means final momentum after collision.
Let x = mass of Ball B.

P_{Before} = P_{After}

Ball A		Ball B		Ball A		Ball B
$m_A v_{Ai}$	+	$m_B v_{Bi}$	=	$m_A v_{Af}$	+	$m_B v_{Bf}$
5.0 kg(20. m/s)	+	x kg(10. m/s)	=	5.0 kg(10. m/s)	+	x kg(15m/s)
100 kg•m/s	+	10.x kg•m/s	=	50. kg•m/s	+	15x kg•m/s
-50. kg•m/s				-50. kg•m/s		
50. kg•m/s	+	10.x kg•m/s	=			15x kg•m/s
		- 10.x kg•m/s				- 10.x kg•m/s
50. kg•m/s						5.0x kg•m/s

Divide by 5.0 kg•m/s

10. = x

Mass of Ball B = 10. kg   Answer 3

Questions 1 & 2: The diagram shows a compressed spring between two carts initially at rest on a horizontal frictionless surface. Cart A has a mass of 2 kg and Cart B has a mass of 1 kg. A string holds the carts together.

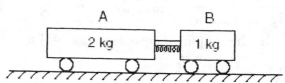

Question 1: What occurs when the string is cut and the carts move apart?

    (1) The magnitude of the acceleration of cart A is one-half the magnitude of the acceleration of cart B.
    (2) The length of time that the force acts on cart A is twice the length of time the force acts on cart B.
    (3) The magnitude of the force exerted on cart A is one-half the magnitude of the force exerted on cart B.
    (4) The magnitude of the impulse applied to cart A is twice the magnitude of the impulse applied to cart B.

Question 2: After the string is cut and the two carts move apart, the magnitude of which quantity is the same for both carts?

  (1) momentum   (2) velocity   (3) inertia (4) kinetic energy

Solution 1:
Given: Mass(m) of cart A= 2 kg   Mass(m) of cart B= 1 kg
Find: Which choice is correct.
When the string is cut, the spring expands and exerts **equal force on cart A and cart B.**

Force(F) on cart A = force(F) on cart B.

Look for an equation on Reference Table: Mechanics that has force and mass

Use the equation **F = ma** (or $a = \dfrac{F}{m}$; cross-multiply and you get F = ma).Since the force on A equals the force on B, set F = ma for both carts equal to each other.

Cart A	**Cart B**
Let m_A = mass of cart A	Let m_B = mass of cart B
Let a_A = acceleration of cart A	Let a_B = acceleration of cart B

$$m_A a_A \quad = \quad F \quad = \quad m_B a_B$$
$$m_A a_A \quad = \quad m_B a_B$$

Substitute for m_A 2 kg;   *substitute for m_B* 1 kg.
$$2 kg \bullet a_A \quad = \quad 1\ kg \bullet a_B$$

Divide both sides of the equation by a_B (the acceleration of Cart B):

$$\frac{2\ kg \bullet a_A}{a_B} = \frac{1\ kg \bullet a_B}{a_B}; \quad \text{simplify:} \quad \frac{2\ kg \bullet a_A}{a_B} = 1\ kg$$

then divide both sides by 2 kg so that you will get $\dfrac{a_A}{a_B}$ (see line below):

$$\frac{2\ kg \bullet a_A}{2\ kg \bullet a_B} = \frac{1\ kg}{2\ kg}; \quad \text{simplify:} \quad \frac{a_A}{a_B} = \frac{1}{2}$$

Cross multiply (the simplified equation): $2\ a_A = 1\ a_B$

Divide by 2: $\dfrac{2\ a_A}{2} = \dfrac{1\ a_B}{2}$

a_A (acceleration of A) = ½ a_B (acceleration of B)

Cart A has one half the acceleration of Cart B.   *Answer 1.*

Solution 2:

$$P_{before} \quad = \quad P_{after}$$
momentum before   =   momentum after

Before the string was cut, the two carts initially were at rest. At rest, velocity = zero, and p = mv = m(0) = 0. **At rest, momentum** (p) = **zero.**

After the string is cut, the two carts move apart.

$P_{before} = P_{after}$ or $P_{after} = P_{before}$

Momentum (of carts A and B)$_{after}$ = Momentum (of carts A and B)$_{before}$

Momentum **before** was **zero**. Therefore, the **momentum after** = **zero**

In this example, momentum (of carts A and B) **after** is **zero**, therefore momentum of carts A and B must be equal, but in opposite directions, so that the momentum of cart A (example:8 kg•m/sec) and momentum of cart B (example:−8 kg•m/sec) **together** must equal zero. (example: 8 + (−8) = 0).

You learned magnitude means number. The magnitude of +8 kg•m/s or −8 kg•m/s is 8 kg•m/s. Cart A and Cart B both have the same magnitude of momentum, 8 kg•m/s. Answer *1*.

Now do Homework Questions #253-259, pages 169-171

PENDULUM

A pendulum consists of a mass (m) at the end of a string (length of the string is ℓ). The beginning of the string is attached to a pivot point that lets it move back and forth.

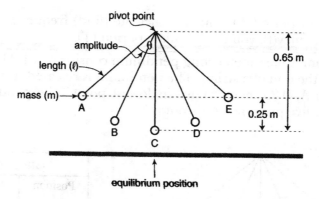

In the diagram above, **C** is the **equilibrium position** because the string is **perpendicular to** the **ground**. The string with the mass at position C (equilibrium position) is raised to a higher position (example: position A) to start the pendulum (string with mass at the end) moving.

Period: The mass is released from A and moves to E and then back to A again. The **time** it takes the mass to make **one complete cycle** (from A to E and back from E to A) equals a period.
Period is the time it takes the pendulum (string with the mass at the end) to make one complete cycle (or one vibration).

The **amplitude** is the **angle between** the **string and** the **equilibrium position**. In the diagram above, angle θ is the angle between the string at position A and the string at position C (equilibrium position).

You learned that **period (T)** is the **time** it takes the pendulum to make **one complete cycle**.

The equation to calculate the period is $T = 2\pi\sqrt{\dfrac{\ell}{g}}$, not given on the reference table.

    T = period
    π = 3.14
    ℓ = length of string
    g = acceleration due to gravity

Frequency (f) is the **number of cycles** the pendulum makes in a unit of time (example: **in one second**). Note: One cycle is when the pendulum moves back and forth from one end (example, A) to the other end (example, E) and back to the first end (example, A). See diagram on the previous page.

There is a relationship between period and frequency.

$$T = \frac{1}{f}$$

f = frequency
T = period

$$\text{Period} = \frac{1}{\text{frequency}}$$

If you know period(T), you can calculate (find) frequency (f). If you know frequency(f), you can calculate period (T).

Question: A 0.65-meter-long pendulum consists of a 1.0 kilogram mass at the end of a string. The pendulum is released from rest at position A, 0.25 meter above its lowest point. The pendulum is timed at five positions, A through E.

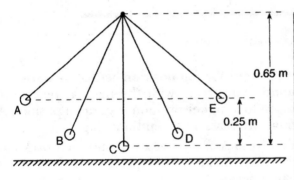

Data Table	
Position	Elapsed Time
A	0.00 s
B	0.20 s
C	0.40 s
D	0.60 s
E	0.80 s

Based on the information in the diagram and the data table, determine the period of the pendulum.

Solution: the period of the pendulum is the time it takes the pendulum (the string with a mass on it) to make one complete cycle (one complete vibration). Look at the data table. It takes 0.80 seconds to go from A to E, and obviously it takes 0.80 second for the pendulum to go from E to A.

```
  0.80
+ 0.80
  1.60
```

1.60 seconds is the period (the time it takes the pendulum to make one complete cycle from A to E and back from E to A).

Questions 1-4: Base your answers to questions 1 through 4 on the information, diagram, and data table below. The diagram shows a light string attached to mass m forming a pendulum of length ℓ. One complete vibration of the pendulum consists of mass m moving from position A to position B and back to position A. The data table shows the results of an experiment measuring the time for 10 complete vibrations of the pendulum for various pendulum lengths.

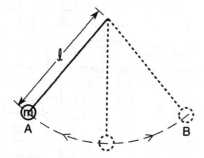

Pendulum Length (meters)	Time for 10 Vibrations (seconds)
0	0
0.2	9
0.5	14
1.0	20.
1.5	25
2.0	28
2.5	32

Copy the grid below on graph paper. Using the information in the data table, construct a graph, following the directions below.

Question 1: Mark an appropriate scale

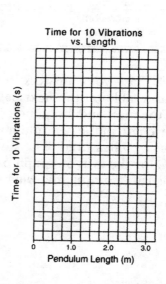

Time for 10 Vibrations vs. Length

Time for 10 Vibrations (s)

Pendulum Length (m)

the axis labeled "Time for 10 Vibrations."

Question 2: Plot the data points for time for 10 vibrations versus length.

Question 3: Draw the best-fit curve.

Question 4: Determine the period of the 1.0 meter pendulum.

Solution 1: Space the lines along the axis equally. There must be an equal number of seconds between each two lines. In the graph here, there are two seconds between each two lines on the y axis (Time for 10 Vibrations).

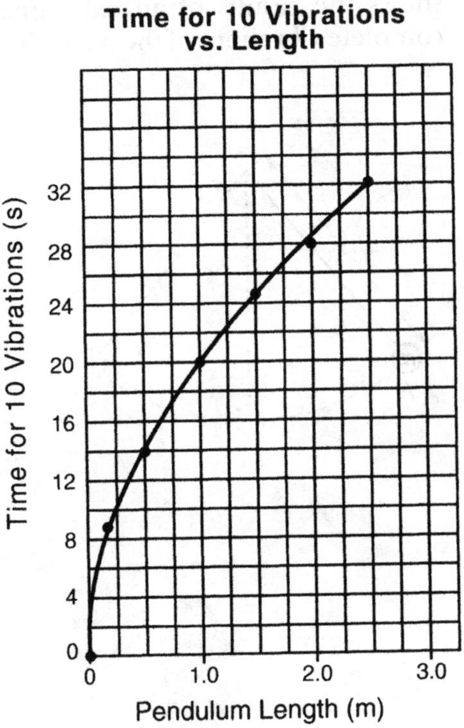

Time for 10 Vibrations vs. Length

Solution 2: Plot the data points from the data table accurately on the graph. You can draw a circle around each point.

Solution 3: Draw the best fit curved line passing (going) through the points as closely as possible. Do not continue the line past the last point.

Solution 4: Period is the **time** for **one vibration (one cycle)**. Look at the data table above. At one meter length, the time for 10 vibrations is 20 seconds. Therefore, the time for one vibration is $\frac{20 \ seconds}{10 \ vibrations} = \frac{2 \ seconds}{1 \ vibration}$. Period is the time for one vibration (one cycle). Period = 2 seconds.

Questions 1-4: Base your answers to questions 1 through 4 on the information and table on the next page. In a laboratory exercise, a student kept the mass and amplitude of swing of a simple pendulum constant. The length of the pendulum was increased and the period of the pendulum was measured. The student recorded the data in the table below. Copy the grid on graph paper. Using the information in the table, construct a graph, following the directions below.

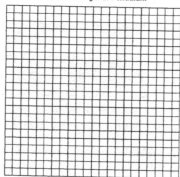

Period vs. Length of Pendulum

Length (meters)	Period (seconds)
0.05	0.30
0.20	0.90
0.40	1.30
0.60	1.60
0.80	1.80

Question 1: Label each axis with the appropriate physical quantity and unit. Mark an appropriate scale on each axis.

Question 2: Plot the data points for period versus pendulum length.

Question 3: Draw the best-fit line or curve for the data graphed.

Question 4: Using your graph, determine the period of a pendulum whose length is 0.25 meter.

Solutions: Solutions to questions 1-3 are on the graph. Read the graph to find the solution to question 4.

Solution 1: On the x axis, put "length, meters (m)." The thing you change (in this case length) is put on the **x axis**. (This is the independent variable). Space the lines along the axis equally. There must be an equal number of meters between each two lines.

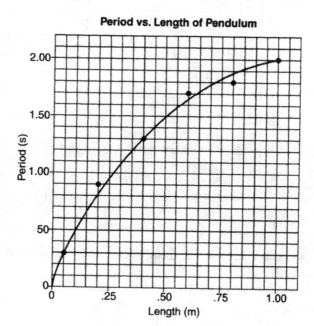

Period vs. Length of Pendulum

On the y axis, put "period, seconds (s)." The result you get is put on the **y axis**. (This is the dependent variable.)Space the lines along the axis equally. There must be an equal number of seconds between each two lines.

Solution 2: Plot the experimental data accurately on the graph. You can draw a circle around each point.

Solution 3: Draw the best-fit curved line passing through the points as closely as possible. Do not continue the line past the last point.

Solution 4: Look at 0.25 m (meters) on the x axis, go up to the curved line, and read the number on the y axis = 1.00 s.

Period of the pendulum = 1.00 s (second) (when the length is 0.25 m).

Question 1-4: Base your answers to questions 1 through 4 on the information and data table below. In an experiment, a student measured the length and period of a simple pendulum. The data table lists the length (ℓ) of the pendulum in meters and the square of the period (T^2) of the pendulum in seconds^2.Copy the grid below on graph paper. Using the information in the data table, construct a graph, following the directions below.

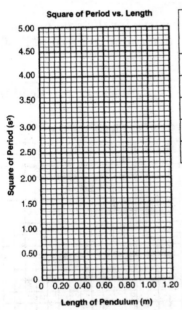

Length (ℓ) (meters)	Square of Period (T^2) (seconds^2)
0.100	0.410
0.300	1.18
0.500	1.91
0.700	2.87
0.900	3.60

Question 1: Plot the data points for the square of period versus length.

Question 2: Draw the best-fit straight line.

Question 3: Using your graph, determine the time in seconds it would take this pendulum to make one complete swing if it were 0.200 meter long.

Question 4: The period of a pendulum is related to its length by the formula:

$$T^2 = (\frac{4\pi^2}{g}) \cdot \ell$$, where g represents the acceleration due to gravity. Explain how the graph you have drawn could be used to calculate the value of g. [You do *not* need to perform any actual calculations.]

Solution 1: Plot the experimental data from the data table accurately on the graph. You can draw a circle around each point.

Solution 2: Connect the points with a straight line that is the best fit between the points.

Solution 3: Period = time (in seconds) it takes pendulum to make one complete swing (cycle or vibration). Since the length of the pendulum (string with mass on it) is 0.200 meter, look at 0.20 meter on the x axis. Go up to the straight line. Read the number on the y axis (**square of period s²**) = 0.80

Square of period = 0.80 second.

Therefore, period (time to make one complete swing when length = 0.200 m) = $\sqrt{0.80}$ = 0.89 second.

Square of Period vs. Length

Square of Period (s²) (y-axis: 0, 0.50, 1.00, 1.50, 2.00, 2.50, 3.00, 3.50, 4.00, 4.50, 5.00)

Length of Pendulum (m) (x-axis: 0, 0.20, 0.40, 0.60, 0.80, 1.00, 1.20)

Solution 4: Choose one point on the straight line and see the length of the pendulum, ℓ (on the x axis) and the square of the period T^2 (on the y axis). For example, from the graph you know that when length (ℓ) = 0.20 m, square of period (T^2) = 0.80 s^2

In the equation $T^2 = (\frac{4\pi^2}{g})\cdot\ell$, *substitute for* ℓ 0.20 m, *substitute for* T^2 0.80 s^2, and *substitute for* π 3.14.

$$0.80 \ s^2 = \frac{4 \times 3.14^2}{g} \cdot 0.20 \ m$$

Solve the equation for g.

PERCENT ERROR

Percent error compares what a student calculated, found, or measured in the lab (measured value) with the accepted value. Equation for percent error is given below:

$$\text{Percent error (\% error)} = \frac{measured\ value - accepted\ value}{accepted\ value} \times 100$$

In solution 4 above, to find g (acceleration due to gravity) we substituted in the equation $T^2 = (\frac{4\pi^2}{g})\cdot\ell$ the measured data from the student's lab experiment: 0.20 m for ℓ and 0.80 s^2 for T^2. In solving the equation above, the **measured value** of **g** = 9.86 m/s².

Find student's percent error in the value of g.

$$\text{Percent error (\% error)} = \frac{measured\ value - accepted\ value}{accepted\ value} \times 100$$

Measured value of g (acceleration due to gravity) in the lab experiment = 9.86 m/s².

The accepted value of g (acceleration due to gravity)= 9.81 m/s², given on Reference Table: List of Physical Constants on page reference tables 2-3.

$$\text{Percent error (\% error)} = \frac{measured\ value - accepted\ value}{accepted\ value} \times 100$$

$$\text{Percent error (\% error)} = \frac{9.86\ m/s^2 - 9.81\ m/s^2}{9.81\ m/s^2} \times 100$$

$$= \frac{0.05\ m/s^2}{9.81\ m/s^2} \times 100 = .00510 \times 100 = 0.51\%$$

Answer: Percent error = 0.51%

When you answer Regents questions on **MECHANICS**, use **Reference Table Mechanics, Reference Table List of Physical Constants, Reference Table Geometry and Trigonometry, Reference Table Approximate Coefficients of Friction, and Reference Table Waves.**

NOW LET'S TRY A FEW HOMEWORK QUESTIONS:
(Regents and Regents-Type Questions)

1. A group of bike riders took at 4.0 hour trip. During the first 3.0 hours, they traveled a total of 50. kilometers, but during the last hour they traveled only 10. kilometers. What was the groups's average speed for the entire trip?
    (1) 15 km/hr (2) 30. km/hr   (3) 40. km/hr   (4) 60. km/hr

2. In a 4.0 kilometer race, a runner completes the first kilometer in 5.9 minutes, the second kilometer in 6.2 minutes, the third kilometer in 6.3 minutes, and the final kilometer in 6.0 minutes. The average speed of the runner for the race is approximately
    (1) 0.16 km/min (2) 0.33 km/min (3) 12 km/min   (4) 24 km/min

3. A car travels between the 100.-meter and 250.-meter highway markers in 10. seconds. The average speed of the car during this interval is
    (1) 10. m/s   (2) 15 m/s   (3) 25 m/s   (4) 35 m/s

4. What is the average velocity of a car that travels 30. kilometers due west in 0.50 hour?
    (1) 15 km/hr (2) 60. km/hr   (3)15 km/hr west (4) 60. km/hr west

5. One car travels 40. meters due east in 5.0 seconds, and a second car travels 64 meters due west in 8.0 seconds. During their periods of travel, the cars definitely had the same
    (1) average velocity   (2) total displacement
    (3) change in momentum   (4) average speed

6. A jogger accelerates at a constant rate as she travels 5.0 meters along a straight track from point A to point B. If her speed was 2.0 meters per second at point A and will be 3.0 meters per second at point B, how long will it take her to go from A to B?
    (1) 1.0 s   (2) 2.0 s   (3) 3.3 s   (4) 4.2 s

7. Two cars, A and B, are 400. meters apart. Car A travels due east at 30. meters per second on a collision course with car B, which travels due west at 20. meters per second. How much time elapses before the two cars collide?
    (1) 8.0 s   (2) 13 s   (3) 20. s   (4) 40. s

8. Which is a vector quantity?
    (1) distance   (2) time   (3) speed   (4) acceleration

9. A manufacturer's advertisement claims that their sports car can accelerate on a level road from 0 to 60.0 miles per hour (0 to 26.8 meters per second) in 3.75 seconds. Determine the acceleration, in meters per second^2, of the car according to the advertisement.

10. A car having an initial velocity of 12 meters per second east slows uniformly to 2 meters per second east in 4.0 seconds. The acceleration of the car during this 4.0-second interval is
    (1) 2.5 m/s^2 west (2) 2.5 m/s^2 east (3) 6.0 m/s^2 west (4) 6.0 m/s^2 east

11. A runner starts from rest and accelerates uniformly to a speed of 8.0 meters per second in 4.0 seconds. The magnitude of the acceleration of the runner is
    (1) 0.50 m/s^2 (2) 2.0 m/s^2 (3) 9.8 m/s^2 (4) 32 m/s^2
    Hint: starts at rest means $v_i = 0$

12. A bicyclist accelerates from rest to a speed of 5.0 meters per second in 10. seconds. During the same 10. seconds, a car accelerates from a speed of 22 meters per second

to a speed of 27 meters per second. Compared to the acceleration of the bicycle, the acceleration of the car is

    (1) less   (2) greater   (3) the same

13. The graph represents the relationship between speed and time for a car moving in a straight line.
The magnitude of the car's acceleration is

    (1) 1.0 m/s^2 (2) 0.10 m/s^2
    (3) 10. m/s^2 (4) 0.0 m/s^2

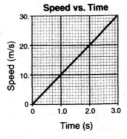

14. A car travels 20. meters east in 1.0 second. The displacement of the car at the end of this 1.0 second interval is

    (1) 20. m   (2) 20. m/s   (3) 20. meters east   (4) 20. m/s east

15. A car is driven from Buffalo to Albany and on to New York City, as shown in the diagram. Compared to the magnitude of the car's total displacement, the distance driven is

    (1) shorter   (2) longer   (3) the same

16. Which terms both represent scalar quantities?

    (1) displacement and velocity   (2) distance and speed
    (3) displacement and speed   (4) distance and velocity

17. Velocity is to speed as displacement is to

    (1) acceleration   (2) time   (3) momentum   (4) distance

18. Which two terms represent a vector quantity and the scalar quantity of the vector's magnitude, respectively?

    (1) acceleration and velocity   (2) weight and force
    (3) speed and time   (4) displacement and distance

19. The map shows the route traveled by a school bus. What is the magnitude of the total displacement of the school bus from the start to the end of its trip?

    (1) 400 m (2) 500 m
    (3) 800 m (4) 1800 M

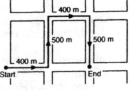

20. What is the total displacement of a student who walks 3 blocks east, 2 blocks north, 1 block west, and then 2 blocks south?

    (1) 0   (2) 2 blocks east (3) 2 blocks west (4) 8 blocks

21. A student walks 40. meters along a hallway that heads due north, then turns and walks 30. meters along another hallway that heads due east. What is the magnitude of the student's resultant displacement?

    (1) 10. m   (2) 35 m   (3) 50. m   (4) 70. m

22. As shown in the diagram, a painter climbs 7.3 meters up a vertical scaffold from A to B and then walks 11.0 meters from B to C along a level platform.
The magnitude of the painter's total displacement

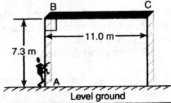

while moving from A to C is
    (1) 3.7 m   (2) 13.2 m   (3) 18.3 m   (4) 25.6 m

23. A car travels 12 kilometers due north and then 8 kilometers due west going from town A to town B. What is the magnitude of the displacement of a helicopter that flies in a straight line from town A to town B/
    (1) 20. km   (2) 14 km   (3) 10. km   (4) 4 km

Base your answers to questions 24 and 25 on the following information. A hiker walks 5.00 kilometers due north and then 7.00 kilometers due east.

24. What is the magnitude of her resultant displacement?

25. What total distance has she traveled?

26. A girl leaves a history classroom and walks 10. meters north to a drinking fountain. Then she turns and walks 30. meters south to an art classroom. What is the girl's total displacement from the history classroom to the art classroom?
    (1) 20. m south (2) 20. m north (3) 40. m south   (4) 40. m north

27. A car travels 90. meters due north in 15 seconds. Then the car turns around and travels 40. meters due south in 5.0 seconds. What is the magnitude of the average velocity of the car during the 20.-second interval?
    (1) 2.5 m/s   (2) 5.0 m/s   (3) 6.5 m/s   (4) 7.0 m/s
    Hint: find (total) displacement.

28. A softball player leaves the batter's box, overruns first base by 3.0 meters, and then returns to first base. Compared to the total distance traveled by the player, the magnitude of the player's total displacement from the batter's box is
    (1) smaller   (2) larger   (3) the same

Base your answers to questions 29 and 30 on the graph, which represents the relationship between the displacement of an object and its time of travel along a straight line.

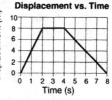

29. What is the magnitude of the object's total displacement after 8.0 seconds?
    (1) 0 m   (2) 2 m   (3) 8 m   (4) 16 m

30. What is the average speed of the object during the first 4.0 seconds?
    (1) 0 m/s   (2) 2 m/s   (3) 8 m/s   (4) 4 m/s
    Hint: Average speed equals total distance/total time.

Base your answers to questions 31 and 32 on the diagram and data table at right. The diagram shows a worker moving a 50.0-kilogram safe up a ramp by applying a constant force of 300. newtons parallel to the ramp. The data table shows the position of the safe as a function of time.

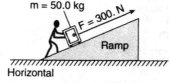

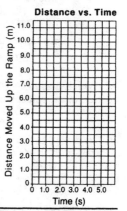

Time (s)	Distance Moved up the Ramp (m)
0.0	0.0
1.0	2.2
2.0	4.6
3.0	6.6
4.0	8.6
5.0	11.0

31. Copy the grid onto separate paper. Using the information in the data table, construct a line graph on the grid. Plot the data points and draw the best-fit line.

32. Using one or more complete sentences, explain the physical significance of the slope of the graph.

33. Which pair of graphs below represent the same motion?

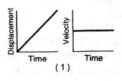

(1)

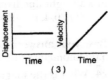

(3)

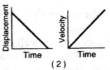

(2)

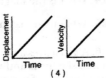

(4)

34. Which pair of graphs represents the same motion of an object?

(1)

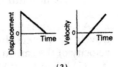

(3)

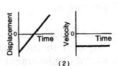

(2)

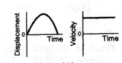

(4)

35. The graph at the right shows speed as a function of time for four cars, A, B, C, and D, in straight-line motion.

Which car experienced the greatest average acceleration during this 6.0 second interval?
    (1) car A   (2) car B
    (3) car C   (4) car D

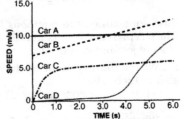

36. The graph shows the velocity of a race car moving along a straight line as a function of time.
What is the magnitude of the displacement of the car from t = 2.0 seconds to t = 4.0 seconds?
    (1) 20. m   (2) 40. m
    (3) 60. m   (4) 80. m

Hint: $\bar{v} = \dfrac{displacement/distance}{time}$

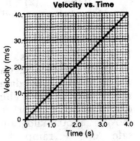

37. Which distance vs time graph below best represents the motion of an object whose speed is increasing?

(1)

(2)

(3)

(4)

38. The displacement-time graph at the right represents the motion of a cart along a straight line.

Displacement vs. Time for a Cart

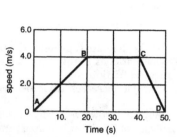

During which interval on the graph, AB, BC, CD, or DE was the cart:

    a. at rest

    b. moving with constant speed in the positive direction

    c. moving with constant speed in the negative direction

    d. accelerating

Base your answers to questions 39-41 on the speed-time graph at the right, which represents the linear motion of a cart.

39. Determine the magnitude of the acceleration of the cart during interval AB. [Show all calculations, including the equation and substitution with units.]

40. Calculate the distance traveled by the cart during interval BC. [Show all calculations, including the equation and substitution with units.]

41. What is the average speed of the cart during interval CD?

42. The displacement-time graph represents the motion of a cart initially moving forward along a straight line. During which interval is the cart moving forward at constant speed?

    (1) AB   (2) BC (3) CD   (4) DE

Displacement vs. Time

43. Which graph best represents the motion of an object that has *no* unbalanced force acting on it?

 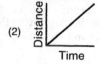

44. Which graph best represents the motion of an object falling from rest near the Earth's surface? [Neglect friction.]

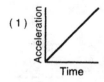 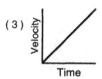

45. A 4.0-kilogram rock and a 1.0-kilogram stone fall freely from rest from a height of 100. meters. After they fall for 2.0 seconds, the ratio of the rock's speed to the stone's speed is

    (1) 1:1   (2) 2:1   (3) 1:2   (4) 4:1

46. A ball dropped from rest falls freely until it hits the ground with a speed of 20 meters per second. The time during which the ball is in free fall is approximately
     (1) 1 s   (2) 2 s   (3) 0.5 s   (4) 10 s

47. An egg is dropped from a third-story window. The distance the egg falls from the window to the ground is closest to
     (1) 10^0 m   (2) 10^1 m   (3) 10^2 m   (4) 10^3 m
     Hint: 1m (meter) = about 39 inches (39.37 inches) or about 3¼ feet (3.28 feet).

48. An 8.0-kilogram rock and a 1.0-kilogram stone fall freely from rest from a height of 100 meters. After they fall for 2.0 seconds, the ratio of the rock's speed to the stone's speed is
     (1) 1:1   (2) 1:2   (3) 2:1   (4) 4:1

49. The diagram represents the path of an object after it was thrown. What happens to the object's acceleration as it travels from A to B [neglect friction]?
     (1) it decreases (2) it increases (3) it remains the same

50. A ball thrown vertically upward reaches a maximum height of 30. meters above the surface of Earth. At its maximum height, the speed of the ball is
     (1) 0.0 m/s   (2) 3.1 m/s   (3) 9.8 m/s   (4) 24 m/s

51. Which two graphs best represent the motion of an object falling freely from rest near Earth's surface?

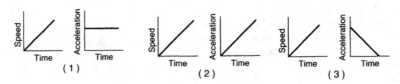

52. Which graph best represents the motion of an object falling from rest near the Earth's surface? [Neglect friction.]

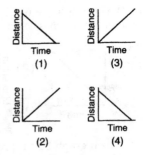

53. A cart moving across a level surface accelerates uniformly at 1.0 meter per second² for 2.0 seconds. What additional information is required to determine the distance traveled by the cart during this 2.0-second interval?
     (1) coefficient of friction between the cart and the surface
     (2) mass of the cart
     (3) net force acting on the cart
     (4) initial velocity of the cart

54. A ball is thrown at an angle of 38° to the horizontal. What happens to the magnitude of the ball's vertical acceleration during the total time interval that the ball is in the air?
     (1) it decreases, then increases (2) it decreases, then remains the same
     (3) it increases, then decreases (4) it remains the same

55. A stone is dropped from a bridge 45 meters above the surface of a river. Approximately how many seconds does the stone take to reach the water's surface?
  (1) 1.0 s   (2) 10. s   (3) 3.0 s   (4) 22 s

56. In an experiment that measures how fast a student reacts, a meter stick dropped from rest falls 0.20 meter before the student catches it. The reaction time of the student is approximately
  (1) 0.10 s   (2) 0.20 s   (3) 0.30 s   (4) 0.40 s

57. A race car traveling at 10. meters per second accelerates at the rate of 1.5 meters per second^2 while traveling a distance of 600. meters. The final speed of the race car is approximately
  (1) 1900 m/s   (2) 910 m/s   (3) 150 m/s   (4) 44 m/s

58. After a model rocket reached its maximum height, it then took 5.0 seconds to return to the launch site. What is the approximate maximum height reached by the rocket?[Neglect air resistance.]
  (1) 49 m   (2) 98 m   (3) 120 m   (4) 250 m

59. An airplane originally at rest on a runway accelerates uniformly at 6.0 meters per second^2 for 12 seconds. During this 12 second interval, the airplane travels a distance of approximately
  (1) 72 meters   (2) 220 meters   (3) 430 m   (4) 860 m

60. A 1000-kilogram car traveling with a velocity of +20. meters per second decelerates uniformly at −5.0 meters per second^2 until it comes to rest. What is the total distance the car travels as it decelerates to rest?
  (1) 10. m   (2) 20. m   (3) 40. m   (4) 80. m

61. A truck with an initial speed of 12 meters per second accelerates uniformly at 2.0 meters per second^2 for 3.0 seconds. What is the total distance traveled by the truck during this 3.0-second interval?
  (1) 9.0 m   (2) 25 m   (3) 36 m   (4) 45 m

Base your answers to questions 62 and 63 on the information and diagram below.
A car is traveling at a constant speed of 14 meters per second along a straight highway. A tree and a speed limit sign are beside the highway. As it passes the tree, the car starts to accelerate. The car is accelerated uniformly at 2.0 meters per second^2 until it reaches the speed limit sign, 5.0 seconds later.

$v = 14$ m/s

SPEED LIMIT 25 m/s

62. Review Question. When the car reaches the sign, the car's speed is
  (1) less than the speed limit   (2) greater than the speed limit
  (3) equal to the speed limit

63. What is the distance between the tree and the sign?
  (1) 10. m   (2) 25 m   (3) 70. m   (4) 95 m

64. A manufacturer's advertisement claims that their 1,250-kg (12,300-newton) sports car can accelerate on a level road from 0 to 60.0 miles per hour (0 to 26.8 meters per second) in 3.75 seconds.
Determine the acceleration, in meters/second^2, of the car according to the advertisement.

65. An object with an initial speed of 4.0 meters per second accelerates uniformly at 2.0 meters per second^2 in the direction of its motion for a distance of 5.0 meters. What is the final speed of the object?
  (1) 6.0 m/s   (2) 10. m/s   (3) 14 m/s   (4) 36 m/s

66. A race car traveling at 10. meters per second accelerates at the rate of 1.5 meters per second^2 while traveling a distance of 600. meters. The final speed of the race car is approximately

    (1) 1900 m/s (2) 910 m/s   (3) 150 m/s   (4) 44 m/s

67. An object falls freely from rest near the surface of the Earth. What is the speed of the object when it has fallen 4.9 meters from its rest position?

    (1) 4.9 m/s   (2) 9.8 m/s   (3) 24 m/s   (4) 96 m/s

68. A car initially traveling at a speed of 16 meters per second accelerates uniformly to a speed of 20. meters per second over a distance of 36 meters. What is the magnitude of the car's acceleration?

    (1) 0.11 m/s^2 (2) 2.0 m/s^2 (3) 0.22 m./s^2 (4) 9.0 m/s^2

69. A skater increases her speed uniformly from 2.0 meters per second to 7.0 meters per second over a distance of 12 meters. The magnitude of this acceleration as she travels this 12 meters is

    (1) 1.9 m/s^2 (2) 2.2 m/s^2 (3) 92.4 m/s^2 (4) 3.8 m/s^2

70. State the *two* general characteristics that are used to define a vector quantity.

71. The diagram at the right shows a worker using a rope to pull a cart.

The worker's pull on the handle of the cart can best be described as a force having

    (1) magnitude, only   (2) direction, only
    (3) both magnitude and direction
    (4) neither magnitude nor direction

72. Which is a vector quantity?

    (1) distance (2) speed   (3) power   (4) force

73. Which term represents a vector quantity?

    (1) work   (2) power   (3) force   (4) distance

74. A 150.-newton force, F_1, and a 200.-newton force, F_2, are applied simultaneously to the same point on a large crate resting on a frictionless, horizontal surface. Which diagram shows the forces positioned to give the crate the greatest acceleration?

75. Which pair of forces acting concurrently on an object will produce the resultant of greatest magnitude? Hint: Which choice has the vectors pointing closest to the same direction?

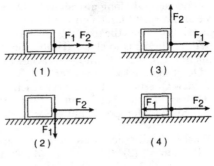

76. A 3.0-newton force and a 4.0-newton force act concurrently on a point. In which diagram below would the orientation of these forces produce the greatest net force on the point?

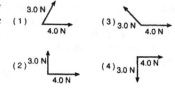

77. A 6-newton force and an 8-newton force act concurrently on a box located on a frictionless horizontal surface. Which top-view diagram shows the forces producing the *smallest* magnitude of acceleration of the box?

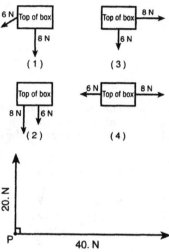

Base your answers to questions 78-81 on the information and vector diagram below.
A 20.-newton force due north and a 40.-newton force due east act concurrently on a 10.-kilogram object, located at point P.

78. Using a ruler, determine the scale used in the vector diagram by finding the number of newtons represented by each centimeter.

79. Copy the vector diagram onto separate paper. On the copy of the diagram, use a ruler and protractor to construct the vector that represents the resultant force.

80. What is the magnitude of the resultant force?

81. What is the measure of the angle (in degrees) between east and the resultant force?

82. The diagram below represents a 5.0-newton force and a 12-newton force acting on point P. The resultant of the two forces has a magnitude of
(1) 5.0 N (2) 7.0 N (3) 12 N (4) 13 N

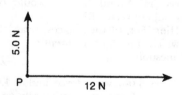

83. A force vector was resolved into two perpendicular components, F_1, and F_2, as shown in the diagram.

Which vector best represents the original force?

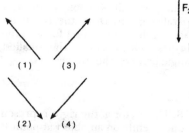

84.Two students push on a sled. One pushes with a force of 30. newtons east and the other exerts a force of 40. newtons south, as shown in the top-view diagram.. Which vector best represents the resultant of these two forces?

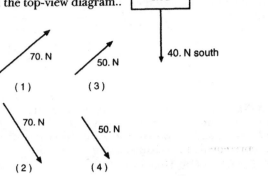

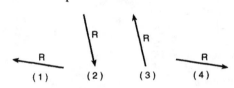

70. N
(1)

50. N
(3)

70. N
(2)

50. N
(4)

85. The vector diagram below represents two forces, F_1 and F_2, simultaneously acting on an object.
Which vector best represents the resultant of the two forces?

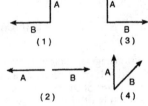

R
(1)

R
(2)

R
(3)

R
(4)

86. The diagram below shows a resultant vector R.

Which diagram best represents a pair of component vectors, A and B, that would combine to form resultant vector R?
Hint: For all the choices, draw the resultant. See which resultant is identical to the one in the question.

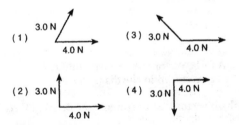

87. A 3.0-newton force and a 4.0-newton force act concurrently on a point. In which diagram below would the orientation of these forces produce the greatest net force on the point?
Hint: For all 4 choices, draw a parallelogram. Draw the resultant. See which resultant (net force) is the biggest. Or, look for the smallest angle between the two vectors.

(1) 3.0 N / 4.0 N

(3) 3.0 N \ 4.0 N

(2) 3.0 N | 4.0 N

(4) 3.0 N | 4.0 N

88. The vector at the right represents the resultant of two forces acting concurrently on an object at point P.

Which pair of vectors best represents two concurrent forces that combine to produce this resultant force vector?

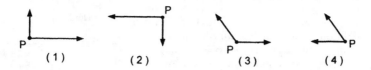

(1)   (2)   (3)   (4)

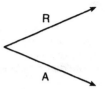

89. Forces A and B have a resultant R. Force A and resultant R are represented in the diagram.
Which vector best represents force B?

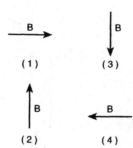

(1)

(3)

(2)

(4)

90. As shown in the diagram, a painter climbs 7.3 meters up a vertical scaffold from A to B and then walks 11.0 meters from B to C along a level platform.
The magnitude of the painter's total displacement while moving from A to C is
(1) 3.7 m   (2) 13.2 m
(3) 18.3 M   (4) 25.6 m

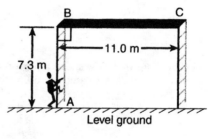

91. An artillery shell is fired at an angle to the horizontal. Its initial velocity has a vertical component of 150 meters per second and a horizontal component of 260 meters per second. What is the magnitude of the initial velocity of the shell?
(1) 9.0×10^4 m/s (2) 4.1×10^2 m/s (3) 3.0×10^2 m/s (4) 1.1×10^2 m/s

92. A 20.-newton force due north and a 40.-newton force due east act concurrently on a 10.-kilogram object, located at point P.
What is the magnitude of the resultant force? (You solved this problem graphically, now solve it algebraically.)

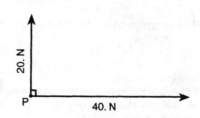

93. Forces F_1 and F_2 act concurrently on point P, as shown in the diagram.
The equilibrant of F_1 and F_2 is

    (1) 14 N southwest   (2) 14 N southeast
    (3) 20. N southwest   (4) 20. N southeast

Hint: Equilibrant is the same magnitude (number) as the resultant, but in the **opposite direction**. Example: If resultant is northeast, equilibrant is southwest, or if resultant is southeast, equilibrant is northwest.

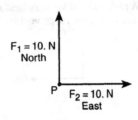

94. A river flows east at 1.5 meters per second. A motorboat leaves the north shore of the river and heads due south at 2.0 meters per second, as shown in the diagram below.

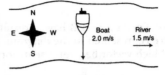

Which vector best represents the resultant velocity of the boat relative to the riverbank?

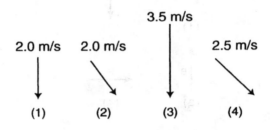

     2.0 m/s   2.0 m/s   3.5 m/s   2.5 m/s

      (1)   (2)   (3)   (4)

95. The diagram below shows a person exerting a 300.-newton force on the handle of a shovel that makes an angle of 60° with the horizontal ground.

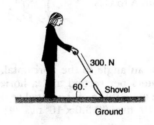

The component of the 300.-newton force that acts perpendicular to the ground is approximately

    (1) 150. N   (2) 260. N   (3)300. N   (4) 350. N

96. A baseball player throws a baseball at a speed of 40. meters per second at an angle of 30° to the ground. The horizontal component of the baseball's speed is approximately

    (1) 15 m/s   (2) 20. m/s   (3) 30. m/s   (4) 35 m/s

97. The handle of a lawn roller is held at 45° from the horizontal. A force, F of 28.0 newtons is applied to the handle as the roller is pushed across a level lawn, as shown in the diagram below.

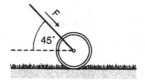

What is the magnitude of the force moving the roller forward?
    (1) 7.00 N   (2) 14.0 N   (3) 19.8 N   (4) 39.0 N
Hint: find horizontal force.

98. A football player kicks a ball with an initial velocity of 25 meters per second at an angle of 53° above the horizontal. The vertical component of the initial velocity of the ball is
    (1) 25 m/s   (2) 20. m/s   (3) 15 m/s   (4) 10. m/s

99. A 100.-newton force acts on point P, as shown in the diagram below. The magnitude of the vertical component of this force is approximately

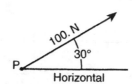

    (1) 30. N   (2) 50. N   (3) 71 N   (4) 87 N

Base your answers to questions 100 and 101 on the information and diagram below.
A golf ball leaves a golf club with an initial velocity of 40.0 meters per second at an angle of 40° with the horizontal.
Hint: **First find horizontal** component of

velocity, then $v = \dfrac{d}{t}$ or d = vt (distance =

velocity times time)

$v_i = 40.0$ m/s

40.°

100. What is the vertical component of the golf ball's initial velocity?
    (1) 25.7 m/s (2) 30.6 m/s   (3) 40.0 m/s   (4) 61.3 m/s

101. What is the total horizontal distance traveled by the golf ball during the first 2.50 seconds of its flight?
    (1) 100. m   (2) 76.6m   (3) 64.3 m   (4) 40.0 m

102. Three forces act on a box on an inclined plane as shown in the diagram. [Vectors are not drawn to scale.]
If the box is at rest, the net force acting on it is equal to
    (1) the weight   (2) the normal force
    (3) friction   (4) zero

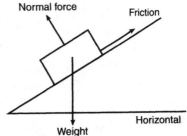

103. Which statement explains why a book resting on a table is in equilibrium?
    (1) there is a net force acting downward on the book
    (2) The weight of the book equals the weight of the table.
    (3) The acceleration due to gravity is 9.8 m/s² for both the book and the table.
    (4) The weight of the book and the table's upward force on the book are equal in magnitude, but opposite in direction.

104. Which two graphs represent the motion of an object on which the net force is zero? Hint: Review graphs in this chapter.

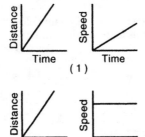

105. Which graph best represents the motion of an object that has *no* unbalanced force acting on it?

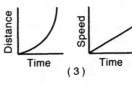

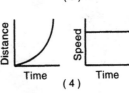

106. A ball rolls through a hollow semi-circular tube lying flat on a horizontal tabletop. Which diagram best shows the path of the ball after emerging from the tube, as viewed from above?

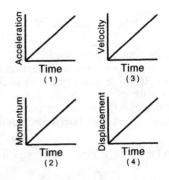

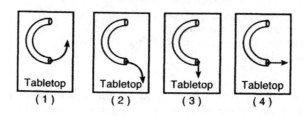

107. Which two graphs represent the motion of an object on which the net force is zero?

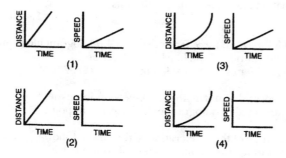

108. A lab cart is loaded with different masses and moved at various velocities. Which diagram shows the cart-mass system with the greatest inertia?

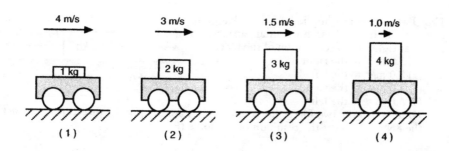

109. Compared to the inertia of a 0.10-kilogram steel ball, the inertia of a 0.20-kilogram Styrofoam ball is
    (1) one-half as great   (3) the same
    (2) twice as great   (4) four times as great

110. Compared to 8 kilograms of feathers, 6 kilograms of lead has
    (1) less mass and less inertia   (2) less mass and more inertia
    (3) more mass and less inertia   (4) more mass and more inertia

111. Which person has the greatest inertia?
    (1) a 110-kg wrestler resting on a mat
    (2) a 90-kg man walking at 2 m/s
    (3) a 70-kg long-distance runner traveling at 5 m/s
    (4) a 50-kg girl sprinting at 10 m/s

112. A mosquito flying over a highway strikes the windshield of a moving truck. Compared to the magnitude of the force of the truck on the mosquito during the collision, the magnitude of the force of the mosquito on the truck is
    (1) smaller   (2) larger   (3) the same

113. A soccer player accelerates a 0.50-kilogram soccer ball by kicking it with a net force of 5.0 newtons. Calculate the magnitude of the acceleration of the ball. [Show all work, including the equation and substitution with units.]

114. A horizontal 8.0-newton force is applied to a 4.0-kilogram block on a frictionless table. What is the magnitude of the block's acceleration?
    (1) 0.50 m/s² (2) 2.0 m/s²   (3) 9.8 m/s²   (4) 32 m/s²

115. A 20.-newton force due north and a 40.-newton force due east act concurrently on a 10.-kilogram object, located at point P.
Calculate the magnitude of the acceleration of the object. [Show all calculations, including the equation and substitution with units.] Hint: First find the resultant force (parallelogram or algebraic method), then use the resultant of the two forces, which is F_{net} (net force).

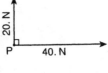

116. A net force of 5.0 x 10² newtons causes an object to accelerate at a rate of 5.0 meters per second². What is the mass of the object?
    (1) 1.0 x 10² kg   (2) 2.0 x 10⁻¹ kg   (3) 6.0 x 10² kg   (4) 2.5 x 10³ kg

117. Two forces are applied to a 2.0-kilogram block on a frictionless, horizontal surface, as shown at right. The acceleration of the block is
    (1) 5.0 m/s² to the right
    (2) 5.0 m/s² to the left
    (3) 3.0 m/s² to the right
    (4) 3.0 m/s² to the left

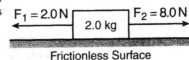

Hint: When the two forces (force vectors←→) are in opposite directions, subtract the 8N – 2N to get the resultant or net force (F_{net})

Base your answers to questions 118-120 on the information and diagram below.
In the scaled diagram, two forces, F_1 and F_2, act on a 4.0-kilogram block at point P. Force F_1 has a magnitude of 12.0 newtons, and is directed toward the right.

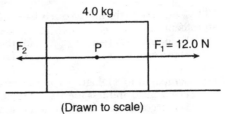

118. Using a ruler and the scaled diagram, determine the magnitude of F_2 in newtons.

(Drawn to scale)

119. Determine the magnitude of the net force acting on the block. Hint: When the two forces (force vectors←→) are in opposite directions, subtract the two forces to get the resultant or net force (F_{net}).

120. Calculate the magnitude of the acceleration of the block. [Show all work, including the equation and substitution with units.]

121. A constant unbalanced force is applied to an object for a period of time. Which graph best represents the acceleration of the object as a function of elapsed time?

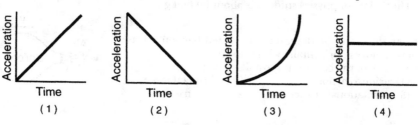

Acceleration   Acceleration   Acceleration   Acceleration

Time   Time   Time   Time

(1)   (2)   (3)   (4)

122. In the diagram, a 10.-kilogram block is at rest on a plane inclined at 15° to the horizontal. As the angle of the incline is increased to 30.°, the mass of the block will
    (1) decrease   (2) increase   (3) remain the same
    Hint: mass is always constant

123. A 1.5-kilogram lab cart is accelerated uniformly from rest to a speed of 2.0 meters per second in 0.50 second. What is the magnitude of the force producing this acceleration?
    (1) 0.70 N   (2) 1.5 N   (3) 3.0 N   (4) 6.0 N

124. What is the magnitude of the net force acting on a 2.0×10^3-kg car as it accelerates from rest to a speed of 15 meters per second in 5.0 seconds?
    (1) 6.0×10^3 N (2) 2.0×10^4 N (3) 3.0×10^4 N   (4) 6.0×10^4 N

125. A 0.60-kilogram softball initially at rest is hit with a bat. The ball is in contact with the bat for 0.20 second and leaves the bat with a speed of 25 meters per second. What is the magnitude of the average force exerted by the ball on the bat?
    (1) 8.3 N   (2) 15 N   (3) 3.0 N   (4) 75 N

126. A man is pushing a baby stroller. Compared to the magnitude of the force exerted on the stroller by the man, the magnitude of the force exerted on the man by the stroller is
    (1) zero   (2) smaller, but greater than zero
    (3) larger   (4) the same

127. A mosquito flying over a highway strikes the windshield of a moving truck. Compared to the magnitude of the force of the moving truck on the mosquito during the collision, the magnitude of the force of the mosquito on the moving truck is
    (1) smaller   (2) larger   (3) the same

128. A tennis ball is hit with a tennis racket. Compared to the magnitude of the force of the racket on the ball, the magnitude of the force of the ball on the racket is
    (1) smaller   (2) larger   (3) the same

129. A person kicks a 4.0-kilogram door with a 48 newton force causing the door to accelerate at 12 meters per second². What is the magnitude of the force exerted by the door on the person?
    (1) 48 N   (2) 24 N   (3) 12 N   (4) 4.0 N

130. How far will a brick starting from rest fall freely in 3.0 seconds?
    (1) 15 m   (2) 29 m   (3) 44 m   (4) 88 m

131. A high school physics student is sitting in a seat reading this question. The magnitude of the force with which the seat is pushing up on the student to support him is closest to
    (1) 0 N   (2) 60 N   (3) 600 N   (4) 6,000 N
    Hint: Mass of physics student is about 60-65 kg

132. As shown in the diagram, an inflated balloon released from rest moves horizontally with velocity v.
The velocity of the balloon is most likely caused by
    (1) action-reaction   (2) centripetal force
    (3) gravitational attraction   (4) rolling friction

133. A person is standing on a bathroom scale in an elevator car. If the scale reads a value greater than the weight of the person at rest, the elevator car could be moving
    (1) downward at constant speed   (2) upward at constant speed
    (3) downward at increasing speed   (4) upward at increasing speed

134. A man weighs 900 newtons standing on a scale in a stationary elevator. If sometime later the reading on the scale is 1200 newtons, the elevator must be moving with
    (1) constant acceleration downward (2) constant speed downward
    (3) constant acceleration upward   (4) constant speed upward

135. A 0.2-kilogram red ball is thrown horizontally at a speed of 4 meters per second from a height of 3 meters. A 0.4-kilogram green ball is thrown horizontally from the same height at a speed of 8 meters per second. Compared to the time it takes the red ball to reach the ground, the time it takes the green ball to reach the ground is
    (1) one-half as great   (3) the same
    (2) twice as great   (4) four times as great

136. A 2-kilogram block is dropped from the roof of a tall building at the same time a 6-kilogram ball is thrown horizontally from the same height. Which statement best describes the motion of the block and the motion of the ball? [Neglect air resistance.]
    (1) The 2-kg block hits the ground first because it has no horizontal velocity.
    (2) The 6-kg ball hits the ground first because it has more mass.
    (3) The 6-kg ball hits the ground first because it is round.
    (4) The block and the ball hit the ground at the same time because they have the same vertical acceleration.

137. A red ball and a green ball are simultaneously thrown horizontally from the same height. The red ball has an initial speed of 40. meters per second and the green ball has an initial speed of 20. meters per second. Compared to the time it takes the red ball to reach the ground, the time it takes the green ball to reach the ground will be
    (1) the same   (2) twice as much
    (3) half as much   (4) four times as much

138. Four different balls are thrown horizontally off the top of four cliffs. In which diagram does the ball have the shortest time of flight?

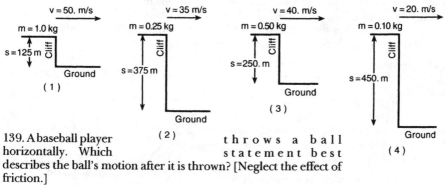

139. A baseball player throws a ball horizontally. Which statement best describes the ball's motion after it is thrown? [Neglect the effect of friction.]

(1) Its vertical speed remains the same, and its horizontal speed increases.
(2) Its vertical speed remains the same, and its horizontal speed remains the same.
(3) Its vertical speed increases, and its horizontal speed increases.
(4) Its vertical speed increases, and its horizontal speed remains the same.

140. A projectile has an initial horizontal velocity of 15 meters per second and an initial vertical velocity of 25 meters per second. Determine the projectile's horizontal displacement if the total time of flight is 5.0 seconds. [Neglect friction.]

Base your answers to questions 141-143 on the following information.
A ball is thrown horizontally with an initial velocity of 20.0 meters per second from the top of a tower 60.0 meters high.

141. What is the initial vertical velocity of the ball?
(1) 0 m/s   (2) 9.8 m/s   (3) 20.0 m/s   (4) 60.0 m/s

142. What is the approximate total time required for the ball to reach the ground? [Neglect air resistance.]
(1) 12.2 s   (2) 2.04 s   (3) 3.00 s   (4) 3.50 s

143. What is the horizontal velocity of the ball just before it reaches the ground? [Neglect air resistance.]
(1) 9.81 m/s   (2) 20.0 m/s   (3) 34.3 m/s   (4) 68.6 m/s

Base your answers to questions 144-146 on the diagram and information below. An object was projected horizontally from a tall cliff. The diagram represents the path of the object, neglecting friction.

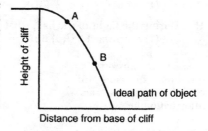

144. How does the magnitude of the horizontal component of the object's velocity at point A compare with the magnitude of the horizontal component of the object's velocity at point B?

145. How does the magnitude of the vertical component of the object's velocity at point A compare with the magnitude of the vertical component of the object's velocity at point B?

146. Copy the diagram on separate paper; sketch a likely path of the horizontally projected object, assuming that it was subject to air resistance.
Hint: air resistance slows down the moving object; less velocity =therefore less distance covered.

Base the answers to questions 147 and 148 on the following:
A student standing on a knoll throws a snowball above the level ground towards a smokestack 4.5 meters away. The snowball hits the smokestack 0.65 seconds after being released (see diagram below). (Neglect air resistance)

147. Approximately how far above the level ground does the snowball hit the smokestack?

    (1) 0.0 m   (2) 0.4 m
    (3) 2.4 m   (4) 4.5 m

Hint: take initial height of snowball above level ground (4.5m) minus vertical distance it drops in 0.65 second.

148. At the instance the snowball is released, the horizontal component of its velocity is approximately

    (1) 6.9 m/s   (2) 9.8 m/s   (3) 17 m/s   (4) 23m/s

Base your answers to questions 149-151 on the following information:
A 10-kilogram sphere A is projected horizontally with a velocity of 30. meters per second due east from a height of 20. meters above level ground. At the same instant, a 20.-kilogram sphere B is projected horizontally with a velocity of 10. meters per second due west from a height of 80. meters above level ground. [Neglect air friction.]

149. Initially, the spheres are separated by a horizontal distance of 100. meters. What is the horizontal separation of the spheres at the end of 1.5 seconds?

    (1) 15 m   (2) 30. m   (3) 40. m   (4) 45 m

150. The magnitude of the horizontal acceleration of sphere A is
    (1) 0.0 m/s^2 (2) 2.0 m/s^2 (3) 9.8 m/s^2 (4) 15 m/s^2

151. Compared to the vertical acceleration of sphere A, the vertical acceleration of sphere B is

    (1) the same   (2) twice as great
    (3) one-half as great   (4) four ties as great

Base your answers to questions 152 and 153 on the following information: A ball is projected horizontally with an initial velocity of 20. meters per second east, off a cliff 100. meters high. [Neglect air resistance.]

152. How many seconds does the ball take to reach the ground?
    (1) 4.5 s   (2) 20. s   (3) 9.8 s   (4) 2.0 s

153. During the flight of the ball, what is the direction of its acceleration?
    (1) downward   (2) upward   (3) westward   (4) eastward

Base your answers to questions 154 and 155 on the diagram and information below.

Elapsed Time = 0.92 s

V_{iy} = 9.0 m/s

154. A machine launches a tennis ball at an angle of 45° with the horizontal, as shown. The ball has an initial vertical velocity of 9.0 meters per second and an initial horizontal velocity of 9.0 meters per second. The ball reaches its maximum height 0.92 second after its launch. [Neglect air resistance and assume the ball lands at the same height above the ground from which it was launched.]

Launcher V_{ix} = 9.0 m/s
45°
Horizontal

The speed of the tennis ball as it leaves the launcher is approximately
    (1) 4.5 m/s   (2) 8.3 m/s   (3) 13 m/s   (4) 18 m/s
(Hint: $c^2 = a^2 + b^2$)

155. The total horizontal distance traveled by the tennis ball during the entire time it is in the air is approximately
    (1) 23 m   (2) 17 m   (3) 8.3 m   (4) 4.1 m

156. A child pulls a 50-kilogram friend on a sled by applying a 300.-newton force on the sled rope at an angle of 40° with the horizontal. The vertical component of the 300. newton force is approximately
    (1) 510 N   (2) 230 N   (3) 190 N   (4) 32 N

157. A golf ball is hit with an initial velocity of 15 meters per second at an angle of 35 degrees above the horizontal. What is the vertical component of the golf ball's initial velocity?
    (1) 8.6 m/s   (2) 9.8 m/s   (3) 12 m/s   (4) 15 m/s

158. A projectile is fired at an angle of 53°to the horizontal with a speed of 80. meters per second. What is the vertical component of the projectile's original capacity?
    (1) 130 m/s   (2) 100 m/s
    (3) 64 m/s   (4) 48 m/s

159. A 100.-newton force acts on point P, as shown in the diagram below. The magnitude of the vertical component of this force is approximately
    (1) 30.N   (2) 50.N
    (3) 71.N   (4) 87.N

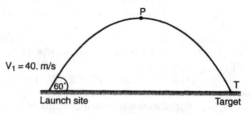

160. A projectile is launched at an angle of 60°above the horizontal at an initial sped of 40. meters per second, as shown in the diagram below. The projectile reaches its highest altitude at point P and strikes a target at point T. [Neglect air resistance.]What is the magnitude of the vertical component of the projectile's initial speed?
    (1) 35 m/s   (2) 20. m/s
    (3) 9.8 m/s   (4) 4.3 m/s

161. A cannon with a muzzle velocity of 500. meters per second fires a cannonball at an angle of 30° above the horizontal. What is the vertical component of the cannonball's velocity as it leaves the cannon?
    (1) 0.0 m/s   (2) 250. m/s   (3) 433 m/s   (4) 500. m/s

Base your answers to questions 162 and 163 on the information below.
A cannon elevated at an angle of 35° to the horizontal fires a cannonball. [Neglect air resistance and assume the ball lands at the same height above the ground from which it was launched.]

162. If the ball lands 7.0 x 10^2 meters from the cannon 10. seconds after it was fired, what is the horizontal component of its initial velocity?
    (1) 70. m/s   (2) 49 m/s   (3) 35 m/s   (4) 7.0 m/s

163. If the ball's time of flight is 10. seconds, what is the vertical component of its initial velocity?

(1) 9.8 m/s   (2) 49 m/s   (3) 70. m/s   (4) 98 m/s

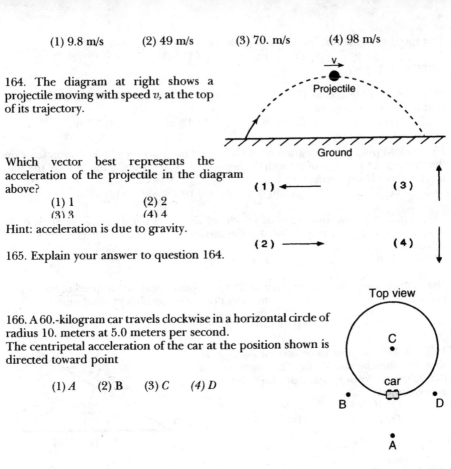

164. The diagram at right shows a projectile moving with speed v, at the top of its trajectory.

Which vector best represents the acceleration of the projectile in the diagram above?

(1) 1   (2) 2
(3) 3   (4) 4

Hint: acceleration is due to gravity.

165. Explain your answer to question 164.

166. A 60.-kilogram car travels clockwise in a horizontal circle of radius 10. meters at 5.0 meters per second.
The centripetal acceleration of the car at the position shown is directed toward point

(1) A   (2) B   (3) C   (4) D

167. A 60.-kilogram adult and a 30.-kilogram child are passengers on a rotor ride at an amusement park. When the rotating hollow cylinder reaches a certain constant speed, v, the floor moves downward. Both passengers stay "pinned" against the wall of the rotor.
The magnitude of the frictional force between the adult and the wall of the spinning rotor is F. What is the magnitude of the frictional force between the child and the wall of the spinning rotor?
        (1) F   (2) 2F   (3) F/2   (4) F/4

168. Compared to the magnitude of the acceleration of the adult, the magnitude of the acceleration of the child is
        (1) less   (2) greater   (3) the same

169. An amusement park ride moves a rider at a constant speed of 14 meters per second in a horizontal circular path of radius 10. meters. What is the rider's centripetal acceleration in terms of g, the acceleration due to gravity?
        (1) 1g (2) 2g (3) 3g (4) 0g
Hint: Acceleration due to gravity, g, $=9.8$ m/s^2. The acceleration you need to find is how many times g (9.8 m/s^2) Example: acceleration of 19.6 m/s^2 = 2 g; acceleration of 29.4 m/s^2 = 3g.

170. A 1200-kilogram car traveling at a constant speed of 9.0 meters per second turns at an intersection. The car follows a horizontal circular path with a radius of 25 meters to point P (see diagram below).

The magnitude of the centripetal force acting on the car as it travels around the circular path is approximately
(1) 1.1×10^4 N   (3) 3.9×10^3 N
(2) 1.2×10^4 N   (4) 4.3×10^2 N

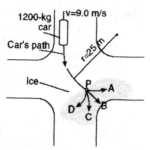

Base your answers to questions 171-174 on the information and diagram below.

In an experiment, a rubber stopper is attached to one end of a string that is passed through a plastic tube before weights are attached to the other end. The stopper is whirled in a horizontal circular path at constant speed.

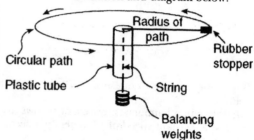

171. Copy the diagram of the top view. Draw the path of the rubber stopper if the string breaks at the position shown.

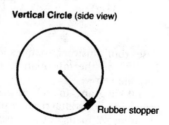

172. Describe what would happen to the radius of the circle if the student whirls the stopper at a greater speed without changing the balancing weights. Hint: Since the balancing weight pulling down on the string is constant, F_c is also constant .

173. List *three* measurements that must be taken to show that the magnitude of the centripetal force is equal to the balancing weights. [Neglect friction.]

174. The rubber stopper is now whirled in a vertical circle at the same speed. Copy the diagram; draw and label vectors to indicate the direction of the weight (*Fg*) and the direction of the centripetal force (*Fc*) at the position shown.

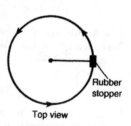

175. A student spins a 0.10-kilogram ball at the end of a 0.50-meter string in a horizontal circle at a constant speed of 10. meters per second. [Neglect air resistance.] If the magnitude of the force applied to the string by the student's hand is increased, the magnitude of the acceleration of the ball in its circular path will
(1) decrease   (2) increase   (3) remain the same

176. The magnitude of the centripetal force required to keep the ball in this circular path is
(1) 5.0 N   (2) 10. N   (3) 20. N   (4) 200 N

177. Which is the best description of the force keeping the ball in the circular path?
    (1) perpendicular to the circle and directed toward the center of the circle
    (2) perpendicular to the circle and directed away from the center of the circle
    (3) tangent to the circle and directed in the same direction that the ball is moving
    (4) tangent to the circle and directed opposite to the direction that the ball is moving

178. A convertible car with its top down is traveling at constant speed around a circular track as shown in the diagram. When the car is at point A, if a passenger in the car throws a ball straight up, the ball could land at point
    (1) A   (2) B
    (3) C   (4) D

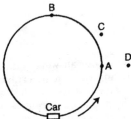

Base your answers to questions 179 through 181 on the information and diagram below.
An athlete in a hammer-throw event throws a 7.0-kilogram hammer in a horizontal circle at a constant speed of 12 meters per second. The radius of the hammer's path is 2.0 meters.

179. At the position shown, the centripetal force acting on the hammer is directed towards point
    (1) A   (2) B
    (3) C   (4) D

180. What is the magnitude of the centripetal acceleration of the hammer?
    (1) 6.0 m/s²   (2) 24 m/s²
    (3) 72 m/s²   (4) 500 m/s²

181. If the hammer is released at the point shown, it will travel towards point
    (1) A   (2) B   (3) C   (4) D

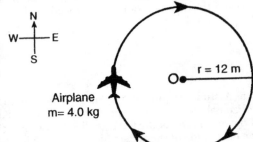

Base your answers to questions 182-183 on the information and diagram below:
A 4.0-kilogram model airplane travels in a horizontal circular path of radius 12 meters at a constant speed of 6.0 meters per second.

182. At the position shown, what is the direction of the net force acting on the airplane?
    (1) North   (2) South
    (3) East   (4) West

183. What is the magnitude of the centripetal acceleration of the airplane?
    (1) 0.5 m/s²   (2) 2.0 m/s²   (3) 3.0 m/s²   (4) 12 m/s²

Base your answers to questions 184-186 on the information and diagram below which shows a 2.0-kilogram cart traveling at a constant speed in a horizontal circle of radius 3.0 meters. The magnitude of the centripetal force of the cart is 24 newtons.

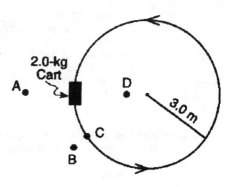

184. In the position shown, the acceleration of the cart is
  (1) 8.0 m/s² directed towards point A
  (2) 8.0 m/s² directed towards point D
  (3) 12.0 m/s² directed towards point A
  (4) 12.0 m/s ²directed towards point D

185. Which statement correctly describes the direction of the cart's velocity and centripetal force in the position shown?
  (1) Velocity is directed towards point *B*, and the centripetal force is directed towards point *A*.
  (2) Velocity is directed towards point *B*, and the centripetal force is directed towards point *D*.
  (3) Velocity is directed towards point *C*, and the centripetal force is directed towards point *A*.
  (4) Velocity is directed towards point *C*, and the centripetal force is directed towards point *D*.

186. What is the speed of the cart?
  (1) 6.0 m/s   (2) 16 m/s   (3) 36 m/s   (4) 4.0 m/s

Base your answers to questions 187 and 188 on the information below.
A vehicle travels at a constant speed of 6.0 meters per second around a horizontal circular curve with a radius of 24 meters. The mass of the vehicle is 4.4 x 10³ kilograms. An icy patch is located at point P on the curve.

187. What is the magnitude of the frictional force that keeps the vehicle on its circular path?
  (1) 1.1 x 10³ N   (2) 6.6 x 10³ N
  (3) 4.3 X 10⁴ N   (4) 6.5 x 10⁴ N

188. On the icy patch of pavement, the frictional force on the vehicle is zero. Which arrow best represents the direction of the vehicle's velocity when it reaches icy patch P?
  (1) →   (2) ←   (3) ↑   (4) ↓

189. As a cart travels around a horizontal circular track, the cart *must* undergo a change in
  (1) velocity   (2) inertia   (3) speed   (4) weight

190. The diagram shows a student seated on a rotating circular platform, holding a 2.0-kilogram block with a spring scale. The block is 1.2 meters from the center of the platform. The block has a constant speed of 8.0 meters per second. [Frictional forces on the block are negligible.]

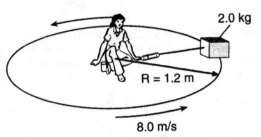

Which statement best describes the block's movement as the platform rotates?

    (1) Its velocity is directed tangent to the circular path, with an inward acceleration.

    (2) Its velocity is directed tangent to the circular path, with an outward acceleration.

    (3) Its velocity is directed perpendicular to the circular path, with an inward acceleration.

    (4) Its velocity is directed perpendicular to the circular path, with an outward acceleration.

191. A 1.50-kilogram cart travels in a horizontal circle of radius 2.40 meters at a constant speed of 4.00 meters per second. Calculate the time required for the cart to make one complete revolution. [Show all work, including the equation and substitution with units.]

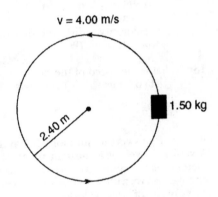

192. A 4.0-kilogram model airplane travels in a horizontal circular path of radius 12 meters at a constant speed of 6.0 meters per second.
If the speed of the airplane is doubled and the radius of the path remains unchanged, the magnitude of the centripetal force acting on the airplane will be

    (1) half as much
    (2) twice as much
    (3) one-fourth as much
    (4) four times as much

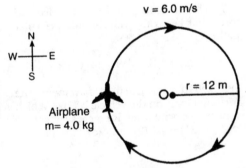

Base your answers to questions 193-196 on the information and diagram below.

The diagram shows a 5.0-kilogram cart traveling clockwise in a horizontal circle of radius 2.0 meters at a constant speed of 4.0 meters per second.

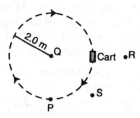

193. At the position shown, the velocity of the cart is directed toward point
    (1) P   (2) Q   (3) R   (4) S

194. At the position shown, the centripetal acceleration of the cart is directed toward point
    (1) P   (2) O   (3) R   (4) S

195. If the mass of the cart was doubled, the magnitude of the centripetal acceleration of the cart would be
    (1) unchanged   (2) doubled   (3) halved   (4) quadrupled

196. What is the magnitude of the centripetal force acting on the cart?
    (1) 8.0 N   (2) 20. N   (3) 40. N   (4) 50. N

197 Which terms represent a vector quantity and its respective unit?
    (1) weight — kilogram
    (2) mass — kilogram
    (3) force — newton
    (4) momentum — newton

    Hint: Force is in newtons

198 As the mass of a body increases, its gravitational force of attraction on the Earth
    (1) decreases   (2) increases   (3) remains the same

    Hint: As mass increases, F_g increases $F_g = \dfrac{Gm_1 m_2}{r^2}$

199 The gravitational force of attraction between two objects would be increased by
    (1) doubling the mass of both objects, only
    (2) doubling the distance between the objects, only
    (3) doubling the mass of both objects and doubling the distance between the objects
    (4) doubling the mass of one object and doubling the distance between the objects

    Hint: F_g increases, then mass and d doubles, etc.

200 The magnitude of the gravitational force between two objects is 20. newtons. If the mass of each object were doubled, the magnitude of the gravitational force between the objects would be
    (1) 5.0 N   (2) 10. N   (3) 20. N   (4) 80.N

---

201 An astronaut weighs 8.00×10^2 newtons on the surface of Earth. What is the weight of the astronaut 6.37×10^6 meters above the surface of Earth?
(1) 0.00 N
(2) 2.00×10^2 N
(3) 1.60×10^3 N
(4) 3.20×10^3 N

Hint: See Reference Table: List of Physical Constants for mean radius of Earth

202 Which combination of fundamental units can be used to express the weight of an object?
(1) kilogram/second
(2) kilogram • meter
(3) kilogram • meter/second
(4) kilogram • meter/second^2

203 The weight of an apple is closest to
(1) 10^{-2} N
(2) 10^{-0} N
(3) 10^2 N
(4) 10^{-4} N

Reminder: $10^0 = 1$, $10^1 = 10$, $10^2 = 100$.

204 Which object weighs approximately 1 newton?
(1) dime
(2) paper clip
(3) physics student
(4) golf ball

205 A 3.0 kilogram mass weighs 15 newtons at a given point in the Earth's gravitational field. What is the magnitude of the acceleration due to the gravity at this point?
(1) 45 m/s^2
(2) 9.8 m/s^2
(3) 5.0 m/s^2
(4) 0.20 m/s^2

206 A 60.-kilogram astronaut weighs 96 newtons on the surface of the Moon. The acceleration due to gravity on the Moon is
(1) 0.0 m/s^2
(2) 1.6 m/s^2
(3) 4.9 m/s^2
(4) 9.8 m/s^2

207 On the surface of Planet X, the acceleration due to gravity is 16 meters per second^2. What is the weight of a 6.0-kilogram mass located on the surface of Planet X?
(1) 2.7N
(2) 59 N
(3) 96 N
(4) 940 N

208 The acceleration due to gravity on the surface of Planet X is 19.6 meters per second^2. If an object on the surface of this planet weighs 980. newtons, the mass of the object is
(1) 50.0 kg
(2) 100. kg
(3) 490. N
(4) 908 N

209 The radius of Mars is approximately one-half the radius of Earth, and the mass of Mars is approximately one-tenth the mass of Earth. Compared to the acceleration due to gravity on the surface of Earth, the acceleration due to gravity on the surface of Mars is
(1) smaller
(2) larger
(3) the same

210 The graph at right shows the relationship between weight and mass for a series of objects on the Moon.
   The acceleration due to gravity on the Moon is approximately
(1) 0.63 m/s^2
(2) 1.6 m/s^2
(3) 9.8 m/s^2
(4) 32 m/s^2

Weight vs. Mass on the Moon
Weight (N) vs. Mass (kg)

Base your answers to question 211 on the information below.

211 Two physics students have been selected by NASA to accompany astronauts on a future mission to the Moon. The students are to design and carry out a simple experiment to measure the acceleration due to gravity on the surface of the Moon. Describe an experiment that the students could conduct to measure the acceleration due to gravity on the Moon. Your description must include:
- the equipment needed [1]
- what quantities would be measured using the equipment [1]
- what procedure the students should follow in conducting their experiment [1]
- what equations and/or calculations the students would need to do to arrive at a value for the acceleration due to gravity on the Moon [1]

Hint: Method 1: Free Fall: Drop object from Moon. Look for an equation on Reference Table: Mechanics that has acceleration (a) (you do not know final velocity). Method 2: Take an object of known mass (m), weigh it (F_g) with a spring scale on the moon. Look for an equation on Reference Table: Mechanics that has F_g and acceleration a.

212 The force required to start an object sliding across a uniform horizontal surface is larger than the force required to keep the object sliding at a constant velocity. The magnitudes of the required forces are different in these situations because the force of kinetic friction
(1) is greater than the force of static friction
(2) is less than the force of static friction
(3) increases as the speed of the object relative to the surface increases
(4) decreases as the speed of the object relative to the surface increases

213 A soccer ball travels in the path shown at the diagram at the right. Which vector best represents the direction of the force of air friction on the ball at point *P*?

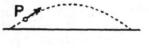

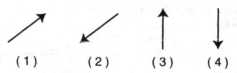

(1)   (2)   (3)   (4)

Hint: Friction (a vector quantity) is in the opposite direction to the object's motion (movement).

214 A box decelerates as it moves to the right along a horizontal surface, as shown in the diagram at the right. Which vector best describes the force of friction on the box?

215 A box is pushed toward the right across a classroom floor. The force of friction on the box is directed toward the
(1) left   (2) right   (3) ceiling   (4) floor

216 A 50.-newton horizontal force is needed to keep an object weighing 500. newtons moving at a constant velocity of 2.0 meters per second across a horizontal surface. The magnitude of the frictional force acting on the object is
(1) 500. N   (2) 450. N   (3) 50. N   (4) 0 N

217 A 1.0×10^2-kilogram box rests on the bed of a truck that is accelerating at 2.0 meters per second². What is the magnitude of the force of friction on the box as it moves with the truck without slipping?
(1) 1.0×10^3 N (2) 2.0×10^2 N (3) 5.0×10^2 N (4) 0.0 N

Hint: Box is at rest; force of friction = applied force.

218 Sand is often placed on an icy road because the sand
(1) decreases the coefficient of friction between the tires of a car and the road
(2) increases the coefficient of friction between the tires of a car and the road
(3) decreases the gravitational force on a car
(4) increases the normal force of a car on the road

219 The table below lists the coefficients of kinetic friction for four materials sliding over steel. A 10.-kilogram block of each of these materials is pulled horizontally across a steel floor at constant velocity. Which block requires the *smallest* applied force to keep it moving at constant velocity?

Material	Coefficient of Kinetic Friction
aluminum	0.47
brass	0.44
copper	0.36
steel	0.57

(1) aluminum   (2) brass   (3) copper   (4) steel

220 A different force is applied to each of four 1-kilogram blocks to slide them across a uniform steel surface at constant speed as shown below. In which diagram is the coefficient of friction between the block and steel smallest?

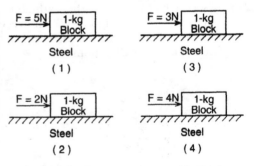

221 The coefficient of kinetic friction between a 780.-newton crate and a level warehouse floor is 0.200. Calculate the magnitude of the horizontal force required to move the crate across the floor at constant speed. [Show all work, including the equation and substitution with units.]

Hint: 780-newton crate means weight of crate = 780 newtons (N)

Base your answers to questions 222A and 222B on the information below. The driver of a car made an emergency stop on a straight horizontal road. The wheels locked and the car skidded to a stop. The marks made by the rubber tires on the dry asphalt are 16 meters long, and the car's mass is 1200 kilograms.

222A Determine the weight of the car. [1]

222B Calculate the magnitude of the frictional force the road applied to the car in stopping it. [Show all work, including the equation and substitution with units.]

223 A 10.-kilogram rubber block is pulled horizontally at constant velocity across a sheet of ice. Calculate the magnitude of the force of friction acting on the block. [Show all work, including the equation and substitution with units].

Base your answers to questions 224 through 227 on the information below:
A manufacturer's advertisement claims that their 1,250 kg (12,300 newton) sports car can accelerate on a level road at 7.15 m/s^2.

224 Calculate the net force required to give the car the acceleration claimed in the advertisement. [Show all work, including the equation and substitution with units.]

225 What is the normal force exerted by the road on the car?

226 The coefficient of friction between the car's tires and the road is 0.80. Calculate the maximum force of friction between the car's tires and the road. [Show all work, including the equation and substitution with units.]

227 Using the values for the forces you have calculated, explain whether or not the manufacturer's claim for the car's acceleration is possible.

228 The diagram at right represents a block sliding down an incline. Which vector best represents the frictional force acting on the block?
(1) A   (2) B   (3) C   (4) D

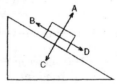

Note that question 229 has only three choices.

229 The diagram at right shows a block sliding down a plane inclined at angle θ with the horizontal. As angle θ is increased, the coefficient of kinetic friction between the bottom surface of the block and the surface of the incline will
(1) decrease   (2) increase   (3) remain the same

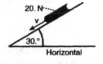

230 A book weighing 20. Newtons slides at a constant velocity down a ramp inclined 30. degrees to the horizontal as shown in the diagram at right.
What is the force of friction between the book and the ramp?
(1) 10. N up the ramp   (3) 10. N down the ramp
(2) 17. N up the ramp   (4) 17. N down the ramp

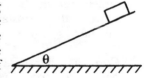

231 The diagram at right represents a 10.-newton block sliding down a 30.° incline at a constant speed. The force of friction on the block is approximately
(1) 5.0 N   (2) 10. N   (3) 49 N   (4) 98 N

Base your answers to questions 232 and 233 on the information and diagram below.

A 10.0-kilogram block slides at constant speed down a plane inclined at 20.º to the horizontal, as shown.

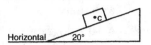

232 Copy the diagram on separate paper. Draw an arrow to represent and identify the direction of each of the *three* forces (weight, friction, normal force) acting on the block. Begin *each* arrow at point *C* and label *each* arrow with the force that it represents.

233 Determine the weight of the block. [Show all calculations, including the equation and substitution with units.]

234 The diagram below shows a sled and rider sliding down a snow-covered hill that makes an angle of 30.° with the horizontal. Which vector best represents the direction of the normal force, F_N, exerted by the hill on the sled?

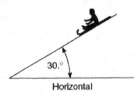

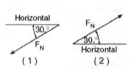 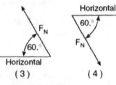

(1)   (2)   (3)   (4)

235 Base your answers to question 235 on the information and diagram at right. A 160.-newton box sits on a 10.-meter-long frictionless plane inclined at an angle of 30.° to the horizontal as shown. Force (*F*) applied to a rope attached to the box causes the box to move with a constant speed up the incline.

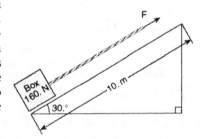

Copy the diagram at right on separate paper. Construct a vector to represent the weight of the box. Use a metric ruler and a scale of 1.0 centimeter = 40. newtons. Begin the vector at point *B* and label its magnitude in newtons.

Hint: 160 newton box means weight of 160 newtons

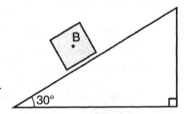

236 Base your answer to question 236 on the information and diagram below.

A 10.0-kilogram block slides at constant speed down a plane inclined at 20.° to the horizontal, as shown.

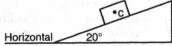

In one or more complete sentences, describe the change in the motion of the block as the angle of inclination is increased to 30°.

237 What is the momentum of a 1,200-kilogram car traveling at 15 meters per second due east?
(1) 80. kg•m/s due east
(2) 80. kg•m/s due west
(3) 1.8 x 10⁴ kg•m/s due east
(4) 1.8 x 10⁴ kg•m/s due west

Hint: If velocity is (15 m/s) due east, momentum is due east.

238 What is the momentum of a 1.5 x 10³-kilogram car as it travels at 30. meters per second due east for 60. seconds?
(1) 4.5 x 10⁴ kg •m/s, east   (3) 2.7 x 10⁶ kg • m, east
(2) 4.5 x 10⁴ kg • m/s, west   (4) 2.7 x 10⁶ kg • m, west

239 The magnitude of the momentum of an object is 64.0 kilogram•meter per second. If the velocity of the object is doubled, the magnitude of the momentum of the object will be
(1) 32.0 kg•m/s   (3) 128 kg•m/s
(2) 64.0 kg•m/s   (4) 256 kg•m/s

240 What is the speed of a 1.0 x 10³ kilogram car that has a momentum of 2.0 x 10⁴ kilogram•meters per second east?
(1) 5.0 x 10⁻² m/s   (3) 1.0 x 10⁴ m/s
(2) 2.0 x 10¹ m/s   (4) 2.0 x 10⁷ m/s

241 In the diagram below, a 60.-kilogram rollerskater exerts a 10.-newton force on a 30.-kilogram rollerskater for 0.20 second. What is the magnitude of the impulse applied to the 30.-kilogram rollerskater?
(1) 50. N•s   (3) 6.0 N•s
(2) 2.0 N•s   (4) 12 N•s

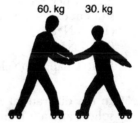

60. kg   30. kg

242 If a net force of 10. newtons acts on a 6.0-kilogram mass for 8.0 seconds, the total change of momentum of the mass is
(1) 48 kg•m/s   (2) 60. kg•m/s   (3) 80. kg•m/s   (4) 480. kg•m/s

243 In a baseball game, a batter hits a ball for a home run. Compared to the magnitude of the impulse imparted to the ball, the magnitude of the impulse imparted to the bat is
(1) less   (2) greater   (3) the same

Hint: Newton's Third Law: Force that bat exerts on ball = Force that ball exerts on bat; time is equal.

244 A 2.0 x 10³.-kg car collides with a tree and is brought to rest in 0.50 seconds by an average force of 6.0 x 10⁴ newtons. What is the magnitude of the impulse on the car during this 0.50-second interval?
(1) 1.0 x 10³ kg•s   (3) 1.2 x 10⁵ N/s
(2) 3.0 x 10⁴ N•s   (4) 6.0 x 10⁷ N•kg•s

245 A 1,000-kilogram car traveling with a velocity of +20. meters per second decelerates uniformly at -5.0. meters/second² until it comes to rest. What is the magnitude of the impulse applied to bring the car to rest?
(1) 1.0×10^4 N•s   (3) 3.9×10^4 N•s
(2) 2.0×10^4 N•s   (4) 4.3×10^4 N•s

246 A bullet traveling at 5.0×10^2 meters per second is brought to rest by an impulse of 50. newton-seconds. What is the mass of the bullet?
(1) 2.5×10^4 kg   (3) 1.0×10^{-1} kg
(2) 1.0×10^1 kg   (4) 1.0×10^{-2} kg

247 A bullet traveling at 5.0×10^2 meters per second is brought to rest by an impulse of 100. newton•seconds. What is the mass of the bullet?
(1) 2.0×10^{-2} kg   (3) 2.0×10^1 kg
(2) 2.0×10^{-1} kg   (4) 5.0×10^4 kg

248 A 2,400-kilogram car is traveling at a speed of 20. meters per second. Compared to the magnitude of the force required to stop the car in 12 seconds, the magnitude of the force required to stop the car in 6.0 seconds is
(1) half as great   (3) the same
(2) twice as great   (4) four times as great

249 A 50.-kilogram student threw a 0.40-kilogram ball with a speed of 20. meters per second. What was the magnitude of the impulse that the student exerted on the ball?
(1) 8.0 N•s   (3) 4.0×10^2 N•s
(2) 78 N•s   (4) 1.0×10^3 N•s

Hint: Change in velocity: before ball was thrown, v was 0.

250 In the diagram at right, a 0.4-kilogram steel sphere and a 0.1-kilogram wooden sphere are located 2.0 meters above the ground. Both spheres are allowed to fall from rest.
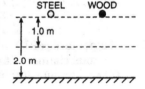
    Which statement best describes the spheres after they have fallen 1.0 meter? (Neglect air resistance.)
(1) Both spheres have the same speed and momentum.
(2) Both spheres have the same speed and the steel sphere has more momentum than the wooden sphere.
(3) The steel sphere has greater speed and has less momentum than the wooden sphere.
(4) The steel sphere has greater speed than the wooden sphere and both spheres have the same momentum.

Hint: In a free fall, velocity of 2 objects is equal when they hit the ground because both fall from the same height, have same acceleration.

Note that question 251 has only three choices.

251 A student drops two eggs of equal mass simultaneously from the same height. Egg *A* lands on the tile floor and breaks. Egg *B* lands intact, without bouncing, on a foam pad lying on the floor. Compared to the magnitude of the impulse on Egg *A* as it lands the magnitude of the impulse on Egg *B* as it lands is
(1) less   (2) greater   (3) the same

252 The velocity-time graph at right represents the motion of a 3.0-kilogram cart along a straight line. What is the magnitude of the change in momentum of the cart between $t=0\ I$ and $t=3$ seconds?
(1) 20 kg• m/s   (3) 60 kg• m/s
(2) 30 kg• m/s   (4) 80 kg• m/s

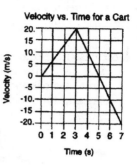

253 In the diagram below, a 100.-kilogram clown is fired from a 500.-kilogram cannon. If the clown's speed is 15 meters per second after the firing, then the recoil speed (v) of the cannon is
(1) 75 m/s   (2) 15 m/s
(3) 3.0 m/s   (4) 0 m/s

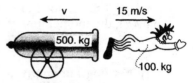

Hint: Before firing, clown and cannon were at rest.

254 A 2.0-kilogram toy cannon is at rest on a frictionless surface. A remote triggering device causes a 0.005-kilogram projectile to be fired from the cannon. Which equation describes this system after the cannon is fired?
(1) mass of cannon + mass of projectile = 0
(2) speed of cannon + speed of projectile = 0
(3) momentum of cannon + momentum of projectile = 0
(4) velocity of cannon + velocity of projectile = 0

255 A 2.0-kilogram cart moving due east at 6.0 meters per second collides with a 3.0-kilogram cart moving due west. The carts stick together and come to rest after the collision. What was the initial speed of the 3.0-kilogram cart?
(1) 1.0 m/s   (2) 6.0 m/s   (3) 9.0 m/s   (4) 4.0 m/s

256 Satellite *A* has a mass of 1.5×10^3 kilograms and is traveling east at 8.0×10^3 meters per second. Satellite *B* is traveling west at 6.0×10^3 meters per second. The satellites collide head-on and come to rest. What is the mass of satellite *B*?
(1) 2.7×10^3 kg   (3) 1.5×10^3 kg
(2) 2.0×10^3 kg   (4) 1.1×10^3 kg

257 The diagram shows two carts on a horizontal, frictionless surface being pushed apart when a compressed spring attached to one of the carts is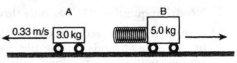
released. Cart *A* has a mass of 3.0-kilograms and Cart *B* has a mass of 5.0 kilograms. The speed of Cart *A* is 0.33 meters per second after the spring is released. If the carts are initially at rest, what is the speed of Cart *B* after the spring is released?
(1) 0.12 m/s   (2) 0.20 m/s   (3) 0.33 m/s   (4) 0.55 m/s

258 Please note question 258 has only three choices.
As shown in the diagrams below, a lump of clay travels horizontally to the right towards a block at rest on a frictionless surface. Upon collision, the clay and the block stick together and move to the right.

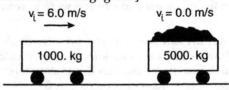

Compared to the total momentum of the clay and the block before the collision, the momentum of the clay and the block after the collision is
(1) less   (2) greater   (3) the same

259 A 1000.-kilogram empty cart moving with a speed of 6.0 meters per second is about to collide with a stationary loaded cart having a total mass of 5000. kilograms, as shown. After the collision, the carts lock and move together. [Assume friction is negligible.]

Calculate the speed of the combined carts after the collision. [Show all work, including the equation and substitution with units.]
Remember: Substitute with units (example: kg•m/s) both in the equation and in the final answer.

CHAPTER 2: ENERGY

Section *1*:

Energy is the ability to do work. Energy is a scalar quantity.

WORK

Work (done) equals the **force** (or the component of the force) which is in the direction the object moves **times** the **distance** the object moves.

$$W = F \quad d$$

Work = Force x distance

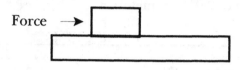

Work done in **LIFTING** a **BOX** = **change in** the (total) **energy** of the box = increase in potential energy, which you will learn about a little later).

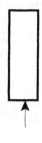

$$W = F \qquad d \quad = \Delta E_T$$

d = displacement/distance
E_T = total energy
F = force
W = work
Δ = change

Work = force x distance = change in total energy.

Work is a scalar quantity. Work = force x distance. Force is in newtons, distance is in meters, and therefore, **work** or ΔE_T is **in newton•meters or joules (J)**.

Table: Mechanics

Question: How much work is done on a downhill skier by an average braking force of 9.8×10^2 newtons to stop her in a distance of 10. meters?

(1) 1.0×10^1 J (2) 9.8×10^1 J (3) 1.0×10^3 J (4) 9.8×10^3 J

Solution:

Given: Average braking force = 9.8×10^2 newtons (N)

Distance = 10 meters (m)

Find: work (W).

Look for an equation on Reference Table: Mechanics that has work (w), force (F) , and distance (d).

Table: Mechanics

$W = \mathrm{Fd} = \Delta E_T$

d = displacement/distance
E_T = total energy
F = force
W = work

Use the equation W = Fd (see above).
Substitute for F (force) 9.8 x 10^2 N (newtons). *Substitute for d* (distance) 10 m (meters) .
$W = (9.8 \times 10^2 \text{ N})(10 \text{ m}) = 9.8 \times 10^3$ N•m (newton•meters) or 9.8 x 10^3 J (joules).   Answer 4

Question: A constant force of 1900 newtons is required to keep an automobile having a mass of 1.0 x 10^3 kilograms moving at a constant speed of 20. meters per second. The work done in moving the automobile a distance of 2.0 x 10^3 meters is

(1) 2.0 x 10^4 J   (2) 3.8 x 10^4 J
(3) 2.0 x 10^6 J   (4) 3.8 x 10^6 J

Solution:
Given: Force = 1900 newtons (N).
       Mass = 1.0 x 10^3 kilograms (kg).
       Speed = 20. meters/second (m/s).
       Distance = 2.0 x 10^3 meters (m).
Find: work (W).

Table: Mechanics

Look for an equation on Reference Table: Mechanics that has work (W), force (F), and distance (d).

$W = \mathrm{Fd} = \Delta E_T$

d = displacement/distance
E_T = total energy
F = force
W = work

You can easily see you need to *use the equation* W = Fd because force (F), and distance (d) are given (and obviously, do not use $W = \Delta E_T$, because ΔE_T is not given). The question gives two extra facts that are not needed to solve the question (speed and mass).

In the equation W = Fd (see above) *substitute for F* (force) 1900 N (newtons). *Substitute for d* (distance) 2.0 x 10^3 m (meters) .
$W = (1900 \text{ N})(2.0 \times 10^3 \text{ m}) = 3.8 \times 10^6$ N•m or 3.8 x 10^6 J (joules).   Answer 4

Question: A student does 60. joules of work pushing a 3.0-kilogram box up the full length of a ramp that is 5.0 meters long. What is the magnitude of the force applied to the box to do this work?
       (1) 20. N   (2) 15 N   (3) 12 N   (4) 4.0 N

Solution:
Given: Work = 60. joules(J).
       3.0 kilogram box.
       Ramp = 5.0 meters (m) long.
Find: Force (F).

Look for an equation on Reference Table: Mechanics that has work (W), force (F), and distance (d).

$$W = Fd = \Delta E_T$$

d = displacement/distance
E_T = total energy
F = force
W = work

Use the equation W = Fd (see above).
Then substitute for W 60. J (joules). *Substitute for d* (distance) 5.0 m (meters).

60. J = F x 5.0 m.

$$\frac{60.\ J}{5.0\ m} = F$$

F = 12 N

or, rearrange the equation:

$$F = \frac{W}{d} = \frac{60.\ J}{5.0\ m} = 12\ N$$

F = 12 N

Answer *3*

Question: Which action would require no work to be done on an object?

    (1) lifting the object from the floor to the ceiling
    (2) pushing the object along a horizontal floor against a frictional force
    (3) decreasing the speed of the object until it comes to rest
    (4) holding the object stationary above the ground

Solution: You learned work = force (in the same direction the object moves) times distance.
Choice *4* is correct. No work is done because the object was held stationary (object did not move any distance). Look at the equation W = F x d. If d (distance) = 0, then W (work) would be 0. Answer *4*

Question: The diagram below shows a 50.-kilogram crate on a frictionless plane at an angle θ to the horizontal. The crate is pushed at constant speed up the incline from point A to point B by force F. If angle θ were increased, what would be the effect on the magnitude of force F and the total work W done on the crate as it is moved from A to B?

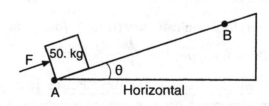

    (1) W would remain the same and the magnitude of F would decrease.
    (2) W would remain the same and the magnitude of F would increase.
    (3) W would increase and the magnitude of F would decrease.
    (4) W would increase and the magnitude of F would increase.

Solution: If angle θ were increased, the ramp would be steeper and it would be harder to push the block up the ramp. Therefore, **more force** would be **needed** to **push** the **block up** the **ramp** the same distance from point A to point B. W (work) = F (force) x d (distance). As you can see from the equation, when F (force) increases (more force is needed to push the crate on the steep slope), W (work) also increases (more work is done). Answer 4

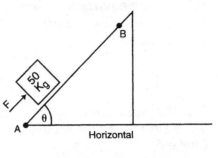

Now Do Homework Questions #1-10, Pages 49-50.

Power (p) is the **rate** at which **work** is done. ($Power = \frac{work}{time}$).

$$P = \frac{W}{t} = \frac{Fd}{t} = F\bar{v}$$

$$Power = \frac{Work}{time} = \frac{Force \; x \; distamce}{time} = Force \; x \; average \; velocity$$

$$P = \frac{W}{t} = \frac{Fd}{t} = F\bar{v}$$

d = displacement/distance
F = force
P = power
t = time
$\bar{v}$ = average velocity/average speed
W = work

Power is work divided by time. You know that work (W) = force (F) x distance (d); therefore, you can **substitute Fd** for W (see equation above) and get the equation $P = \frac{Fd}{t}$. You know $\bar{v} = \frac{d}{t}$, Reference Table: Mechanics therefore you can **substitute** $\bar{v}$ **for** $\frac{d}{t}$ and get $P = F\bar{v}$.

To summarize, $P = \frac{W}{t} = \frac{Fd}{t} = F\bar{v}$

Power is a scalar quantity. **Power** is **in watts** or in $\frac{joules \; (work)}{seconds \; (time)}$ or in $\frac{newton \cdot meters \; (force \; in \; newtons \; x \; distance \; in \; meters)}{seconds \; (time)}$.

Work is in joules.
time is in seconds.
Power is in joules per second or watts.
1 watt = 1 joule per second (1 J/s).

Question: A 3.0 kilogram block is initially at rest on a frictionless, horizontal surface. The block is moved 8.0 meters in 2.0 seconds by the application of a 12-newton horizontal force, as shown in the diagram.

below.

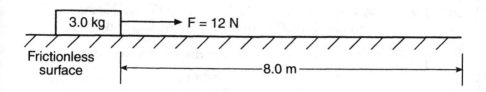

What is the average power developed while moving the block?

    (1) 24 W   (2) 32 W   (3) 48 W   (4) 96 W

Solution:

Given: Force = 12 newtons (N)

        distance = 8.0 meters (m)(block moved 8.0 meters)

        time = 2.0 seconds (s)

        mass = 3.0 kilogram block means mass = 3.0 kg

Find: Power (P)

Look for an equation for power (P) on Reference Table: Mechanics that has power (P) and also force (F), distance (d), and time (t).

$$P = \frac{W}{t} = \frac{Fd}{t} = F\bar{v}$$

                                     d = displacement/distance

                                     F = force

                                     P = power

                                     t = time interval

                                     $\bar{v}$= average velocity/average speed

                                     W = work

Use the equation

    $P = \frac{Fd}{t}$ (see above).

You can solve this equation because three things are known, force (F), distance(d), and time(t), and you have only one unknown, power (P).

In the equation $P = \frac{Fd}{t}$, *then substitute for F* 12 N (newtons). *Substitute for d* 8.0 m (meters). *Substitute for t* 2.0 s (seconds).

    $P = \frac{(12\ N)(8.0\ m)}{2.0\ s} = \frac{96\ N \cdot m}{2.0\ s} = \frac{48\ N \cdot m}{s}$ P = 48 W (watts)

Question: A 4.0 x 10³-watt motor applies a force of 8.0 x 10² newtons to move a boat at constant speed. How far does the boat move in 16 seconds?

    (1) 3.2 m   (2) 5.0 m   (3) 32 m   (4) 80. m

Solution:

Given: 4.0 x 10⁹-watt (W) motor

      Force = 8.0 x 10² newtons (N)

      Time = 16 seconds (s)

Find: How far boat moves in 16 seconds (means find distance).

You learned **power** is in **watts**, therefore, 4.0×10^3 watts means power is 4.0×10^3 watts (W).

Look for an equation for power (P) on Reference Table: Mechanics that has power (P) and also force(F) , time (t) and distance (d).

Table: Mechanics

$$P = \frac{W}{t} = \frac{Fd}{t} = F\bar{v}$$

d = displacement/distance
F = force
P = power
t = time interval
$\bar{v}$ = average velocity/average speed
W = work

Use the equation
$$P = \frac{Fd}{t} .$$

Then substitute for P (power) 4.0×10^3 W (watts). **Substitute for F** (force) 8.0×10^2 N (newtons). **Substitute for t** (time) 16 s (seconds).

4.0×10^3 W $= \dfrac{8.0 \times 10^2 \ N{\cdot}d}{16 \ s}$	Or, rearrange the equation:
Cross multiply	$P = \dfrac{Fd}{t}$
8.0×10^2 N${\cdot}$d$=(4.0 \times 10^3$ W$)(16$ s$)$	Pt = Fd
Divide by 8.0×10^2 N	$d = \dfrac{Pt}{F}$
$\dfrac{8.0 \times 10^2 \ N{\cdot}d}{8.0 \times 10^2 \ N} = \dfrac{(4.0 \times 10^3 \ W)(16 \ s)}{8.0 \times 10^2 \ N}$	$d = \dfrac{(4.0 \times 10^3 \ W)(16 \ s)}{8.0 \times 10^2 \ N}$
d = 80 m	d = 80 m

Answer 4

Question: A motor having a power rating of 500. watts is used to lift an object weighing 100. newtons. How much time does the motor take to lift the object a vertical distance of 10.0 meters?
 (1) 0.500 s   (2) 2.00 s   (3) 5.00 s   (4) 50.0 s

Solution:
Given: Power = 500. watts (W)
    weight of object = 100. newtons (N)
    vertical distance = 10.0 meters (m)
Find: How much time (t) to lift object 10.0 meters (m).
You learned weight = force (force of gravity). Weight of object = 100. newtons means force (F) = 100. N.

Look for an equation for power (P) on Reference Table: Mechanics that has power (P) and also force (F), time (t) and distance (d).

$$P = \frac{W}{t} = \frac{Fd}{t} = F\bar{v}$$

Use the equation
$$P = \frac{Fd}{t}$$

Substitute for P (power) 500. W (watts). **Substitute for F** (force) 100. N (newtons). **Substitute for d** (distance) 10.0 m (meters).

$$P = \frac{Fd}{t}$$

$$500. \text{ W} = \frac{(100. \text{ N})(10.0 \text{ m})}{t}$$

Cross multiply:

$500.\text{W}t = (100. \text{ N})(10.0 \text{ m})$

$$\frac{500. \text{ W}t}{500. \text{ W}} = \frac{(100. \text{ N})(10.0 \text{ m})}{500. \text{ W}}$$

$$t = \frac{(100. \text{ N})(10.0 \text{ m})}{500. \text{ W}} = \frac{1000 \text{ N} \cdot m}{500. \text{ W}}$$

$t = 2.00$ s (seconds)   Answer 2

Or, rearrange the equation:

$$P = \frac{Fd}{t}$$

Cross multiply

$Pt = Fd$

$$t = \frac{Fd}{P}$$

$$t = \frac{(100. \text{ N})(10.0 \text{ m})}{500. \text{ W}} = \frac{1000 \text{ N} \cdot m}{500. \text{ W}}$$

$t = 2.00$ s (seconds)   Answer 2

In the question above, you are given weight and **vertical distance**. When you use the equation $P = \frac{Fd}{t}$ and the only force (F) you have is **weight,** which is force of gravity ($\mathbf{F_g}$, **downward force**), you must **use** only **vertical distance** (distance object is lifted vertically).

Question: What is the average power developed by a motor as it lifts a 400. kilogram mass at constant speed through a vertical distance of 10.0 meters in 8.0 seconds?

(1) 320 W   (2) 500 W   (3) 4,900 W   (4) 32,000 W

Solution:

Given: mass = 400. kilograms (kg)
      vertical distance = 10.0 meters (m)
      time = 8.0 seconds (s)
Find: power (P)

Look for an equation for power (P) on Reference Table: Mechanics that has power (P) and also time (t) and distance (d).

$$P = \frac{W}{t} = \frac{Fd}{t} = F\bar{v}$$

Use the equation

$$P = \frac{Fd}{t} \text{ (see above)}.$$

Distance and time are given. In the equation $P = \frac{Fd}{t}$, you have two unknowns, force (F) and power (P), therefore, first find force (F) and then substitute F in the equation $P = \frac{Fd}{t}$ to find P (power).

The motor lifts a 400. kilogram mass (example: 400. kilogram box) a vertical distance. The motor needs to **lift** the weight of the mass (box). The **force** used in **lifting** the box is **equal** but in the opposite direction to $\mathbf{F_g}$ (force of gravity or force due to gravity), which pulls the box down; therefore, find $\mathbf{F_g}$ or weight.

First find F_g. Look for an equation on Reference Table: Mechanics that has F_g.

$$g = \frac{F_g}{m}$$

F_g = weight (force due to gravity)
m = mass
g = acceleration due to gravity
   or gravitational field strength

Solve for F_g (weight, or force due to gravity)
Cross multiply:

F_g	=	m	x	g
weight or **force** due to gravity		mass		acceleration due to gravity

In the equation above, *substitute* for g (acceleration due to gravity) 9.81 m/s² given on Reference Table: List of Physical Constants and *substitute* for m (mass) 400. kg (given).

$$F_g = (400.\ kg)(9.81\ m/s^2) = 3924\ \frac{kgm}{s^2} = \textbf{3924 N (newtons)}$$

Then, substitute weight F_g (3924 N) for F in the equation $P = \frac{Fd}{t}$.

Now you can solve the equation because three things are known, force (F), distance (d) and time (t), and you have only one unknown, power (P).

$$P = \frac{Fd}{t}$$

$$P = \frac{(3924\ N)(10.0\ m)}{8.0\ s} = 4905\ \frac{N \cdot m}{s} = 4905\ W\ (watts) \qquad \text{Answer 3}$$

Work vs. Time

Question: The graph shows the relationship between the work done by a student and the time of ascent as the student runs up a flight of stairs. The slope of the graph would have units of
(1) joules (2) seconds (3) watts (4) newtons

Work (joules) vs. Time (seconds)

Solution: *Look for an equation* on Reference Table: Mechanics for $\frac{work}{time}$.

$$P = \frac{W}{t} = \frac{Fd}{t} = F\bar{v}$$

d = displacement/distance
F = force
P = power
t = time interval
$\bar{v}$ = average velocity/average speed
W = work

Use the equation

$$\text{Power} = \frac{Work}{time}$$

In a graph of work versus time, the slope of the line is power. Power is in **watts** (W). Answer 3

Question: A motor having a maximum power rating of 8.1×10^4 watts is used to operate an elevator with a weight of 1.8×10^4 newtons. What is the maximum weight this motor can lift at an average speed of 3.0 meters per second?

      (1) 6.0×10^3 N   (2) 1.8×10^4 N

      (3) 2.4×10^4 N   (4) 2.7×10^4 N

Solution:

Given: Power = 8.1×10^4 watts (W). Speed = 3.0 meters/second.
(Note: weight of the elevator is an extra fact, not needed to solve the problem.)
Find: Maximum weight the motor can lift.

Look for an equation for power (P) on Reference Table: Mechanics that has power (P), force (F) (because weight is force of gravity, F_g) and speed (v).

$$P = \frac{W}{t} = \frac{Fd}{t} = F\bar{v}$$

d = displacement/distance
F = force
P = power
t = time interval
$\bar{v}$ = average velocity/average speed
W = work

Use the equation

    $P = F\bar{v}$

Then substitute for P (power) 8.1×10^4 W (watts). *Substitute* for $\bar{v}$ (average speed) 3.0 m/s (meters per second).

$P = F\bar{v}$	Or, rearrange the equation:
8.1×10^4 W = F(3.0 m/s)	$P = F\bar{v}$
$\dfrac{8.1 \times 10^4 \text{ W}}{3.0 \text{ m/s}} = F$	$\dfrac{P}{\bar{v}} = F$
F = 2.7×10^4 N	$\dfrac{8.1 \times 10^4 \text{ W}}{3.0 \text{ m/s}} = F$
	F = 2.7×10^4 N

                               Answer *4*

Question: If the time required for a student to swim 500 meters is doubled, the power developed by the student will be

      (1) halved   (2) doubled   (3) quartered (4) quadrupled

Solution:

Given: Time for a student to swim 500 meters is doubled. (500 meters means a distance of 500 meters).
Find: Power developed by the student.

Look for an equation for power (P) on Reference Table: Mechanics that has power (P), distance (d) and time (t).

$$P = \frac{W}{t} = \frac{Fd}{t} = F\bar{v}$$

d = displacement/distance
F = force
P = power
t = time interval
$\bar{v}$ = average velocity/average speed
W = work

Use the equation
$$P = \frac{Fd}{t} \text{ (see above).}$$

OLD	**NEW**
$P = \dfrac{Fd}{t}$	Time is doubled. Let new time equal 2t. $$\text{New } P = \frac{Fd}{2t}$$
Old $P = \dfrac{Fd}{t}$ Old Power	New $P = \dfrac{1Fd}{2t} = \dfrac{1}{2}\dfrac{Fd}{t}$ New Power **when time is doubled**

Look at the new power and the old power.
New power = 1/2 old power.   Answer *1*.

Now Do Homework Questions #11-25, pages 50-51.

POTENTIAL ENERGY AND GRAVITATIONAL POTENTIAL ENERGY

Potential energy (PE): the energy an object possesses (has) due to its position (how high up the object is) or condition (example, stretched out or compressed spring).

Gravitational Potential Energy--the **energy** an object has **because** of its **height. the higher up** the object (example: rock) is, the **more potential energy** the object has.

PE	=	m	g	h
potential energy		mass	acceleration due to gravity	height

The potential energy an object has equals mass (m) of the object times acceleration due to gravity (g) (9.81 meters per second^2 on Earth's surface) times height (how high up the object is, example: rock or ball).

$$\Delta PE = m \quad g \quad \Delta h \qquad \begin{array}{l} m = \text{mass} \\ g = \text{acceleration} \\ \quad \text{due to gravity} \\ h = \text{height} \\ \Delta = \text{change} \end{array}$$

change in   mass   acceleration   change in
potential energy   due to gravity   height

The **change** in (**gravitational**) **potential energy** is because there is a **change** in **height** (how high the object is lifted or how far down the rock falls).

Change in potential energy (ΔPE) is in joules or $\dfrac{kg \cdot m^2}{s^2}$.

Mass (m) is in kilograms (kg).   g (acceleration due to gravity) is in $\dfrac{m}{s^2}$. Δh is in meters (m).

You learned $\Delta PE = mg\Delta h$. Since m(mass) is in kg, g is in $\dfrac{m}{s^2}$, and Δh is in m (meters) (see above), therefore ΔPE, which equals $mg\Delta h$, is in $\dfrac{kg \cdot m}{s^2} \cdot m$ or $\dfrac{kg \cdot m^2}{s^2}$.

Work (Fd) done in lifting a box (moving the box higher up) = change (**increase**) in **potential energy of the box ($mg\Delta h$)**.

Change in height–change in gravitational potential energy.

A rock falls off the top of a cliff from a height of 40 meters, dropping to 30 meters, to 20 meters, to 10 meters, and to zero meters.

40 meters	↓	maximum potential energy (highest up)	
30 meters	↓	3/4 height of cliff	3/4 potential energy
20 meters	↓	½ height of cliff	½ potential energy
10 meters	↓	1/4 height of cliff	1/4 potential energy
0 meters	↓	0 height	0 potential energy

As you can see, when the rock is highest up, it has maximum potential energy. When the rock goes down and is at 20 meters high (½ the height of the cliff), it has ½ the potential energy. The rock at 1/4 the height of the cliff (10 meters high) has 1/4 the potential energy, and the rock on the ground (zero height) has zero potential energy.

Energy (E) cannot be created or destroyed. You saw that the potential energy (PE) of the rock decreased as it went down the cliff (from maximum potential energy to 3/4 potential energy to ½ potential energy to 1/4 potential energy to zero potential energy).

When the PE (potential energy) of the rock was changed from maximum (1 PE) to 3/4 PE, 1/4 of the PE was changed into (KE) kinetic energy (energy of motion-rock moving down the cliff).

Question: An object weighing 15 newtons is lifted from the ground to a height of 0.22 meter. The increase in the object's gravitational potential energy is approximately

      (1) 310 J   (2) 32 J   (3) 3.3 J   (4) 0.34 J

Solution:

Given: Δh = 0.22 meters–lifted (changed in height) 0.22 meters from the ground.

      Weight = 15 newtons

Find: Increase (change) in gravitational potential energy.

Look for an equation on Reference Table: Mechanics that has change in (gravitational) potential energy (ΔPE). There is only one equation on Reference Table: Mechanics with change in potential energy (ΔPE).

Use the equation

Table: Mechanics

$$\Delta PE \quad = \quad mg\Delta h$$

    change in
potential energy

g = acceleration due to gravity or gravitational field strength
h = height
m = mass
PE = potential energy
Δ = change

Δh = 0.22 meters, lifted 0.22 meters from the ground.
ΔPE = mgΔh. You know Δh, but you also need to find mg.

The object weighs 15 newtons (N) (given). You learned that the **weight** of an object = **force of gravity (F_g)**.

Look for an equation on Reference Table: Mechanics with force of gravity (F_g) and one mass (m) (one object).

Table: Mechanics

$$g = \frac{F_g}{m}$$

F_g = weight/force due to gravity

g = acceleration due to gravity or gravitational field strength
m = mass

Cross-multiply F_g = mg. **Weight** of an object (example, 15 N) = force of gravity (F_g), and **F_g = mg** (see above). Therefore, **weight** of an object (example 15 N) = **mg (15 N).**

In the equation $\Delta PE = mg\Delta h$, *then substitute* for mg 15 N (newtons) and *substitute* for Δh (given) 0.22 m (meters).
$\Delta PE = (15 \text{ N})(0.22 \text{ m}) = 3.3 \text{ N}\bullet\text{m}$ (newton•meters) = 3.3 J (joules).
Increase (change) in gravitational potential energy = 3.3 J   Answer 3

Questions 1 & 2: Base your answers to questions 1 and 2 on the information and diagram below. A 160.-newton box sits on a 10.-meter-long frictionless plane inclined at an angle of 30° to the horizontal as shown. Force (F) applied to a rope attached to the box causes the box to move with a constant speed up the incline.

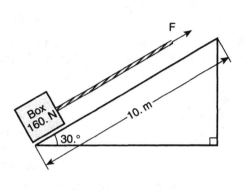

Question 1: Copy the diagram on a sheet of paper. On the diagram, construct a vector to represent the weight of the box. Use a metric ruler and a scale of 1.0 centimeter = 40. newtons. Begin the vector at point B and label its magnitude in newtons.

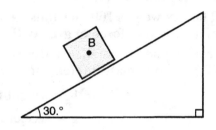

Question 2: Calculate the amount of work done in moving the box from the bottom to the top of the inclined plane.[Show all work, including the equation and substitution with units.]

Solution 1: 160. N box means the weight of the box is 160. N (newtons). F_g = weight of box = 160 N. F_g (force of gravity) is a downward force. Draw a line straight down from point B, which is in the center of the block. Let 1 cm = 40 newtons; therefore, draw a 4 cm line

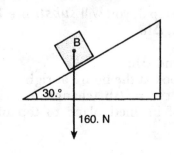

(vector) to represent 160. newtons. Put an arrow at the end of the vector.

Solution 2:

Given: 160. N box means the weight of the box is 160. N (newtons).

The box moved from the bottom to the top of an inclined plane.

Find: amount of work done in moving the box from the bottom to the top of the inclined plane.

Note: Box is higher up, increase in height Δh.

Work done equals **increase in potential energy**.

Therefore, *look for an equation* on Reference Table: Mechanics for change in potential energy (ΔPE).

Use the equation

$$\Delta PE = mg\Delta h$$

g = acceleration due to gravity
h = height
m = mass
Δ = change

By looking at the equation above, you see, to find work done or change (increase) in potential energy ΔPE, you need to **find mg** and **Δh**.

In step 1, you will find mg, in step 2 find Δh, and in step 3, substitute mg and Δh in the equation $\Delta PE = mg\Delta h$ to find ΔPE (change in potential energy or work done).

Step 1: The box weighs 160. newtons (N)(given). You learned that the **weight** of an object = **force of gravity (F_g)**.

Look for an equation on Reference Table: Mechanics with force of gravity (F_g) and one mass (m) (example, one box).

$$g = \frac{F_g}{m}$$

F_g = weight/force due to gravity

g = acceleration due to gravity or gravitational field strength

m = mass

Cross-multiply $F_g = mg$. **Weight** of an object (example, 160 N, given)= force of gravity (F_g), and $F_g = mg$ (see above). Therefore, **weight** of an object (example 160 N) = **mg (160 N).**

Later, in step 3, you will *substitute* **160. N** for **mg** in the equation $\Delta PE = mg\Delta h$.

Step 2: Find Δh:

Look at the figure at right.

Let y = Δh (change in height from bottom of inclined plane to top of inclined plane).

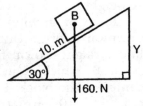

Sin θ for a right triangle $= \dfrac{opposite}{hypotenuse}$, given on Reference Table: Geometry and Trigonometry.

$$\sin 30° = \dfrac{opposite}{hypotenuse}$$

$$\sin 30° = \dfrac{y}{10.\ m}$$

$\sin 30° = 0.50$; (use calculator: press 30, then press sin) substitute for sin 30° 0.50

$$0.50 = \dfrac{y}{10.\ m}$$

$(0.50)(10.m) = y$

$5.0m = y$; $y = 5.0\ m = \Delta h$

$\Delta h = 5.0\ m$

Or

Find Δh, change in height, by using the equation $A_y = A \sin \theta$
Look at the figure. $A = 10.\ m$ $\theta = 30°$.

$A_y = A \sin \theta$ $A =$ any vector
In this case, A_y means change in height.
$A_y = 10.m \sin 30°$ $\sin 30° = 0.50$
$A_y = (10.\ m)(0.50) = 5.0m = \Delta h$
$\Delta h = 5.0\ m$

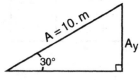

Step 3: You had in the beginning of solution 2, $\Delta PE = mg\Delta h$
Then substitute for mg 160. N (from step 1) and substitute for Δh 5.0 m (from step 2).

$$\Delta PE = (160.N)(5.0m) = 800\ N\bullet m = 800\ J = 8.0 \times 10^2\ J$$

The answer should have two significant figures, 8.0×10^2 J.

Rule: All numbers from 1 to 9 count as significant figures (example: 239 has three significant figures). When there is no decimal point, zeros at the end do not count. (If, in a different example, there is the number 160 with no decimal point, zeros at the end do not count and there would be only 2 significant figures.) If there is a decimal point, zeros at the end do count. In this question, 160. N has three significant figures. 5.0 has two significant figures.

If a number with three significant figures, example 160., is multiplied by a number with two significant figures, 5.0, the product (example: 8.0×10^2), has the least number of significant figures, which is two significant figures.

Also, another rule: start counting from the first non-zero digit. .0007 has 1 significant digit; start counting from the 7.   .0025 has two.

Question: a 650-kilogram roller coaster car starts from rest at the top of the first hill of its track and glides freely. [Neglect friction.] Height of the first hill is 24 meters. Determine the gravitational potential energy of a car at the top of the first hill. [Show all calculations, including the equation and substitution with units.]

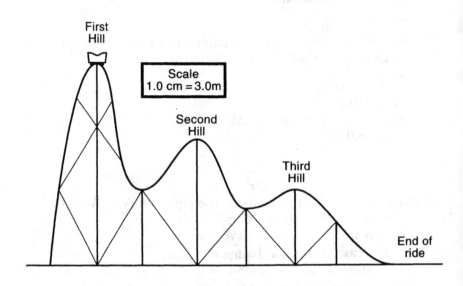

Solution:
Given: 650-kilogram (kg) roller coaster car. Height of first hill is 24 meters (m).
Find: Gravitational potential energy.
650-kilogram car (given) means m (mass) of the car equals 650 kilograms; kilogram is a unit of mass.

Look for an equation on Reference Table: Mechanics that has PE (potential energy) , m (mass), and h (height).

Use the equation

$$\Delta PE = mg\Delta h$$
g = acceleration due to gravity
h = height
m = mass
Δ = change

Then substitute for m (mass) 650 kg (kilograms). *Substitute for g* (acceleration due to gravity) 9.81 m/s², given on Reference Table: List of Physical Constants on page reference tables 2-3. *Substitute for Δh* 24 m (meters) (change in height from top of the first hill (24 meters) to ground (0 meters at the end of the ride)).
$\Delta PE = (650\,kg)(9.81\,m/s^2)(24\,m) = 153036\,kg \cdot m^2/s^2 = 153036\,J$ (joules).

Question: Which graph best represents the relationship between the gravitational potential energy of a freely falling object and the object's height above the ground near the surface of Earth?

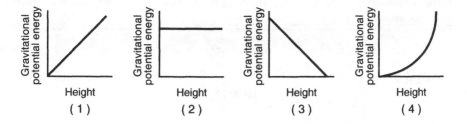

Height (1) Height (2) Height (3) Height (4)

Solution: *Look for an equation* on Reference Table: Mechanics that has PE (potential energy) and height (h).

Use the equation
   ΔPE = mgΔh.
When height increases (Δh), the gravitational potential energy increases (ΔPE).

Example: A. A ball is thrown 3 m high into the air. The ball has m(mass) = 2 kilograms (kg), g (acceleration due to gravity) = 9.81 m/s², and **h (height) = 3 meters.**
ΔPE = mgΔh ΔPE = (2 kg)(9.81 m/s²)(**3 m**)= 58.9 J
                           ΔPE = 58.9 J

Example: B. **Increase** the **h (height)** of the ball to **6 meters** (2x the height or double the height of example A), then the potential energy (PE) will also increase and double (2x the potential energy or double the potential energy) from 58.8 joules (in example A) to 117.6 joules (in example B-see below).
   ΔPE = mgΔh
   ΔPE = (2 kg)(9.81 m/s²)(6 m)
   ΔPE = 117.7 joules

Height and potential energy (PE) are directly proportional (when height increased and doubled, potential energy also increased and doubled).

Graph 1 is correct. As you can see in the graph, as height increases, gravitational potential energy increases. As height decreases, gravitational potential energy decreases. The line is a straight line, which shows that height and gravitational potential energy are directly proportional.   Answer *1*

Question: As an object falls freely, the kinetic energy of the object
      (1) decreases   (2) increases   (3) remains the same
Solution: You learned when a rock (or ball) is falling off the top of a cliff, when the potential energy (PE) of the rock is changed from maximum potential energy (1PE) to 3/4 PE, 1/4 of the potential energy is changed into kinetic energy (rock moving down the cliff). As an

---

object falls freely (free fall), potential energy decreases while **kinetic energy increases.** Answer 2

Now Do Homework Questions #26-31, pages 51-53.

Section 2:

SPRINGS

Work done in making the spring longer (stretching it) or compressing it (making the spring shorter) causes the spring to have more stored potential energy. Look at the figure. The force you use to pull down on the spring causes the spring to become longer, or the force you use to push up on the spring causes the spring to become shorter.

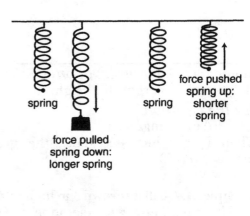

spring

force pulled
spring down:
longer spring

spring

force pushed
spring up:
shorter
spring

Hooke's Law: (See equation below.) The force (F) you put on the spring equals the spring constant (k) times the number of meters the spring got longer or shorter (change in length of the spring from the equilibrium position, also called rest position). See figure at right. The equilibrium position (rest position) (see figure at right) is where the free end of the spring is when no force is on it.

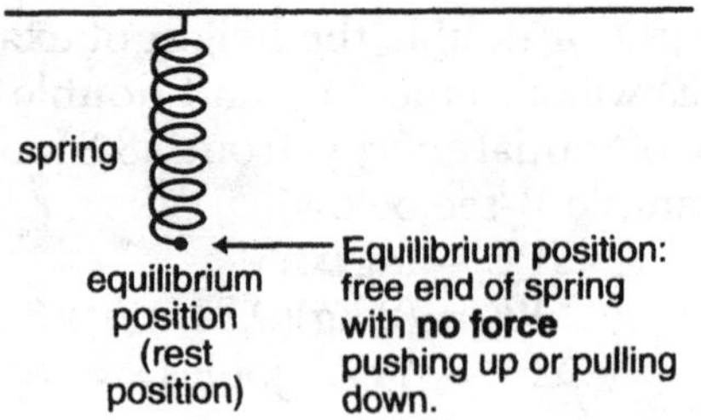

spring

equilibrium
position
(rest
position)

Equilibrium position:
free end of spring
with **no force**
pushing up or pulling
down.

$$F_s = k \qquad x$$

F_s = force on a spring
k = spring constant
x = change in spring
 length from
 equilibrium position

Force on spring	spring constant	change in length of spring from equilibrium position

Table: Mechanics (vertical label)

Force on the spring = spring constant (a specific number for that particular spring) times number of meters the spring got longer or shorter. The subscript **s** in F_s (force on a spring) means **spring**.

F force) is in newtons, k is in $\dfrac{newtons}{meter}$, and x is in meters.

Question: A 10-newton force is required to hold a stretched spring 0.20 meters from its rest position. What is the spring constant?

     (1) 10 N/m   (2) 20 N/m   (3) 50 N/m   (4) 200 N/m

Solution:
Given: 10 newton (N) force
        Spring stretched 0.20 meter (m)
Find: Spring constant (k)
Look for an equation on Reference Table: Mechanics that has **force** on a spring (F_s). There is only one equation for F_s (force on a spring), $F_s = kx$. Spring stretched 0.20 m from rest position (equilibrium position)(given), therefore x (change in length of spring) = **0.20 m**.

Use the equation
    $F_s = kx$ F_s = force on a spring
                        k = spring constant
                        x = change in spring length
                                from the equilibrium position

Look at the figure. *Then substitute for F_s* (force on spring) 10 N (given). *Substitute for x* (change in length of spring from rest position) 0.20 m.

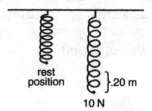

    $F_s = kx$
    $10N = k\,(0.20m)$
Divide both sides by 0.20 m

rest position $\}$.20 m
10 N

$$\frac{10\ N}{0.20\ m} = \frac{k(0.20\ m)}{0.20\ m}$$

$50\ \dfrac{N}{m} = k,\ \ k = 50\ \dfrac{N}{m}$

The spring constant (k) = $50\ \dfrac{N}{m}$.   Answer *3*

Note: If you have a **weight** (example, a watermelon that weighs 10 N) at the end of a spring, the 10 N weight is the **force** pulling the spring down. Weight = force of gravity.

If you are **given mass** (example 10 kg) at the **end of** a **spring**, to **find force** pulling down **on** the **spring**, use the equation $g = \dfrac{F_g}{m}$ or $F_g = mg$.

Multiply mass (m), (example 10 kg) times acceleration of gravity (g) ($9.81\ m/s^2$ on Earth, given on Reference Table: List of Physical Constants), to get force (F), ($10\ kg\ \times\ 9.81\ m/s^2 = 98\ kg \bullet m/s^2$ or 98 N).

Question: A spring has a spring constant of 10 N/m. Find the force to stretch the spring 0.25 m from its equilibrium position.

Solution:
Given: Spring constant = 10 N/m. Spring stretched 0.25 m (meters).
Find: Force on a spring (F_s).
Look for an equation on Reference Table: Mechanics to find F_s.
Use the equation $F_s = kx$ k = spring constant
                                                 x = change in spring length
                                                      from the equilibrium position
Substitute for k (spring constant) 10 N/m. *Substitute for x* (spring stretched) 0.25 m.
$F_s = (10 \text{ N/m})(0.25 \text{ m}) = 2.5 \text{ N}$.

Table: Mechanics

USING GRAPHS TO FIND SPRING CONSTANT AND POTENTIAL ENERGY

Finding Spring Constant by Using a Point on the Graph:

Question: A student performed a laboratory investigation to determine the spring constant of a spring. The force applied to the spring was varied and the resulting elongation of the spring measured. The student graphed the data collected, as shown. According to the student's graph, what is the spring constant for this spring?

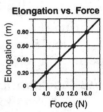

(1) 0.050 m/N   (2) 9.8 N/kg   (3) 13 N•m   (4) 20.N/m

Solution: *Look for an equation* on Reference Table: Mechanics that has **force** on a spring (F_s). There is only one equation for F_s (force on a spring). Or, you can *look for an equation* on Reference Table: Mechanics that has force on a spring (F_s), elongation of a spring (change in length of a spring)(x), and spring constant (k).

Use the equation
         $F_s = kx$ F_s = force on a spring
                              k = spring constant
                              x = change in spring length
                                     from the equilibrium position

Choose any point on the graph, such as force (F) = 4.0 N, elongation = 0.20 m (or you can choose a different point where force F = 8.0 N, elongation = 0.40 m, etc.).
In the equation $F_s = kx$, *then substitute for F_s* 4.0 N. *Substitute for x* (change in length of spring from equilibrium position, example: elongation, which means spring gets longer) 0.20 m.

F_s = k x	Or, rearrange the
4.0 N = k (0.20 m)	equation:
Divide by 0.20 m:	$F_s = kx$
$\dfrac{4.0 \text{ N}}{0.20 \text{ m}} = \dfrac{k(0.20) \text{ m}}{0.20 \text{ m}}$	$k = \dfrac{F_s}{x}$
$\dfrac{4.0 \text{ N}}{0.20 \text{ m}} = k$	$k = \dfrac{4.0 \text{ N}}{0.20 \text{ m}}$
$\dfrac{20. \text{ N}}{\text{m}} = k$ (spring constant)	$k = \dfrac{20. \text{ N}}{\text{m}}$ Answer *4*
Spring constant (k) = $\dfrac{20. \text{ N}}{\text{m}}$ Answer *4*	

Question: The graph shows elongation as a function of the applied force for two springs, A and B. Compared to the spring constant for spring A, the spring constant for spring B is
    (1) smaller
    (2) larger
    (3) the same.

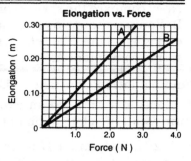

Elongation vs. Force

Table: Mechanics

Solution: *Look for an equation* on Reference Table: Mechanics that has force on a spring (F_s). There is only one equation for F_s (force on a spring).
Use the equation
    $F_s = kx$.

F_s = force on a spring
k = spring constant
x = change in spring length from the equilibrium position

Look on the graph. Choose one point on line A, such as force (F) = 2.2 N, elongation = 0.24 m (or you can choose a different point where force = 1.0 N, elongation = 0.109 m). In the equation $F_s = kx$, *then substitute for F* 2.2 N. *Substitute for x* (change in length of spring from equilibrium position, example: elongation, which means spring gets longer) 0.24 m.

$F_s = kx$	Or, rearrange the equation:
2.2 N = k 0.24	$k = \dfrac{F_s}{x}$
$k = \dfrac{2.2\ N}{0.24\ m}$	
	$k = \dfrac{2.2\ N}{0.24\ m}$
$k = 9.1$ N/m	$k = 9.1$ N/m

Look at the graph again. Choose one point on line B such as force (F) = 3.0 N, elongation = 0.195 m (or you can choose a different point where force = 1.0 N, elongation = 0.65 m). In the equation $F_s = kx$, *then substitute for F* 3.0 N. *Substitute for x* (change in length of spring from equilibrium position, example: elongation, which means spring gets longer) 0.195 m.

$F_s = kx$	Or, rearrange the equation:
3.0 N = k 0.195	$k = \dfrac{F_s}{x}$
$k = \dfrac{3.0\ N}{0.195\ m}$	
	$k = \dfrac{3.0\ N}{0.195\ m}$
$k = 15.4$ N/m	$k = 15.4$ N/m

Now, compare the spring constant (k) of A with the spring constant of B. You saw the spring constant of A is 9.1 N/m and the spring constant of B is 15.4 N/m. Therefore, the spring constant of B is larger than the spring constant of A. **Answer 2**

Finding Spring Constant by Using Slope:

Students in a class did an experiment and compared force applied to a spring with the elongation of the spring:

1 N, 2 N, 3 N, and 4 N forces were applied to a spring. The elongation (change in length–number of centimeters the spring got longer) is in column 2. For example, when a 2 newton force was put on the spring, the spring stretched and became 6 cm (centimeters) longer. (6 cm = 0.06 m (meter)).

Data Table	
Force, newtons	Elongation, cm
0	0
1	3
2	6
3	9
4	12

As you can see, as **force increases**, **elongation** of spring (number of cm the spring gets longer) **increases proportionately**. The change in the length of the spring is directly proportional to the force.

You learned $F_s = kx$ or (rearranged) k(spring constant) $= \frac{F_s}{x}$.

In a graph showing force and change of length of a spring (example: elongation of spring), when using the slope method (explained below) to find spring constant, it is easier when force is written on the y axis and elongation (change in length) on the x axis. See graph at right.

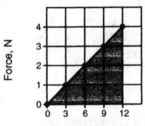

Elongation, cm
(change in length from equilibrium point)

You can use the graph to find k (spring constant).

Spring constant (k) = slope of the line.

The slope of a graph is $\frac{\Delta y}{\Delta x}$ $\frac{(change\ in\ y)}{(change\ in\ x)}$. Choose any two points on the line. (See the graph above.)

Examples:

1. (3,1) and (6,2).

Slope $= \frac{\Delta y}{\Delta x} = \frac{2\ N\ -\ 1\ N}{6\ cm\ -\ 3\ cm} = \frac{1\ N}{3\ cm} = \frac{1\ N}{0.03\ m}$

2. (9,3) and (12,4)

Slope $= \frac{\Delta y}{\Delta x} = \frac{4\ N\ -\ 3\ N}{12\ cm\ -\ 9\ cm} = \frac{1\ N}{3\ cm} = \frac{1\ N}{0.03\ m}$

Spring constant (k) = slope $= \frac{1\ N}{3\ cm} = \frac{1\ N}{0.03\ m}$

Finding Potential Energy of a Spring from the Area Under a Graph:
You can use the graph (see previous page) to find PE_s (potential energy of the spring).
The area under the line in the graph, which is shaded, equals the potential energy of the spring.
Area of triangle = ½ b x h
Look at the graph on the previous page.
With a 4 N force, base = 12 cm (centimeters) = .12 m (meters), and height = 4 N
Area (A) = ½bh, given on Reference Table: Geometry & Trigonometry
Area = ½ x .12m x 4N = .24 N•m = .24 joules (J) = potential energy of spring.

In the next section, you will learn how to calculate the PE (potential energy) of a spring using an equation.

Now Do Homework Questions #32-43, pages 53-55

POTENTIAL ENERGY

$PE_s = \dfrac{1}{2}kx^2$ PE_s = potential energy stored in a spring

k = spring constant

x = change in spring length from the equilibrium position

| PE_s | = | $\dfrac{1}{2}k$ | x^2 |

| potential energy of a spring | $\dfrac{1}{2}$ | spring constant | x | (change in length of spring from equilibrium position)² |

The subscript **s** in PE_s (potential energy stored in a spring) means **spring**.
PE_s (potential energy stored in a spring) is in newton•meters or joules.
k (spring constant) is in newtons per meter and
x (change in spring length from equilibrium position) is in meters
Note: Spring constant depends on the material that the spring is made of.

Question: A 10.-newton force is required to hold a stretched spring 0.20 meter from its rest position. What is the potential energy stored in the stretched spring?

　　　(1) 1.0 J　　　(2) 2.0 J　　　(3) 5.0 J　　　(4) 50. J

Solution:

Given: F_s = 10. newtons (N)

　　　Spring stretched 0.20 meters from rest position (equilibrium position). You learned x is change in spring length from equilibrium position, therefore x = 0.20 meters

Find: **potential energy** stored in the stretched spring (PE_s).

Look for an equation on Reference Table: Mechanics for potential energy stored in a stretched spring,. There is only one equation on Reference Table: Mechanics for PE_s (potential energy stored in a spring).

Use the equation

$$PE_S = \frac{1}{2}kx^2$$

You have two unknowns, PE_s and k, therefore, **first find k** and then *substitute k in* the equation $PE_s = \frac{1}{2}kx^2$ to find PE_s.

First find k. You see on Reference Table: Mechanics, that there are only two equations that have k (spring constant), $F_s = kx$ and $PE_s = \frac{1}{2}kx^2$. Use $F_s = kx$ to find k because you know F_s and x and there is only one unknown, k.

Use the equation:

				F_s = force on a spring
F_s	=	k	x	k = spring constant

x = change in spring length from the equilibrium position

Then substitute for F_s (force on a spring) 10. N (newtons) (given) and *substitute* for x (change in spring length-in this example, spring stretched) 0.20 m (meters).

$$F_s = k \ x$$
$$10.N = k \ (0.20 \text{ m})$$

Divide both sides by 0.20 m

$$\frac{10. \ N}{0.20 \ m} = \frac{k(0.20 \ m)}{0.20 \ m}$$

$$\frac{50. \ N}{m} = k$$

$$\frac{50. \ N}{m} = k \text{ (spring constant)}$$

Then in the equation $PE_S = \frac{1}{2}kx^2$ *substitute for k* $\frac{50. \ N}{m}$ (answer from first part of the solution). *Substitute for x* 0.20 m (given)

$$PE_S = \frac{1}{2} \ k \ x^2.$$
$$PE_S = \frac{1}{2}(\frac{50. \ N}{m})(0.20 \text{ m})^2$$
$$PE_S = \frac{25 \ N}{m}(0.04\text{m}^2)$$
$$PE_S = 1.0 \ N \bullet m = 1.0 \text{ J (joule)} \qquad \text{Answer } 1$$

Question: A spring of negligible mass has a spring constant of 50. newtons per meter. If the spring is stretched 0.40 meter from its equilibrium position, how much potential energy is stored in the spring?

(1) 20. J (2) 10. J (3) 8.0 J (4) 4.0 J

Table: Mechanics

Table: Mechanics

Solution:

Given: spring constant $= \dfrac{50.\ newtons\ (N)}{meter\ (m)}$

spring stretched 0.40 meter (m) from its equilibrium position. You learned x is change in spring length from equilibrium position, therefore x = 0.40 m.

Find: Potential energy stored in the spring (PE_s).

Look for an equation on Reference Table: Mechanics that has potential energy stored in a spring (PE_s).

There are only two equations that have to do with springs, and only one equation for potential energy stored in a spring (PE_s):

F_s (force on a spring) = kx

PE_s (potential energy stored in a spring) = ½kx².

Use the equation

$PE_S = \dfrac{1}{2}kx^2.$ k = spring constant

PE_s = potential energy stored in a spring

x = change in spring length from the equilibrium position

Then substitute for k (spring constant) $\dfrac{50.\ N}{m}$ (given).

Substitute for x (change in spring length from the equilibrium position example: spring stretched) 0.40 m (meters) given

$$PE_S = \dfrac{1}{2}kx^2.$$

$$= \dfrac{1}{2}(\dfrac{50.\ N}{m})(0.40\ m)^2$$

$$= \dfrac{25\ N}{m}(0.16m^2)$$

$$PE_S = 4.0\ N \bullet m = 4.0\ J\ (joules) \qquad Answer\ 4$$

Question: A student compresses the spring in a pop-up toy 0.020 meter.

If the spring has a spring constant of 340 newtons per meter, how much energy is being stored in the spring?

(1) 0.068 J   (2) 0.14 J   (3) 3.4 J   (4) 6.8 J

Solution:

Given: spring constant $= \dfrac{340\ newtons\ (N)}{meter\ (m)}$

spring was compressed 0.020 meter (m) from its equilibrium position. You learned x is change in spring length from equilibrium position, therefore x = 0.020 meter.

Find: **Potential energy** stored in the **spring (PE_s).**

Look for an equation on Reference Table: Mechanics that has energy stored in a spring.

There are only two equations that have to do with springs and only one equation for potential energy stored in a spring (PE_s):

F_s (force on a spring) = kx

PE_s (potential energy stored in a spring) = $\frac{1}{2}kx^2$.

Use the equation

$$PE_S = \frac{1}{2}kx^2.$$

PE_s = potential energy stored
in a spring
k = spring constant
x = change in spring length
from the equilibrium position

Then substitute for k $\frac{340\ N}{m}$ (given).

Substitute for x (change in spring length from the equilibrium position, example: spring compressed) 0.020 meters (m) given

$$PE_S = \frac{1}{2}kx^2.$$

$$= \frac{1}{2}(\frac{340\ N}{m})(0.020\ m)^2$$

$$= \frac{170\ N}{m}(0.0004m^2)$$

$$PE_S = 0.068\ N\bullet m = 0.068\ J \qquad \text{Answer } 1$$

Question: A s a spring is stretched, its elastic potential energy
(1) decreases (2) increases (3)remains the same

Solution: Look for an equation on Reference Table: Mechanics for the potential energy of a spring (PE_s).

$$PE_S = \frac{1}{2}kx^2.$$

PE_s = potential energy stored
in a spring
k = spring constant
x = change in spring length
from the equilibrium position

When the distance the spring stretches (x) increases, PE_S (potential energy of the spring) also increases (see equation above).

Question: As shown in the diagram below, a 0.50-meter-long spring is stretched from its equilibrium position to a length of 1.00 meter by a weight. If 15 joules of energy are stored in the stretched spring, what is the value of the spring constant?
(1) 30. N/m   (2) 60. N/m
(3) 120 N/m   (4) 240 N/m

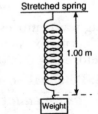

Unstretched spring   Stretched spring

0.50 m

1.00 m

Weight

Solution:

Given: 0.50 meter long spring. Spring is stretched from 0.50 meter to 1.00 meter by a weight. 15 joules of energy is stored in the stretched spring.

Find: Value of spring constant (k).

Look for an equation on Reference Table: Mechanics that has energy stored in a spring (PE_s,) spring constant (k), and spring stretched from its equilibrium position, (x).

Use the equation

$$PE_s = \frac{1}{2}kx^2.$$

Then substitute for PE_s 15 J (joules) (given). *Substitute for x* (change in spring length from the equilibrium position) 0.50 m, as explained below:

> Equilibrium position = 0.50 m (meters).
> Spring stretched to 1.00 m (see diagram in question), therefore, change in spring length (x) = 0.50 m. Substitute for x 0.50 m.

$PE_s = \frac{1}{2}kx^2.$	Or, rearrange the equation
$15\,J = \frac{1}{2}k\,(0.50m)^2$	$k = \dfrac{2\,PE_s}{x^2}$
$15\,J = \frac{1}{2}k\,(0.25\ m^2)$	$k = \dfrac{(2)(15J)}{(0.50\ m)^2} = \dfrac{30\ J}{(0.25\ m^2)}$ or $\dfrac{30\ N\bullet m}{(0.25\ m^2)}$
Cross multiply	$k = \dfrac{120\ N}{m}$ \qquad Answer *3*
$30J = k\,(0.25\ m^2)$	
$\dfrac{30\ J}{0.25\ m^2} = k$	
$k = \dfrac{30\ J}{0.25\ m^2}$ or $\dfrac{30\ N\bullet m}{0.25\ m^2}$	
$k = \dfrac{120\ N}{m}$ \qquad Answer *3*	

Question: Which graph best represents the elastic potential energy stored in a spring (PE_S) as a function of its elongation, x?

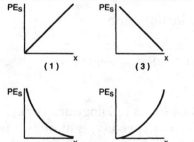

Solution: *Look for an equation* on Reference Table: Mechanics that has PE_S (potential energy stored in a spring) and x (change in length from equilibrium position, example elongation).

$PE_s = \frac{1}{2}kx^2$.

Since PE_s (potential energy stored in a spring) is proportional to x^2 (elongation squared)(see equation above), the graph has the equation $y = kx^2$, which is a curve (parabola). When x (elongation) increases, PE_s (potential energy of the spring) increases. The curve is rising (going up).   Answer 4

Wrong choices:

Choice 1: The graph is a **straight line** (not a curve), which shows that PE_s (potential energy stored in a spring) is directly proportional to x (elongation). When x increases, PE_s increases proportionately (example, when x doubles, PE_s also doubles).

Choices 2 and 3. The graph shows PE_s decreases when x (elongation) increases. By looking at the equation $PE_s = \frac{1}{2}kx^2$, you see PE_s increases when x (elongation) increases.

Now Do Homework Questions #44-52, pages 55-56.

Section 3:

KINETIC ENERGY

Kinetic energy is energy of motion (movement). Kinetic energy is the energy that an object has when it **moves** (example: a ball has kinetic energy when it moves.)

A boy is playing baseball. He takes his bat and swings at (hits) the ball. The ball moves. Work done by the bat gives the ball its kinetic energy, making the ball move.

Work done in **accelerating** (speeding up) an **object** (example: car) = change **(increase)** in **kinetic energy** of the **object**.

The equation for kinetic energy (KE) is

KE	=	$\frac{1}{2}$		m		v^2
kinetic energy	=	$\frac{1}{2}$	x	mass	x	velocity squared

$KE = \frac{1}{2}mv^2$ KE = kinetic energy
                                 m = mass
                                 v = velocity/speed

Mass (m) is in kilograms (kg).

Velocity/speed (v) is in meters per second (m/s), and

kinetic energy is in $\frac{kilogram \cdot meter^2}{second^2}$ ($\frac{kg \cdot m^2}{s^2}$) or joules (J).

Question: The kinetic energy of a 980-kilogram race car traveling at 90. meters per second is approximately

(1) 4.4×10^4 J (2) 8.8×10^4 J (3) 4.0×10^6 J (4) 7.9×10^6 J

Solution:

Given: 980-kilogram car means mass (m) of the car = 980 kilograms (kg)

Speed = 90. meters per second (m/s)

Find: kinetic energy (KE)

Look for an equation on Reference Table: Mechanics that has kinetic energy (KE), mass (*m*) and speed (v).

Use the equation

$$KE = \tfrac{1}{2}mv^2$$ KE = kinetic energy

m = mass

v = velocity/speed

Then substitute for m (mass) 980 kg. *Substitute for v* (velocity/speed) 90. m/s.

$KE = \dfrac{1}{2}(980 \text{ kg})(90. \text{ m/s})^2$

$KE = \dfrac{1}{2}(980 \text{ kg})(8100 \text{ m}^2/\text{s}^2)$

$KE = (490 \text{ Kg})(8100 \text{ m}^2/\text{s}^2)$

$KE = 3.969 \times 10^6 \text{ kg} \bullet \text{m}^2/\text{s}^2$ or 3.969×10^6 J (joules)

KE is approximately 4.0×10^6 J   Answer *3*

Question: An object moving at a constant speed of 25 meters per second possesses 450 joules of kinetic energy. What is the object's mass?

(1) 0.72 kg   (2) 1.4 kg   (3) 18 kg   (4) 36 kg

Solution:

Given: Speed = 25 meters per second (m/s)

Kinetic energy = 450 joules (J)

Find: mass (*m*)

Look for an equation on Reference Table: Mechanics that has kinetic energy (KE), speed (v) and mass (*m*).

Use the equation

$$KE = \dfrac{1}{2}mv^2$$ KE = kinetic energy

m = mass

v = velocity/speed

Then substitute for v (velocity or speed) 25 m/s. *Substitute for KE* (kinetic energy) 450 J.

$$KE = \frac{1}{2} m v^2$$

$$450 \text{ J} = \frac{1}{2} m (25 \text{ m/s})^2$$

$$450 \text{ J} = \frac{1}{2} m (625 \text{ m}^2/\text{s}^2)$$

$$450 \text{ J} = m \; 312.5 \text{ m}^2/\text{s}^2$$

Divide both sides by $312.5 \text{ m}^2/\text{s}^2$

$$\frac{450 \text{ J}}{312.5 \text{ m}^2/\text{s}^2} = \frac{m \; 312.5 \text{ m}^2/\text{s}^2}{312.5 \text{ m}^2/\text{s}^2}$$

$$\frac{450 \text{ J}}{312.5 \text{ m}^2/\text{s}^2} = m$$

$$m = \frac{450 \text{ J}}{312.5 \text{ m}^2/\text{s}^2} = \frac{1.4 \text{ J}}{\text{m}^2/\text{s}^2} = 1.4 \text{ kg}$$

m (mass) $= 1.4 \text{ kg}$ Answer 2

Or, rearrange the equation

$$m = \frac{KE}{\frac{1}{2}v^2}$$

Substitute for KE (kinetic energy) 450 J (given).
Substitute for v (speed or velocity) 25 m/s (given).

$$m = \frac{KE}{\frac{1}{2}v^2} = \frac{2KE}{v^2} = \frac{2(450 \text{ J})}{(25 \text{ m/s})^2}$$

$$= \frac{900 \text{ J}}{625 \text{ m}^2/\text{s}^2} = \frac{1.4 \text{ J}}{\text{m}^2/\text{s}^2} = 1.4 \text{kg}$$

m (mass) $= 1.4 \text{ kg}$ Answer 2

Question: A 60.0-kilogram runner has 1920 joules of kinetic energy. At what speed is she running?

    (1) 5.66 m/s   (2) 8.00 m/s   (3) 32.0 m/s   (4) 64.0 m/s

Solution:
Given: 60.0-kilogram runner means mass (m) = 60.0 kilogram (kg)
      Kinetic energy = 1920 joules (J)
Find: speed (v)

Look for an equation on Reference Table: Mechanics that has kinetic energy (KE), mass (*m*) and speed (v).

Use the equation

$$KE = \frac{1}{2}mv^2$$

KE = kinetic energy

m = mass
v = velocity/speed

Then substitute for m (mass) 60.0 kg. *Substitute for KE* (kinetic energy) 1920 J.

$1920 \text{ J} = \frac{1}{2}(60.0 \text{ kg}) \text{ v}^2$

$1920 \text{ J} = 30.0 \text{ kg} \cdot \text{v}^2$

Divide both sides by 30.0 kg

$\dfrac{1920 \text{ J}}{30.0 \text{ kg}} = \dfrac{30.0 \text{ kg} \cdot \text{v}^2}{30.0 \text{ kg}}$

$\dfrac{1920 \text{ J}}{30.0 \text{ kg}} = \text{v}^2$

$\text{v}^2 = \dfrac{1920 \text{ J}}{30.0 \text{ kg}} = \dfrac{64 \text{ J}}{\text{kg}} = \dfrac{64 \text{ m}^2}{\text{s}^2}$

$\text{v} = \sqrt{\dfrac{64 \text{ m}^2}{\text{s}^2}} = \dfrac{8.0 \text{ m}}{\text{s}}$

v = 8.0 m/s

Speed = 8.0 m/s   Answer 2

Or, rearrange the equation KE = ½mv².

$\text{v}^2 = \dfrac{KE}{\frac{1}{2} \text{ m}}$

$\text{v} = \sqrt{\dfrac{KE}{\frac{1}{2} \text{ m}}}$

Substitute for KE (kinetic energy) 1920 J (given). Substitute for m (mass) 60.0 kg (given).

$\text{v} = \sqrt{\dfrac{KE}{\frac{1}{2} \text{ m}}} = \sqrt{\dfrac{1920 \text{ J}}{\frac{1}{2} (60.0 \text{ kg})}}$

$= \sqrt{\dfrac{1920 \text{ J}}{30.0 \text{ kg}}} = \sqrt{\dfrac{64 \text{J}}{\text{kg}}} = \sqrt{\dfrac{64 \text{ m}^2}{\text{s}^2}}$

v = 8.0 m/s

Speed = 8.0 m/s   Answer 2

Question: If the speed of a car is doubled, the kinetic energy of the car is
    (1) quadrupled   (2) quartered   (3) doubled   (4) halved

Solution:

Given: Speed (v) of car is doubled.

Find: kinetic energy (KE).

Look for an equation on Reference Table: Mechanics that has kinetic energy (KE) and speed (v).

Use the equation

$$KE = \frac{1}{2} \text{ mv}^2.$$

KE = kinetic energy

m = mass

v = velocity/speed

Table: Mechanics

OLD	NEW
$KE = \dfrac{1}{2} \text{mv}^2$	Speed (v) is doubled. New speed = 2v
	Substitute 2v for v in $KE = \dfrac{1}{2} \text{ mv}^2$
	New $KE = \dfrac{1}{2} \text{ m}(2\text{v})^2 =$
	$\dfrac{1}{2} \text{ m}(2\text{v})(2\text{v}) = \dfrac{1}{2}\text{m}(4\text{v}^2) \text{ } rearrange = 4(\dfrac{1}{2}\text{mv}^2)$
	New $KE = 4(\dfrac{1}{2} \text{ mv}^2)$
Old $KE = \dfrac{1}{2} \text{ mv}^2$ Old kinetic energy	New $KE = 4(\dfrac{1}{2} \text{ mv}^2)$ New kinetic energy

---

Look at the new KE and the old KE. New KE = 4 times the old KE, which means the new KE is quadrupled.   Answer *1*

Question: A cart of mass m traveling at speed v has kinetic energy KE. If the mass of the cart is doubled and its speed is halved, the kinetic energy of the cart will be

(1) half as great	(2) twice as great
(3) one-fourth as great	(4) four times as great

Solution:

Given: Mass (m) of cart is doubled. Speed (v) of cart is halved.
Find: kinetic energy (KE).

Look for an equation on Reference Table: Mechanics that has kinetic energy (KE), mass (m) and speed (v).

Use the equation

$$KE = \frac{1}{2} mv^2$$

KE = kinetic energy

m = mass

v = velocity/speed

Table: Mechanics

OLD	**NEW**
$KE = \frac{1}{2} mv^2$	Mass (m) is doubled. New mass = $2m$. Speed (v) is halved. New speed $= \frac{1}{2} v$ *Substitute* $2m$ for m and *substitute* $\frac{1}{2}v$ for v in $KE = \frac{1}{2} mv^2$ New KE $= \frac{1}{2} (2m)(\frac{1}{2} v)^2 = \frac{1}{2} (2m)(\frac{1}{2} v)(\frac{1}{2} v)$ $= \frac{1}{2} (2m)(\frac{1}{4}v^2)$ *rearrange* $= (2 \times \frac{1}{4})(\frac{1}{2} mv^2)$ $= \frac{1}{2} (\frac{1}{2} mv^2)$ New KE $= \frac{1}{2}(\frac{1}{2} mv^2)$ Note: You need to keep $\frac{1}{2} mv^2$ together so you can see that the new KE is $\frac{1}{2}$ times the old KE, which means the new KE is half as great.
Old KE $= \frac{1}{2} mv^2$ Old kinetic energy	New KE $= \frac{1}{2}(\frac{1}{2} mv^2)$ New kinetic energy

Look at the new KE and the old KE. New KE $= \frac{1}{2}$ times the old KE, which means the new KE is half as great.   Answer *1*

Question: Which quantity and unit are correctly paired?
    (1) velocity–m/s²   (2) momentum–kg•m/s²
    (3) energy–kg•m²/s²   (4) work–kg/m

Solution: You can use the kinetic energy equation to see what units are used to measure energy.

$$KE = \frac{1}{2}mv^2 \qquad\qquad KE = \text{kinetic energy}$$

$$m = \text{mass}$$
$$v = \text{velocity/speed}$$

Mass (**m**) is in **kg**
Velocity (v) is in m/s (meters/second), therefore velocity²(v^2) is in (m/s)²
= **m²/s²**
In the **kinetic energy** (KE) equation, put in kg for mass and m²/s² for v^2.

$$KE = \frac{1}{2}mv^2$$

$$KE = \frac{1}{2}\textbf{kg}\bullet\textbf{m}^2/\textbf{s}^2$$

Choice *3* is correct; energy is in kg•m²/s²   Answer *3*

Or, you can use the change in potential **energy** (ΔPE) equation to see what units are used to measure energy.

ΔPE = m g Δh   g = acceleration due to gravity or
                                    gravitational field strength
                          h = height
                          m = mass
                          PE = potential energy

m (mass) is in kg (kilograms)
g (acceleration due to gravity) is in m/s² (meters/second²)
h (height) is in m (meters)
In the **potential energy** (PE) equation, put in kg for *m*, m/s² for g, and m for h.

$$\Delta PE = m \quad g \quad \Delta h$$
$$\Delta PE = \text{kg}\bullet\text{m/s}^2\bullet\text{m} = \textbf{kg}\bullet\textbf{m}^2/\textbf{s}^2$$

Choice *3* is correct; energy is in kg•m²/s²   Answer *3*

Wrong choices:
1. Velocity equals $\frac{distance}{time}$ ($v = \frac{d}{t}$), given on Reference Table: Mechanics.
Distance (d) is in meters (m), and time (t) is in seconds (s), therefore, velocity (v) is in meters/second (m/s).
2. Momentum (p) equals mass (m) times velocity (v).
       p = mv given on Reference Table: Mechanics. Mass (m) is in kilograms (kg), and velocity (v) is in meters/second (m/s), therefore p (momentum) is in kg•m/s.

Table: Mechanics

4. Work (W) = force (F) times distance (d).
Let's find units for force and units for distance.

$$a = \frac{F}{m}$$ given on Reference Table: Mechanics or cross multiply and you have F = ma. F (Force) = m (mass) times a (acceleration). Mass (m)is in kilograms (kg), and acceleration (a) is in meters/second^2 (m/s^2), therefore F (force) is in kg•m/s^2.
Put kg•m/s^2 for force (F) in the equation W = Fd. Put m (meters) for distance (d).

$W =$ F   x   d
Work = kg•m/s^2 x   m = kg•m^2/s^2

Question: Which graph best represents the relationship between the kinetic energy, KE, and the velocity of an object accelerating in a straight line?

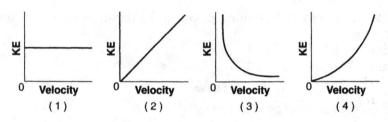

(1)   (2)   (3)   (4)

Solution: Look for an equation on Reference Table: Mechanics that has kinetic energy (KE) and velocity (v).
KE = ½ mv^2.
Since KE (kinetic energy) is proportional to v^2 (velocity squared) (see equation above), the graph has the equation y = kx^2, which is a curve (a parabola). When velocity increases, kinetic energy increases. The curve is rising (going up).   Answer *4*

Wrong choices:
Choice *1*: The graph shows that kinetic energy is constant at all velocities.
Choice *2*: The graph is a straight line (not a curve), which shows that KE (kinetic energy) is directly proportional to v (velocity). When velocity increases, kinetic energy increases proportionately (example, when velocity doubles, kinetic energy also doubles).
Choice *3*: The graph shows, as velocity (v) increases, kinetic energy (KE) decreases; it shows kinetic energy is inversely proportional to velocity. The graph is a hyperbola with the equation xy = k.

Questions 1-4: Base your answers to questions 1 through 4 on the information and table below. The table lists the kinetic energy of a 4.0-kilogram mass as it travels in a straight line for 12.0 seconds.

Time (seconds)	Kinetic Energy (joules)
0.0	0.0
2.0	8.0
4.0	18
6.0	32
10.0	32
12.0	32

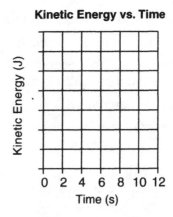

Using the information in the data table, construct a graph on the grid provided following the directions below.

Question 1: Mark an appropriate scale on the axis labeled "Kinetic Energy (J)".

Question 2: Plot the data points for kinetic energy versus time.

Question 3: Calculate the speed of the mass at 10.0 seconds. [Show all work, including the equation and substitution with units.]

Question 4: Compare the speed of the mass at 6.0 seconds to the speed of the mass at 10.0 seconds.

Solution 1: Space the **lines** along the axis **equally**; there must be an **equal number of J (joules) between each two lines.** On the y axis, the graph must show the kinetic energy from 0 J (joules) to 32 J (joules), evenly spaced between the lines. The graph should use a large part of the grid provided .

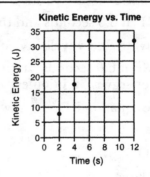

Since there are seven lines available above the zero, a possible spacing is to mark the lines 5, 10, 15, 20, 25, 30, 35 J (joules).

Solution 2: (See graph).

Solution 3:

Given: Mass = 4.0 kg. Data table of time (seconds) with kinetic energy (joules).

Find: Speed at 10.0 seconds (s).

Look for an equation on Reference Table: Mechanics that has kinetic energy (KE), speed (v) and mass (m).

Use the equation

$$KE = \frac{1}{2} mv^2.$$

Table: Mechanics

First find KE at 10.0 seconds and then substitute KE in the equation
$KE = \frac{1}{2} mv^2$ to find v (velocity) at 10.0 seconds.

First find KE at 10.0 seconds. In the data table and the graph, you see the kinetic energy is 32 J (joules) at 10.0 s (seconds).

Then, in the equation $KE = \frac{1}{2} mv^2$, *substitute* for KE 32 J. *Substitute* for m (mass) 4.0 kg (given).

$32\,J = \frac{1}{2}(4.0\ kg)v^2$.

$32\,J = (2.0\ kg)v^2$.

$$v^2 = \frac{32\ J}{2.0\ kg} = \frac{16\ J}{kg} = \frac{16\ kg \cdot m^2/s^2}{kg} = \frac{16\ m^2}{s^2}.$$

$v = 4.0$ m/s.

Solution 4: In question 3, you calculated the speed at 10.0 seconds is 4.0 meters/second (m/s). Now compare speed of the mass at 6.0 seconds to speed of the mass at 10.0 seconds.

Given: Mass = 4.0 kg. Data table of time (s) with kinetic energy (j).
Find: Speed at 6.0 seconds (s).

Look for an equation on Reference Table: Mechanics that has kinetic energy (KE), speed (v) and mass (m).

Use the equation $KE = \frac{1}{2} mv^2$.

First find KE at 6.0 seconds and then substitute KE in the equation
$KE = \frac{1}{2} mv^2$ to find v (velocity) at 6.0 seconds.

First find KE at 6.0 seconds. In the data table and the graph, you see the kinetic energy is 32 J (joules) at 6.0 s (seconds).

Then, in the equation $KE = \frac{1}{2} mv^2$, *substitute* for KE 32 J. *Substitute* for m (mass) 4.0 kg (given).

$32\,J = \frac{1}{2}(4.0\ kg)v^2$.

$32\,J = (2.0\ kg)v^2$.

$$v^2 = \frac{32\ J}{2.0\ kg} = \frac{16\ J}{kg} = \frac{16\ kg \cdot m^2/s^2}{kg} = \frac{16\ m^2}{s^2}.$$

$v = 4.0$ m/s.

Answer: As you can see, the speed at 6.0 seconds and the speed at 10.0 seconds are the same, 4.0 m/s.

Or

since the kinetic energy is the same at 6.0 seconds and 10.0 seconds, and the mass is also the same, therefore the speed at 6.0 seconds and 10.0 seconds must be the same (see equation below).

$KE = ½ \quad m \quad v^2$
same   same

Answer: Speed is the same at 6.0 seconds and 10.0 seconds

Now Do Homework Questions #53-61, pages 56-57

WORK CHANGES INTO ENERGY

Work changes into potential energy or kinetic energy. When there is friction, work also changes into internal energy. You learned work done lifting a box (example 30 joules of work) causes an increase in potential energy (30 joules of potential energy).

A boy hits a ball with a bat. The work done by the bat gives the ball kinetic energy, causing the ball to move.

raised box on shelf

increase in potential energy = 30 J

work done to lift a box = 30J

Question: In the diagram below, an average force of 20. newtons is used to pull back the string of a bow 0.60 meter.

0.60 m

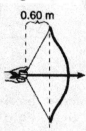

As the arrow leaves the bow, its kinetic energy is

    (1) 3.4 J   (2) 6.0 J   (3) 12 J   (4) 33 J

Solution:

Given: Force = 20. newtons (N). String was pulled back 0.60 meter (m), which means distance string was pulled back = 0.60 m.

Find: kinetic energy.

Obviously, we cannot find kinetic energy directly by using the equation $KE = \frac{1}{2} mv^2$ because we do not know (and cannot find) the velocity (v) of the arrow.

Work done by pulling back the bow **string** is **changed** to (equals) **kinetic energy**(KE) of the arrow (**arrow moved**). Therefore, find the work done by the string, because it equals the kinetic energy of the arrow.

Look for an equation on Reference Table: Mechanics that has force, distance, work, and energy.

Use the equation

    $W = Fd = \Delta E_T$ d = displacement/distance
                                      E_T = total energy
                                      F = force
                                      W = work
                                      Δ = change

Table: Mechanics

Then, in the equation W = Fd, *substitute for F* (force) 20 N. *Substitute for d* (distance) 0.60 m.

$W = (20. \text{ N})(0.60 \text{ m}) = 12 \text{ N} \cdot \text{m} = 12 \text{ J}$

W (work) = 12 J.
The 12 J of work (done pulling back the string) was changed into
12 J of kinetic energy (arrow moves).   Answer 3

CHANGING WORK INTO ENERGY

No Friction: When there is **no friction**, all the **work** done (in a system) becomes **potential energy** or **kinetic energy**. Work done (example 30 joules) of work) in lifting a box causes an increase in potential energy (30 joules of potential energy).

Friction: Friction opposes motion. Therefore work is (needed) used to overcome the friction and this work becomes **heat** or **internal energy** (Q). **Work done** (example 30 joules) in **dragging** a **box** on a **bumpy** (there is **friction**) steep road (box is raised **higher up**) **changes into** two types of energy, **internal energy** (because of friction) and **potential energy** (box is raised higher up). In the example above, 30 joules of work change into 10 joules of internal energy (Q) and 20 joules of potential energy.

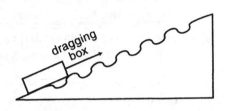

NOTE: A rough track or a bumpy track has friction.

CONSERVATION OF ENERGY

Conservation of energy – energy cannot be created or destroyed. The **total** amount of **energy** of an object or a system is **constant** (stays the same). For example, potential energy (PE) can change into kinetic energy (KE) and kinetic energy can change into potential energy, but the total energy is conserved (constant). See examples below.

Mechanical energy is the sum of the potential energy and kinetic energy of an object or a system.

In an **ideal mechanical system**, (where there is no friction and no air resistance), the **total energy** is **made** up **of potential energy** and **kinetic energy**; the total energy is constant (remains the same). For example, some potential energy is changed to kinetic energy, causing a decrease in potential energy and an increase in kinetic energy, but the **total energy remains constant** (the same).

In a **nonideal mechanical system**, there is **friction** or air **resistance**, etc. (a nonconservative force). Air resistance opposes motion (movement) and slows down a feather falling to the ground. You learned that friction opposes motion. The frictional force converts some kinetic energy into internal energy (Q). When you rub your hands together, some kinetic energy (KE) is changed into internal energy (Q) and you feel your hands are warmer (increase in temperature). **Total energy** of a nonideal system remains **constant.** Total energy of a nonideal system is:

$$E_t \quad = \quad PE \quad + \quad KE \quad + \quad Q$$

| Total energy | Potential energy | Kinetic energy | Internal energy |

The **total energy** of a **nonideal mechanical system** is **made up of** the **potential energy, kinetic energy,** and **internal energy.**

Energy is in joules. Potential energy, kinetic energy, internal energy and total energy are in joules.

PENDULUM: RELATIONSHIP OF POTENTIAL AND KINETIC ENERGY

The Law of Conservation of Energy states that the total energy is constant (stays the same). When a pendulum (string with a mass at the end) moves, some potential energy (PE) is converted (changed) into kinetic energy (KE), and some kinetic energy (KE) is converted into potential energy (PE), but the total energy remains the same.

At A, **potential energy** is **maximum (highest from the ground);** there is **zero kinetic** energy because, for an instant, the pendulum is not moving.

When the pendulum goes to **B, some potential energy** is **converted to kinetic energy.** At B, potential energy = kinetic energy.

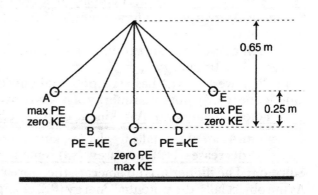

At **point C (lowest down),** all potential energy has been converted to kinetic energy. **Point C** is **lowest down;** there is **zero potential** energy and **maximum kinetic** energy.

At **point D, some kinetic** energy is **converted to potential** energy. Kinetic energy = potential energy.

At **point E,** there is **zero kinetic** energy. All kinetic energy is converted to potential energy, **maximum potential** energy (highest from the ground).

In short, potential energy at points A and E is the same (**maximum potential, highest,** same height).

Potential energy equals kinetic energy at points B and D (same height).

C has the **maximum kinetic energy** and zero potential energy (**lowest down).**

Question: The diagram below shows three positions, A, B and C, in the swing of a pendulum, released from rest at point A. [Neglect friction]. Which statement is true about this swinging pendulum?

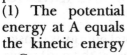

(1) The potential energy at A equals the kinetic energy at C.

(2) The speed of the pendulum at A equals the speed of the pendulum at B.

(3) The potential energy at B equals the potential energy at C.

(4) The potential energy at A equals the kinetic energy at B.

Solution: Answer 4. Potential energy of A was converted to kinetic energy of B.

Point A (highest from the ground) has the maximum potential energy and zero kinetic energy.

Point B (lowest down) has zero potential energy and the maximum kinetic energy. All potential energy of A was converted to kinetic energy of B. Potential energy of A = kinetic energy of B.   Answer 4

Question: As an object falls freely, the kinetic energy of the object

(1) decreases   (2) increases   (3) remains the same

Solution: The higher up the object is, the more potential energy it has. As the object falls, the potential energy (PE) changes into kinetic energy (KE); kinetic energy increases.   Answer 2

Question: A 650-kilogram roller coaster car starts from rest at the top of the first hill of its track and glides freely.[Neglect friction.]

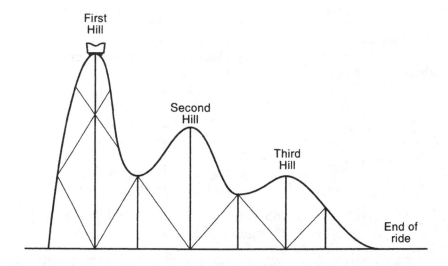

First
Hill

Second
Hill

Third
Hill

End of
ride

If the heights of the three hills are 10 m, 6 m and 3 m, find the kinetic energy of the car at the top of the third hill.

Solution:

Given: 650-kilogram roller coaster means mass (m) = 650 kilogram(kg).
     Heights of hills are 10 m, 6 m, and 3 m.

Find: Kinetic energy of car at top of third hill.

The Law of Conservation of Energy states that the total energy is constant. Potential energy (PE) can be changed into kinetic energy (KE), but the total energy (of a system you are dealing with) remains constant.

The question has to do with mass (m), height (h) and energy (E).

Look for an equation on Reference Table: Mechanics that has to do with mass (m), height (h) and energy (E).

Use the equation
$$\Delta PE = mg\Delta h.$$

PE = potential energy
g = acceleration due to gravity or
     gravitational field strength
h = height
m = mass
Δ = change

Table: Mechanics

First find potential energy (ΔPE) of the first hill and find potential energy (ΔPE) of the third hill. (The potential energies of both hills are compared to ground level.)Then PE of the first hill minus PE of the third hill = PE which is changed into (converted into) kinetic energy. Total energy of the system is constant.

PE of First Hill	PE of Third Hill
$\Delta PE = mg\Delta h$.	$\Delta PE = mg\Delta h$.
Substitute 650 kg for m (mass).	*Substitute* 650 kg for m (mass).
Substitute 9.81 m/s² for g (acceleration due to gravity, given on Reference Table: List of Physical Constants)	*Substitute* 9.81 m/s² for g (acceleration due to gravity, given on Reference Table: List of Physical Constants)
Substitute 10 m for Δh.	*Substitute* 3 m for Δh.
$\Delta PE =$ m g Δh.	$\Delta PE =$ m g Δh.
$\Delta PE = (650\ kg)(9.81\ m/s^2)(10\ m)$	$\Delta PE = (650\ kg)(9.81\ m/s^2)(3\ m)$
$\Delta PE = 63765\ J$ for first hill.	$\Delta PE = 19130\ J$ for third hill.

ΔPE of the first hill (63765 J) $-\Delta PE$ of the third hill (19130 J) = potential energy which is changed into kinetic energy of the car at the top of the third hill (44635 J).

Question: The diagram below shows a 0.1-kg apple attached to a branch of a tree 2 meters above a spring on the ground below. The apple falls and hits the spring, compressing it 0.1 meter from its rest position. If all of the gravitational potential energy of the apple on the tree is transferred to the spring when it is compressed, what is the spring constant of this spring?

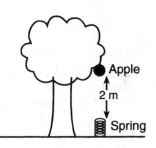

Solution:
Given: 0.1-kilogram (kg) apple, means mass = 0.1 kg. Apple 2 meters above spring on ground means height of apple above spring on ground is 2 m (meters). Apple compresses spring 0.1 m (meters).
Find: Spring constant of the spring.

The question says all the gravitational potential energy is transferred to the spring when it is compressed.

Look for an equation on Reference Table: Mechanics for gravitational potential energy PE. Hint: The equation for gravitational potential energy has g (gravitational field strength or acceleration due to gravity) and also has h (height).

Use the equation
$$\Delta PE = mg\Delta h$$

PE = potential energy
g = gravitational field strength or acceleration due to gravity
h = height
m = mass
Δ = change

Substitute for m 0.1 kg. Substitute for g 9.81 m/s²(given on Reference Table: List of Physical Constants on page reference tables 2-3). Substitute for h 2m.

$\Delta PE = (0.1 \text{ kg})(9.81 \text{ m/s}^2)(2m) = 1.96 \text{ kg} \bullet \text{m}^2/\text{s}^2 = 1.96 \text{ J}.$

$\Delta PE = 1.96 \text{ J}.$

Gravitational potential energy is transferred to the spring (given),therefore **$\Delta PE = PE_s$**. (potential energy stored in a spring) . $\Delta PE = 1.96 \text{ J}$, therefore $PE_s = 1.96 \text{ J}.$

The question is to find spring constant (k). There are only two equations on the reference table for spring constant (k).

Look for an equation on Reference Table: Mechanics that has k (spring constant) and PE_s (potential energy of a spring).

Use the equation

$PE_s = \frac{1}{2} kx^2.$

k = spring constant
x = change in spring length from the equilibrium position

Table: Mechanics

Then substitute 1.96 J for PE_s, *Substitute* 0.1 m for x (change in spring length-spring compressed).

$1.96 \text{ J} = \frac{1}{2} k(0.1 \text{ m})^2$

$k = \dfrac{1.96 \text{ J}}{\frac{1}{2} (0.1 \text{ m})^2}$ or approximately 400 N/ m.

Or, rearrange the equation:

$k = \dfrac{PE_s}{\frac{1}{2} x^2} = \dfrac{1.96 \text{ J}}{\frac{1}{2} (0.1 \text{ m})^2}$

approximately 400 N/m.

Questions 1 & 2: Base your answers to questions 1 and 2 on the information below and on your knowledge of physics. Using a spring toy like the one shown in the diagram, a physics teacher pushes on the toy, compressing the spring, causing the suction cup to stick to the base of the toy. When the teacher removes her hand, the toy pops straight up and just brushes against the ceiling. She does this demonstration five times, always with the same result. When the teacher

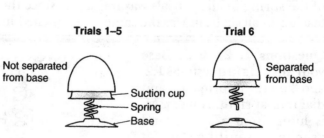

Trials 1–5

Not separated from base

Suction cup
Spring
Base

Trial 6

Separated from base

repeats the demonstration for the sixth time, the toy crashes against the ceiling with considerable force. The students notice that in this trial, the spring and toy separated from the base at the moment the spring released. The teacher puts the toy back together, repeats the demonstration, and the toy once again just brushes against the ceiling.

Question 1: Describe the conversions that take place between pairs of the three forms of mechanical energy, beginning with the work done by the teacher on the toy and ending with the form(s) of energy possessed by the toy as it hits the ceiling. [Neglect friction].

Question 2: Explain, in terms of mass and energy, why the spring toy hits the ceiling in the sixth trial and not in the other trials.

Solution 1: Mechanical energy includes gravitational potential energy, potential energy of a spring (elastic potential energy), and kinetic energy.

1. Work done by the teacher (pushes on toy) becomes potential energy of the compressed spring(PE$_S$).

$$PE_S = \tfrac{1}{2}kx^2$$

Elastic potential energy is the potential energy in a spring (PE$_S$).
Work is changed into (converted to) **elastic potential energy.**

2. Teacher lets go. The toy goes straight up. When the toy goes straight up, the **elastic potential energy** of the spring is changed (is **converted)** into **kinetic energy** of the spring. (The kinetic energy is energy of motion (movement)– example, spring is moving).

3. As the toy goes up, **some kinetic energy** (KE) changes into (is **converted** into) **gravitational potential energy** (PE).

Note: The higher up the toy goes, the more gravitational potential energy it has. Look at the equation $\Delta PE = mg\Delta h$. The higher up the toy goes, h(height) is bigger, therefore PE (potential energy) is bigger.

Solution 2: In the sixth trial, the toy separates from the base and only the toy (not the base) goes up. therefore, the mass is less.

Look at the equation: $KE = \tfrac{1}{2}mv^2$

Since the kinetic energy (KE) in all trials is the same and the mass in the sixth trial is less (no base), therefore the velocity must be more and the toy goes up higher.

Note: The KE in all six trials was the same because the potential energy of the spring in all six trials was the same, since the work done by the teacher in all six trials was the same (as explained in points 1, 2 above.)

Questions 1, 2, & 3: Base your answers to questions 1,2, and 3 on the information and diagram at right. A mass, M, is hung from a spring and reaches equilibrium at position B. The mass is then raised to position A and released. The mass oscillates between positions A and C. [Neglect friction.]

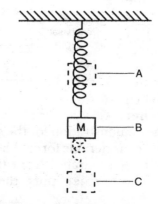

Question 1: At which position, A, B, or C, is mass M located when the kinetic energy of the system is at a maximum? Explain your choice.

Question 2: At which position, A, B, or C, is mass M located when the gravitational potential energy of the system is at a maximum? Explain your choice.

Question 3: At which position, A, B, or C, is mass M located when the elastic potential energy of the system is at a maximum? Explain your choice.

Solution 1: Energy cannot be created or destroyed, only changed from one form to another. Example: potential energy (stored energy) changes to kinetic energy (energy of motion-movement).

Position A has the most gravitational **potential** energy (higher up) and has (spring) elastic **potential** energy.

A **compressed** spring (example: at position A) or an **elongated** spring (example: at position C) has elastic **potential energy.**

When the compressed spring (at A) **moves to B**, some of the potential energy at A changes into kinetic energy (energy of motion - movement). B has more **kinetic energy** than A. Similarly, when the elongated spring (at C) **moves to B**, some of the potential energy at C changes into kinetic energy (energy of motion- movement). B has more kinetic energy than C. **B has the maximum kinetic energy** (most kinetic energy).   *Answer B*

Solution 2: As was explained in solution 1 above, A has the most gravitational potential energy because it is highest (the higher up, the more gravitational potential energy it has).   *Answer A*

Solution 3: The system has the same amount of energy at every point. The spring stops moving for an instant at A and C (kinetic energy is zero); therefore, all the energy at A and C is potential energy, and both A and C have equal potential energy.

A has both gravitational potential energy (high up) and elastic potential energy.

C is lower down and has less gravitational potential energy, therefore, C has the most elastic potential energy (maximum elastic potential energy).   *Answer C*

Note: B has the most kinetic energy (answer to question 1) and therefore the least potential energy.

Question: A 0.10 kilogram ball dropped vertically from a height of 1.00 meter above the floor bounces back to a height of 0.80 meter. The mechanical energy lost by the ball as it bounces is

    (1) 0.080 J   (2) 0.20 J   (3) 0.30 J   (4) 0.78 J

Solution: Mechanical energy equals potential energy and kinetic energy. At the top, when the ball is dropped (free fall), and when the ball bounces back to a height of 0.80 meters (stops before falling down again), in both cases velocity (v) is zero, therefore **kinetic energy** $(KE = \frac{1}{2}mv^2)$ **also equals zero. All** the **mechanical energy is potential energy.**

Step 1: Find potential energy when the ball is dropped:
Given: mass (m) = 0.10 kilogram (kg).
      height (h) = 1.00 meter.
      acceleration of gravity (g) = 9.81 m/s^2, given on Reference Table:
List of Physical Constants on page reference tables 2-3.
Find: potential energy when the ball is dropped vertically from a
height of one meter.
Look for an equation for (gravitational) potential energy (PE) on
Reference Table: Mechanics.
$\Delta PE = mg\Delta h$
Then substitute for m 0.10 kg.
Substitute for g 9.81 m/s^2. *Substitute*
for h 1.00 m (meter).
$\Delta PE = (0.10 \text{ kg})(9.81 \text{ m/s}^2)(1.00 \text{ m})$
$\Delta PE = 0.98 \text{ J}$

0.10 Kg ball
1.00 meter

0.10 Kg ball
0.80 meter

Step 2: Find potential energy when
the ball bounces back to a height of
0.80 meters:
Given: mass (m) = 0.10 kilogram (kg).
      height (h) = 0.80 meter.
      acceleration of gravity (g) = 9.81 m/s^2, given on Reference Table:
List of Physical Constants on page reference tables 2-3.
Find: potential energy when the ball bounces back from the floor to a
height of 0.80 meter.
$\Delta PE = mg\Delta h$
Then substitute for m 0.10 kg. *Substitute for g* 9.81 m/s^2. *Substitute*
for h 0.80 m (meter).
$\Delta PE = (0.10 \text{ kg})(9.81 \text{ m/s}^2)(0.80 \text{ m})$
$\Delta PE = 0.78 \text{ J}$

Step 3: Potential energy (PE), 0.98 J at a height of 1.00 meter (Step 1)
minus potential energy (PE), 0.78 J, when it bounced back to a height
of 0.80 meters (Step 2) equals potential energy lost or **mechanical
energy lost, 0.20 J.**

    0.98 J   –   0.78 J   =   0.20 J

PE at 1.00 m   PE at 0.80 m   mechanical energy lost
                                         Answer 2
Note: Mechanical energy or potential energy lost by the ball was
converted (changed) into internal energy. The total amount of energy
stays the same.

Question: In the diagram below, 400. joules of work is done raising a
72-newton weight a vertical distance of 5.0 meters.

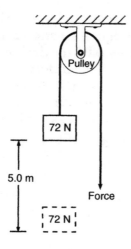

Pulley

72 N

5.0 m

Force

72 N

How much work is done to overcome friction as the weight is raised?
  (1) 40. J   (2) 360 J   (3) 400. J   (4) 760 J

Solution:
Given: Work = 400. J. Weight =72 Newtons. Distance = 5.0 meters.
Find: Work done to overcome friction.

Look for an equation on Reference Table: Mechanics that has work(W),
weight/force due to gravity (F_g), and distance (d).
$W = Fd = \Delta E_T$

Use the equation
        $W = Fd$ (see above)   d = displacement/distance
                                        F = force
                                        W = work
Substitute for d 5.0 m. *Substitute for F* 72 N.
$W = 72$ N $(5.0$ m$) = 360$ N•m $= 360$ J.
360 J (of work) raises a 72-Newton weight (force) 5.0 m (distance).
But, **in this example, 400 J (of work) was needed** to raise the 72-
newton weight the 5.0 m distance. The extra 40 J of work (400 J −360
J) was needed to overcome friction.   Answer *1*

Question: A 1.0 kilogram mass gains kinetic energy as it falls freely
from rest a vertical distance d. How far would a 2.0-kilogram mass have
to fall freely from rest to gain the same kinetic energy?
  (1) d   (2) 2d   (3) d/2   (4) d/4

Solution:
Given : 1kilogram mass and 2 kilogram mass. 1 kilogram mass falls
distance d.
Find: distance 2 kg mass must fall to have same kinetic energy as the 1
kg mass has.

1 kilogram (kg) mass falls a distance d. The question asks how far does
a 2 kg mass have to fall so that the kinetic energy (KE) of the 1 kg mass
and the 2 kg mass will be the same? When the 1 kg mass and the 2 kg

mass fall freely, the gravitational potential energy is changed into kinetic energy. To get **equal kinetic energy** for both masses, the **change in potential energy ΔPE** (or the loss of potential energy) **must be equal** for **both masses.** Therefore, look for a potential energy equation for both masses (1 kg mass and 2 kg mass) and set the potential energies equal to each other.

Look for an equation on Reference Table: Mechanics for a change in gravitational potential energy (ΔPE) (which has g and h in it).

Use the equation

$$\Delta PE = mg\Delta h.$$

PE = potential energy
g = acceleration due to gravity or gravitational field strength
h = height
m = mass
Δ = change

Table: Mechanics

1 kg mass	2 kg mass
ΔPE = mgΔh	ΔPE = mgΔh
Let m (mass) = 1 kg.	Let m (mass) = 2 kg
Let Δh = d	Let Δh = x
ΔPE = 1 kg g d	ΔPE = 2 kg g x

The change in potential energy must be equal, therefore set the two equations equal to one another. Then solve for x (the height of the 2 kg mass, which means the distance the 2 kg mass falls):

$$1 \text{ kg } g \, d = 2 \text{ kg } g \, x$$

$$\frac{1 \text{ kg } g \, d}{2 \text{ kg } g} = x$$

$$\frac{1 \, d}{2} = x \quad \text{ or } \quad \frac{d}{2} = x$$

x (distance the 2 kg mass must fall) = $\frac{d}{2}$.   Answer 3

Now Do Homework Questions #62-74, pages 58-60.

When you answer Regents questions on **ENERGY**, use **Reference Table Mechanics, Reference Table List of Physical Constants,** and **Reference Table Geometry and Trigonometry.**

(Regents and Regents-Type Questions)

1 The work done in moving a block across a rough surface and the heat energy gained by the block can both be measured in
(1) watts   (2) degrees   (3) newtons   (4) joules

2 Which action would require no work to be done on an object?
(1) lifting the object from the floor to the ceiling
(2) pushing the object along a horizontal floor against a frictional force
(3) decreasing the speed of the object until it comes to rest
(4) holding the object stationary above the ground

3 A constant force of 2.0 newtons is used to push a 3.0-kilogram mass 4.0 meters across the floor. How much work is done on the mass?
(1) 6.0 J   (2) 8.0 J   (3) 12 J   (4) 24 J

4 The diagram below shows a worker moving a 50.0 kilogram safe up a ramp by applying a constant force of 300. newtons parallel to the ramp. The data table shows the position of the safe as a function of time.

Time (s)	Distance Moved Up the Ramp (m)
0.0	0.0
1.0	2.2
2.0	4.6
3.0	6.8
4.0	8.6
5.0	11.0

m = 50.0 kg

F = 300. N

Ramp

Horizontal

Calculate the work done by the worker in the first 3.0 seconds [Show all calculations, including the equation and substitution with units.]

5 A 500.-newton girl lifts a 10.-newton box vertically upward a distance of 0.50 meter. The work done on the box is
(1) 5.0 J   (2) 50. J   (3) 250. J   (4) 2500. J

6 Two weightlifters, one 1.5 meters tall and one 2.0 meters tall, raise identical 50.-kilogram masses above their heads. Compared to the work done by the weightlifter who is 1.5 meters tall, the work done by the weightlifter who is 2.0 meters tall is
(1) less   (2) greater   (3) the same
Hint: 50 kg masses are raised from the floor.

7 A student pulls a block 3.0 meters along a horizontal surface at constant velocity. The diagram shows the components of the force exerted on the block by the student.
How much work is done against friction?
(1) 18 J   (2) 24 J
(3) 30. J   (4) 42 J

6.0 kg

String

Block   8.0 kg

Horizontal Surface

3.0 m

Hint: When an object moves at constant velocity, applied force = frictional force.

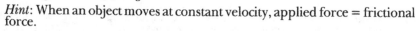

8 A student pulls a box across a horizontal floor at a constant speed of 4.0 meters per second by exerting a constant horizontal force of 45 newtons. Approximately how much work does the student do against friction in moving the box 5.5 meters across the floor?
(1) 45 J   (2) 180 J   (3) 250 J   (4) 740 J

Hint: Speed is extra fact, not needed to solve.
Force of friction (F_f) = Applied force (F_a).

9A A student applies a 20.-newton force to move a crate at a constant speed of 4.0 meters per second across a rough floor. How much work is done by the student on the crate in 6.0 seconds?
(1) 80. J   (2) 120 J   (3) 240 J   (4) 480 J

9B A student does 300. joules of work pushing a cart 3.0 meters due east and then does 400. joules of work pushing the cart 4.0 meters due north. The total amount of work done by the student is
(1) 500. J   (2) 100. J   (3) 2500. J   (4) 700 J

Hint : Add all joules of work and get total number of joules of work.

10 A box is pushed to the right with a varying horizontal force. The graph represents the relationship between the applied force and the distance the box moves. What is the total work done in moving the box 6.0 meters?
(1) 9.0 J   (3) 27 J
(2) 18 J   (4) 36 J
Hint: Similar to pages 1:13-1:15.

Force vs. Distance

11 Which unit is equivalent to a watt, the SI unit of power?
(1) joule/second   (3) joule/ohm
(2) joule/volt   (4) joule/coulomb

12 One watt is equivalent to one
(1) N•m   (2) N/m   (3) J•s   (4) J/s

13 The graph at right represents the relationship between the work done by a student running up a flight of stairs and the time of ascent. What does the slope of this graph represent?
(1) impulse   (3) speed
(2) momentum   (4) power

Work vs. Time

14 A 1.0×10^3-newton crate is to be lifted at constant speed from the ground to a loading dock 1.5 meters high in 5.0 seconds. What power is required to lift the crate?
(1) 1.5×10^3 W   (2) 2.0×10^2 W   (3) 3.0×10^2 W   (4) 7.5×10^3 W

15 A 10.-newton force is required to move a 3.0-kilogram box at constant speed. How much power is required to move the box 8.0 meters in 2.0 seconds?
(1) 40. W   (2) 20. W   (3) 15 W   (4) 12 W

16 A 5.0×10^2-newton girl takes 10. seconds to run up two flights of stairs to a landing, a total of 5.0 meters vertically above her starting point. What power does the girl develop during her run?
(1) 25 W   (2) 50. W   (3) 250 W   (4) 2,500 W

Hint: 5.0×10^2 newton girl means force (force of gravity F_g) = 5.0×10^2 N.

17 A 45-kilogram bicyclist climbs a hill at a constant speed of 2.5 meters per second by applying an average force of 85 newtons. Approximately how much power does the bicyclist develop?
(1) 110W   (2) 210 W   (3) 1100 W   (4) 1400 W

18 In raising an object vertically at a constant speed of 2.0 meters per second, 10. watts of power is developed. The weight of the object is
(1) 5.0 N   (2) 20. N   (3) 40. N   (4) 50. N

19 A 10.-newton force is required to move a 3.0-kilogram box at constant speed. How much power is required to move the box 8.0 meters in 2.0 seconds?
(1) 40. W   (2) 20. W   (3) 15 W   (4) 12 W

20 A 3.0-kilogram block is initially at rest on a frictionless, horizontal surface. The block is moved 8.0 meters in 2.0 seconds by the application of a 12-newton horizontal force, as shown in the diagram below.

What is the average power developed while moving the block?
(1) 24 W   (2) 32 W   (3) 48 W   (4) 96 W

21 What is the maximum height to which a 1200.-watt motor could lift an object weighing 200. newtons in 4.0 seconds?
(1) 0.67 m   (2) 1.5 m   (3) 6.0 m   (4) 24 m

Hint: Watt is a unit of power.

22 A motor used 120. watts of power to raise a 15-newton object in 5.0 seconds. Through what vertical distance was the object raised?
(1) 1.6 m   (2) 8.0 m   (3) 40. m   (4) 360 m

23 A 40.-kilogram student runs up a staircase to a floor that is 5.0 meters higher than her starting point in 7.0 seconds. The student's power output is
(1) 29 W   (2) 280 W   (3) 1.4×10^3 W   (4) 1.4×10^4 W

24 A 45-kilogram bicyclist climbs a hill at a constant speed of 2.5 meters per second by applying an average force of 85 newtons. Approximately how much power does the bicyclist develop?
(1) 110W   (2) 210 W   (3) 1100 W   4) 1400 W

25 A 2000.-watt motor working at full capacity can vertically lift a 400.-newton weight at a constant speed of
(1) 2×10^5 m/s   (2) 50 m/s   (3) 5 m/s   (4) 0.2 m/s

26 Which variable expression is paired with a corresponding unit?

(1) $\dfrac{mass \bullet distance}{time}$ and watt   (3) $\dfrac{mass \bullet distance^2}{time^2}$ and joule

(2) $\dfrac{mass \bullet distance^2}{time}$ and watt   (4) $\dfrac{mass \bullet distance}{time^3}$ and joule

27 Which graph best represents the relationship between gravitational potential energy (PE) and height (h) above the ground for an object near the surface of Earth?

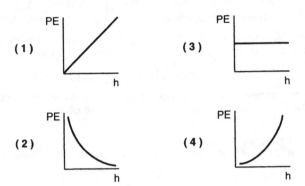

28 Which graph best represents the relationship between the gravitational potential energy of a freely falling object and the object's height above the ground near the surface of Earth?

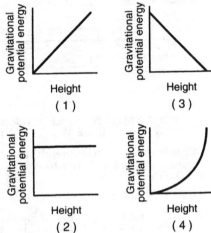

29 A box weighing 1.0×10^2 newtons is dragged to the top of an incline, as shown in the diagram at right. The gravitational potential energy of the box at the top of the incline is approximately
(1) 1.0×10^2 J   (3) 8.0×10^2 J
(2) 6.0×10^2 J   (4) 1.0×10^3 J

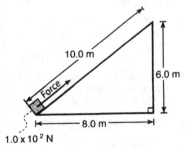

30 The diagram below shows a 1.5-kilogram kitten jumping from the top of a 1.80-meter-high refrigerator to a 0.90-meter-high counter.

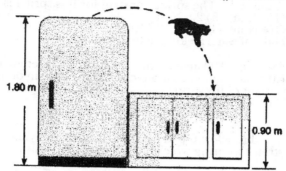

Compared to the kitten's gravitational potential energy on top of the refrigerator, the kitten's gravitational potential energy on top of the counter is
(1) half as great
(2) twice as great
(3) one-fourth as great
(4) four times as great

31 A 650.-kilogram roller coaster car starts from rest at the top of the first hill of its track and glides freely. (Neglect friction.) (The diagram below is drawn to a scale of 1.0 centimeters = 3.0 meters.)

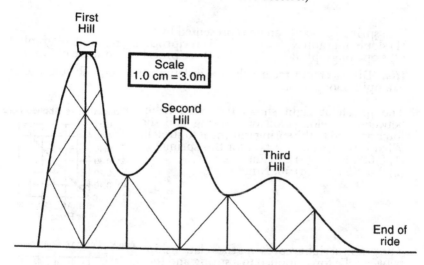

a. Using a metric ruler and a scale of 1.0 cm = 3.0 meters, determine the height of the first hill and the second hill.
b. Determine the gravitational potential energy of the car at the top of the first hill.

32 A spring has a spring constant of 25 newtons per meter. The minimum force required to stretch the spring 0.25 meter from its equilibrium position is approximately
(1) 1.0×10^{-4} N
(2) 0.78 N
(3) 6.3 N
(4) 1.0×10^{2} N

33a The spring in a scale in the produce department of a supermarket stretches 0.025 meter when a watermelon weighing 1.0×10^2 newtons is placed on the scale. The spring constant for this spring is
(1) 3.2×10^5 N/m   (3) 2.5 N/m
(2) 4.0×10^3 N/m   (4) 3.1×10^{-2} N/m
Hint: Weight of watermelon is a force.

33b A vertical spring 0.100 meter long is elongated to a length of 0.119 meter when a 1.00-kilogram mass is attached to the bottom of the spring. The spring constant of his spring is
(1) 9.8 N/m   (3) 82 N/m
(2) 520 N/m   (4) 98 N/m

34 Graphs A and B below represent the results of applying an increasing force to stretch a spring which did not exceed its elastic limit.

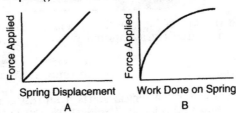

The spring constant can be represented by the
(1) slope of graph A (3) reciprocal of the slope of graph A
(2) slope of graph B (4) reciprocal of the slope of graph B

Hint: Displacement means change in length from equilibrium position, example: Elongation.

35 The graph at right shows the relationship between the elongation of a spring and the force applied to the spring causing it to stretch. What is the spring constant for this spring?
(1) 0.020 N/m   (3) 25 N/m
(2) 2.0 N/m   (4) 50. N/m

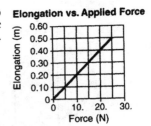

36 The graph at right represents the relationship between the force applied to a spring and the compression (displacement) of the spring. What is the spring constant for this spring?
(1) 1.0 N/m   (3) 0.20 N/m
(2) 2.5 N/m   (4) 0.40 N/m

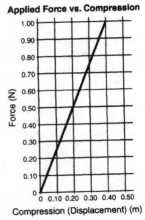

Base your answers to questions 37-40 on the information in the data table at right. The data were obtained by varying the force applied to a spring and measuring the corresponding elongation of the spring. *Directions*: Copy the grid provided onto separate paper. Using the information in the table, construct a graph on the grid following the directions below.

Applied Force (N)	Elongation of Spring (m)
0.0	0.00
4.0	0.16
8.0	0.27
12.0	0.42
16.0	0.54
20.0	0.71

37 Mark an appropriate scale on the axis labeled "Elongation (m)."

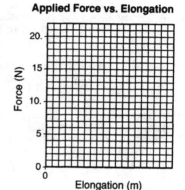

38 Plot the data points for force versus elongation.

39 Draw the best-fit line.

40 *Using the best-fit line*, determine the spring constant of the spring. [Show all calculations, including the equation and substitution with units.]

Base your answers to questions 41-43 on the information and data table below.

In an experiment, a student applied various forces to a spring and measured the spring's corresponding elongation. The table at right shows his data.

Force (newtons)	Elongation (meters)
0	0
1.0	0.30
3.0	0.67
4.0	1.00
5.0	1.30
6.0	1.50

41 Copy the grid onto separate paper. Plot the data points for force versus elongation.

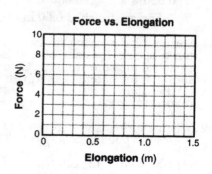

42 Draw the best-fit line.

43 Using your graph, calculate the spring constant of the spring. [Show all work, including the equation and substitution with units.]

44 A force of 0.2 newton is needed to compress a spring a distance of 0.02 meter. The potential energy stored in this compressed spring is
(1) 8×10^{-5} J   (2) 2×10^{-3} J   (3) 2×10^{-5} J   (4) 4×10^{-5} J

45 A 10.-newton force is required to hold a stretched spring 0.20 meter from its rest position. What is the potential energy stored in the stretched spring?
(1) 1.0 J   (2) 2.0 J   (3) 5.0 J   (4) 50. J

46 A 5-newton force causes a spring to stretch 0.2-meter. What is the potential energy stored in the stretched spring?
(1) 1 J   (2) 0.5 J   (3) 0.2 J   (4) 0.1 J

47 A spring has a spring constant of 120 newtons per meter. How much potential energy is stored in the spring as it is stretched 0.20 meter?
(1) 2.4 J   (2) 4.8 J   (3) 12 J   (4) 24 J

48 A spring has a spring constant of 240 newtons per meter. How much potential energy is stored in the spring as it is stretched 0.20 meter?
(1) 4.8 J   (2) 9.6 J   (3) 24 J   (4) 48 J

49 A catapult with a spring constant of 1.0×10^4 newtons per meter is required to launch an airplane from the deck of an aircraft carrier. The plane is released when it has been displaced 0.50 meter from its equilibrium position by the catapult. The energy acquired by the airplane from the catapult during takeoff is approximately
(1) 1.3×10^3 J   (2) 2.0×10^4 J   (3) 2.5×10^3 J   (4) 1.0×10^4 J

50 The unstretched spring in the diagram below has a length of 0.40 meter and spring constant of k. A weight is hung from the spring, causing it to stretch to a length of 0.60 meter.

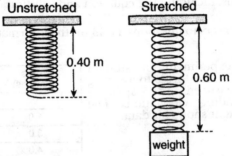

How many joules of elastic potential energy are stored in this stretched spring?
(1) $0.020 \times k$ (2) $0.080 \times k$ (3) $0.18 \times k$ (4) $2.0 \times k$

Hint: Spring stretched 0.60 m − 0.40 m.

51 Spring A has a spring constant of 140 newtons per meter, and spring B has a spring constant of 280 newtons per meter. Both springs are stretched the same distance. Compared to the potential energy stored in spring A, the potential energy stored in spring B is
(1) the same   (3) half as great
(2) twice as great   (4) four times as great

52 When a spring is stretched 0.200 meter from its equilibrium position, it possesses a potential energy of 10.0 joules. What is the spring constant for this spring?
(1) 100. N/m   (2) 125 N/m   (3) 250. N/m   (4) 500. N/m

53 A 60.-kilogram student running at 3.0 meters per second has a kinetic energy of
(1) 180 J   (2) 270 J   (3) 540 J   (4) 8100 J

54 A 1.0×10^3-kilogram car is moving at a constant speed of 4.0 meters per second. What is the kinetic energy of the car?
(1) 1.6×10^3 J   (2) 2.0×10^4 J   (3) 8.0×10^3 J   (4) 4.0×10^3 J

55 A 45.0-kilogram boy is riding a 15.0-kilogram bicycle with a speed of 8.00 meters per second. What is the combined kinetic energy of the boy and the bicycle?
(1) 240. J   (2) 480. J   (3) 1440. J   (4) 1920. J
Hint: Add masses together to get total mass.

56 An electron is accelerated from rest to a speed of 2.0×10^6 meters per second. How much kinetic energy is gained by the electron as it is accelerated to this speed? [Show all calculations, including the equation and substitution with units.]

Hint: Mass of an electron is given on Reference Table: List of Physical Constants on page Reference Tables:2-3.

57 An object with a speed of 20. meters per second has a kinetic energy of 400. joules. The mass of the object is
(1) 1.0 kg   (2) 2.0 kg   (3) 0.50 kg   (4) 40. kg

58 An object moving at a constant speed of 25 meters per second possesses 450 joules of kinetic energy. What is the object's mass?
(1) 0.72 kg   (2) 1.4 kg   (3) 18 kg   (4) 36 kg

59 The diagram below shows block A, having mass $2m$ and speed v, and block B having mass m and speed $2v$.

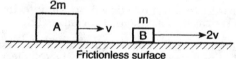

Compared to the kinetic energy of block A, the kinetic energy of block B is
(1) the same   (3) one-half as great
(2) twice as great   (4) four times as great

60 Which graph best represents the relationship between the kinetic energy, KE, and the velocity of an object accelerating in a straight line?

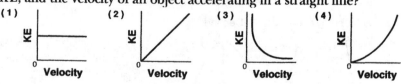

61 Which graph best represents the relationship between the kinetic energy of a moving object and its velocity?

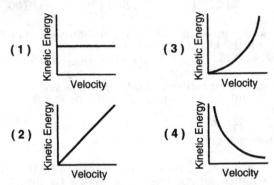

(1)   (3)

(2)   (4)

62 A force is applied to a block, causing it to accelerate along a horizontal, frictionless surface. The energy gained by the block is equal to the
(1) work done on the block   (3) impulse applied to the block
(2) power applied to the block (4) momentum given to the block

63 A constant force is used to keep a block sliding at constant velocity along a rough horizontal track. As the block slides, there could be an increase in its
(1) gravitational potential energy, only
(2) internal energy, only
(3) gravitational potential energy and kinetic energy
(4) internal energy and kinetic energy

Hint: A rough track is like a bumpy track.

Base your answers to questions 64-66 on the information and diagram below, which is drawn to a scale of 1.0 centimeters = 3.0 meters.

A 650.-kilogram roller coaster car starts from rest at the top of the first hill of its track and glides freely. (Neglect friction.)

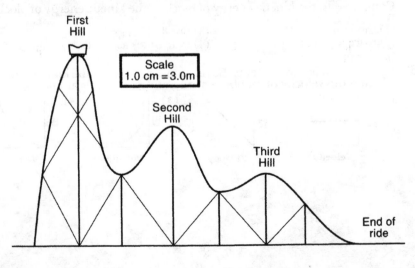

First
Hill

Scale
1.0 cm = 3.0m

Second
Hill

Third
Hill

End of
ride

64 Using a metric ruler and a scale of 1.0 cm = 3.0 meters, determine the height of the first hill.

65 Determine the gravitational potential energy of the car at the top of the first hill. [Show all calculations, including the equation and substitution with units.]

66 Using one or more complete sentences, compare the kinetic energy of the car at the top of the second hill to its kinetic energy at the top of the third hill.

67 A cart of mass M on a frictionless track starts from rest at the top of a hill having height h_1, as shown in the diagram below.

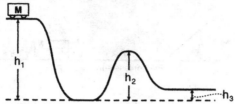

What is the kinetic energy of the cart when it reaches the top of the next hill, having height h_2?
(1) Mgh_1 (2) $Mg(h_1-h_2)$ (3) $Mg(h_2-h_3)$ (4) 0

68 The diagram below shows a moving, 5.00-kilogram cart at the foot of a hill 10.0 meters high.

For the cart to reach the top of the hill, what is the minimum kinetic energy of the cart in the position shown? [Neglect energy loss due to friction.]
(1) 4.91 J   (2) 50.0 J   (3) 250. J   (4) 491 J

69 A 0.50-kilogram ball is thrown vertically upward with an initial kinetic energy of 25 joules. Approximately how high will the ball rise? [Neglect air resistance.]
(1) 2.6 m   (2) 5.1 m   (3) 13 m   (4) 25 m

Hint: 25 joules of kinetic energy was changed into 25 joules of potential energy (PE).

Base your answers to questions 70-71 on the information and diagram below.

A block of mass m starts from rest at height h on a frictionless incline. The block slides down the incline across a frictionless level surface and comes to rest by compressing a spring through distance x, as shown in the diagram below.

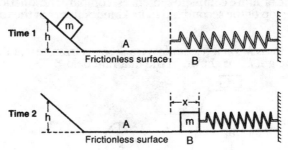

70 Name the forms of mechanical energy possessed by the system when the block is in position A and in position B.

71 Determine the spring constant, k, in terms of g, h, m, and x. [Show all work including formulas and an algebraic solution for k.]

Hint: Gravitational potential energy at the beginning equals energy at the end (at B).

72 As a ball falls freely (without friction) toward the ground, its total mechanical energy
(1) decreases   (2) increases   (3) remains the same

73A In the diagram at right, 400. joules of work is done raising a 72-newton weight a vertical distance of 5.0 meters. How much work is done to overcome friction as the weight is raised?
(1) 40. J   (3) 400. J
(2) 360 J   (4) 760. J

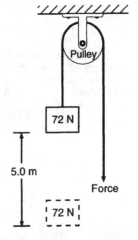

73B A 2.0-kilogram block sliding down a ramp from a height of 3.0 meters above the ground reaches the ground with a kinetic energy of 50. joules. The total work done by friction on the block as it slides down the ramp is approximately
(1) 9 J   (2) 44 J   (3) 6 J   (4) 18 J

74 In the diagram at right, an ideal pendulum released from point A swings freely through point B. Compared to the pendulum's kinetic energy at A, its potential energy at B is
(1) half as great
(2) twice as great
(3) the same
(4) four times as great

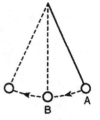

CHAPTER 3: ELECTRICITY

Section *1*:

ELECTROSTATICS

Electrostatics is the study of electric charges at rest (not moving through a wire). It deals with electric fields and potential differences (explained later in the chapter).

THE ATOM

The nucleus is in the center of the atom and has protons and neutrons. The electrons go around the nucleus. Most of the atom is empty space. Since protons, electrons, and neutrons are inside the atom, they are called subatomic particles.

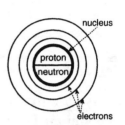

	PROTON	NEUTRON	ELECTRON
CHARGE	positive	none	negative
MASS	1 atomic mass unit	1 atomic mass unit	hardly any: 1/1836 atomic mass unit

An electron has a negative charge and a proton has a positive charge (see table above). In an atom, the number of protons (positive charges) equals the number of electrons (negative charges).

An atom or object that **loses electrons** (negative charges) becomes positive (**positively charged**). An atom or object that **gains electrons** (negative charges) becomes negative (**negatively charged**).

One **coulomb** (C) has **6.25 x 10^18 (elementary) charges**. One elementary charge is the charge of one proton, which is positive, or the charge of one electron, which is negative. Look below or on Reference Table: List of Physical Constants on page Reference Tables 2-3 for 1 coulomb.

1 coulomb (C)		6.25 x 10^18 elementary charges

One **elementary charge** (example charge of one electron or one proton) is **1.60 x 10^{-19} C**. See table on next page or on Reference Table: List of Physical Constants, on page reference tables 2-3. One proton has one positive (+) charge of +1.60 x 10^{-19} C and one electron has one negative (−) charge of −1.60 x 10^{-19} C.

1 elementary charge	e	1.60×10^{-19} C

An object can gain 3 electrons, 3 elementary charges which are negative, and get a charge of 3 times -1.60×10^{-19} C $= -4.8 \times 10^{-19}$C, or it can gain 10 electrons, 10 elementary charges which are negative, and get a charge of 10 times -1.60×10^{-19} C $= -16.0 \times 10^{-19}$C. An object **cannot** gain 1½ or 2½ elementary charges; it must be a **whole number** (example: 1, 2, 3, etc.) of elementary charges. Charge is quantized, which means an object can only gain or lose a whole number of elementary charges. Therefore, a charged object can have a charge of 6.4×10^{-19}C (4 elementary charges) or 8.0×10^{-19}C (5 elementary charges), etc, but **NOT** 2.4×10^{-19}C (1½ elementary charges).

Question: An object possessing an excess of 6.0×10^{6} electrons has a net charge of
(1) 2.7×10^{-26} C (2) 5.5×10^{-24} C (3) 3.8×10^{-13}C (4) 9.6×10^{-13} C
Solution: Look at Reference Table: List of Physical Constants for (elementary) charge (example charge of one electron or charge of one proton).

1 elementary charge	e	1.60×10^{-19} C

1 electron has one (elementary) charge of 1.60×10^{-19} C. Therefore, 6×10^{6} electrons have a charge of $(6 \times 10^{6})(1.60 \times 10^{-19}C) =$
9.6×10^{-13} C.   Answer 4

Question: A metal sphere having an excess of $+5$ elementary charges has a net electric charge of
(1) 1.6×10^{-19} C   (2) 8.0×10^{-19} C
(3) 5.0×10^{0} C   (4) 3.2×10^{19} C

Solution:
Given: Excess of $+5$ elementary charges.
Find: Net electric charge.
Look at Reference Table: List of Physical Constants for elementary charge below or on page Reference Tables 2-3.

1 elementary charge	e	1.60×10^{-19} C

One elementary charge (example charge of one electron or charge of one proton) is **1.60 x 10^{-19} C**. One proton has one positive $(+)$ charge of $+ 1.60 \times 10^{-19}$ C. $+5$ elementary charges (5 elementary charges which are positive) have a charge of $5 \times +1.60 \times 10^{-19}$ C $=$
$+ 8.00 \times 10^{-19}$ C.   Answer 2

Question: An object can *not* have a charge of
(1) 3.2×10^{-19} C (2) 4.5×10^{-19} C (3) 8.0×10^{-19} C (4) 9.6×10^{-19} C
Solution: The charge on an object must be a **whole number** times one elementary charge (e) **1.60 x 10^{-19}C**, given on Reference Table: List of Physical Constants.

1 elementary charge	e	1.60×10^{-19} C

For example: An **object can have a charge** of:

2 elementary charges = $2(1.60 \times 10^{-19}$ C) = **3.20 x 10^{-19} C**

3 elementary charges = $3(1.60 \times 10^{-19}$ C) = **4.80 x 10^{-19} C**, etc.

An object cannot have a charge of 4.5×10^{-19} C because it is about $2\frac{4}{5}$ elementary charges, $2\frac{4}{5}$ times 1.60×10^{-19} C; it is not a whole number times 1.60×10^{-19} C.   Answer 2

CHARGE AND MASS OF PROTON AND ELECTRON

Charge and mass of proton and electron: You learned the **charge** of **one proton** or **charge** of **one electron** (one elementary charge) = **1.60 x 10^{-19} C**, given on Reference Table: List of Physical Constants.

1 elementary charge	e	1.60×10^{-19} C

Mass of an **electron** or **proton** is also given on Reference Table: List of Physical Constants.

Rest mass of the electron	m_e	9.11×10^{-31} kg
Rest mass of the proton	m_p	1.67×10^{-27} kg

1. Find the **charge to mass ratio** (which is $\frac{charge}{mass}$) of an **electron.**

In the ratio $\frac{charge}{mass}$, *substitute* 1.60×10^{-19} C *for charge of an electron* (one elementary charge) and *substitute* 9.11×10^{-31} kg *for mass of an electron*, both given on Reference Table: List of Physical Constants.

$$\frac{charge}{mass} = \frac{1.60 \times 10^{-19}\ C}{9.11 \times 10^{-31}\ kg} = 1.76 \times 10^{11}\ \text{C/kg}.$$

Charge to mass ratio ($\frac{charge}{mass}$) of an electron = 1.76×10^{11} C/kg Answer

2. Find the **charge to mass ratio,** (which is $\frac{charge}{mass}$) of a **proton.**

In the ratio $\frac{charge}{mass}$, *substitute* 1.60×10^{-19} C *for charge of a proton* (one elementary charge) and *substitute* 1.67×10^{-27} kg *for mass of a proton*, both given on Reference Table: List of Physical Constants.

$$\frac{charge}{mass} = \frac{1.60 \times 10^{-19}\ C}{1.67 \times 10^{-27}\ kg} = 9.58 \times 10^{7}\ \text{C/kg}.$$

Charge to mass ratio ($\frac{charge}{mass}$) of a proton = 9.58×10^{7} C/kg Answer

Now Do Homework Questions #1-5, page 127

CHARGES AND CHARGED OBJECTS

Charges: A positive charge (+) attracts a negative charge (−). A negative charge (−) attracts a positive charge (+). Unlike charges attract each other.
A positive charge (+) repels (moves away from) a positive charge (+). A negative charge (−) repels (moves away from) a negative charge (−). Like charges repel each other.

An object loses or gains electrons and becomes a **charged object**. For example, electrons can be removed by friction, heat, or light. **Electrostatic forces** are forces **between charged objects**; these forces cause unlike charges to attract each other and like charges to repel each other.

Question: The diagram below shows the arrangement of three charged hollow metal spheres, A, B, and C. The arrows indicate the direction of the electric (electrostatic) forces acting between the spheres. At least two of the spheres are positively charged.
Which sphere, if any, could be negatively charged?

    (1) sphere A   (2) sphere B
    (3) sphere C   (4) no sphere

Solution:
Given: Two spheres are positively charged.
Find: Sphere that could be negatively charged.
Two spheres (out of three spheres) are positively charged (same charge). Spheres B and C repel each other (arrows go in opposite directions), therefore these two spheres, B and C, must be positively (+) charged. A is attracted to both B and to C

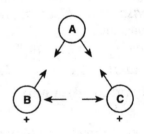

(B and C are positively charged), therefore A must be negatively charged.

                                             Answer 1

ELECTROSTATIC FORCES BETWEEN OBJECTS NEAR EACH OTHER
(attract, do not attract, or repel):

    1. A positively charged object (+) is attracted to a negatively charged object (−) or a negatively charged object (−) is attracted to a positively charged object (+). (**Opposite charges attract** by an electrostatic (electrical) force of attraction.)

2. A positively charged object (+) repels a positively charged object (+) and a negatively charged object (−) repels a negatively charged object(−). (**Like charges repel each other** by an electrostatic force of repulsion.)

3. A **charged object** (example positive rod or negative rod) is **attracted** to a **neutral object** (an object with an equal number of positive and negative charges; its total charge or net charge equals zero).

The electrons (−) in the neutral object are attracted to the positively charged rod (see figure at right) and the electrons move closer to the positively charged rod. The object is attracted to the positive rod.

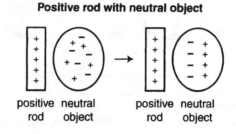

Positive rod with neutral object

positive neutral   positive neutral
rod   object   rod   object

The electrons (−) in the neutral object are repelled by the electrons in the negatively charged rod (see figure at right). Electrons in the object move away from the negative rod, leaving the **positive charges closer to** the (negative) **rod**. The object now is attracted to the negative rod.

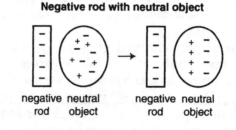

Negative rod with neutral object

negative neutral   negative neutral
rod   object   rod   object

4. A **neutral object** is **not attracted** to a **neutral object**.

Question: The diagram shows three neutral metal spheres, x, y, and z, in contact and on insulating stands.

Which diagram best represents the charge distribution on the spheres when a positively charged rod is brought near sphere x, but does not touch it?

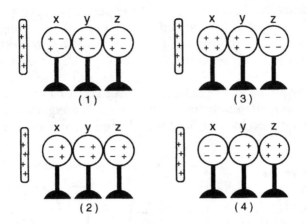

(1) (3) (2) (4)

Solution: The positively charged rod attracts the electrons from spheres *x*, *y*, and *z*, causing the six electrons (two electrons from each sphere) to move closest to the positively charged rod.

Answer *4*

Question: An electroscope is a device with a metal knob, a metal stem, and freely hanging metal leaves used to detect charges. The diagram below shows a positively charged leaf electroscope.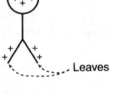

As a positively charged glass rod is brought near the knob of the electroscope, the separation of the electroscope leaves will

(1) decrease   (2) increase   (3) remain the same

Solution: A positively charged glass rod is placed near the knob. Electrons (negatively charged particles) in the leaves are attracted to the positively charged glass rod, causing some electrons (negative) to go away from the leaves to the knob; the leaves become more positive and separate more.

Answer *2*

Now Do Homework Questions #6-12, pages 127-128.

ELECTROSTATIC FORCES BETWEEN OBJECTS IN CONTACT
(touching one another):

Some **neutral objects** in contact with other neutral objects (rubbing) **become charged objects**.

Example 1: When fur is rubbed with a rubber rod, the fur loses electrons and becomes positively (+) charged; the rubber rod gains the electrons and becomes negatively (−) charged.

Example 2: When a glass rod is rubbed with silk, the glass loses electrons and becomes positively charged (+); the silk gains the electrons and becomes negatively charged (−).

Example 3: When a balloon is rubbed on hair, in this case the hair is the one that loses electrons and becomes positively (+) charged. The balloon gains the electrons and becomes negatively (−) charged.

Question: An inflated balloon which has been rubbed against a person's hair is touched to a neutral wall and remains attracted to it. Which diagram best represents the charge distribution on the balloon and wall?

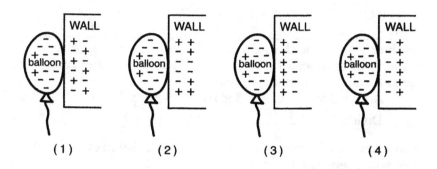

(1)   (2)   (3)   (4)

Solution: Balloon was rubbed against a person's hair. The hair lost (loses) electrons and the balloon gained (gains) electrons and **becomes negative.**

Look at choice 3. The negatively charged balloon repels the electrons in the wall, causing the electrons in the wall to go further away from the balloon. The part of the wall that touches the balloon (next to the balloon) becomes slightly positive. The negative balloon is attracted to the positive part of the wall by electrostatic force between charged objects.   Answer 3

LAW OF CONSERVATION OF CHARGE
Charge cannot be created or destroyed-the total charge in the system remains constant. In the example above, fur loses negative charges and the rubber rod gains the negative charges; therefore the total charge (in the fur and the rubber rod) remains constant.

FINDING CHARGES ON EACH OBJECT WHEN THE OBJECTS ARE IN CONTACT (touching):
When charged objects are put in contact with each other, to find the final charge on each object, **add** up the **total charge** and **divide by** the **number of objects.** The answer you get is the charge on each object; all the objects have the same charge.

Question: The diagram shows two identical metal spheres, A and B, on insulated stands. Each sphere possesses a net charge of -3×10^{-6} coulomb. If the spheres are brought into contact with each other and then separated, the charge on sphere A will be

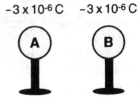

-3×10^{-6} C -3×10^{-6} C

(1) 0 C   (2) $+3 \times 10^{-6}$ C
(3) -3×10^{-6} C   (4) -6×10^{-6} C

Solution: To find the charge on each object (example sphere A) add up the total number of charges and divide it by the number of objects (example 2 metal spheres).

Add: -3×10^{-6} C $+ -3 \times 10^{-6}$ C $= -6 \times 10^{-6}$ C

Divide: $\dfrac{-6 \times 10^{-6} \ C}{2} = -3 \times 10^{-6} \ C$

Metal sphere A and metal sphere B each has a charge of -3×10^{-6} C (even when separated).

Charge on sphere A will be -3×10^{-6} C.   Answer 3

Question: The diagram shows two identical metal spheres, A and B, on insulated stands. One sphere has a net charge of -4×10^{-6} coulomb; the other sphere has a net charge of -6×10^{-6} coulomb.
If the spheres are brought into contact with each other and then separated, the charge on sphere A will be

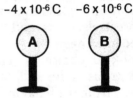

-4×10^{-6} C -6×10^{-6} C

(1) 0 C   (2) $+5 \times 10^{-6}$ C
(3) -5×10^{-6} C   (4) -10×10^{-6} C

Solution: To find the charge on each object (example sphere A) add up the total number of charges and divide it by the number of objects (example 2 metal spheres).

Add: -4×10^{-6} C $+ -6 \times 10^{-6}$ C $= -10 \times 10^{-6}$ C

Divide: $\dfrac{-10 \times 10^{-6} \ C}{2} = -5 \times 10^{-6} \ C$

Metal sphere A and metal sphere B each has a charge of -5×10^{-6} C (even when separated).

Charge on sphere A is -5×10^{-6} C.   Answer 3

Question: The diagram below shows the initial charge and position of three metal spheres, X, Y, and Z, on insulating stands.

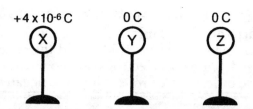

+4 x 10⁻⁶ C   0 C   0 C

Sphere X is brought into contact with sphere Y and then removed. Then sphere Y is brought into contact with sphere Z and removed. What is the charge on sphere Z after this procedure is completed?

(1) $+1 \times 10^{-6}$ C   (2) $+2 \times 10^{-6}$ C

(3) $+3 \times 10^{-6}$ C   (4) $+4 \times 10^{-6}$ C

Solution:

Given: Sphere X is brought into contact with sphere Y and then removed (separated). Sphere Y is brought into contact with sphere Z and then removed (separated).

Find: charge of sphere Z.

Step 1: Sphere X in contact with Sphere Y. To find the charge on each sphere (example sphere X or sphere Y), add up the total number of charges and divide by the number of objects in contact or touching each other (example 2 spheres). Sphere X has $+4 \times 10^{-6}$ C. Sphere Y has 0 C.

Add: $+4 \times 10^{-6}$ C $+ 0$ C $= +4 \times 10^{-6}$ C

Divide: $\dfrac{+4 \times 10^{-6} \ C}{2} = +2 \times 10^{-6} \ C.$

Metal sphere X and metal sphere Y each now has a charge of $+2 \times 10^{-6}$ C (even when removed (separated)).

Step 2: Sphere Y in contact with Sphere Z. Again add up the total number of charges and divide by the number of objects in contact or touching each other (example 2 spheres).

Sphere Y now has $+2 \times 10^{-6}$ C (answer from step 1). Sphere Z has 0 C.

Add: $+ 2 \times 10^{-6}$ C $+ 0$ C $= +2 \times 10^{-6}$ C

Divide: $\dfrac{+2 \times 10^{-6} \ C}{2} = +1 \times 10^{-6} \ C$

Metal sphere Y and metal sphere Z each now has a charge of $+1 \times 10^{-6}$ C (even when removed (separated)).

Metal sphere Z now has a charge of $+1 \times 10^{-6}$ C (the charge on sphere Z is $+1 \times 10^{-6}$ C) after the procedure is completed.

Answer *1*

Question: When a neutral metal sphere is charged by contact with a positively charged glass rod, the sphere

(1) loses electrons   (2) gains electrons

(3) loses protons   (4) gains protons

Solution: When you have a positively charged rod and a neutral sphere in contact, the total charge is positive; the positive charge is divided between the rod and the sphere and the sphere becomes positively charged. Since only electrons can move easily, the sphere becomes positive by losing electrons (which are negative).Answer *1*

Now Do Homework Questions #13-19, pages 128-129.

COULOMB'S LAW

Electrostatic force is the force of attraction between opposite charges (+ and −)(opposite charges move toward each other + →   ← −) and the force of repulsion between like charges (+ and + or − and −) (charges move away from each other ←+ +→ or ← − − −→).Force of attraction and force of repulsion will be explained on the following pages.

Look at the equation below or on Reference Table: Electricity on page reference tables 14-15.

$$F_e = \frac{kq_1q_2}{r^2}$$

$$\text{Electrostatic force} = \frac{\text{electrostatic constant} \times \text{charge of one object} \times \text{charge of other object}}{(\text{distance between the centers})^2}$$

$$F_e = \frac{kq_1q_2}{r^2}$$

F_e = electrostatic force

k = electrostatic constant
q = charge
r = distance between centers

Note: r means distance between the centers of the charged objects.

This equation holds for point charges, which means charged objects that are much smaller than the distance between them.

This equation represents Coulomb's Law.

As you can see from the equation above, F_e (electrostatic force) is directly proportional to the product of the charges (q_1 times q_2) and inversely proportional to the square of the distance between the charges. The charges q_1 and q_2 have equal force on one another.

F_e, electrostatic force, is in newtons
q_1, q_2 charges are in coulombs
r distance between the charged particles is in meters
k, electrostatic constant (given on Reference Table: List of Physical Constants) = 8.99×10^9 N·m²/C²

Question: The diagram below shows two metal spheres suspended by strings and separated by a distance of 3.0 meters. The charge on sphere A is $+5.0 \times 10^{-4}$ coulomb and the charge on sphere B is $+3.0 \times 10^{-5}$ coulomb.

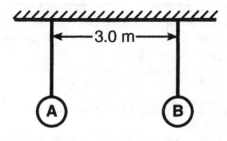

Which statement best describes the electrical (electrostatic) force between the spheres?

       (1) It has a magnitude of 15 N and is repulsive.
       (2) It has a magnitude of 45 N and is repulsive.
       (3) It has a magnitude of 15 N and is attractive.
       (4) It has a magnitude of 45 N and is attractive.

Solution:

Given: Charge on sphere A is $+5.0 \times 10^{-4}$ C. Charge on sphere B is $+3.0 \times 10^{-5}$ C. Distance separated is 3.0 meters.

Find: Electrical force (electrostatic force) F_e .

Look for an equation on Reference Table: Electricity that has electrostatic force (electrical force)(F_e) , charge (q), and distance (r). *Use the equation*

$$F_e = \frac{kq_1q_2}{r^2}$$

    F_e = electrostatic force

    k = electrostatic constant
    q = charge
    r = distance between centers

Look below or on Reference Table: List of Physical Constants on page reference tables 2-3 to find k (electrostatic constant).

Electrostatic constant	k	$8.99 \times 10^9 N \cdot m^2/C^2$

In the equation $F_e = \dfrac{kq_1q_2}{r^2}$, *substitute for k* 8.99×10^9 N•m²/C². *Substitute for q_1* (charge on sphere A) $+5.0 \times 10^{-4}$C. *Substitute for q_2* (charge on sphere B) $+3.0 \times 10^{-5}$ C. *Substitute for r* (distance between centers) 3.0 m.

$$F_e = \frac{kq_1q_2}{r^2}$$

$$F_e = \frac{8.99 \times 10^9 N \cdot m^2/C^2 (+5.0 \times 10^{-4} C)(+3.0 \times 10^{-5} C)}{(3.0 \ m)^2}$$

F_e = 15 N. Sphere A and sphere B are both positive (+); like charges repel each other. The electrostatic force F_e is 15 N and is repulsive (charges repel).   **Answer 1**

Question: What is the approximate electrostatic force between two protons separated by a distance of 1.0×10^{-6} meter?

    (1) 2.3×10^{-16} N and repulsive
    (2) 2.3×10^{-16} N and attractive
    (3) 9.0×10^{21} N and repulsive
    (4) 9.0×10^{21} N and attractive

Solution:

Given: Two protons separated by a distance of 1.0×10^{-6} meter (m).
Find: Electrostatic force (F_e).

Look for an equation on Reference Table: Electricity that has electrostatic force (F_e) and distance (r).

Use the equation

$$F_e = \frac{kq_1q_2}{r^2}$$

F_e = electrostatic force

k = electrostatic constant
q = charge
r = distance between centers

1. Look below or at Reference Table: List of Physical Constants to find k (electrostatic constant).

Electrostatic constant	k	8.99×10^9 N·m²/C²

In the equation above, *then substitute for k:* 8.99×10^9 N·m²/C²

2. q = charge. In this question there are two protons, therefore first find the charge of one proton. **One proton** (or one electron) has **one elementary charge.**
Look below or at Reference Table: List of Physical Constants.

1 elementary charge	e	1.60×10^{-19} C

1 proton or 1 electron has a charge of 1.60×10^{-19} C (one elementary charge).

    Note: 1 proton has a charge of $+ 1.60 \times 10^{-19}$ C.
           1 electron has a charge of $- 1.60 \times 10^{-19}$ C.

Because there are **two protons,** *substitute for q_1* (charge of 1 proton) 1.60×10^{-19} C and *substitute for q_2* (charge of the other proton) 1.60×10^{-19} C in the equation above.

3. In the equation above, substitute for r (distance between charged objects, in this example protons) 1.0×10^{-6} m (given).

$$F_e = \frac{kq_1q_2}{r^2}$$

$$= \frac{8.99 \times 10^9 \ N \cdot m^2/C^2 \ (1.60 \times 10^{-19} \ C)(1.60 \times 10^{-19} \ C)}{1.0 \times 10^{-6} \ m^2}$$

Electrostatic force (F_e) = 2.3×10^{-16} N

Protons are positive and two protons (both have the same, positive charge) repel each other; the electrostatic force is repulsive.
Electrostatic force equals 2.3 x 10^{-16} N, repulsive   Answer 1

Rule: $F_e = \dfrac{kq_1q_2}{r^2}$

If both charges q_1 and q_2 are positive (example: two protons) or both charges q_1 and q_2 are negative (example: two electrons), the two positive charges or two negative charges repel one another (objects and arrows (or you can say arrowheads) go away from each other) (electrostatic force of repulsion).

Note:——►⋯⋯arrowhead

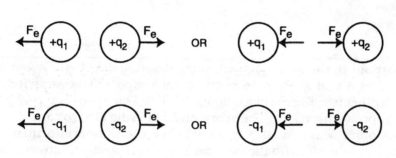

Electrostatic Force of Repulsion

But, if charge q_1 is positive (example: a proton) and charge q_2 is negative (example: an electron), see figure below, they attract one another (objects and arrows (or you can say arrowheads) go toward each other)(electrostatic force of attraction).

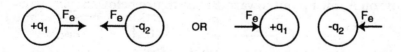

Electrostatic Force of Attraction

Question: In the diagram below, two positively charged spheres, A and B, of masses m_A and m_B, are located a distance d apart.
Which   diagram   best   represents   the

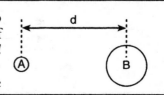

directions of the gravitational force, F_g, and the electrostatic force, F_e, acting on sphere A due to the mass and charge of sphere B? [Vectors are not drawn to scale.]

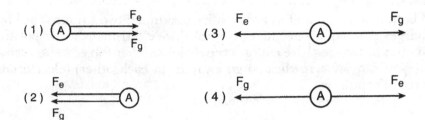

(1) A $\xrightarrow{F_e}$ F_g

(2) $\overset{F_e}{\underset{F_g}{\longleftarrow}}$ A

(3) $\overset{F_e}{\longleftarrow}$ A $\overset{F_g}{\longrightarrow}$

(4) $\overset{F_g}{\longleftarrow}$ A $\overset{F_e}{\longrightarrow}$

Solution: In the question, look at the diagram of spheres A and B. Spheres A and B are **both positive** ;they **repel** (move away from) each other because the electrostatic force (F_e) on A moves away from B (opposite direction). The arrow on A (showing electrostatic force) must point away from B. See figure below. (Additional information: Similarly, the electrostatic force on B, which is positive, moves away from A, which is positive.)

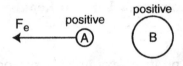

positive

F_e $\quad$ positive

$\longleftarrow$ (A) $\qquad$ (B)

Look again at the diagram in the question. There is a gravitational force of attraction (F_g) between A and B (or any two objects), therefore the gravitational force (F_g) on A moves toward B. The arrow on A must point toward B. See figure below.

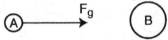

(A) $\xrightarrow{\quad F_g \quad}$ (B)

Now look at the diagrams above and combine the F_e and F_g forces on A.

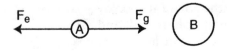

F_e $\qquad$ F_g

$\longleftarrow$ (A) $\longrightarrow$ (B)

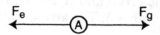

Question: The diagram below shows two identical metal spheres, A and B, separated by distance d. Each sphere has mass m and possesses charge q.

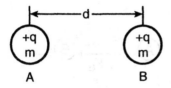

Which diagram best represents the electrostatic force F_e and the gravitational force F_g acting on sphere B due to sphere A?

F_g $\leftarrow$ (B) F_e $\leftarrow$	F_g $\longrightarrow$ (B) F_e $\longrightarrow$	F_g $\longrightarrow$ (B) F_e $\leftarrow$	F_g $\longrightarrow$ (B) F_e $\longrightarrow$
(1)	(2)	(3)	(4)

Solution: In the question, look at the diagram of spheres A and B. Spheres A and B are **both positive**; they **repel** (move away from) each other because the electrostatic force (F_e) on B moves away from A (opposite direction). The **arrow on B** (showing electrostatic force) must **point away from A.** See figure below.

(A) $\xrightarrow{\quad F_e \quad}$ (B)

Note: The arrow showing B moving away from A can also be drawn

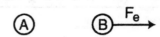

Look again at the diagram in the question. There is a gravitational force of attraction (F_g) between the two objects A and B, therefore the gravitational force (F_g) on B moves towards A. The arrow on B must point toward A. See figure below.

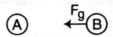

Now look at the diagrams above and combine the F_e and F_g forces on B.

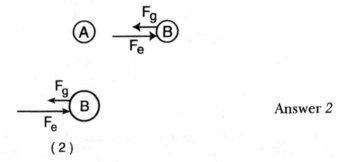

Answer 2

(2)

Question: Two protons are located one meter apart. Compared to the gravitational force of attraction between the two protons, the electrostatic force between the protons is

 (1) stronger and repulsive (2) weaker and repulsive
 (3) stronger and attractive (4) weaker and attractive

Solution: Protons are positive and two protons (both have the same, positive charge) repel each other; the electrostatic force is repulsive. Electrostatic force is much stronger than gravitational force. Electrostatic force is stronger and repulsive. Answer 1

Now Do Homework Questions #20-23, pages 129-130.

Question: If the charge on each of two small charged metal spheres is doubled and the distance between the spheres remains fixed, the magnitude of the electric force between the spheres will be

 (1) the same   (2) two times as great
 (3) one half as great (4) four times as great

Solution:
Given: the charge (q) on each sphere is doubled, new charge on each sphere equals 2q, and the distance is fixed. (See new F_e below.)
Find: Compare the new F_e (electric force, also called electrostatic force) with the old F_e (electric force or electrostatic force).

Look for an equation on Reference Table: Electricity on page reference tables 14-15 that has electric force (electrostatic force) (F_e), charge (q), and distance (r).

Use the equation

$$F_e = \frac{kq_1q_2}{r^2}$$

F_e = electrostatic force

k = electrostatic constant

q = charge

r = distance between centers

Table: Electricity

OLD	**NEW**
	Charge of each sphere is doubled. Look at the equation above. Charges q_1 and q_2 are doubled. New charges are $2q_1$ and $2q_2$.

$$F_e = \frac{kq_1q_2}{r^2}$$

$$F_e = \frac{k(2q_1)(2q_2)}{r^2}$$

$$F_e = \frac{kq_1q_2}{r^2}$$

$$F_e = \frac{k4q_1q_2}{r^2} \text{ or } \frac{4kq_1q_2}{r^2}$$

Old electrostatic force

New electrostatic force

Look at the new F_e and the old F_e. New F_e equals 4 times the old F_e.

Answer *4*

Question: The magnitude of the electrostatic force between two point charges is F. If the distance between the charges is doubled, the electrostatic force between the charges will become

(1) $\dfrac{F}{4}$ (2) 2F   (3) $\dfrac{F}{2}$ (4) 4F

Solution:
Given: Distance (r) between the charges is doubled. New distance equals 2r.
Find: Compare the new F_e (electrostatic force) with the old F_e (electrostatic force).
Look for an equation on Reference Table: Electricity with electrostatic force (F_e), charge (q), and distance (r).

Use the equation

$$F_e = \frac{kq_1q_2}{r^2}$$

F_e = electrostatic force

k = electrostatic constant
q = charge
r = distance between centers

OLD	NEW
	When distance (r) between charges is doubled, new distance is 2r.
$$F_e = \frac{kq_1q_2}{r^2}$$	$$F_e = \frac{(1)kq_1q_2}{(2r)^2}$$
$$F_e = \frac{kq_1q_2}{r^2}$$ Old electrostatic force	$$F_e = \frac{(1)kq_1q_2}{4r^2}$$ New electrostatic force

Look at the new F_e and the old F_e. The new F_e is ¼ the old F_e.

Old force is F (given in the question); new force is $\frac{1}{4}F$ or $\frac{F}{4}$.

Answer *1*

As you saw in the previous example, when r (distance between the charges) was doubled, the new F_e was $\frac{1}{4}$ the old F_e.

If r (distance) is tripled, replace r with 3r in the equation $F_e = \frac{kq_1q_2}{r^2}$

OLD	NEW
	When distance (r) between charges is tripled new distance is 3r.
$$F_e = \frac{kq_1q_2}{r^2}$$	$$F_e = \frac{(1)kq_1q_2}{(3r)^2 \text{ or } 9r^2}$$
$$F_e = \frac{kq_1q_2}{r^2}$$ Old electrostatic force	$$F_e = \frac{(1)kq_1q_2}{9r^2} \text{ or } \frac{1}{9}\frac{kq_1q_2}{r^2}$$ New electrostatic force

Look at the new F_e and the old F_e. The new F_e is 1/9 the old F_e. When r (distance between the charges) is tripled, the new F_e is 1/9 the old F_e.

Question: Which graph best represents the electrostatic force between an alpha particle with a charge of +2 elementary charges and a positively charged nucleus as a function of their distance of separation?

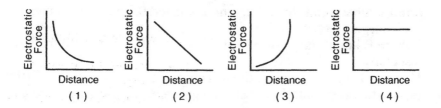

Distance	Distance	Distance	Distance
(1)	(2)	(3)	(4)

Solution: *Look for an equation* on Reference Table: Electricity that has electrostatic force (F_e) and distance between the charges(r).
Use the equation

$$F_e = \frac{kq_1q_2}{r^2}$$

F_e = electrostatic force

k = electrostatic constant
q = charge
r = distance between centers

When r (distance) is bigger, F_e (electrostatic force) is smaller. If the equation above is rearranged, you would get $F_e r^2 = kq_1q_2$ (a constant); this type of equation gives a curved graph that does not touch the axes. **Answer 1**

Wrong choices:
Choice 2: The graph shows as distance gets bigger (increases), electrostatic force gets smaller (decreases). The graph is a straight line that (if continued) will hit the axes; a graph of $F_e r^2 = kq_1q_2$ gives a curve that does not touch the axes (see above).
Choice 3: The graph shows as distance increases, electrostatic force increases.
Choice 4: As distance increases, force is constant (does not change).

Question: In the diagram below, a positive test charge is located between two charged spheres, A and B. Sphere A has a charge of $+2q$ and is located 0.2 meter from the test charge. Sphere B has a charge of $-2q$ and is located 0.1 meter from the test charge.

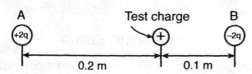

If the magnitude of the force on the test charge due to sphere A is F, what is the magnitude of the force on the test charge due to sphere B?

(1) $\dfrac{F}{4}$ (2) 2F   (3) $\dfrac{F}{2}$ (4) 4F

Solution:
Given: Diagram shows positive test charge is located between two charged spheres, A and B.

Sphere A has a charge of $+2q$ and is located 0.2 meter (m) from the test charge.

Sphere B has a charge of $-2q$ and is located 0.1 meter (m) from the test charge.

Magnitude of the force on the test charge due to sphere A is F (this means the electrostatic force between sphere A and the test charge is F).

Find: What is the magnitude of the force (F_e) on the test charge due to sphere B (this means find the electrostatic force between sphere B and the test charge).

Look for an equation on Reference Table: Electricity that has electrostatic force (F_e), distance between charges (r) and charge (q).

F_e between A and test charge:

$$F_e = \frac{kq_1q_2}{r^2}$$

Substitute for r 0.2 m

$$F_e = \frac{kq_1q_2}{(0.2m)^2}$$

$$F_e = \frac{1kq_1q_2}{0.04m^2}$$

Cross multiply

$0.04m^2F_e = 1kq_1q_2$

$4m^2F_e = 100\ kq_1q_2$

$F_e = 25\ kq_1q_2/m^2$

F_e between the test charge and sphere A = F (given).

$F_e = 25\ kq_1q_2/m^2 = F$

F_e between B and test charge:

$$F_e = \frac{kq_1q_2}{r^2}$$

Substitute for r 0.1 m

$$F_e = \frac{kq_1q_2}{(0.1m)^2}$$

$$F_e = \frac{1kq_1q_2}{0.01m^2}$$

Cross multiply

$0.01m^2F_e = 1kq_1q_2$

$1m^2F_e = 100kq_1q_2$

$F_e = 100kq_1q_2/m^2$

$F_e = 100kq_1q_2/m^2 = 4 \times 25\ kq_1q_2/m^2$
$= 4F$

F_e between B and the test charge = 4F. Answer *4*

Now Do Homework Questions #24-30, pages 130-131, and #148-149, page 145.

Section 2:

ELECTRIC FIELD

You have a charged particle (+ or −). You bring another charged particle (positive + or negative −) near it. Any place where there is an **electrostatic force** (either attractive or repulsive) **between** the two **charged particles**, we say that there **is an electric field** between them.

$$E = \frac{F_e}{q}$$

Electric field strength = $\dfrac{electrostatic\ force}{charge\ (in\ coulombs,\ C)}$

Electric field strength tells how strong an electric field is.

$$E = \frac{F_e}{q}$$

E = electric field strength

F_e = electrostatic force

q = charge

Electrostatic force (F_e) is in newtons, charge (q) is in coulombs, and electric field strength (E) is in newtons/coulomb.

Electric field strength is a vector quantity because it has both magnitude (a number) and direction.

Question: An electrostatic force of 20. newtons is exerted on a charge of 8.0 x 10^{-2} coulomb at point P in an electric field. The magnitude of the electric field intensity at P is
(1) 4.0 x 10^{-3} N/C   (2) 1.6 N/C   (3) 20. N/C   (4) 2.5 x 10^2 N/C

Solution:

Given: electrostatic force = 20. N
charge = 8.0 x 10^{-2} coulomb (C)

Find: E (electric field intensity, also called electric field strength).

Look for an equation on Reference Table: Electricity that has electrostatic force (F_e), charge (q), and electric field intensity (electric field strength) (E).

Use the equation

$$E = \frac{F_e}{q}$$

E = electric field strength

F_e = electrostatic force

q = charge

Then substitute for F_e (electrostatic force) 20. N (newtons).

Substitute for q (charge), 8.0 x 10^{-2} C (coulombs). When you see the number 8.0 x 10^{-2} **coulombs**, you know that number is charge, **q**. Charge (q) is in **coulombs (c)**.

$$E = \frac{F_e}{q} = \frac{20. \text{ N}}{8.0 \ x \ 10^{-2} \ C} = 2.5 \ x \ 10^2 \text{ N/C}$$

Electric field intensity (E) = 2.5 x 10^2 N/C   Answer *4*

As you can see from the equation above, electric field strength (E) is the electrostatic force (F_e) divided by charge (q) in coulombs (coulombs of charge), which gives you force for one coulomb of charge.

Question: At point P in an electric field, the magnitude of the electrostatic force on a proton is 4.0 x 10^{-10} newton. What is the magnitude of the electric field intensity at point P?
(1) 6.4 x 10^{-29} N/C   (2) 1.6 x 10^{-19} N/C
(3) 4.0 x 10^{-10} N/C   (4) 2.5 x 10^9 N/C

Solution:

Given: Electrostatic force = 4.0 x 10^{-10} newton (N).
Electrostatic force is on a proton.

Find: E (electric field intensity, also called electric field strength).
Look for an equation on Reference Table: Electricity that has electrostatic force (F_e) and electric field intensity (electric field strength) (E).

Use the equation

$$E = \frac{F_e}{q}$$

E = electric field strength

F_e = electrostatic force

q = charge

Then substitute for F_e (electrostatic force) 4.0×10^{-10} N (newton).

The question says that there is an electrostatic force on a proton. For q, find the charge of a proton in C (coulombs). Charge of a proton equals one elementary charge.

Look below or at Reference Table: List of Physical Constants page reference tables 2-3, to find one elementary charge.

1 elementary charge	e	1.60×10^{-19} C

In the equation $E = \frac{F_e}{q}$, *substitute for q* (charge), in this example charge of a proton, 1.60×10^{-19} C.

Remember: charge (q) is in coulombs (C).

$$E = \frac{F_e}{q} = \frac{4.0 \times 10^{-10} \ N}{1.60 \times 10^{-19} \ C} = 2.5 \times 10^9 \ N/C \quad \text{Answer 4}$$

Question: What is the magnitude of the electrostatic force experienced by one elementary charge at a point in an electric field where the electric field intensity is 3.0×10^3 newtons per coulomb?

    (1) 1.0×10^3 N   (2) 1.6×10^{-19} N

    (3) 3.0×10^3 N   (4) 4.8×10^{-16} N

Solution:
Given: Electric field intensity (E) = 3.0×10^3 newtons per coulomb.
       One elementary charge (e)
Find: electrostatic force (F_e)
Look for an equation on Reference Table: Electricity that has electric field intensity (electric field strength)(E), electrostatic force (F_e), and charge (q).

Use the equation

$$E = \frac{F_e}{q}$$

E = electric field strength

F_e = electrostatic force

q = charge

Then substitute for E (electric field strength) 3.0×10^3 N/C (newtons per coulomb).

The question says that there is an electrostatic force on one elementary charge.

Look below or at the Reference Table: List of Physical Constants to find one elementary charge.

| 1 elementary charge | e | 1.60×10^{-19} C |

Substitute for q (charge), in this example one elementary charge, 1.60×10^{-19} C (coulombs).

Remember: charge (q) is in coulombs (C).

$$E = \frac{F_e}{q}$$

3.0×10^3 N/C $= \dfrac{F_e}{1.60 \times 10^{-19} \ C}$

Cross multiply

$F_e = (3.0 \times 10^3 \text{ N/C})(1.60 \times 10^{-19} \text{ C})$

$F_e = 4.8 \times 10^{-16}$ N

Or, rearrange the equation:

$F_e = Eq$

$F_e = (3.0 \times 10^3 \text{ N/C})(1.60 \times 10^{-19} \text{ C})$

$F_e = 4.8 \times 10^{-16}$ N

Answer 4

Question: Which graph best represents the relationship between electric field intensity and distance from a point charge?

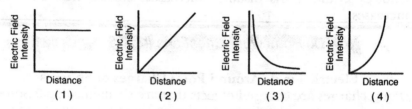

Electric Field Intensity — Distance (1)

Electric Field Intensity — Distance (2)

Electric Field Intensity — Distance (3)

Electric Field Intensity — Distance (4)

Solution:

Given: Four graphs of electric field intensity and distance.

Find: Which graph shows the relationship between electric field intensity and distance.

Look for equations on Reference Table: Electricity that have electric field intensity (electric field strength) and distance.

$$E = \frac{F_e}{q}$$

E = electric field strength

F_e = electrostatic force

q = charge

Since F_e (electrostatic force) is part of the equation above, look for an equation for F_e. (Note: The F_e equation has distance in it).

$$F_e = \frac{kq_1q_2}{r^2}$$

F_e = electrostatic force

k = electrostatic constant

q = charge

r = distance between centers

In the equation $E = \dfrac{F_e}{q}$, *substitute for* F_e $\dfrac{kqq_2}{r^2}$ (which equals $\dfrac{kq_1q_2}{r^2}$).

$$E = \frac{F_e}{q} = \frac{\dfrac{kqq_2}{r^2}}{q} = \left(\frac{kqq_2}{r^2}\right)\left(\frac{1}{q}\right) = \frac{kq_2}{r^2}$$

$E = \dfrac{kq_2}{r^2}$. By looking at the equation, you see E (electric field strength, also called electric field intensity) is inversely proportional to r^2 (distance squared). As distance (r) increases, electric field intensity (E) decreases.

The graph in choice 3 shows as distance increases, electric field intensity decreases. Answer 3

To explain further: In the equation above, E is inversely proportional to r^2 (inverse square relationship); the graph is a curve, which does not touch the axes, as shown in choice 3.

Wrong choices: Choice 1: As distance increases, electric field intensity is constant.

Choices 2 and 4: As distance increases, electric field intensity increases.

Now Do Homework Questions #31-35, pages 131.

Electric Fields Around Point Charges or Spheres
(Point charges are charged objects that are small in comparison to the distance between them.)

Electric field lines (lines of force) show where an electric field is. The closer together the lines are, the stronger is the electric field.

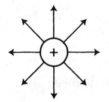   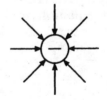

Electric field lines (lines of force) go **away** from a **positive** point **charge** or **positive sphere**. (Electric field lines are perpendicular or at right angles to the sphere.)

Electric field lines (lines of force) go **toward** a **negative** point **charge** or negative **sphere**. (Electric field lines are perpendicular or at right angles to the sphere.)

Electric Fields Around Point Charges or Spheres (continued)

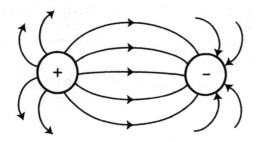

An electric field (electric field lines or lines of force) goes **away** from **positive** and goes **toward** the **negative**. Electric field lines never intersect (never cross) each other. (See figure above.)

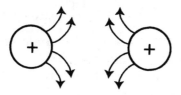 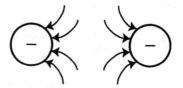

You learned electric field lines (lines of force) go away from a positive charge. Field lines between two **positively** charged **particles** (same charge) **go away** from each other (not toward each other). (See figure above).

You learned electric field lines (lines of force) go toward a negative charge. Field lines between two **negatively** charged **particles** (same charge) **go away** from each other (not toward each other). (See figure above.)

Question: Which diagram best represents the electric field around a negatively charged conducting sphere?

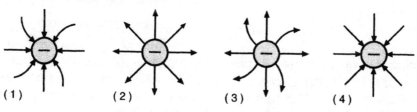

(1)   (2)   (3)   (4)

Solution: The sphere (−) is negatively charged. The electric field goes toward the negative. The line with the **arrow** goes toward the negative and is at right angles to the sphere. _Answer 4_

Note: In choice _4_, all the lines with the arrows are at right angles to the sphere, but in choice _1_, some of the lines with the arrows are not at right angles to the sphere.

Question: A positive test charge is placed between an electron, e, and a proton, p, as shown in the diagram below.

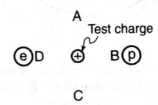

When the test charge is released, it will move toward
     (1) A   (2) B   (3) C   (4) D

Solution: A positive test charge (+) is attracted to the negative (electron) and moves toward the negative (electron). The electron is at D; the test charge moves toward D, where the electron is.
                                                   Answer 4

Question: An object with a net charge of 4.80×10^{-6} coulomb experiences an electrostatic force having a magnitude of 6.00×10^{-2} newton when placed near a negatively charged metal sphere. What is the electric field strength at this location?
     (1) 1.25×10^4 N/C directed away from the sphere
     (2) 1.25×10^4 N/C directed toward the sphere
     (3) 2.88×10^{-8} N/C directed away from the sphere
     (4) 2.88×10^{-8} N/C directed toward the sphere

Solution:
Given: electrostatic force = 6.00×10^{-2} newton (N)
         charge = 4.80×10^{-6} coulomb (C)
Find: E (electric field strength, also called electric field intensity).

Look for an equation on Reference Table: Electricity that has electrostatic force (F_e), charge (q), and electric field strength (E).

Use the equation

$$E = \frac{F_e}{q}$$

                                     E = electric field strength
                                     F_e = electrostatic force
                                     q = charge

Substitute for F_e (electrostatic force) 6.00×10^{-2} N (newtons).
Substitute for q (charge), 4.80×10^{-6} C (coulombs) (given). When you see the number 4.80×10^{-6} **coulombs**, you know that number is charge, **q**. **Charge (q)** is in **coulombs (c).**

$$E = \frac{F_e}{q} = \frac{6.00 \times 10^{-2}\ N}{4.80 \times 10^{-6}\ C} = 1.25 \times 10^4\ N/C$$

Electric field strength (E) = 1.25×10^4 N/C
Electric field (lines of force) go away from the positive and go toward the negative. The sphere is negatively charged; therefore, the electric field goes toward the (negatively charged) sphere.
Electric field strength (E) = 1.25×10^4 N/C toward the sphere.

Answer 2

Now Do Homework Questions 36-41, pages 131-132, and #150-151, page 146.

Electric Field Lines Between Two Parallel Plates

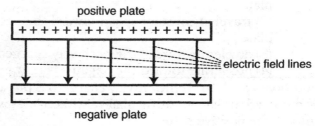

Electric Field Lines Between Two Parallel Plates

Electric field lines go **away from** the **positive** plate and go **toward** the **negative** plate. **Electric field strength** (strength of the electric field) is the **same everywhere between** the **plates**. (See figure above).
A **proton** (positively charged particle) would **accelerate** (speed up) **toward** (near) the **negative plate**, while an **electron** (negatively charged particle) would **accelerate** (speed up) **toward** (near) the **positive plate**.

Question: The diagram below represents a source of potential difference connected to two large, parallel metal plates separated by a distance of 4.0 x 10^{-3} meter. Which statement best describes the electric field strength between the plates?

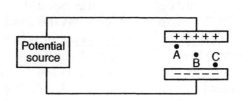

(1) It is zero at point B.
(2) It is a maximum at point B
(3) It is a maximum at point C.
(4) It is the same at points A, B, and C

Solution: Any point between the two plates has the same electric field strength. The electric field strength is the same at points A, B, and C. **Answer 4**

Question: The diagram below shows a point, P, located midway between two oppositely charged parallel plates.

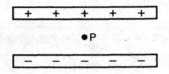

If an electron is introduced at point P, the electron will
    (1) travel at constant speed toward the positively charged plate
    (2) travel at constant speed toward the negatively charged plate
    (3) accelerate toward the positively charged plate
    (4) accelerate toward the negatively charged plate

Solution: An electron (negatively charged) is put at P. An electron is attracted to the positive plate and accelerates (moves faster) toward the positive plate. **Answer 3**

Question: In the diagram below, proton p, neutron n, and electron e are located as shown between two oppositely charged plates. The magnitude of acceleration will be greatest for the

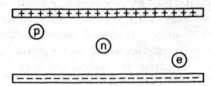

    (1) neutron, because it has the greatest mass.
    (2) neutron, because it is neutral
    (3) electron, because it has the smallest mass
    (4) proton, because it is farthest from the negative plate

Solution: There is an electric field between a positive plate and a negative plate. **Neutrons** have **no charge**, therefore they **cannot be accelerated in** an **electric field** (choices 1 and 2 are wrong).

The electric field strength (E) is the same everywhere between the parallel plates. E is constant. $E = \dfrac{F_e}{q}$. The charge, q, is the same for a proton and an electron (one elementary charge), but the sign is opposite. Look at the equation above. Since E and q are the same, F (force) is the same for protons and electrons.

The question asks about acceleration. Look for an equation on Reference Table: Mechanics that has acceleration (a) and force (F). Look at the equation $a = \dfrac{F}{m}$ or $F = ma$.

Since force (F) is constant, the smaller mass (m) has the bigger acceleration (a). The electron has the smallest mass (m) and therefore has the biggest acceleration (a). (Masses of the electron, proton, and neutron are given in Reference Table: List of Physical Constants on page reference tables 2-3).   **Answer 3**

Question: A moving electron is deflected by two oppositely charged parallel plates, as shown in the diagram below.

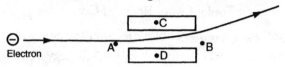

The electric field between the plates is directed from
          (1) A to B   (2) B to A   (3) C to D   (4) D to C

Solution: Electrons have a negative charge; they are attracted to the positive plate and repelled by the negative plate. In the drawing, the electron (which is negative) is attracted to (moves toward) plate C, which must be positive. The electron is repelled by (moves away from) plate D, which must be negative. An electric field is always directed from (goes from) the positive plate (C) to the negative plate (D). Therefore, the field goes from C to D.   **Answer 3**

Now Do Homework Questions #42-45, page 133.

POTENTIAL DIFFERENCES

Opposite charges attract (+ and −). Same charges repel, (+ and + or − and −). As you learned, a **positively** charged particle is **attracted to** a **negative**ly charged particle and a positively charged particle is **repelled by** (goes away from) a **positive**ly charged particle .

Similarly, a **negative**ly charged particle is **attracted to** a **positive**ly charged particle and a negatively charged particle is **repelled by** (goes away from) a **negative**ly charged particle.

Potential difference: The equation for potential difference (potential drop) is

$$V = \frac{W}{q}$$

$$\text{Potential difference} = \frac{work\ (in\ joules)}{charge\ (number\ of\ coulombs)}$$

Potential difference (potential drop) (V) is:
how much **work (W)** or energy (amount of work or energy) is needed to move a **positively** charged particle **(positive** charge +) **toward** a **positively** charged particle **(positive** charge +)

or

how much **work (W)** or energy (amount of work or energy) is needed to move a **negatively** charged particle **(negative** charge −) **toward** a **negatively** charged particle **(negative** charge −)

divided by

charge (q) in coulombs. See equation below.
Note: You learned one coulomb = 6.25 x 10^{18} elementary charges, given on Reference Table: List of Physical Constants.

Look below or at Reference Table: Electricity

$$V = \frac{W}{q}$$

V = potential difference
W = work (electrical energy)
q = charge

$$\text{Potential difference} = \frac{work\ (electrical\ energy)}{charge}$$

Work (or electrical energy) (W) is in joules, charge (q) is in coulombs, and potential difference (V) is in $\dfrac{joules}{coulombs}$ (see equation above).
When 1 joule of work (W) moves one coulomb (q) of charge, there is a **potential difference** of 1 volt (V).

Question: The unit "volts per meter" measures the same quantity as
    (1) joules per volt
    (2) newtons per ampere•meter
    (3) newton•meters^2 per coulomb^2
    (4) newtons per coulomb

Solution: The question is which choice equals $\dfrac{volts}{meter}$.

$$V = \frac{W}{q}$$

$$potential\ difference\ (in\ volts) = \frac{joules\ (of\ work)}{coulombs\ (of\ charge)}$$

The question asks for $\dfrac{volts}{meter}$; **meters** is **distance**.
You learned work = force x distance.
$$W = Fd$$
W (work) in **joules** = F (force) in **newtons** x d (distance) in **meters**.
Therefore you can substitute newton•meters for joules in
$$volt = \frac{joule}{coulomb}.$$

Tbl: List of Phys Cons

Tbl: Electricity

Tbl: Electricity

Table: Mechanics

$$volt = \frac{newton \cdot meter}{coulomb}$$

But, the question asks for $\frac{volts}{meter}$, therefore, divide both sides of the equation ($volt = \frac{newton \cdot meter}{coulomb}$) by 1 meter:

$$\frac{volt}{meter} = \frac{\frac{newton \cdot meter}{coulomb}}{meter} = \frac{newton}{coulomb}$$

Volts per meter   =   newtons per coulomb   Answer *4*

Question: Moving 2.5 x 10^{-6} coulomb of charge from point A to point B in an electric field requires 6.3 x 10^{-4} joules of work. The potential difference between points A and B is approximately
      (1) 1.6 x 10^{-9} volt   (2) 4.0 x 10^{-3} volt
      (3) 2.5 x 10^{2} volt   (4) 1.0 x 10^{14} volt

Solution:
Given: Work = 6.3 x 10^{-4} joule; charge = 2.5 x 10^{-6} coulomb.
Find: Potential difference (V).
Look for an equation on Reference Table: Electricity that has potential difference (V), work (W), and charge (q).
Use the equation:

$$V = \frac{W}{q}$$
                                    V = potential difference

W = work (electrical energy)
                                  q = charge
Then substitute for W (work) 6.3 x 10^{-4} J (joules).
Substitute for q (charge) 2.5 x 10^{-6} C (coulombs).

$$V = \frac{6.3 \ x \ 10^{-4} \ J}{2.5 \ x \ 10^{-6} \ C} = 2.5 \ x \ 10^{2} \ V \ (volts)$$ Answer *3*

In the equation above, when work (W) is in joules, charge (q) must be in coulombs to get V in volts.

Tbl: Electricity

When you use the equation V = W/q, if charge is given in microcoulombs or millicoulombs, etc, change microcoulombs or millicoulombs to coulombs (C):

4 microcoulombs = 4 x 10^{-6} coulomb (C)
7 millicoulombs = 7 x 10^{-3} coulomb (C)

Prefixes for Powers of 10		
Prefix	Symbol	Notation
milli	m	10^{-3}
micro	μ	10^{-6}
nano	n	10^{-9}

Table: Prefixes for Powers of 10

Question: If 4.8 x 10^{-17} joule of work is required to move an electron between two points in an electric field, what is the electric potential difference between these points?
(1) 1.6 x 10^{-19} V (2) 4.8 x 10^{-17} V (3) 3.0 x 10^{2} V (4) 4.8 x 10^{2} V
Solution:
Given: Work = 4.8 x 10^{-17} joules; moving an electron.
Find: electric potential difference (V).

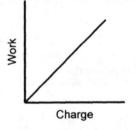

One **electron** has one elementary **charge**.
Look for an equation that has potential difference (V), work (W), and charge (q).
Use the equation

$$V = \frac{W}{q}$$

V = potential difference

W = work (electrical energy)

q = charge

Then substitute for W (work) 4.8×10^{-17} J

Find q (charge, in this example charge of one electron in coulombs). One electron has one elementary charge. Look below or at Reference Table: List of Physical Constants for one elementary charge (in coulombs).

1 elementary charge	e	1.60×10^{-19} C

One elementary charge (means the charge of one electron or one proton) = 1.60×10^{-19} C. *Substitute for q* (**charge**, in this example charge of an **electron**) **1.60 x 10^{-19} C** (coulombs).

$$V = \frac{W}{q} = \frac{4.8 \times 10^{-17} \ J}{1.60 \times 10^{-19} \ C} = 3.0 \times 10^2 \ V \ (volts)$$

Note: $\dfrac{J \ (joules)}{C \ (coulombs)} = V \ (volts)$ 　　　　　Answer 3

Question: The graph shows the relationship between the work done on a charged body in an electric field and the net charge on the body.
What does the slope of this graph represent?
(1) power 　　　(2) potential difference
(3) force 　　　(4) electric field intensity

Solution: *Look for an equation* on Reference Table: Electricity that has work (W) and charge (q). The equation is

$$V = \frac{W}{q}.$$

q = charge

V = potential difference

W = work (electrical energy)

You learned slope $= \dfrac{\Delta y}{\Delta x}$ which means $\dfrac{change \ in \ y}{change \ in \ x}$

On the graph, $slope = \dfrac{\Delta y}{\Delta x} = \dfrac{\Delta \ work \ (\Delta W)}{\Delta \ charge \ (\Delta q)} = potential \ difference \ (V)$

therefore potential difference (V) is the slope. 　　　Answer 2

Question: How much work is required to move a single electron through a potential difference of 100. volts?

(1) 1.6×10^{-21} J   (2) 1.6×10^{-19} J

(3) 1.6×10^{-17} J   (4) 1.0×10^{2} J

Solution:

Given: Potential difference = 100. volts; 1 electron (moving)

Find: Work (W)

One **electron** has one elementary **charge**.

Look for an equation on Reference Table: Electricity that has potential difference (V), work (W), and charge (q).

Use the equation

$$V = \frac{W}{q}$$

V = potential difference

W = work (electrical energy)

q = charge

Then substitute for V (potential difference) 100.V (100. volts)

Find q (charge, in this example charge of one electron in coulombs). One electron has one elementary charge. Look below or at Reference Table: List of Physical Constants on page reference tables 2-3 for one elementary charge (in coulombs).

1 elementary charge	e	1.60×10^{-19} C

One elementary charge (means the charge of one electron or one proton) = 1.60×10^{-19} C. Therefore, *substitute for q* (**charge**, in this example charge of an **electron**) **1.60×10^{-19} C** (coulombs).

$V = \dfrac{W}{q}$

$100.V = \dfrac{W}{1.60 \; x \; 10^{-19} \; C}$

Cross multiply

$W = (100.V)(1.60 \times 10^{-19}$ C)

$W = 1.60 \times 10^{-17}$ J Answer *3*

Or, rearrange the equation

$W = Vq$

$W = (100.V)(1.60 \times 10^{-19}$C)

$W = 1.60 \times 10^{-17}$ J

Answer *3*

Question: The energy required to move one elementary charge through a potential difference of 5.0 volts is

(1) 8.0 J   (2) 5.0 J

(3) 8.0×10^{-19} J   (4) 1.6×10^{-19} J

Solution:

Given: potential difference = 5.0 volts

One elementary charge (moving)

Find: Energy (W) W means work (electrical energy).

Look for an equation on Reference Table: Electricity that has potential difference (V), energy (W), and charge (q).

Use the equation

$$V = \frac{W}{q}$$

V = potential difference

W = work (electrical energy)
q = charge

As you can see from above, W = work (electrical energy).

Then substitute for V (potential difference) 5.0 V (volts).

Find q (charge, in this example one elementary charge in coulombs).

Look below or at **Reference Table: List of Physical Constants** for one elementary charge (in coulombs).

1 elementary charge	e	1.60×10^{-19} C

Substitute for q (charge, in this example, 1 elementary charge) 1.60×10^{-19}C (coulombs).

$V = \dfrac{W}{q}$ $$5.0\ V = \frac{W}{1.60 \ x \ 10^{-19}\ C}$$ Cross multiply $W = (5.0\ V)(1.60 \times 10^{-19}\ C)$ $W = 8.0 \times 10^{-19}$ J Answer 3	Or, rearrange the equation $W = Vq$ $W = (5.0V)(1.60 \times 10^{-19}C)$ $W = 8.0 \times 10^{-19}$ J Answer 3

Question: The energy required to move one elementary charge through a potential difference of 5.0 volts, is
(1) 5×10^{19} eV   (2) 3.1×10^{19} eV   (3) 5 eV   (4) 1 eV

Solution:

Given: potential difference = 5.0 volts (V); 1 elementary charge
Find: energy (W) in electronvolts (eV) (because choices in the question are given in eV). W means work (electrical energy).

Look for an equation on Reference Table: Electricity that has potential difference (V), energy (W), and charge (q).

Use the equation

$$V = \frac{W}{q}$$

V = potential difference

W = work (electrical energy)
q = charge

Rule: Since the question asks for **energy** (W) **in eV (electronvolts)**, q must be **number of elementary charges (e)**, which is the **number of electrons or protons**.

You can understand the rule by looking at the equation: $V = \dfrac{W}{q}$,

cross multiply and you get **Vq = W**. When q = number of elementary charges **(e)** (example, **electrons**) and V is in **volts** (V), work or energy (W) is in **electron volts** (eV).

Then in the equation $V = \dfrac{W}{q}$ *substitute for q* (charge) 1e (one elementary charge). *Substitute for V*(volts) 5.0 V.

$V = \dfrac{W}{q}$	Or, rearrange the equation
$5.0V = \dfrac{W}{1e}$	W = qV
Cross multiply	W =(1e)(5.0 V)
W =(1e)(5.0V)	W = 5eV Answer *3*
W = 5 eV Answer *3*	

RULE: Look at the equation $V = \dfrac{W}{q}$.

When **W** (work or energy) is in **joules**, **q** must be in **coulombs**.
When **W** (work or energy) is in **electronvolts**, **q** is **number** of elementary charges **(e)** (example, number of **electrons**).

Now Do Homework Questions #46-59, pages 133-134

Section *3*:

CONDUCTIVITY

Metals are good conductors of electricity. Wires are made of metals (example: copper) because electrons (negative charges) can easily flow through the metals.
Nonmetals are poor conductors (insulators) because electrons cannot move easily through nonmetals.

ELECTRIC CURRENT

Current-the **number of charges** that reach a point (example: Point P) or go past that point in the wire **in one second**.
Look below or at Reference Table: Electricity on page reference tables 14-15.

$$I = \frac{\Delta q}{t}$$

I = current
q = charge
t = time
Δ = change

$$\text{Current} = \frac{number\ of\ charges\ (that\ reach\ a\ certain\ point)}{time}$$

Current (I) is in **amperes** (A), example: 1 ampere, 2 amperes, etc.

Tbl: Electricity

Charge (q) is in **coulombs;** 1 coulomb is 6.25×10^{18} elementary charges (which is the charge of 6.25×10^{18} electrons), given on Reference Table: List of Physical Constants. **Time (t)** is in **seconds.**

You learned current (I) is in amperes.

$$I = \frac{\Delta q}{t}$$

Current

One ampere means **one coulomb** of charge (6.25×10^{18} charges) passing a point **in one second** (see equation above) or **one coulomb** of charge **per second.** Two amperes means two coulombs of charge ($2 \times 6.25 \times 10^{18}$ charges) passing a point in one second (see equation above).

Question: Two coulombs of charge ($2 \times 6.25 \times 10^{18}$ charges) pass a point in four seconds. How much current (I) flows through the wire?

Solution:
Given: Two coulombs of charge; four seconds.
Find: Current (I).

Look for an equation on Reference Table: Electricity that has current (I), charge (q) and time (t).

Use the equation:

$$I = \frac{\Delta q}{t}$$

I = current
q = charge
t = time
Δ = change

Rule: If a number is in **coulombs (C)**, substitute it for q.
In the examples dealing with current (I), (see equation above) you can substitute the number of coulombs for Δq, because there is a change in charge (charge passing or being transferred).
If a number is in **seconds (s)**, substitute it for **t**.
If a number is in **amperes (A)**, substitute it for **I**.

In the equation $I = \frac{\Delta q}{t}$, *substitute* 2C (coulombs) for Δq and *substitute* 4 s(seconds) for t.

$$I = \frac{2C}{4s} = 0.5 \ A \ (ampere)$$

Current (I) = 0.5 A.

An **ammeter** is an instrument that **measures current**.

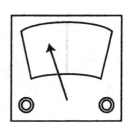

Question: If 10. coulombs of charge are transferred through an electric circuit in 5.0 seconds, then the current in the circuit is
      (1) 0.50 A   (2) 2.0 A   (3) 15A   (4) 50. A

Solution:
Given: Charge transferred = 10. coulombs (C)
Time = 5.0 seconds (s)
Find: Current (I)
Look for an equation on Reference Table: Electricity on page reference tables 14-15 that has current (I), charge (q) and time (t).
Use the equation:

$$I = \frac{\Delta q}{t}$$

    I = current

    q = charge
    t = time
    Δ = change

Then substitute 10. C (coulombs)for Δq. *Substitute 5.0 s* (seconds) for t (time).

$$I = \frac{10.\ C}{5.0\ s} = 2.0\ A\ (amperes)$$

    I (current) = 2.0 A   Answer 2

Question: An operating lamp draws a current of 0.50 ampere. The amount of charge passing through the lamp in 10. seconds is
      (1) 0.050 C   (2) 2.0 C   (3) 5.0 C   (4) 20. C

Solution:
Given: Current = 0.50 ampere; time = 10. seconds
Find: charge passing (Δq)
Look for an equation on Reference Table: Electricity that has current (I), charge (q), and time (t).

Use the equation $I = \dfrac{\Delta q}{t}$

    I = current

    q = charge
    t = time
    Δ = change

Then substitute 0.50 A (amperes) for I (current). *Substitute 10. s* (seconds) for t (time).

Tbl: Electricity

Tbl: Electricity

$$I = \frac{\Delta q}{t}$$

$$0.50 \ A = \frac{\Delta q}{10. \ s}$$

Cross multiply
$(0.50 \text{ A})(10. \text{ s}) = \Delta q$
$5.0 \text{ C} = \Delta q$
Charge passing $(\Delta q) = 5.0$ C

Answer 3

Or, rearrange the equation:
$\Delta q = It$
$\Delta q = (0.50 \text{ A})(10. \text{ s})$
$\Delta q = 5.0$ C
Charge passing $(\Delta q) = 5.0$ C

Answer 3

Question: In a lightning flash, a charge of 10. coulombs was transferred from the base of a cloud to the ground. The current was 1.0×10^4 amperes. Find the amount of time it took for this flash to travel.

(1) 1.0×10^{-5} s (2) 1.0×10^{-3} s (3) 1.0×10^{-1} s (4) 1.0×10^{1} s

Solution:

Given: charge transferred = 10. coulombs; current = 1.0×10^4 amperes.

Find: Time (t) for the lightning flash to travel.

Look for an equation on Reference Table: Electricity that has charge (q), current (I), and time (t).

Use the equation:

$$I = \frac{\Delta q}{t}$$

I = current
q = charge
t = time
Δ = change

Then substitute 1.0×10^4 A (amperes) *for I* (current). *Substitute* 10. C (coulombs) *for* Δq.

$1.0 \times 10^4 \ A = \dfrac{10. \ C \ or \ 1.0 \times 10^1 \ C}{t}$

Cross multiply
$(1.0 \times 10^4 \text{ A})(t) = 1.0 \times 10^1$ C
Note: $1.0 \times 10^0 = 1$,
$1.0 \times 10^1 = 10., 1.0 \times 10^2 = 100$
Divide both sides of the
equation above by 1.0×10^4 A:

$t = \dfrac{1.0 \times 10^1 \ C}{1.0 \times 10^4 \ A}$

$t = 1.0 \times 10^{-3}$ s Answer 2

Or, rearrange the equation:

$$t = \frac{\Delta q}{I}$$

$$t = \frac{10. \ C \ or \ 1.0 \times 10^1 \ C}{1.0 \times 10^4 \ A}$$

$t = 1.0 \times 10^{-3}$ s Answer 2

Question: The current traveling from the cathode to the screen in a television picture tube is 5.0×10^{-5} ampere. How many electrons strike the screen in 5.0 seconds?

Solution:
Given: Current = 5.0×10^{-5} ampere; time = 5.0 seconds
Find: number of electrons that strike screen in 5.0 seconds (s).
An electron is an elementary charge.
Look for an equation on Reference Table: Electricity that has current (I), time (t) and charge (q).
Use the equation

$$I = \frac{\Delta q}{t}$$

I = current

q = charge
t = time
Δ = change

Then, substitute 5.0×10^{-5} A (amperes) *for I* (current). *Substitute* 5.0 s (seconds) *for t* (time).

$5.0 \times 10^{-5} A = \dfrac{\Delta q}{5.0 \ s}$

Cross multiply
$(5.0 \times 10^{-5}$ A)$(5.0$ s$) = \Delta q$
$\Delta q = 25 \times 10^{-5}$ C (coulombs)

Or, rearrange the equation:
$\Delta q = It$
$\Delta q = (5.0 \times 10^{-5}$ A)$(5.0$ s$)$
$\Delta q = 25 \times 10^{-5}$ C (coulombs)

To convert **coulombs** of charge to **number of elementary charges** (in this example electrons), first look below or at **Reference Table: List of Physical Constants** for an equation with coulombs (C) and elementary charge (e).

1 elementary charge	e	1.60×10^{-19} C

(This equation is used to convert coulombs (C) to elementary charges (electrons or protons) or elementary charges to coulombs.)
Next, multiply coulombs (C) of charge

$$25 \times 10^{-5} \ C \ \times \frac{1 \ \textit{elementary charge (in this example 1 electron)}}{1.60 \times 10^{-19} \ C} = 1.6 \times$$

10^{15} electrons.   Answer *3*
Note: Since 25×10^{-5} C is on top, 1.60×10^{-19} C must be on the bottom of the fraction; therefore, coulombs (C) cancel out and you get electrons.

Now Do Homework Questions #60-69, pages 134-135, and questions #152-153, page 146.

POTENTIAL DIFFERENCE

Potential difference pushes the **charges** and **causes them to flow**. A battery (many cells) or 1 cell provides the potential difference, pushing the charges and causing them to flow.
Potential difference (V) is in volts and is measured with a voltmeter.

There are two different ways to describe a current:
Conventional current: Positive charges flow to negative.
Electron flow: Electrons flow from negative to positive.

RESISTANCE

Resistance: it **resists** or **hinders** the **flow** of **charges**, which **means** the **flow of current (I).**
Look at the equation for resistance below or on Reference Table: Electricity:

$$R = \frac{V}{I}$$

I = current
R = resistance
V = potential difference

$$\text{Resistance} = \frac{potential\ difference}{current}$$

V (potential difference) is in volts, I (current) is in amperes, and R (resistance) is in ohms, Ω.
Resistance of 1 ohm, Ω, = 1 volt per ampere (see equation above or below).

$$R = \frac{V}{I}$$ is Ohm's Law.

Resistance (R) (of a wire) is affected by temperature.
The **higher** the temperature, the **more resistance** (R) it has.
The **lower** the temperature, the **less resistance** (R) it has.

Question: In a simple electric circuit, a 110 volt electric heater draws 2.0 amperes of current. The resistance of the heater is
    (1) 0.018 Ω (2) 28 Ω (3) 55 Ω (4) 220 Ω

Solution:
Given: 110 volts (V). Current = 2.0 amperes (A).
Find: Resistance (R).
When you see volts, such as 110 volts (V), you know it is potential difference (*V*). **V** is **potential difference** (potential drop) in **volts.**
Look for an equation on Reference Table: Electricity that has resistance (R), potential difference (V), and current (I).

Use the equation:

$$R = \frac{V}{I}$$

R = resistance
V = potential difference
I = current

Then substitute for V 110V (volts). *Substitute for I* (current) 2.0 A (amperes).

$$R = \frac{110 \ V}{2.0 \ A} = 55 \ \Omega \ \text{(ohms)} \qquad \text{Answer } 3$$

Question: How much current flows through a 12 ohm flashlight bulb operating at 3.0 volts?

    (1) 0.25 A   (2) 0.75 A   (3) 3.0 A   (4) 4.0 A

Solution:

Given: 12 ohms (Ω). 3.0 volts (V).

Find: current (I)

When you see ohms (example 12 Ω) you know it is resistance, (R)
When you see volts, such as 3.0 volts (V), you know it is potential difference (V).

Look for an equation on Reference Table: Electricity that has resistance (R), potential difference (V), and current (I).

Use the equation:

$$R = \frac{V}{I}$$

R = resistance
V = potential difference
I = current

Then substitute for R 12 Ω (ohms). *Substitute for V* 3.0 V (volts).

$12 \ \Omega = \dfrac{3.0 \ V}{I}$ Cross multiply $I(12 \ \Omega) = 3.0 \ V$ Divide by 12 Ω $I = \dfrac{3.0 \ V}{12 \ \Omega} = 0.25 \ \dfrac{V}{\Omega} = 0.25 \ A$ I (current) = 0.25 A (ampere) current = 0.25 A Answer *1*	Or, rearrange the equation $I = \dfrac{V}{R}$ $I = \dfrac{3.0 \ V}{12 \ \Omega} = 0.25 \ \dfrac{V}{\Omega} = 0.25 \ A$ I (current) = 0.25 A (ampere) current = 0.25 A Answer *1*

Question: What is the potential difference across a 2.0-ohm resistor that draws 2.0 coulombs of charge per second?

    (1) 1.0 V   (2) 2.0 V   (3) 3.0 V   (4) 4.0 V

Solution:

Given : 2.0-ohm resistor. Draws (lets go through) 2.0 coulombs of charge per second.

Find: potential difference(V)

When you see **ohms,** you know it is **resistance**. 2.0-ohm resistor has a resistance of 2.0 ohms.

You learned $I = \dfrac{\Delta q}{t}$. You learned **one ampere** means **one coulomb** of charge (6.25×10^{18} elementary charges) passing a point in **1 second**. The question has **two coulombs of charge per second**, which is **two amperes**. When you see coulombs of charge per second, you know it is amperes of current (I). For another way to realize coulombs of charge per second is current, see note at end of problem.

Look for an equation on Reference Table: Electricity that has resistance (R), potential difference (V), and current (I).
Use the equation:

$$R = \frac{V}{I}$$

I = current
R = resistance
V = potential difference

Tbl: Electricity

Then substitute for R 2.0 Ω (ohms). **Substitute for I** 2.0 A (amperes).

$2.0\ \Omega = \dfrac{V}{2.0\ A}$

Cross multiply
(2.0 A)(2.0 Ω) = V
V = 4.0 V (volts)
V (potential difference) = 4.0 V

Answer 4

Or, rearrange the equation:
V = IR
V = (2.0 A)(2.0 Ω)
V = 4.0 V (volts)
V (potential difference) = 4.0 V

Answer 4

Note: Since you are given charge (q) and time (t), you can use the equation $I = \dfrac{\Delta q}{t}$ and find current (I) . Given: Draws (lets go through) 2 coulombs of charge per second. **Substitute** 2C (coulombs) for **Δq.. Substitute** 1s (second) **for t.** I (current) = $\dfrac{2\ C}{1\ s} = 2\ A$ (amperes).

A wire is a conductor that lets charges flow through the wire. As you learned before, resistance (R) of a wire is affected by temperature. The **higher** the **temperature,** the **more resistance** (R) the wire has: the **lower** the **temperature, the less resistance** the wire has.

Look at the equation below. When **V** (potential difference) is **constant,** the **higher** the **temperature** means there is more resistance (R), (**bigger R**), and therefore I (current) is less (**smaller I**). See equation below.

$$bigger\ R = \frac{V\ constant}{I\ smaller}$$

Question: An incandescent light bulb is supplied with a constant potential difference of 120 volts. As the filament of the bulb heats up, its resistance

(1) increases and the current through it decreases
(2) increases and the current through it increases
(3) decreases and the current through it decreases
(4) decreases and the current through it increases

Solution: Current is in all four choices in the question. Look for an equation on Reference Table: Electricity that has potential difference (V), resistance (R), and current (I). $R = \dfrac{V}{I}$. V is constant (120 volts). Bulb heats up, temperature increases. When temperature increases, R(resistance) increases and I (current) decreases (see equation below).

$$increases \ R = \frac{V \ constant}{I \ decreases}$$

R becomes bigger   I becomes smaller

Answer *1*

Table: Electricity

Now Do Homework Questions #69-72, page 135.

Question: A metallic conductor obeys Ohm's Law. Which graph best represents the relationship between the potential difference (V) across the conductor and the resulting current (I) through the conductor?

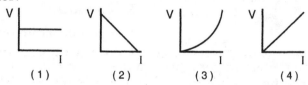

Solution: Look at the equation for Ohm's Law $R = \dfrac{V}{I}$. The resistance (R) of a conductor is constant; when V (potential difference) increases, I (current) increases (directly proportional, which means when V is doubled, I doubles). Since V and I are **directly proportional**, the **line** on the graph **must be a straight line** (a straight line has constant slope).

Look at the graphs:

Choice *4*: When V (potential difference) increases, I (current) increases. The graph is a **straight line** ; with both V and I increasing, it shows that **I is directly proportional to V**.

Wrong choices: Answer *4*

Choice *1*: When V is constant, I increases.

Choice *2*: When V decreases, I increases (inverse relationship).

Choice *3*: When V increases, I increases. The line is curved. In Ohm's Law, V and I are directly proportional, therefore, the line on the graph must be straight, not curved.

Question: The graph below represents the relationship between the potential difference across a metal conductor and the current through the conductor at a constant temperature.

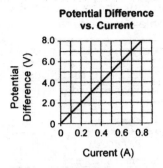

Potential Difference vs. Current

What is the resistance of the conductor?

    (1) 1 Ω   (2) 0.01 Ω   (3) 0.1 Ω   (4) 10 Ω

Solution: *Look for an equation* on Reference Table: Electricity that has potential difference (V), current (I) and resistance (R).
Use the equation

$$R = \frac{V}{I}$$

                            R = resistance

                            V = potential difference

                            I = current

The line on the graph goes through (0,0). Therefore, choose any point on the line drawn on the graph. Substitute values for V (potential difference) and I (current).
For example:

$$R = \frac{V}{I}$$

$$R = \frac{6.0\ V}{0.6\ A}$$

R = 10 Ω   *Answer 4*

Question: The graph below shows the relationship between the potential difference across a metallic conductor and the electric current through the conductor at constant temperature T_1.

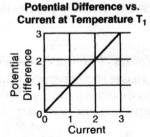

Potential Difference vs. Current at Temperature T_1

Which graph best represents the relationship between potential difference and current for the same conductor maintained at a higher constant temperature, T_2 ?

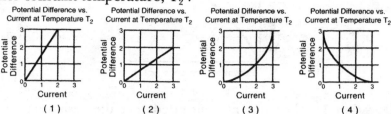

Potential Difference vs. Current at Temperature T_2	Potential Difference vs. Current at Temperature T_2	Potential Difference vs. Current at Temperature T_2	Potential Difference vs. Current at Temperature T_2
(1)	(2)	(3)	(4)

Table: Electricity

Solution: At a higher temperature, the conductor has more resistance (R). *Look for an equation* on Reference Table: Electricity that has resistance (R), potential difference (V), and current (I). *Use the equation* $R = \dfrac{V}{I}$. At constant temperature, R (resistance) is constant, then $\dfrac{V}{I}$ is constant. V (potential difference) and I (current) are directly proportional (I is directly proportional to V). Therefore, the graph must be a straight line. (Only choices 1 and 2 are possible).

When temperature increases, resistance increases and less current flows (see equation above). Look at the graph in the question and the graphs in the choices. Choose a graph where, at the same potential difference as in the question, the current is less.

Choice (1): In the graph in the question, at a potential difference of 3 volts, current is 3 amperes. In the graph for choice 1, at a potential difference of 3 volts, the current is less, 2 amperes.

Also, in the graph in the question, at a potential difference of 2 volts, current is 2 amperes. In choice 1, at 2 volts, the current is less, 1.3 amperes. Choice *1* is correct because the current is less.

Answer *1*

Wrong choices:

Choice 2: in the graph in the question, at a potential difference of 2 volts, current is 2 amperes. In choice 2, at 2 volts, the current is more, 3 amperes. Choice *2* is wrong because the current is more.

Choices 3 and 4 are wrong; at constant temperature, resistance (R) is constant, then $\dfrac{V}{I}$ is constant. V and I are directly proportional, therefore the line of the graph must be straight, not curved.

Questions 1, 2, and 3: A student conducted an experiment to determine the resistance of a lightbulb. As she applied various potential differences to the bulb, she recorded the voltages and corresponding currents and constructed the graph below.

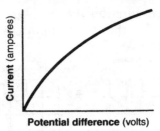

Current vs. Potential Difference

Current (amperes)

Potential difference (volts)

Question 1: The student concluded that the resistance of the lightbulb was not constant. What evidence from the graph supports the student's conclusion?

Question 2: According to the graph, as the potential difference increased, the resistance of the lightbulb

    (1) decreased   (2) increased

    (3) changed, but there is not enough information to know which way

Question 3: While performing the experiment, the student noticed that the lightbulb began to glow and became brighter as she increased the voltage. Of the factors affecting resistance, which factor caused the greatest change in the resistance of the bulb during her experiment?

Solution 1: *Look for an equation* on Reference Table: Electricity that has resistance (R), potential difference (V), and current (I). *Use the equation* $R = \dfrac{V}{I}$. Constant resistance (R) gives a straight line on a graph (dashed line on the graph at right). The line on the graph is curved, therefore the resistance is not constant.

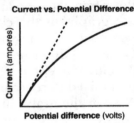

Current vs. Potential Difference

Current (amperes)

Potential difference (volts)

Solution 2: $R = \dfrac{V}{I}$. If R (resistance) was constant, V (potential difference) and I (current) would be directly proportional, and the graph would be a straight line. The graph curves downward (compared to a straight line), which means current (I) does not increase proportionately with potential difference (V) (I is less than predicted by a straight line), therefore $\dfrac{V}{I}$ is bigger (increases), and, since $R = \dfrac{V}{I}$ (Ohm's Law), R increases.   Answer 2

Solution 3: The light bulb glows (gives off light) because it gets hotter. The higher the temperature of the bulb, the more resistance it has.

Do Homework Questions 73-77, page 136, and #154, page 146.

Table: Electricity

Variable resistor: The resistance can be adjusted by using a variable resistor. A resistor ⋀⋀ is an object that has a specific amount of resistance. In a variable resistor ⋀⋀ , as more of the coil of wire is used, there is more resistance.

Symbols for resistor ⋀⋀ , and variable resistor ⋀⋀ , are given on Reference Table: Circuit Symbols.

You learned resistance resists or hinders the flow of charges, which means the flow of current (I). As you know from the equation $R = \dfrac{V}{I}$, when the resistance (R) increases, current (I) decreases.

Resistance-affected by length, area, resistivity and temperature

The resistance (R) of a conductor (example wire) is affected by its length (L), area (A), and resistivity (ρ), as explained below. The **longer** the **wire**, the **more resistance** it has; there is more distance for the electrons (negative charges) to travel. The **shorter** the **wire**, the **less resistance** it has. The larger (bigger) the width (diameter) of the wire, the **larger** the **cross-sectional area**, and the **easier** it is **for charges to flow**; there is **less resistance**.

$$R = \frac{\rho \; x \; L}{A}$$

$$\text{Resistance} = \frac{resistivity \; times \; length}{area}$$

$$R = \frac{\rho L}{A}$$

A = cross-sectional area
L = length of conductor
R = resistance
ρ = resistivity

Resistivity (ρ): The resistivity (ρ) for various materials is given on the next page or on Reference Table: Resistivities on page reference tables 17. The letter ρ (resistivity) is pronounced row (like in row your boat). Resistivity is a characteristic of a material at a specific temperature. Resistivity is in $\Omega \cdot m$(ohm·meter), as shown in the table on the next page.

Resistivities at 20°C	
Material	**Resistivity ($\Omega \cdot$m)**
Aluminum	2.82×10^{-8}
Copper	1.72×10^{-8}
Gold	2.44×10^{-8}
Nichrome	$150. \times 10^{-8}$
Silver	1.59×10^{-8}
Tungsten	5.60×10^{-8}

From the equation $R = \dfrac{\rho L}{A}$ you can see **R**(resistance) is **directly proportional to L**(length). The longer the wire, the more resistance it has; the shorter the wire, the less resistance it has.

From the equation above you can see **R** (resistance) is **inversely proportional to A** (area). The larger the area, the smaller is R (resistance). Area (A) of a circle $= \pi r^2$, given on Reference Table: Geometry and Trigonometry (under the heading Circle) on page reference tables 21. The bigger the area (πr^2) or the bigger the radius (r), the smaller is the resistance. Since two radii equal one diameter (d), you can say the bigger the radius or the bigger the diameter, the smaller is the resistance.

Resistance (R) is also affected by temperature. The higher the temperature of a wire, the more resistance it has; the lower the temperature of a wire, the less resistance it has. Increasing temperature increases the resistance; decreasing temperature decreases the resistance.

Question: A copper wire is connected across a constant voltage source. The current flowing in the wire can be increased by increasing the wire's

(1) cross-sectional area (2) length (3) resistance (4) temperature

Solution: The larger (**bigger**) the **width** (diameter) of the wire, the larger is the radius (r), and the larger is the cross-sectional area (πr^2). The **larger** the **cross-sectional area** (wire has less resistance), the easier it is for charges (example, electrons have a negative charge) to flow, and **more current** (charges) can **flow** through the wire. Current flowing through the wire can be increased by increasing the wire's cross-sectional area.   Answer *1*

Question: The diagram below shows a circuit in which a copper wire connects points A and B.

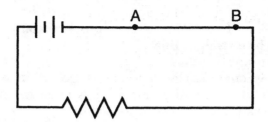

The electrical resistance between points A and B can be decreased by

(1) replacing the wire with a thicker copper wire of the same length

(2) replacing the wire with a longer copper wire of the same thickness

(3) increasing the temperature of the copper wire

(4) increasing the potential difference supplied by the battery

Solution: Look at the equation $R = \dfrac{\rho L}{A}$. A bigger area (A) has a **smaller resistance (R).**
You can decrease the resistance (R), which means make the resistance smaller, by using a thicker (bigger radius or diameter) copper wire, which has a bigger cross-sectional area (A). Area of a circle $= \pi r^2$. By looking at the equation you see a thicker wire, which has a bigger radius (r), has a bigger cross-sectional area.

Answer 1

Question: A copper wire is part of a complete circuit (path) through which current flows. Which graph best represents the relationship between the wire's length and its resistance?

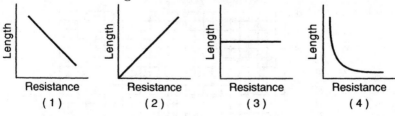

Solution: *Look for an equation* on Reference Table: Electricity that has resistance and length.

Use the equation $R = \dfrac{\rho L}{A}$.

From the equation, you see as L (length) increases, R (resistance) increases (directly proportional, which means when L is doubled, R doubles). Since L and R are **directly proportional**, the **line** on the graph **must be a straight line.**

Look at the graphs:

Choice (2): As length (L) increases, resistance (R) increases. This is the only correct choice. Also, the graph is a straight line with both L and R increasing (directly proportional).   Answer 2

Wrong choices:

(1) The graph shows as length (L) increases, resistance (R) decreases. Length and resistance have an inverse relationship.

(3) The graph shows when length (L) is constant (stays the same), resistance (R) increases.

(4) The graph shows as length (L) increases, resistance (R) decreases (inversely proportional).

Questions 1-4: An experiment was performed using various lengths of a conductor of uniform cross-sectional area. The resistance of each length was measured and the data recorded in the table below.

Length (meters)	Resistance (ohms)
5.1	1.6
11.0	3.8
16.0	4.6
18.0	5.9
23.0	7.5

Copy the grid below onto separate paper. Using the information in the data table, construct a graph on the grid, following the directions below.

Resistance vs. Length

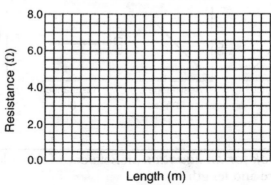

Question 1: Mark an appropriate scale on the axis labeled "Length, (m)".

Question 2: Plot the data points for resistance versus length.

Question 3: Draw the best-fit line.

Question 4: Calculate the slope of the best-fit line. [Show all work, including the equation and substitution with units.]

Solution 1: On the x axis is "Length (m)". The **thing you change** (in this case length) is always put on the **x axis**. What you change is called the independent variable. Space the lines along the axis

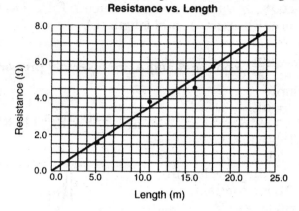

Resistance vs. Length

equally; there must be an equal number of meters between each two lines.

Solution 2: Plot the data points for resistance vs. length on the graph. You can draw a circle around each point.

Solution 3: Connect the points with the best fit line. (A best fit line is a straight line or curve that is closest to all the points.) Do not continue the line past the last point.

Solution 4: The slope of a graph is $\frac{\Delta y \ (change \ in \ y)}{\Delta x \ (change \ in \ x)}$. **Choose** any **two points on** the best-fit **line.** Don't use points (from the table/graph) that are off the line.

Possible points used to find the slope:

1. (0,0) and (14.0, 4.5).

$$Slope = \frac{\Delta y}{\Delta x} = \frac{(4.5 \ \Omega - 0.0 \ \Omega)}{(14.0 \ m - 0.0 \ m)} = \frac{4.5 \ \Omega}{14.0 \ m} = 0.32 \ \frac{\Omega}{m}$$

2. (11.0, 3.6) and (17.0, 5.5)

$$Slope = \frac{\Delta y}{\Delta x} = \frac{(5.5 \ \Omega - 3.6 \ \Omega)}{(17.0 \ m - 11.0 \ m)} = \frac{1.9 \ \Omega}{6.0 \ m} = 0.32 \ \frac{\Omega}{m}$$

Question: Several pieces of copper wire, all having the same length but different diameters, are kept at room temperature. Which graph best represents the resistance, R, of the wires as a function of their cross-sectional areas, A?

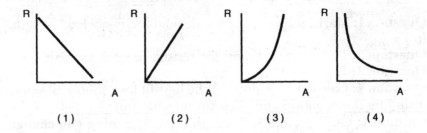

(1)   (2)   (3)   (4)

Solution: *Look for an equation* on Reference Table: Electricity that has resistance (R), area (A), and length (L).
Use the equation

$$R = \frac{\rho L}{A}.$$ You see **R** and **A** are **inversely proportional**.

Cross multiply

$$RA = \rho L$$

ρ (resistivity) for copper is a constant, $1.72 \times 10^{-8}\ \Omega \cdot m$, given on Reference Table: Resistivities; L is a constant, (all the wires in this question have the same length), therefore ρL is a constant.
In the equation $RA = \rho L$, substitute constant for ρL.
RA = constant.

You learned the graph of xy = constant is always a hyperbola. See figure at right.

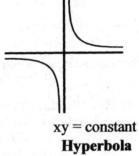

xy = constant
Hyperbola

The **graph of RA** = constant is also a **hyperbola** (see figure at right), but obviously R (resistance) and A (area) must be positive numbers, therefore the second part of the hyperbola, which has negative numbers, cannot happen.
                    Answer *4*

As you can see in the figures, a **hyperbola does not touch the axes.**

RA=constant
Hyperbola
(choice *4*)

Now Do Homework Questions #78-87, pages 137-138.

Question: A 1.00 meter length of nichrome wire with a cross-sectional area of 7.85×10^{-7} meter^2 is connected to a 1.50 volt battery. Calculate the resistance of the wire.

Solution:

Given: nichrome wire; length of wire = 1.00 meter (m)
area (cross-sectional)= 7.85×10^{-7} meter^2 (m^2)
Find: resistance (R)

Look for an equation on Reference Table: Electricity that has resistance (R), length (L), and cross-sectional area (A).

Use the equation:

$$R = \frac{\rho L}{A}$$

A = cross-sectional area
L = length of conductor
R = resistance
ρ = resistivity

In the equation above, you have two unknowns, R (resistance) and ρ (resistivity) therefore, first find ρ (resistivity) for nichrome wire, then substitute ρ, L and A in the equation $R = \frac{\rho L}{A}$ to find R (resistance).

First find ρ (resistivity) for nichrome wire. Look below or on Reference Table: Resistivities on page reference tables 17.

Resistivities at 20°C	
Material	**Resistivity ($\Omega \cdot$m)**
Nichrome	$150. \times 10^{-8}$
Silver	1.59×10^{-8}

Resistivity (ρ) of nichrome wire = $150. \times 10^{-8} \, \Omega\bullet$m .

Next: In the equation $R = \frac{\rho L}{A}$, *substitute* $150. \times 10^{-8} \, \Omega\cdot$m (from first part of the solution) for ρ*(resistivity). Substitute* 1.00 m (meters) given *for L* (length) . *Substitute* 7.85×10^{-7} m^2 (meters^2) given *for A* (area).

$$R = \frac{(150. \times 10^{-8} \, \Omega m)(1.00m)}{7.85 \times 10^{-7} m^2} = 1.91\Omega$$

Resistance = 1.91 Ω

Question: A 10. meter length of wire with a cross-sectional area of 3.0×10^{-6} square meter has a resistance of 9.4×10^{-2} ohm at 20° Celsius. The wire is most likely made of

(1) silver   (2) copper   (3) aluminum   (4) tungsten

Solution:
Given: length = 10. meters (m)

cross-sectional area = 3.0×10^{-6} square meter (m^2)

resistance = 9.4×10^{-2} ohm (Ω)

Find: Which material is the wire most likely made of?

Look for an equation on Reference Table: Electricity that has resistance (R), length (L), and cross-sectional area (A).

Use the equation:

$$R = \frac{\rho L}{A}$$

A = cross-sectional area

L = length of conductor

R = resistance

ρ = resistivity

If you know the resistivity (ρ) of a material, then you can look at Reference Table: Resistivities to tell which material it is.

Therefore, first find ρ (resistivity) by using the equation above.

In the equation $R = \dfrac{\rho L}{A}$ *substitute for R* (resistance) 9.4×10^{-2} Ω (ohm). *Substitute for L* (length) 10. m (meters). *Substitute for A* (cross-sectional area) $3.0 \times 10^{-6} m^2$ (meters^2 or square meters).

$$R = \frac{\rho L}{A}$$

$$9.4 \times 10^{-2}\Omega = \frac{\rho(10.\ m)}{3.0 \times 10^{-6}\ m^2}$$

Cross-multiply:

$(9.4 \times 10^{-2}\Omega)(3.0 \times 10^{-6}m^2) = \rho 10.m$

Divide by 10.m:

$$\frac{(9.4 \times 10^{-2}\ \Omega)(3.0 \times 10^{-6}\ m^2)}{10.\ m} = \rho$$

ρ(resistivity) = 2.82×10^{-8} $\Omega \cdot$m.

Or, rearrange the equation:

$$R = \frac{\rho L}{A}$$

$$\frac{RA}{L} = \rho$$

$$\rho = \frac{RA}{L}$$

$$\rho = \frac{(9.4 \times 10^{-2}\ \Omega)(3.0 \times 10^{-6}\ m^2)}{10.\ m}$$

ρ(resistivity)= $2.82 \times 10^{-8}\Omega \cdot$m

Next, look on the next page or on Reference Table: Resistivities on page reference tables 17 to see which material has a resistivity of 2.82×10^{-8} $\Omega \cdot$m.

Resistivities at 20°C	
Material	**Resistivity($\Omega \cdot$m)**
Aluminum	2.82×10^{-8}
Copper	1.72×10^{-8}

As you can see, aluminum has a resistivity of 2.82×10^{-8} $\Omega \cdot$m.

Answer 3

Question: A 12.0 meter length of copper wire has a resistance of 1.50 ohms. How long must an aluminum wire with the same cross-sectional area be to have the same resistance?

    (1) 7.32 m   (2) 8.00 m   (3) 12.0 m   (4) 19.7 m

Solution:

Given: Length of copper wire = 12.0 meters (m). Copper and aluminum wires have a resistance of 1.50 ohms (Ω). Copper and aluminum wires have the same cross-sectional area.

Find: Length of aluminum wire with the same cross-sectional area to have the same resistance as the copper wire.

Look for an equation on Reference Table: Electricity that has resistance (R), length (L), and cross-sectional area (A).

Use the equation:

$$R = \frac{\rho L}{A}$$

A = cross-sectional area

L = length of conductor
R = resistance
ρ = resistivity

In the equation above, *substitute for R* (resistance) 1.50 Ω (ohms) for both copper and aluminum wires.

For copper wire
$$1.50 \ \Omega = \frac{\rho L}{A}$$

For aluminum wire
$$1.50 \ \Omega = \frac{\rho L}{A}$$

(Both have the same resistance, 1.50 Ω, therefore both are equal to each other.) $\dfrac{\rho L}{A}$ (for copper) $= \dfrac{\rho L}{A}$ (for aluminum)

Since area is the same on both sides of the equation, area can be crossed out. ρ**L** (for copper) $=$ ρ**L** (for aluminum)

Find ρ (resistivity) of copper and aluminum; then put the resistivities into the equation ρL (for copper) = ρL (for aluminum), to find L (length) for the aluminum wire.

Find ρ (resistivity) of copper and aluminum. Look at Reference Table: Resistivities on the next page or on page reference tables 17.

Resistivities at 20°C	
Material	**Resistivity ($\Omega \cdot m$)**
Aluminum	2.82×10^{-8}
Copper	1.72×10^{-8}

In the equation ρL (for copper) = ρL (for aluminum), *then substitute for* ρ (of copper) $1.72 \times 10^{-8} \Omega \cdot m$ and ρ (of aluminum) $2.82 \times 10^{-8} \Omega \cdot m$. Also *substitute for L* (length) of the copper wire, 12.0 m (given).

$$\rho L \text{ (for copper)} = \rho L \text{(for aluminum)}$$
$$(1.72 \times 10^{-8} \Omega \cdot m)(12.0 \text{ m}) = 2.82 \times 10^{-8} \Omega \cdot m \, L$$

Divide both sides of the equation by $2.82 \times 10^{-8} \Omega \cdot m$

$$\frac{(1.72 \times 10^{-8} \Omega \cdot m)(12.0 \text{ m})}{2.82 \times 10^{-8} \Omega \cdot m} = L \text{ (length of aluminum wire)}$$

7.32 m = L   L(length of aluminum wire) = 7.32 m Answer *1*

Question: The table below lists various characteristics of two metallic wires, A and B.

Wire	Material	Temperature (°C)	Length (m)	Cross-Sectional Area (m^2)	Resistance (Ω)
A	silver	20.	0.10	0.010	R
B	silver	20.	0.20	0.020	???

If wire *A* has resistance *R*, then wire *B* has resistance

          (1) R   (2) 2R   (3)R/2   (4) 4R

Solution:
Given: data table for wires A and B
          Wire A has resistance R
Find: resistance of wire B
Look for an equation on Reference Table: Electricity that has length (L), cross-sectional area (A), and resistance (R).
Use the equation

$$R = \frac{\rho L}{A}$$

A = cross-sectional area
L = length of conductor
R = resistance
ρ = resistivity

Wire A and wire B both are silver, therefore they have the same ρ (resistivity) of $1.59 \times 10^{-8} \Omega \cdot m$, given on Reference Table: Resistivities on page reference tables 17.

Wire A	Wire B
$R = \dfrac{\rho L}{A}$	$R = \dfrac{\rho L}{A}$
Look at the data table in the question.	Look at the data table in the question.
Resistance (R) = R	Resistance (R) = ???
Length (L) = 0.10 m (meter)	Length (L) = 0.20 m (meter)
Cross-sectional area = 0.010 m²	Cross-sectional area = 0.020 m²
In the equation above, *substitute* R *for R.*	In the equation above, *substitute* ??? *for R.*
Substitute 0.10 m *for L*	*Substitute* 0.20 m *for L*
Substitute 0.010 m² *for A* (area)	*Substitute* 0.020 m² *for A* (area)
$R = \dfrac{\rho\ 0.10\ m}{0.010\ m^2} = \dfrac{10\ \rho}{m}$	$??? = \dfrac{\rho\ 0.20\ m}{0.020\ m^2} = \dfrac{10\ \rho}{m}$
Resistance of wire A	Resistance of wire B

As you can see, resistance of wire A is the same as the resistance of wire B. Resistance of wire A = R (given), therefore resistance of wire B = R.   Answer 1

Now Do Homework Questions #88-90, page 138, and #155-156, page 146.

Section 4:

CIRCUITS

A circuit is a closed path where current flows (charges flow). A circuit has a **source** of **potential difference** (cell or battery), a **resistance** (example: bulb), and **wires** (see figure A).

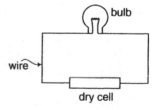

Figure A

To review: Look at figure A. The source of **potential difference** (cell or battery) pushes the charges and causes the charges to move. The wires connect the battery or cell to the resistor (example, bulb) and then back to the cell or battery, so there is a complete path for the charges to travel through. The resistor (examples: bulb, toaster, resistor) hinders the flow of charges.

A switch is added to the circuit (see figure B). If you open the switch,

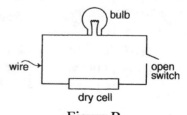

Figure B

---

the circuit is no longer a complete path and no current (no charge) can flow.

Circuit symbols are given below or on Reference Table: Circuit Symbols on page reference tables 16.

Circuit Symbols			
⊥⊤	cell	–(A)–	ammeter
⊥	battery	⋀⋀	resistor
∕	switch	⋀⋀	variable resistor
–(V)–	voltmeter	–(lll)–	lamp

As you can see in Reference Table: Circuit Symbols above, ⋀⋀ = resistor (has resistance).

There are two types of circuits: series and parallel.

SERIES CIRCUITS

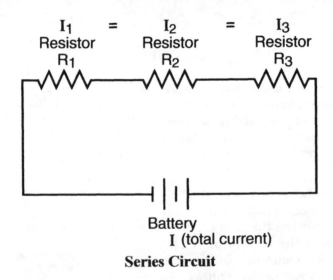

$$I_1 = I_2 = I_3$$

Resistor R_1 Resistor R_2 Resistor R_3

Battery
I (total current)

Series Circuit

A series circuit has **only 1** path for the current (electrons) to flow. You learned, and you can see on Reference Table: Electricity on page reference tables 14-15 what I, R, and V are.

$$R = \frac{V}{I}$$

I = current
R = resistance
V = potential difference

Look at the diagram of the series circuit on the previous page. The current flows from the battery to R_1 (example: bulb) to R_2 (example: resistor or toaster) to R_3 (example: bell) and then back to the battery.

Look below or at Reference Table: Electricity Series Circuits on page reference tables 14-15.

Series Circuits

$I = I_1 = I_2 = I_3 = ...$
$V = V_1 + V_2 + V_3 + ...$
$R = R_1 + R_2 + R_3 + ...$

In a **series circuit**, the **current** (I) is the same in all parts of the circuit (see diagram of series circuit on the previous page).
I_1, (which means the current at R_1) = I_2, (current at R_2) = I_3, (current at R_3). Current at any point in the circuit is the same as the current (I) coming out of the battery.

$$I \qquad = \quad I_1 \; = \; I_2 \; = \; I_3$$

current from battery or
   cell or power source

In a series circuit (see diagram below),

V	=	V_1	+	V_2	+	V_3
Potential difference from power source or cell or battery		Potential difference across R_1		Potential difference across R_2		Potential difference across R_3

Potential difference, V, is given in volts.

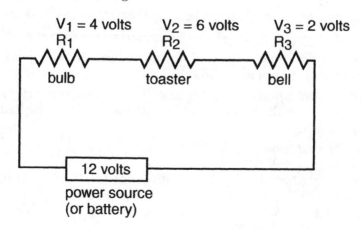

$V_1 = 4$ volts $V_2 = 6$ volts $V_3 = 2$ volts
R_1 (bulb) R_2 (toaster) R_3 (bell)

12 volts
power source
(or battery)

Look at the diagram on the previous page:

| V | = | V₁ | + | V₂ | + | V₃ |

$$V = V_1 + V_2 + V_3$$

12 volts from the power = 4 volts + 6 volts + 2 volts
source or battery   across R_1 across R_2 across R_3

The total number of volts from the power source (battery or cell) (example: 12 volts)= sum of the voltages (sum of all the volts) across all the resistances (example: 4 volts + 6 volts + 2 volts).

A voltmeter is an instrument that measures potential difference (volts).

Question: The diagram below shows three resistors, R_1, R_2, and R_3, connected to a 12-volt battery.

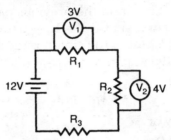

If voltmeter V_1 reads 3 volts and voltmeter V_2 reads 4 volts, what is the potential drop (potential difference) across resistor R_3?

    (1) 12 V   (2) 5 V   (3) 0 V   (4) 4 V

Solution:

Given: V_1 is 3 V (volts), V_2 is 4 V (volts), battery is 12 V (volts).
Find: Potential drop across resistor R_3, which means find V_3.
Look at the figure in the question. You know it is a **series circuit** because there is only **one path** for the current (charges) to flow.

On Reference Table: Circuit Symbols, ─(v)─ = voltmeter, given on

page reference tables 16. In the figure in the question, a voltmeter ─(v)─

and another voltmeter ─(v)─ are added to the circuit to measure potential difference (volts). The voltmeters are added on to the circuit; they do not affect whether the circuit is series or parallel.

Look for an equation on Reference Table: Electricity series circuits having to do with V_1, V_2, V_3 and total volts (V) from the battery or power source.

Use the equation
$V = V_1 + V_2 + V_3 + ...$
Then substitute for V_1 3 V. *Substitute for V_2* 4 V. *Substitute for V* (which is total volts from the battery) 12 V.

    $12\ V = 3\ V + 4\ V + V_3$
    $12\ V - 7\ V = V_3$

$V_3 = 5$ V

Potential drop (potential difference) across resistor R_3 is 5 V.

Answer 2

Similarly, in a series circuit,

R_{eq}	=	R_1	+	R_2	+	R_3
Equivalent resistance (total resistance)		Resistance of R_1		Resistance of R_2		Resistance of R_3

R_{eq} = equivalent resistance, given on Reference Table: Electricity.
In the equation above, R means resistance (examples: resistance of bulb, toaster, resistor $\mathcal{W}$, bell, etc). Resistance hinders (slows down) the flow of current (charge).

Question: R_1 (bulb) = 100 Ω; R_2 (toaster) = 12 Ω; and R_3 (bell) = 4 Ω in the series circuit diagram on page 3:59. Find the total (equivalent) resistance.

Solution:
Given: Series circuit; $R_1 = 100$ Ω; $R_2 = 12$ Ω; $R_3 = 4$ Ω.
Find: R_{eq} Equivalent resistance (total resistance).
Look for an equation on Reference Table: Electricity series circuits for equivalent resistance (R_{eq}).

Use the equation

R_{eq}	=	R_1	+	R_2	+	R_3
Equivalent resistance (total resistance)		Resistance of R_1		Resistance of R_2		Resistance of R_3

In the equation above, *substitute for R_1 100 Ω. Substitute for R_2 12 Ω. Substitute for R_3 4 Ω.*
$R_{eq} = R_1 + R_2 + R_3$
$\mathbf{R_{eq}} = 100$ $\Omega + 12$ $\Omega + 4$ $\Omega = \mathbf{116}$ $\mathbf{\Omega}$.
Equivalent
resistance
(total
resistance)

Total resistance (equivalent resistance R_{eq}) = 116 Ω
In a series circuit, total resistance (equivalent resistance, R_{eq}) = sum of all the resistances.

As you can see from Reference Table: Electricity series circuits

Series Circuits
$I = I_1 = I_2 = I_3...$
$V = V_1 + V_2 + V_3 +...$
$R_{eq} = R_1 + R_2 + R_3 +...$

Series Circuits: The current (I) is the same in all parts of the circuit. The total volts (from the power source, cell, or battery) = the sum of all the voltages (volts)in the circuit. The total resistance (R_{eq}) equals the sum of all the resistances in the circuit.

An ammeter -Ⓐ- is an instrument that measures current. A voltmeter -Ⓥ- is an instrument that measures voltage(volts) (potential difference). Symbols for ammeter -Ⓐ-, voltmeter -Ⓥ-, cell ⊣⊢, and battery ⊣⊢ are given on **Reference Table: Circuit Symbols** on page reference tables 16.

Now Do Homework Questions #91-94, pages 138-139.

Question: The diagram shows a circuit with two resistors.
What is the reading on ammeter A?
(1) 1.3 A   (2) 1.5 A
(3) 3.0 A   (4) 0.75 A

8.0 Ω   8.0 Ω

12-volt source   Ⓐ

Solution:
Given: ⋀⋀ = 8.0 Ω, ⋀⋀ = 8.0 Ω.
    Diagram has 12 volt source (total volts = 12 volts).
Find: reading on ammeter A. An ammeter measures current; therefore, find I (current).

⋀⋀ = resistor (has resistance), given on **Reference Table: Circuit Symbols**.
Look at the diagram below.

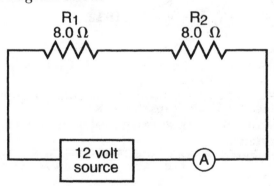

R_1 R_2
8.0 Ω   8.0 Ω

12 volt source   Ⓐ

Label one resistor R_1; R_1 = 8.0 Ω. Label the other resistor R_2; R_2 = 8.0 Ω.
Look for an equation on Reference Table: Electricity that has

resistance (R), volts (potential difference V, which is in volts V), and current (I).

Use the equation:

$$R = \frac{V}{I}.$$

I = current
R = resistance
V = potential difference

In the equation above, you have two unknowns, I (current) and R_{eq} (total resistance); therefore, first find the total resistance (R_{eq}) and then substitute R_{eq} and V in the equation $R = \frac{V}{I}$ to find current (I).

First find the total resistance R_{eq}. By looking at the figure in the question, you know that it is a series circuit, because there is only one path for the current to flow. Look for an equation on Reference Table: Electricity Series Circuits that has total resistance R_{eq}, R_1 and R_2. Use the equation:

$R_{eq} = R_1 + R_2 + R_3...$
Substitute for R_1 8.0 Ω. Substitute for R_2 8.0 Ω.
$R_{eq} = 8.0\,Ω + 8.0\,Ω = 16\,Ω$
R_{eq} (total resistance) = 16 Ω

Then, in the equation $R = \frac{V}{I}$, *substitute for R* (total resistance) 16 Ω. *Substitute for V* (potential difference, which equals total number of volts) 12 V (volts).

$R = \frac{V}{I}$

$16\,Ω = \frac{12\ V}{I}$

Cross multiply
I(16 Ω) = 12V

$I = \frac{12\ V}{16\ Ω} = 0.75\ A$ Answer 4

Or rearrange the equation

$I = \frac{V}{R}$

$I = \frac{12\ V}{16\ Ω} = 0.75A$ Answer 4

Note: In a series circuit, the current (I) is the same in all parts of the circuit and is equal to the total current (from battery or power source). $I = I_1 = I_2 = I_3 = ...$

Question: A 30. ohm resistor and a 60. ohm resistor are connected in an electric circuit as shown at right.

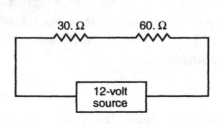

Compared to the electric current through the 30. ohm resistor, the current through the 60. ohm resistor is
      (1) smaller   (2) larger   (3) the same

Solution: By looking at the figure in the question, you know it is a series circuit, because there is only one path for the current to flow. In a series circuit, the current is the same in all parts of the circuit. $I = I_1 = I_2 = I_3 = ...$, given on Reference Table: Electricity Series Circuits.
Therefore, I (current) through the 30. Ω resistor equals I (current) through the 60. Ω resistor.   **Answer 3**

Question: A 5.0-ohm resistor, a 15.0-ohm resistor, and an unknown resistor R are connected as shown with a 15-volt source. The ammeter reads a current of 0.50 ampere.

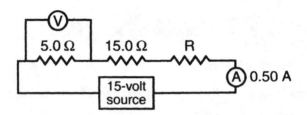

Determine the reading of the voltmeter connected across the 5.0-ohm resistor. [Show all calculations, including the equation and substitution with units.]

Solution:
Given: 5.0-ohm (5.0 Ω) resistor
      15.0-ohm (15.0 Ω) resistor
      Unknown resistor R
      15-volt (V) source (total volts = 15 volts)
      Ammeter reads current of 0.50 amperes (A)
Find: Reading of voltmeter across the 5.0-ohm resistor.

ᴠᴠᴠ = resistor (has resistance), given on Reference Table: Circuit Symbols.

Look for an equation on Reference Table: Electricity that has resistance (R), volts (potential difference) (V), and current (I).

Use the equation

$$R = \frac{V}{I}.$$

Look at the figure above. It is a series circuit because there is only one path for the current to flow.

The **question** is to **find** the **reading** of the **voltmeter (V) across** the **5.0-Ω resistor.** **Look** at the **part** of the **circuit with** the **5.0-Ω resistor,** and use the values of R and I across the 5.0 Ω resistor to find V across the 5.0 Ω resistor, in the equation $R = \dfrac{V}{I}$.

In the equation $R = \dfrac{V}{I}$, *then substitute for R* 5.0 Ω. *Substitute for I* (current) 0.50 A. In a series circuit, current (I) is the same in all parts of the circuit and equals the total current coming from the power source or battery.

Table: Electricity

$R = \dfrac{V}{I}$

$5.0 \ \Omega = \dfrac{V}{0.50 \ A}$

Cross multiply
$(0.50 \ A)(5.0 \ \Omega) = V$
$V = 2.5 \ A\,\Omega = 2.5 \ V$ (volts)

Or, rearrange the equation
$V = IR$
$V = (0.50 \ A)(5.0 \ \Omega)$
$V = 2.5 \ A\,\Omega = 2.5 \ V$ (volts)

Note: $R = \dfrac{V}{I}$

$ohms \ (\Omega) = \dfrac{volts \ (V)}{amperes \ (A)}$

Cross multiply: Amperes (A) x ohms(Ω) = volts (V) or A Ω= V.

Question: The diagram below represents an electric circuit consisting of a 12-volt battery, a 3.0-ohm resistor, R_1, and a variable resistor, R_2.

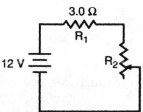

At what value must the variable resistor be set to produce a current of 1.0 ampere through R_1?

    (1) 6.0 Ω   (2) 9.0 Ω   (3) 3.0 Ω   (4) 12 Ω

Solution:
Given: 12-volt (V) battery (total volts = 12 volts)
         3.0 ohm (Ω) resistor (R_1)
         variable resistor (R_2)
Find: variable resistor (R_2) when current = 1.0 ampere (1.0 A) through R_1.

‑W̸ = resistor (has resistance), given on Reference Table: Circuit Symbols.

You know this is a series circuit because there is only one path for the current (charges) to flow.

Look at Reference Table: Electricity Series Circuits.

$$R_{eq} = R_1 + R_2 + R_3 + ...$$

total resistance = sum of the resistances.

Since in this question there is **no R_3** (only R_1 and R_2), cross off R_3 from the equation above and **you have $R_{eq} = R_1 + R_2$.**

You know R_1 but you have two unknowns R_{eq} and R_2, therefore first find R_{eq} (by using the equation $R = \dfrac{V}{I}$); then substitute R_{eq} in the equation $R_{eq} = R_1 + R_2$ to find R_2.

First find R_{eq}. The question deals with resistance (R), volts (potential difference) (V), and current (I).

Use the equation

$$R = \frac{V}{I}, \text{ given on Reference Table: Electricity.}$$

Since you need to find R_{eq} (total resistance), look at total volts (V) and total current (I). Total volts (V) = 12 V. Total current (I) = 1.0 A (ampere) because in a series circuit the total current equals the current in any part of the circuit and the current through R_1 in this circuit equals 1.0 A.

Substitute for V 12 V and substitute for I 1.0 A in the equation

$$R = \frac{V}{I}.$$

$$R_{eq} = \frac{12 \; V}{1.0 \; A} = 12 \; \Omega.$$

Next: *Use the equation*

$R_{eq} = R_1 + R_2 + R_3$, given on Reference Table: Electricity Series Circuits.

Since in the question there is no R_3 (only R_1 and R_2) cross off R_3 from the equation and you have $R_{eq} = R_1 + R_2$.

Substitute for R_{eq} 12 Ω. Substitute for R_1 3.0 Ω.

$R_{eq} = R_1 + R_2$	Or, rearrange the equation
$12 \, \Omega = 3.0 \, \Omega + R_2$	$R_2 = R_{eq} - R_1$
$9.0 \, \Omega = R_2$	$R_2 = 12 \, \Omega - 3.0 \, \Omega$
$R_2 = 9.0 \, \Omega$	$R_2 = 9.0 \, \Omega$

Resistance across the variable resistor (R_2) = 9.0 Ω   Answer 2

Question: In the circuit shown on the next page, voltmeter V_2 reads 80. volts.

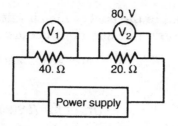

What is the reading of voltmeter V_1?

    (1) 160 V   (2) 80. V   (3) 40. V   (4) 20. V

Solution: There are two methods to solve this question. Choose whichever method is easier.

Method 1:

Given: V_2 = 80. V across 20. Ω $\wedge\!\!\wedge\!\!\wedge$, given in diagram above.

   V_1 is across 40. Ω $\wedge\!\!\wedge\!\!\wedge$, given in diagram above.

Find: reading of V_1 (voltmeter 1).

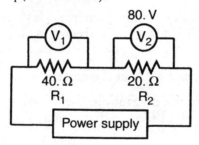

By looking at the figure in the question, you know it is a series circuit because there is only one path for the current to flow through the resistors (example R_1 and R_2).

In the circuit diagram above, $\wedge\!\!\wedge\!\!\wedge$ = resistor (has resistance R).

Look for an equation on Reference Table: Electricity that has resistance (R) and volts (or potential difference) (V).

Use the equation

$$R = \frac{V}{I}.$$

   I = current

   R = resistance
   V = potential difference

You need to find V_1. You know R_1 (given) but you have two unknowns, V_1 and I_1 (current at R_1).

Therefore, **first find I** (in a series circuit, I is the same in all parts of the circuit: $I = I_1 = I_2 = I_3 = ...$, given on Reference Table: Electricity

Series Circuits) and then substitute I in the equation $R = \frac{V}{I}$ to

find V_1.

First find I (current) in the **part** of the **circuit** with V_2 (**80. V**) and R_2 (**20. Ω**) (see diagram in question) because, when you use the equation $R = \dfrac{V}{I}$, R and V are given and there is only one unknown, I (current).

In the equation $R = \dfrac{V}{I}$, *substitute for R* 20. Ω. *Substitute for V* 80. V.

$R = \dfrac{V}{I}$	Or, rearrange the equation
$20. \ \Omega = \dfrac{80. \ V}{I}$	$I = \dfrac{V}{R}$
Cross multiply	$I = \dfrac{80. \ V}{20. \ \Omega} = 4.0 \ A$
$I(20. \ \Omega) = 80. \ V$	
$I = \dfrac{80. \ V}{20. \ \Omega} = 4.0 \ A$ (amperes)	

You learned in a series circuit, I (current) is the same in all parts of the circuit, therefore **4.0 A** is **I (current)** in **all parts** of the **circuit.**

Then substitute for I 4.0 A in the equation $R = \dfrac{V}{I}$ to find V_1.
Look at the part of the diagram in the question at V_1.
Substitute for R 40. Ω(see the diagram at V_1).

$R = \dfrac{V}{I}$	Or, rearrange the equation
$40. \ \Omega = \dfrac{V}{4.0 \ A}$	$V = IR$
Cross multiply	$V = (4.0 \ A)(40. \ \Omega) = 160 \ A\Omega$
$V = (4.0 \ A)(40. \ \Omega) = 160A \ \Omega$	$= 160 \ V$
$= 160 \ V$	Answer *1*
Answer *1*	

Note: $R = \dfrac{V}{I}$

$$ohms \ (\Omega) = \dfrac{volts \ (V)}{amperes \ (A)}$$

Cross multiply: Amperes (A) x ohms(Ω) = volts (V) or A Ω= V.

Method 2:
Given: $V_2 = 80. \ V$ across 20. Ω ⋀⋀⋁, see diagram on next page.

V_1 is across 40. Ω ⋀⋀⋁, see diagram on next page.
Find: reading of V_1.

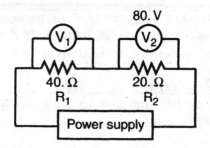

By looking at the figure in the question, you know it is a series circuit because there is only one path for the current to flow through the resistors (example R_1 and R_2).

Look for an equation on Reference Table: Electricity that has resistance (R) and volts (potential difference) (V).

Use the equation

$$R = \frac{V}{I}.$$

I = current
R = resistance
V = potential difference

Current (I) is the same in all parts of a series circuit.

$$I = I_1 = I_2 = I_3$$

Rearrange the equation $R = \frac{V}{I}$ and you get:

$$I = \frac{V}{R}$$

Current I_1 is the current at V_1, where resistance (R_1) = 40 Ω.

$$I_1 = \frac{V_1}{R_1}$$

Current I_2 is the current at V_2 (80 V), where resistance (R_2) = 20 Ω.

$$I_2 = \frac{V_2}{R_?}$$

Current at all parts of a series circuit is equal. Therefore, set both equations equal to each other:

$$\frac{V_1}{R_1} = \frac{V_2}{R_?}$$

Find V_1:
Cross multiply

$$V_1 R_2 = V_2 R_1$$

$$V_1 = \frac{V_2 R_1}{R_2}$$

Substitute for V_2 80. V. **Substitute for R_1** 40. Ω. **Substitute for R_2** 20. Ω.

$$V_1 = \frac{(80. \ V)(40. \ \Omega)}{20. \ \Omega} = 160 \text{ V}$$

Question: A 100.-ohm resistor and an unknown resistor are connected in series to a 10.0-volt battery. If the potential drop across the 100.-ohm resistor is 4.00 volts, the resistance of the unknown resistor is

(1) 50.0 Ω   (2) 100. Ω   (3) 150. Ω   (4) 200. Ω

Solution: There are two methods to solve this question. Choose whichever method is easier.

Method 1:

Given: 100.-ohm resistor and unknown resistor in series.

      10.0-volt battery (total volts = 10.0 volts).

      potential drop (potential difference) across 100.-ohm resistor is 4.00 volts.

Find: resistance (R) of unknown resistor.

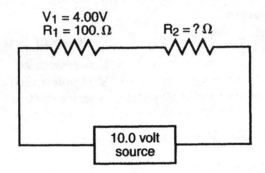

$V_1 = 4.00V$
$R_1 = 100. Ω$ $R_2 = ? Ω$

10.0 volt source

Look for an equation on Reference Table: Electricity that has resistance (R) and volts (potential difference) (V).

Use the equation

$$R = \frac{V}{I}$$

Let R_1 = 100. Ω (ohm) resistor

Let R_2 = unknown resistor

Potential difference across 100.-ohm resistor is 4.00 volts, which means V_1 = 4.00 V (volts).

The question asks to find R_2 (resistance of unknown resistor); first you need to find I_2 and V_2 (current and number of volts at R_2) and then substitute I_2 and V_2 in the equation $R = \dfrac{V}{I}$ to find R_2.

In a series circuit, current is the same at any point in the circuit. You can find I_1 by using the equation above, because V_1 and R_1 are given (but you cannot solve for I_2 using the equation above because you do not know R_2). Therefore, first find **I_1 (current at the R_1 100. Ω resistor)**, which **equals** the **current (I_2) at R_2** (the unknown resistor).

$$R = \frac{V}{I}$$

Look at the part of the diagram in the question with V_1.
Then, iin the equation above, substitute for R_1 100. Ω (ohms).
Substitute for V_1 4.00 V (volts).

$100.\ \Omega = \dfrac{4.00\ V}{I_1}$	Or, rearrange the equation $I = \dfrac{V}{R}$
$I_1\ (100.\ \Omega) = 4.00\ V$	
$I_1 = \dfrac{4.00\ V}{100.\ \Omega} = 0.040\ \dfrac{V}{\Omega}$	$I_1 = \dfrac{4.00\ V}{100.\ \Omega} = 0.040\ \dfrac{V}{\Omega}$
$I_1 = 0.040$ A (amperes)	$I_1 = 0.040$ A (amperes)

In a series circuit, current (I) is the same in all parts of the circuit.
Since current I_1 is 0.040 A, therefore current I_2 is also 0.040 A.

Now find V_2:
Look at Reference Table: Electricity-Series Circuits:
$$V \quad = \quad V_1 + V_2 + V_3.$$
Total volts = sum of the volts at all the resistors
In the equation above, substitute for V (total volts) 10.0 V (10.0-volt battery). Substitute for V_1 4.00 V. Note: There is no V_3.

$10.0\ V = 4.00\ V + V_2$
total volts
$10.0\ V - 4.00\ V = V_2$
$V_2 = 10.0\ V - 4.00\ V = 6.00\ V$

Since you now know V_2 and I_2, find R_2 by using the equation
$$R = \frac{V}{I}.$$

In the equation $R = \dfrac{V}{I}$ *then substitute* for V_2 6.00 V. *Substitute*
for I_2 0.040 A.

$$R_2 = \frac{V_2}{I_2}$$

$$R_2 = \frac{6.00\ V}{0.040\ A} = 150.\ \Omega \qquad\qquad \text{Answer 3}$$

Method 2:
Given: 100.-ohm resistor and unknown resistor in series.
      10.0-volt battery (total volts = 10.0 volts)
      potential drop (potential difference) across 100.-ohm resistor is 4.00 volts.
Find: resistance (R) of unknown resistor.

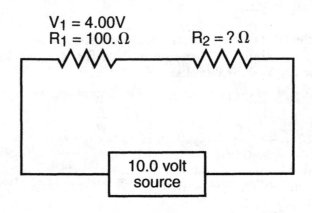

$V_1 = 4.00V$
$R_1 = 100.\,\Omega$ $R_2 = ?\,\Omega$

10.0 volt
source

Look for an equation on Reference Table: Electricity that has resistance (R) and volts or potential difference (V).

$$R = \frac{V}{I}.$$

I = current
R = resistance
V = potential difference

Current (I) is the same in all parts of a series circuit.

$$I = I_1 = I_2 = I_3$$

Rearrange the equation $R = \dfrac{V}{I}$ and you get:

$$I = \frac{V}{R}$$

Current I_1 is the current at V_1, where resistance (R_1) = 100. Ω.

$$I_1 = \frac{V_1}{R_1}$$

Current I_2 is the current at V_2 (unknown voltage), where resistance (R_2) is also unknown.

$$I_2 = \frac{V_2}{R_2}$$

Current at all parts of a series circuit is equal. Therefore, set both equations equal to each other:

$$\frac{V_1}{R_1} = \frac{V_2}{R_2}$$

Find R_2:

Cross multiply

$$V_1R_2 = V_2R_1$$

$$R_2 = \frac{V_2R_1}{V_1}$$

In the equation above, R_2 and V_2 are two unknowns, therefore first find V_2, then substitute V_2 in $R_2 = \dfrac{V_2R_1}{V_1}$ to find R_2.

First find V_2:

Look at Reference Table: Electricity Series Circuits:

$$V = V_1 + V_2 + V_3$$

Total volts is equal to the sum of the volts at all the resistors.
In the equation above, **substitute for** *V* (total volts) 10.0 V and **substitute for** *V₁* 4.00 V (volts). Note: There is no V_3.
10.0 V = 4.00 V + V_2.
V_2 = 10.0 V − 4.00 V = 6.00 V.

Next:

In the equation $R_2 = \dfrac{V_2R_1}{V_1}$, *substitute for* V_2 6.00 V. *Substitute* for R_1 100. Ω. *Substitute for* V_1 4.00 V.

$$R_2 = \frac{(6.00\ V)(100.\ \Omega)}{4.00\ V} \qquad R_2 = 150.\ \Omega$$

Now Do Homework Questions #95-98, page 139.

PARALLEL CIRCUITS

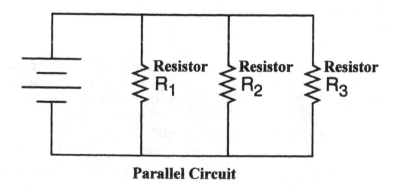

Parallel Circuit

Note: ⊹ means battery (given on Reference Table: Circuit Symbols).

A parallel circuit has **more than one path** (2 or 3, etc.) for the current (charges) to flow.

In the diagram on the previous page:

there
are
three
paths
$\left\{\rule{0pt}{140pt}\right.$

1. Current can flow from the battery to R_1 and then back to the battery.

and

2. Current can flow from the battery to R_2 and then back to the battery.

and

3. Current can flow from the battery to R_3 and then back to the battery.

Look below or on Reference Table: Electricity Parallel Circuits on page reference tables 14-15:

Parallel circuit:
$$I = I_1 + I_2 + I_3$$
$$V = V_1 = V_2 = V_3$$
$$\frac{1}{R_{eq}} = \frac{1}{R_1} + \frac{1}{R_2} + \frac{1}{R_3}$$

Table: Electricity Parallel Circuits

In a **parallel circuit**, the **total current (I)** equals the **sum of all the currents in the circuit** (the current in path 1 through resistor 1 plus the current in path 2 through resistor 2 plus the current in path 3 through resistor 3). See diagram on previous page.

$$I \quad = \quad I_1 \quad + \quad I_2 \quad + \quad I_3$$

total current	current through R_1	current through R_2	current through R_3

Total current = sum of all the currents.

In a **parallel circuit**, the **potential difference** (V), the **number of volts**, is the **same** in **all parts of** the circuit and also is the **same** as the **total** number of **volts** (example, from the battery).

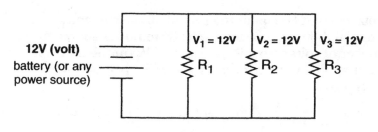

Parallel Circuit

Look below or on Reference Table: Electricity Parallel Circuits.

$$V \quad = \quad V_1 \quad = \quad V_2 \quad = \quad V_3$$

| Potential difference or total volts from power source (battery or cell) | Potential difference or volts across R_1 | Potential difference or volts across R_2 | Potential difference or volts across R_3 |

All the voltages (volts) are equal.

In a **parallel circuit**, to find **resistance**, use the equation given on Reference Table: Electricity Parallel Circuits.

$$\frac{1}{R_{ea}} \quad = \quad \frac{1}{R_1} \quad + \quad \frac{1}{R_2} \quad + \quad \frac{1}{R_3}$$

| $\frac{1}{equivalent\ resistance}$ | $\frac{1}{resistance\ at\ resistor\ 1}$ | $\frac{1}{resistance\ at\ resistor\ 2}$ | $\frac{1}{resistance\ at\ resistor\ 3}$ |

$\frac{1}{number}$ is called the reciprocal of the number. Therefore, you can say the reciprocal of the equivalent resistance ($\frac{1}{R_{eq}}$) equals the sum of the reciprocals of all the resistances ($\frac{1}{R_1} + \frac{1}{R_2} + \frac{1}{R_3}$).

SUMMARY: As you can see from Reference Table: Electricity Parallel Circuits

$$I = I_1 + I_2 + I_3$$
$$V = V_1 = V_2 = V_3$$
$$\frac{1}{R_{ea}} = \frac{1}{R_1} + \frac{1}{R_2} + \frac{1}{R_3}$$

The total current (I) equals the sum of all the currents.

V (potential difference or total volts from power source or battery) = V_1(number of volts across R_1 resistor) = V_2 (number of volts across R_2 resistor) = V_3 (number of volts across R_3 resistor) See diagram on previous page.

Reciprocal of the equivalent resistance ($\frac{1}{R_{eq}}$) = sum of the reciprocals of the resistances = $(\frac{1}{R_1} + \frac{1}{R_2} + \frac{1}{R_3})$.

Question: In the circuit diagram, what are the correct readings of voltmeters V_1 and V_2?

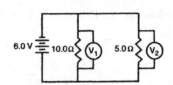

(1) V_1 reads 2.0 V and V_2 reads 4.0 V
(2) V_1 reads 4.0 V and V_2 reads 2.0 V
(3) V_1 reads 3.0 V and V_2 reads 3.0 V
(4) V_1 reads 6.0 V and V_2 reads 6.0 V

Solution:

Given: ⊣⊢ has 6.0 V (volts),therefore, battery is 6.0 V (volts).

Find: V_1 and V_2.

Battery has 6.0 V (volts), which means total volts V = 6.0 V

Look at the circuit diagram in the question. You know it is a parallel circuit because there is more than one path (there are two paths) for the current (charges) to flow.

Look for an equation on Reference Table: Electricity Parallel Circuits on page reference tables 14-15 that has V (volts).

Use the equation
$$V = V_1 = V_2 = V_3$$
In a parallel circuit, all volts (voltages) are equal. Since total volts = 6.0 V, therefore V_1 = 6.0 V and V_2 = 6.0 V.
$$V = V_1 = V_2$$
$$6.0 \text{ V} = 6.0 \text{ V} = 6.0 \text{ V}$$ Answer 4

Note: If there was a V_3, V_3 would also equal 6.0 V.

Question: What is the total resistance of the circuit segment shown in the diagram?
(1) 1.0 Ω   (2) 9.0 Ω
(3) 3.0 Ω   (4) 27 Ω

Solution:
Given: 〜 3.0 Ω

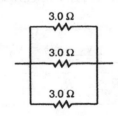

3.0 Ω
3.0 Ω
3.0 Ω

〰 3.0 Ω
〰 3.0 Ω

Find: total resistance (R_{eq}).

〰 = resistor (has resistance), given on Reference Table: Circuit Symbols.

R_{eq} = equivalent resistance, given on Reference Table: Electricity.

Look at the circuit diagram in the question. You know it is a parallel circuit because there is more than one path for the current (charges) to flow.

Look for an equation on Reference Table: Electricity Parallel Circuits for resistance (R) and total resistance (R_{eq}).

Use the equation:

$$\frac{1}{R_{ea}} = \frac{1}{R_1} + \frac{1}{R_2} + \frac{1}{R_3}$$

Resistance (R) is given in ohms Ω. When you see a number such as 3 Ω, 5 Ω, or 9 Ω, you know it is resistance (R).

3.0 Ω 〰 means resistance of 3.0 ohms. Label 3.0 Ω 〰 R_1. Label 3.0 Ω 〰 R_2. Label 3.0 Ω 〰 R_3 (see diagram below).

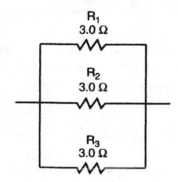

In the equation $\frac{1}{R_{eq}} = \frac{1}{R_1} + \frac{1}{R_2} + \frac{1}{R_3}$, *then substitute for R_1 3.0 Ω.*
Substitute for R_2 3.0 Ω. Substitute for R_3 3.0 Ω.

$$\frac{1}{R_{eq}} = \frac{1}{3.0 \; \Omega} + \frac{1}{3.0 \; \Omega} + \frac{1}{3.0 \; \Omega}$$

$$\frac{1}{R_{eq}} = \frac{3}{3.0 \; \Omega}$$

Cross multiply
$3 \, R_{eq} = 3.0$ Ω
R_{eq} (total resistance) = 1.0 Ω   Answer 1

Now Do Homework Questions #99-100, page 139.

PLACEMENT OF AMMETERS AND VOLTMETERS IN CIRCUITS

An **ammeter** -(A)- , which measures current, is connected in **series**.

A **voltmeter** -(V)- , which measures potential difference (volts), is connected in **parallel** across the resistor, power source, dry cell or battery. Look at the diagram below. Voltmeter -(V)- in parallel means current (charges) can flow through the resistors and through the voltmeter (only a little current flows through the voltmeter).

Hint: The connected voltmeter -(V)- forms a box-like shape across the resistor, power source, dry cell or battery.

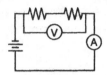 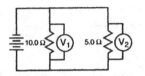

The circuit symbols -(A)- ammeter, -(V)- voltmeter, ⋀⋀ resistor and ⎓ battery in the diagrams above are given on Reference Table: Circuit Symbols on page reference tables 16.

Table: Circuit Symbols

Question: Which circuit diagram shows voltmeter V and ammeter A correctly positioned to measure the total potential difference of the circuit and the current through each resistor?

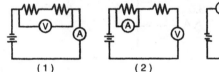 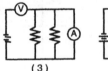

(1)   (2)   (3)   (4)

Solution:

Choice 1: Ammeter -(A)- , which measures current, is connected in series. Voltmeter -(V)- , which measures potential difference (volts) is connected in parallel across the two resistors.

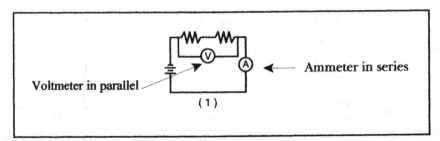

Voltmeter in parallel ⟶

Ammeter in series ⟵

(1)

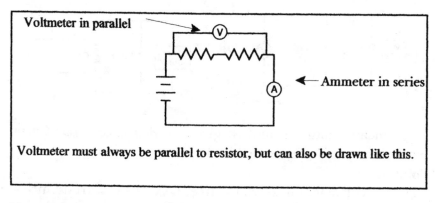

Voltmeter in parallel

Ammeter in series

Voltmeter must always be parallel to resistor, but can also be drawn like this.

Note: A voltmeter can be drawn across one resistor, two or more resistors, a dry cell or battery (see diagrams at top of previous page).

Wrong choices:
Choice 2 and Choice 3: In both choices the ammeter and voltmeter both are placed incorrectly. Ammeter must be in series and voltmeter must be in parallel.
Choice 4: Voltmeter is placed incorrectly. Voltmeter must be in parallel. Answer *1*

Now Do Homework Questions #101-102, page 139.

Questions: Base your answers to questions 1 and 2 on the circuit diagram below, which shows two resistors connected to a 24 volt source of potential difference.

Question 1: Copy the diagram on separate paper. On the diagram, use an appropriate circuit symbol to indicate a correct placement of a voltmeter to determine the potential difference across the circuit.

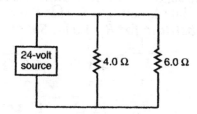

Question 2: What is the total resistance of the circuit?
    (1) 0.42 Ω   (2) 2.4 Ω   (3) 5.0 Ω   (4) 10. Ω

Solution 1: A voltmeter is always connected in **parallel** across the resistor, power source, or battery. In this parallel circuit, the voltmeter can be placed across the power source or either resistor, because in a parallel circuit there is the same number of volts at any place in the circuit.

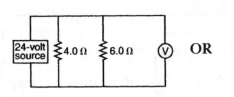 OR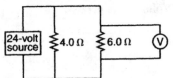

—Ⓥ— means voltmeter and is given on Reference Table: Circuit Symbols on page reference tables 16.

Solution 2:

Given: circuit diagram, 24-volt source, ⋀⋁ = 4.0 Ω (resistance = 4.0 Ω), ⋀⋁ = 6.0 Ω (resistance = 6.0 Ω)

Find: Total resistance (R_{eq}).

⋀⋁ = resistor (has resistance) given on Reference Table: Circuit Symbols.

You know it is a parallel circuit because there is more than one path (there are two paths) for current (charges) to flow through the resistors.

Look for an equation on Reference Table: Electricity Parallel Circuits for resistance (R) and total resistance (R_{eq}), on page reference tables 14-15.

Use the equation:

$$\frac{1}{R_{ea}} = \frac{1}{R_1} + \frac{1}{R_2} + \frac{1}{R_3}$$

Resistance (R) is given in ohms Ω. When you see a number such as 4.0 Ω, 6.0 Ω, or 8.0 Ω, you know it is resistance (R).

Let R_1 = 4.0 Ω. Let R_2 = 6.0 Ω. There is no R_3 in this circuit.

Then substitute for R_1 4.0 Ω. Substitute for R_2 6.0 Ω

$$\frac{1}{R_{ea}} = \frac{1}{4.0 \ \Omega} + \frac{1}{6.0 \ \Omega}$$

$$\frac{1}{R_{ea}} = \frac{3}{12 \ \Omega} + \frac{2}{12 \ \Omega} = \frac{5}{12 \ \Omega}$$

$$\frac{1}{R_{ea}} = \frac{5}{12 \ \Omega}$$

Cross multiply

$$5 \ R_{eq} = 12 \ \Omega$$

$$R_{eq} = \frac{12 \ \Omega}{5}$$

$$R_{eq} = 2.4 \ \Omega$$

Total resistance (R_{eq}) = 2.4 Ω   Answer 2

Side tabs: "Table: Circuit Symbols" and "Tbl: Elect Parallel Circ"

Table: Circuit Symbols

Tbl: Elect Parallel Circ

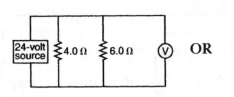 OR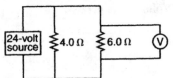

Table: Circuit Symbols

Tbl: Elect Parallel Circ

—Ⓥ— means voltmeter and is given on Reference Table: Circuit Symbols on page reference tables 16.

Solution 2:

Given: circuit diagram, 24-volt source, ⋀⋁ = 4.0 Ω (resistance = 4.0 Ω), ⋀⋁ = 6.0 Ω (resistance = 6.0 Ω)

Find: Total resistance (R_{eq}).

⋀⋁ = resistor (has resistance) given on Reference Table: Circuit Symbols.

You know it is a parallel circuit because there is more than one path (there are two paths) for current (charges) to flow through the resistors.

Look for an equation on Reference Table: Electricity Parallel Circuits for resistance (R) and total resistance (R_{eq}), on page reference tables 14-15.

Use the equation:

$$\frac{1}{R_{ea}} = \frac{1}{R_1} + \frac{1}{R_2} + \frac{1}{R_3}$$

Resistance (R) is given in ohms Ω. When you see a number such as 4.0 Ω, 6.0 Ω, or 8.0 Ω, you know it is resistance (R).

Let R_1 = 4.0 Ω. Let R_2 = 6.0 Ω. There is no R_3 in this circuit.

Then substitute for R_1 4.0 Ω. Substitute for R_2 6.0 Ω

$$\frac{1}{R_{ea}} = \frac{1}{4.0 \ \Omega} + \frac{1}{6.0 \ \Omega}$$

$$\frac{1}{R_{ea}} = \frac{3}{12 \ \Omega} + \frac{2}{12 \ \Omega} = \frac{5}{12 \ \Omega}$$

$$\frac{1}{R_{ea}} = \frac{5}{12 \ \Omega}$$

Cross multiply

$$5 \ R_{eq} = 12 \ \Omega$$

$$R_{eq} = \frac{12 \ \Omega}{5}$$

$$R_{eq} = 2.4 \ \Omega$$

Total resistance (R_{eq}) = 2.4 Ω   Answer 2

Question: Two identical resistors connected in parallel have an equivalent resistance of 40. ohms. What is the resistance of each resistor?

      (1) 20. Ω (2) 40. Ω (3) 80. Ω (4) 160 Ω

Solution:

Given: parallel circuit; two identical resistors;
      Equivalent resistance (R_{eq}) = 40. ohms
Find: resistance of each resistor.

Look for an equation on Reference Table: Electricity Parallel Circuits for resistance (R) and equivalent resistance (R_{eq}).

Use the equation:
$$\frac{1}{R_{eq}} = \frac{1}{R_1} + \frac{1}{R_2} + \frac{1}{R_3}$$

R_{eq} = total resistance. R_1 is one resistor; R_2 is the other identical resistor.

Then, substitute for R_{eq} (equivalent resistance) 40. Ω. *Substitute for R_1 and R_2* just R (resistance), because both R_1 and R_2 are identical resistors (same number of ohms). There is no third resistor in this question (there is no R_3).

$$\frac{1}{40.\ \Omega} = \frac{1}{R} + \frac{1}{R}$$

$$\frac{1}{40.\ \Omega} = \frac{2}{R}$$

Cross multiply

R (resistance of each resistor) = 80. Ω **Answer *3***

In a parallel circuit, the **equivalent resistance R_{eq} is less than any individual resistance** (R_1 or R_2, etc.). See question and solution above.

For example: R_1 = 4 Ω and R_2 = 4 Ω.
Substitute for R_1, 4 Ω. Substitute for R_2 4 Ω.

$$\frac{1}{R_{eq}} = \frac{1}{R_1} + \frac{1}{R_2}$$

$$\frac{1}{2\ \Omega} = \frac{1}{4\ \Omega} + \frac{1}{4\ \Omega}$$

As you can see, equivalent resistance R_{eq}, which is 2 Ω, is less than R_1, which is 4 Ω, and also less than R_2, which is 4 Ω.

Question: Resistors R_1 and R_2 have an equivalent resistance of 6 ohms when connected in the circuit shown below.
The resistance of R_1 could be

      (1) 1 Ω (2) 5 Ω (3) 8 Ω (4) 4 Ω

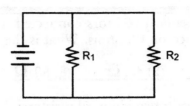

Solution:
Given: circuit diagram
 equivalent resistance = 6 ohms (Ω).
Find: resistance of R_1.
You know it is a parallel circuit because there is more than one path for the current (charges) to flow.

Look for an equation on Reference Table: Electricity Parallel Circuits for resistance (R) or equivalent resistance (R_{eq}). The equation is $\frac{1}{R_{eq}} = \frac{1}{R_1} + \frac{1}{R_2} + \frac{1}{R_3}$. Since $\frac{1}{R_{eq}}$ is found by adding up the reciprocals of all the resistances ($\frac{1}{R_1} + \frac{1}{R_2} + \frac{1}{R_3}$), $\frac{1}{R_{eq}}$ must be bigger than $\frac{1}{R_1}$ or $\frac{1}{R_2}$ or $\frac{1}{R_3}$, therefore R_{eq} (which is in the denominator) **must be smaller than** any of the resistances, R_1 or R_2 or R_3 (see equation above).

The equivalent resistance R_{eq} is 6 Ω and must be smaller than any of the resistances, which means 6 Ω must be less than resistance R_1; therefore, R_1 could be 8 ohms. See "For example" on previous page. **Answer 3**

Now Do Homework Questions #103-106, pages 140-141, and #157, page 146.

Question: In the diagram below of a parallel circuit, ammeter A measures the current supplied by the 110-volt source.

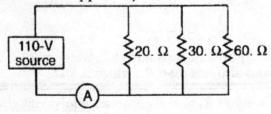

The current measured by ammeter A is
  (1) 1.0 A   (2) 0.10 A   (3) 5.5 A   (4) 11 A

30. Ω $\mathsf{\Lambda\Lambda\Lambda}$ (30.-ohm resistor)

60. Ω $\mathsf{\Lambda\Lambda\Lambda}$ (60.-ohm resistor)

Find: current (I)

Label the diagram in the question:
label the 20. Ω $\mathsf{\Lambda\Lambda\Lambda}$ (resistor) R_1;
label the 30. Ω $\mathsf{\Lambda\Lambda\Lambda}$ R_2; label the
60. Ω$\mathsf{\Lambda\Lambda\Lambda}$ R_3.

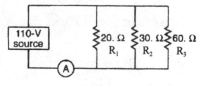

Look for an equation on Reference Table: Electricity that has resistance (R), volts (potential difference)(V), and current (I).

Use the equation

$$R = \frac{V}{I}$$

Look at the figure in the question. An ammeter measures current. Where the ammeter $-\!\text{\textcircled{A}}\!-$ is located, **all** the **current** (**total current**) leaving the 110-V source (110-volt source) must go through $-\!\text{\textcircled{A}}\!-$ before going to the other resistors. Therefore, find the total current.

To find **total current,** you must use **total volts** and **total resistance** in the equation $R = \dfrac{V}{I}$. You know total volts from the 110-volt source, but you do not know total resistance and total current; therefore, *first* **find total resistance (R_{eq})** and *then substitute* total resistance *for R* in the equation $R = \dfrac{V}{I}$ to **find current (I)**

Look at the diagram. You know it is a parallel circuit because there is more than one path for the current (charges) to flow through the resistors.

Look for an equation for total resistance (R_{eq}) of a parallel circuit. First use the equation

$$\frac{1}{R_{eq}} = \frac{1}{R_1} + \frac{1}{R_2} + \frac{1}{R_3}$$

When you have ohms (Ω) you know it is resistance (R).
Substitute for R_1 2 0. Ω. *Substitute for R_2* 30. Ω. *Substitute for R_3* 60. Ω (see diagram above.)

$$\frac{1}{R_{eq}} = \frac{1}{20.\ \Omega} + \frac{1}{30.\ \Omega} + \frac{1}{60.\ \Omega}$$

$$\frac{1}{R_{eq}} = \frac{3}{60.\ \Omega} + \frac{2}{60.\ \Omega} + \frac{1}{60.\ \Omega} = \frac{6}{60.\ \Omega} = \frac{1}{10.\ \Omega}$$

$$\frac{1}{R_{eq}} = \frac{1}{10.\ \Omega}$$

Cross multiply

R_{eq} (total resistance) = 10. Ω

Now you know total resistance and total volts and can find total current.

Then, in the equation $R = \dfrac{V}{I}$ *substitute for V* (volts) 110 V.

Substitute for R 10. Ω (from first part of the solution).

$R = \dfrac{V}{I}$

10. $\Omega = \dfrac{110\ V}{I}$

Cross multiply

I(10. Ω) = 110 V

Divide by 10. Ω

$I = \dfrac{110\ V}{10.\ \Omega} = \dfrac{11\ V}{\Omega} = 11A$

Answer 4

Rearrange the equation

$I = \dfrac{V}{R}$

$I = \dfrac{110\ V}{10.\ \Omega} = \dfrac{11\ V}{\Omega} = 11\ A$

Answer 4

Question: In which circuit would ammeter A show the greatest current?

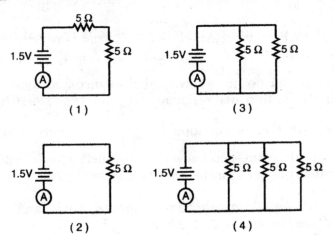

(1)   (3)

(2)   (4)

Solution:

Given: Four circuit diagrams with 〰 (resistors) and –Ⓐ– (ammeter). V = 1.5 V (volts), the same in all four choices.

Find: Greatest current (I).

Look for a equation on Reference Table: Electricity that has resistance (R), volts (potential difference) (V), and current (I).

Use the equation

$R = \dfrac{V}{I}$

I = current

R = resistance

V = potential difference

Cross multiply: V = IR. Look at the equation V = IR. V is 1.5 V (volts), a constant in all 4 choices; the **smaller R** is, the **bigger is I** (current). **Find** the choice with the **smallest R**. *Look for an equation* for resistance (R) on Reference Table: Electricity Series Circuits (when it is a series circuit) or on Reference Table: Electricity Parallel Circuits (when it is a parallel circuit).

Choice 1: You know it is a series circuit because there is only one path for the current (charges) to flow. In a series circuit, R_{eq} is the sum of all the resistances. Find R_{eq}.
Use the equation

$$R_{eq} = R_1 + R_2 + R_3 + ...$$

(Let the 5 Ω resistor be R_1. Let the other 5 Ω resistor be R_2. There is no other resistor, which means there is no R_3.)
$R_{eq} = R_1 + R_2$.
Substitute for R_1 5 Ω. Substitute for R_2 5 Ω.
$R_{eq} = 5\,\Omega + 5\,\Omega = 10\,\Omega$

Choice 2: There is one 5 Ω resistor. R = 5 Ω.

Choices 3 and 4: You know it is a parallel circuit because there is more than one path (there are two or three paths) for the current (charges) to flow. **In a parallel circuit, the more resistors** you add, the **smaller is R_{eq}.** (See note at end of problem.)
Choice 3: There are two resistors:
The two resistors are ⋀⋀ 5 Ω (means R_1 = 5 Ω) and ⋀⋀ 5 Ω (means R_2 = 5 Ω). Find equivalent resistance (R_{eq}).

Use the equation $\dfrac{1}{R_{eq}} = \dfrac{1}{R_1} + \dfrac{1}{R_2} + \dfrac{1}{R_3}$

(Let the 5 Ω resistor be R_1. Let the other 5 Ω resistor be R_2. There is no other resistor, which means there is no R_3.)

The equation becomes $\dfrac{1}{R_{eq}} = \dfrac{1}{R_1} + \dfrac{1}{R_2}$.
Substitute for R_1 5 Ω. Substitute for R_2 5 Ω.
$\dfrac{1}{R_{eq}} = \dfrac{1}{5\Omega} + \dfrac{1}{5\Omega} = \dfrac{2}{5\Omega}$; in short, $\dfrac{1}{R_{eq}} = \dfrac{2}{5\Omega}$.
Cross multiply
$2\,R_{eq} = 5\,\Omega \qquad R_{eq} = 2.5\,\Omega$

Choice 4: There are three resistors (more resistors than in choice 3):
⋀⋀ 5 Ω (means R_1 = 5 Ω). ⋀⋀ 5 Ω (means R_2 = 5 Ω). ⋀⋀ 5 Ω (means R_3 = 5 Ω). Find equivalent resistance (R_{eq}).
Use the equation
$\dfrac{1}{R_{eq}} = \dfrac{1}{R_1} + \dfrac{1}{R_2} + \dfrac{1}{R_3}$ *Substitute for R_1 5 Ω. Substitute for R_2 5 Ω.*

Substitute for R_3 5 Ω. $\dfrac{1}{R_{eq}} = \dfrac{1}{5\Omega} + \dfrac{1}{5\Omega} + \dfrac{1}{5\Omega} = \dfrac{3}{5\Omega}$; in short, $\dfrac{1}{R_{eq}} = \dfrac{3}{5\Omega}$.

Cross multiply

$3 R_{eq} = 5 \, \Omega$ $R_{eq} = 1.67 \, \Omega$

Choice 4 is the answer. Choice 4 has the smallest R. Now look at the equation: $R = \dfrac{V}{I}$. Cross multiply: V = IR. Look at the equation V = IR. V is 1.5 V (volts), a constant in all 4 choices; the **smaller R** is, the **larger is I** (current). **Choice 4 has the smallest R**, 1.67 Ω (the more resistors in parallel, the smaller is R), **therefore the largest** (or greatest) **current (I).**   Answer 4

In a parallel circuit, the more resistors you add, the smaller is R_{eq}; and in a parallel circuit, R_{eq} is less than any of the resistors (R_1, R_2, R_3). You can also answer this question by finding the current (I) of all four circuits (using the equations $R = \dfrac{V}{I}$, $R_{eq} = R_1 + R_2 + R_3 + ...$ in a series circuit, and $\dfrac{1}{R_{eq}} = \dfrac{1}{R_1} + \dfrac{1}{R_2} + \dfrac{1}{R_3} + ...$ in a parallel circuit). See which circuit has the greatest current.

Note: You can see what happens to R_{eq} in a parallel circuit when you add more resistors. Try it out:

Circuit with two resistors: R_1 = 10 Ω, R_2 = 10 Ω.	Add three resistors (Total: five resistors): R_1 = 10 Ω, R_2 = 10 Ω, R_3 = 10 Ω, R_4 = 10 Ω, R_5 = 10 Ω.
$\dfrac{1}{R_{eq}} = \dfrac{1}{R_1} + \dfrac{1}{R_2}$	$\dfrac{1}{R_{eq}} = \dfrac{1}{R_1} + \dfrac{1}{R_2} + \dfrac{1}{R_3} + \dfrac{1}{R_4} + \dfrac{1}{R_5}$
$\dfrac{1}{R_{eq}} = \dfrac{1}{10\,\Omega} + \dfrac{1}{10\,\Omega} = \dfrac{2}{10\,\Omega} = \dfrac{1}{5\,\Omega}$	$\dfrac{1}{R_{eq}} = \dfrac{1}{10} + \dfrac{1}{10} + \dfrac{1}{10} + \dfrac{1}{10} + \dfrac{1}{10} = \dfrac{5}{10} = \dfrac{1}{2}$
$\dfrac{1}{R_{eq}} = \dfrac{1}{5\,\Omega}$ Cross multiply	$\dfrac{1}{R_{eq}} = \dfrac{1}{2\,\Omega}$ Cross multiply
$R_{eq} = 5 \, \Omega$	$R_{eq} = 2 \, \Omega$

As you can see, when you add more resistors, R_{eq} is less.

Question: A 20.-ohm resistor and a 30.-ohm resistor are connected in parallel to a 12-volt battery as shown. An ammeter is connected as shown. What is the current reading of the ammeter?

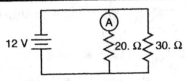

(1) 1.0 A   (2) 0.60 A   (3) 0.40 A   (4) 0.20 A

Solution:

Given: parallel circuit

      20.-ohm resistor (20. Ω 〰)

      30.-ohm resistor (30. Ω 〰)

      12-volt (V) battery

Find: What is the current reading of the ammeter –(A)–, which means find the current (I) at or going to the 20. Ω $\sim\!\!\sim$ (resistor).

$\sim\!\!\sim$ = resistor (has resistance), given on Reference Table: Circuit Symbols on page reference tables 16.

Look at the diagram in the question. You know it is a parallel circuit because there is more than one path for the current (charges) to flow.

Look for an equation on Reference Table: Electricity that has to do with resistance (R), volts (potential difference) (V) and current (I).
Use the equation

$$R = \frac{V}{I}$$

Look at the diagram. The **ammeter (A) measures** the **current** only **going to** the **20. Ω** $\sim\!\!\sim$ (20-ohm resistor), not the total current of the circuit; therefore, you need to **find** the **current (I) going to** the **20. Ω** $\sim\!\!\sim$ (**20-ohm resistor).**

Note: If, in a different example (see diagram below) the ammeter (A) is near the battery (or any power source) and the current through the ammeter goes to both resistors (R_1 and R_2), then the ammeter (A) would measure the total current of the circuit.

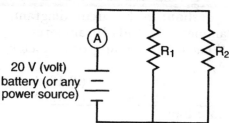

20 V (volt)
battery (or any power source)

This question asks to find current (I) going to the 20 ohm resistor.

As we said before, use the equation $R = \dfrac{V}{I}$.

When you use the equation above to **find I (going to** the **20. Ω resistor)**, obviously also **use** the values of **R and V at** the **20. Ω** $\sim\!\!\sim$ (resistor). You know R (resistance, 20. Ω at the 20. Ω resistor), but you do not know I (current) and V (volts, potential difference) at the 20 Ω resistor; therefore, **first find volts (V)**, **then** *substitute* volts **(V)** *for V* in the equation $R = \dfrac{V}{I}$ to find current (I) at the 20. Ω $\sim\!\!\sim$ (resistor).

First find V: Look for an equation on Reference Table: Electricity Parallel Circuits for volts (potential difference)(V).
$$V = V_1 = V_2 = V_3$$
Total Volts

This means, in a parallel circuit, the total volts (in this example 12 V, from the 12-volt battery) equals the number of volts (12 V) at any place in the circuit; this means the total volts (12 V) equals the number of volts at the 20. Ω resistor (also 12 V).

The question asks for the current reading of the ammeter, which means to find current (I) going to the 20. Ω 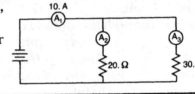 (20 ohm resistor); therefore, in the equation $R = \dfrac{V}{I}$, *then substitute for V* 12 V and *substitute for R* 20. Ω (at the 20 Ω $\wedge\wedge$).

$R = \dfrac{V}{I}$	Or, rearrange the equation
20. $\Omega = \dfrac{12\ V}{I}$	$I = \dfrac{V}{R}$
Cross multiply $I(20.\ \Omega) = 12\ V$	$I = \dfrac{12\ V}{20.\ \Omega} = \dfrac{12}{20.}\ A = 0.60\ A$
$I = \dfrac{12\ V}{20.\ \Omega} = \dfrac{12}{20.}\ A = 0.60\ A$	
Reading of ammeter = 0.60 A	Reading of ammeter = 0.60 A
Answer 2	Answer 2

Question: In the circuit diagram, ammeter A₁ reads 10. amperes. What is the reading of ammeter A₂?

    (1) 6.0 A   (2) 10. A
    (3) 20. A   (4) 4.0 A

Solution:
METHOD 1:
Given: circuit with diagram.
        Ammeter A₁ reads 10. amperes, A₁ = 10. A (amperes)
        20. Ω $\wedge\wedge$ (20. Ω resistor)
        30. Ω $\wedge\wedge$ (30. Ω resistor)
Find: reading of A₂.
$\wedge\wedge$ = resistor (has resistance), given on Reference Table: Circuit Symbols on page reference tables 16.
You know this is a parallel circuit because there is more than one path for the current (charges) to flow through the resistors.
An ammeter (A) measures current. Ammeter A₁ reads 10. A (amperes), which means current (I) at A₁ = 10. A (amperes). Find reading of ammeter A₂, which measures current at A₂, that only goes to the 20 Ω $\wedge\wedge$.
Look for an equation on Reference Table: Electricity that has resistance (R) and current (I).
Use the equation $R = \dfrac{V}{I}$

Since you need to find current (I) at the 20. Ω ⋀⋀ (resistor), obviously use the values of R and V at the 20. Ω ⋀⋀ (resistor) in the equation $R = \dfrac{V}{I}$.

At the 20. Ω resistor, you know R (resistance) but you don't know I (current) and V (volts, potential difference) at the 20. Ω resistor; therefore, first find volts (V) and then *substitute* volts (V) *for V* in the equation $R = \dfrac{V}{I}$ to find current (I) at the 20. Ω ⋀⋀ (resistor).

First find volts: Look at the equation on Reference Table: Electricity Parallel Circuits for potential difference (volts) in a parallel circuit.

$$V = V_1 = V_2 = V_3$$

Total volts = volts at any place in the circuit. This means volts at the 20.-ohm resistor = total volts.

At the 20. Ω resistor, you cannot find V directly by using the equation $R = \dfrac{V}{I}$, because you do not know both V and I at the 20 Ω resistor.

Therefore, find total volts by using the equation $R = \dfrac{V}{I}$. We know total current (I) = 10. A (ammeter A_1 reads 10. A), and we can find total resistance (R_{eq}) by using the equation $\dfrac{1}{R_{eq}} = \dfrac{1}{R_1} + \dfrac{1}{R_2} + \dfrac{1}{R_3}$.

Note: From the diagram, you see the current measured by ammeter A_2 goes through the 20. Ω resistor; therefore, call the 20. Ω resistor R_2. Let the 30. Ω resistor be R_3. In the equation $\dfrac{1}{R_{eq}} = \dfrac{1}{R_1} + \dfrac{1}{R_2} + \dfrac{1}{R_3}$ **substitute for R_2** 20. Ω and **substitute for R_3** 30. Ω. (There are only two resistors in this circuit, which we called R_2 and R_3. There is no other resistor, which means there is no R_1.)

$$\frac{1}{R_{eq}} = \frac{1}{20.\ \Omega} + \frac{1}{30.\ \Omega}$$

$$\frac{1}{R_{eq}} = \frac{3}{60.\ \Omega} + \frac{2}{60.\ \Omega} = \frac{5}{60.\ \Omega} \ ;$$

in short, $\dfrac{1}{R_{eq}} = \dfrac{5}{60.\ \Omega}$

Cross multiply: $5R_{eq} = 60.\ \Omega$

R_{eq} (total resistance) = 12 Ω

In the equation $R = \dfrac{V}{I}$, **substitute** 12 Ω (total resistance) **for R.**
Substitute 10. A (total current from battery) **for I.**

$$12\ \Omega = \frac{V}{10.\ A}$$

Cross multiply

Total V = (10 A)(12 Ω) = 120 V

10. A
(A₁)

(A₂)   (A₃)

R_2 R_3
20. Ω 30. Ω

Total volts = volts at any place in the circuit. Since the total volts = 120 V, volts at the 20.-ohm $\wedge\!\!\wedge\!\!\wedge$ (20 ohm resistor) = 120 V.

The question asks to find current (I_2) going to the 20. Ω $\wedge\!\!\wedge\!\!\wedge$ (resistor). In the equation $R = \dfrac{V}{I}$, *then substitute for V* 120 V (volts) at the 20. Ω $\wedge\!\!\wedge\!\!\wedge$ (resistor). *Substitute for R* 20. Ω (resistance at the 20. Ω $\wedge\!\!\wedge\!\!\wedge$).

$$R = \frac{V}{I}$$

$$20.\ \Omega = \frac{120\ V}{I}$$

Cross multiply

$$I(20.\ \Omega) = 120\ V$$

$$I = \frac{120\ V}{20.\ \Omega} = 6.0\ A$$

I(current at the 20 Ω $\wedge\!\!\wedge\!\!\wedge$)= 6.0 A **Ammeter A$_2$ reads** the current at the 20 Ω resistor, which = **6.0 A.**   Answer *1*

Or, rearrange the equation

$$I = \frac{V}{R}$$

$$I = \frac{120\ V}{20.\ \Omega} = 6.0\ A$$

I(current at the 20 Ω $\wedge\!\!\wedge\!\!\wedge$)= 6.0 A **Ammeter A$_2$ reads** the current at the 20 Ω resistor, which = **6.0 A.**   Answer *1*

METHOD 2:

You know it is a parallel circuit because there is more than one path for the current (charges) to flow through the resistors. There are three equations for parallel circuits on Reference Table: Electricity Parallel Circuits:

$$I = I_1 + I_2 + I_3 + \ldots$$
$$V = V_1 = V_2 = V_3 = \ldots$$
$$\frac{1}{R_{ea}} = \frac{1}{R_1} + \frac{1}{R_2} + \frac{1}{R_3} + \ldots$$

Look for an equation that has resistance (R) and current (I).

Use the equation

$$R = \frac{V}{I}$$

You realize A$_1$ measures total current (I) coming from the battery, equals 10. A, A$_2$ measures current I$_2$ going through the 20. Ω resistor, and A$_3$ measures current I$_3$ going through the 30. Ω resistor. Let R$_2$ = 20. Ω resistor because ammeter A$_2$ is at the 20. Ω resistor. Let R$_3$ = 30. Ω resistor because ammeter A$_3$ is at the 30. Ω resistor.

From Reference Table: Electricity Parallel Circuits you see that V = V$_1$ = V$_2$ = V$_3$. The total volts equals the volts at any point in the circuit. As stated before, use the equation $R = \dfrac{V}{I}$.

Total resistance (R_{eq})	R_2(Resistance at A_2)	R_3(Resistance at A_3)
$R_{total} = \dfrac{V_{total}}{I_{total}}$	$R_2 = \dfrac{V_2}{I_2}$	$R_3 = \dfrac{V_3}{I_3}$
Cross multiply	Cross multiply	Cross multiply
$V_{total} = I_{total}R_{total}$	$V_2 = I_2R_2$	$V_3 = I_3R_3$

$V = V_1 = V_2 = V_3$, given on Reference Table: Electricity Parallel Circuits
Total volts = volts at any place in the circuit.

Since $V_{total} = V_2 = V_3$ (see above)
the rest of each equation is equal to one another:
$$I_{total}R_{total} = I_2R_2 = I_3R_3.$$

Use the equation $I_{total}R_{total} = I_2R_2$. Since ammeter A_1 measures total current going from the battery, you know total current $(I) = 10$. A (amperes). You know R_2 (resistance at A_2) = 20. Ω. You do not know both I_2 and R_{total}; therefore, first find R_{total} and then substitute R_{total} in the equation $I_{total}R_{total} = I_2R_2$ to find I_2.

Look for an equation on Reference Table: Electricity Parallel Circuits for resistance (R) or total resistance (equivalent resistance R_{eq})

Use the equation $\dfrac{1}{R_{eq}} = \dfrac{1}{R_1} + \dfrac{1}{R_2} + \dfrac{1}{R_3}$. Let R_2 equal 20. Ω resistor and let R_3 equal 30. Ω resistor (explained on the previous page). (There is no other resistor in this example, which means there is no R_1). $\dfrac{1}{R_{eq}} = \dfrac{1}{R_2} + \dfrac{1}{R_3}$.

Substitute for R_2 20. Ω. Substitute for R_3 30. Ω.

$$\frac{1}{R_{eq}} = \frac{1}{20.\ \Omega} + \frac{1}{30.\ \Omega} = \frac{3}{60.\ \Omega} + \frac{2}{60.\ \Omega} = \frac{5}{60.\ \Omega}$$

$$\frac{1}{R_{eq}} = \frac{5}{60.\ \Omega}$$

Cross multiply
$5R_{eq} = 60.\ \Omega$
$R_{eq} = 12\ \Omega$
$R_{total}\ (R_{eq}) = 12\ \Omega$

Next: Find I_2
Set the equations equal to one another.
$I_{total}R_{total} = I_2R_2$.
Substitute for I_{total}. 10. A. **Substitute for** R_{total} 12 Ω (see above). **Substitute for** R_2 20. Ω.
$(10.\ A)(12\ \Omega) = I_2(20.\ \Omega)$
$$I_2 = \frac{(10.\ A)(12\ \Omega)}{20.\ \Omega} = \frac{120\ A\Omega}{20.\ \Omega} = 6.0\ A. \qquad \text{Answer } 1$$

Note: It is a little harder to solve for I_2 using $I_2R_2 = I_3R_3$. You know R_2 and R_3; you cannot find I_2 or I_3 directly by using $I = I_2 + I_3$, because you have two unknowns, I_2 and I_3, in the same equation.

Question: Base your answers to these two questions on the circuit diagram below.

Question 1: If switch S_1 is open, the reading of ammeter A is

(1) 0.50 A   (2) 2.0 A

(3) 1.5 A   (4) 6.0 A

Question 2: If switch S_1 is closed, the equivalent resistance of the circuit is

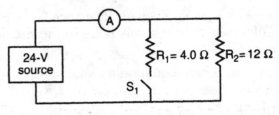

    (1) 8.0 Ω (2) 2.0 Ω (3) 3.0 Ω (4) 16 Ω

Solution 1:

Given: 24-V source (24 volts); $R_1 = 4.0\ \Omega$; $R_2 = 12\ \Omega$

Find: Reading of ammeter when S_1 is open. An ammeter measures current, (I); therefore, find current (I).

$\wedge\!\!\wedge\!\!\wedge$ = resistor (has resistance), given on Reference Table: Circuit Symbols on page Reference Tables 16.

Look for an equation on Reference Table: Electricity on page reference tables 14-15 that has R (resistance), V (potential difference, volts), and I (current).

Use the equation

$$R = \frac{V}{I}$$

I = current

R = resistance

V = potential difference

You know it is a parallel circuit because there is more than one path for the current to flow. Since switch S_1 is open, current cannot flow through the 4.0 Ω resistor (see diagram above), but only flows through the 12 Ω $\wedge\!\!\wedge\!\!\wedge$ (resistor), therefore the resistance (R) of the circuit is 12 Ω.

Then, in the equation above *substitute for R* 12 Ω. *Substitute for* V (potential difference, volts) 24 V.

$$R = \frac{V}{I}$$

$$12\ \Omega = \frac{24\ V}{I}$$

Cross multiply

$$I(12\ \Omega) = 24\ V$$

$$I = \frac{24\ V}{12\ \Omega} = 2.0\ A$$

I = 2.0 A (amperes)

Ammeter measures current, therefore, the reading of ammeter A is 2.0 A.

Answer 2

Solution 2:

Given: V (volts) = 24 V; R_1 = 4.0 Ω; R_2 = 12 Ω; S_1 is closed.

Find: equivalent resistance (R_{eq})

You know it is a parallel circuit because there is more than one path for the current to flow. Since the switch is closed the current flows in both paths, through the 4.0 Ω 〰 (resistor) and through the 12 Ω resistor (where the 4.0 Ω resistor is and where the 12 Ω resistor is).

Look for an equation on Reference Table: Electricity Parallel Circuits that has equivalent resistance (R_{eq}).

Use the equation:

$$\frac{1}{R_{eq}} = \frac{1}{R_1} + \frac{1}{R_2} + \frac{1}{R_3} + \ldots$$

$$\frac{1}{R_{eq}} = \frac{1}{R_1} + \frac{1}{R_2} \quad \text{(because there is no } R_3 \text{ in this example).}$$

Substitute for R_1 4.0 Ω. Substitute for R_2 12 Ω.

$$\frac{1}{R_{eq}} = \frac{1}{4.0 \ \Omega} + \frac{1}{12 \ \Omega}$$

$$\frac{1}{R_{eq}} = \frac{3}{12 \ \Omega} + \frac{1}{12 \ \Omega} = \frac{4}{12 \ \Omega} = \frac{1}{3.0 \ \Omega},$$

$$\frac{1}{R_{eq}} = \frac{1}{3.0 \ \Omega}$$

Cross multiply

R_{eq} = 3.0 Ω

Equivalent resistance (R_{eq}) = 3.0 Ω

Answer 3

Note: As you can see in the parallel circuit, equivalent resistance R_{eq} 3.0 Ω, is less than any of the resistances, R_1 4.0 Ω or R_2 12 Ω.

Now Do Homework Questions #107-109, page 141.

Question: An electric circuit contains two 3.0 ohm resistors connected in parallel with a battery. The circuit also contains a voltmeter that reads the potential difference across one of the resistors. On separate paper, draw a diagram of this circuit, using the symbols from the Reference Tables for Physical Setting/Physics. [Assume availability of any number of wires of negligible resistance.]

Solution: Look below or on Reference Table: Circuit Symbols on page reference tables 16. Use the symbols in the circuit.

⇶	〰	–Ⓥ–
battery	resistor	voltmeter

Draw a parallel circuit.

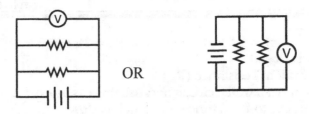

OR

Remember, a parallel circuit has more than one path and a voltmeter is always in parallel across a resistor or battery.

Note: If the question above asked for lamps connected in parallel, you would use the lamp symbol ⎯(ℓℓℓ)⎯ given on Reference Table: Circuit Symbols instead of the resistor symbol ⋀⋀⋁ .

Removing A Lamp or Resistor in a Parallel Circuit

In a parallel circuit, let's see what happens to the other lamps when one (or more) lamps (or resistors) is removed.

Question: In the diagram below, lamps L_1 and L_2 are connected to a constant voltage power supply. If lamp L_1 burns out, the brightness of L_2 will

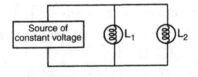

      (1) decrease   (2) increase   (3) remain the same

Solution: In a parallel circuit, if one lamp burns out, the other lamp is **not affected.** Lamp 2 still has the **same current, same volts,** and **same resistance** (even after lamp 1 burns out), and therefore the **same brightness.**   Answer *3*

Questions 1 and 2: Three lamps were connected in a circuit with a battery of constant potential. The current, potential difference, and resistance for each lamp are listed in the data table on the next page. [There is negligible resistance in the wires and the battery.]

	Current (A)	Potential difference (V)	Resistance (Ω)
lamp 1	0.45	40.1	89
lamp 2	0.11	40.1	365
lamp 3	0.28	40.1	143

Question 1: If lamp 3 is removed from the circuit, what would be the value of the potential difference across lamp 1 after lamp 3 is removed?

Question 2: If lamp 3 is removed from the circuit, what would be the value of the current in lamp 2 after lamp 3 is removed?

Solution 1: Look below or at Reference Table: Electricity Parallel Circuits on page reference tables 14-15. $V = V_1 = V_2 = V_3$. Note : V means volts or potential difference. When volts are equal, you know that it is a parallel circuit. Look at the table above. For the three lamps, current is not equal, but the potential difference (volts) are equal; therefore, you know that it is a parallel circuit.

In a parallel circuit, if one lamp is removed, the other lamps are **not affected**. Lamp 1 still has the **same volts (potential difference)**, same current, and same resistance (even after lamp 3 is removed). Lamp 1 still has a potential difference of 40.1 V (volts) (see table above).   Answer *40.1 volts*

Solution 2: As you learned, in a parallel circuit, if one lamp is removed, the other lamps are **not affected**. Lamp 2 still has the **same current**, same volts and same resistance (even after lamp 3 is removed). Lamp 2 still has a current of 0.11 A (see table above).

Answer *0.11A*

The wires in your house are connected in parallel. If one light bulb goes out, the other light bulbs and electrical appliances (example TV, VCR) in your house are not affected; they still have the same current, voltage, and resistance.

Rule: In a **parallel circuit**, if **one** or more **lamps** (or **resistors**) are **removed**, the **other lamps** are **not affected**. They still have the **same current, same voltage,** and **same resistance**, (even after one lamp is removed).

You learned about series and parallel circuits. Let's see how you would find the resistance of an unknown resistor in the laboratory.

Question: Your school's physics laboratory has the following equipment available for conducting experiments:

accelerometers	lasers	stopwatches
ammeters	light bulbs	thermometers
bar magnets	meter sticks	voltmeters
batteries	power supplies	wires
electromagnets	spark timers	

Explain how you would find the resistance of an unknown resistor in the laboratory. Your explanation must include:
a. measurements required   b. equipment needed
c. complete circuit diagram   d. any equations needed to calculate
                          the resistance

Solution:
Given: Physics laboratory with equipment available.
Find: Resistance (R) of an unknown resistor.

Look for an equation on Reference Table: Electricity to find R (resistance). By using the equation $R = \dfrac{V}{I}$, you can find R because V can be measured by a voltmeter and I can be measured by an ammeter; therefore, you have only one unknown, R.

Use the equation:

$$R = \frac{V}{I}$$

I = current

R = resistance

V = potential difference

First find (measure) V and I; *then* substitute the (measurements) numbers in the equation $R = \dfrac{V}{I}$ to find R.

Step 1. Set up a circuit as shown on the next page. Use a battery, wire, resistor, ammeter, and voltmeter. Use the circuit symbols for battery ⏚, resistor ⋁⋁⋁, ammeter –Ⓐ– , and voltmeter –Ⓥ– , given on Reference Table: Circuit Symbols on page reference tables 16.
Put an **ammeter** in **series** and a **voltmeter** in **parallel** across the resistor. Remember: always put (draw) –Ⓐ– ammeter in series and –Ⓥ– voltmeter in parallel. The ammeter is an instrument that measures current (I) and the voltmeter measures potential difference or number of volts (V).
Read the ammeter and voltmeter and record the measurements (numbers).

Tbl: Electricity

Step 2. Find resistance (R): use the equation $R = \dfrac{V}{I}$. *Substitute for V* the voltmeter reading. *Substitute for I* the ammeter reading.

a. measurements required: As you saw above, potential difference (number of volts) V and current I are measured.

b. equipment needed: battery or power source, ammeter, voltmeter, connecting wires, unknown resistor.

c. complete circuit diagram:

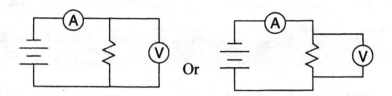

Or

d. equations needed to calculate the resistance: $R = \dfrac{V}{I}$

Question: A 5.0-ohm resistor, a 20.0-ohm resistor, and a 24-volt source of potential difference are connected in parallel. A single ammeter is placed in the circuit to read the total current.
Draw a diagram of this circuit, using the symbols with labels shown here.

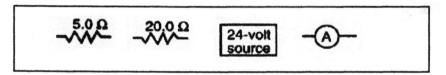

Solution: In a parallel circuit there is more than one path for the current (charges) to flow. Draw a parallel circuit with two paths. Look at the diagram in the question and the parallel circuit on the next page. Connect the wires from the 24-volt source (or, in a different example, power source, cell, or battery) to and through the ammeter (the ammeter —Ⓐ— is connected in series), to the resistors, and back to the source, forming a complete circuit. Put in the circuit the symbols with labels shown above in the question: ⌇ⱳ⌇ (resistor of 5.0 Ω), ⌇ⱳ⌇ (resistor of 20.0 Ω), 24-volt source , and —Ⓐ— (ammeter).

Draw this circuit:

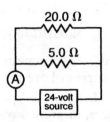

20.0 Ω

5.0 Ω

(A)

24-volt source

Now Do Homework Questions #110-111, page 141, and #158-165, pages 146-147

Placement of two or more Ammeters and Voltmeters in a Parallel Circuit

Ammeter: An ammeter, which measures current, is connected in **series** with the resistor. Look at the wire from the voltage source (power source) to the ammeter (A_1), to the resistor (R_1) and back to the voltage source. As you can see, the ammeter (A_1) and the resistor (R_1) are in series (one path). Now look at the wire from the voltage source to the ammeter (A_1) directly to resistor R_2 (not going to R_1) and back to the voltage source. The ammeter (A_1) and the resistor (R_2) are in series (one path). The symbol for ammeter is ⊸(A)⊸ , given on Reference Table: Circuit Symbols.

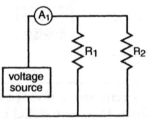

A_1

R_1 R_2

voltage source

Look at the diagram on the next page:

The ammeter at A_1 or A_2 measures total current coming from the voltage source (power source).

The ammeter at A_3 or A_4 measures current only going to and from resistor R_1 (does not measure current to and from R_2 and does not measure total current from the voltage source.)

The ammeter at A_5, A_6, A_7, or A_8 measures only current going to and from R_2 (does not measure current going to and from R_1 and does not measure total current from the voltage source).

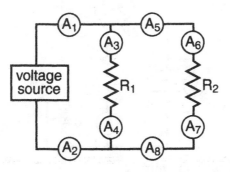

Voltmeter: The symbol for voltmeter is $-\!\widehat{V}\!-$, given on Reference Table: Circuit Symbols. A voltmeter, which measures potential difference (volts), is connected in **parallel** across the resistor (or dry cell or battery). See diagrams below. The voltmeter can be drawn as shown in Figure A or Figure B below. Parallel means there is more than one path for current (charges) to flow. Current from the power source (or battery) can flow through the path of the resistors or (a little current) through the path of the voltmeter. (A voltmeter has high resistance; very little current flows through the voltmeter.)

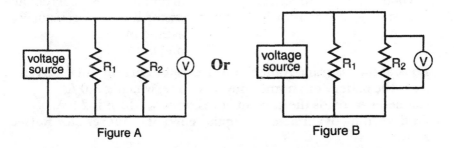

Note: The diagram in the question on the next page shows a voltmeter $-\!\widehat{V}\!-$ across a battery.

Question: Ammeters A_1, A_2, and A_3 are placed in a circuit as shown on the next page.

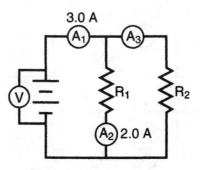

What is the reading on ammeter A_3?s

Solution:

Given: Circuit diagram with ⊒ (battery), ⩘ (resistor), –Ⓐ– (ammeter) and –Ⓥ– (voltmeter).

      A_1 = 3.0 A (given in circuit diagram)

      A_2 = 2.0 A (given in circuit diagram)

Find: Reading of ammeter A_3.

An ammeter measures current (I). You know it is a parallel circuit because there is more than one path for the current (charges) to flow.

Look for an equation on Reference Table: Electricity Parallel Circuits on page reference tables 14-15 that deals with current (I).

Use the equation

I	=	I_1	+	I_2	+	I_3
Total current	=	current at resistor R_1	+	current at resistor R_2; reading of ammeter A_3	+	current at resistor R_3

Look at the diagram. Ammeter A_1 reads the current (total current) from the battery or another power source, which is 3.0 A.

Ammeter A_2 reads the current at resistor R_1, which is 2.0 A.

Find: reading of **ammeter A_3, equals current (I_2) at resistor R_2** (see above).

In the equation $I = I_1 + I_2 + I_3$, *then substitute for I* (total current) 3.0 A. *Substitute for I_1* (current at resistor R_1) 2.0 A and solve for I_2 (reading of ammeter A_3, which is the current at resistor R_2).

Note: There is no I_3 because there is no resistor R_3.

$I = I_1 + I_2$	Or, rearrange the equation:
3.0 A = 2.0 A + I_2	$I_2 = I - I_1$
3.0 A −2.0 A = I_2	I_2 = 3.0 A - 2.0 A
1.0 A = I_2	I_2 (reading of ammeter A_3)=
I_2 (reading of ammeter A_3) =	1.0 A *Answer 1*
1.0 A *Answer 1*	

Tbl: Elect Parallel Circ

Section 5:

CONSERVATION OF CHARGE IN AN ELECTRIC CIRCUIT

Total number of amperes (A) going toward the black dot (junction) equals total number of amperes (A) going away from the black dot (junction). Look at the diagram. There are 10 A (amperes) going toward the black dot, which means there are 10 amperes of current going into (entering) the dot (junction). There must then be 10 A (amperes) of current leaving the black dot (junction). There is always conservation of charge. In the example above, there is 10 amperes of current (8 A + 2 A) entering the junction (black dot)= 10

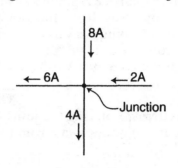

Lines in the diagram are wires in an electric circuit. At the junction, wires bringing current in and out meet.

amperes of current (6 A + 4 A) leaving the junction (black dot). Sum of the currents (amperes A of current) entering the junction (black dot) equals sum of the currents (amperes A of current) going away from the junction.

Question: The diagram below shows currents in a segment of an electric circuit.

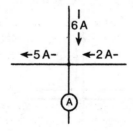

What is the reading of ammeter A?
            (1) 8 A   (2) 2 A   (3) 3A   (4) 13 A
Solution: Look at the diagram in the question.

Given: 6A (amperes) and 2A (amperes) enter the junction (arrows going toward the black dot or junction). 5A (amperes) leave the junction (arrow going away from the black dot or junction).

Find: reading of ammeter A –Ⓐ– (which means find the number of A (amperes) at –Ⓐ–).

6 A and 2 A = 8 A are going toward the black dot (junction). There must be a total of 8 A going away from the dot (junction). You have 5 A going away from the dot (junction); therefore, you need another 3 A going away from the dot (so that the total current going away from the dot = 8 A).

Reading of ammeter A = 3 A.   Answer 3

OR

Total current entering the junction (going toward the dot) equals total current going away from the junction (going away from the dot).

Let x = number of A (amperes) at –Ⓐ– .

Total current (I) going in	=	Total current (I) going out
6 A + 2 A	=	5 A + x A
8 A	=	5 A + x A

Solve for x:

8A − 5A	=	xA
3 A	=	x A
3	=	x

Reading of ammeter A –Ⓐ– (number of A (amperes) at –Ⓐ–) = 3 A.   Answer 3

Question: The diagram shows the current in three of the branches of a direct current electric circuit. The current in the fourth branch, between junction P and point W, must be

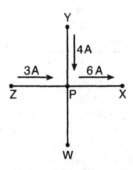

(1) 1 A toward point W   (2) 1 A toward point P
(3) 7 A toward point W   (4) 7 A toward point P

Solution:
Given: 4 A (amperes) and 3 A (amperes) entering the junction (arrows going toward the black dot or junction P).
6 A (amperes) leaving the junction (arrow going away from the black dot or junction P).
Find: Current (which means number of amperes) in the fourth branch between junction P and point W.
4 A and 3 A are going toward the dot (junction P). 6 A are going away from junction P. There must be a total of 7 A going away from the dot (junction P), therefore, there must be another 1 A going away from the dot (junction P).
Choice *1*   1 A going toward point W, which is the same as saying 1 A going away from junction P (see diagram in question).

Question: Which diagram below correctly shows currents traveling near junction P in an electric circuit?

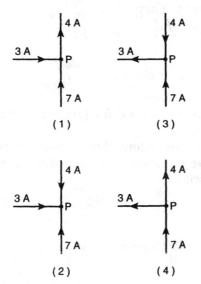

Solution: Look at the diagram. In choice 4, 7 A goes toward the dot which is junction P (arrow goes toward P) and 3 A and 4 A go away from junction P (arrows going away from P). **The total A (amperes) entering the junction (arrows going toward the junction (dot)) must equal the total A (amperes) leaving the junction (dot).**

Wrong choices:
Choice 1: 3 A and 7 A = 10 A entering the dot which is junction P. 4 A leaving junction P. (10 A is not the same as 4 A.)The total A (amperes) entering the junction (arrows going toward the junction (dot)) must equal the total A (amperes) leaving the junction (dot).

Choice 2: 4 A and 3 A and 7 A = 14 A entering the dot which is junction P.
No A or 0 A leaving junction P. (14 A is not the same as 0 A.)The total A (amperes) entering the junction (arrows going toward the junction (dot)) must equal the total A (amperes) leaving the junction (dot).
Choice 3: 7 A and 4 A = 11 A entering the dot which is junction P. 3 A leaving junction P. (11 A is not the same as 3 A.).The total A (amperes) entering the junction (arrows going toward the junction (dot)) must equal the total A (amperes) leaving the junction (dot).

Now Do Homework Questions #113-114, page 141.

POWER

You learned, in the energy chapter,

$$P = \frac{W}{t} = \frac{Fd}{t} = F\bar{v}$$

$$Power = \frac{work}{time} = \frac{force \ x \ distance}{time} = force \ x \ average \ velocity$$

Power is the rate at which work is done (energy is used).

Electrical power (P) equals potential difference (V) times current (I), and is also equal to the equations shown below, which are given on Reference Table: Electricity:

$$P = VI = I^2R = \frac{V^2}{R}$$

$$Power = \frac{potential}{difference} \ x \ current = current^2 \ x \ resistance = \frac{(potential \, difference)^2}{resistance}$$

Power is scalar.
Power (P) is in watts.
Potential difference (V) is in volts (V).
Current is in amperes (A).
Resistance is in ohms (Ω).

Question: A microwave oven operating at 120 volts is used to heat a hot dog. If the oven draws 12.5 amperes of current for 45 seconds, what is the power dissipated by the oven?

(1) 33 W	(2) 1.5×10^3 W
(3) 5.4×10^3 W	(4) 6.8×10^4 W

Solution:
Given: 120 volts (V)
       12.5 amperes (A) of current
       Time = 45 seconds (s).

Tbl: Mechanics (side tab)

Tbl: Electricity (side tab)

Find: power (P).

Look for an equation on Reference Table: Electricity that has power (P), volts (potential difference) (V) and current (I).

Time (t) is an extra fact not needed to solve the question.

Use the equation

$$P = VI$$

I = current
P = electrical power
V = potential difference

V and I are given and you have only one unknown, power (P).
In the equation P = VI, *then substitute for V* (volts, potential difference) 120 V. *Substitute for I* (current) 12.5 A.

P = 120 V (12.5 A) = 1500 VA = 1500 W (watts).

P = 1500 W = 1.5×10^3 W(watts)   Answer 2

Question: If the potential drop (potential difference) across an operating 300-watt floodlight is 120 volts, what is the current through the floodlight?

(1) 0.40 A   2.5 A   (3) 7.5 A   (4) 4.8 A

Solution:

Given: Potential drop (potential difference) = 120 volts (V)
          300 watt (W) floodlight

Find: Current (I)

When you see **watts,** it means **power (P)**.

Look for an equation on Reference Table: Electricity that has power (P), potential drop (potential difference) or volts (V) and current (I).

Use the equation

$$P = VI$$

In the equation P = VI, *then substitute for P* (power) 300 W.
Substitute for V (potential difference, potential drop, or volts) 120 V (volts).

P = VI	Or, rearrange the equation
300 W = 120 VI	$I = \dfrac{P}{V}$
$\dfrac{300 \ W}{120 \ V} = I$	
$I = \dfrac{300 \ W}{120 \ V} = 2.5 \ \dfrac{W}{V} = 2.5 \ A$	$I = \dfrac{300 \ W}{120 \ V} = 2.5 \ \dfrac{W}{V} = 2.5 \ A$
Current (I) = 2.5 A Answer 2	Current (I) = 2.5 A Answer 2

Now Do Homework Questions #115-118, pages 141-142.

Question: Which graph best represents the relationship between the electrical power and the current in a resistor that obeys Ohm's Law?

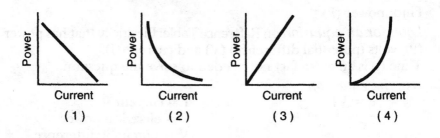

(1)	(2)	(3)	(4)

Solution:

Given: 4 graphs.

Find: Which graph best shows the relationship between electrical power and current in a resistor.

A resistor has a constant resistance (R).

Look for an equation on Reference Table: Electricity that has to do with power (P), current (I) and resistance (R).

Use the equation
$$P = I^2R$$

I = current
P = electrical power
R = resistance

Table: Electricity

In a resistor, resistance (R) is constant. Look at the equation. Since resistance (R) is constant, when I (current) increases, P (power) increases. When there is a square like $P = I^2R$, the line on the graph is curved.

Look at the graphs. Choice 4 is the only correct answer. When current increases, power increases, and the line is curved.

Answer *4*

Wrong choices:

Choices 1 and 2:, When current (I) increases, power (P) decreases.
Choice 3: When there is a square like $P = I^2R$, the line must be curved. Choice 3 is incorrect because the line is a straight line.

Question: A potential drop of 50. volts is measured across a 250-ohm resistor. What is the power developed in the resistor?
    (1) 0.20 W   (2) 5.0 W   (3) 10. W   (4) 50. W

Solution:

Given: potential drop (potential difference) of 50. volts (V)
    250-ohm (Ω) resistor

Find: power (P)

You know a resistor has resistance (R).

Look for an equation on Reference Table: Electricity that has power (P), volts (potential drop or potential difference) (V), and resistance (R).

Use the equation

$$P = \frac{V^2}{R}$$

P = electrical power
R = resistance
V = potential difference

Then Substitute for V 50. V (volts). **Substitute for R** 250 Ω.

$$P = \frac{(50.\ V)^2}{250\ \Omega} = \frac{2500\ V^2}{250\ \Omega} = \frac{10.\ V^2}{\Omega} = 10.\ W\text{(watts)}\text{Answer 3}$$

When you see W (watts), you know it is power.

Question: The heating element on an electric stove dissipates 4.0 x 10^2 watts of power when connected to a 120-volt source. What is the electrical resistance of this heating element?

      (1) 0.028 Ω   (2) 0.60 Ω   (3) 3.3 Ω   (4) 36 Ω

Solution:

Given: power = 4.0 x 10^2 watts (W)
        120-volt (V) source
Find: electrical resistance (R)

Look for an equation on Reference Table: Electricity that has power (P), volts (or potential difference) (V) and resistance (R).

Use the equation

$$P = \frac{V^2}{R}$$

Substitute for P (power) 4.0 x 10^2 W (watts). **Substitute for V** 120 V (volts).

$$4.0 \times 10^2\ W = \frac{(120\ V)^2}{R}$$

Cross multiply

$$4.0 \times 10^2\ WR = (120\ V)^2$$

$$R = \frac{(120\ V)^2}{4.0 \times 10^2\ W} = \frac{14400\ V^2}{4.0 \times 10^2\ W}$$

$$= \frac{36\ V^2}{W} = 36\ \Omega$$

Answer 4

Or, rearrange the equation

$$R = \frac{V^2}{P}$$

$$R = \frac{(120\ V)^2}{4.0 \times 10^2\ W} = \frac{14400\ V^2}{4.0 \times 10^2\ W}$$

$$= \frac{36\ V^2}{W} = 36\ \Omega$$

Answer 4

Note: When you see ohms Ω (example 36 Ω), you know it is resistance (R).

Now Do Homework Questions #119-122, page 142.

Question: As the potential difference across a given resistor is increased, the power expended in moving charge through the resistor

      (1) decreases   (2) increases   (3) remains the same

Table: Electricity

Table: Electricity

Solution: You know a resistor has resistance. *Look for an equation* on Reference Table: Electricity that has power (P), potential difference (V) and resistance (R).

Use the equation

$$P = \frac{V^2}{R}$$

P = electrical power

R = resistance

V = potential difference

The question says a given resistor; a given resistor means resistance (R) is constant.

By looking at the equation above, you see, when R is a constant, if V (potential difference) **increases** (obviously V² increases), then P (power) must also increase. **Answer 2**

Question: Base your answer on the diagram below, which shows two resistors connected in parallel across a 6.0 - volt source.

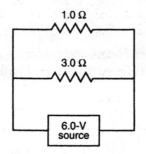

1.0 Ω

3.0 Ω

6.0-V source

Compared to the power dissipated in the 1.0 - ohm resistor, the power dissipated in the 3.0 - ohm resistor is

(1) less   (2) greater   (3) the same

Solution:

Given: circuit diagram

6.0-volt (V) source

Find: Power dissipated (used up) in the 3.0-ohm (3.0 Ω) resistor is less, greater, or the same as the power dissipated in the the 1.0-ohm (1.0 Ω) resistor.

 = resistor (has resistance) given on Reference Table: Circuit Symbols on page reference tables 16.

Look for an equation on Reference Table: Electricity that has power (P), volts (potential difference) (V) and resistance (R).

Use the equation

$$P = \frac{V^2}{R}$$

P = electrical power

R = resistance

V = potential difference

In 1.0 Ω Resistor	In 3.0 Ω Resistor
$P = \dfrac{V^2}{R}$	$P = \dfrac{V^2}{R}$
Then, substitute for V 6.0 V (volts). Substitute for R (resistance)1.0 Ω	Then, substitute for V 6.0 V (volts). Substitute for R 3.0 Ω
$P = \dfrac{(6.0\ V)^2}{1.0\ \Omega} = \dfrac{36\ V^2}{1.0\ \Omega} = 36W$	$P = \dfrac{(6.0\ V)^2}{3.0\ \Omega} = \dfrac{36\ V^2}{3.0\ \Omega} = 12W$

As you can see, the power (P) dissipated in the 3.0 Ω resistor is **12 W**, which is **less** than the power in the 1.0 Ω resistor (36 W).

Answer 1

Question: If the potential difference applied to a fixed resistance is doubled, the power dissipated by that resistance
(1) remains the same   (2) doubles   (3) halves   (4) quadruples
Solution:
Given: fixed resistance (R)
     Potential difference is doubled
Find: power dissipated by the resistance when the potential difference (V) is doubled.

Look for an equation on Reference Table: Electricity that has potential difference (V), resistance (R) and power (P).

Use the equation
$$P = \frac{V^2}{R}$$

OLD	**NEW**
$P = \dfrac{V^2}{R}$	Potential difference (V) is doubled. New potential difference = 2V. In $P = \dfrac{V^2}{R}$, substitute 2V for V. New $P = \dfrac{(2V)^2}{R}$
Old $P = \dfrac{V^2}{R}$ Old power	New $P = \dfrac{4V^2}{R}$ New power

Look at the new P and the old P. New P = 4 times the old P, which means the new P is quadrupled.   Answer 4

Question: The potential difference applied to a circuit element remains constant as the resistance of the element is varied. Which graph best represents the relationship between power (P) and resistance (R) of this element?

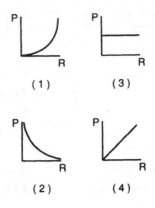

(1)   (3)

(2)   (4)

Solution:

Given: potential difference is constant (which means V is constant); resistance is varied

Find: What graph shows the relationship between power (P) and resistance (R).

Look for an equation on Reference Table: Electricity that has to do with power (P), resistance (R) and potential difference (V).

Use the equation

$$P = \frac{V^2}{R}$$

Potential difference (V) is constant, therefore obviously V^2 is constant.

Look at the equation above. Since V^2 is constant, you see when R (resistance) increases, P (power) decreases.

It might be easier to see as R increases, P decreases, when you look at the equation $P = \frac{V^2}{R}$, then cross multiply, and you get $V^2 = PR$. Since V^2 is a constant, when R (resistance) increases, P (power) decreases. Power is inversely proportional to resistance.

Look at the graphs. Choice 2 is the only graph that shows when R (resistance) increases, P (power) decreases.   Answer 2

Wrong choices: From the equation above, you see as resistance (R) increases, power (P) decreases. Choice 1, choice 3, and choice 4 do not show as resistance (R) increases, power (P) decreases:

Choice 1: As resistance (R) increases, power (P) increases.
Choice 3: As resistance (R) increases, power (P) is constant.
Choice 4: As resistance (R) increases, power (P) increases. Power is directly proportional to resistance.

Now Do Homework Questions #123-125, page 142

WORK

You learned energy is the ability to do work.
Work (electrical energy)W is equal to power (P) times time (t) and is also equal to the equations shown below, which are given on Reference Table: Electricity.

$$W \quad = Pt \quad = VIt \quad = I^2Rt \quad = \frac{V^2t}{R}$$

| work (electrical energy) | = power x time | = potential difference x current x time | = current squared x resistance x time | = potential difference squared x time divided by resistance |

$$W = Pt = VIt = I^2Rt = \frac{V^2t}{R}$$

I= current
P= electrical power
R= resistance
t = time
V= potential difference
W= work (electrical energy)

Table: Electricity

The unit for **work (electrical energy)** is the **joule (J)**. In the equations above, **time** must be in **seconds** (units then cancel out).

Question: A toaster dissipates 1500 watts of power in 90. seconds. The amount of electric energy used by the toaster is approximately
(1) 1.4×10^5 J (2) 1.7×10^1 J (3) 5.2×10^8 J (4) 6.0×10^{-2} J

Solution:
Given: power is 1500 watts (W)
      time is 90. seconds (s)
Find: electrical energy (W)

Look for an equation on Reference Table: Electricity that has power (P), time (t), and electrical energy (W).

Use the equation
$$W = Pt$$

P = electrical power
t = time
W = work (electrical energy)

Then, substitute for P (power) 1500 W (watts). *Substitute for t* (time) 90. s (seconds).
$W = Pt$
$W = 1500W(90.s) = 135000 \text{ Ws} = 135000 \text{ J} = 1.35 \times 10^5$ J (joules)
Electrical energy (W) used by the toaster is about 1.4×10^5 J.
                                                    Answer 1

Table: Electricity

Question: An electric iron operating at 120 volts draws 10. amperes of current. How much heat energy is delivered by the iron in 30. seconds?

(1) 3.0×10^2 J (2) 1.3×10^3 J (3) 3.6×10^3 J (4) 3.6×10^4 J

Solution:

Given: 120 volts (V)

Current 10. amperes (A)

Time 30. seconds (s)

Find: heat energy. Note: All the electrical energy (*W*) changes into heat energy, therefore, find electrical energy (*W*).

Look for an equation that has energy (*W*), volts (potential difference)(V), current (I) and time (t).

Use the equation

$W = VIt$ I = current

t = time

V = potential difference

W = work (electrical energy)

Then substitute for V (potential difference, volts) 120 V. *Substitute for I* (current) 10. A. *Substitute for t* (time) 30. s.

$W = VIt$

$W = 120$ V $(10.$ A$) (30.$ s$) = 36000$ VAs $= 36000$ J $= 3.6 \times 10^4$ J

Answer *4*

When you see joules (J), you know it is work or energy.

Question: An electric dryer consumes 6.0×10^6 joules of energy when operating at 220 volts for 30. minutes (1800 seconds). During operation, the dryer draws a current of approximately

(1) 10. A   (2) 15 A   (3) 20. A   (4) 25 A

Solution:

Given: energy $= 6.0 \times 10^6$ joules (J)

220 volts (V)

30. minutes (1800 seconds)

Find: current (I)

Look for an equation on Reference Table: Electricity that has energy (*W*), volts (potential difference) (V), time (t), and current (I).

Use the equation

$W = VIt$ I = current

t = time

V = potential difference

W = work (electrical energy)

Then substitute for V (volts, potential difference) 220 V. *Substitute for t* (time) 1800 s. *Substitute for energy* (*W*) 6.0×10^6 J (joules).

$$W = V \ I \ t$$
$$6.0 \times 10^6 \, J = (220 \, V)I(1800 \, s)$$
$$I = \frac{6.0 \times 10^6 \, J}{(220 \, V)(1800 \, s)} = 15 \, A$$
Current (I) = 15 A (amperes)

Answer 2

Or, rearrange the equation
$$I = \frac{W}{Vt}$$
$$I = \frac{6.0 \times 10^6 \, J}{(220 \, V)(1800 \, s)} = 15 \, A$$
Current (I) = 15 A (amperes)

Answer 2

<u>Work (electrical energy) is in joules (J); time must be in seconds (s).</u>

Question: An operating electric heater draws a current of 10. amperes and has a resistance of 12 ohms. How much energy does the heater use in 60. seconds?

    (1) 120 J   (2) 1200 J   (3) 7200 J   (4) 72000 J

Solution:
Given: current = 10. amperes (A)
       Resistance = 12 ohms (Ω)
       Time = 60. seconds (s)
Find: energy (W)

Look for an equation on Reference Table: Electricity that has that has electrical energy (W), current (I), resistance (R), and time (t).

Use the equation
        $W = I^2Rt$
                  I = current
                  R = resistance
                  t = time
                  W = work (electrical energy)

Then substitute for I 10. A (amperes). *Substitute for R* 12 Ω (ohms). *Substitute for t* 60. s (seconds).

$W = I^2Rt$
$W = (10. \, A)^2(12 \, \Omega)(60. \, s)$
$W = 7200 \, A^2\Omega s = 7200 \, J$ Energy (W) = 7200 J   Answer 3

Question: The diagram below represents an electric circuit.

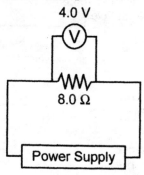

4.0 V

8.0 Ω

Power Supply

The total amount of energy delivered to the resistor in 10. seconds is
(1) 3.2 J   (2) 5.0 J   (3) 20. J   (4) 320 J

Solution:

Given: 4.0 V (volts) in diagram

     ⋀⋀⋎ (resistor) of 8.0 Ω (ohms) in diagram

     10. seconds (s)

Find: energy (W)

⋀⋀⋎ = resistor (has resistance), given on Reference Table: Circuit Symbols. You know Ω (example 8.0 Ω) is resistance (R).

Look for an equation on Reference Table: Electricity that has electrical energy (W), volts (potential difference) (V), resistance (R) and time (t).

Use the equation

$$W = \frac{V^2 t}{R}$$

     R = resistance

     t = time

     V = potential difference

     W = work (electrical energy)

Then substitute for V 4.0 V(volts). *Substitute for t* (time) 10. s. *Substitute for R* (resistance) 8.0 Ω.

$$W = \frac{(4.0 \ V)^2 (10. \ s)}{8.0 \ \Omega} = \frac{(16 \ V^2)(10. \ s)}{8.0 \ \Omega} = \frac{160 \ V^2 s}{8.0 \ \Omega} = \frac{20. \ V^2 s}{\Omega} = 20. \ J$$

Energy (W) = 20. J   Answer 3

Note: Work and energy are in joules (J).

Now Do Homework Questions #126-137, pages 142-143, and #169, page 147.

Section 6:

MAGNETISM

A magnet attracts iron and has two ends, north pole and south pole.

The electrons of the atoms of a magnet all spin in one direction and this produces a magnetic force.

A magnetic field is the region around the magnet that has the magnetic force.

Take a magnet. Put a piece of paper on top of the magnet. Put iron filings on the paper. The iron filings

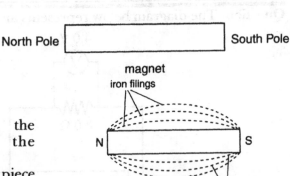

North Pole   South Pole

magnet

iron filings

N   S

iron filings

Figure 1: Iron Filings Show Magnetic Field

Table: Electricity

on the paper show (line up along) the magnetic field. The iron filings arrange themselves in curved lines around the magnet (magnetic field lines, also called flux lines or lines of force), which show where the magnetic field is. (See Figure 1.)

The magnetic field lines (lines of force, lines of flux) can also be shown by drawing curved lines (with arrows running from north pole to south pole) (see Figure 2).

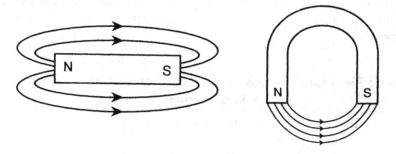

Figure 2: Magnetic Field Lines (Flux Lines, Lines of Force)

A magnetic field is strongest at the poles (north pole and south pole). Look at the diagrams above. At the north and south poles, the magnetic field lines are closest together, therefore the magnetic field is strongest. When you draw a magnetic field, draw the curved lines from north pole to south pole and closest together at the poles.

Question: A student sprinkled iron filings around a bar magnet and observed that the filings formed the pattern shown below.

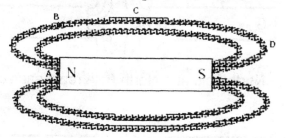

The magnetic field is strongest at point
        (1) A   (2) B   (3) C   (4) D

Solution: The magnetic field is strongest where the lines (magnetic field lines, also called magnetic flux lines or magnetic lines of force) are closest together; therefore, the magnetic field is strongest at A because the lines are closest together.   Answer *1*

Look at the diagram on the next page. Where there are two magnets, the **north pole** of one magnet **attracts** the **south pole** of the other magnet (unlike poles, north and south poles, attract each other). The magnetic field lines or lines of force are closest together directly between the north pole and south pole (see middle three lines in the diagram) and the magnetic field is strongest directly between the north pole and south pole.

When there are two magnets (see diagram below), the **north pole** of one magnet **repels** (goes away from) the **north pole** of the other magnet, or the **south pole** of one magnet **repels** (goes away from) the **south pole** of the other magnet (like poles, north and north or south and south, repel each other).

Magnetic Field Lines (Lines of Magnetic Force or Flux Lines) Between Two Magnets

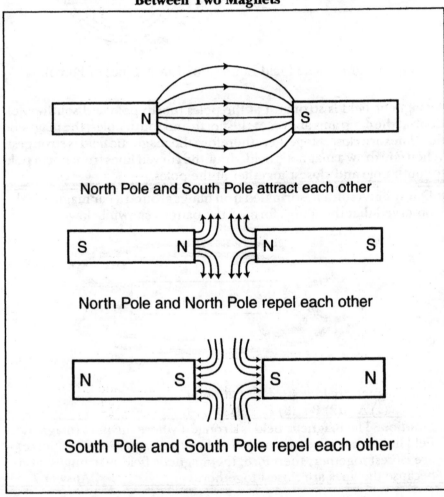

North Pole and South Pole attract each other

North Pole and North Pole repel each other

South Pole and South Pole repel each other

Magnetic field lines (magnetic flux lines or magnetic lines of force) go **from north pole to south pole** and **never cross.**

Question: Which diagram best represents magnetic flux lines around a bar magnet?

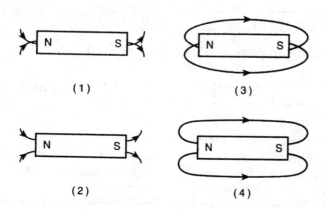

(1)   (3)

(2)   (4)

Solution: Magnetic field lines (magnetic flux lines) go **from north pole to south pole** and **do not cross.** Arrows showing magnetic field lines go from north pole to south pole.   **Answer 4**
Wrong choices:

Choice 1: Magnetic field lines should not cross. Arrows should go away from the north pole and go toward the south pole. In choice 1, field lines cross and arrows go in the wrong direction.

Choice 2:
A r r o w s
should go
away from
the north
pole and go
toward the
south pole,

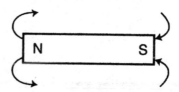

as shown at the right. In choice 2, the arrows go in the wrong direction.

Choice 3: Magnetic field lines (magnetic flux lines) should not cross. In choice 3, the magnetic field lines (magnetic flux lines) cross.

Question: A student is given two pieces of iron and told to determine if one or both of the pieces are magnets. *First,* the student touches an end of one piece to one end of the other. The two pieces of iron attract. *Next,* the student reverses one of the pieces and again touches the ends together. The two pieces attract again. What does the student definitely know about the initial magnetic properties of the two pieces of iron?

Solution: Since the two pieces of iron attract each other, the student definitely knows that at least one is a magnet. A magnet attracts a piece of iron (that is not a magnet) or can attract a magnet.
Or, you can add the following to the answer above:
If the second piece was also a **magnet** (both pieces were magnets):

| S | N | | S | N | 2 pieces attract each other |

And when one piece (magnet) was reversed:

| S | N | | N | S | The pieces (magnets) would repel each other |

In this example, when one piece was reversed, the pieces were still attracted to each other, therefore you know the second piece cannot be a magnet (see second drawing above).

Compass: A compass is a magnet. The north pole of the compass is attracted to (points to) the south pole of a magnet.
The Earth has its own magnet (Earth's magnet). The north pole of a compass is attracted to the south pole of Earth's magnet. Strange as it may seem, the south pole of the Earth's magnet is near the geographic North Pole (the North Pole on a map).

North Pole

South Pole

Compass

Question: The diagram below represents the magnetic field near point P.
If a compass is placed at point P in the same plane as the magnetic field, which arrow represents the direction the north end of the compass needle will point?

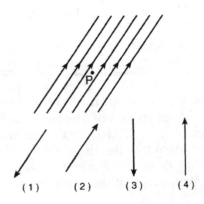

Solution:
Given: A compass is placed on point P.
Find: Which arrow shows the direction the compass needle (north pole of the compass) will point.

Magnetic lines of force (magnetic field lines) go from north pole to south pole. Arrows showing the magnetic field always point toward the south pole (see figure at right

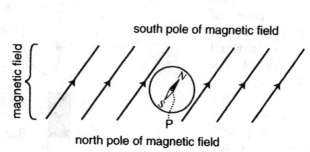

and figure in the question). The compass is placed at point P. The north pole of the compass will point to the south pole of the magnetic field. The compass needle will point like the arrow in

choice 2, ↗ .

Answer 2

Question: The diagram below shows a bar magnet.

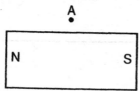

Which arrow best represents the direction of the needle of a compass placed at point A?

(1) ↑   (2) ↓   (3) →   (4) ←

Solution:
Given: A compass is placed on point A.
Find: Which arrow shows the direction the compass needle (north pole of the compass) will point.

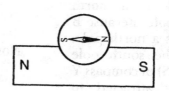

The **north pole** of a **compass** is **attracted to** (points to) the **south pole** of a **magnet**. The compass needle, which is the north pole of the compass, follows the magnetic field lines, which go from the north pole of the magnet to the south pole of the magnet (see page 3:115, Figure 2). The compass needle will point like this arrow →.

Answer 3

Question: The diagram below shows two compasses located near the ends of a bar magnet. The north pole of compass X points toward end A of the magnet.

Copy the diagram on separate paper. On your drawing, draw the correct orientation of the needle of compass Y and label its polarity.

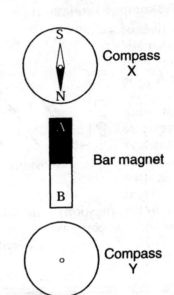

Compass X

Bar magnet

B

Compass Y

Solution: The north pole (N) of a compass is attracted to the south pole of a bar magnet, therefore, A must be a south pole. If A is a south pole, then **B** is a **north pole**. Because B is a north pole, the south pole (S) of compass Y is attracted to (points to) B.

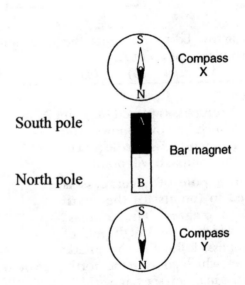

Compass X

South pole

North pole

Bar magnet

B

Compass Y

MAGNETIC FIELD STRENGTH

You learned the closer together the magnetic field lines or lines of flux, the stronger is the magnetic field
Magnetic field strength is determined by the number of lines of flux per unit area (magnetic flux density).

Question: The diagram below represents lines of magnetic flux within a region of space.

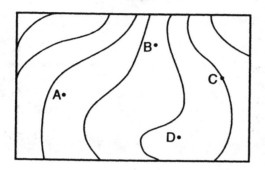

The magnetic field strength is greatest at point
     (1) A   (2) B   (3) C   (4) D

Solution: Magnetic field strength is greatest (magnetic field is strongest) where the flux lines are closest together. At point B the lines are closest together, therefore the magnetic field strength is greatest at point B.   Answer 2

Question: Two bar magnets of equal strength are positioned as shown.`

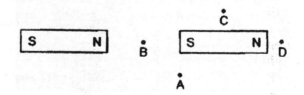

At which point is the magnetic flux density due to the two magnets greatest?
     (1) A   (2) B   (3) C   (4) D

Solution: Point B is between the north pole and the south pole (see diagram above). Magnetic flux density (magnetic field strength) is greatest between the north pole and south pole, where the lines are closest together. Since point B is between the poles, where the lines are closest together, it has maximum magnetic flux density.

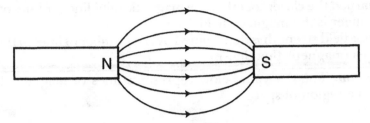

North Pole and South Pole attract each other

Answer 2

The number of lines of flux is measured in webers. Magnetic field strength (magnetic flux density) is measured in webers/m^2, which is called teslas. Magnetic field strength is a vector quantity.

Now Do Homework Questions #143-146, pages 144-145.

ELECTROMAGNETIC INDUCTION

A wire cuts across magnetic field lines. Let's compare the magnetic field lines to a carrot on a plate or cutting board. A knife chops the carrot like the wire or conductor cuts across the magnetic field lines. When a conductor or **wire cuts across magnetic field lines**, (electromagnetic forces cause charges in the wire or conductor to move from one end of the wire to the other end), one end of the wire becomes more negative and one end of the wire is more positive, **producing a potential difference.** See figure below.

Magnetic field goes from left to right

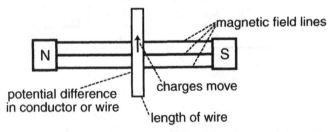

Figure 1

Electromagnetic induction is moving a wire across a magnetic field, producing a potential difference, also called induced potential difference. The **greatest potential difference** is made (see Figure 1) when the **wire** is moved **perpendicular** both **to** the **magnetic field** and to the length of the wire. This means, when the **magnetic field** is **from left to right** (or right to left), the **wire must go into or out of the page**.

But if the wire is moved parallel to the magnetic field, there is no potential difference. In the picture below, magnetic field is from left to right; if the wire moves parallel to the magnetic field, moving from left to right, there would be no potential difference.

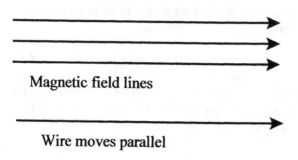

Magnetic field lines

Wire moves parallel

Question: The diagram below represents a wire conductor, RS, positioned perpendicular to a uniform magnetic field directed (that goes) into the page.

Magnetic Field Goes into the Page

```
        R
 x  x  ⌈⌐⌉  x  x   Magnetic
 x  x  |  |  x  x   field
 x  x  |  |  x  x   directed
 x  x  ⌊⌐⌋  x  x   into the page
        S
```

Figure 2

Describe the direction in which the wire could be moved to produce the maximum potential difference across its ends, R and S.

Solution: The magnetic field in this example is different than in the previous illustration. The **magnetic field goes into the page**. To get the **maximum potential difference**, the **wire** must move **perpendicular** to the **magnetic field** and perpendicular to the length of the wire. Therefore, the **wire** must **move** from **left to right** or from **right to left.**

In short: To get the maximum potential difference, if the magnetic field goes from left to right, the wire cuts across the field and goes into or out of the page (shown in Figure 1, page 3:122). If the magnetic field goes into the page, the wire cuts across and goes from left to right (shown in Figure 2 on the previous page).

The **potential difference increases** when a **wire** or conductor **moves faster** (cuts across a magnetic field faster) or when the wire moves across more field lines in a given area, which means the field lines are closer together (stronger magnetic field).

You learned, when a wire cuts across magnetic field lines, the wire has a potential difference (like a battery). When additional wires are attached to the ends of the wire or conductor, a circuit is formed. The potential difference in the wire or conductor causes a current to flow, which means it produces electricity which can light a bulb, etc. See figure below.

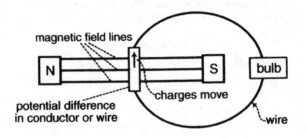

Question: The diagram on the next page shows a wire moving to the right at speed v through a uniform magnetic field that is directed into the page. As the speed of the wire is increased, the induced potential difference will

      (1) decrease   (2) increase   (3) remain the same

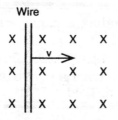

Wire

Magnetic field directed into page

Solution: As the speed of the wire increases, the induced potential difference increases. **Answer 2**

Generator: A generator produces electricity. Look at the diagram on the previous page, which is similar to how a generator works. In a generator, steam or falling water hitting a turbine, which is a device with blades (like a fan) that move (all have mechanical or moving energy), turns a coil of wire in a magnetic field, producing electricity (electrical energy). In the generator, mechanical (moving) energy from the steam or falling water is changed (converted) into electrical energy (electricity).

Now Do Homework Question #147, page 145

ELECTROMAGNETS

Electric current (charges) going through (moving through) a wire creates a magnetic field around the wire. If the wire is made into a coil and a piece of iron is placed inside the coil, the iron becomes a strong magnet, but only when the current goes through (moves through) the wire. In short, an electromagnet is an iron core (piece of iron) inside a coil of wire, with a current (charges) moving through the wire.

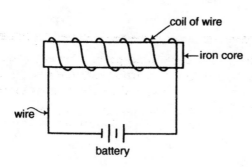

Question: In order to produce a magnetic field, an electric charge must be

    (1) stationary   (2) moving   (3) positive   (4) negative

Solution: Electric current (charges) **moving** through a wire in a circuit produces a magnetic field.   Answer 2

When you answer Regents questions on **ELECTRICITY,** use **Reference Table Electricity, Reference Table List of Physical Constants, Reference Table Resistivities, Reference Table Electricity Series Circuits, Reference Table Electricity Parallel Circuits, and Reference Table Circuit Symbols.**

1 Compared to the charge on a proton, the charge on an electron has the
(1) opposite sign and a smaller magnitude
(2) opposite sign and the same magnitude
(3) same sign and a smaller magnitude
(4) same sign and the same magnitude
Hint: Magnitude is number or amount. Compare number of elementary charges or number of coulombs in a proton and in an electron .

2 A glass rod becomes positively charged when it is rubbed with silk. This net positive charge accumulates because the glass rod
(1) gains electrons   (3) loses electrons
(2) gains protons   (4) loses protons

3 A sphere has a net excess charge of -4.8×10^{-19} coulomb. The sphere must have an excess of
(1) 1 electron   (3) 3 electrons
(2) 1 proton   (4) 3 protons

4A What is the net static electric charge on a metal sphere having an excess of +3 elementary charges?
(1) 1.6×10^{-19} C   (3) 3.0×10^{0} C
(2) 4.8×10^{-19} C   (4) 4.8×10^{19} C

4B What is the net electrical charge on a magnesium ion that is formed when a neutral magnesium atom loses two electrons?
(1) $+1.6 \times 10^{-19}$ C   (3) -3.2×10^{-19} C
(2) $+3.2 \times 10^{-19}$ C   (4) $+1.6 \times 10^{-19}$ C

5 The charge-to-mass ratio of an electron is
(1) 5.69×10^{-12} C/kg   (3) 1.76×10^{11} C/kg
(2) 1.76×10^{-11} C/kg   (4) 5.69×10^{12} C/kg

6 An inflated balloon which has been rubbed against a person's hair is touched to a neutral wall and remains attracted to it. Which diagram best represents the charge distribution on the balloon and wall?

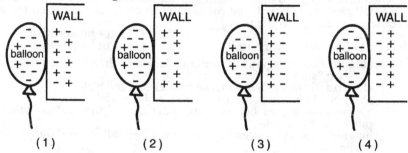

      (1)   **(2)**   **(3)**   **(4)**

7 The diagram below shows the arrangement of three charged hollow metal spheres, *A*, *B*, and *C*, the arrows indicate the direction of the electric forces acting between the spheres. At least two of the spheres are positively charged.
Which sphere, if any, could be negatively charged?
(1) sphere *A*   (3) sphere *C*
(2) sphere *B*   (4) no sphere

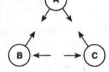

8 Which part of an atom is most likely to be transferred as a body acquires a static electric charge?
(1) proton   (2) neutron   (3) electron   (4) positron

9 An object with +10 elementary charges is grounded and becomes neutral. What is the best explanation for this occurrence?
(1) The object gained 10 electrons from the ground.
(2) The object lost 10 electrons to the ground
(3) The object gained 10 protons from the ground.
(4) The object lost 10 protons to the ground.
Hint: Neutral means zero charge.

10 A positively charged rod is held near the knob of a neutral electroscope. Which diagram best represents the distribution of charge in the electroscope?

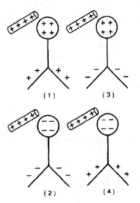

11 If a positively charged rod is brought near the knob of a positively charged electroscope, the leaves of the electroscope will
(1) converge, only
(2) diverge, only
(3) first diverge, then converge
(4) first converge, then diverge

12 A negatively charged plastic comb is brought close to, but does not touch, a small piece of paper. If the comb and the paper are attracted to each other, the charge on the paper
(1) may be negative or neutral
(2) may be positive or neutral
(3) must be negative
(4) must be positive

13 A balloon is rubbed against a student's hair and then touched to a wall. The balloon "sticks" to the wall due to
(1) electrostatic forces between the particles of the balloon
(2) magnetic forces between the particles of the wall
(3) electrostatic forces between the particles of the balloon and the particles of the wall
(4) magnetic forces between the particles of the balloon and the particles of the wall

14 Two metal spheres having charges of $+4.0 \times 10^{-6}$ coulomb and $+2.0 \times 10^{-5}$ coulomb, respectively, are brought into contact and then separated. After separation, the charge on each sphere is
(1) 8.0×10^{-11} C
(2) 8.0×10^{-6} C
(3) 2.1×10^{-6} C
(4) 1.2×10^{-5} C

15 Two identical spheres carry charges of +0.6 coulomb and -0.2 coulomb, respectively. If these spheres touch, the resulting charge on the first sphere will be
(1) +0.8 C
(2) +0.2 C
(3) -0.3C
(4) +0.4 C

16 Sphere A has a charge of $+2 \times 10^{-6}$ coulomb and is brought into contact with a similar sphere, B, which has charge of -4×10^{-6} coulomb. After it is separated from sphere B, sphere A will have a charge of
(1) -1×10^{-6} C
(2) -2×10^{-6} C
(3) $+2 \times 10^{-6}$ C
(4) $+6 \times 10^{-6}$ C

17 The diagram at right shows four charged metal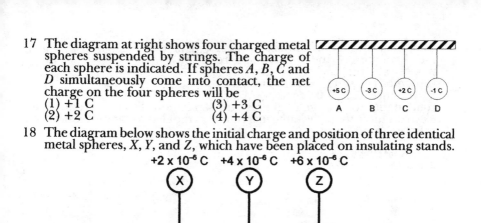
spheres suspended by strings. The charge of
each sphere is indicated. If spheres A, B, C and
D simultaneously come into contact, the net
charge on the four spheres will be
(1) +1 C   (3) +3 C
(2) +2 C   (4) +4 C

18 The diagram below shows the initial charge and position of three identical
metal spheres, X, Y, and Z, which have been placed on insulating stands.

$$+2 \times 10^{-6} \text{ C} \quad +4 \times 10^{-6} \text{ C} \quad +6 \times 10^{-6} \text{ C}$$

All three spheres are simultaneously brought into contact with each other
and then returned to their original positions. Which statement best
describes the charge of the spheres after this procedure is completed?
(1) All the spheres are neutral
(2) Each sphere has a net charge of $+4 \times 10^{-6}$ coulomb.
(3) Each sphere retains the same charge that it had originally
(4) Sphere Y has a greater charge than spheres X or Z.
Hint: Realize the number of objects is three (three spheres).

19 Three identical metal spheres are mounted on insulating stands. Initially,
sphere A has a net charge of q and spheres B and C are uncharged.
Sphere A is touched to sphere B and removed. then sphere A is touched
to sphere C and removed. What is the final charge on sphere A?

(1) q (2) $\dfrac{q}{2}$ (3) $\dfrac{q}{3}$ (4) $\dfrac{q}{4}$

20 A point charge of $+3.0 \times 10^{-7}$ coulomb is placed 2.0×10^{-2} meter from a
second point charge of $+4.0 \times 10^{-7}$ coulomb. then magnitude of the
electrostatic force between the charges is
(1) 2.7 N   (3) 3.0×10^{-10} N
(2) 5.4×10^{-2} N   (4) 6.0×10^{-12} N

21 The diagram at right shows two metal spheres $+1.0 \times 10^{-6}$ C $+3.0 \times 10^{-6}$ C
charged to $+1.0 \times 10^{-6}$ coulomb and $+3.0 \times$
10^{-6} coulomb, respectively, on insulating stands
separated by a distance of 0.10 meter.
    The spheres are touched together and then
returned to their original positions. As a result,
the magnitude of the electrostatic force between
the spheres changes from 2.7 N to
(1) 1.4 N   (3) 3.6 N
(2) 1.8 N   (4) 14 N

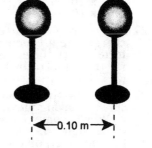

$\leftarrow$0.10 m$\rightarrow$

22 An electron is located 1.0 meter
from a $+2.0$ coulomb charge, as
shown in the diagram at right.
The electrostatic force acting on
the electron is directed toward
point
(1) A (3) C
(2) B (4) D

$\bullet$ A

+2.0 C   D$\bullet$ (e$^-$) $\bullet$ B

$\longmapsto$ ——— 1.0 m ——— $\dashv$

$\bullet$ C

23 The diagram at right shows two small metal spheres, *A* and *B*. Each sphere possesses a net charge of 4.0 x 10^{-6} coulomb. The spheres are separated by a distance of 1.0 meter. Which

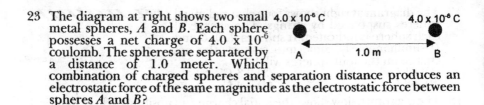

combination of charged spheres and separation distance produces an electrostatic force of the same magnitude as the electrostatic force between spheres *A* and *B*?

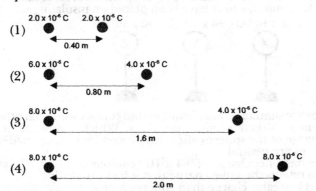

(1)
(2)
(3)
(4)

24 If the charge on each of two small spheres a fixed distance apart is doubled, the force of attraction between the spheres will be
(1) quartered (2) doubled (3) halved (4) quadrupled

25 The diagram at right represents two charges, q_1 and q_2, separated by distance *d*. Which change would produce the greatest increase in the electrical force between the two charges?
(1) doubling charge q_1, only
(2) doubling *d*, only
(3) doubling *d* and charge q_1, only
(4) doubling *d* and charges q_1 and q_2

26 Two charges that are 2 meters apart repel each other with a force of 2 x 10^{-5} newton. If the distance between the charges is decreased to 1 meter, the force of repulsion will be:
(1) 1 x 10^{-5} N   (3) 8 x 10^{-5} N
(2) 5 x 10^{-6} N   (4) 4 x 10^{-5} N

27 The electrostatic force between two positive point charges is *F* when the charges are 0.1 meter apart. When these point charges are placed 0.05 meter apart, the electrostatic force between them is
(1) 4F, and attracting   (3) 4F, and repelling
(2) F/4, and attracting   (4) F/4, and repelling

28 A repulsive electrostatic force of magnitude *F* exists between two metal spheres having identical charge *q*. The distance between their centers is *r*. Which combination of changes would produce *no* change in the electrostatic force between the spheres?
(1) doubling *q* on one sphere while doubling *r*
(2) doubling *q* on both spheres while doubling *r*
(3) doubling *q* on one sphere while halving *r*
(4) doubling *q* on both spheres while halving *r*

29 An electrostatic force of magnitude *F* exists between two metal spheres having identical charge *q*. The distance between their centers is *r*. Which combination of changes would produce *no* change in the electrostatic force between the spheres?
(1) doubling *q* on one sphere while doubling *r*
(2) doubling *q* on both spheres while doubling *r*
(3) doubling *q* on one sphere while halving *r*
(4) doubling *q* on both spheres while halving *r*

30 Two similar metal spheres possessing +1.0 coulomb of charge and –1.0 coulomb of charge, respectively, are brought toward each other. Which graph best represents the relationship between the magnitude of the electric force between the spheres and the distance between them?

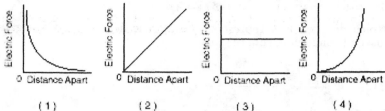

(1)   (2)   (3)   (4)

Hint: Magnitude means number, disregarding plus or minus.

31 An electrostatic force of 20. newtons is exerted on a charge of 8.0×10^{-2} coulomb at point P in an electric field. The magnitude of the electric field intensity at P is
(1) 4.0×10^{-3} N/C   (3) 20. N/C
(2) 1.6 N/C   (4) 2.5×10^2 N/C

32 What is the magnitude of the electrostatic force acting on an electron located in an electric field having a strength of 5.0×10^3 newtons per coulomb?
(1) 3.1×10^{22} N   (3) 8.0×10^{-16} N
(2) 5.0×10^3 N   (4) 3.2×10^{-23} N

33 What is the magnitude of the electric force acting on an electron located in an electric field with an intensity of 5.0×10^3 newtons per coulomb?
(1) 3.2×10^{-23} N   (3) 5.0×10^3 N
(2) 8.0×10^{-16} N   (4) 3.2×10^{22} N

34 What is the magnitude of the electric field intensity at a point in the field where an electron experiences a 1.0-newton force?
(1) 1.0 N/C   (3) 6.3×10^{18} N/C
(2) 1.0×10^{-19} N/C   (4) 9.1×10^{-31} N/C

35 Which graph best represents the relationship between the magnitude of the electric field strength, E, around a point charge and the distance, r, from the point charge?

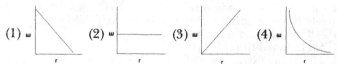

(1)   (2)   (3)   (4)

36 Which diagram best represents the electric field of a point charge?

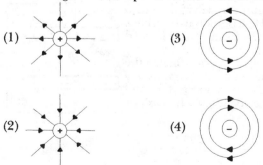

(1)   (3)

(2)   (4)

37 In the diagram at right, *A* is a point near a positively charged sphere. Which vector best represents the direction of the electric field at point *A*?

(1) →   (2) ↑   (3) ←   (4) ↓

38 Which diagram best represents the electric field around a negatively charged conducting sphere?

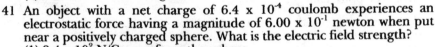

(1)   (3)

(2)   (4)

39 The diagram at right represents the electric field lines in the vicinity of two isolated electrical charges, *A* and *B*. Which statement identifies the charges of *A* and *B*?
(1) *A* is negative and *B* is positive.
(2) *A* is positive and *B* is negative.
(3) *A* and *B* are both positive.
(4) *A* and *B* are both negative.

40 The diagram at right shows the electric field in the vicinity of two charged conducting spheres, *A* and *B*. What is the static electric charge on each of the conducting spheres?
(1) *A* is negative and *B* is positive.
(2) *A* is positive and *B* is negative.
(3) Both *A* and *B* are positive.
(4) Both *A* and *B* are negative.

41 An object with a net charge of 6.4×10^{-4} coulomb experiences an electrostatic force having a magnitude of 6.00×10^{-1} newton when put near a positively charged sphere. What is the electric field strength?
(1) 9.4×10^{2} N/C away from the sphere
(2) 9.4×10^{2} N/C toward the sphere
(3) 9.2×10^{-6} N/C away fSrom the sphere
(4) 9.2×10^{-6} N/C toward the sphere

42 Two parallel plates separated by a distance of 2.0×10^{-2} meter are charged to a potential difference of 1.0×10^{2} volts. Points *A*, *B*, and *C* are located in the region between the plates.

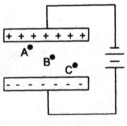

    Copy the diagram on separate paper. Sketch the electric field lines between the oppositely charged parallel plates through points *A*, *B*, and *C*. [Draw lines with arrowheads in the proper direction.]

43 The electric field between the plates in question 42 will cause an alpha particle, starting from rest at point B, to
(1) accelerate toward the positive plate
(2) accelerate toward the negative plate
(3) move at constant speed toward the positive plate
(4) move at constant speed toward the negative plate

44 The diagram at the right represents a source of potential difference connected to two large, parallel metal plates separated by a distance of 3.0×10^{-3} meter.
Which statement best describes the electric field strength between the plates?
(1) It is a maximum at point X.
(2) The strength is equal at points X, Y, and Z.
(3) It is a maximum at point Y.
(4) It is zero at point Z.

45 A moving electron is deflected by two oppositely charged parallel plates, as shown in the diagram at right.
The electric field between the plates is directed from
(1) W to X   (2) X to W   (3) Y to Z   (4) Z to Y

46 If 20. joules of work is done in transferring 5.0 coulombs of charge between two points, the potential difference between these two points is
(1) 100 V   (2) 50. V   (3) 0.25 V   (4) 4.0 V

47 Moving +2.0 coulombs of charge from infinity to point P in an electric field requires 8.0 joules of work. What is the electric potential at point P?
(1) 0.25 V   (2) 8.0 V   (3) 16 V   (4) 4.0 V

48 If 15 joules of work is required to move 3.0 coulombs of charge between two points, the potential difference between these two points is
(1) 45 V   (2) 15 V   (3) 3.0 V   (4) 5.0 V

49 If 1.0 joule of work is required to move a charge of 1.0 coulomb between two points in an electric field, the potential difference between these two points is
(1) 1.0 V   (2) 1.6×10^{-19} V   (3) 9.0×10^{9} V   (4) 6.3×10^{18} V

50 Moving 2.5×10^{-6} coulomb of charge from point A to point B in an electric field requires 6.3×10^{-4} joule of work. The potential difference between points A and B is approximately
(1) 1.6×10^{-9} V   (3) 2.5×10^{2} V
(2) 4.0×10^{-3} V   (4) 1.0×10^{14} V

51 Moving a point charge of 3.2×10^{-19} coulomb between points A and B in an electric field requires 4.8×10^{-19} joule of energy. What is the potential difference between these two points?
(1) 0.67 V   (2) 2.0 V   (3) 3.0 V   (4) 1.5 V

52 In an electric field, 0.90 joule of work is required to bring 0.45 coulomb of charge from point A to point B. What is the electric potential difference

between points A and B?
(1) 5.0 V   (2) 2.0 V   (3) 0.50 V   (4) 0.41 V

53 The energy required to move one elementary charge through a potential difference of 5.0 volts is
(1) 8.0 J   (2) 5.0 J   (3) 8.0×10^{-19} J   (4) 1.6×10^{-19} J

54 How much energy is needed to move one electron through a potential difference of 1.0×10^2 volts?
(1) 1.0 J
(2) 1.0×10^2 J
(3) 1.6×10^{-19} J
(4) 1.6×10^{-17} J

55 If a 1.5-volt cell is to be completely recharged, each electron must be supplied with a minimum energy of
(1) 1.5 eV   (2) 1.5 J   (3) 9.5×10^{18} eV   (4) 9.5×10^{18} J

56 The diagram at right shows proton P located at point A near a positively charged sphere. If 6.4 x 10^{-19} joule of work is required to move the proton from point A to point B, the potential difference between A and B is
(1) 6.4×10^{-19} V
(2) 4.0×10^{-19} V
(3) 6.4 V
(4) 4.0 V

57 In the diagram, proton P located at point A near a positively charged sphere.
If 6.4×10^{-19} joule of work is required to move the proton from point A to point B, the potential difference between A and B is
(1) 6.4×10^{-19} V
(2) 4.0×10^{-19} V
(3) 6.4 V
(4) 4.0 V

58 How much energy is needed to move one electron through a potential difference of 2.0×10^2 volts?
(1) 2.0 J   (2) 2.0×10^2 J   (3) 3.2×10^{-10} J   (4) 3.2×10^{-17} J

59 An alpha particle with a charge of 2 elementary charges is accelerated by a potential difference of 1.0×10^6 volts. The energy acquired by the particle is
(1) 0.50×10^6 eV
(2) 2.0×10^6 eV
(3) 1.6×10^{-19} eV
(4) 3.2×10^{-13} eV

60 A lightning bolt transfers 6.0 coulombs of charge from a cloud to the ground in 2.0×10^{-3} second. What is the average current during this event?
(1) 1.2×10^{-2} A
(2) 3.0×10^2 A
(3) 3.0×10^3 A
(4) 1.2×10^4 A

61 During a thunderstorm, a lightning strike transfers 12 coulombs of charge in 2.0×10^{-3} second. What is the average current produced in this strike?
(1) 1.7×10^{-4} A
(2) 2.4×10^{-2} A
(3) 6.0×10^3 A
(4) 9.6×10^3 A

62 A charge of 5.0 coulombs moves through a circuit in 0.50 second. The current in the circuit is
(1) 2.5 A   (2) 5.0 A   (3) 7.0 A   (4) 10. A

63 In a lightning strike, a charge of 18 coulombs is transferred between a cloud and the ground in 2.0×10^{-2} seconds at a potential difference of 1.5 $\times 10^6$ volts. What is the average current produced by this strike:
(1) 3.6×10^{-1} A
(2) 9.0×10^2 A
(3) 3.0×10^4 A
(4) 7.5×10^7 A

64A If 10 coulombs of charge passes a given point in a conductor every 2 seconds, the current at that point is

(1) 0.2 A   (2) 5 A   (3) 10 A   (4) 20 A

64B If 10. coulombs of charge are transferred through an electric circuit in 5.0 seconds, then the current through the circuit is
(1) 0.50 A   (2) 2.0 A   (3) 15 A   (4) 50. A

65 The diagram shows two resistors, R_1 and R_2, connected in parallel in a circuit having a 120-volt power source. Resistor R_1 develops 150 watts and resistor R_2 develops an unknown power. Ammeter A in the circuit reads 0.50 ampere.
The amount of charge passing through resistor R_2 in 60. seconds is

(1) 1.25 C   (3) 25 C
(2) 30. C   (4) 0.50 C
Hint: What does the question ask?
Extra facts are given.

66 A current of 3.0 amperes is flowing in a circuit. How much charge passes a given point in the circuit in 30. seconds?
(1) 0.10 C   (2) 10. C   (3) 33 C   (4) 90. C
Hint: Electric circuit is a path where electrons flow.

67 A wire carries a current of 6.0 amperes. How much charge passes a point in the wire in 120 seconds?
(1) 6.0 C   (2) 20. C   (3) 360 C   (4) 720 C

68 A charge of 20 coulombs was transferred through a wire. The current was 1.0×10^3 amperes. The time it took the current to travel was
(1) 0.2 second   (3) 0.02 seconds
(2) 20 seconds   (4) 10 seconds

69 A complete circuit is left on for several minutes, causing the connecting copper wire to become hot. As the temperature of the wire increases, the electrical resistance of the wire
(1) decreases
(2) increases
(3) remains the same

70 In a simple electric circuit, a 110-volt electric heater draws 2.0 amperes of current. The resistance of the heater is
(1) 0.018 Ω   (2) 28 Ω   (3) 55 Ω   (4) 220 Ω

71 In a flashlight, a battery provides a total of 3.0 volts to a bulb. If the flashlight bulb has an operating resistance of 5.0 ohms, the current through the bulb is
(1) 0.30 A   (2) 0.60 A   (3) 1.5 A   (4) 1.7 A

72 A 20.-ohm resistor has 40. coulombs passing through it in 5.0 seconds. The potential difference across the resistor is
(1) 8.0 V   (2) 100 V   (3) 160 V   (4) 200 V

73 Which graph best represents the relationship between potential difference across a metallic conductor and the resulting current through the conductor at a constant temperature?

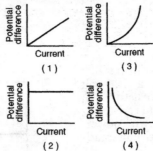

74 Which graph best represents the relationship between the potential difference across a conductor and the current through the conductor at constant temperature?

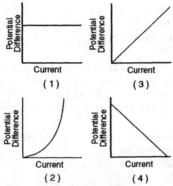

75 The graph at right shows the relationship between current and potential difference for four resistors, A, B, C, and D. Which resistor has the least resistance?
(1) A (2) B (3) C (4) D

76 The slope of the line on the graph at the right represents:
(1) resistance of a material
(2) electric field intensity
(3) power dissipated in a resistor
(4) electrical energy

77 A student conducted an experiment to determine the resistance of a lightbulb. As she applied various potential differences to the bulb, she recorded the voltages and corresponding currents and constructed the graph below.

Current vs. Potential Difference

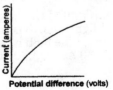

The student concluded that the resistance of the lightbulb was not constant. What evidence from the graph supports the student's conclusion?

Hint: Straight line shows R is constant; the line on the graph is not straight.

78 Plastic insulation surrounds a wire having diameter d and length ℓ as shown below.

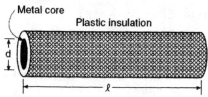

Metal core

Plastic insulation

A decrease in the resistance of the wire would be produced by an increase in the
(1) thickness of the plastic insulation
(2) length ℓ of the wire
(3) diameter d of the wire
(4) temperature of the wire

79 If the diameter of a wire were decreased, its electrical resistance would
(1) decrease
(2) increase
(3) remain the same

80 Which graph below best represents how the resistance (R) of a series of copper wires of uniform length and temperature varies with cross-sectional area (A)?

(1) R

A

(2) Resistance

Length

(3) Resistance

Length

(4) Resistance

Length

81 If the diameter of a wire were to increase, its electrical resistance would
(1) decrease
(2) increase
(3) remain the same

82 A copper wire has a resistance of 100 ohms. A second copper wire with twice the cross-sectional area and the same length would have a resistance of
(1) 25 Ω   (2) 50 Ω   (3) 100 Ω   (4) 200 Ω

83 A manufacturer recommends that the longer the extension cord used with an electric drill, the thicker (heavier gauge) the extension cord should be. This recommendation is made because the resistance of a wire varies
(1) directly with length and inversely with cross-sectional area
(2) inversely with length and directly with cross-sectional area
(3) directly with both length and cross-sectional area
(4) inversely with both length and cross-sectional area

84 In the diagram at right, ℓ represents a unit length of copper wire and A represents a unit cross-sectional area. Which copper wire has the *smallest* resistance at room temperature?

(1) A

(3) 2A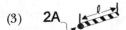

(2) A

(4) 2A

85 Which graph best represent the relationship between the resistance of a copper wire of uniform cross-sectional area and the wire's length at constant temperature?

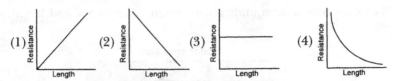

(1) Resistance / Length (2) Resistance \ Length (3) Resistance — Length (4) Resistance ⌐ Length

86 A metal conductor is used in an electric circuit. The electrical resistance provided by the conductor could be increased by
 (1) decreasing the length of the conductor
 (2) decreasing the applied voltage to the circuit
 (3) increasing the temperature of the conductor
 (4) increasing the cross-sectional area of the conductor

87 When an incandescent light bulb is turned on, its thin wire filament heats up quickly. As the temperature of this wire filament increases, its electrical resistance
 (1) decreases   (2) increases   (3) remains the same

88 A 0.500-meter length of wire with a cross-sectional area of 3.14×10^{-6} meters squared is found to have a resistance of 2.53×10^{-3} ohms. According to the resistivity chart, the wire could be made of
 (1) aluminum   (3) nichrome
 (2) copper   (4) silver

89 A 10.-meter length of wire with a cross-sectional area of 3.0×10^{-6} square meter has a resistance of 9.4×10^{-2} ohm at 20° Celsius. The wire is most likely made of
 (1) silver   (2) copper   (3) aluminum (4) tungsten

90 A copper wire has a resistance of 200 ohms. A second copper wire with twice the cross-sectional area and the same length would have a resistance of
 (1) 50 Ω   (2) 100 Ω   (3) 200 Ω   (4) 400 Ω

 Hint: Area and resistance are inversely proportional (double area, half the resistance).

91 A 10.-ohm resistor and a 20.-ohm resistor are connected in series to a voltage source. When the current through the 10.-ohm resistor is 2.0 amperes, what is the current through the 20.-ohm resistor?
 (1) 1.0 A   (2) 2.0 A   (3) 0.50 A   (4) 4.0 A

92 The diagram at right shows two resistors connected in series to a 20.-volt battery. If the current through the 5.0-ohm resistor is 1.0 ampere, the current through the 15.0-ohm resistor is
 (1) 1.0 A   (2) 0.33 A   (3) 3.0 A   (4) 1.3 A

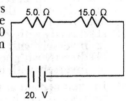

93 The diagram at right represents a sample electric circuit. How much charge passes through the resistor in 2.0 seconds?
 (1) 6.0 C   (3) 8.0 C
 (2) 2.0 C   (4) 4.0 C

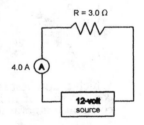

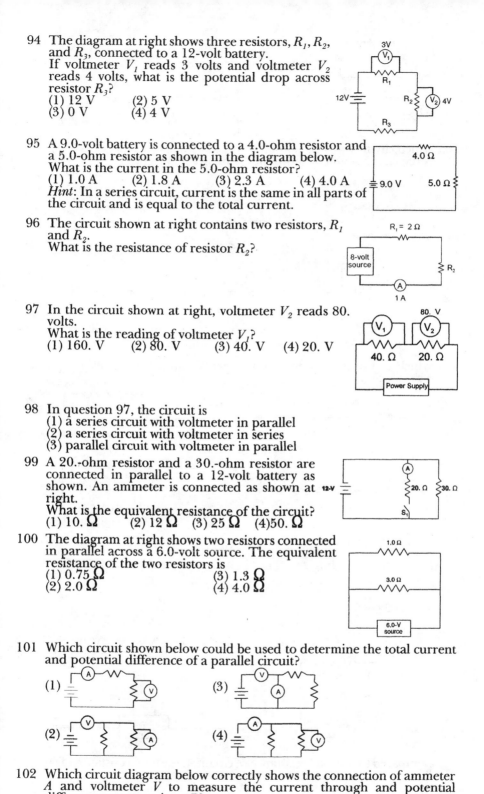

94 The diagram at right shows three resistors, R_1, R_2, and R_3, connected to a 12-volt battery. If voltmeter V_1 reads 3 volts and voltmeter V_2 reads 4 volts, what is the potential drop across resistor R_3?
(1) 12 V   (2) 5 V
(3) 0 V   (4) 4 V

95 A 9.0-volt battery is connected to a 4.0-ohm resistor and a 5.0-ohm resistor as shown in the diagram below. What is the current in the 5.0-ohm resistor?
(1) 1.0 A   (2) 1.8 A   (3) 2.3 A   (4) 4.0 A
Hint: In a series circuit, current is the same in all parts of the circuit and is equal to the total current.

96 The circuit shown at right contains two resistors, R_1 and R_2.
What is the resistance of resistor R_2?

97 In the circuit shown at right, voltmeter V_2 reads 80. volts.
What is the reading of voltmeter V_1?
(1) 160. V   (2) 80. V   (3) 40. V   (4) 20. V

98 In question 97, the circuit is
(1) a series circuit with voltmeter in parallel
(2) a series circuit with voltmeter in series
(3) parallel circuit with voltmeter in parallel

99 A 20.-ohm resistor and a 30.-ohm resistor are connected in parallel to a 12-volt battery as shown. An ammeter is connected as shown at right.
What is the equivalent resistance of the circuit?
(1) 10. Ω   (2) 12 Ω   (3) 25 Ω   (4)50. Ω

100 The diagram at right shows two resistors connected in parallel across a 6.0-volt source. The equivalent resistance of the two resistors is
(1) 0.75 Ω   (3) 1.3 Ω
(2) 2.0 Ω   (4) 4.0 Ω

101 Which circuit shown below could be used to determine the total current and potential difference of a parallel circuit?

102 Which circuit diagram below correctly shows the connection of ammeter A and voltmeter V to measure the current through and potential difference across resistor R?

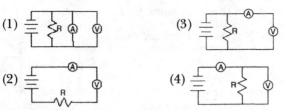

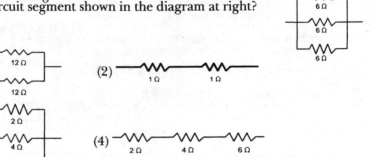

103 Which circuit segment below has the same total resistance as the circuit segment shown in the diagram at right?

(1) 12 Ω / 12 Ω (parallel)   (2) —WW— 1 Ω —WW— 1 Ω

(3) 2 Ω / 4 Ω / 6 Ω (parallel)   (4) —WW— 2 Ω —WW— 4 Ω —WW— 6 Ω

Hint: Review finding resistance in both series and parallel circuits.

104 Which two of the resistor arrangements shown below have equivalent resistance?

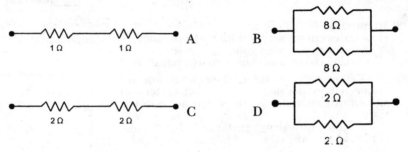

(1) A and B   (2) B and C   (3) C and D   (4) D and A

Hint: Review finding resistance in both series and parallel circuits.

105 Circuit A and circuit B are shown below.

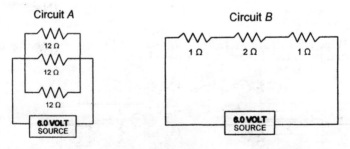

Compared to the total resistance of circuit A, the total resistance of circuit B is
(1) less   (2) greater   (3) the same

---

106 A physics student is given three 12-ohm resistors with instructions to create the circuit that would have the lowest possible resistance. The correct circuit would be a
(1) series circuit with a total resistance of 36 Ω
(2) series circuit with a total resistance of 4 Ω
(3) parallel circuit with a total resistance of 36 Ω
(4) parallel circuit with a total resistance of 4 Ω

107 In the circuit diagram at right, ammeter A measures the current supplied by the 10.-volt battery. The current measured by the ammeter A is
(1) 0.13 A   (3) 0.50 A
(2) 2.0 A   (4) 4.0 A

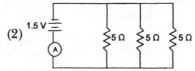

Base your answers to questions 108 and 109 on the circuit drawings below.

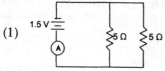

108 Find the current in circuit 1 and in circuit 2.

109 By looking at the two circuits, how can you tell which circuit has more current?

110 An electric circuit contains an operating heating element and a lit lamp. Which statement best explains why the lamp remains lit when the heating element is removed from the circuit?
(1) The lamp has less resistance than the heating element.
(2) The lamp has more resistance than the heating element.
(3) The lamp and heating element were connected in series.
(4) The lamp and heating element were connected in parallel.

Hint: A heating element is a resistor, just like a bulb is a resistor.

111 Four lamps are connected in parallel. If one lamp burns out, the current and brightness of the other lamps
(1) increase   (2) decrease   (3) remain the same

112 Two resistors are connected to a source of voltage as shown in the diagram at right. At which position should an ammeter be placed to measure the current passing only through resistor R_1?
(1) 1   (2) 2   (3) 3   (4) 4

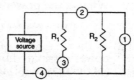

113 Which diagram shows correct current direction in a segment of an electric circuit?

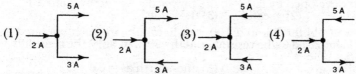

114 The figure at right represents a segment of a circuit. What is the current in ammeter A?
(1) 1 ampere   (3) 3.5 amperes
(2) 0 amperes   (4) 7 amperes

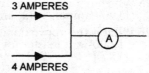

115 A light bulb operating at 120. volts draws a current of 0.50 ampere for 240. seconds. The power rating of the light bulb is
   (1) 30. W   (2) 60. W   (3) 75 W   (4) 120. W

116A What is the current in a 1,200-watt heater operating on 120 volts?
   (1) 0.10 ampere   (2) 5.0 amperes   (3) 10. amperes   (4) 20. amperes

116B What is the total current in a circuit consisting of six operating 100-watt lamps connected in parallel to a 120-volt source?
   (1) 20 A   (2) 600 A   (3) 5 A   (4) 12000 A

117 A toaster having a power rating of 1050. watts is operated at 120. volts. It is connected in a circuit protected by a 15-ampere fuse. (The fuse will shut down the circuit if it carries more than 15 amperes.) Is it possible to simultaneously operate the toaster and a microwave oven that requires a current of 10.0 amperes on this circuit? Justify your answer mathematically.
   Hint: First find how many amperes the toaster requires.

118 To increase the brightness of a desk lamp, a student replaces a 60-watt light bulb with a 100-watt bulb. Compared to the 60-watt bulb, the 100-watt has
   (1) less resistance and draws more current
   (2) less resistance and draws less current
   (3) more resistance and draws more current
   (4) more resistance and draws less current
   Hint: Lamp in the socket has constant V (volts). First use $P = VI$, then $R = \dfrac{V}{I}$.

119 While operating at 120 volts, an electric toaster has a resistance of 15 ohms. The power used by the toaster is
   (1) 8.0 W   (2) 120 W   (3) 960 W   (4) 1,800 W

120 The potential difference across a 100.-ohm resistor is 4.0 volts. What is the power dissipated in the resistor?
   (1) 0.16 watt   (2) 25 watts   (3) 4.0×10^2 watts   (4) 4.0 watts

121 A toaster having a power rating of 1050. watts is operated at 120. volts. Calculate the resistance of the toaster. [Show all work, including the equation and substitution with units.]

122 A 20.-ohm resistor and a 30.-ohm resistor are connected in parallel to a 12-volt battery as shown. An ammeter is connected as shown at right.
   What is the power of the 30.-ohm resistor?

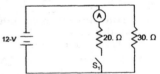

   (1) 4.8 W   (2) 12 W   (3) 30. W   (4) 75 W

123 As the resistance of a lamp operating at a constant voltage increases, the power dissipated by the lamp
   (1) decreases   (2) increases   (3) remains the same

124A The same potential difference is applied to two lamps, A and B. The resistance of lamp A is twice the resistance of lamp B. Compared to the power developed by lamp B, the power developed by lamp A is
   (1) less   (2) greater   (3) the same

124B A 50-watt lightbulb and a 100-watt lightbulb are each operated at 110 volts. Compared to the resistance of the 50-watt bulb, the resistance of the 100-watt bulb is
   (1) half as great   (3) one-fourth as great
   (2) twice as great   (4) four times as great

125 Which is a unit of electrical power?
   (1) volt/ampere   (2) ampere/ohm   (3) ampere²/ohm   (4) volt²/ohm

126 What is the approximate amount of electrical energy needed to operate a 1,600-watt toaster for 60. seconds?
   (1) 27 J   (2) 1,500. J   (3) 1,700. J   (4) 96,000. J

127 A light bulb attached to a 120.-volt source of potential difference draws a current of 1.25 amperes for 35.0 seconds. Calculate how much electrical energy is used by the bulb. [Show all work, including the equation and substitution with units.]

128 An electric fan draws 1.7 amperes of current when operated at a potential difference of 120. volts. How much electrical energy is needed to run this fan for 1 hour? (1 hour = 3600 seconds)
(1) 7.1×10^1 J   (3) 2.5×10^5 J
(2) 2.0×10^2 J   (4) 7.3×10^5 J

Hint: Time should be in seconds (s).

129 The circuit represented in the diagram at the right is a series circuit. The energy delivered to resistor R in 2.0 seconds is
(1) 20. J   (3) 80. J
(2) 40. J   (4) 120 J

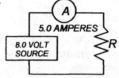

130 A clothes dryer connected to a 240-volt line draws 30. amperes of current for 20 minutes (1,200 seconds). Approximately how much electrical energy is consumed by the dryer?
(1) 4.8×10^3 J   (2) 7.2×10^3 J   (3) 1.4×10^5 J   (4) 8.6×10^6 J

131 An electric fan draws 3.4 amperes of current when operated at a potential difference of 120. volts. How much electrical energy is needed to run this fan for 1 hour? (1 hour = 3600 seconds)
(1) 1.4×10^2 J   (2) 4.0×10^2 J   (3) 5.0×10^5 J   (4) 1.5×10^6 J

132 An operating electric iron draws a current of 5 amperes and has a resistance of 20 ohms. The amount of energy used by the iron in 40 seconds is
(1) 1×10^2 J   (2) 5×10^2 J   (3) 4×10^3 J   (4) 2×10^4 J

133 An electric iron draws a current of 5 amperes and has a resistance of 20. ohms. The amount of energy used by the iron in 40 seconds is
(1) 100. J   (2) 500. J   (3) 4,000. J   (4) 20,000. J

134 A 12-ohm resistor is connected to a 26-volt source of electricity. How much energy is used by te circuit in ½ hour?
(1) 48 joules   (3) 3.6×10^3 joules
(2) 8.64×10^4 joules   (4) 1.1×10^4 joules
Hint: Time must be in seconds.

Base your answers to questions 135-137 on the information below:
An electric heater rated at 4,800 watts is operated on 120 volts.

135 An electric heater rated at 4,800 watts is operated on 120 volts. What is the resistance of the heater?
(1) 576,000 Ω (2) 120 Ω (3) 3.0 Ω (4) 40. Ω

136 An electric heater rated at 4,800 watts is operated on 120 volts. How much energy is used by this heater in 10.0 seconds?
(1) 1.15 J   (2) 40. J   (3) 4.8×10^3 J   (4) 4.8×10^4 J

137 If a heater were replaced by one having a greater resistance, the amount of heat produced each second would:
(1) decrease   (2) increase   (3) remain the same
Hint: New heater also operates on 120 V (volts); time (t) is constant.

138 Which diagram below best represents the magnetic field near a bar magnet?

(1)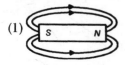

(3) [diagram]

(2) 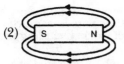   (4)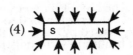

139 The diagram at right represents the
magnetic lines of force around a bar
magnet.
At which point is the magnitude of the
magnetic field strength of the bar magnet
the greatest?
(1) A   (3) C
(2) B   (4) D

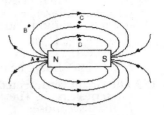

140 Which diagram correctly shows a
magnetic field configuration?

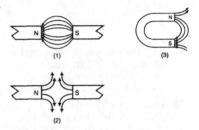

141 Which diagram best represents the magnetic field between two
magnetic north poles?

(1)    (3)

(2)    (4)

Compass

142 The diagram at right shows a compass

placed near the north pole, N, of a bar magnet. Which diagram best
represents the position of the needle of the compass as it responds to
the magnetic field of the bar magnet?

143 The diagram at right represents magnetic lines of force within a region
of space.
The magnetic force is strongest at point
(1) A   (2) B   (3) C   (4) D

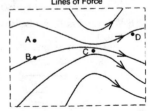

144 In the diagram at right, a steel paper clip is attached to a string, which is attached to a table. The clip remains suspended beneath a magnet.
   As the magnet is lifted, the paper clip begins to fall as a result of
   (1) an increase in the potential energy of the clip
   (2) an increase in the gravitational field strength near the magnet
   (3) a decrease in the magnetic properties of the clip
   (4) a decrease in the magnetic field strength near the clip.

145 In which diagram below is the magnetic flux density at point *P* greatest?

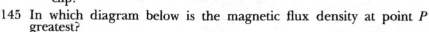

146 A volt is to electric potential as a tesla is to
   (1) electrical energy
   (2) electric field intensity
   (3) magnetic flux density
   (4) charge density

147 The two ends of a wire are connected to a galvanometer, forming a complete electric circuit. The wire is then moved through a magnetic field, as shown in the diagram at right.
   The galvanometer is being used to measure
   (1) current
   (2) potential difference
   (3) temperature change
   (4) resistance

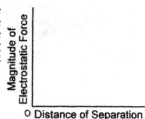

CONSTRUCTED RESPONSE QUESTIONS: Parts B-2 and C of NYS Regents Exam

Base your answers to questions 148-150 on the information and diagram below.

Two small charged spheres, *A* and *B*, are separated by a distance of 0.50 meter. The charge on sphere *A* is $+2.4 \times 10^{-6}$ coulomb and the charge on sphere *B* is -2.4×10^{-6} coulomb.

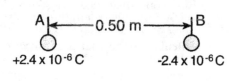

148 Calculate the magnitude of the electrostatic force that sphere *A* exerts on sphere *B*. [Show all calculations, including the equation and substitution with units.]

149 Using the axes, sketch the general shape of the graph that shows the relationship between the magnitude of the electrostatic force between the two charged spheres and the distance separating them. The charge on each sphere remains constant as the distance separating them is varied.

150 Two small charged spheres, *A* and *B*, are separated by a distance of 0.50 meter. The charge on sphere *A* is $+2.4 \times 10^{-6}$ coulomb and the charge on sphere *B* is -2.4×10^{-6} coulomb.

A $\longleftarrow$ 0.50 m $\longrightarrow$ B

$+2.4 \times 10^{-6}$ C -2.4×10^{-6} C

Copy sphere A, with its charge of $+2.4 \times 10^{-6}$ coulomb, and sphere B, with its charge of -2.4×10^{-6} coulomb, on separate paper. Sketch *three* electric field lines to represent the electric field in the region between sphere *A* and sphere *B*. [Draw an arrowhead on each field line to show the proper direction.]

151 A proton starts from rest and gains 8.35×10^{-14} joule of kinetic energy as accelerates between points *A* and *B* in an electric field. Calculate the potential difference between points *A* and *B* in the electric field. [Show all work including the equation and substitution with units.]

Base your answers to questions 152 and 153 on the information below.
A scientist set up an experiment to collect data about lightning. In one lightning flash, a charge of 25 coulombs was transferred from the base of a cloud to the ground. The scientist measured a potential difference of 1.8×10^{6} volts between the cloud and the ground and an average current of 2.0×10^{4} amperes.

152 Determine the time interval over which this flash occurred. [Show a calculations, including the equation and substitution with units.]

153 Determine the amount of energy, in joules, involved in the transfer of th electrons from the cloud to the ground. [Show all calculations, including th equation and substitution with units.]

154 A long copper wire was connected to a voltage source. The voltage was varied and the current through the wire measured, while temperature was held constant. The collected data are represented by the graph below.
Using the graph, determine the resistance of the copper wire.

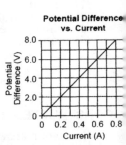

Potential Difference vs. Current

155 Calculate the resistance of the wire. [Show all work, including the equation an substitution with units.]

Base your answers to questions 155 and 156 on the information below.
A 1.00-meter length of nichrome wire with a cross-sectional area of 7.85×10^{-7} meter^2 is connected to a 1.50-volt battery.

155 Calculate the resistance of the wire. [Show all work, including the equation an substitution with units.]

156 Determine the current in the wire.

157 An electric circuit contains two 3.0-ohm resistors connected in parallel with battery. The circuit also contains a voltmeter that reads the potential differenc across one of the resistors. Calculate the total resistance of the circuit. [Sho all work, including the equation and substitution with units.]

Base your answers to questions 158-160 on the information below.
A 5.0-ohm resistor, a 20.0-ohm resistor, and a 24-volt source of potential difference are connected in parallel. A single ammeter is placed in the circuit to read the total current.

158 In the space provided *on your answer paper*, draw a diagram of this circuit, using the symbols with labels given below. [Assume availability of any number of wires of negligible resistance.]

159 Determine the total resistance. [Show all calculations, including the equation and substitution with units.]

160 Determine the total circuit current. [Show all calculations, including the equation and substitution with units.]

Base your answers to questions 161-165 on the information and data table below.

Three lamps were connected in a circuit with a battery of constant potential. The current, potential difference, and resistance for each lamp are listed in the data table below. [There is negligible resistance in the wires and the battery.]

	Current (A)	Potential Difference (V)	Resistance (Ω)
lamp 1	0.45	40.1	89
lamp 2	0.11	40.1	365
lamp 3	0.28	40.1	143

Hint: Use symbol for lamp given on **Reference Table: Circuit Symbols**.

161 Using the circuit symbols found in the *Reference Tables for Physical Setting/Physics*, draw a circuit showing how the lamps and battery are connected.

162 What is the potential difference supplied by the battery?

163 Calculate the equivalent resistance of the circuit. [Show all work, including the equation and substitution with units.]

164 If lamp *2* is removed from the circuit, what would be the value of the potential difference across lamp *1* after lamp *2* is removed?

165 If lamp *2* is removed from the circuit, what would be the value of the current in lamp *1* after lamp *2* is removed?

Base your answers to questions 166-168 on the information below.

You are given a 12-volt battery, ammeter *A*, voltmeter *V*, resistor R_1, and resistor R_2. Resistor R_2 has a value of 3.0 ohms.

166 Using appropriate symbols from the *Reference Tables for Physical Setting/Physics*, draw and label a complete circuit showing:
   • resistors R_1 and R_2 connected in parallel with the battery
   • the ammeter connected to measure the current through resistor R_1, only
   • the voltmeter connected to measure the potential drop across resistor R_1

167 If the total current in the circuit is 6.0 amperes, determine the equivalent resistance of the circuit.

168 If the total current in the circuit is 6.0 amperes, determine the resistance of resistor R_1. [Show all calculations, including the equation and substitution with units.]

169 A 5.0-ohm resistor, a 15.0-ohm resistor, and an unknown resistor, R, are connected as shown with a 15-volt source. The ammeter reads a current of 0.50 ampere.

Determine the total electrical energy used in the circuit in 600. seconds. [Show all calculations, including the equation and substitution with units.]

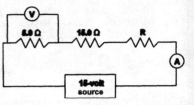

CHAPTER 4: WAVES

Section *1*:

Light waves, sound waves, water waves, microwaves, radio waves, etc., are examples of different kinds of waves.

A **wave** (example: sound wave, water wave) is produced by particles vibrating (which means particles shaking (moving) back and forth), causing the particles' surroundings (example air, water) to vibrate. A wave is a vibratory disturbance.

Pulses and Periodic Waves: Waves can be one pulse or periodic waves, as explained below.

A **pulse** is a **single vibratory disturbance** (one vibration) that moves from one point to another point. It moves horizontally and vertically.

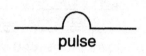
pulse

Periodic wave - A periodic wave is the same pulse, which means **one pulse, repeated many times** (or you can say, **several identical repeating pulses** that are **evenly spaced**). Pulse 1 moves on and a new identical pulse (pulse 2) follows it.

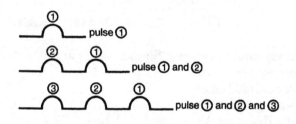
pulse ①
pulse ① and ②
pulse ① and ② and ③

Periodic Wave

Pulse 1 and 2 move on and a new identical pulse (pulse 3) follows them. As you can see, a periodic wave is several identical repeating pulses that are evenly spaced.

If a pulse (or wave, example, light wave in air) hits a new medium (example, water) (see diagram) light goes from air to water; parts of the wave can be absorbed, transmitted (example: light wave goes through the

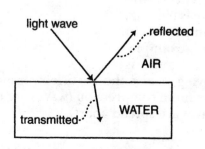
light wave
reflected
AIR
transmitted
WATER

water), or reflected (lightwave bounces back into the air).

If the wave hits a solid wall (see diagram), the wave is reflected (nothing is absorbed or transmitted). The reflected wave would be inverted (upside down).

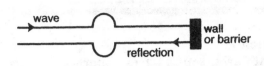

If sound waves hit drapes or carpets, they absorb some of the energy of the sound waves and the sound is lower.

When waves (example: sound, light, radio waves) move, **they transfer energy (not mass)**.

Question: A periodic wave transfers

    (1) energy, only   (2) mass, only

    (3) both energy and mass   (4) neither energy nor mass

Solution: Waves transfer energy but not mass   Answer *1*

Mechanical waves (examples: sound waves or water waves) need a **medium** (example, air) to travel in. Sound waves cannot travel in a vacuum (where there is no air). However, electromagnetic waves (example, light waves) can travel in a vacuum (where there is no air).

LONGITUDINAL AND TRANSVERSE WAVES

Longitudinal waves: Sound waves and compression waves in a spring are examples of longitudinal waves. Look at the diagram. In a **longitudinal** wave, the particles vibrate **parallel** to the motion of the wave (the direction the wave is moving, example →). In this example, the wave is

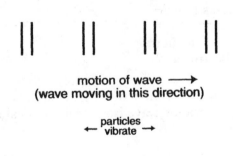

moving → and the particles vibrate parallel, ↔. The wave has places of maximum compression (waves are compressed) and maximum expansion (waves are spread apart).

Transverse waves: Light waves, electromagnetic waves (which include light waves), water waves, and earthquake S-waves are transverse waves. Look at the diagram. In a **transverse wave,** the particles vibrate **perpendicular** to the motion of the wave (the direction the wave is moving).

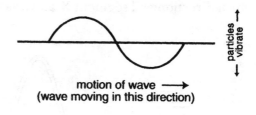

motion of wave ⟶
(wave moving in this direction)

particles
vibrate

This is **one wave** (example, light wave). The **top** of the **wave** is called the **crest.** The **bottom** of the **wave** is called a **trough.**

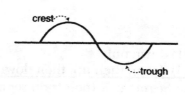

crest

trough

One wave

In the figure below there are three waves. The waves keep on repeating themselves.

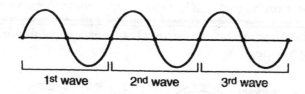

1st wave   2nd wave   3rd wave

The waves keep moving (see figure below).

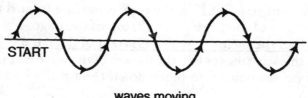

START

waves moving

Question: As shown in the diagram below, a transverse wave is moving with velocity v along a rope.
In which direction will segment X move as the wave passes through it?

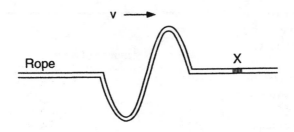

(1) down only   (2) up only
(3) down, then up, then down   (4) up, then down, then up

Solution: Segment X (points on segment X) will move up or down as each part of the wave goes through segment X of the rope. X starts along the middle line. As the wave moves to the right, first a crest reaches X and X moves upward; then a trough arrives, and X moves down. Finally, as the wave has passed, X moves back up to the middle line.   **Answer** *4*

When the crest of a wave meets a point (example, a point on Segment X), it causes the point to move up. When a trough of a wave meets a point (example, a point on Segment X), it causes the point to move down.

Question: The diagram below shows a transverse wave moving toward the left along a rope.

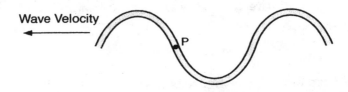

At the instant shown, point P on the rope is moving toward the
(1) bottom of the page   (2) top of the page
(3) left of the page   (4) right of the page

Solution: As the wave moves left, the trough of the wave is approaching point P and causes point P to move down toward the bottom of the page.   **Answer** *1*

Now Do Homework Questions 1-11, pages 81-82.

CHARACTERISTICS OF WAVES

AMPLITUDE is the **height** of the **wave from** the **rest position** (equilibrium position) **to** the **top** (crest) of the **wave or from** the **rest position to** the **bottom** (trough) of the **wave** (see figure below).

Amplitude in a transverse wave (example: light, water) is the **m a x i m u m displacement** of a particle (biggest distance the particle moves from its rest position to the very top or very bottom of the wave).

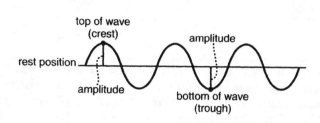

The more energy a wave has, the bigger (greater) the amplitude. In a sound wave, the bigger (greater) the amplitude, the louder the sound; the smaller the amplitude, the lower the sound. In a light wave, the bigger (greater) the amplitude, the brighter the light; the smaller the amplitude, the dimmer the light.

Question: An electric guitar is generating a sound of constant frequency. An increase in which sound wave characteristic would result in an increase in loudness?

　　　　(1) speed　　　(2) period　　　(3) wavelength　(4) amplitude

Solution: The bigger (greater) the amplitude, the louder the sound. An increase in amplitude causes an increase in loudness. Answer *4*

WAVE LENGTH (lambda, λ) is **how long** the **wave is(length of** the **wave).**

Length of the wave is t h r e e m e t e r s . Wavelength (λ) is three meters. Wavelength is the horizontal length of one complete wave (one cycle, one wave cycle).

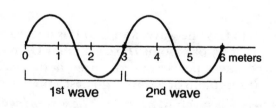

½ wavelength (½ λ) is one half the length of one wave. If the length of one wave is three meters long, obviously ½ wavelength (½ λ) is 11/2 meters long.

Question: The diagram below shows two points, A and B, on a wave train.

How many wavelengths separate point A and point B?
(1) 1.0 (2) 1.5
(3) 3.0 (4) 0.75

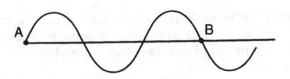

Solution: One wavelength is from A to #1, the length of one wave; one wave has one complete crest and one complete trough. ½ of a wavelength is from #1 to B (one half the length of the wave). Therefore, the number of wavelengths from A to B = **1 wavelength (from A to #1) + ½ wavelength** (from #1 **to B**) = 1½ **wavelengths** (1.5 wavelengths).

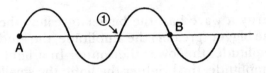

Answer 2

FREQUENCY (f) is the **number of waves** that pass a point (reach a point) **in a unit of time (in one second).**

Three waves reach a point (example point D) in one second (see figure) or go past a point in one second.

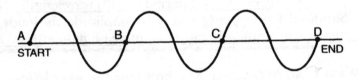

A to B is one wave, B to C is one wave, and C to D is one wave, therefore, A to D is three waves that go past point D (reach point D) in one second. The frequency is three waves per second or three hertz (Hz). Frequency is how many waves (example, 3 or 4 waves) go past a point (reach a point) in one second.

Frequency is given **in hertz** (Hz) **or waves (cycles) per second** (1/s or s^{-1}). When a **number** is **in hertz (Hz)** (example 3 hertz or 512 hertz), you know it **means frequency.**

Question: A motor is used to produce 4.0 waves each second in a string. What is the frequency of the waves?
(1) 0.25 Hz (2) 15 Hz (3) 25 Hz (4) 4.0 Hz

Solution: Four waves travel in one second; the frequency is 4 waves/second or 4 Hz.

Answer 4

Question: A physics student notices that 4.0 waves arrive at the beach every 20. seconds. The frequency of these waves is

(1) 0.20 Hz   (2) 5.0 Hz   (3) 16 Hz   (4) 80. Hz

Solution: Frequency (f) is the number of waves that pass (reach) a point in one second. Frequency is given in waves per second or Hz.

$$f = \frac{4\ waves}{20\ seconds} = \frac{1\ wave}{5\ seconds} = \frac{0.20\ waves}{second} = 0.20\ Hz \qquad \text{Answer } 1$$

Question: The diagram below represents a periodic wave generated during a 1.5-second interval.

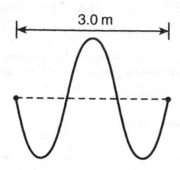

The frequency of the wave is

(1) 1.0 Hz   (2) 2.0 Hz   (3) 0.50 Hz   (4) 4.5 Hz

Solution: One wave has one complete crest and one complete trough. In the diagram above, there is one crest and two troughs, which equals **1½ waves (1.5 waves).** 1½ waves (1.5 waves) are in 1½ seconds (1.5 seconds), therefore 1.0 wave is in 1.0 second. Frequency = 1.0 wave/second = 1.0 Hz.   Answer *1*

PERIOD (T): the **time** it takes for **one wave** (one complete vibration, one cycle). Period (T) is given in seconds.

The period (T) of a wave is inversely proportional to frequency (f).

$$T = \frac{1}{f} \qquad\qquad T = \text{period}$$
$$\qquad\qquad\qquad f = \text{frequency}$$
$$\text{Period} = \frac{1}{frequency}$$

If the frequency (f) is 3 waves/second or 3 hertz (Hz), what is the period (T)? Use the equation

$$T = \frac{1}{f}$$

Substitute for f (frequency) 3 Hz.

$$T = \frac{1}{3\ Hz} \qquad Hz = \frac{1}{s} \qquad T = \frac{1}{3}s$$

$$\text{Period (T)} = \frac{1}{3}\ s$$

If the question says three waves travel (pass a point) in one second, it means frequency is 3 Hz; then the period T (time for one wave) is ⅓ second, as shown on the previous page.

Note: $T = \frac{1}{f}$ and $f = \frac{1}{T}$

Relationship between Period and Frequency

$T = \frac{1}{f}$ can be used to find T (period) or f (frequency). If you are given period (T), you can find frequency. If you are given frequency, you can find period.

Question: What is the frequency of a wave if its period is 0.25 second?
    (1) 1.0 Hz   (2) 0.25 Hz   (3) 12 Hz   (4) 4.0 Hz

Solution:
Given: Period = 0.25 second (s).
Find: Frequency.
Look for an equation on Reference Table: Waves that has frequency (f) and period (T).
Use the equation

$$T = \frac{1}{f} \qquad \begin{array}{l} T = \text{period} \\ f = \text{frequency} \end{array}$$

Substitute 0.25s for T (period).

$0.25s = \frac{1}{f}$	Or, rearrange the equation: Tf = 1
Cross multiply	$f = \frac{1}{T}$
$0.25s\ f = 1$	
$f = \frac{1}{0.25\ s} = 4.0\ \frac{1}{s}$ $Hz = \frac{1}{s}$	$f = \frac{1}{0.25\ s} = 4.0\ \frac{1}{s}$ $Hz = \frac{1}{s}$
$f = 4.0\ Hz$ Answer *4*	$f = 4.0\ Hz$ Answer *4*

Question: If the frequency of a periodic wave is doubled, the period of the wave will be
        (1) halved   (2) doubled   (3) quartered   (4) quadrupled

Solution:
Given: Frequency is doubled.
Find: New period
Look for an equation on Reference Table: Waves having to do with period (T) and frequency (f).
Use the equation

$$T = \frac{1}{f} \qquad \begin{array}{l} T = \text{period} \\ f = \text{frequency} \end{array}$$

Table: Waves

Table: Waves

OLD	NEW
$T = \dfrac{1}{f}$	Frequency is doubled. Let new frequency = 2f. New T = $\dfrac{1}{2f}$
$T = \dfrac{1}{f}$ Old Period	$T = \dfrac{1}{2f}$ or $\dfrac{1}{2} \cdot \dfrac{1}{f}$ New Period when frequency is doubled.

Look at the new period and the old period. New period = ½ old period, which means period is halved.   **Answer** *1*

Now Do Homework Questions #12-19, pages 82-83, and #132-134, page 100.

PHASE: Transverse waves travel (move) like this:

Phase: Points **A and B** are **in phase- same distance above axis** (rest or equilibrium position) and **moving in the same direction.**

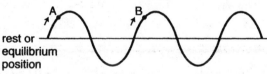

Points **C and D** are **in phase- same distance** (displacement) **below** the **axis** (rest or equilibrium position) and **moving in** the **same direction**.

In short, points on the wave that are **either** the

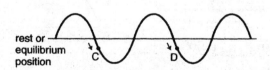

same distance (displacement) above the axis (A and B) or the same distance below the axis (C and D) and moving in the same direction are in phase.

All crests are **in phase** (points **E, F**)-same distance (displacement) above the axis and moving in the same direction. **All troughs**

---

are **in phase** (points **G, H**) same distance (displacement) below the axis and moving in the same direction.

When waves are in phase, both waves are the same, and the first wave can be put exactly on top of the second wave.

Question: The diagram below represents a periodic wave.

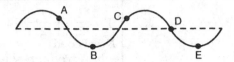

Which two points on the wave are in phase?
    (1) A and C   (2) B and D   (3) A and D   (4) B and E

Solution: Points B and E are in phase. B and E are the same distance below the axis (the dashed line) and moving in the same direction (moving upward).

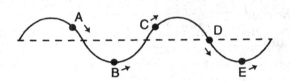

Answer *4*

One complete wave cycle (example, A to F) can be **considered** as having **360°** (like a circle).

$\frac{1}{2}$ wave cycle (example, A to G) can be considered as having $\frac{1}{2}$ (360°) = 180°.

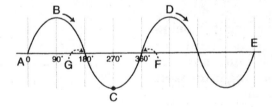

Wavelength (λ, lambda) is the **horizontal length of a wave**, which is **360°**.

Wavelength (λ) is from crest to crest, which is 360°. B (crest) is at 90°. D (crest) is at (360 +

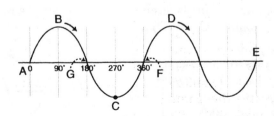

90)°. Therefore, wavelength = 360°.

Phase: Points B and D are **in phase** because they are the same distance above the x axis (or you can say, the same amplitude or height), and are moving in the same direction. Points B and D are also in phase because they are **360° apart**. Any two points 0° apart or 360° apart are in phase.

You learned one complete wave cycle can be considered as having 360°; therefore, $\frac{1}{2}$ wave cycle can be considered as having $\frac{1}{2}$ (360°) = 180°.

Any two points **180° apart** are **out of phase**. Example: Point A (0°) and point G (180°) are out of phase because point A and point G are 180° different. Point B (90°) and Point C (270°) are out of phase because (270° − 90° = 180°) there is a difference of 180°.

Note: Since one wave (cycle) or the distance of one wavelength is considered as having 360°, $\frac{1}{2}$ wave (cycle) or $\frac{1}{2}$ wavelength is considered as having 180°.

Question: A periodic transverse wave has an amplitude of 0.20 meter and a wavelength of 3.0 meters. Copy the grid below onto separate paper. On the grid, draw at least one cycle of this periodic wave.

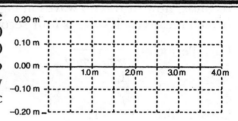

Solution:
Given: Amplitude = 0.20 meters, wavelength = 3.0 meters.
Find: Draw at least one cycle of the periodic wave.
Amplitude is 0.20 meters (m), which means height of wave = 0.20 meters. Wavelength is 3.0 meters, which means length of one wave is 3.0 meters.

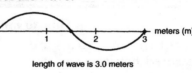

length of wave is 3.0 meters

Look at the figure below. Draw one wave with a height of 0.20 meters (above and below the line) and a length of 3.0 meters (m). The wave crosses the axis at 1½ meters, which is one half the length of the wave. Waves always cross the axis at a point that is one half (example, 1½ meters) of the length of the wave (example, 3.0 meters).

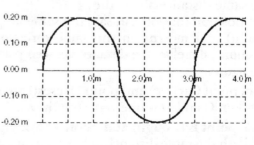

Question: Given wave A. Draw wave B with twice the amplitude and twice the frequency of wave A.

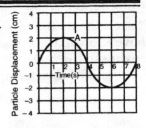

Solution: Amplitude: Since the amplitude (height) of wave A is 2 cm, draw **wave B** with an amplitude (height) of 4 cm (twice the amplitude of wave A). Draw wave B 4 cm above the axis and 4 cm below the axis.

Frequency (f): Twice the frequency means two times the number of waves in the same time. The figure above has one wave (A) in eight seconds; now draw two waves in eight seconds (which means each wave is four seconds).

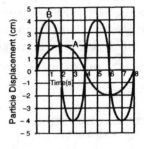

Or: Period $= \dfrac{1}{frequency}$

$$T = \dfrac{1}{f}$$

Cross multiply fT = 1;

In **wave B**, f is doubled (2f), then T (period, time for one wave) is ½T, so that (2f)(½T)= 1.

T (period) for wave A is 8 seconds (s), therefore period (time) for wave B is 4 seconds (s). In 8 seconds, there are two wave B. Draw two wave B.

How to measure wavelength

Wavelength can be measured between any two points that are in phase. **Points A and B** are **in phase** because A and B are both the same distance above the rest position (or you can say, the same amplitude, which means the same

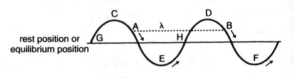

height) and moving in the same direction (downward toward the rest position), therefore the **distance between points A and B** is **one wavelength (λ)** (see figure).

Also, point C (crest) and point D (crest) are in phase, therefore the distance between C and D is one wavelength (λ).

Also, **point E (trough) and point F (trough)** are **in phase** because E and F are both the same distance below the rest position (or you can say, the same amplitude (height)) and moving in the same direction (upward toward the rest position), therefore the **distance between E and F** is **one wavelength (λ)** (see figure).

Also, points **G and H are in phase,** because G and H are both on the axis (rest position) and moving in the same direction (upward), therefore the **distance between G and H** is **one wavelength (λ)** (see figure).

In short, wavelength can be measured between any two points in phase (examples: points A and B, points E and F, or points G and H).

Note: Any two points in phase are 360° apart.

Wavelength can also be **defined** as the horizontal length of **one complete crest and one complete trough.** The distance between G and H is one wavelength; there is one complete crest and one complete trough.

Question: In the diagram below, the distance between points A and B on a wave is 5.0 meters.

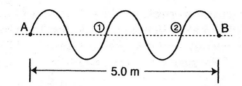

The wavelength of this wave is
    (1) 1.0 m   (2) 2.0 m   (3) 5.0 m   (4) 4.0 m

Solution:
Given: Distance between points A and B on a wave is 5.0 meters (m).
Find: Wavelength of this wave.

Look at the diagram at right. A to 1 is one wavelength (one complete crest and one complete trough), 1 to 2 is another wavelength, and 2 to B is ½ wavelength; therefore, A to B is 2½

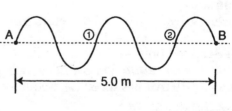

wavelengths. A to B (2½ wavelengths) is (has a distance of) 5.0 meters (given), therefore, $\dfrac{5.0 \text{ meters}}{2\frac{1}{2} \text{ wavelengths}} = \dfrac{2.0 \text{ meters}}{1 \text{ wavelength}}$.

Wavelength = 2.0 m (meters)

Or

you can set a proportion:

$\dfrac{2\frac{1}{2} \text{ wavelengths}}{5.0 \text{ meters}} = \dfrac{1 \text{ wavelength}}{x \text{ meters}}$ or $\dfrac{5.0 \text{ meters}}{2\frac{1}{2} \text{ wavelengths}} = \dfrac{x \text{ meters}}{1 \text{ wavelength}}$

Cross multiply   Cross multiply
    2½ x = 5.0   2½ x = 5.0
       x = 2.0 meters (m)   x = 2.0 meters (m)
  Wavelength = 2.0 m   Wavelength = 2.0 m
                                         Answer 2

Now Do Homework Questions #20-29, pages 83-84.

SPEED OF WAVES, FREQUENCY AND WAVELENGTH

$$v = f \lambda$$

f = frequency
v = velocity or speed
λ = wavelength

velocity or speed = frequency x wavelength

The velocity or speed of waves = frequency (number of waves per second) times wavelength (length of one wave).

Velocity is in meters/second (m/s); frequency is in hertz (Hz) or cycles (waves) per second, wavelength λ is in meters (m), and therefore velocity is in meters/second (m/s).

Speed of light in a vacuum (represented by the letter c) or in air = 3.00×10^8 m/s. (Speed of light in air is actually a little less than in a vacuum.) Speed of light in a vacuum and speed of sound in air are given on Reference Table: List of Physical Constants.

Speed of light in a vacuum	c	3.00×10^8 m/s
Speed of sound in air at STP		3.31×10^2 m/s

Question: A periodic transverse wave has an amplitude of 0.20 meter and a wavelength of 3.0 meters. If the frequency of this wave is 12 Hz, what is its speed?
(1) 0.25 m/s   (2) 12 m/s   (3) 36 m/s   (4) 4.0 m/s

Solution:
Given: wavelength = 3.0 meters (m)
　　　　frequency = 12 Hz
Find: speed (v)

Look for an equation on Reference Table: Waves on page reference tables 18-19 that has speed (v), frequency (f), and wavelength (λ).

Use the equation

$$v = f \lambda$$

f = frequency
v = velocity or speed
λ = wavelength

velocity or speed = frequency x wavelength

Then substitute for f (frequency) 12 Hz. *Substitute for λ* (wavelength) 3.0 m (meters).

$v = 12$ Hz (or $12 \frac{1}{s}$) x 3.0 m   Note: 1 Hz = $\frac{1}{s}$

v (speed) = 36 m/s   speed = 36 m/s
Note: Amplitude is an extra fact, not needed to solve the problem.

Answer 3

Question: Orange light has a frequency of 5.0×10^{14} hertz in a vacuum. What is the wavelength of this light?
(1) 1.5×10^{23} m (2) 1.7×10^6 m (3) 6.0×10^{-7} m (4) 2.0×10^{-15} m

Solution:
Given: Frequency (f) = 5.0 x 10^{14} hertz(Hz) in a vacuum.
Find: Wavelength (λ)

Look for an equation on Reference Table: Waves that has frequency (f) and wavelength (λ).

Use the equation

$$v = f\lambda$$

    f = frequency
    v = velocity or speed
    λ = wavelength

You have two unknowns, wavelength (λ) and speed (v). First find v (speed) of (orange) light and then substitute v in v = fλ to find λ (wavelength).

First find v (velocity/speed of light).
Look at Reference Table: List of Physical Constants for speed of light (in a vacuum).
Note: The specific symbol for speed of light is c.

Speed of light in a vacuum   c   3.00 x 10^8 m/s
Speed of light in a vacuum (any color **light**-example: red, **orange**) **equals 3.00 x 10^8 m/s.**

Then in the equation v = fλ, *substitute for v* 3.00 x 10^8 m/s and *substitute for f* 5.0 x 10^{14} Hz (given).

v = f λ	Or, rearrange the equation
3.00 x 10^8 m/s = (5.0 x 10^{14} Hz)λ	$\lambda = = \dfrac{v}{f}$
$\lambda = \dfrac{3.00 \times 10^8 \ m/s}{5.0 \times 10^{14} \ Hz \ (or \ 1/s)}$	$\lambda = = \dfrac{3.00 \times 10^8 \ m/s}{5.0 \times 10^{14} \ Hz \ (or \ 1/s)}$
λ = 0.60 x 10^{-6} m or 6.0 x 10^{-7} m	λ = 0.60 x 10^{-6} m or 6.0 x 10^{-7} m
Wavelength = 6.0 x 10^{-7} m	Wavelength = 6.0 x 10^{-7} m

Answer *3*

Question: A surfacing whale in an aquarium produces water wave crests having an amplitude of 1.2 meters every 0.40 second. If the water wave travels at 4.5 meters per second, the wavelength of the wave is
         (1) 1.8 m   (2) 2.4 m   (3) 3.0 m   (4) 11 m

Solution:
Given: wave travels at 4.5 m/sec (which means velocity = 4.5 m/s)
Crest produced every **0.40 second** means the time for one wave to pass is 0.40 second or the **period (T) = 0.40 second.**
Find: wavelength (λ).

Look for an equation on Reference Table: Waves that has speed (v), wavelength (λ), and period (T). There is no one equation on Reference Table: Waves that has v, λ, and T. Therefore, use two equations,
v = fλ and T = $\dfrac{1}{f}$.

Use the equation
$$v = f\lambda$$
In the equation $v = f\lambda$, you have two unknowns, frequency and wavelength. First find f (frequency), then *substitute f* in the equation $v = f\lambda$ to find λ (wavelength).

First find f (frequency). To find frequency, realize you know period (T); *look for an equation* on Reference Table: Waves that relates period and frequency.

Use the equation
$$T = \frac{1}{f} \qquad\qquad f = \text{frequency}$$
$$T = \text{period}$$

$$\text{Period} = \frac{1}{frequency}$$

Cross multiply
$$Tf = 1$$
$$f = \frac{1}{T}$$

Then, in the equation $v = f\lambda$ *substitute for f* (frequency) $\frac{1}{T}$.

Therefore $v = \frac{1}{T}\lambda$ (use this equation)

Substitute for v 4.5m/s (given). *Substitute for T* 0.40 s (given)

$$4.5 \text{ m/s} = \frac{1}{0.40 \text{ s}}\lambda$$

Cross multiply
$$(4.5 \text{ m/s})(0.40 \text{ s}) = \lambda$$
$$1.8 \text{ m} = \lambda \qquad\qquad \text{Wavelength} = 1.8 \text{ m} \qquad\qquad \text{Answer } 1$$

Remember: $T = \frac{1}{f}$ (given on reference table), $f = \frac{1}{T}$

Question: Determine the frequency of a ray of light with a wavelength of 6.21×10^{-7} meter.

Solution:
Given: Wavelength $= 6.21 \times 10^{-7}$m
Find: Frequency of a ray of light.

Look for an equation on Reference Table: Waves that has wavelength (λ) and frequency (f).

Use the equation
$$v = f\lambda \qquad\qquad f = \text{frequency}$$
$$v = \text{velocity or speed}$$
$$\lambda = \text{wavelength}$$

You have two unknowns, f (frequency) and v (speed). First find v (speed) of (orange) light and then substitute v in $v = f\lambda$ to find f (frequency).

First find v (velocity/speed of light).

Look at Reference Table: List of Physical Constants for speed of light. Note: The specific symbol for speed of light is c.

Speed of light in a vacuum   c   3.00 x 10⁸ m/s

Speed of light in a vacuum (any color **light**-example: red, **orange**) **equals 3.00 x 10⁸** m/s.

Then, in the equation, v = fλ, *substitute for v* (speed), 3.00 x 10⁸ m/s. *Substitute for* λ (wavelength), 6.21 x 10⁻⁷ m (given).

$v = f\lambda$	Or, rearrange the equation:
$3.00 \times 10^8 \text{ m/s} = f(6.21 \times 10^{-7} \text{ m})$	$f = \dfrac{v}{\lambda}$
$\dfrac{3.00 \times 10^8 \ m/s}{6.21 \times 10^{-7} \ m} = f$	$f = \dfrac{3.00 \times 10^8 \ m/s}{6.21 \times 10^{-7} \ m}$
$4.83 \times 10^{14} \text{ Hz} = f$	$f = 4.83 \times 10^{14} \text{ Hz}$
Note: Hz = 1/s	

To determine the frequency of a sound wave (instead of light) when the wavelength is given, use the equation v = fλ and substitute for v (speed of sound) 3.31 x 10² m/s, given on Reference Table: List of Physical Constants.

Now Do Homework Questions #30-34, page 85, and #135-139, pages 100-101.

Section 2:

PROPERTIES OF WAVES

Wave Fronts

Wave front: A pebble is dropped into a lake. Starting from the pebble, waves spread out in concentric circles.

Each **circle** represents the **crest** of a wave (**top** of a **wave**). All **points** on **one crest** of one wave (one circle) are a **wave front**.

At the beach, you have seen waves come to shore and then waves go back to the ocean. All points on one crest of the wave (top of the wave) that together come to shore make up the **wave front**. Similarly, all points on one wave that are in phase (example: 45° above the axis) that together come to shore also make up a **wave front**.

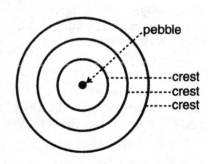

Doppler Effect

If a police car with a **siren** is approaching (**moving closer** to) a person or the person is moving closer to the police car with the siren, , the **frequency** of the siren **appears to increase.** In sound (with sound waves), if the

frequency increases, the **pitch** of the sound is **higher**. In music notes, the pitch increases as one plays do re mi fa so la ti do.

If a police car with a **siren** is **moving away** from a person **or** if a **person** is **moving away** from the police car with a siren, the **frequency** of the siren **appears to decrease**. If frequency appears to decrease, the **pitch** is **lower**.

Doppler effect:

Moving closer: When either the **object making** a **sound** (example, siren) is **moving closer** to the person **or** the **p e r s o n** i s **moving closer** to the sound, the **frequency** a p p e a r s t o **increase** (gets h i g h e r) a n d **p i t c h** g e t s **higher**. Look at the equation v = fλ, velocity = frequency times w a v e l e n g t h . Velocity (v) of s o u n d i s constant. If the object making sound (example siren), is moving closer to the person, the sound waves get

Source moving at constant velocity towards the lady and away from the man

··source

Waves are spread out, wavelength is longer, and frequency appears to decrease.

Waves are closer together, wavelength is shorter, and frequency appears to increase.

squashed together (closer together)(see figure), therefore the length of the wave (wavelength, λ) is shorter (distance from one circle [crest] to the next circle [crest] is less). Since v = fλ (or f = $\frac{v}{\lambda}$) and v is constant, the shorter the wavelength λ, the higher the frequency (f). When frequency (f) is higher, pitch is higher.

Moving further away: When either the **object making** a **sound** (example, siren) is **moving away** from the person **or** the **person** is **moving away** from the sound, the **frequency** appears to **decrease** (gets lower) and **pitch** gets **lower**. If the object making the sound is moving away from a person, the sound waves get further apart (see figure), therefore, the length of the wave (wavelength λ) is longer.

Since $v = f\lambda$ (or $f = \frac{v}{\lambda}$) and v is constant, the longer the wavelength λ, the lower (smaller) the frequency (f). When frequency (f) is lower, pitch is lower.

Look at the equation $v = f\lambda$ and the figure on the previous page. Speed of sound (v) is constant. If a **person** is **moving** at **constant speed toward** a car **alarm**, the sound waves are squashed together by a constant amount (same amount), therefore the wavelength is shorter by a constant amount; v (speed of sound) is constant, therefore f (frequency) or pitch is higher by a constant amount.

But, if a police car with a siren is **moving toward a person** and **speeding up** (increasing speed, accelerating), the sound waves keep being squashed more and more, therefore wavelength keeps getting shorter and shorter, and (because $v = f\lambda$, and v is constant) the frequency or pitch keeps increasing (getting higher and higher). Note: if the police car is **accelerating away** from the person, the **frequency or pitch keeps decreasing** (getting lower and lower).

Question: A 2.00×10^6 hertz radio signal is sent a distance of 7.30×10^{10} meters from Earth to a spaceship orbiting Mars. The spaceship is moving away from Earth when the radio signal is received. Compared to the frequency of the signal sent from Earth, the frequency of the signal received by the spaceship is
    (1) lower   (2) higher   (3) the same

Solution: The spaceship receiving the radio signal is **moving away** from Earth, therefore the **frequency** appears to **decrease** (frequency **gets lower**).
                                      Answer 1

Question: A sound of constant frequency is produced by the siren on top of a firehouse. Compared to the frequency produced by the siren, the frequency observed by a firefighter approaching the firehouse is
    (1) lower   (2) higher   (3) the same

Solution: The firefighter is **approaching** (**moving closer to**) the siren on the firehouse, therefore the **frequency** appears to **increase** (frequency **gets higher**).
                                        Answer 2

The **doppler effect,** similarly, **also** happens **with light.** When either the **person** is **moving closer to** the **light or** the object making the **light** (example, flashlight, headlight of a car) is **moving closer** to the person, the **frequency** appears to **increase.**

Just like in sound, when either the **person** is **moving further away from** the **light or** the object making the **light** (example, flashlight, headlight of a car) is **moving further away** from the person, the **frequency** (of the light waves) appears to **decrease.**

As the person and the source of light **move closer** together, the **frequency** appears to **increase** and the **color of light** appears to change **from red** (**lowest frequency**) to orange, yellow, green, blue, indigo, and to **violet** (**highest frequency** of visible light).

Obviously, as the person or the source of light **moves further** apart (recede), the **frequency decreases** and the **color of light** appears to change **from violet (highest frequency)** to indigo, blue, green, yellow, orange, and to **red (lowest frequency** of visible light).

Relationship Between Frequency and Wavelength

Table: Waves

The velocity of sound is constant in any medium (example, in air or in water) and the velocity of light is constant in any medium.

You know   velocity = frequency x wavelength

$$v = f \quad \lambda$$

Since in any medium (in air or water, etc.) **velocity (v)** is **constant**, if frequency (f) decreases, wavelength (λ) increases, and if frequency (f) increases, then wavelength (λ) decreases.

Question: A source of sound waves approaches a stationary observer through a uniform medium. Compared to the frequency and wavelength of the emitted sound, the observer would detect waves with a
  (1) higher frequency and shorter wavelength
  (2) higher frequency and longer wavelength
  (3) lower frequency and shorter wavelength
  (4) higher frequency and longer wavelength

Solution: As you learned with the doppler effect, when the sound approaches the observer, the frequency appears to increase (higher frequency).

Table: Waves

You know velocity = frequency x wavelength

$$v = f \quad \lambda$$

Since velocity (v) of sound is constant (in any medium), if frequency (f) increases, wavelength (λ) decreases (shorter wavelength). Answer *1*

The **doppler effect** is used by the police to see if a car is speeding. A radar gun shoots radar waves at a car; the waves are reflected back (bounce back) to the radar gun. If the car is moving toward the radar gun, the frequency of the reflected waves (from the car) appears higher (than the waves from the radar gun); if the car is moving away, the frequency of the reflected waves appears lower (than the waves from the radar gun). If the driver is moving toward the radar gun at a normal speed, the reflected radar waves are squashed, wavelength (λ) becomes shorter, and frequency (f) is higher. See the equation $v = f\lambda$. But if the driver is **speeding** at a high speed, the **reflected radar waves** are **squashed even more**, wavelength (λ) is even shorter, and the **frequency** (f) is **even much higher**. The **bigger** the **difference** between the frequency of the radar waves from the radar gun and the reflected radar waves, the **higher** the **speed.**

Question: A radar gun can determine the speed of a moving automobile by measuring the difference in frequency between emitted and reflected radar waves. This process illustrates

(1) resonance (2) the Doppler effect (3) diffraction (4) refraction

Solution: The Doppler effect can be used to determine the speed of the car, as explained on the previous page.   **Answer 2**

Now Do Homework Questions #35-46, pages 85-86, and #140-142, page 101.

SUPERPOSITION

Superposition is when two or more waves travel through the same medium (example: air) at the same time. The **resultant displacement** is the **sum total** of (**add**) how much each wave was displaced (**how much each wave** is **above or below** the **axis**).

Example 1: the highest point on wave **X** (height of wave X) is **2 cm above** the **axis** or a displacement (distance) of 2 cm above the axis. The highest point on Wave **Y** (height of wave Y) is **3 cm above** the **axis** or a displacement (distance) of 3 cm above the axis. Add how much each wave is above or below the axis and you get the resultant displacement. Add **2 cm**

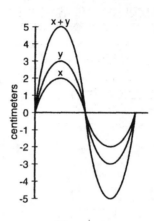

Figure 1

+ 3 cm = 5 cm (5 cm is the maximum height of X plus Y). 5 cm is the **resultant displacement.** The result of superposition is interference. Interference is a combined wave (example, wave X + Y) that is a different height than either wave (wave X or wave Y). See Figure 1 above.

Example 2: Look at the figure. Wave X = 2 cm above the axis (+2 cm) and wave Y is 4 cm below the axis (−4 cm). Add how much each wave is above or below the axis and you get the **resultant displacement.** Add **+2 cm + (−4 cm) = −2 cm.** −2 cm is the **resultant displacement.**

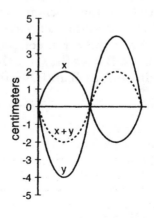

Figure 2

The result of superposition is interference. Interference is a combination of waves (example, wave X + wave Y) that will give a different height than either wave (wave X or wave Y). See figure 2.

Question: The diagram below shows two pulses, A and B, approaching each other in a uniform medium.

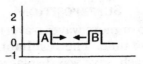

Which diagram best represents the superposition of the two pulses?

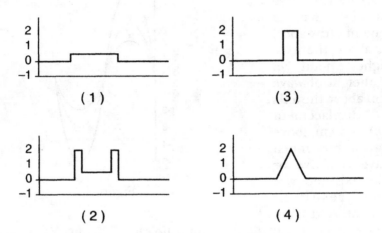

Solution: Superposition: when two or more waves travel in the same medium, add the amount each wave was displaced above or below the axis. When pulse A and pulse B meet, pulse A and pulse B are **added** together. Pulse A and pulse B have the same shape. The combined pulse should have the same width as A or B and the combined height. Only choice 3 has this appearance.   Answer 3

Constructive interference is when the displacements (heights) of both waves are above the axis (example, +2 and +3). Add +2 and +3 together and you get the resultant displacement +5, which is a bigger distance (further) away from the x axis than either +2 or

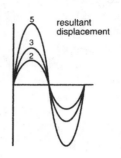

Constructive Interference

+3. Obviously, then, the amplitude (height) of the resultant wave is bigger than the amplitudes (heights) of each wave.

Constructive interference is also when the displacements (heights) of both waves are below the axis (example, −2 and −3). Add −2 and −3 together and you get the resultant displacement −5. which is a bigger distance (further) away from the x axis than either −2 or −3.

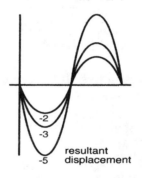

Constructive Interference

Maximum constructive interference is when the **phase difference is 0°**; the crests of the two waves overlap. One crest is directly above or below the other crest. The point of maximum displacement is called an **antinode**.

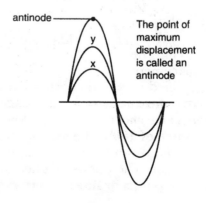

Maximum Constructive Interference

Destructive Interference is when, in the same place, the **displacement** of part of **one wave** (example, wave X) is **above** the **axis,** and the displacement of **part** of the **other wave** (example, wave Y) is **below** the **axis.**

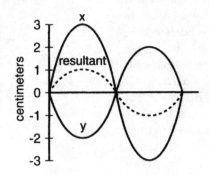

Destructive Interference

Look at the figure at right. One wave (X) is 3 cm above the axis (+3 cm) and the other wave (Y) is 2 cm below the axis (−2 cm). Add how much each wave is above or below the axis and you get the resultant displacement. Add: + 3 cm + (−2 cm) = +1 cm. The resultant displacement is +1 cm above the axis. The displacement (distance away from the axis) of the resultant, 1 cm, is less than the displacement (distance away from the axis) of the bigger wave (X, which is 3 cm above).

Maximum Destructive Interference- You learned that the resultant displacement is equal to the sum of the displacements of all the waves. Look at the figure. One wave is 1 cm above the axis (rest position or equilibrium position) (+1 cm) and the other wave is 1 cm below the axis or equilibrium position (−1 cm). Add: + 1 cm + (−1 cm) = 0 cm. The **resultant displacement** is **zero.** This is called maximum destructive interference.

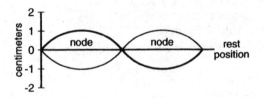

Maximum Destructive Interference

In **maximum destructive interference**, the waves have **equal displacements** (1 cm above axis, 1 cm below axis), the **same frequency,** and a **phase difference of 180°.** The **waves cancel each other** and have zero displacement. Sound would be silent; light waves would combine to give a black (dark) point. The points or lines of zero displacement are called nodes. **Nodes** are **points or lines** of **zero displacement.**

Question: The diagram below represents two waves of equal amplitude and frequency approaching point P as they move through the same medium. **WAVE A**   **WAVE B**

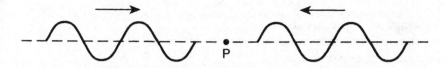

As the two waves pass through each other, the medium at point P will
    (1) vibrate up and down   (2) vibrate left and right
    (3) vibrate into and out of the page   (4) remain stationary

Solution: The crest (top of a wave) moves the medium upward; the trough (bottom of a wave) moves the medium downward. Two waves in the same medium move at the same speed. In this example, the crest and trough both have the same height and shape. The trough of wave A closest to point P and the crest of wave B closest to point P are both the same horizontal distance from point P. As they move toward each other, they will be above and below each other at point P (or both on the line) and cancel each other out. The medium at point P does not move; it remains stationary.   **Answer** *4*

WAVES FROM TWO SOURCES IN PHASE.

The figure shows waves coming from two point sources A and B(small points or openings that waves go through). Waves in phase travel up to the barrier (from the bottom of the drawing to the barrier); the waves pass through two small openings A and B and remain in phase.
The solid lines in the diagram represent crests; the dashed lines are troughs.

Destructive interference: At point C, the **dashed line** (trough) of one wave meets the **solid line** (crest) of the other wave, which causes destructive interference; there is destructive interference at point C (see figure).

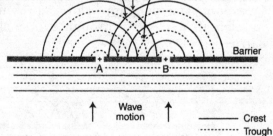

Constructive interference: At point D, the **solid line** (crest) of one wave meets (crosses) the **solid line** (crest) of the other wave, which causes constructive interference; there is constructive interference at point D. At point E, the **dashed line** (trough) of one wave meets (crosses) the **dashed line** (trough) of the other wave, which causes constructive interference; there is constructive interference at point E (see figure above).

In short, when a dashed line (representing a trough) crosses a solid line (representing a crest), it causes destructive interference. When a solid line crosses a solid line, or a dashed line crosses a dashed line, it causes constructive interference.

By looking at a picture of waves, there is another way of seeing if it is constructive or destructive interference. A wavelength is made of two parts, a crest and a trough. A crest is shown by a solid line in the drawing; a trough is shown by a dashed line.
From source A, there are six half wavelengths (six semicircles, 3 dashed and 3 solid) to Point D. From source B,

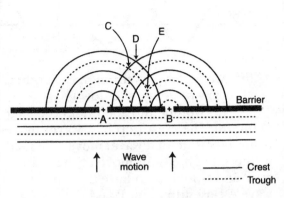

there are six half wavelengths (six semi-circles, three dashed and three solid) to Point D. Subtract the number of half wavelengths from one source (source A) to point D (which is 6 half wavelengths) from the number of half wavelengths from the other source (source B) to point D (6 half wavelengths). $6 - 6 = 0$. When the difference is an **even number** of **half wavelengths,** it is **constructive interference** (because crest meets crest or trough meets trough)(in this example, crest meets crest at point D).

From source A, there are 5 half wavelengths to Point C.
From source B, there are 6 half wavelengths to Point C.
The difference between the number of half wavelengths is $6 - 5 = 1$. When the difference (in number of **half wavelengths**) is an **odd number**, it is **destructive interference** (because crest meets trough(in this example crest meets trough at point C).

Question: The diagram below represents shallow water waves of wavelength λ passing through two small openings, A and B, in a barrier.

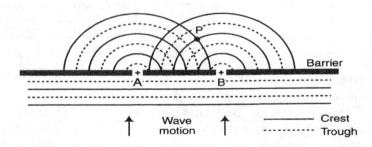

How much longer is the length of path AP than the length of path BP?

    (1) 1λ   (2) 2λ   (3) 3λ   (4) 4λ

Solution:
Path AP is 6 half wavelengths (6 semicircles) or **3 wavelengths (3λ).**
Path BP is 4 half wavelengths (4 semicircles) or **2 wavelength (2λ).**

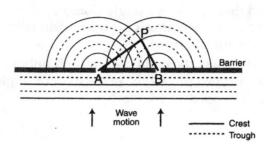

Path AP (3 wavelengths, 3λ) is one wavelength more (or longer) than path BP (which is 2 wavelengths, 2λ).   **Answer 1**

Question: The diagram below represents the wave pattern produced by two sources located at points A and B.

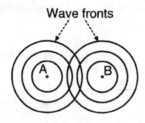

Which phenomenon occurs at the intersections of the circular wave fronts?

    (1) diffraction   (2) interference
    (3) refraction   (4) reflection

Solution: When waves intersect (meet or cross) each other, interference takes place.   **Answer 2**

Question: Two monochromatic, coherent light beams of the same wavelength converge on a screen. The point at which the beams converge appears dark. Which wave phenomenon best explains this effect?

Solution: When the crest of a light wave meets the trough of another light wave, there is destructive interference and it appears dark on the screen (light is cancelled out).

Now Do Homework Questions # 47-50, page 87, and #143-145, page 101.

PULSES

You learned that a pulse is a single vibratory disturbance that moves from one point to another point. It moves horizontally (example, left to right) and vertically (up and down).

Type I –both pulses above the axis or both pulses below the axis.
When you have two pulses above the axis, example +2 and +4, add the pulses together: +2 and +4 = +6.

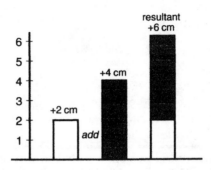

Similarly, if both pulses are below the axis, example −1 and −4, add the pulses together: −1 + (−4) = −5.

Type II- One pulse above the axis and one pulse below the axis.

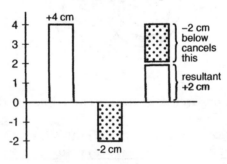

When you have two pulses, one pulse above the axis (+4 cm) and one pulse below the axis (−2 cm), add the pulses together and you get the resultant displacement: +4 and −2= +2

Type III- Different shapes above and below the axis.
When you have two pulses with different shapes, one pulse above the axis and one pulse below the axis,

---

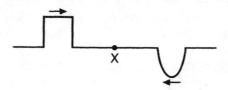

X

See figure 1. Add the pulses together; waves cancel where they overlap (dotted area cancels).

See Figure 2. What is left over is the resultant displacement.

Figure 1

Figure 2

Question: The diagram below represents a rope along which two pulses of equal amplitude, each one cm, approach point P.

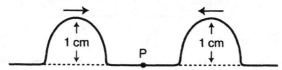

When the two pulses meet at P, the vertical displacement (height) of the rope at point P will be

    (1) 1 cm   (2) 2 cm   (3) 0   (4) ½ cm

Solution: The two pulses move toward each other. **Pulse 1** is **above** the axis and pushes the rope vertically up. The other pulse, **pulse 2,** is also **above** the axis and also pushes the rope up. When the **pulses meet** at point P, it is **constructive interference** and you **add** the amounts pulse 1 and pulse 2 push the rope up or you add the **heights of both pulses.** You add **1 cm** (height of pulse 1) **plus 1 cm** (height of pulse 2) (see Figure 1 below) and the resultant displacement **is 2 cm.** (see Figure 2 below).

Figure 1

Figure 2

Answer 2

Question: The diagram below shows two pulses traveling toward each other in a uniform medium.

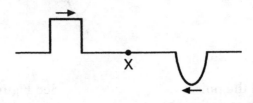

Which diagram best represents the medium when the pulses meet at point X?

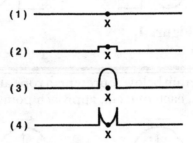

Solution: The pulse on the **left** pushes **vertically up. The pulse** on the **right** pushes **vertically down.** Add the pulses together and you get the resultant displacement (see figure 1 and figure 2 below). Since one pulse in the question is above the axis and one pulse is below the axis, when they meet at point X, there is **destructive interference**, and the **pulses partially cancel** each other. Because they have different shapes, they do not cancel completely. What is left over is the resultant displacement (figure 2).

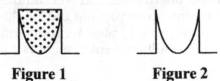

Figure 1   **Figure 2**

See Figure 1. Add the pulses together; waves cancel where they overlap (dotted area cancels).

See Figure 2. What is left over is the resultant displacement.

Answer *4*

How **pulses** appear (**look**) **after** they **pass each other**:

Question: The figure below shows two waves approaching each other in the same uniform medium.

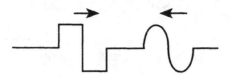

Which diagram best represents the appearance of the medium after the waves have passed through each other?

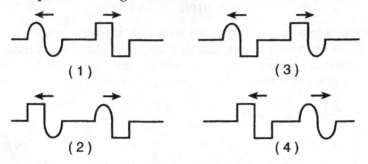

Solution: There is constructive and destructive interference only when two waves meet (are) at a point. **After** the **pulses pass** the **point,** the **pulses keep** their own **shape.**

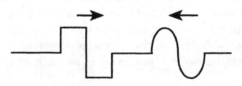

Before pulses pass each other

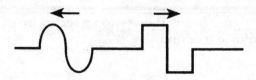

After pulses pass each other

Answer *1*

Now Do Homework Questions #51-58, pages 87-89.

STANDING WAVES

Standing waves are made when two waves of the same amplitude (height) and frequency travel in opposite directions in the same medium. In a standing wave, crest and trough, antinodes and nodes are stationary (they stay at the same place along the length of the string).

Examples of standing waves:

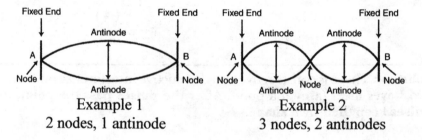

Example 1
2 nodes, 1 antinode

Example 2
3 nodes, 2 antinodes

The **nodes, caused by destructive interference,** are the points that do not move. Example 1 has two nodes and example 2 has three nodes. The nodes are on the x axis (equilibrium line), not above the axis or below the axis (zero displacement). Nodes are at both ends of the string; there can also be nodes along the string on the x axis (see figure above). The **distance between two successive nodes** (nodes next to each other) **equals ½ λ (½ wavelength).**

The antinodes vibrate with the maximum amplitude (height) above and below the axis. Example 1 has one antinode, vibrating above and below the axis; example 2 has two antinodes, vibrating above and below the axis.

In a **standing wave,** the waves **hit the border** (fixed end) and are **reflected back** at the **same amplitude and frequency.** In the figures above, a standing wave is produced when the **waves go from A to B** and are **reflected back from B to A.**

Question: Standing waves in water are produced most often by periodic water waves

    (1) being absorbed at the boundary with a new medium
    (2) refracting at a boundary with a new medium
    (3) diffracting around a barrier
    (4) reflecting from a barrier

Solution: Standing waves are reflected back from a barrier (example wall or cliff, which is a fixed end).   *Answer 4*

Question: A standing wave pattern is produced when a guitar string is plucked. Which characteristic of the standing wave immediately begins to decrease?

    (1) speed   (2) wavelength   (3) frequency   (4) amplitude

Solution: The more energy a string has, the bigger (greater) the amplitude. When a guitar string or rubber band is plucked, the amplitude (height) that the string moves up or down decreases because the string loses energy (energy decreases) as it is moving up or down.

      Answer 4

Question: The diagram below shows a standing wave.

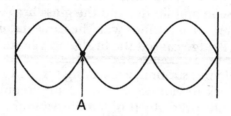

A

Point A on the standing wave is

    (1) a node resulting from constructive interference.
    (2) a node resulting from destructive interference.
    (3) an antinode resulting from constructive interference.
    (4) an antinode resulting from destructive interference.

Solution: Nodes are caused by destructive interference. Answer 2

Now Do Homework Questions #59-63, pages 89-90, and #146-149 page 102.

RESONANCE

Objects vibrate at a specific frequency when the object is hit, touched, etc. For example, this tuning fork has a natural frequency of 512 Hz.

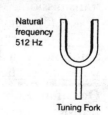

Natural frequency 512 Hz

Tuning Fork

Hit the tuning fork. The tuning fork will vibrate at 512 Hz (vibrations per second). A tuning fork nearby which has the same **natural frequency of 512 Hz** will begin to **vibrate** at 512 Hz without being touched.

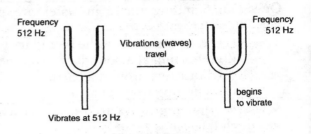

Let's explain. Two tuning forks have the same natural frequency, in this example 512 Hz. Hit one tuning fork. The vibrating tuning fork has energy. The **vibrations** from the first tuning fork (with a frequency of 512 Hz) make the air vibrate. The vibrations (sound waves) in the air, with their energy, **travel** to the **second tuning fork**, which causes the **second tuning fork** to **vibrate** at 512 Hz. The energy causes the vibrations of the second tuning fork to increase in amplitude (loudness).

Resonance is when one **object vibrates** and **causes** another **object** with the **same frequency** to **vibrate** (even without touching it). When an opera singer **sings at** the **natural frequency** of a **glass**, the energy of the sound waves from the singer reaches the glass and **causes** the **glass to vibrate** (vibrations increase in amplitude) and the **glass breaks**. Another example of resonance is when strong winds with the **same natural frequency** as the Tacoma Narrows Bridge caused the bridge to vibrate and collapse.

Question: In a demonstration, a vibrating tuning fork causes a nearby second tuning fork to vibrate with the same frequency. Which wave phenomenon is illustrated by this demonstration?
    (1) the Doppler effect (2) nodes (3) resonance (4) interference
Solution: One tuning fork vibrates (example at 512 Hz) and causes a second tuning fork (with the same natural frequency of 512 Hz) to vibrate at the same frequency (512 Hz). This is resonance. Answer 3

Question: A tuning fork oscillates with a frequency of 256 hertz after being struck by a rubber hammer. Which phrase best describes the sound waves produced by this oscillating tuning fork?
    (1) electromagnetic waves that require no medium for transmission.
    (2) electromagnetic waves that require a medium for transmission.
    (3) mechanical waves that require no medium for transmission.
    (4) mechanical waves that require a medium for transmission.
Solution: You learned that **mechanical waves** (example: **sound** or water waves) need a **medium** (example: air) to travel in. Answer 4

Question: Rubbing a moistened finger around the rim of a water glass transfers energy to the glass at the natural frequency of the glass. Which wave phenomenon is responsible for this effect?

Solution: Resonance is the transfer of energy between two objects with the same natural frequency.

Question: A nearby object may vibrate strongly when a specific frequency of sound is emitted from a loudspeaker. This phenomenon is called

    (1) resonance (2) the Doppler effect (3)reflection (4) interference

Solution: The loudspeaker emits a specific frequency of sound
A nearby object vibrates strongly because it has the same natural frequency emitted by the loudspeaker. Resonance is when one object vibrates (example, loudspeaker) and causes another object with the same natural frequency to vibrate.   **Answer 1**

Remember: In **resonance**, both objects must have the **same natural frequency**.

Now Do Homework Questions #64-70, pages 90-91 and # 150-151, page 102.

DIFFRACTION

Diffraction is spreading of a wave into a region behind a barrier.

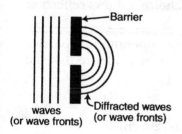 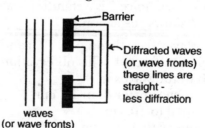

Narrow opening in barrier	Large opening in barrier
Waves go through the narrow opening in the barrier and form semi-circles (behind the barrier).	If the **opening** in the barrier is **larger** than the wavelength (of the entering wave), there is little or no diffraction. Or, you can say, if the wavelength (of the entering wave) is smaller than the opening, it can go through without being diffracted.

Question: The diagram below shows a plane wave passing through a small opening in a barrier.
Copy the diagram on separate paper and sketch four wave fronts after they have passed through the barrier.

Solution: Waves go through the narrow opening in the barrier and form semi-circles (behind the barrier). Draw four semi-circles behind the barrier.

Each semi-circle is a diffracted wave front.

Question: Which diagram represents the phenomenon of diffraction?

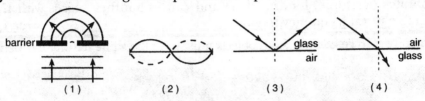

Solution: Choice *1* illustrates diffraction through a small opening. Waves go through the narrow opening in the barrier and form semi-circles behind the barrier.   **Answer** *1*

(Wrong choices: Choice *2* is a standing wave, choice *3* shows reflection and choice *4* shows refraction.)

Question: Waves pass through a 10. centimeter opening in a barrier without being diffracted. This observation provides evidence that the wavelength of the waves is

    (1) much shorter than 10. cm

    (2) equal to 10. cm

    (3) longer than 10. cm, but shorter than 20. cm

    (4) longer than 20. cm

Solution: If the wavelength is smaller than the opening (example, 10 cm) the waves can go without being diffracted. **Answer** *1*

Now Do Homework Questions # 71-80, pages 91-93.

Section *3:*

REFLECTION

A ray shows how (the direction) the light waves are traveling. A ray is perpendicular to the crest of the wave or the wave front (see figure).

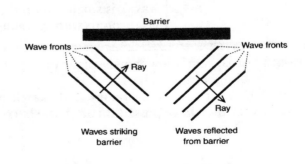

Look at the figure at the right. An incident ray is the ray (representing light waves) that hits the mirror or table top.

The reflected ray is the ray of light that bounces off the mirror or table top or floor, etc.

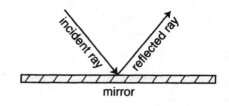

mirror

To generalize, an incident ray starts in a medium (example: air) and hits a surface or boundary (example: mirror, floor, table, etc.). The reflected ray bounces off the surface (example: mirror, table, floor) and goes into the medium (example: air). The incident ray and the reflected ray both must be in one medium; in this example, both rays are in air.

Look at the figure.

At the point where the incident ray hits the mirror (or table, etc.) draw a line perpendicular to the mirror (or table, etc.). The line perpendicular to the mirror is called the NORMAL.

Angle of incidence = Angle of reflection

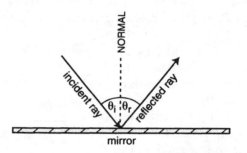

mirror

The **angle between the incident ray** (hitting the mirror) and **the normal** is called the **angle of incidence.** In the figure, the angle of incidence is θ_i.

The **angle between the reflected ray** (bouncing off the mirror) and **the normal** is called the **angle of reflection.** In the figure, the angle of reflection is θ_r.

These two angles are equal; the angle of incidence (θ_i) equals the angle of reflection (θ_r). Look below or on Reference Table: Waves on page reference tables18.

$$\theta_i \qquad = \qquad \theta_r$$

θ_i = incident angle
θ_r = reflected angle

Table: Waves

angle of incidence   =   angle of reflection
(incident angle)   (reflected angle)

The Law of Reflection states that the angle of incidence equals the angle of reflection.

Question: A ray of light passes from air into a block of transparent material X as shown in the diagram. The refracted light ray (which is ray A-P) is reflected from the material X-air boundary at point P. Copy the diagram on separate paper. Using a protractor and straight edge, draw the reflected ray from point P.

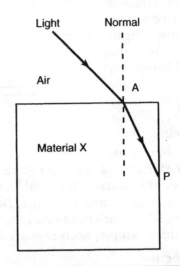

Solution:

Given: Ray A-P (ray 1, the incident ray) hits the side of the block at point P. At point P, the light ray is reflected from the side of the block (see diagram) into the block. (The light ray is reflected from the material X-air boundary at point P).

Find: Draw the reflected ray from point P.

Draw the normal to the side of the block through point P.

Measure θ_i (angle of incidence), the angle between the incident ray and the normal. Put the line drawn on the

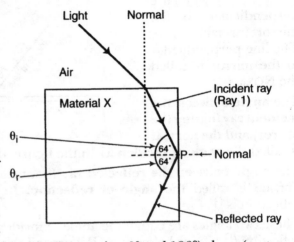

bottom of the protractor (the line connecting 0° and 180°) along (on top of) the normal at point P. The curved part of the protractor is toward the incident ray because we are measuring the angle of incidence. Put the reference point (hole or marker on the bottom of the protractor) at point P (where incident ray and normal meet). θ_i (angle of incidence) = 64°, therefore θ_r (angle of reflection), the angle between the reflected ray and the normal, must = 64°.

Angle of incidence (θ_i) = angle of reflection (θ_r). $\theta_i = \theta_r$, given on Reference Table: Waves.

The question is to draw the reflected ray. Put the line drawn on the bottom of the protractor (the line connecting 0° and 180°) along (on top of) the normal at point P; turn the curved part of the protractor the opposite way, toward the reflected ray that you will draw. Put the reference point (hole or marker on the bottom of the protractor) at point P (where incident ray and normal meet). Measure the angle of reflection, θ_r, which is 64°. Draw the reflected ray 64° from the normal.

Question: A light ray is incident on a plane mirror as shown in the diagram below.
Which ray best represents the reflected ray?

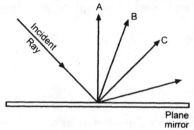

    (1) A   (2) B
    (3) C   (4) D

Solution: Measure the angle of incidence (angle between the incident ray and the normal). Put the **line** on the **bottom** of the **protractor** (the line connecting 0° and 180°) along (**on top** of) the **normal,** with the curved part of the protractor toward the incident ray; **put** the reference point (**hole** or marker which is **on** the **line** on the **bottom**) of the **protractor where** the normal and the incident ray meet the mirror. Angle of incidence = 45°. Angle of incidence = angle of reflection. Therefore, angle of reflection (angle between reflected ray and normal) must = 45°. Again put the **line** on the **bottom** of the **protractor** (the line connecting 0° and 180°) along (**on top** of) the **normal;** turn the curved part of the protractor the opposite way, toward the reflected ray (the side of the drawing with lines A, B, C, and D); **put** the reference point (**hole** or marker which is **on** the **line** on the **bottom**) of the **protractor where** the normal and the reflected ray meet the mirror. Choose the reflected ray that is 45° away from the normal. Answer C

REGULAR REFLECTION AND DIFFUSE REFLECTION

Regular reflection - incident rays hitting a mirror (smooth surface) are parallel to each other (like parallel lines) (the normals are also all parallel) and therefore the reflected rays are also all parallel to each other.

Diffuse reflection- when incident rays hit a rough surface, incident rays are parallel to each other (normals are not parallel),

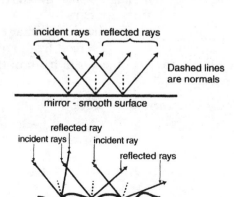

---

therefore the reflected rays are not parallel to each other and are **scattered all over**, in all directions.

Images Formed in a Mirror

Images formed in a mirror- Stand in front of a mirror. Your image is how your face and body appear in the mirror.

Each object is made up of millions of points. Stand in front of a mirror. One point of light from the object (your face and body) hits the mirror at a 0° angle to the normal (normal is a line

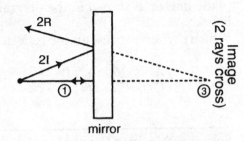

perpendicular to the mirror). This is ray 1 ——▶. The ray is reflected back to your eye: ray 1 ◀——.

Another point of light from the object hits the mirror at a slant. This is ray 2I (incident ray). This ray is reflected back to your eye (ray 2R). When ray 2R reaches your eye, you assume the ray traveled in a straight line. You can see from the picture, the rays (dashed lines from light ray 1 and light ray 2R) meet behind the mirror at point 3, so the object appears (seems) to be at 3.

At the point where the light ray from 1 meets (crosses) the reflected light ray from 2, an image (picture) is formed. When you stand in front of a plane (flat, not curved) mirror, your image appears the same size as you are. In a plane mirror, size of the image is the same as the size of the object.

In a plane (flat, not curved) mirror, your image is erect (standing), but reversed from left to right. (If you move your left hand, it looks like your right hand is moving.) Your image appears behind the mirror the same distance as you are standing in front of the mirror.

This is a virtual image, which means the picture of you is not really behind the mirror. It only appears to be.

In short, in a plane mirror, the **image** (behind the mirror) is the same size as the object, erect, reversed from left to right, the same distance behind the mirror as the object is in front of the mirror, and the image is a virtual image.

Now Do Homework Questions #81-85, pages 93-94 and # 152-157, page 103.

REFRACTION OF LIGHT

Light can travel in a vacuum and in a medium (examples: air, water, flint glass, glycerol, etc.).

Case I: Shine a flashlight at an angle; the light rays go from air into water.
Light rays travel in air at about 3.00×10^8 m/s. Light travels slower in water.
The normal line is perpendicular (at right angles) to the surface of the water. When light goes from air into water, it **bends toward the normal** (because light travels slower in water).

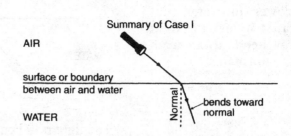

The light rays bend toward the normal.

Rule: When **light** travels **from** a less dense medium (like **air**) **to** a more optically dense medium (like **water**), the **light** ray **bends toward** the **normal** (instead of continuing the straight line from the flashlight).

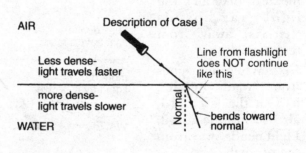

The bending of light when it goes from one medium (example: air) to a different medium (example: water) is called **refraction. Light rays bend (are refracted)** when they go from one medium (example: air) to a different medium (example: water).

Hint: When light goes from "air to wa**ter**", look at the last word, wa**ter**. wa**ter ends in "ter"**; it sounds like **toward** the normal. When light goes from air to wa**ter**, light bends **toward** the normal.

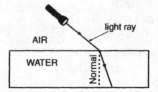

Case II: This is the reverse way, **opposite way**. When **light** at an angle **goes from water to air**, (light travels slower in water and faster in air), the **light** ray **bends away from** the **normal**.

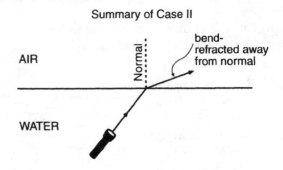

Summary of Case II

AIR

Normal

bend-refracted away from normal

WATER

The light rays bend away from the normal

When light travels from a more dense medium (like water) to a less optically dense medium (like air), the light ray bends (refracts) away from the normal.

Hint: When light goes from "water to air", look at the last word, **air**. Air has the **a** in it. Light bends **away** from the normal.

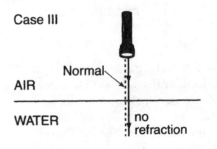

Description of Case II

AIR

Less dense-light travels faster

Normal

Line from flashlight does NOT continue like this

bends away from normal

more dense-light travels slower

WATER

Case III: Shine a flash**light** from air **straight down** on the water (the light ray is on the normal line). Angle of incidence (angle between the incident ray and the normal) is 0°. Light slows down in water but the **light** ray is **not bent (not refracted)**.

Case III

Normal

AIR

WATER

no refraction

ANGLE OF REFRACTION

The angle of refraction is the angle between the refracted ray (bent ray) and the normal.

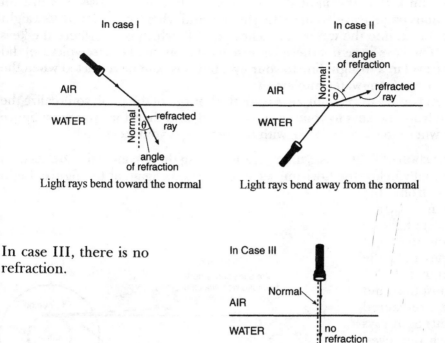

In case I

Light rays bend toward the normal

In case II

Light rays bend away from the normal

In case III, there is no refraction.

In Case III

no refraction

EFFECTS OF REFRACTION

If you lost your keys, money, or diamond ring in the bottom of a lake or pool you would try to get them back. How would you do it? Get a stick or pole with a net on the end. You would put the net where you think the keys are (appear to be).

You think the keys are here (where you put the net) but they are not there. Let's understand why.

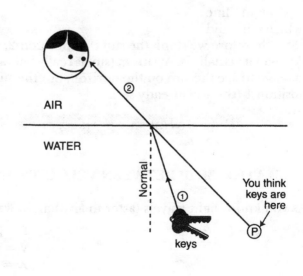

Ray 1 is the light ray that went from the keys to the top of the water. Ray 2 is the light ray that went from the top of the water to your eye. Light bent (was refracted) when light went from water to air.

You think that the light that reached your eye (ray 2-see picture on previous page) traveled in a straight line, and when you follow the straight line, ray 2, into the water, it reaches point P, which is not where the keys are. The keys were not there because light from the keys (see picture) did not travel in a straight line to your eye, but was bent or refracted when the light went from water into air.

When you try to get your keys from the bottom of the pool, you realize the light from the keys to your eye is refracted, and therefore you must figure out where to place the stick with the net to get your keys back.

Refraction of light causes mirages and seeing the sun after the sun set (sun is actually below the horizon, see figure). Look again at the figure. Light rays from the sun are refracted (bent) when the light comes near the Earth's atmosphere and the refracted (bent) light rays reach our eyes. We think the light from the sun that reached our eyes traveled in a straight line (which it did not), therefore we think the sun is at position 2, which is higher up in the sky than it actually is. At sunset (sun is really below the horizon) you still can manage to see the sun on the horizon, but the sun is really lower down, at position 1 (the sun already set).

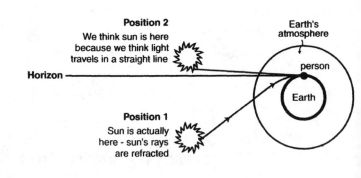

Now Do Homework Questions # 86-88, page 94

RELATIONSHIP BETWEEN VELOCITY AND WAVELENGTH

As you know, light travels faster in air than in water.

$$v = f \lambda$$

f = frequency
v = velocity or speed
λ = wavelength

The **same number** of light waves per second (example: from the flashlight) go from one medium (example: air) to the next medium (example: water), therefore, the **frequency** of the light waves is **constant** (see figure). Look at the equation

$$v = f \lambda$$

Since frequency (f) of the light waves is constant, when speed (v) of light in water is slower, wavelength (λ) of light is shorter (smaller).

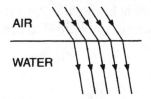

AIR

WATER

Frequency is constant

Question: A change in the speed of a wave as it enters a new medium produces a change in

    (1) frequency (2) period   (3) wavelength   (4) phase

Solution: *Look for an equation* on Reference Table: Waves, on page reference tables 18, for speed (v) of a wave.

Use the equation

         v   =   f λ

velocity or speed =   frequency x wavelength

A certain number of waves (example: 100 waves per second) go from the first medium (example: air) to the new medium (example: water); the number of waves per second in both media (example: air and water) are the same, which means the frequency (f) is constant.

Look at the equation **v = fλ**. Since frequency (f) is constant,

    when velocity or **speed (v) decreases, wavelength (λ) decreases**;

    when velocity or **speed (v) increases, wavelength (λ) increases**.

As you can see, a change in velocity or speed produces a change in wavelength.   Answer *3*

ABSOLUTE INDEX OF REFRACTION (n)

Absolute index of refraction (n) is the **ratio** of the **speed of light in a vacuum (c) to** the **speed of light in** a **medium** (material such as water, corn oil, flint glass, lucite, diamond, etc.) (v).

$$n = \frac{c}{v}$$

    n = absolute index of refraction

    c = speed of light in a vacuum

    v = velocity or speed

absolute index of refraction = $\dfrac{\text{speed of light in a vacuum}}{\text{speed of light in a medium (ex. in water, etc.)}}$

Note: Speed of light in air is approximately the same as the speed of light in a vacuum, 3.00×10^8 m/s.

Find the absolute index of refraction (n) of lucite.
Look below or on Reference Table: Absolute Indices of Refraction on page
reference tables 8-9 to find the index of refraction (n) of lucite.

Absolute Indices of Refraction ($f = 5.09 \times 10^{14}$ Hz)	
Air	1.00
Diamond	2.42
Glass, flint	1.66
Lucite	1.50
Water	1.33
Zircon	1.92

The absolute index of refraction (n) of lucite = 1.50.

Look at the equation $\quad n = \dfrac{c}{v}$

$$index\ of\ refraction = \frac{speed\ of\ light\ in\ vacuum}{speed\ of\ light\ in\ medium\ (lucite)}$$

n (index of refraction of lucite) = 1.50 (see above), which means 1.50 = the
ratio of the speed of light in a vacuum (c) to the speed of light in lucite (v).
Light travels 1½ times as fast in a vacuum (c) (or air) as it travels in lucite (v).

For diamond, n (index of refraction) = 2.42 (see table above), which means
2.42 =the ratio of the speed of light in a vacuum or air to the speed of light
in diamond (v).

By looking at the equation $n = \dfrac{c}{v}$ or (cross multiply) nv = c, since c is
constant, 3.00 x 10^8 m/s (given on Reference Table: List of Physical
Constants), **the bigger n** (index of refraction) is, **the smaller is v** (speed of
light in the medium); the smaller n is, the bigger is v (speed of light in the
medium).

Example: lucite, n = 1.50

$n = \dfrac{c}{v}$

$1.50 = \dfrac{3.00 \times 10^8 \ m/s}{v}$

Cross multiply

$1.50 \ v = 3.00 \times 10^8 \ m/s$

$v = \dfrac{3.00 \times 10^8 \ m/s}{1.50} = 2.00 \times 10^8 \ m/s$

Example: diamond, n = 2.42

$n = \dfrac{c}{v}$

$2.42 = \dfrac{3.00 \times 10^8 \ m/s}{v}$

Cross multiply

$2.42 \ v = 3.00 \times 10^8 \ m/s$

$v = \dfrac{3.00 \times 10^8 \ m/s}{2.42} = 1.24 \times 10^8 \ m/s$

Diamond has a **bigger index of refraction** (n = 2.42) than lucite (n = 1.50); therefore, in diamond, light has a **smaller speed(v).**

Lucite has a **smaller index of refraction (n** = 1.50) than diamond (n = 2.42); therefore in lucite, light has a bigger speed (v).

Rule: By looking at the equation $n = \dfrac{c}{v}$ or (cross multiply) nv = c, you see the bigger n (index of refraction) is, the smaller is v (speed of light in the medium); the smaller n is, the bigger is v (speed of light in the medium).

By looking at the equation $n = \dfrac{c}{v}$, you learned, the **bigger n** (index of refraction) is, the **smaller** is **v** (speed of light in the medium).

You also learned, by looking at the equation **v** =fλ, f (frequency) is constant and the **smaller v** (speed of light) is, the **smaller** is λ (wavelength). Therefore, you can **combine both equations**, the **bigger n** is, the **smaller** is v, and the smaller v is, the **smaller** is λ **(wavelength).**

By looking at both equations you can also say the **smaller n**, the **bigger v** (from the first equation) and the bigger v, the **bigger** λ (from the second equation).

Later you will see there is also another equation which shows the relationship among n, v, and λ.

Compare Absolute Index of Refraction to See if Light Bends Toward or Away from the Normal, or Does Not Bend

You learned when light goes from air to water, light bends toward the normal. An easy way to know if **light bends toward** the **normal or away from** the **normal** is to **compare** the **index of refraction (n)** of each medium, (example: air and water), as explained below.

Look at Reference Table: Absolute Indices of Refraction on the next page. Light goes from air (index of refraction 1.00) to water (index of refraction 1.33).

Absolute Indices of Refraction	
Air	1.00
Corn oil	1.47
Glass, flint	1.66
Glycerol	1.47
Water	1.33

Rule: When light goes from a **lower index of refraction** (example: **air**, 1.00) (or higher speed) **to a higher index of refraction** (example: **water**, 1.33) (smaller speed), **light bends toward the normal**.

When light goes from a **higher index of refraction** (example: **water**, 1.33) (or smaller speed) **to a lower index of refraction** (example: **air**, 1.00) (higher speed), **light bends away from the normal**.

But, when light goes from corn oil (n = 1.47) to glycerol (n = 1.47), both have the **same index of refraction (n),** and **light does not bend**.

Helpful Hint: You learned, when light goes from air, lower index of refraction (index of refraction 1.00) to water, higher index of refraction (index of refraction 1.33) light bends toward the normal. You can now generalize when light goes from a lower index of refraction to a higher index of refraction, light bends toward the normal.

Now Do Homework Questions #89-97, pages 94-96.

Question: A beam of monochromatic light (light of one color or one frequency) travels through flint glass, crown glass, Lucite, and water. The speed of the light beam is slowest in

    (1) flint glass   (2) crown glass   (3) Lucite   (4) water

Solution:

Given: Light travels through flint glass, crown glass, Lucite, and water.

Find: In which material does light have the slowest speed.

As you know, each material (flint glass, crown glass, Lucite, and water) has its own index of refraction (n), given on Reference Table: Absolute Indices of Refraction.

Look for an equation on Reference Table: Waves on page reference tables 18-19 that has index of refraction (n) and speed of light in the material (v).

Use the equation

$$n = \frac{c}{v}$$

                            n = absolute index of refraction

                            c = speed of light in a vacuum

                            v = velocity or speed

c (speed of light in a vacuum)= 3.00×10^8 m/s, a constant, given on Reference Table: List of Physical Constants.

In the equation above, since c is constant, when n (index of refraction) is bigger, v (velocity/speed) is smaller or slower.

Look below or on Reference Table: Absolute Indices of Refraction on page reference tables 8-9 for the material with the biggest n :

Absolute Indices of Refraction $(f = 5.09 \times 10^{14}$ Hz)	
Ethyl alcohol	1.36
Glass, crown	1.52
Glass, flint	1.66
Lucite	1.50
Water	1.33

The absolute index of refraction (n) of flint glass is 1.66, crown glass 1.52, lucite 1.50, and water 1.33. Flint glass has the biggest index of refraction (n), therefore the smallest speed (slowest speed). Answer *1*

Question: A ray of monochromatic light passes through a flint glass prism. What is the speed of the light ray in flint glass?
    (1) 5.53×10^{-9} m/s   (2) 1.81×10^{8} m/s
    (3) 3.00×10^{8} m/s   (4) 4.98×10^{8} m/s

Solution:
Given: Light travels in flint glass.
Find: Speed of a light ray in flint glass.
As you know, a material such as flint glass has its own absolute index of refraction (n), given on Reference Table: Absolute Indices of Refraction.

Look for an equation on Reference Table: Waves that has absolute index of refraction (n) and speed of light in flint glass (v).

Use the equation

$$n = \frac{c}{v}$$
                    n = absolute index of refraction

                    c = speed of light in a vacuum
                    v = velocity or speed

absolute index of refraction $= \dfrac{speed\ of\ light\ in\ a\ vacuum}{speed\ of\ light\ in\ a\ medium\ (such\ as\ flint\ glass)}$

First find c (speed of light in a vacuum) and find n (absolute index of refraction) of flint glass, then substitute n and c in the equation $n = \dfrac{c}{v}$ to find v.

First find c (speed of light in a vacuum). Look below or on Reference Table: List of Physical Constants for speed of light.

Speed of light in a vacuum   c   3.00 x 10^8 m/s

Find n (absolute index of refraction) of flint glass. Look below or on Reference Table: Absolute Indices of Refraction.

Absolute Indices of Refraction	
Air	1.00
Glass, flint	1.66

The index of refraction (n) for flint glass = 1.66.

Then, in the equation $n = \dfrac{c}{v}$, *substitute for n* (index of refraction) of flint glass 1.66. *Substitute for c* 3.00 x 10^8 m/s.

$$n = \frac{c}{v}$$

$1.66 = \dfrac{3.00 \times 10^8 \; m/s}{v}$

Cross multiply

1.66 v = 3.00 x 10^8 m/s

$v = \dfrac{3.00 \times 10^8 \; m/s}{1.66} = 1.81 \times 10^8 \; m/s$

Speed of light in flint glass =
1.81 x 10^8 m/s   Answer 2

or, rearrange the equation:

$$v = \frac{c}{n}$$

$v = \dfrac{3.00 \times 10^8 \; m/s}{1.66} = 1.81 \times 10^8 \; m/s$

Speed of light in flint glass =
1.81 x 10^8 m/s   Answer 2

Question: In a certain material, a beam of monochromatic light ($f = 5.09 \times 10^{14}$ hertz) has a speed of 2.25 x 10^8 meters per second. The material could be

(1) crown glass   (2) flint glass   (3) glycerol   (4) water

Solution:

Given: Speed of light in the material is 2.25 x 10^8 m/s.

Find: Which material.

Different materials (example: crown glass, flint glass, etc.) have different absolute indices of refraction (n).

You need to find index of refraction (n) of the material in this question and then you can look at Reference Table: Absolute Indices of Refraction to see what material it is.

Look for an equation on Reference Table: Waves that has index of refraction (n) and speed of light in material (v).

Use the equation

$$n = \frac{c}{v}$$

n = absolute index of refraction
c = speed of light in a vacuum
v = velocity or speed

First find c (speed of light in a vacuum) then substitute c and v (given) in the equation $n = \dfrac{c}{v}$ to find n.

First find c (speed of light in a vacuum). Look below or on Reference Table: List of Physical Constants on page reference tables 2 for speed of light.

Speed of light in a vacuum c 3.00×10^8 m/s

In the equation $n = \dfrac{c}{v}$, **then substitute for c** 3.00×10^8 m/s. **Substitute for v** (speed of light in the material) 2.25×10^8 m/s (given).

$$n = \frac{3.00 \times 10^8 \ m/s}{2.25 \times 10^8 \ m/s}$$

n = 1.33

Look below or on Reference Table: Absolute Indices of Refraction on page reference tables 8-9.

Absolute Indices of Refraction	
Air	1.00
Glass, crown	1.52
Glass, flint	1.66
Glycerol	1.47
Water	1.33

When n = 1.33, the material could be water.   Answer *4*

Question: The speed of light ($f = 5.09 \times 10^{14}$ Hz) in a transparent material is 0.75 times its speed in air. The absolute index of refraction of the material is approximately

  (1) 0.75   (2) 1.3   (3) 2.3   (4) 4.0

Solution:

Given: Speed of light in material is 0.75 times the speed of light in air.

 f (frequency) of light = 5.09×10^{14} Hz, which you will learn later is yellow light.

Find: Absolute index of refraction of the material.

Look for an equation on Reference Table: Waves that has absolute index of refraction (n) and speed of light in the material (v).

Use the equation

$$n = \frac{c}{v}$$

n = absolute index of refraction

c = speed of light in a vacuum
v = velocity or speed

First find c and v, then substitute c and v in the equation $n = \dfrac{c}{v}$ to find n.

First find c. **Speed** of **light** in **air** is approximately the same as **speed of light** in a **vacuum (c) 3.00 x 10⁸ m/s**, given on Reference Table: List of Physical Constants on page reference tables 2-3.

Find v. The speed of light in the material (v) is 0.75 times the speed of light in air (speed of light in air is about 3.00 x 10⁸ m/s). Speed of light in the material (v) = **0.75 (3.00 x 10⁸ m/s).**

Then in the equation $n = \dfrac{c}{v}$ *substitute for c* 3.00 x 10⁸ m/s. *Substitute for v* 0.75 x (3.00 x 10⁸ m/s).

$$n = \frac{3.00 \times 10^8 \ m/s}{0.75(3.00 \times 10^8 \ m/s)} = 1.3$$

Answer 2

Question: The diagram below represents a ray of monochromatic light ($f = 5.09 \times 10^{14}$ Hz) passing from medium X (n = 1.46) into fused quartz. Which path will the ray follow in the quartz?

    (1) A   (2) B
    (3) C   (4) D

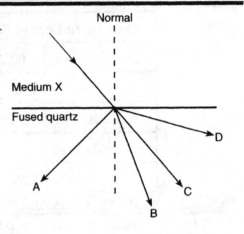

Solution:
Given: In medium X, n = 1.46, which means absolute index of refraction = 1.46.
Find: Which path will the light ray follow (travel) in quartz.

You learned when you compare the absolute index of refraction of two media (in this example medium X and quartz) you can tell if light bends toward the normal, away from the normal, or does not bend. The absolute index of refraction (n) of medium X is n = 1.46 (given), but you need to find the absolute index of refraction (n) of quartz.

Look on the next page or at Reference Table: Absolute Indices of Refraction on page reference tables 8-9 to find the absolute index of refraction (n) of quartz.

Absolute Indices of Refraction	
Air	1.00
Lucite	1.50
Quartz, fused	1.46

The absolute index of refraction **(n)** of **fused quartz = 1.46.**

The absolute index of refraction **(n)** of **medium X = 1.46** (given). Since medium X and fused quartz have the **same absolute index of refraction**, 1.46, **light** does **not bend** (does not refract).

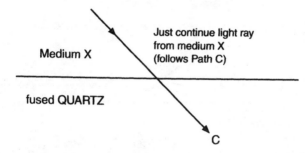

Light ray from medium X continues to go in the same direction

Medium X

Just continue light ray from medium X (follows Path C)

fused QUARTZ

C

The light ray from medium X continues to move in the same direction (path C).   Answer 3

Now Do Homework Questions #98-104, pages 96-97.

RELATIONSHIP OF INDEX OF REFRACTION (n), VELOCITY (v), AND WAVELENGTH (λ)

You learned $n = \dfrac{c}{v}$.

$$absolute\ index\ of\ refraction = \frac{speed\ of\ light\ in\ a\ vacuum}{speed\ of\ light\ in\ a\ medium\ (ex.\ in\ water,\ etc.)}$$

When n (index of refraction) is bigger, v (speed) is smaller or slower.
When n (index of refraction) is smaller, v (speed) is bigger.

You learned $v = f\lambda$

velocity = frequency x wavelength

Frequency of light waves (number of waves per second that go from one medium, example air, to another medium, example water) does not change (is constant). Look at the equation $v = f\lambda$. Since f (frequency of the light waves) is constant, when v (velocity/speed) of the light waves decreases (slows down), then λ (wavelength) decreases; when v (velocity/speed) of the light waves increases then λ (wavelength) increases.

Or

You can also see the relationship among n (index of refraction), velocity, and wavelength by using the equation below, given on Reference Table: Waves.

$$\frac{n_2}{n_1} = \frac{v_1}{v_2} = \frac{\lambda_1}{\lambda_2}$$

n = absolute index of refraction

v = velocity or speed

λ = wavelength

Example: Light goes from air (medium 1) to water (medium 2).

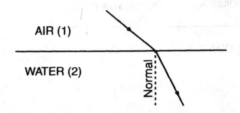

AIR (1)

WATER (2)

Normal

In the equation above, n_1, v_1, and λ_1 mean index of refraction, velocity, and wavelength of light in medium 1 (in this example air); n_2, v_2, and λ_2 mean index of refraction, velocity, and wavelength of light in medium 2 (in this example water).

$$\frac{n_2}{n_1} = \frac{v_1}{v_2} = \frac{\lambda_1}{\lambda_2}$$

n = absolute index of refraction

v = velocity or speed

λ = wavelength

Look at $\dfrac{n_2}{n_1} = \dfrac{v_1}{v_2}$ from the equation above.

Cross multiply

$n_2 v_2 = n_1 v_1$

Therefore, if n_2 (index of refraction of second medium) is **bigger**, v_2 (velocity in second medium) must be **smaller**, so that $n_2 v_2 = n_1 v_1$.

bigger smaller

Table: Waves

If n_2 (index of refraction of second medium) is **smaller**, v_2 (velocity in second medium) must be **bigger**, so that $n_2v_2 = n_1v_1$.

smaller bigger

Look at $\dfrac{n_2}{n_1} = \dfrac{\lambda_1}{\lambda_2}$ which is part of $\dfrac{n_2}{n_1} = \dfrac{v_1}{v_2} = \dfrac{\lambda_1}{\lambda_2}$ given on Reference Table: Waves and Optics.

Cross multiply

$n_2\lambda_2 = n_1\lambda_1$

Therefore, if n_2 (index of refraction in second medium) is bigger, λ_2 (wavelength in second medium) must be smaller (shorter), so that

$n_2\lambda_2 = n_1\lambda_1$

bigger smaller

If n_2 (index of refraction in second medium) is smaller, λ_2 (wavelength in second medium) must be bigger (longer), so that

$n_2\lambda_2 = n_1\lambda_1$

smaller bigger

Look at the example below (when one increases, the other decreases):
Area equals length times width. Let's see what happens to width when length is increased (or becomes bigger) and area is kept constant ($24\ m^2$).

	Length x width	= area
Area = length x width.	6 m x 4 m	= $24\ m^2$.
Increase length to 8 m:	8 m x 3 m	= $24\ m^2$
Increase length to 12 m:	12 m x 2 m	= $24\ m^2$

As you can see, as length increases, width decreases. Similarly, in the equation $n_2\lambda_2 = n_1\lambda_1$, as n_2 **increases**, λ_2 **decreases**. Notice: In the area problem, you can change the length or change the width, but length x width must always equal $24\ m^2$. In this equation $n_2\lambda_2 = n_1\lambda_1$, you can increase or decrease n_2 or λ_2, but n_2 x λ_2 must always equal to $n_1\lambda_1$ (n_1 times λ_1).

By just looking at the equation $\dfrac{n_2}{n_1} = \dfrac{v_1}{v_2} = \dfrac{\lambda_1}{\lambda_2}$, you see **n** (index of refraction) is **inversely proportional to v** (velocity) **and** λ (wavelength); n_2 is on the top of the fraction, v_2 and λ_2 are on the bottom of the fraction. This means if **n_2** (index of refraction in the second medium) is **bigger**, v_2 (velocity in the second medium) and λ_2 (wavelength in the second medium) must be **smaller**.
If **n_2** (index of refraction in the second medium) is **smaller**, v_2 (velocity in the second medium) and λ_2 (wavelength in the second medium) must be **bigger**.

Question: As a monochromatic beam of light passes obliquely from flint glass into water, how do the characteristics of the beam of light change?

(1) Its wavelength decreases and its frequency decreases.
(2) Its wavelength decreases and its frequency increases.
(3) Its wavelength increases and it bends toward the normal.
(4) Its wavelength increases and it bends away from the normal.

Solution:

Given: A beam of light passes obliquely from flint glass into water.
Find: How do the characteristics (wavelength, frequency, and bending) of the beam of light change.

By comparing the absolute indices of refraction of flint glass and water, you can see which direction light bends and how frequency and wavelength change.

Compare the absolute index of refraction of flint glass and water. Look at Reference Table: Absolute Indices of Refraction.

Absolute Indices of Refraction	
Glass, flint	1.66
Water	1.33

The index of refraction of flint glass is 1.66; the index of refraction of water is 1.33.

You learned, as a **light** ray **goes** from a **bigger index of refraction** (flint glass, n =1.66) **to a smaller index of refraction** (water, n = 1.33) light **bends away from** the **normal.**

A light ray goes from a bigger index of refraction (flint glass, n =1.66) to a smaller index of refraction (water, n = 1.33). The index of refraction, n, decreases. From the equation $n = \dfrac{c}{v}$, or (cross multiply) $nv = c$, you see **when n decreases, v increases** (gets bigger), and by looking at the equation $v = f\lambda$, you know **when v is bigger, λ is bigger** (increases).

In short, when light goes from flint glass to water, its wavelength (λ) increases and the light ray bends away from the normal.   *Answer 4*

Or

Use the equation $\dfrac{n_2}{n_1} = \dfrac{v_1}{v_2} = \dfrac{\lambda_1}{\lambda_2}$. You can notice, in the equation, that the small 2 next to the n (n_2) is on the top, while the small 2 next to v and λ (v_2 and λ_2) is on the bottom, which shows that n is inversely proportional to v and λ.

When light goes from flint glass (medium 1, n = 1.66) to water (medium 2, n = 1.33), the index of refraction (n) gets smaller (decreases). When n_2 is smaller, v_2 and λ_2 are bigger.

When light goes from a **bigger index of refraction** (n) (flint glass, n = 1.66) **to a smaller index of refraction** (n) (water, n = 1.33), light **bends away from** the **normal.**

In short, when light goes from flint glass to water, its wavelength in water (λ_2) increases (gets bigger) and the light ray bends away from the normal (see above).   Answer 4

Question: Light travels from air to water. Find the speed of light in water.

Solution:
Given: light travels from air to water.
Find: speed of light in water.

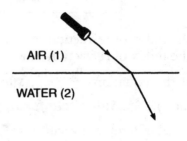

Look at the figure. In this example, let n_1, v_1, λ_1 represent index of refraction, velocity/speed, and wavelength in medium 1 (air); let n_2, v_2, λ_2 represent index of refraction, velocity/speed, and wavelength in medium 2 (water).

You know v_1 (speed of light in air) is almost the same as speed of light in a vacuum, 3.00×10^8 m/s, given on Reference Table: List of Physical Constants. You need to find v_2 (speed of light in water).

Look for an equation on Reference Table: Waves that has v_1 and v_2.

$$\frac{n_2}{n_1} = \frac{v_1}{v_2} = \frac{\lambda_1}{\lambda_2}$$ n = absolute index of refraction

                                                    v = velocity
                                                    λ = wavelength

By looking at Reference Table: Absolute Indices of Refraction, you know the absolute index of refraction of air (n_1) and water (n_2). You know n_1 and n_2; you know v_1 (speed of light in air). Therefore, you have three knowns (n_1, n_2, v_1) and only one unknown, v_2 (speed of light in water). Use the part of the equation above that has three knowns (n_1, n_2, v_1) and one unknown v_2.

Use the equation
$$\frac{n_2}{n_1} = \frac{v_1}{v_2}$$

Look at part of Reference Table: Absolute Indices of Refraction on the next page or on page reference tables 8-9. Find index of refraction of air (n_1) and water (n_2).

Absolute Indices of Refraction $(f = 5.09 \times 10^{14}$ Hz)	
Air	1.00
Water	1.33
Lucite	1.50

The index of refraction of air (n_1) equals 1.00.
The index of refraction of water (n_2) equals 1.33.

In the equation $\dfrac{n_2}{n_1} = \dfrac{v_1}{v_2}$, **substitute for n_2** (index of refraction of water) 1.33. **Substitute for n_1** (index of refraction of air) 1.00.

Speed of light in a vacuum = 3.00×10^8 m/s, given on Reference Table: List of Physical Constants. Speed of light in air is about the same, 3.00×10^8 m/s. **Substitute for v_1** (speed of light in air) 3.00×10^8 m/s and find v_2 (speed of light in water).

$$\frac{1.33}{1.00} = \frac{3.00 \times 10^8 \ m/s}{v_2}$$

Cross multiply
$$1.33 \, v_2 = 1.00 \, (3.00 \times 10^8 \ m/s)$$

$$v_2 = \frac{3.00 \times 10^8 \ m/s}{1.33} = 2.26 \times 10^8 \ m/s$$

Speed of light in water (v_2) = 2.26×10^8 m/s.

If you know n_2, n_1, and one λ (wavelength, ex: in air), you can find the other λ (ex: in water) by using the equation
$$\frac{n_2}{n_1} = \frac{v_1}{v_2} = \frac{\lambda_1}{\lambda_2}.$$

Example: light goes from air into water.
λ_1 (wavelength of light in medium 1, air) is given.
Find λ_2 (wavelength of light in medium 2, water).

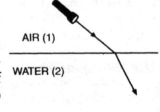

AIR (1)

WATER (2)

By looking at Reference Table: Absolute Indices of Refraction, you know the index of refraction (n) (example, of air, n_1, and water, n_2). You know n_1 and n_2; you know λ_1 (given). Therefore, you have three knowns (n_1, n_2, λ_1) and only one unknown, λ_2. Use the part of the equation above that has three knowns (n_1, n_2, λ_1) and one unknown, λ_2.

Use

$$\frac{n_2}{n_1} = \frac{\lambda_1}{\lambda_2}.$$

$$\frac{\text{index of refraction of second medium (water)}}{\text{index of refraction of first medium (air)}} = \frac{\text{wavelength in first medium (air)}}{\text{wavelength in second medium (water)}}$$

Use the equation above to find λ_2 when n_2, n_1, and λ_1 are given,

or

use the equation above to find λ_1 when n_2, n_1, and λ_2 are given.

Now Do Homework Questions #105-107, Page 97.

SNELL'S LAW: $n_1 \sin \theta_1 = n_2 \sin \theta_2$

Snell's Law describes the bending (refraction) of light when it goes from one medium, example air, to another medium, example lucite (see figure below). It shows the relationship between the absolute **index of refraction** of medium 1 (n_1), the absolute index of refraction of medium 2 (n_2), **and** the **sines** of the **angles** (θ_1 and θ_2).

n_1	$\sin \theta_1$	=	n_2	$\sin \theta_2$
Index of refraction of first medium	x sin of angle of incidence		Index of refraction of second medium	x sin of angle of refraction

Example: Light goes from air to a lucite block at an angle of 33° (see figure). Look at the equation above and the figure below. The 1 in $n_1 \sin \theta_1$ means the first medium that light goes through (in this example, air); the 2 in $n_2 \sin \theta_2$ means the second medium that light goes through (in this example, lucite).

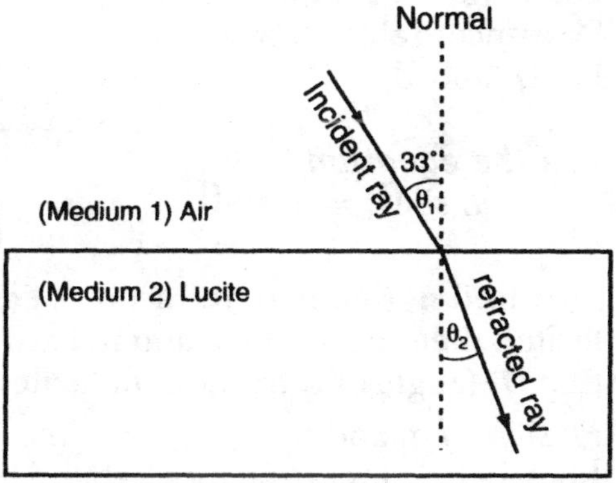

In $n_1 \sin \theta_1 = n_2 \sin \theta_2$:
n_1 = **index of refraction** of the **first medium** (example, air),
θ_1 = **angle of incidence** (angle between incident ray and the normal, example, 33°)
$\sin \theta_1$ = **sin of angle of incidence** (example, sin 33°),
n_2 = **index of refraction** of the **second medium** (example, lucite)
θ_2 = **angle of refraction** (angle between refracted ray and the normal).

sin θ_2 = **sin of angle of refraction** (angle between refracted ray and normal).
$n_1 \sin \theta_1 = n_2 \sin \theta_2$ is used when light goes from one medium, example air to another medium, example lucite (see figure). From the equation you see $n_1 \sin \theta_1$ describes one medium, $n_2 \sin \theta_2$ describes the second medium.

Question: A beam of light is incident on a lucite block in air at an angle of 33°. Calculate the angle of refraction. Show all work, including the equation and substitution with units.

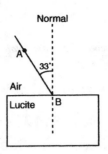

Normal

A

33°

Air

Lucite   B

Solution: Review the previous example (with the figure) under Snell's Law (which is the same as this question). Know the meaning of n_1, n_2, $\sin \theta_1$, $\sin \theta_2$.

You learned θ_1 is the **angle of incidence, angle between** the **incident ray and** the **normal**.

You learned θ_2 is the **angle of refraction, angle between** the **refracted ray and** the **normal**.

Given: Light goes from air to lucite. The angle between the incident beam (ray) and the normal = 33° (which means $\theta_1 = 33°$).

Find: angle of refraction, (angle between the refracted ray and the normal), θ_2.

Look for an equation on Reference Table: Waves that has θ_1 and θ_2.

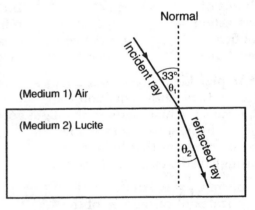

Normal

Incident ray

33° θ_1

(Medium 1) Air

(Medium 2) Lucite

refracted ray

θ_2

Use the equation
$$n_1 \sin\theta_1 = n_2 \sin\theta_2$$

n = absolute index of refraction
θ = angle

First find n_1 (index of refraction of air) and n_2 (index of refraction of lucite), then substitute n_1 and n_2 in the equation $n_1 \sin \theta_1 = n_2 \sin \theta_2$ to find θ_2 (angle of refraction) in lucite. (*Note:* θ_1 is given).

First find n_1 and n_2.
Look below or at Reference Table: Absolute Indices of Refraction.

Absolute Indices of Refraction	
Air	1.00
Lucite	1.50

absolute index of refraction of air (n_1) = 1.00
absolute index of refraction of lucite (n_2) = 1.50

Then, in the equation $n_1 \sin\theta_1 = n_2 \sin\theta_2$, **substitute for n_1** (index of refraction of air), 1.00 and **substitute for n_2** (index of refraction of lucite), 1.50. **Substitute for θ_1,** 33° (given) which is the angle of incidence (angle between the incident ray and the normal). (See figure on previous page.)

$$n_1 \; \sin\theta_1 \;\; = \;\; n_2 \; \sin\theta_2$$
$$1.00 \, (\sin 33°) = 1.50 \, (\sin \theta_2)$$
$$1.00(0.545) \;\; = 1.50 \, (\sin \theta_2)$$
$$\frac{1.00 \; (0.545)}{1.50} = \sin \theta_2$$
$$0.363 = \sin \theta_2$$

Find θ_2: On a calculator: 0.363 2nd sin = 21.28°
Angle of refraction (θ_2) = 21°.

Question: A ray of light passes from air into a block of transparent material X as shown in the diagram at right. The angle between the incident ray and the normal is 45°. The angle between the refracted ray and the normal is 26°. Calculate the absolute index of refraction of material X.

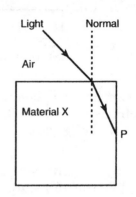

Solution:
Given: Light goes from air to material X. The angle between the incident ray and the normal (angle of incidence) is 45° (which means $\theta_1 = 45°$). The angle between the refracted ray and the normal (angle of refraction) is 26° (which means $\theta_2 = 26°$).
Find: absolute index of refraction of material X.

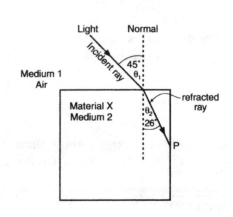

Absolute index of refraction is n. Look at the figure. In medium 1 (air) absolute index of refraction is n_1. In medium 2 (material X), absolute index of refraction is n_2. **Look for an equation** on Reference Table: Waves that has θ_1, θ_2, and n_2 (absolute index of refraction of material X).

Use the equation
$$n_1 \sin\theta_1 = n_2 \sin\theta_2$$

n = absolute index of refraction
θ = angle.

First find n_1 (absolute index of refraction of air), then substitute n_1 in the equation $n_1 \sin\theta_1 = n_2 \sin\theta_2$ to find n_2 (absolute index of refraction of material X). (*Note:* θ_1 and θ_2 are given.)

First find n_1 (absolute index of refraction of air). Look below or on Reference Table: Absolute Indices of Refraction on page reference tables 8-9.

Absolute Indices of Refraction	
Air	1.00
Lucite	1.50

absolute index of refraction of air $(n_1) = 1.00$

Then, in the equation $n_1 \sin\theta_1 = n_2 \sin\theta_2$, **substitute for n_1** (index of refraction of air) 1.00. **Substitute for θ_1** 45° (given) and **substitute for θ_2** 26°(given).

$$n_1\sin\theta_1 = n_2 \sin\theta_2$$
$$1.00\,(\sin 45°) = n_2\,(\sin 26°)$$
$$1.00\,(0.707) = n_2\,(0.438)$$
$$\frac{0.707}{0.438} = n_2$$
$$n_2 = 1.61$$

Absolute index of refraction of material X (n_2) is 1.61.

Or, rearrange the equation:
$$\frac{n_1 \sin\theta_1}{\sin\theta_2} = n_2$$
$$\frac{n_1\,(\sin 45°)}{\sin 26°} = n_2$$
$$\frac{1.00 \times 0.707}{0.438} = n_2$$
$$\frac{0.707}{0.438} = n_2$$
$$n_2 = 1.61$$

Absolute index of refraction of material X (n_2) is 1.61.

Note: θ_1 (45°) is a **bigger** angle **than** θ_2 (26°), see figure on previous page, then **sin 45°**, which equals 0.707, is **bigger than sin 26°**, which equals 0.438.

SUMMARY:
Use the equation $n_1\sin\theta_1 = n_2 \sin\theta_2$
1. to find the angle of incidence (θ_1) or angle of refraction (θ_2).
2. to find the absolute index of refraction $(n_1$ or $n_2)$ when it is not given on Reference Table: Absolute Indices of Refraction.

Questions 1 and 2:

Base your answers to questions 1 and 2 on the diagram, which represents a light ray traveling from air to lucite to medium Y and back into air.

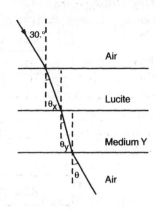

Question 1: The sine of θ_x is
(1) 0.333 (2) 0.500
(3) 0.707 (4) 0.886

Solution 1:

Given: Light travels from air to lucite to medium Y to air. The angle between the incident ray and the normal (angle of incidence) is 30° (which means $\theta_1 = 30°$)

Find: sine θ_x. θ_x is the angle between the refracted ray and the normal (angle of refraction).

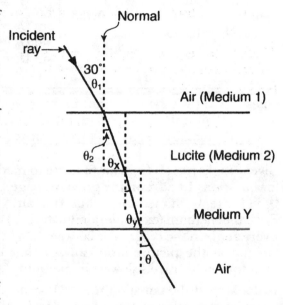

Look at the figure in the question. (Note: 30°is the angle of incidence.)
θ_x = **angle of refraction** = θ_2. Obviously, **sin θ_x = sin θ_2.** Find sin θ_2.

Look for an equation on Reference Table: Waves that has θ_1 and θ_2 and realize that light goes from one medium to another medium.

Use the equation
$$n_1 \sin\theta_1 = n_2 \sin\theta_2$$

n = absolute index of refraction
θ = angle

Or, the question is to find sin θ_x; the only equation on the reference table with sin θ is $n_1\sin\theta_1 = n_2 \sin\theta_2$. Use the equation $n_1\sin\theta_1 = n_2 \sin\theta_2$.

First find n_1 (absolute index of refraction of air) and n_2 (absolute index of refraction in lucite), and then substitute n_1 and n_2 in the equation $n_1\sin\theta_1 = n_2\sin\theta_2$ to find sin θ_2 (which is sin θ_x).

First find n_1 and n_2.

Look below or at Reference Table: Absolute Indices of Refraction.

Absolute Indices of Refraction	
Air	1.00
Lucite	1.50

$$n_1 = 1.00. \quad n_2 = 1.50$$

Then, in the equation $n_1 \sin \theta_1 = n_2 \sin \theta_2$, *substitute for n_1* (absolute index of refraction of air) 1.00 and *substitute for n_2* (absolute index of refraction of lucite) 1.50. *Substitute for θ_1* 30°(given).

$n_1 \sin \theta_1 = n_2 \sin \theta_2$

$1.00 (\sin 30°) = 1.50 \sin \theta_2$

$1.00 (0.500) = 1.50 \sin \theta_2$

$\dfrac{1.00\ (0.500)}{1.50} = \sin \theta_2$

$0.333 = \sin \theta_2$

$\sin \theta_2$ (which is $\sin \theta_x$) = **0.333**

$\sin \theta_x = 0.333$

Or, rearrange the equation

$\sin \theta_2 = \dfrac{n_1 \ \sin \theta_1}{n_2}$

$\sin \theta_2 = \dfrac{1.00\ \sin 30°}{1.50}$

$\sin \theta_2 = \dfrac{1.00\ (0.500)}{1.50}$

$\sin \theta_2 = 0.333$

$\sin \theta_2$ (which is $\sin \theta_x$) = **0.333**

$\sin \theta_x = 0.333$

Answer *1*

Question 2: (Review Question) Light travels slowest in
    (1) air only   (2) lucite, only
    (3) medium Y, only   (4) air, lucite, and medium Y

Solution 2:

Given: Light travels from air to lucite to medium Y to air (see diagram for questions 1 and 2 on the previous page). The angles are 30° in air, θ_x in lucite, θ_y in medium Y, and θ in air.

Find: the medium (example: air, lucite, etc.) where light travels slowest. Every angle in the diagram is between the light ray and the normal. By looking at the picture, you can see that θ_y **is the smallest angle,** therefore light travels slowest in medium Y, as explained below.

By looking at the equation $n_1 \sin \theta_1 = n_2 \sin \theta_2$, you see a **smaller θ** means **n, the index of refraction,** must be **bigger,** so that n times $\sin \theta$ on one side of the equation equals n times $\sin \theta$ on the other side of the equation.

Look at the equation

    bigger   n = absolute index of refraction

    $n = \dfrac{c}{v}$ c = speed of light in a vacuum

    smaller   v = velocity or speed

Since **medium Y** has a **bigger n** (index of refraction) and c (speed of light in a vacuum, 3.00×10^8 m/s) is a constant, therefore **v** (speed) in medium Y **must be smaller (slower).**   Answer *3*

Look at the diagram for questions 1 and 2 on page 4:63. In **medium Y**, the light ray is **bent more** (angle between light ray and normal is smaller-see diagram) than in air or lucite. More bending (more refraction) means a **bigger index of refraction (n)**. Medium Y has a bigger index of refraction (n).

Look at the equation below (given on Reference Table: Waves).

bigger	n = absolute index of refraction
$$n = \frac{c}{v}$$	c = speed of light in a vacuum
smaller	v = velocity or speed

Medium Y has a **bigger n** (index of refraction); c is constant, and therefore **v** (speed) in medium Y **must be smaller (slower).** Answer 3

Note: Biggest index of refraction, most bending, travels the slowest (smallest speed).

Now Do Homework Questions #108-114, pages 97-98 and #159-164, pages 104-105.

Question: A beam of monochromatic light ($f = 5.09 \times 10^{14}$ hertz)passes through parallel sections of glycerol, medium X, and medium Y as shown in the diagram at right.

Note: Monochromatic light means light of one color ($f = 5.09 \times 10^{14}$ hertz means yellow light).

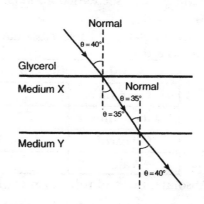

What could medium X and medium Y be?
    (1) X could be flint glass and Y could be corn oil.
    (2) X could be corn oil and Y could be flint glass.
    (3) X could be water and Y could be glycerol.
    (4) X could be glycerol and Y could be water.

Solution:
Given: A light ray goes from glycerol to medium X and then to medium Y. In glycerol, $\theta = 40°$ (we will call this angle θ_1). In medium X, $\theta = 35°$ (we will call this angle θ_2). See figure on next page.

Find: What could X and Y be.
Each medium (example, glycerol, medium X or medium Y) has its own absolute index of refraction (n).

Look for an equation on Reference Table: Waves that has θ_1, θ_2, and n.

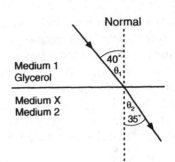

Use the equation
$$n_1 \sin\theta_1 = n_2 \sin\theta_2 \quad \text{n = absolute index of refraction}$$
$$\theta = \text{angle}$$
Or, look for an equation on Reference Table: Waves that has θ_1 and θ_2. θ_1 is in one medium (glycerol) and θ_2 is in another medium (medium X). *Use the equation* $n_1 \sin\theta_1 = n_2 \sin\theta_2$. This equation is used when light goes from one medium to another medium.
First find n_1 (absolute index of refraction of glycerol) and then substitute n_1 in the equation $n_1 \sin\theta_1 = n_2 \sin\theta_2$ to find n_2 (absolute index of refraction of medium X). (*Note:* θ_1 and θ_2 are given.) After that, use Reference Table: Absolute Indices of Refraction to see what material medium X is (see explanation below).

First find n_1.
Look below or at Reference Table: Absolute Indices of Refraction on page reference tables 8-9.

Absolute Indices of Refraction	
Corn oil	1.47
Glass, flint	1.66
Glycerol	1.47
Water	1.33

Absolute index of refraction of glycerol (n_1) = 1.47.

Then, in the equation $n_1 \sin\theta_1 = n_2 \sin\theta_2$ *substitute for n_1* (absolute index of refraction for glycerol) 1.47. *Substitute for* θ_1 40° (given) and *substitute for* θ_2 35° (given). See figure above.

$$
\begin{array}{ccc}
n_1 \quad \sin\theta_1 & = & n_2 \quad \sin\theta_2 \\
\text{For glycerol } 1.47 \, (\sin 40) & = & n_2 \, (\sin 35) \text{ For medium X} \\
1.47 \, (.643) & = & n_2 \, (.574) \\
\dfrac{1.47 \, (.643)}{.574} & = & n_2 \\
\end{array}
$$

$$n_2 = 1.66$$
n_2 (absolute index of refraction of medium X) = 1.66.

After that, look at Reference Table: Absolute Indices of Refraction on the previous page to see what material has **absolute index of refraction (n) = 1.66**. Flint glass has an absolute index of refraction = 1.66; therefore, medium X can be flint glass.

Note: By looking at Reference Table: Absolute Indices of Refraction, you see index of refraction (n) of corn oil, water, and glycerol is not equal to 1.66, therefore, medium X cannot be corn oil, water, or glycerol. Choice *1* is the only choice that medium X could be flint glass.

Choice *1*: X could be flint glass and Y could be corn oil.   Answer *1*

Or

Use the equation $n_1 \sin \theta_1 = n_2 \sin \theta_2$.

Glycerol   Medium   X

n_1 $\sin \theta_1$ $=$ n_2 $\sin \theta_2$ n = absolute index
                                                        of refraction
                                                θ = angle

n_1 40° n_2 larger   35°
                  than n_1

Look at Reference Table: Absolute Indices of Refraction and the diagram of light going from glycerol to medium X, both on the previous page. θ_2 (35°) is smaller than θ_1(40°), sin 35° is smaller than sin 40°; n_2 must be larger than n_1, so that n_1 times sin 40° = n_2 times sin 35°. θ_2 (angle in medium X) is smaller than the angle in glycerol, sin of the angle in medium X is smaller than the sin of the angle in glycerol, therefore n_2 in medium X must be larger than n_1 in glycerol. Find a choice that has a larger n than glycerol.

Look again at Reference Table: Absolute Indices of Refraction. The index of refraction of glycerol is 1.47. Find a choice that has a larger n (index of refraction) than glycerol. Of the four choices in this question for medium X, only flint glass (n = 1.66) has a bigger n (index of refraction) than glycerol (n = 1.47).

Therefore, the answer must be *1*, X could be flint glass.

Choice *1*: X could be flint glass and Y could be corn oil.

Extra information about medium Y not necessary to solve:
In **glycerol**, θ = 40° Index of refraction **(n) = 1.47**.
In **medium Y**, θ = 40° (just like in glycerol), therefore, index of refraction **(n)** is also equal to **1.47**.
By looking at Reference Table: Absolute Indices of Refraction, you see **corn oil** (like **glycerol**) has an index of refraction **(n) = 1.47**, therefore, medium Y can be either glycerol or corn oil.

Note: By looking at the diagram, you see the angle is smaller in medium X than in glycerol, the light bends more in medium X (more refraction), and medium X has a bigger index of refraction.

Now Do Homework Questions #115-117, page 98.

High Marks: Regents Physics Made Easy   *Waves*   **Chap. 4:67**

Questions 1 and 2: Base your answers to questions 1 and 2 on the diagram below which shows a ray of monochromatic yellow light (f = 5.09 x 10^{14} hertz) passing through a flint glass prism.

Question 1: Calculate the angle of refraction (in degrees) of the light ray as it enters the air from the flint glass prism.

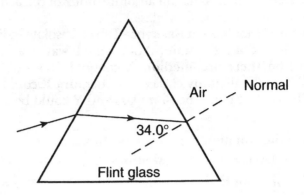

Question 2: Copy the diagram in the previous question on separate paper. Using a protractor and a straightedge, construct the refracted light ray in the air.

Solution 1:

Given: Light goes from a flint glass prism to air. The angle between the light ray and the normal is 34°.

Find: The angle of refraction (in degrees) of the light ray as it enters the air from the flint glass prism.

Look for an equation on Reference Table: Waves that has two angles, θ_1 and θ_2. Realize that light goes from one medium (flint glass) to another medium (air).

Use the equation

$$n_1 \sin \theta_1 = n_2 \sin \theta_2.$$ n = absolute index of refraction
θ = angle

The question is about light rays from the flint glass prism entering the air; the flint glass is medium 1 and the air is medium 2.

First find n_1 (absolute index of refraction of flint glass) and n_2 (absolute index of refraction of air) and then substitute n_1 and n_2 in the equation $n_1 \sin \theta_1 = n_2 \sin \theta_2$ to find $\sin \theta_2$. (*Note:* θ_1 is given.)

First find n_1 and n_2.

Look below or on Reference Table: Absolute Indices of Refraction.

Absolute Indices of Refraction	
Air	1.00
Flint glass	1.66

absolute index of refraction of flint glass (n_1) = 1.66
absolute index of refraction of air (n_2) = 1.00

Table: Waves

Table: Absolute Indices of Refraction

Then, in the equation $n_1 \sin \theta_1 = n_2 \sin \theta_2$, **substitute for** n_1 (absolute index of refraction of flint glass) 1.66 and **substitute for** n_2 (absolute index of refraction of air) 1.00. **Substitute for** θ_1 (angle of incidence, angle between incident ray and normal) 34° and find θ_2 (angle of refraction, angle between refracted ray and normal).

$$n_1 \sin \theta_1 = n_2 \sin \theta_2$$

For flint glass
$$1.66 (\sin 34°) = 1.00 \sin \theta_2 \quad \text{For air}$$
$$1.66 (.5592) = \sin \theta_2$$
$$0.9283 = \sin \theta_2$$
$$68.2° = \theta_2$$

To find θ_2 on a calculator: 0.9283, 2nd, sin = 68.2°
Answer: Angle of refraction (angle between refracted ray and normal θ_2) = 68.2°.

Solution 2:

Given: Light goes from a flint glass prism to air. The angle of refraction is 68.2° or 68° (from answer to question 1). Find: Construct the refracted light ray in air on the diagram. Look at figure 1. Put the **line** on the **bottom** of the **protractor** (the line connecting 0° and 180°) along (**on top** of) the **normal; put** the reference point (**hole** or marker which is **on the line** on the **bottom**) of the **protractor where** the ray of **light leaves** the **prism**.

Look at Figure 2. The ray of **light crosses** (goes over) the **normal.** The ray of light bends 68.2° (or 68°) away from the normal.

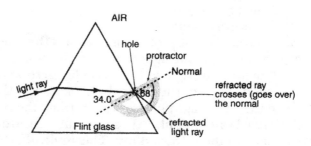

Figure 1

Figure 2

Look at the protractor in Figure 2. The angle of refraction (angle between the normal and the refracted ray) equals 68° (from answer to question 1). Using the protractor (see Figure 2 on previous page), measure a 68° angle from the normal and draw the refracted ray.

Question: A monochromatic beam of yellow light, AB, is incident upon a lucite block in air at an angle of 33°. Using the equation $n_1\sin \theta_1 = n_2\sin \theta_2$, the angle of refraction was calculated to be 21°.

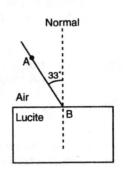

Using a straightedge and a protractor, draw an arrow to represent the path of the refracted beam.

Solution:
Given: Light goes from air to lucite. The angle of refraction is 21°.
Find: Draw an arrow to represent the path of the refracted beam.
Look at the figure at right. Put the line on the bottom of the protractor (the line connecting 0° and 180°) along (on top of) the normal; put

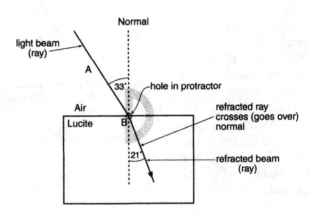

the reference point (hole or marker on the line on the bottom) of the protractor where the light ray enters the new medium (example lucite). Look again at the figure. The ray of light crosses (goes over) the normal and bends toward the normal. Look at how the protractor is placed. Since the ray of light crosses the normal, the protractor is placed like the letter D and not like Ɑ , so we can measure the angle between the normal and the refracted ray. The angle of refraction (angle between normal and refracted ray) = 21°(given). Using the protractor (see figure above), measure a 21° angle from the normal and draw the refracted ray.

Question: A ray of light passes from air into a block of transparent material X as shown in the diagram.

Measure the angles of incidence and refraction to the nearest degree at the air into material X boundary.

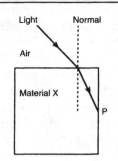

Solution:

Given: Light passes from air into material X as shown in the diagram.

Find: Angle of incidence and angle of refraction to the nearest degree. See figure 1.

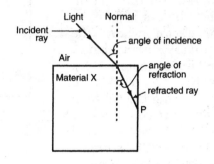

Figure 1

Find the angle of incidence. Look at Figure 2 below. Put the line on the bottom of the protractor (the line connecting 0° and 180°) along (on top of) the normal; put the reference point (hole or marker on the line on the bottom) of the protractor where the light ray enters the new medium (material X). Since you are measuring the angle of incidence (angle between the incident ray and the normal), make sure that some of the numbers on the protractor are between the incident ray and the normal. Place the protractor as shown in the diagram. Measure the angle of incidence

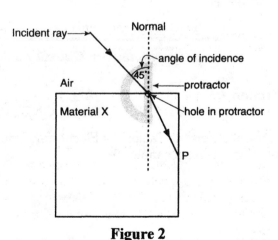

Figure 2

(angle between the incident light ray and the normal) to the nearest degree. Angle of incidence equals 45°.

Find angle of refraction. Look at Figure 3 below. Put the line on the bottom of the protractor (the line connecting 0° and 180°) along (on top of) the normal; put the reference point (hole or marker on the line on the bottom) of the protractor where the light ray enters the new medium (material X). Since you are measuring the **angle of refraction** (angle between the refracted ray and the normal), make sure that some of the numbers on the protractor are between the refracted ray and the normal. Place the protractor as shown in Figure 3. Measure the angle of refraction (angle **between the refracted ray and the normal), to the nearest degree. Angle** of refraction equals 26°.

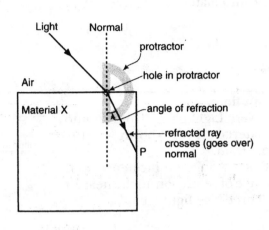

Figure 3

Answer: The angle of incidence is 45°. The angle of refraction is 26°.

Now Do Homework Questions #118-120, page 99.

Section 4:

THE ELECTROMAGNETIC SPECTRUM

Look at Reference Table: The Electromagnetic Spectrum on the next page or on page reference tables 6-7.

The Electromagnetic Spectrum

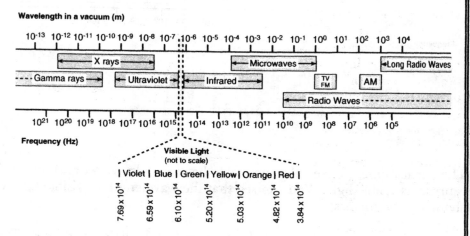

The electromagnetic spectrum is made of different kinds of waves: gamma rays, x rays, ultraviolet, visible light, infrared, microwaves, radio waves, and long radio waves. The waves in the electromagnetic spectrum are called electromagnetic waves (electromagnetic radiation). The **velocity** or **speed** of the waves in the **electromagnetic spectrum** in a vacuum is **3.00 x 10⁸ m/s** (**just like** the **speed** of **light in** a **vacuum, 3.00 x 10⁸ m/s,** given on Reference Table: List of Physical Constants).

Look at Reference Table: The Electromagnetic Spectrum above or on page Reference Tables 6-7. The word **wavelength** (m) is **written above** the **waves** (gamma rays, x rays, etc.). The word **frequency** (Hz) is **written below** the **waves** (gamma rays, x rays, etc.). The top half shows the wavelength of gamma rays, x rays, ultraviolet, infrared, and the rest of the electromagnetic spectrum. The bottom half shows the frequency of gamma rays, x rays, ultraviolet, infrared, and the rest of the electromagnetic spectrum, and further below are the frequencies of the different colors of visible light (see reference table above).

Look again at wavelength, which is at the top of the reference table above. The length of the longest waves, biggest wavelength, is more than 10^4 m (meters), which is long radio waves and radio waves. The shortest wavelength is less than 10^{-13} m (meters), which is gamma rays.

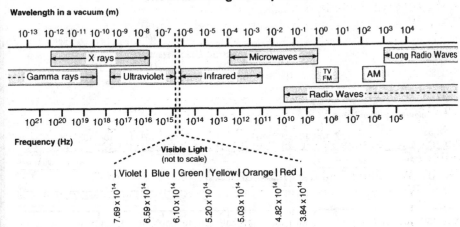

The Electromagnetic Spectrum

The vertical line on the reference table between ultraviolet and infrared represents visible light. You can see that the wavelength of visible light is about 10^{-6} m (meters).

Look at frequency, which is at the bottom half of Reference Table: The Electromagnetic Spectrum. The smallest frequency is less than 10^5 Hz (hertz), which is radio waves and long radio waves. The highest frequency (biggest frequency) is more than 10^{21} Hz, which is gamma rays.

Look further down on the reference table for **frequency** for **visible light**.

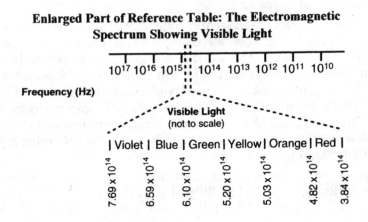

Enlarged Part of Reference Table: The Electromagnetic Spectrum Showing Visible Light

The frequency of visible light goes from 3.84×10^{14} Hz, which is red light, to 7.69×10^{14} Hz, which is violet light.

If the frequency of the light wave is between 3.84×10^{14} Hz and 4.82×10^{14} Hz, the color of the light is red (see reference table on the previous page or below). If the frequency is between 4.82×10^{14} Hz and 5.03×10^{14} Hz, the color is orange. You know light with a frequency of 5.0×10^{14} Hz is orange, because 5.0×10^{14} Hz is between 4.82×10^{14} Hz and 5.03×10^{14} Hz.

If the frequency is between 6.59×10^{14} Hz and 7.69×10^{14} Hz, the color is violet.

Question: The wavelength of a helium nucleus moving with a speed of 2×10^6 m/s is 4.9×10^{-14} m. The wavelength of this particle is of the <u>same order of magnitude as which type of electromagnetic radiation?</u>

Solution:
Given: Wavelength of a helium nucleus = 4.9×10^{-14} m.

Find: What type of electromagnetic radiation has a wavelength of 4.9×10^{-14} m.

You need to find type of electromagnetic radiation, therefore, look at Reference Table: The Electromagnetic Spectrum below or on page reference tables 6-7.

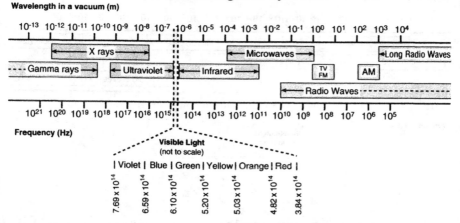

The Electromagnetic Spectrum

You need to find an electromagnetic radiation having a wavelength similar to the wavelength (4.9×10^{-14} m given) of the helium nucleus. Look at the top of Reference Table: The Electromagnetic Spectrum, at wavelength.

Gamma rays are the only rays shown in the electromagnetic spectrum that have a wavelength of 10^{-13} m or less (wavelengths of 10^{-14} m, 10^{-15} m, etc.).

The **wavelength** of the **helium nucleus**, 4.9×10^{-14} **m** (given in the question), is just like the **wavelength** of some **gamma rays, 10^{-14} m**.

Answer: *gamma ray*

Question: Base your answer on the data table below. The data table lists the energy and corresponding frequency of two photons.

Photon	Energy (J)	Frequency (Hz)
A	6.63×10^{-15}	1.00×10^{19}
B	1.33×10^{-20}	2.00×10^{13}

In which part of the electromagnetic spectrum would photon B be found?

(1) infrared   (2) visible   (3) ultraviolet (4) x ray

Solution:
Given: Frequency of photon B = 2.00×10^{13} Hz.
Find: Which part of the electromagnetic spectrum has the frequency of photon B, 2.00×10^{13} Hz.
You need to find a part of the electromagnetic spectrum, therefore, look on Reference Table: the Electromagnetic Spectrum below or on page Reference Tables 6-7.

The Electromagnetic Spectrum
You need to find which part of the electromagnetic spectrum has the

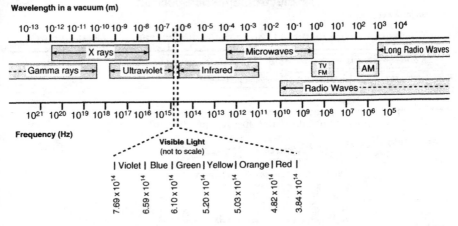

frequency of photon B (2.00×10^{13} Hz given). Look at the bottom half of Reference Table: The Electromagnetic Spectrum, at frequency.
Infrared rays are the only rays shown in the electromagnetic spectrum that have a frequency of 10^{13} Hz or 2.00×10^{13} Hz, which is the same frequency as photon B.

Answer *1*

Find Frequency or Wavelength of an Electromagnetic Wave
The **electromagnetic spectrum** is **made of** different kinds of **waves**: gamma rays, x rays, radio waves, etc. (see reference table above). The waves on the electromagnetic spectrum are called **electromagnetic waves**.

To find the frequency or wavelength of an electromagnetic wave (x rays, ultraviolet, visible light, radio waves, etc.), you can use the equation

$$v \quad = \quad f \quad\quad \lambda$$

speed $\quad=\quad$ frequency $\quad$ x $\quad$ wavelength

Look at Reference Table: The Electromagnetic Spectrum. Light is part of the electromagnetic spectrum. The speed of light in a vacuum equals 3.00×10^8 m/s, given on Reference Table: List of Physical Constants. The speed of light in air is about the same, 3.00×10^8 m/s. The **speed (v)** of all the **waves** in the **electromagnetic spectrum**(examples: gamma rays, x rays, ultraviolet, visible light, infrared, microwave, radio waves, and long radio waves) **also equals** the **speed of light** in a vacuum, **3.00×10^8 m/s**. Therefore, for electromagnetic waves (example gamma rays, infrared, radio waves, etc.), you can write either v (speed/velocity) $= f\lambda$, or you can write c (speed of light) $= f\lambda$, because $v = c = 3.00 \times 10^8$ m/s.

Using the equation $v = f\lambda$, if the frequency (f) of an electromagnetic wave in a vacuum is given and you know v (always 3.00×10^8 m/s), you have two knowns, v and f, then you can find λ (one unknown).

In the equation $v = f\lambda$, if wavelength (λ) of an electromagnetic wave in a vacuum is given and you know v (always 3.00×10^8 m/s), you have two knowns v and λ, then you can find f (one unknown).

Question: Calculate the wavelength in a vacuum of a radio wave having a frequency of 2.2×10^6 hertz.

Solution:

Given: Frequency of radio wave $= 2.2 \times 10^6$ hertz.

Find: Wavelength (λ) in a vacuum of the radio wave.

Look for an equation on Reference Table: Waves that has frequency (f) and wavelength (λ).

Use the equation
$$v = f\lambda$$

f = frequency
v = velocity or speed
λ = wavelength

velocity or speed $=$ frequency x wavelength.

Look at Reference Table: The Electromagnetic Spectrum on the previous page or on the next page. The **electromagnetic spectrum** includes **radio waves, visible light**, gamma rays, etc. The speed of light in a vacuum equals 3.00×10^8 m/s, given on Reference Table: List of Physical Constants. Radio waves (and all electromagnetic waves) in a vacuum have a speed of 3.00×10^8 m/s, just like the speed of light. In the equation $v = f\lambda$, *then substitute for v* (speed of radio waves) 3.00×10^8 m/s. *Substitute for f* (frequency) 2.2×10^6 Hz (Hertz).

$v = f\ \lambda$

$3.00 \times 10^8 \text{ m/s} = 2.2 \times 10^6 \text{ Hz } \lambda$

$\dfrac{3.00 \times 10^8 \ m/s}{2.2 \times 10^6 \ Hz} = \lambda$ Note: Hz $= 1/s$

$1.4 \times 10^2 \text{ m} = \lambda$

Wavelength (λ) = 1.4×10^2 m or 140 m.

Or, rearrange the equation

$\lambda = \dfrac{v}{f}$

$\lambda = \dfrac{3.00 \times 10^8 \ m/s}{2.2 \times 10^6 \ Hz}$

$\lambda = 1.4 \times 10^2$ m

Wavelength (λ) = 1.4×10^2 m or 140 m.

Part of Table: The Electromagnetic Spectrum

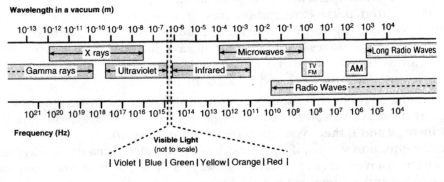

Table: The Electromagnetic Spectrum

Question: Determine the color of a ray of light with a wavelength of 6.21×10^{-7} meter.

Solution:

Given: Wavelength $= 6.21 \times 10^{-7}$ m

Find: Color of a ray of light.

The question asks to find the color of light. The only reference table with colors of light is Reference Table: The Electromagnetic Spectrum. Look at the table above and on the following page, which shows the colors of visible light with their frequencies. You need to find the frequency of the light ray and then look at Reference Table: The Electromagnetic Spectrum to see which color has that frequency.

Look for an equation on Reference Table: Waves that has to do with frequency and wavelength.

Use the equation

$$v \qquad = \qquad f \qquad \qquad \lambda$$

velocity or speed   =   frequency   x   wavelength

First find speed of light and then substitute speed of light in the equation $v = f\lambda$ to find f (frequency).

Note: The symbol (c) is used for speed (v) of light.

Table: Waves

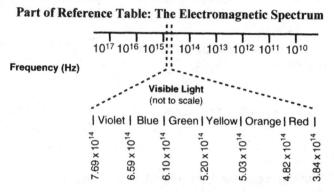

First find speed of light.

Look below or on Reference Table: List of Physical Constants on page reference tables 2-3 to find speed of light.

Speed of light in a vacuum   c 3.00×10^8 m/s

In the equation, $v = f\lambda$, *then substitute for v* (speed of light), 3.00×10^8 m/s. *Substitute for λ* (wavelength), 6.21×10^{-7} m (given).

$v = f\lambda$

3.00×10^8 m/s $= f(6.21 \times 10^{-7}$ m$)$

$\dfrac{3.00 \times 10^8 \ m/s}{6.21 \times 10^{-7} \ m} = f$

$4.83 \times 10^{14}\dfrac{1}{s} = f$ Note: Hz = 1/s

4.83×10^{14} Hz $= f$

f (frequency) $= 4.83 \times 10^{14}$ Hz

Or, rearrange the equation:

$f = \dfrac{v}{\lambda}$

$f = \dfrac{3.00 \times 10^8 \ m/s}{6.21 \times 10^{-7} \ m}$

$f = 4.83 \times 10^{14}\dfrac{1}{s}$ Note:Hz = 1/s

f (frequency) $= 4.83 \times 10^{14}$ Hz

Look below or on Reference Table: The Electromagnetic Spectrum on page Reference Tables 6-7. On the reference table, the color between the frequencies 4.82×10^{14} Hz and 5.03×10^{14} Hz is **orange**. The frequency of the light in this example is 4.83×10^{14} Hz; 4.83×10^{14} Hz is between 4.82×10^{14} Hz and 5.03×10^{14} Hz, therefore the color is orange.

Part of Reference Table: The Electromagnetic Spectrum

Finding Distance or Time An Electromagnetic Wave Travels
(examples: radio wave, light wave, etc.)

Question: A 2.00×10^6 hertz radio signal is sent a distance of 7.30×10^{10} meters from Earth to a spaceship orbiting Mars. Approximately how much time does it take the radio signal to travel from Earth to the spaceship?

(1) 4.11×10^{-3} s   (2) 2.43×10^2 s   (3) 2.19×10^8 s   (4) 1.46×10^{17} s

Solution:

Given: distance from Earth to spaceship orbiting Mars is 7.30×10^{10} meters. Find: time it takes the radio signal to go from Earth to spaceship orbiting Mars.

Look at Reference Table: The Electromagnetic Spectrum on the next page or on page reference tables 6-7. The **electromagnetic spectrum** includes **radio waves, light,** infrared, gamma rays, etc. The speed of light in a vacuum equals 3.00×10^8 m/s, given on **Reference Table: List of Physical Constants.**

Speed of light in a vacuum   c 3.00×10^8 m/s
Similarly, **radio waves** (and all electromagnetic waves) have a speed of 3.00×10^8 m/s, just like the speed of light.

The Electromagnetic Spectrum

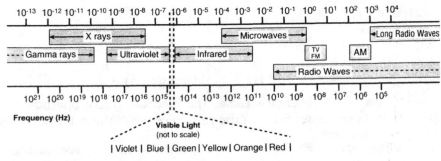

Look for an equation on Reference Table: Mechanics that has distance (d), time (t), and speed (v).

Use the equation
$$\bar{v} = \frac{d}{t}$$

d= displacement/distance

t = time interval
$\bar{v}$ = average velocity/average speed

Then substitute for v (speed of radio waves) 3.00×10^8 m/s. *Substitute for d* (distance) 7.30×10^{10} m(meters).

$$\bar{v} = \frac{d}{t}$$

$$3.00 \times 10^8 \text{ m/s} = \frac{7.30 \times 10^{10} \ m}{t}$$

Cross multiply
$(3.00 \times 10^8 \text{m/s})t = 7.30 \times 10^{10}$ m

$$t = \frac{7.30 \times 10^{10} \ m}{3.00 \times 10^8 \ m/s} = 2.43 \times 10^2 \ s$$

Answer 2

Or, rearrange the equation:
$$t = \frac{d}{\bar{v}}$$

$$t = \frac{7.30 \times 10^{10} \ m}{3.00 \times 10^8 \ m/s} = 2.43 \times 10^2 \ s$$

Answer 2

Now Do Homework Questions #121-131, pages 98-100 and #165-167, page 105.

When you answer Regents questions on **WAVES,** use **Reference Table Waves, Reference Table Absolute Indices of Refraction, Reference Table The Electromagnetic Spectrum, and Reference Table List of Physical Constants.**

1 Which phrase best describes a periodic wave?
   (1) a single pulse traveling at constant speed
   (2) a series of pulses at irregular intervals
   (3) a series of pulses at regular intervals
   (4) a single pulse traveling at different speeds in the same medium

2 As a wave travels between two points in a medium, the wave transfers
   (1) energy, only
   (2) mass, only
   (3) both energy and mass
   (4) neither energy nor mass

3 A periodic wave travels through a rope, as shown in the diagram at right. As the wave travels, what is transferred between points A and B?
   (1) mass, only
   (2) energy, only
   (3) both mass and energy
   (4) neither mass nor energy

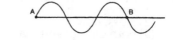

4 A ball dropped from rest falls freely until it hits the ground with a speed of 20 meters per second. The time during which the ball is in free fall is approximately
   (1) 1 s   (2) 2 s   (3) 0.5 s   (4) 10. s

5 A tuning fork vibrating in air produces sound waves. These waves are best classified as
   (1) transverse, because the air molecules are vibrating parallel to the direction of wave motion
   (2) transverse, because the air molecules are vibrating perpendicular to the direction of wave motion
   (3) longitudinal, because the air molecules are vibrating parallel to the direction of wave motion
   (4) longitudinal, because the air molecules are vibrating perpendicular to the direction of wave motion

6 The diagram below shows a tuning fork vibrating in air. The dots represent air molecules as the sound wave moves toward the right. Which diagram best represents the direction of the air molecules?

(1)   (2)   (3)   (4)

7 The diagram below shows a person shaking the end of a rope up and down, producing a disturbance that moves along the length of the rope.

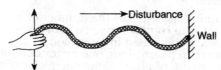

   Which type of wave is traveling in the rope?
   (1) torsional   (2) longitudinal (3) transverse   (4) elliptical

8 What type of wave is sound traveling in water?
   (1) torsional   (2) transverse   (3) elliptical   (4) longitudinal
   Hint: What type of wave is a sound wave?

9 A student strikes the top rope of a volleyball net, sending a single vibratory disturbance along the length of the net, as shown in the diagram at right. This disturbance is best described as

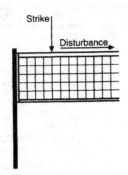

(1) a pulse
(2) a periodic wave
(3) a longitudinal wave
(4) an electromagnetic wave

10 A periodic wave transfers
   (1) energy, only
   (2) mass, only
   (3) both energy and mass
   (4) neither energy nor mass

11 The diagram at right shows a transverse wave moving to the right along a rope. As the wave passes point X, the motion of X will be
   (1) up, then down
   (2) down, then up
   (3) left, then right
   (4) in a circle

12 The energy of a water wave is most closely related to its
   (1) frequency　(2) wavelength　(3) period　(4) amplitude

13 An electric guitar is generating a sound of constant frequency. An increase in which sound wave characteristic would result in an increase in loudness?
   (1) speed　(2) period　(3) wavelength　(4) amplitude

14 The amplitude of a sound wave is to its loudness as the amplitude of a light wave is to its
   (1) brightness　(2) frequency　(3) color　(4) speed

15 Which wave diagram has both wavelength (λ) and amplitude (A) labeled correctly?

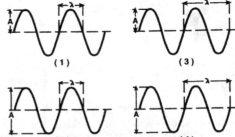

(1)　(3)

(2)　(4)

16 The hertz is a unit that describes the number of
   (1) seconds it takes to complete one cycle of a wave
   (2) cycles of a wave completed in one second
   (3) points that are in phase along one meter of a wave
   (4) points that are out of phase along one meter of a wave

17 The graph below shows displacement versus time for a particle of uniform medium as a wave passes through the medium.

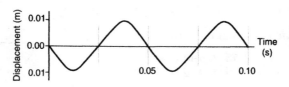

What is the frequency of the wave?
(1) 10 Hz   (2) 20 Hz   (3) 50 Hz   (4) 100 Hz

Hint; Method 1: Realize how many waves are in 0.05 s (second) or in 0.10 s, therefore how many waves are in 1 s; or, Method 2: First find T (period), then find f (frequency)

18 The frequency of a light wave is 5.0×10^{14} hertz. What is the period of the wave?
(1) 1.7×10^6 s   (2) 2.0×10^{-15} s   (3) 6.0×10^{-7} s   (4) 5.0×10^{-14} s

19 The diagram below represents waves A, B, C, and D traveling in the same medium.

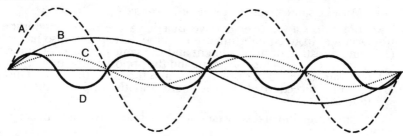

Which wave has the longest period?
(1) A (2) B (3) C (4) D

20 The diagram below shows a periodic wave. Which two points on the wave are in phase?
(1) A and C (2) B and D
(3) C and F (4) E and G

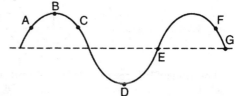

21 The diagram represents wave movement. Which two points are in phase?
(1) A and G   (2) B and F
(3) C and E   (4) D and F

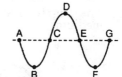

22 The diagram on the right represents a periodic wave. Which two points on the wave are in phase?
(1) A and C (3) A and D
(2) B and D (4) B and E

23 The diagram at right represents a periodic wave. Which two points on the wave are in phase?
(1) A and E (3) B and D
(2) A and C (4) D and F

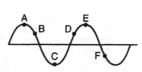

24 The diagram at right shows a periodic wave.
    Which two points on the wave are in phase?
    (1) A and C   (3) C and F
    (2) B and D   (4) E and G

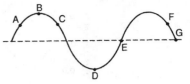

25 The diagram below represents a wave traveling in a uniform medium.

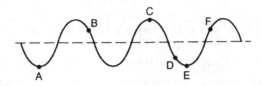

    Which two points on the wave are in phase?
    (1) A and C   (2) A and E   (3) B and D   (4) B and F

    Hint: Must be same distance above or below axis.

26 Two points on a transverse wave that have the same magnitude of displacement from equilibrium are in phase if the points also have the
    (1) same direction of displacement and the same direction of motion
    (2) same direction of displacement and the opposite direction of motion
    (3) opposite direction of displacement and the same direction of motion
    (4) opposite direction of displacement and the opposite direction of motion

    Hint: Same direction of displacement means both above or both below the axis .

27 The diagram below shows two waves, A and B.

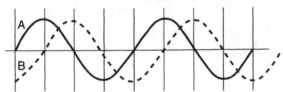

    The phase difference between A and B is
    (1) 0°   (2) 45°   (3) 90°   (4) 180°

    Hint: One wavelength = 360°. How many degrees apart are the crests?

28 The diagram below represents waves A, B, C, and D traveling in the same medium.

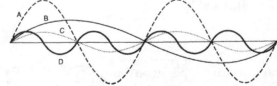

    Which two waves have the same wavelength?
    (1) A and B   (2) A and C   (3) B and D   (4) C and D

29 The diagram below shows a parked car with a siren on top. The siren is producing a sound with a frequency of 680 hertz, which travel first through point A then through point B, as shown. The speed of sound is 340 meters per second.

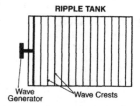

A   B

(not drawn to scale)

If the sound waves are in phase at points A and B, the distance between the points could be

(1) 1λ (2) $\frac{1}{2}\lambda$ (3) $\frac{3}{2}\lambda$ (4) $\frac{1}{4}\lambda$

Base your answers to questions 30 through 31 on the information and diagram below.
The diagram represents a wave generator having a constant frequency of 12 hertz, producing parallel wave fronts in a ripple tank. The velocity of the waves is v.

RIPPLE TANK

Wave Generator   Wave Crests

30 Using a ruler, measure the wavelength of the waves shown and record the value *to the nearest tenth of a centimeter*. [1]

Hint: Wavelength is from one crest to the next crest. Answer must have units. Examples of units: Grams, centimeters (cm), joules.

31 Determine the speed of the waves in the ripple tank. [Show all calculations, including the equations and substitutions with units.] [2]

32 In a vacuum, light with a frequency of 5.0×10^{14} hertz has a wavelength of
(1) 6.0×10^{-21} m (2) 6.0×10^{-7} m (3) 1.7×10^{6} m (4) 1.5×10^{23} m

33 The periodic wave in the diagram below has a frequency of 40. hertz.

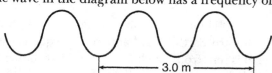

|← 3.0 m →|

What is the speed of the wave?
(1) 13 m/s   (2) 27 m/s   (3) 60. m/s   (4) 120 m/s

34 What is the frequency of a light wave with a wavelength of 6.0×10^{-7} meter traveling through space?
(1) 2.0×10^{-15} Hz (2) 5.0×10^{1} Hz (3) 1.8×10^{14} Hz (4) 5.0×10^{14} Hz

35 A sound of constant frequency is produced by the siren on top of a firehouse. Compared to the frequency produced by the siren, the frequency observed by a firefighter approaching the firehouse is
(1) lower   (2) higher   (3) the same

36 The driver of a car sounds the horn while traveling toward a stationary person. Compared to the sound of the horn heard by the driver, the sound heard by the stationary person has
(1) lower pitch and shorter wavelength
(2) lower pitch and longer wavelength
(3) higher pitch and shorter wavelength
(4) higher pitch and lower wavelength

37 A source of sound waves approaches a stationary observer through a uniform medium. Compared to the frequency and wavelength of the emitted sound, the observer would detect waves with a
(1) higher frequency and shorter wavelength
(2) higher frequency and longer wavelength
(3) lower frequency and shorter wavelength

38 A train sounds a whistle of constant frequency as it leaves the train station. Compared to the sound emitted by the whistle, the sound that the passengers standing on the platform hear has a frequency that is
(1) lower, because the sound-wave fronts reach the platform at a frequency lower than the frequency at which they are produced
(2) lower, because the sound waves travel more slowly in the still air above the platform than in the rushing air near the train
(3) higher, because the sound-wave fronts reach the platform at a frequency higher than the frequency at which they are produced
(4) higher, because the sound waves travel faster in the still air above the platform than in the rushing air near the train

39 A system consists of aan oscillator and a speaker that emits a 1000.-hertz sound wave. A microphone detects the sound wave.
The microphone is moved at a constant speed from the 0.50-meter position back to 1.00 meter from the speaker. Compared to the 1,000.-hertz frequency emitted by the speaker, the frequency detected by the moving microphone is
(1) lower   (2) higher   (3) the same

40 A source of waves and an observer are moving relative to each other. The observer will detect a steadily increasing frequency if
(1) he moves toward the source at a constant speed
(2) the source moves away from him at a constant speed
(3) he accelerates toward the source
(4) the source accelerates away from him

41 An astronomer on Earth studying light coming from a star notes that the observed light frequencies are lower than the actual emitted frequencies. The astronomer concludes that the distance between the star and Earth is
(1) decreasing   (2) increasing   (3) not changing

42 An astronomical body emitting high-intensity pulses of green light is moving toward Earth at high velocity. To an observer on Earth, this light may appear
(1) red   (2) blue   (3) orange   (4) yellow

Hint: moves toward Earth, what happens to frequency and color

43 A radio signal is sent from Earth to a spaceship orbiting Mars.
The spaceship is moving away from Earth when the radio signal is received. Compared to the frequency of the signal sent from Earth, the frequency of the signal received by the spaceship is
(1) lower   (2) higher   (3) the same

44 Compared to the wavelength of red light, the wavelength of yellow light is
(1) shorter   (2) longer   (3) the same

45 A radar gun can determine the speed of a moving automobile by measuring the difference in frequency between emitted and reflected radar waves. This process illustrates
(1) resonance   (3) diffraction
(2) the Doppler effect   (4) refraction

46 Base your answer on the diagram below which shows a parked car with a siren on top. The siren is producing a sound with a frequency of 680 hertz, which travel first through point *A* then through point *B*, as shown. The speed of sound is 340 meters per second.

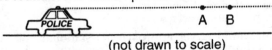

(not drawn to scale)

If the car were to accelerate toward point *A*, the frequency of the sound heard by an observer at point *A* would
(1) decrease   (2) increase   (3) remain the same

---

47 Two waves having the same amplitude and the same frequency pass simultaneously through a uniform medium. Maximum destructive interference occurs when the phase difference between the two waves is
(1) 0°   (2) 90°   (3) 180°   (4) 360°

48 Two waves having the same amplitude and the same frequency pass simultaneously through a uniform medium. Maximum destructive interference occurs when the phase difference between the two waves is
(1) 0°   (2) 90°   (3) 180°   (4) 360°

49 The diagram at right represents shallow water waves of wavelength λ passing through two small openings, A and B, in a barrier. Compared to the length of path BP, the length of path AP is
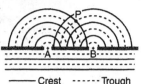
(1) 1λ longer   (3) ½λ longer
(2) 2λ longer   (4) the same

—— Crest - - - - - Trough

50 Two monochromatic, coherent light beams of the same wavelength converge on a screen. The point at which the beams converge appears dark. Which wave phenomenon best explains this effect?

51 The diagram below shows two pulses, each of length λ, traveling toward each other at equal speed in a rope.

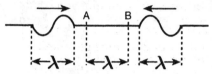

    Which diagram best represents the shape of the rope when both pulses are in region AB?

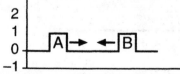

52 The diagram represents a rope along which two pulses of equal amplitude, A, approach point P.

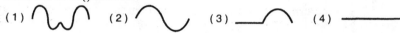

As the two pulses pass through point P, the maximum vertical displacement of the rope at point P will be
(1) A   (2) 2A   (3) 0   (4) A/2.

53 The diagram below shows two pulses, A and B, approaching each other in a uniform medium.

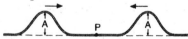

Which diagram best represents the superposition of the two pulses?

(1) ⌐_□_   (2) ⌐□□⌐

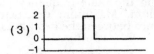 (3) 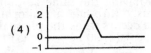 (4)

54 The diagram below shows two pulses, each of length ℓ, traveling toward each other at equal speed in a rope.

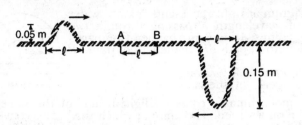

Which diagram best represents the shape of the rope when both pulses are in region *AB*?

 (1) 0.10 m   (3) 0.10 m

 (2) 0.20 m   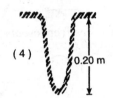 (4) 0.20 m

55 The diagram below shows two pulses traveling toward each other in a uniform medium.

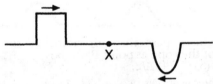

Which diagram best represents the medium when the pulses meet at point *X*?

 (1)

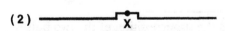 (2)

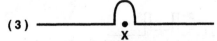 (3)

(4)

56 The diagram below shows two pulses of equal amplitude, A, approaching point P along a uniform string.

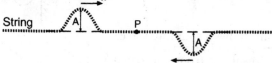

   When the two pulses meet at P, the vertical displacement of the string at P will be

(1) A   (2) 2A   (3) 0   (4) $\frac{A}{2}$

57 The diagram below shows two waves approaching each other in the same uniform medium.

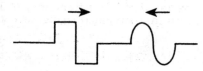

   Which diagram best represents the appearance of the medium after the waves have passed each other?

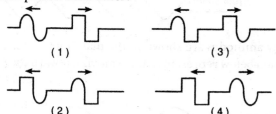

58 The diagram below shows two pulses approaching each other from opposite directions in the same medium. Pulse A has an amplitude of 0.20 meter and pulse B has an amplitude of 0.10 meter.
   After the pulses have passed through each other, what will be the amplitude of each of the two pulses?

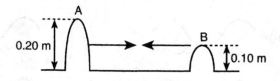

(1) A = 0.10 m; B = 0.20 m   (3) A = 0.30 m; B = 0.30 m
(2) A = 0.20 m; B = 0.10 m   (4) A = 0.15 m; B = 0.15 m

59 The superposition of two waves traveling in the same medium produces a standing wave pattern if the two waves have
   (1) the same frequency, the same amplitude, and travel in the same direction
   (2) the same frequency, the same amplitude, and travel in opposite directions
   (3) the same frequency, different amplitudes, and travel in the same direction
   (4) the same frequency, different amplitudes, and travel in opposite directions

60 How many nodes are represented in the standing wave diagram at right?
(1) 1   (3) 3
(2) 6   (4) 4

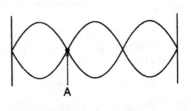

61 The diagram shows a standing wave. Point A on the standing wave is
(1) a node resulting from constructive interference
(2) a node resulting from destructive interference
(3) an antinode resulting from constructive interference
(4) an antinode resulting from destructive interference

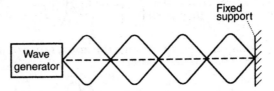

62 A wave generator having a constant frequency of 15 hertz produces a standing wave pattern in a stretched string, as shown in the diagram below.

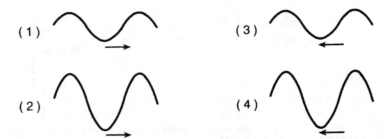

How many antinodes are shown in the diagram?

63 The diagram below represents a wave moving toward the right side of this page.

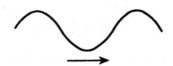

Which wave shown below could produce a standing wave with the original wave?

(1)   (3)

(2)   (4)

64 In a demonstration, a vibrating tuning fork causes a nearby second tuning fork to begin to vibrate with the same frequency. Which wave phenomenon is illustrated by this demonstration?
(1) the Doppler effect   (3) resonance
(2) nodes   (4) interference

---

65 When an opera singer hits a high-pitched note, a glass on the opposite side of the opera hall shatters. Which statement best explains this phenomenon?
(1) The frequency of the note and natural vibration frequency of the glass are equal.
(2) The vibrations of the note are polarized by the shape of the opers hall.
(3) The amplitude of the note increases before it reaches the glass.
(4) The singer and glass are separated by an integral number of wavelengths.

66 An opera singer's voice is able to break a thin crystal glass when the singer's voice and the vibrating glass have the same
(1) frequency   (3) amplitude
(2) speed   (4) wavelength

67 Two identical guitar strings are tuned to the same pitch. If one string is plucked, the other nearby string vibrates with the same frequency. This phenomenon is called
(1) resonance   (3) refraction
(2) reflection   (4) destructive interference

68 A girl on a swing may increase the amplitude of the swing's oscillations if she moves her legs at the natural frequency of the spring. This is an example of
(1) resonance   (3) destructive interference
(2) the Doppler effect   (4) wave transmission

69 A student in a band notices that a drum vibrates when another instrument emits a certain frequency note. This phenomenon illustrates
(1) reflection   (2) resonance   (3) refraction   (4) diffraction

70 Which phenomenon occurs when an object absorbs wave energy that matches the object's natural frequency?
(1) reflection   (2) diffraction   (3) resonance   (4) interference

71 The diagram at right shows a wave phenomenon. The pattern of waves shown behind the barrier is the result of
(1) reflection   (3) diffraction
(2) refraction   (4) interference

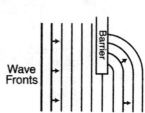

72 The diagram at right shows straight wave fronts passing through an opening in a barrier. This wave phenomenon is called
(1) reflection   (2) refraction
(3) polarization (4) diffraction

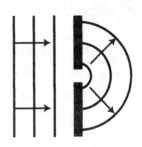

73 Which diagram best illustrates wave diffraction?

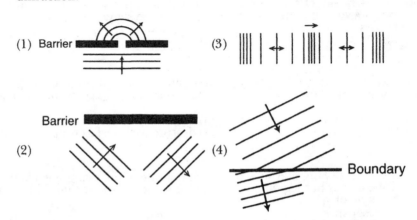

74 The diagram below shows straight wave fronts passing through an opening in a barrier.
    This wave phenomenon is called
(1) reflection   (3) polarization
(2) refraction   (4) diffraction

75 The diagram at right shows a wave phenomenon.
    The pattern of waves shown behind the barriers is the result of
(1) reflection   (3) refraction
(2) diffraction   (4) absorption

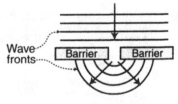

76 The spreading of a wave into the region behind an obstruction is called
(1) diffraction (2) absorption (3) reflection (4) refraction

77 Which diagram below best represents the phenomenon of diffraction?

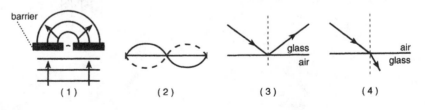

78 The diagram at right shows wave fronts spreading into the region behind a barrier.
Which wave phenomenon is represented in the diagram?
(1) reflection   (3) diffraction
(2) refraction   (4) standing waves

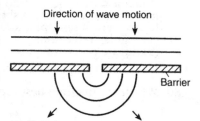

Direction of wave motion

Barrier

79 Which wave phenomenon makes it possible for a player to hear the sound of a referee's whistle in an open field even when standing behind the referee?
(1) diffraction   (2) Doppler effect   (3) reflection   (4) refraction

80 A wave is diffracted as it passes through an opening in a barrier. The amount of diffraction that the wave undergoes depends on both the
(1) amplitude and frequency of the incident wave
(2) wavelength and speed of the incident wave
(3) wavelength of the incident wave and the size of the opening
(4) amplitude of the incident wave and the size of the opening

81 A ray of monochromatic light traveling in air is incident on a plane mirror at an angle of 30.°, as shown in the diagram at right.
The angle of reflection for the light ray is
(1) 15.° (3) 60.°
(2) 30.° (4) 90.°

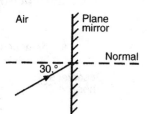

Air

Plane mirror

Normal

30.°

82 The diagram at right shows a light ray being reflected from a plane mirror.
What is the angle of incidence?
(1) 20.°   (3) 55.°
(2) 35.°   (4) 70.°

Hint: Draw normal

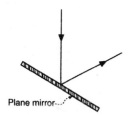

Plane mirror

83 A ray of light strikes a plane mirror at an angle of incidence equal to 35°. The angle between the incident ray and the reflected ray is
(1) 0°   (2) 35°   (3) 55°   S(4) 70.°

84 Which diagram best represents the reflection of light from an irregular surface?

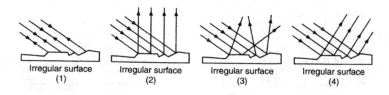

Irregular surface (1)   Irregular surface (2)   Irregular surface (3)   Irregular surface (4)

85 When a student looks into a plane mirror, she sees a virtual image of herself. However, when she looks into a sheet of paper, no such image forms. Which light phenomenon occurs at the surface of the paper?
(1) regular reflection   (3) polarization
(2) diffuse reflection   (4) resonance

Hint: Paper is a rough surface.

86 Which ray diagram best represents the phenomenon of refraction?

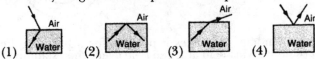

87 A ray of light traveling in air is incident on an air-water boundary as shown at the right.
    Copy the diagram on separate paper. Draw the path of the ray in the water.

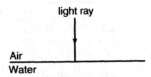

88 The diagram below shows how an observer located at point *P* on Earth can see the Sun when it is below the observer's horizon.

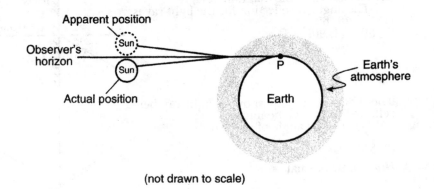

(not drawn to scale)

This observation is possible because of the ability of Earth's atmosphere to
(1) reflect light   (3) refract light
(2) diffract light   (4) polarize light

89 In the diagram at right, monochromatic light ($\lambda = 5.9 \times 10^{-7}$ meter) in air is about to travel through crown glass, water, and diamond. In which substance does the light travel the slowest?
(1) air   (3) water
(2) diamond   (4) crown glass

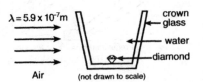

90 What occurs as a ray of light passes from air into water?
    (1) The ray must decrease in speed.
    (2) The ray must increase in speed.
    (3) The ray must decrease in frequency.
    (4) The ray must increase in frequency.

91 A beam of monochromatic light travels through flint glass, crown glass,
    Lucite, and water. The speed of the light beam is slowest in
    (1) flint glass   (2) crown glass   (3) Lucite   (4) water

92 A monochromatic beam of yellow light, *AB*, is incident upon a Lucite
    block in air at an angle of 33°.

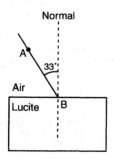

    Compare the speed of the yellow light in air to the speed of the yellow
    light in Lucite.

93 What happens to the frequency and the speed of an electromagnetic
    wave as it passes from air into glass?
    (1) The frequency decreases and the speed increases.
    (2) The frequency increases and the speed decreases.
    (3) The frequency remains the same and the speed increases.
    (4) The frequency remains the same and the speed decreases.

94 A beam of light crosses a boundary between two different media.
    Refraction can occur if
    (1) the angle of incidence is 0°
    (2) there is no change in the speed of the wave
    (3) the media have different indices of refraction
    (4) all of the light is reflected

95 The diagram at right shows a ray of
    monochromatic light incident on an alcohol-
    flint glass interface. What occurs as the light
    travels from alcohol into flint glass?
    (1) The speed of the light decreases and the
    ray bends toward the normal.
    (2) The speed of the light decreases and the
    ray bends away from the normal.
    (3) The speed of light increases and the ray
    bends toward the normal.
    (4) The speed of light increases and the ray bends away from the
    normal.

96 A ray of monochromatic light traveling in air enters a rectangular glass
    block obliquely and strikes a plane mirror at the bottom. Then the ray
    travels back through the glass and strikes the air-glass interface. Which
    diagram below best represents the path of this light ray? [*N* represents
    the normal to the surface.]

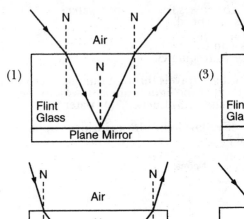

(1)

(3)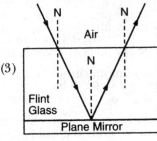

(2)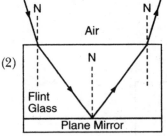

(4)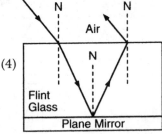

97 The diagram at right shows a light ray in air incident on a crown glass block. As the light ray enters the crown glass block, it will
(1) slow down and bend toward the normal
(2) slow down and bend away from the normal
(3) speed up and bend toward the normal
(4) speed up and bend away from the normal

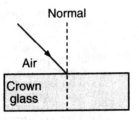

98 The speed of light in Lucite is
(1) 1.5×10^8 m/s
(2) 2.0×10^8 m/s
(3) 3.0×10^8 m/s
(4) 4.5×10^8 m/s

99 The speed of light in glycerol is approximately
(1) 1.6×10^7 m/s
(2) 2.0×10^8 m/s
(3) 3.0×10^8 m/s
(4) 4.4×10^8 m/s

100 The diagram at right shows a ray of monochromatic light ($f = 5.09 \times 10^{14}$ hertz) passing through a flint glass prism.
What is the speed of the light ray in flint glass?
(1) 5.53×10^{-9} m/s
(2) 1.81×10^8 m/s
(3) 3.00×10^8 m/s
(4) 4.98×10^8 m/s

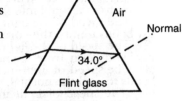

101 The speed of light in a material is 2.5×10^8 meters per second. What is the absolute index of refraction of the material?
(1) 1.2   (2) 2.5   (3) 7.5   (4) 0.83

102 The speed of light in a material is 2.50×10^8 meters per second. What is the absolute index of refraction of the material?
(1) 1.20   (2) 2.50   (3) 7.50   (4) 0.833

103 A beam of light travels through medium X with a speed of 1.80×10^8 meters per second. Calculate the absolute index of refraction of medium X.[Show all work, including the equation and substitution with units.]

104 Which quantity is equivalent to the product of the absolute index of refraction of water and the speed of light in water?
(1) wavelength of light in a vacuum
(2) frequency of light in water
(3) sine of the angle of incidence
(4) speed of light in a vacuum

105 As a monochromatic beam of light passes obliquely from flint glass into water, how do the characteristics of the beam of light change?
(1) Its wavelength decreases and its frequency decreases.
(2) Its wavelength decreases and its frequency increases.
(3) Its wavelength increases and it bends toward the normal.
(4) Its wavelength increases and it bends away from the normal.

106 A change in the speed of a wave as it enters a new medium produces a change in
(1) frequency   (2) period   (3) wavelength   (4) phase

107 What occurs when light passes from water into flint glass?
(1) Its speed decreases, its wavelength becomes shorter, and its frequency remains the same.
(2) Its speed decreases, its wavelength becomes shorter, and its frequency increases.
(3) Its speed increases, its wavelength becomes longer, and its frequency remains the same.
(4) Its speed increases, its wavelength becomes longer, and its frequency decreases.

108 A beam of monochromatic light ($\lambda = 5.9 \times 10^{-7}$ meter) crosses a boundary from air into Lucite at an angle of incidence of 45°. The angle of refraction is approximately
(1) 63°   (2) 56°   (3) 37°   (4) 28°

109 A ray of monochromatic light ($\lambda = 5.9 \times 10^{-7}$ meter) traveling in air is incident on an interface with a liquid at an angle of 45°.
If the absolute index of refraction of a liquid is 1.4, the angle of refraction for the light ray is closest to
(1) 10.°   (2) 20.°   (3) 30.°   (4) 40.°

110 A ray of light ($\lambda = 5.9 \times 10^{-7}$) traveling in air is incident on an interface with medium X at an angle of 30°. The angle of refraction for the light ray in medium X is 12°. Medium X could be
(1) alcohol   (2) corn oil   (3) diamond   (4) flint glass

111 A light ray passes from air into glass as shown in the diagram at right. Which relationship represents the index of refraction of the glass?

(1) $\dfrac{\sin A}{\sin C}$ (3) $\dfrac{\sin B}{\sin C}$

(2) $\dfrac{\sin A}{\sin D}$ (4) $\dfrac{\sin B}{\sin D}$

Hint: Use Snell's Law. Index of Refraction of Air (n_1) = 1.0.

112 The diagram at right shows a ray of light passing from medium X into air.
    What is the absolute index of refraction of medium X?
    (1) 0.500   (3) 1.73
    (2) 2.00   (4) 0.577

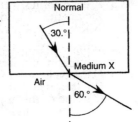

113 A monochromatic beam of yellow light, AB, is incident upon a Lucite block in air at an angle of 33°. Calculate the angle of refraction for incident beam AB. [Show all work, including the equation and substitution with units.]

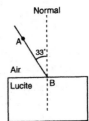

114 A ray of monochromatic light ($f = 5.09 \times 10^{14}$ hertz) in air is incident at an angle of 30.° on a boundary with corn oil. What is the angle of refraction, to the nearest degree, for this light ray in the corn oil?
    (1) 6°   (2) 20.°   (3) 30.°   (4) 47°

115 A ray of light ($\lambda = 5.9 \times 10^{-7}$) traveling in air is incident on an interface with medium X at an angle of 30°. The angle of refraction for the light ray in medium X is 12°. Medium X could be
    (1) alcohol   (2) corn oil   (3) diamond   (4) flint glass

116 The diagram at right shows a ray of light ($\lambda = 5.9 \times 10^{-7}$ meter) traveling from air into medium X.
    If the angle of incidence is 30.° and the angle of refraction is 19°, medium X could be
    (1) air   (3) crown glass
    (2) alcohol   (4) glycerol

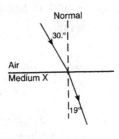

117 A monochromatic ray of light ($f = 5.09 \times 10^{14}$ hertz) traveling in air is incident upon medium A at an angle of 45°. If the angle of refraction is 29°, medium A could be
    (1) water   (3) Lucite
    (2) fused quartz   (4) flint glass

118 Base your answers to questions 118 and 119 on the diagram below, which shows a light ray in water incident at an angle of 60° on a boundary with plastic. Using a protractor, measure the angle of refraction to the *nearest degree*.

119 Determine the absolute index of refraction for the plastic. [Show all calculations, including the equation and substitution with units.]

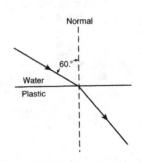

120 The diagram at right represents a beam of monochromatic light ($\lambda = 5.9 \times 10^{-7}$ meter) traveling from Lucite into air.
What is the measure of the angle of refraction? [Use a protractor or a mathematical calculation.]
(1) 19°   (3) 49°
(2) 30.°   (4) 60.°

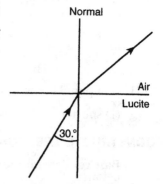

121 In a vacuum, all electromagnetic waves have the same
(1) wavelength   (2) frequency   (3) speed   (4) amplitude

122 Radio waves and gamma rays traveling in space have the same
(1) frequency   (2) wavelength   (3) period   (4) speed

123 In a vacuum, a monochromatic beam of light has a frequency of 6.3×10^{14} hertz. What color is the light?
(1) red   (2) yellow   (3) green   (4) blue

124 A monochromatic beam of light has a frequency of 6.5×10^{14} hertz. What color is the light?
(1) yellow   (2) orange   (3) violet   (4) blue

125 A ray of monochromatic light of frequency 5.00×10^{14} hertz is incident on a mirror and reflected. What is the color of the ray of light?

126 When an electron in an excited hydrogen atom falls from a higher to a lower energy level, a photon having a wavelength of 6.58×10^{-7} meter is emitted. Is this photon an x ray photon? Justify your answer.

Base your answers to questions 127 and 128 on the data table below. The data table lists the energy and corresponding frequency of five photons.

Photon	Energy (J)	Frequency (Hz)
A	6.63×10^{-15}	1.00×10^{19}
B	1.99×10^{-17}	3.00×10^{16}
C	3.49×10^{-19}	5.26×10^{14}
D	1.33×10^{-20}	2.00×10^{13}
E	6.63×10^{-26}	1.00×10^{8}

127 In which part of the electromagnetic spectrum would photon E be found?
(1) infrared   (2) visible   (3) ultraviolet   (4) radio waves

128 A ray of monochromatic light of frequency 5.00×10^{14} hertz is incident on a mirror and reflected. Determine the wavelength of the ray of light. [Show all work, including the equation and substitution with units.]

129 In a vacuum, light with a frequency of 5.0×10^{14} hertz has a wavelength of

(1) 6.0×10^{-21} m   (3) 1.7×10^{6} m
(2) 6.0×10^{-7} m   (4) 1.5×10^{23} m

130 What is the frequency of a light wave with a wavelength of 6.0×10^{-7} meter traveling through space?
(1) 2.0×10^{-15} Hz   (3) 1.8×10^{14} Hz
(2) 5.0×10^{1} Hz   (4) 5.0×10^{14} Hz

131 Compared to the wavelength of red light, the wavelength of yellow light is
(1) shorter   (2) longer   (3) the same

CONSTRUCTED RESPONSE QUESTIONS: Parts B-2 and C of NYS Regents Exam

Base your answers to questions 132-134 on the information and diagram below.

Three waves, *A*, *B*, and *C*, travel 12 meters in 2.0 seconds through the same medium, as shown in the diagram below.

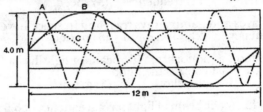

132 What is the amplitude of wave *C*?

133 What is the period of wave *A*?

134 What is the speed of wave *B*?

135 A ray of monochromatic light of frequency 5.00×10^{14} hertz is incident on a mirror and reflected, as shown at right.
Determine the wavelength of the ray of light. [Show all calculations, including the equation and substitution with units.]

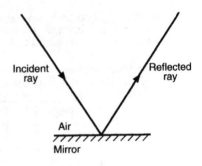

Base your answers to questions 136 and 137 on the following information:
A transverse wave with an amplitude of 0.20 meter and wavelength of 3.0 meters travels toward the right in a medium with a speed of 4.0 meters per second.

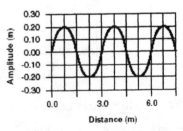

136 Review question: Copy the diagram on separate paper. Place an *X* at each of two points that are in phase with each other.

137 Calculate the period of the wave. [Show all work, including the equation and substitution with units.]

Base your answers to questions 138 and 139 on the information below.
A student plucks a guitar string and the vibrations produce a sound wave with a frequency of 650 hertz.

138 The sound wave produced can best be described as a
(1) transverse wave of constant amplitude
(2) longitudinal wave of constant frequency
(3) mechanical wave of varying frequency
(4) electromagnetic wave of varying wavelengths

139 Calculate the wavelength of the sound wave in air at STP. [Show all work, including the equation and substitution with units.]

Base your answers to questions 140-142 on the information below:
A 0.12-meter-long electromagnetic (radar) wave is emitted by a weather station and reflected from a nearby thunderstorm.

140 Determine the frequency of the radar wave. [Show all calculations, including the equation and substitution with units.]
Hint: Radar waves travel at the speed of light

141 Using one or more complete sentences, define the Doppler effect.

142 The thunderstorm is moving toward the weather station. Using one or more complete sentences, explain how the Doppler effect could have been used to determine the direction in which the storm is moving.

Base your answers to questions 143-145 on the information and diagram below.
Two waves, *A* and *B*, travel in the same direction in the same medium at the same time.

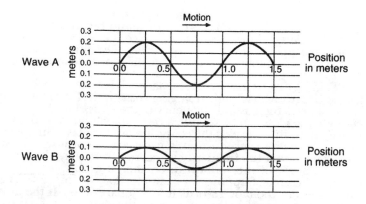

143 Copy the grid provided on separate paper. Draw the resultant wave produced by the superposition of waves *A* and *B*.

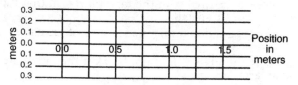

144 What is the amplitude of the resultant wave?
Hint: Answer must include units (example: meters, grams, etc.)

145 What is the wavelength of the resultant wave?
Hint: answer must include units (example: meters, grams, etc.)

Base your answers to questions 146-149 on the information and diagram below.

A wave generator having a constant frequency of 15 hertz produces a standing wave pattern in a stretched string.

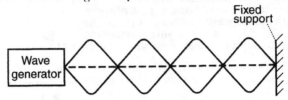

146 Using a ruler, measure the amplitude of the wave shown. Record the value to the *nearest tenth of a centimeter* on your answer paper.
Hint: Review characteristics of waves.

147 Using a ruler, measure the wavelength of the wave shown. Record the value to the *nearest tenth of a centimeter* on your answer paper.
Hint: Review characteristics of waves.

148 State what would happen to the wavelength of the wave if the frequency of the wave were increased.
Hint: Review characteristics of waves.

149 How many antinodes are shown in the diagram?

Base your answers to questions 150-151 on the passage below.

Shattering Glass

An old television commercial for audio recording tape showed a singer breaking a wine glass with her voice. The question was then asked if this was actually her voice or a recording. The inference is that the tape is of such high quality that the excellent reproduction of the sound is able to break glass.

This is a demonstration of resonance. It is certainly possible to break a wine glass with an amplified singing voice. If the frequency of the voice is the same as the natural frequency of the glass, and the sound is loud enough, the glass can be set into a resonant vibration whose amplitude is large enough to surpass the elastic limit of the glass. But the inference that high-quality reproduction is necessary is not justified. All that is important is that the frequency is recorded and played back correctly. The waveform of the sound can be altered as long as the frequency remains the same. Suppose, for example, that the singer sings a perfect sine wave, but the tape records it as a square wave. If the tape player plays the sound back at the right speed, the glass will still receive energy at the resonance frequency and will be set into vibration leading to breakage, even though the tape reproduction was terrible. Thus, this phenomenon does not require high-quality reproduction and, thus, does not demonstrate the quality of the recording tape. What it does demonstrate is the quality of the tape player, in that it played back the tape at an accurate speed!

150 List *two* properties that a singer's voice must have in order to shatter a glass.

151 Explain why the glass would not break if the tape player did not play back at an accurate speed.

Base your answers to questions 152 and 153 on the information and diagram below.

A ray of monochromatic light of frequency 5.00×10^{14} hertz is incident on a mirror and reflected, as shown.

152 Copy the diagram onto separate paper. Using a protractor and ruler, construct and label the normal to the mirror at the point of incidence.

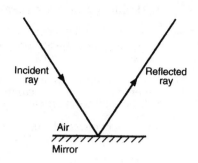

153 Using a protractor, measure the angle of incidence to the nearest degree and record the value *on your answer paper*.

154 The diagram at right represents a wave generator having a constant frequency of 12 hertz, producing parallel wave fronts in a ripple tank. The velocity of the waves is v.
A barrier is placed in the ripple tank as shown in the diagram. Use a protractor and ruler to construct an arrow to represent the direction of the velocity of the reflected waves.

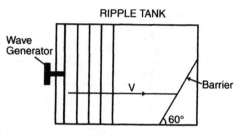

Base your answers to questions 155 and 156 on the information and diagram below.
In the diagram, a light ray, R, strikes the boundary of air and water.

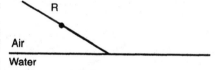

155 Using a protractor, determine the angle of incidence.

156 Copy the diagram on separate paper. Using a protractor and straight edge, draw the reflected ray.

157 Base your answers to parts *A* through *C* on the information and diagram below.
A ray of light *AO* is incident on a plane mirror, as shown

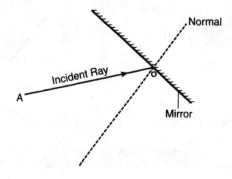

A. Using a protractor, measure the angle of incidence for light ray *AO*

B. What is the angle of reflection of the light ray?

C. Copy the diagram on separate paper. Using a protractor and straightedge, construct the reflected ray on the diagram.

158 A beam of light travels through medium *X* with a speed of 1.80×10^8 meters per second. Calculate the absolute index of refraction of medium *X*. [Show all work, including the equation and substitution with units.]

159 A monochromatic beam of yellow light, *AB*, is incident upon a Lucite block in air at an angle of $33°$.
  Calculate the angle of refraction for incident beam *AB*. [Show all work, including the equation and substitution with units.]

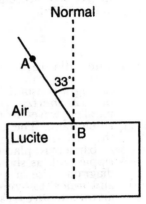

Base your answers to questions 160 and 161 on the diagram below, which shows a light ray in water incident at an angle of 60.° on a boundary with plastic.

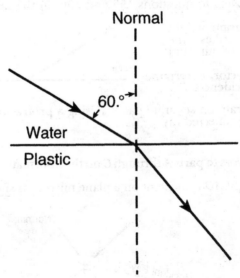

160 Using a protractor, measure the angle of refraction to the *nearest degree*.

161 Determine the absolute index of refraction for the plastic. [Show all calculations, including the equation and substitution with units.]

Base your answers to questions 162-164 on the information and diagram below:

A light ray with a frequency of 5.09×10^{14} hertz traveling in air is incident at an angle of 40.° on an air-water interface as shown. At the interface, part of the ray is refracted as it enters the water and part of the ray is reflected from the interface.

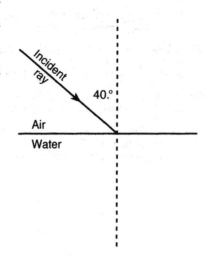

162 Calculate the angle of refraction of the light ray as it enters the water. [Show all work, including the equation and substitution with units.]

163 Copy the diagram on separate paper. Using a protractor and straightedge, draw the refracted ray. Label this ray "Refracted ray."

164 Copy the diagram on separate paper. Using a protractor and straightedge, draw the reflected ray. Label this ray "Reflected ray."
Hint: review reflection

Base your answers to questions 165 and 166 on the information and diagram.

A ray of monochromatic light of frequency 5.00×10^{14} hertz is incident on a mirror and reflected, as shown. [The diagram below is provided for practice purposes only.]

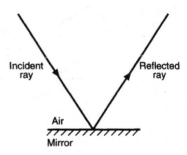

165 What is the color of the ray of light?

166 Determine the wavelength of the ray of light. [Show all calculations, including the equation and substitution with units.]

167 When an electron in an excited hydrogen atom falls from a higher to a lower energy level, a photon having a wavelength of 6.58×10^{-7} meter is emitted.
Is this photon an x-ray photon? Justify your answer.

CHAPTER 5:
MODERN PHYSICS

Section 1:

You learned about light waves and other electromagnetic waves, also called electromagnetic radiation (examples x-rays, radio waves, etc.), which are given on Reference Table: the Electromagnetic Spectrum.

Light (and other **electromagnetic waves**, such as x-rays, microwaves, etc.) are actually both **waves** and **particles**.

1. **Wave characteristics** (showing electromagnetic waves are waves): Light (and other electromagnetic waves) have **diffraction,** page 4:35, **interference,** page 4:23, and **doppler effects**, page 4:18, which are explained in terms of waves (wave model). Diffraction, interference, and doppler effect are explained in the chapter on waves.

2. **Particle characteristics** (showing electromagnetic waves are particles). The particles are called photons. Photons have no mass and no charge; they move at the speed of light. Photons are a specific amount of energy. **Photoelectric effect:** A photon (example x-ray photon) hits a piece of metal or graphite, which gives off electrons. Look at the figure. The incident x-ray photon (called incident because it hits the electron) strikes or collides with an electron (e⁻) of the metal. The **x-ray photon puts** some of its **energy into** the **electron,** causing the electron to be given off (goes away from the atom of the metal); the rest of the energy of the x-ray photon is released as a **photon of lower energy.** *Note:* When an incident **visible light** photon , which has less energy (lower frequency) than x-ray, hits an electron (e⁻) of a metal, an electron is sometimes emitted. There is no extra energy to produce a new photon.

Recoiling electron
Incident photon
Scattered photon

The total **energy and** total **momentum** (mass times velocity) of the x-ray photon and the electron **before** the **collision** (before the x-ray photon and the electron collide) **equal** the total **energy and** total **momentum** of the photon and electron **after** the **collision.** Energy and momentum are conserved (stay the same).

Energy is a **scalar** quantity. Energy has magnitude (a number and a unit, example 40 joules), but no direction. Momentum is a **vector** quantity. Momentum has magnitude (a number and a unit, example 40 kg·m/s) and direction (east); an example of momentum is 40 kg·m/s east.

Similarly, **matter** (anything that has mass and takes up space) is both **particles** and **waves.** When matter (example electrons) goes through an opening (slit), the **matter** (example **electrons**) is **diffracted** (electron diffraction), **showing** that **matter** is a **wave**. Large objects have wavelengths too small (10^{-34} meter) to show diffraction.

QUANTUM THEORY

Atoms (example hydrogen) can only give off or absorb **specific amounts** (discrete amounts) of **energy** called a **quantum** of energy (or a **photon** of **energy**). Energy is given off or absorbed as light or other electromagnetic waves.

Questions 1 and 2: Base your answers on the information and diagram. The diagram shows the collision of an incident photon having a frequency of 2.00×10^{19} hertz with an electron initially at rest.

Before collision   **After collision**

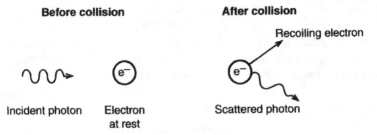

Incident photon   Electron   Scattered photon
                   at rest

Question 1: Calculate the initial energy of the photon. (Show all calculations, including the equation and substitution with units.)
Question 2: What is the total energy of the two particle system after the collision?

Solution 1:
Given: Frequency (f) of the incident photon = 2.00×10^{19} hertz.
Find: Energy (E) of the photon.

Look for an equation on Reference Table: Modern Physics on page reference tables 20 that has energy of the photon (E_{photon}) and frequency (f).

Use the equation:

$$E_{photon} \qquad = \qquad h \qquad\qquad f$$
energy of a photon = Planck's constant x frequency

First find h, then substitute h and f in $E_{photon} = hf$ to find E_{photon}.

First find h (Planck's constant). Look below or at Reference Table: List of Physical Constants on page Reference Tables 2-3.

Planck's constant h 6.63×10^{-34} J•s

Then, in the equation $E_{photon} = hf$, *substitute for h*, 6.63×10^{-34} J•s. *Substitute for f*, 2.00×10^{19} Hz (given).

$$E_{photon} \quad = \qquad h \qquad\qquad\qquad f$$
$$E_{photon} \quad = \quad 6.63 \times 10^{-34} \text{ J•s} \quad \times \quad 2.00 \times 10^{19} \text{ Hz}$$
$$E_{photon} \quad = \quad 1.326 \times 10^{-14} \text{ J•s•Hz} = 1.33 \times 10^{-14} \text{ J•s•Hz}$$

$Hz = \dfrac{1}{s}$; therefore, you can substitute $\dfrac{1}{s}$ for Hz (see below).

$E_{photon} = 1.33 \times 10^{-14}\,J\bullet s\bullet \dfrac{1}{s}$

$E_{photon} = 1.33 \times 10^{-14}\,J$ (joules)

Solution 2: You learned that energy is conserved.

Total energy before collision = total energy after collision.

Before collision:

Initial energy of photon = $1.33 \times 10^{-14}\,J$ (answer to question 1).

Energy of electron **at rest = zero.**

Total energy before collision = $1.33 \times 10^{-14}\,J$, therefore, total energy after collision is the same, $1.33 \times 10^{-14}\,J$ (joules).

Let's look at the first equation given on reference table modern physics.

$$E_{photon} = h \qquad f \qquad = \qquad \dfrac{hc}{\lambda}$$

c = speed of light in a vacuum
E = Energy
f = frequency
h = Planck's constant
λ = wavelength

$$E_{photon} = h \qquad f \qquad = \qquad \dfrac{hc}{\lambda}$$

energy of a photon = Planck's constant × frequency = $\dfrac{Planck's\ constant \times speed\ of\ light\ in\ a\ vacuum}{wavelength}$

Energy is in joules (J), f is in Hz (= 1/s), h is in J•s, c is in m/s, and λ is in meters (m).

Questions 1 and 2: Base your answers to questions 1 and 2 on the information below. The light of the "alpha line" in the Balmer series of the hydrogen spectrum has a wavelength of 6.58×10^{-7} meter.

Question 1: Calculate the energy of an "alpha line" photon in joules.(Show all work, including the equation and substitution with units.)

Question 2: What is the energy of an "alpha line" photon in electron volts?

Solution 1:

Given: Wavelength = 6.58×10^{-7} meter.

Find: Energy of the photon (E_{photon}) in joules.

Look for an equation on Reference Table: Modern Physics on page reference tables 20 that has energy of a photon (E_{photon}) and wavelength (λ).

$$E_{photon} = h \qquad f = \frac{hc}{\lambda}$$

E =	Energy
h =	Planck's constant
f =	frequency
c =	speed of light in a vacuum
λ =	wavelength

$$E_{photon} = h \qquad f = \frac{hc}{\lambda}$$

energy of a photon $=$ Planck's constant $\times$ frequency $= \dfrac{\textit{Planck's constant} \times \textit{speed of light in a vacuum}}{\textit{wavelength}}$

Use the equation $E_{photon} = \frac{hc}{\lambda}$ (see above).

You have three things you do not know, E_{photon}, h, and c; therefore, first find h and c, and then **substitute** h and c in the equation $E_{photon} = \frac{hc}{\lambda}$ to find E_{photon}. *Note:* λ (wavelength) is given.

First find h and c. Look at the List of Physical Constants below or on Reference Table: List of Physical Constants, on page reference tables 2-3.

Reference Table: List of Physical Constants		
Name	**Symbol**	**Value**
Universal gravitational constant	G	$6.67 \times 10^{-11}\,N\bullet m^2/kg^2$
Speed of light in a vacuum	c	3.00×10^8 m/s
Planck's constant	h	$6.63 \times 10^{-34}\,J\bullet s$

Then, in the equation $E_{photon} = \frac{hc}{\lambda}$, **substitute for h** (Planck's constant), 6.63×10^{-34} J•s and **substitute for c** (speed of light in a vacuum), 3.00×10^8 m/s (from reference table above). **Substitute for** λ (wavelength) 6.58×10^{-7} m (given).

(In this equation, $E_{photon} = hf = \frac{hc}{\lambda}$, you substituted for h, 6.63×10^{-34} J•s (joule•seconds), therefore E_{photon} must also be in J (joules)).

$$E_{photon} = \frac{hc}{\lambda}$$

$$E_{photon} = \frac{(6.63 \times 10^{-34} J \bullet s)(3.00 \times 10^8 m/s)}{6.58 \times 10^{-7} m}$$

E_{photon} (Energy of the photon) $= 3.02 \times 10^{-19}$ J (joule)

Solution 2:

Given: Energy of an "alpha line" photon = 3.02×10^{-19} joule (J) (answer from question 1).

Find: Energy of an "alpha line" photon in electronvolts (eV).

To **convert joules of energy to electronvolts** of energy, **first** look below or on Reference Table: List of Physical Constants on page reference tables 2-3.

$\qquad$ 1 electronvolt (eV) $\qquad = \qquad 1.60 \times 10^{-19}$ J.

(This equation is used to convert joules into electronvolts (or electronvolts into joules).)

Next, multiply energy in joules:

$$3.02 \times 10^{-19} \text{ J} \times \frac{1 \text{ eV}}{1.60 \times 10^{-19} J} = 1.89 \text{ eV}$$

Energy of an "alpha line" photon = 1.89 eV (electronvolts)

Note: Since 3.02×10^{-19} J is on top, then 1.6×10^{-19} J must be on the bottom of the fraction; therefore, the J's cancel out and you get eV (electronvolts).

SOLVING PROBLEMS ON ENERGY OF A PHOTON

There are only two equations given on Reference Table: Modern Physics for energy of a photon (E_{photon}).

Use the equation $E_{photon} = h f = \frac{hc}{\lambda}$ when the question has energy of a photon and frequency (f) or energy of a photon and wavelength (λ).

BUT, when the question has **two different energy levels**, such as when an electron of an atom drops from energy level 4 to energy level 2, and asks to **find energy**, use

$$E_{photon} = E_i - E_f.$$

In this question, E_i is energy at starting (initial) energy level 4, and E_f is energy at final energy level 2. You will learn how to use this equation later in the chapter.

Note: When a question gives two different energy levels and **also gives** the **energy**, obviously, you do not need to use the equation $E_{photon} = E_i - E_f$ to find energy, because energy was given in the question. You will learn about this later in the chapter.

Question: A photon of which electromagnetic radiation has the most energy?

(1) ultraviolet (2) x ray (3) infrared (4) microwave

Solution:

Given: A photon of electromagnetic energy.

Find: Which electromagnetic radiation (electromagnetic waves) has the most energy.

Use either method below to find which equation to use to solve the problem.

Method 1: *Look for an equation* on Reference Table: Modern Physics that has energy of a photon (E_{photon}).

Since the question asks about **electromagnetic** radiation (with the most energy), look at Reference Table: Electromagnetic Spectrum; it has frequency and wavelength. Different kinds of electromagnetic radiation (examples ultraviolet, microwave) have different frequencies. Therefore, choose the equation for energy of a photon with frequency and wavelength:

$$E_{photon} = hf = \frac{hc}{\lambda}.$$

Or

Easy Method 2: *Look for an equation* on Reference Table: Modern Physics that has energy of a photon (E_{photon}). On Reference Table: Modern Physics, there are only two equations for the energy of a photon. Obviously, the equation $E_{photon} = E_i - E_f$ (given on Reference Table: Modern Physics) **cannot** be used, because this question has **nothing to do with two different energy levels** (nothing to do with energy at starting energy level E_i and nothing to do with energy at final energy level E_f); therefore, use the equation $E_{photon} = hf = \frac{hc}{\lambda}$.

After using **method 1 or method 2, look at the equation** $E_{photon} = hf$. Since h is constant, energy (E) is directly proportional to frequency (f). The higher the frequency (f) of the electromagnetic wave (examples of electromagnetic waves are x ray, visible light, etc.) the more energy (E) it has.

Look at Reference Table: The Electromagnetic Spectrum on the next page or on page reference tables 6-7. See which choice in the question has the highest frequency.

Reference Table: The Electromagnetic Spectrum

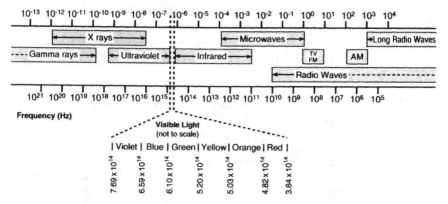

Of the four choices in the question, x-rays have the highest frequency, therefore x-rays have the most (highest) energy.

Answer 2

Question: Compared to a photon of red light, a photon of blue light has a

    (1) greater energy   (2) longer wavelength

    (3) smaller momentum   (4) lower frequency

Solution:

Given: A photon of red light and a photon of blue light.

Find: Which of the four choices is correct.

Look for an equation on Reference Table: Modern Physics that has to do with photons. (This question has nothing to do with energy levels.)

Use the equation

$$E_{photon} = hf = \frac{hc}{\lambda}.$$

    c = speed of light in a vacuum

    E = energy

    f = frequency

    h = Planck's constant

    λ = wavelength

In the equation above, h is Planck's constant. By looking at the equation $E_{photon} = hf$, you know the **higher** the **frequency** (f) of the electromagnetic wave, the **more energy** (*E*) it has.

Table: Modern Physics

Since the question has red light and blue light, look below or on Reference Table: The Electromagnetic Spectrum on page reference tables 6-7 to see what are the frequencies of red light and blue light.

Part of Reference Table: The Electromagnetic Spectrum

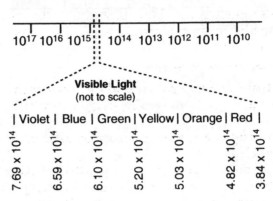

On Reference Table: The Electromagnetic Spectrum, red light (or a photon of red light) has a frequency between 3.84×10^{14} Hz- 4.82×10^{14} Hz. Blue light (or a photon of blue light) has a frequency between 6.10×10^{14} Hz- 6.59×10^{14} Hz. Blue light has a higher frequency than red light. By looking at the equation $E_{photon} = hf$, you know the higher the frequency (f) of the electromagnetic wave, the more energy it has; blue light (or a photon of blue light) has a higher frequency than red light, therefore blue light has more energy.   Answer *1*

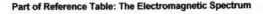

Section 2:

MODELS OF THE ATOM

An atom is the **smallest part** of **an element** (example: oxygen) that has the characteristics of the element.

Atomic Models

1. **Thomson Model** Thomson's model is known as the plum pudding model. The atom is made up of evenly spread out positive charge, with electrons embedded in (inside) it. Thomson discovered electrons, particles with a negative charge.

2. Ernest Rutherford **bombarded gold foil** with **alpha particles** (nuclei of helium atoms). Most of the alpha particles **went straight through** the foil, **showing** that most of the **atom** is **empty space**.

Alpha particles are **positively charged**. Some alpha particles (positively charged) hit the **nucleus (positively charged)** of the gold atoms in the gold foil. Positive charge repels positive charge (also called electrostatic repulsion), making the positive charges go in opposite directions. Alpha particles (positively charged) that come close to a nucleus (positively charged) are repelled and have their path (hyperbolic path) bent (deflected) to the side; **alpha particles** that hit a nucleus are also repelled and **bounce back**. This shows that most of the **mass** of the atom is in the **center**, the **nucleus**, which is **positive**.

Rutherford's model: Most of the mass of the atom is in the center, the nucleus, which is positive. Most of the atom is empty space. Electrons go around the nucleus.

3. **Bohr model** (of the atom):

   a. Electrons revolve (go) around the nucleus in concentric circular orbits (see circles in diagram).

   b. Each orbit is a specific distance away from the nucleus.

   c. All forms of **energy** are **quantized**. An electron can gain or lose energy only **by changing orbits** (energy levels); **it gains or loses specific amounts** of energy called **quanta** of energy. Therefore, we can say **energy** is **quantized** (explained below).

   d. You learned that electrons revolve (go) around the nucleus. An electron that stays in the same orbit (energy level) does not lose energy, even though the negative electron is accelerating (being pulled) toward the positive nucleus.

An electron can jump from a lower energy level (closer to the nucleus) to a higher energy level (further away from the nucleus) by absorbing a specific amount of energy, a quantum of energy (photon of energy) [see diagram above]. Electrons can also go the reverse way, from higher energy level (further away from the nucleus) to a lower energy level (closer to the nucleus), by giving off a specific amount of energy, a quantum of energy (photon of energy) [see diagram above].

The orbit (energy level) nearest the nucleus has the least energy. For example, when the electron of hydrogen is in the lowest possible energy level (closest or nearest to the nucleus), the electron is in the **ground state**. If the electron (example: of hydrogen) jumps ahead to a higher orbit (energy level) further away from the nucleus, the electron is excited (**excited state**). You will learn more about this later in this chapter.

An electron is in a stationary state when it is in any energy level (closer to the nucleus or further away from the nucleus).

4. **Electron Cloud Model** Electrons are not in specific energy levels (differs from Bohr) but are spread out as a cloud of negative charge (electrons have a negative charge). The thickest (most dense) part of the cloud is the most probable place to find the electron.

ENERGY LEVELS OF HYDROGEN

Look below or on Reference Table: Energy Level Diagrams, for hydrogen, on page Reference Tables 10-11. When $n = 1$, first energy level, closest to the nucleus, the energy is -13.60 eV. When $n = 2$, second energy level, a little further away from the nucleus, energy $= -3.40$ eV. When $n = 3$, third energy level, further away from the nucleus, energy $= -1.51$ eV. When the electron from the atom went away (left) the atom (ionized), the electron is far away from the nucleus, and the energy $= 0$.

When an electron goes from a higher energy level (example: $n = 6$) to a lower energy level (example: $n = 2$), it gives off one photon of energy (a specific amount of energy). When an electron goes from a lower energy level (example: $n = 3$) to a higher energy level (example: $n = 6$) it absorbs one photon of energy (a specific amount of energy). You will learn later how to answer questions using Reference Table: Energy Level Diagrams.

Part of Table:
Energy Level Diagrams

Hydrogen

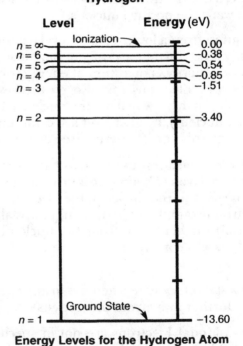

Energy Levels for the Hydrogen Atom

Chap. 5:10   Modern Physics   **High Marks: Regents Physics Made Easy**

Let's continue with questions using the equation $E_{photon} = hf = \dfrac{hc}{\lambda}$.

Question: An electron in a hydrogen atom drops from the $n = 3$ energy level to the $n = 2$ energy level. Energy of the emitted photon = $1.89\,eV$ or $3.02 \times 10^{-19}\,J$. Calculate the frequency of the emitted radiation. [Show all work, including the equation and substitution with units.]

Solution :

Given: An electron in a hydrogen atom drops from the $n = 3$ energy level to the $n = 2$ energy level. Energy of the emitted photon = $1.89\,eV$ or $3.02 \times 10^{-19}\,J$.

Find: Frequency (f) of the emitted radiation.

The question gives you energy of the photon. The fact that the electron drops from n = 3 to n = 2 is extra information, not necessary to solve the problem.

Look for an equation below or on Reference Table: Modern Physics that has energy of the photon (E_{photon}) and frequency (f).

$$E_{photon} \quad = \quad h \quad\quad f \quad = \quad \frac{hc}{\lambda}$$

$$\begin{array}{ccc} \text{energy of} \\ \text{a photon} \end{array} = \begin{array}{c} \text{Planck's} \\ \text{constant} \end{array} \times \text{frequency} = \frac{\textit{Planck's constant} \times \textit{speed of light in a vacuum}}{\textit{wavelength}}$$

Use the equation $E_{photon} = hf$. You have two unknowns, h and f; therefore, first find h (Planck's constant) and then substitute h and E_{photon} (given) in the equation $E_{photon} = hf$ to find f (frequency).

First find h. Look at the list of physical constants below or on Reference Table: List of Physical Constants.

Reference Table: List of Physical Constants		
Name	**Symbol**	**Value**
Universal gravitational constant	G	$6.67 \times 10^{-11}\,N \cdot m^2/kg^2$
Speed of light in a vacuum	c	$3.00 \times 10^8\,m/s$
Planck's constant	h	$6.63 \times 10^{-34}\,J \cdot s$

Then, in the equation $E_{photon} = hf$, *substitute for h* (Planck's constant) = $6.63 \times 10^{-34}\,J \cdot s$. *Substitute for E_{photon}* (energy of the photon) = $3.02 \times 10^{-19}\,J$ (given).

(In this equation, $E_{photon} = hf = \dfrac{hc}{\lambda}$, remember, **energy must be in joules** (J) because h, given on Reference Table: List of Physical Constants, is $6.63 \times 10^{-34}\,J \cdot s$ (joule•seconds).)

$$E_{photon} = h \quad f$$
$$3.02 \times 10^{-19}\,J = 6.63 \times 10^{-34}\,J \cdot s \cdot f$$
$$\frac{3.02 \times 10^{-19}\,J}{6.63 \times 10^{-34}\,J \cdot s} = f$$
$$4.56 \times 10^{14} \cdot \frac{1}{s} = f \qquad Hz = \frac{1}{s};$$
$$4.56 \times 10^{14}\,Hz = f$$
$$frequency\ (f) = 4.56 \times 10^{14}\,Hz$$
answer

Or, rearrange the equation:
$$f = \frac{E_{photon}}{h}$$
$$f = \frac{3.02 \times 10^{-19}\,J}{6.63 \times 10^{-34}\,J \cdot s}$$
$$f = 4.56 \times 10^{14} \cdot \frac{1}{s} \qquad Hz = \frac{1}{s};$$
$$f = 4.56 \times 10^{14}\,Hz$$
$$frequency\ (f) = 4.56 \times 10^{14}\,Hz$$
answer

Question : An electron in a hydrogen atom drops from the $n = 3$ energy level to the $n = 2$ energy level. The energy of the emitted photon is 1.89 eV or 3.02×10^{-19} J and its frequency is 4.56×10^{14} Hz. Calculate the wavelength of the emitted radiation. [Show all work, including the equation and substitution with units.]

Solution:
METHOD 1:

Given: An electron in a hydrogen atom drops from the $n = 3$ energy level to the $n = 2$ energy level. Energy of the emitted photon = 1.89 eV or 3.02×10^{-19} J. Frequency = 4.56×10^{14} Hz.

Find: Wavelength (λ) of emitted radiation (photon).

The question gives you energy of the photon. The fact that the electron drops from n = 3 energy level to n = 2 energy level is extra information, not necessary to solve the problem.

Look for an equation below or on Reference Table: Modern Physics on page reference tables 20 that has energy of a photon (E_{photon}) and wavelength (λ).

$$E_{photon} = h \quad f = \frac{hc}{\lambda}$$

$c =$ speed of light in a vacuum
$E =$ Energy
$f =$ frequency
$h =$ Planck's constant
$\lambda =$ wavelength

$$\begin{array}{l} energy \\ of\ a \\ photon \end{array} = \begin{array}{l} Planck's \\ constant \end{array} \times frequency = \frac{Planck's\ constant \times speed\ of\ light\ in\ a\ vacuum}{wavelength}$$

Use the equation $E_{photon} = \frac{hc}{\lambda}$ (see above) because the question asks to find wavelength (λ).

You have three unknowns, h, c, and λ; therefore, first find h and c,

---

and then substitute h and c in the equation $E_{photon} = \frac{hc}{\lambda}$ to find λ (wavelength). (*Note:* E_{photon} is given.)

First find h and c. Look at the List of Physical Constants below or on Reference Table: List of Physical Constants on page Reference Table 2-3.

Reference Table: List of Physical Constants		
Name	Symbol	Value
Universal gravitational constant	G	6.67×10^{-11} N•m^2/kg^2
Speed of light in a vacuum	c	3.00×10^8 m/s
Planck's constant	h	6.63×10^{-34} J•s

Then, in the equation $E_{photon} = \frac{hc}{\lambda}$ *substitute for h* (Planck's constant), 6.63×10^{-34} J•s and *substitute for c* (speed of light in a vacuum), 3.00×10^8 m/s. *Substitute for E_{photon}* 3.02×10^{-19} J (given).

Remember, in the equation, $E_{photon} = hf = \frac{hc}{\lambda}$, E_{photon} (**energy of a photon**) **must be in joules (J) because** h (Planck's constant) is in **J•s (joule•seconds)**.

$$E_{photon} = \frac{hc}{\lambda}$$

$$3.02 \times 10^{-19} \text{ J} = \frac{(6.63 \times 10^{-34} \text{ J•s})(3.00 \times 10^8 \text{ m/s})}{\lambda}$$

Cross multiply

$$3.02 \times 10^{-19} \text{ J•}\lambda = (6.63 \times 10^{-34} \text{ J•s})(3.00 \times 10^8 \text{ m/s})$$

$$\lambda = \frac{(6.63 \times 10^{-34} \text{ J•s})(3.00 \times 10^8 \text{ m/s})}{3.02 \times 10^{-19} \text{ J}}$$

$$\lambda = 6.59 \times 10^{-7} \text{ m(meters)}$$

$$\text{wavelength } (\lambda) = 6.59 \times 10^{-7} \text{ m}$$

METHOD 2:

Given: An electron in a hydrogen atom drops from the $n = 3$ energy level to the $n = 2$ energy level. Energy of the emitted photon = 1.89 eV or 3.02×10^{-19} J. Frequency of emitted radiation = 4.56×10^{14} Hz.

Find: Wavelength (λ) of emitted radiation.

Electromagnetic radiation is both a particle and a wave. A photon (particle form) travels at the speed of light in a vacuum.

Look for an equation on Reference Table: Waves that has frequency (f) and wavelength (λ).

Use the equation:

$$v = f \lambda$$

f = frequency
v = velocity
λ = wavelength

velocity = frequency x wavelength

First find v (speed) of a photon and then substitute v and f in the equation $v = f\lambda$ to find λ (wavelength).

First find v (speed) of a photon.

A photon travels at the speed of light. The speed of light in a vacuum is 3.00×10^8 m/s, given on Reference Table: List of Physical Constants; therefore the speed of a photon is 3.00×10^8 m/s.

Then, in the equation $v = f\lambda$, **substitute for v** 3.00×10^8 m/s. **Substitute for f** 4.56×10^{14} Hz (given).

$$v = f \lambda$$

$$3.00 \times 10^8 \text{ m/s} = 4.56 \times 10^{14} \text{ Hz} \lambda$$

$$\frac{3.00 \times 10^8 \text{ m/s}}{4.56 \times 10^{14} \text{ Hz (or 1/s)}} = \lambda$$

Note: Hz $= \dfrac{1}{s \text{ (second)}}$

$\lambda = 6.58 \times 10^{-7}$ m(meters)

Wavelength (λ) = 6.58×10^{-7} m.

Now do Homework Questions #36-37, page 48.

Part of Table:
Energy Level Diagrams

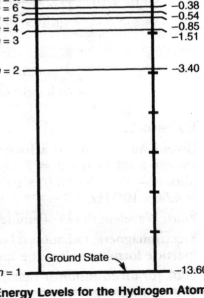

Hydrogen

Energy Levels for the Hydrogen Atom

REVIEW OF ENERGY LEVELS OF HYDROGEN Look at the right or on Reference Table: Energy Level Diagrams, for hydrogen, on page reference tables 10-11. When $n = 1$, first energy level, closest to the nucleus, the energy is -13.60 eV (electronvolts). When $n = 2$, second energy level, a little further away from the nucleus, energy = -3.40 eV (electronvolts). When $n = 3$, third energy level, further away from the nucleus, energy = -1.51 eV. When the electron from the atom went away (left) the atom (ionized), the electron is far away from the nucleus, and the energy = 0.

When an electron goes from a higher energy level (example: $n = 6$) to a lower energy level (example: $n = 2$), it gives off one photon of energy (a specific amount of energy). When an electron goes from a lower energy level (example: $n = 3$) to a higher energy level (example: $n = 6$) it absorbs one photon of energy (a specific amount of energy).

Questions 1-2: Base your answers on the information below.
An electron in a hydrogen atom drops from the $n = 3$ energy level to the $n = 2$ energy level.
Question 1: What is the energy, in electron volts, of the emitted photon?
Question 2: What is the energy, in joules, of the emitted photon?

Solution 1:
Given: The electron of the hydrogen atom drops from the $n = 3$ energy level to the $n = 2$ energy level.
Find: energy of the emitted photon in electronvolts (eV).

Look for an equation on Reference Table: Modern Physics, on page reference tables 20 that has to do with energy of the photon (E_{photon}). There are two equations for E_{photon} on Reference Table: Modern Physics. The question says that the electron drops from the $n = 3$ energy level to the $n = 2$ energy level; therefore, choose the equation with two different energy levels, $E_{photon} = E_i - E_f$.
Use the equation:

$$E_{photon} = E_i - E_f$$

Energy of photon	Initial energy (beginning energy) of the electron	Final energy of the electron

The electron drops from $n = 3$ energy level (beginning, **initial energy level**) to $n = 2$ energy level (**final energy level**). Look on Reference Table: Energy Level Diagrams for Hydrogen on the previous page or on page reference tables 10-11 to find E_i (initial energy) and E_f (final energy).

First find E_i and E_f. Follow the line connecting $n = 3$ (initial, starting energy level) to -1.51 eV (**initial energy E_i**). Follow the line connecting $n = 2$ (final energy level) to -3.40 eV (**final energy E_f**).

Then, in the equation $E_{photon} = E_i - E_f$, *substitute for E_i* (initial energy) -1.51 eV and *substitute for E_f* (final energy) -3.40 eV (see above).

$$E_{photon} = E_i - E_f$$
$$E_{photon} \quad -1.51eV \; - \; -3.40eV \; = 1.89 \text{ eV}$$

When the electron dropped from $n = 3$ to $n = 2$, a photon of energy was given off. Energy of the photon (E_{photon}) = 1.89 eV.

In general, to find the energy at any level (initial energy level, final energy level, $n = 2$, level j, etc.), use Reference Table: Energy Level Diagrams. Follow the line connecting the level (on the left side) to energy (eV) (on the right side).

Solution 2:
Given: Energy of the emitted photon = 1.89 eV (answer to Question 1 above).

Find: Energy of the emitted photon in joules (J).

To convert **electronvolts** of energy **to joules, first** look below or on Reference Table: List of Physical Constants on page reference tables 2.

$$1 \text{ electronvolt (eV)} = 1.60 \times 10^{-19} \text{ J.}$$

(This equation is used to convert electronvolts into joules (or joules into electronvolts).)

Next, multiply energy in electronvolts (eV)

$$1.89 \text{ eV} \times \frac{1.60 \times 10^{-19} \, J}{1 \, eV} = 3.02 \times 10^{-19} \text{ J.}$$

Energy of emitted photon = 3.02×10^{-19} J (joules).

Note: Since 1.89 eV is on top, 1 eV must be on the bottom of the fraction; therefore, eV cancels out and you get joules (J).

Or,

From Reference Table: List of Physical Constants, you see

$$1 \text{ eV} = 1.60 \times 10^{-19} \text{ J}$$

therefore,

$$10 \text{ eV} = 10 \times 1.60 \times 10^{-19} \text{ J,} \qquad \text{and}$$

$$20 \text{ eV} = 20 \times 1.60 \times 10^{-19} \text{ J,} \qquad \text{and}$$

$$1.89 \text{ eV} = 1.89 \times 1.60 \times 10^{-19} \text{ J} = 3.02 \times 10^{-19} \text{ J}$$

Answer: *1.89 eV = 3.02 x 10⁻¹⁹ J (joules)*

Now Do Homework Questions #16-21, pages 46-47, and # 38-42, page 49.

Questions 1-3: Base your answers to Questions 1-3 on the information below.

An electron in a hydrogen atom drops from the $n = 4$ energy level to the $n = 2$ energy level.

Question 1: What is the energy, in electron volts, of the emitted photon?

Question 2: What is the energy, in joules, of the emitted photon?

Question 3: Calculate the frequency of the emitted radiation.

Solution 1:

Given: The electron of the hydrogen atom drops from the $n = 4$ energy level to the $n = 2$ energy level.

Find: energy of the emitted photon in electronvolts (eV).

Look for an equation on Reference Table: Modern Physics, on page reference tables 20 that has to do with energy of the photon (E_{photon}). There are two equations for E_{photon} on Reference Table: Modern Physics. The question says that the electron drops from the $n = 4$ energy level to the $n = 2$ energy level; therefore, choose the equation with two different energy levels, $E_{photon} = E_i - E_f$.

Use the equation:

E_{photon}	=	E_i	–	E_f
Energy of photon		**Initial energy (beginning energy)of the electron**		**Final energy of the electron**

The electron drops from $n = 4$ energy level (beginning, **initial energy level**) to $n = 2$ energy level (**final energy level**). Look on Reference Table: Energy Level Diagrams for Hydrogen on page 5:14 or on page reference tables 10-11 to find E_i (initial energy) and E_f (final energy).

First find E_i and E_f. Follow the line connecting $n = 4$ (initial, starting energy level) to $-$**0.85 eV** (**initial energy E_i**). Follow the line connecting $n = 2$ (final energy level) to $-$**3.40 eV** (**final energy E_f**).

Then, in the equation $E_{photon} = E_i - E_f$ *substitute for E_i* (initial energy) -0.85 eV and *substitute for E_f* (final energy) -3.40 eV (see above).

$$E_{photon} = E_i - E_f$$
$$E_{photon} = -0.85eV - -3.40eV = 2.55 \text{ eV}$$

When the electron dropped from $n = 4$ to $n = 2$, a photon of energy was given off. Energy of the photon (E_{photon}) = 2.55 eV.

In general, to find the energy at any level (initial energy level, final energy level, $n = 2$, level a, etc.), use Reference Table: Energy Level Diagrams. Follow the line connecting the level (on the left side) to energy (eV) (on the right side).

Solution 2:

Given: Energy of the emitted photon = 2.55 eV (answer to Question 1 above).

Find: Energy of the emitted photon in joules (J).

To convert **electronvolts** of energy **to joules, first** look below or at Reference Table: List of Physical Constants on page reference tables 2.

$$1 \text{ electronvolt (eV)} = 1.60 \times 10^{-19} \text{ J.}$$

(This equation is used to convert electronvolts into joules (or joules into electronvolts).)

Next, multiply energy in electronvolts (eV)

$$2.55 \text{ eV} \times \frac{1.60 \times 10^{-19} \text{ } J}{1 \text{ } eV} = 4.08 \times 10^{-19} \text{ J}.$$

Energy of emitted photon = 4.08×10^{-19} J (joules).

Note: Since 2.55 eV is on top, 1 eV must be on the bottom of the fraction; therefore, eV cancels out and you get joules (J).

Or,

From Reference Table: List of Physical Constants, you see

1 electronvolt (eV)   = 1.60×10^{-19} J

therefore,

$$10 \text{ eV} = \quad 10 \quad \times \quad 1.60 \times 10^{-19} \text{ J}, \qquad \text{and}$$

$$20 \text{ eV} = \quad 20 \quad \times \quad 1.60 \times 10^{-19} \text{ J}, \qquad \text{and}$$

$$2.55 \text{ eV} = 2.55 \quad \times \quad 1.60 \times 10^{-19} \text{ J} \quad = \quad 4.08 \times 10^{-19} \text{ J}$$

Answer: *2.55 eV = 4.08 x 10⁻¹⁹ J (joules)*

Solution 3:

Given: An electron in a hydrogen atom drops from the $n = 4$ energy level to the $n = 2$ energy level. Energy of the emitted photon = 2.55 eV or 4.08×10^{-19} J (answers to questions 1 and 2).

Find: Frequency (f) of the emitted radiation.

Answers to questions 1 and 2 give you energy of the photon. The fact that the electron drops from n = 4 to n = 2 is extra information, not necessary to solve question 3.

Look for an equation on Reference Table: Modern Physics that has energy of the photon (E_{photon}) and frequency (f).

$$E_{photon} \quad = \quad h \qquad f \quad = \quad \frac{hc}{\lambda}$$

energy of   =   Planck's   x frequency = $\dfrac{\text{x \textit{speed of light in a vacuum}}}{\textit{wavelength}}$
a photon   constant

Planck's constant

Use the equation $E_{photon} = hf$. You have two unknowns, h and f; therefore, first find h and then substitute h and E_{photon} in the equation $E_{photon} = hf$ to find f (frequency).

First find h. Look at the list of physical constants on the next page or on Reference Table: List of Physical Constants.

Table: Modern Physics

Reference Table: List of Physical Constants		
Name	**Symbol**	**Value**
Universal gravitational constant	G	$6.67 \times 10^{-11} \, N \cdot m^2/kg^2$
Speed of light in a vacuum	c	$3.00 \times 10^8 \, m/s$
Planck's constant	h	$6.63 \times 10^{-34} \, J \cdot s$

Then, in the equation $E_{photon} = hf$, *substitute for h* (Planck's constant), $6.63 \times 10^{-34} \, J \cdot s$. *Substitute for E_{photon}* (energy of the photon) $4.08 \times 10^{-19} \, J$ (given).

Remember, in the equation, $E_{photon} = hf = \frac{hc}{\lambda}$, E_{photon} (**energy of a photon) must be in joules (J) because** h (Planck's constant) is in **J**•s (**joule•**seconds).

E_{photon}	=	h	f
$4.08 \times 10^{-19} \, J$	=	$(6.63 \times 10^{-34} \, J \cdot s)f$	
$\dfrac{4.08 \times 10^{-19} \, J}{6.63 \times 10^{-34} \, J \cdot s}$	=	f	
$(6.11 \times 10^{14})\dfrac{1}{s}$	=	f	$Hz = \dfrac{1}{s}$
$6.11 \times 10^{14} \, Hz$	=	f	
f (frequency)	=	$6.11 \times 10^{14} \, Hz$	
		answer	

Or, rearrange the equation:

$$f = \frac{E_{photon}}{h}$$

$$f = \frac{4.08 \times 10^{-19} \, J}{6.63 \times 10^{-34} \, J \cdot s}$$

$$f = (6.11 \times 10^{14})\frac{1}{s} \qquad Hz = \frac{1}{s}$$

$$f = 6.11 \times 10^{14} \, Hz$$

f (frequency) $= 6.11 \times 10^{14} \, Hz$

answer

Rule: If you have energy levels and you need to find frequency, do these three steps:

1. first **find energy** of the photon **in electronvolts (eV)**,
2. **then find energy** of the photon **in joules** (J)(by converting eV to J)
3. **then** find **frequency** (f) from the equation $E = hf = \frac{hc}{\lambda}$; **use $E = hf$.**

Question: Excited hydrogen atoms are all in the $n = 3$ state. How many different photon energies could possibly be emitted as these atoms return to the ground state?

   (1) 1   (2) 2   (3) 3   (4) 4

Solution:

Given: Excited atoms are in $n = 3$

Find: How many different photon energies could be emitted (given off) as the atoms return to the ground state ($n = 1$)?

Look at energy levels $n = 3$ to ground state on Reference Table: Energy Level Diagrams for hydrogen on the next page or on page reference tables 10-11.

Different energies can be emitted when an electron goes:

From $n = 3$ to $n = 2$
From $n = 2$ to $n = 1$ (ground state)
From $n = 3$ to $n = 1$ (ground state).

Three different (photon) energies can be emitted.   Answer *3*

Question: After electrons in hydrogen atoms are excited to the $n = 3$ energy state, how many different frequencies of radiation can be emitted as the electrons return to the ground state?

   (1) 1   (2) 2   (3) 3   (4) 4

Solution:

Given: Excited electrons are in $n = 3$ energy state.

Find: How many different frequencies of radiation can be emitted.

You saw in the last example when excited electrons were in $n = 3$, there were three different (photon) energies emitted as the electrons returned to the ground state.

Look for an equation on Reference Table: Modern Physics that has energy (E) and frequency (*f*).

Use the equation

   $E_{photon} = hf$.

Look at the equation $E_{photon} = hf$. h is a constant (Planck's constant), given on Reference Table: List of Physical Constants. When E_{photon} (energy) changes, f (frequency) changes.

Excited electrons can go from:

$n = 3$ to $n = 2$
$n = 2$ to $n = 1$
$n = 3$ to $n = 1$

Each energy level change ($n = 3$ to $n = 2$, $n = 2$ to $n = 1$, $n = 3$ to $n = 1$) produces a different amount of energy ,therefore a different frequency (see equation above).Since there are three different energy level changes, producing three different amounts of energy, therefore three different frequencies are emitted.   Answer *3*

Question: An excited hydrogen atom returns to its ground state. A possible energy change for the atom is a

   (1) loss of 10.20 eV   (2) gain of 10.20 eV
   (3) loss of 3.40 eV   (4) gain of 3.40 eV

Solution: An excited hydrogen atom returns to its ground state means an electron goes from a higher energy level (**excited atom**) **to** the ground state (a lower energy level) and **gives off** a **photon of energy** (which is always **equal to** the **difference between** the **two energy levels**).

Look below or at Reference Table: Energy Level Diagrams for hydrogen on page reference tables 10-11.

Part of Table:
Energy Level Diagrams

Hydrogen

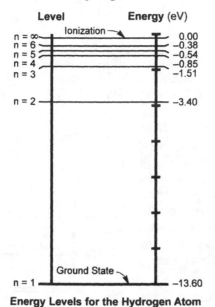

Energy Levels for the Hydrogen Atom

Use your calculator. When the electron of the excited atom goes from $n = 2$, -3.40 eV, to $n = 1$ (ground state), -13.60 eV, the **difference** between the two energy levels is 10.20 eV:

$(-3.40$ eV$) - (-13.60$ eV$) = 10.20$ eV.

Since the electron went from a higher energy level ($n = 2$), to a lower energy level ($n=1$, ground state), the atom gives off (loses) **10.20 eV.**

Answer *1*: Loss of 10.20 eV

Note: There is no difference of 3.40 eV between any excited level ($n = 2, 3, 4, 5, 6$) and the ground state. (Choice 3 and Choice 4 are wrong.)

Now Do Homework Question #22, page 47, and #43-49, pages 48-49.

Question: An electron in a mercury atom drops from energy level i to the ground state by emitting a single photon. This photon has an energy of

(1) 1.56 eV   (2) 8.82 eV   (3) 10.38 eV   (4) 11.94 eV

Solution:
Given: An electron in a mercury atom drops from energy level i to the ground state by emitting a single photon.

Find: energy of the photon.

Look for an equation on Reference Table: Modern Physics, on page reference tables 20 that has to do with energy of the photon (E_{photon}). The question says that the electron drops from energy level *i* to the ground state; therefore, choose the equation with two different energy levels, $E_{photon} = E_i - E_f$.

Use the equation:

$$E_{photon} \quad = \quad E_i \quad - \quad E_f$$

| Energy of photon | Initial energy(beginning energy) of the electron | Final energy of the electron |

The electron drops from energy level *i* to the ground state by emitting a single photon. **Energy level *i*** is the **beginning energy level** (initial energy level) of the electron. The **ground state** (energy level *a*, see diagram at right) is the **final energy level**.

Look at the energy level diagram for mercury at right or on Reference Table: Energy Level Diagrams on page reference tables 10-11 to find E_i (initial energy) and E_f (final energy).

First find E_i and E_f. Follow the line connecting **level *i*** (initial, starting energy level) to -1.56 eV (**initial energy E_i**). Follow the line connecting **level *a*, ground state** (final energy level) to -10.38 eV (**final energy E_f**).

Part of Table: Energy Level Diagrams Mercury

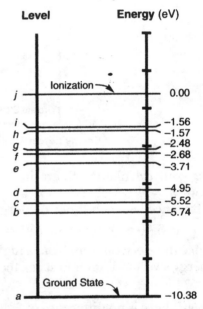

A Few Energy Levels for the Mercury Atom

Then, in the equation $E_{photon} = E_i - E_f$, *substitute for E_i* (initial energy of electron) -1.56 eV and *substitute for E_f* (final energy of electron) -10.38 eV. *Use a calculator* to solve the equation below.

$$E_{photon} \quad = \quad E_i \quad - \quad E_f$$

$$E_{photon} \quad = \quad -1.56 \text{ eV} \quad - \quad (-10.38 \text{ eV}) \quad = 8.82 \text{ eV}$$

$$E_{photon} = 8.82 \text{ eV (electronvolts)} \qquad \text{Answer 2}$$

In general, to find the energy at any level (initial energy level, final energy level, $n = 3$, level j, etc.), use Reference Table: Energy Level Diagrams. Follow the line connecting the level (on the left side) to the energy (eV) (on the right side).

Bright line spectrum: When an **electron goes from a higher energy level to a lower** energy level, it **gives off a photon** of energy. Electrons can fall back from a higher level (example: n =5) to different lower levels ($n = 1, 2, 3, 4$). Each change ($5 \longrightarrow 1$, $5 \longrightarrow 2$, $5 \longrightarrow 3$, $5 \longrightarrow 4$) gives off (produces) a different amount of energy. Since $E_{photon} = hf$, and h is a constant, each different amount of energy given off produces a different frequency. The energy given off (example: light energy) can be made to enter and **go through** a **spectroscope** (an instrument that separates the different frequencies, example: frequencies of light). Each frequency of light produces a bright line when it comes out of the spectroscope. The light that comes out of the spectroscope is a **bright line spectrum,** which is a number of **bright lines against a dark background.**

In short, when an **electron goes from** a **higher energy level to** a **lower energy level**, it gives off a photon of energy, which **produces** a **bright line spectrum** (bright lines against a dark background).

Question: The diagram represents the bright-line spectra of four elements, A, B, C, and D, and the spectrum of an unknown gaseous sample.

Based on comparisons of these spectra, which two elements are found in the unknown sample?

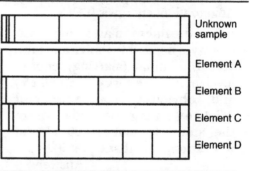

Solution: If you want to know which elements are in the unknown, compare the spectral lines from the other elements to the unknown sample. All the lines in element B and in element C are also in the unknown sample, therefore the unknown sample has elements B and C. Wrong choices: Some lines in A and D are not in the sample.

Now do Homework Questions #50-52, page 49.

Let's now learn what happens when an **electron goes from** a **lower energy level to** a **higher energy level.** An electron must take in (absorb) energy (energy of a photon) when the electron goes from a lower energy level (example: $n = 1$) to a higher energy level (example: $n = 5$).

Question: What is the minimum energy needed to ionize a hydrogen atom in the $n = 2$ energy state?

    (1) 13.6 eV   (2) 10.2 eV   (3) 3.40 eV   (4) 1.89 eV

Solution:

Given: Atom is in $n = 2$ energy state.

Find: Minimum energy needed to ionize a hydrogen atom. Ionization means removing an electron from an atom.

The question asks for the minimum energy needed to ionize a hydrogen atom in the $n = 2$ energy state (level). Therefore, look for an energy level diagram for hydrogen on Reference Table: Energy Level Diagrams.

Look right or on Reference Table: Energy Level Diagrams for hydrogen on page reference tables 10-11; find the initial (starting) energy at $n = 2$, and the final energy at ionization.

Follow the line connecting $n = 2$ (initial energy) to number of eV, which is -3.40 eV. Follow the line connecting $n = \infty$ (ionization) to number of eV, which is 0.00 eV.

When $n = 2$, energy is -3.40 eV. At ionization, energy is 0 eV.

When the question asks how much **energy** is **needed to ionize** an **atom**, **take** the initial (**starting**) energy level (at $n = 2$, **energy = -3.40 eV**) and, obviously, you **must add +3.40 eV** (energy needed to ionize the atom) **to make 0.00 eV** (at ionization, eV **must equal 0**).

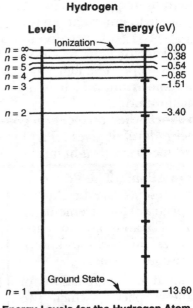

Part of Table: Energy Level Diagrams

Hydrogen

Energy Levels for the Hydrogen Atom

Answer *3*

When a question asks how much energy is needed to ionize an atom:

* If the **initial (starting) energy** = **-1.51 eV**, obviously you must **add +1.51 eV** (energy needed to ionize an atom) **to make 0.00 eV (at ionization, eV must = 0)**. To ionize an atom, it must absorb enough energy to reach 0.0 eV(it can also absorb more energy).

* If the initial (starting) energy = -13.60 eV, obviously you must add $+13.60$ eV (energy needed to ionize an atom) to make 0.00 eV (at ionization, eV must = 0).

Question: Explain why a hydrogen atom in the ground state can absorb a 10.2 electronvolt photon, but can *not* absorb an 11.0 electronvolt photon.

Solution: When an electron goes from a lower energy level to a higher energy level, it **absorbs** a **photon of energy** (which is **always**

equal to the **difference between** the **two energy levels**).

Look right or at Reference Table: Energy Level Diagrams for hydrogen on the previous page.

The **difference** between the two energy levels, $n = 1$, -13.60 eV and $n = 2$, -3.40 eV, is 10.2 eV, therefore, the atom **can absorb 10.2 eV** (electronvolts).

When you take the **difference** between (subtract) any **two energy levels** of hydrogen, you do **NOT** get 11.0 eV; therefore, an atom of hydrogen **cannot absorb 11.0 eV** (electronvolts).

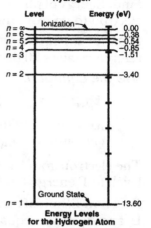

Hydrogen

Level		Energy (eV)
$n = \infty$	Ionization	0.00
$n = 6$		-0.38
$n = 5$		-0.54
$n = 4$		-0.85
$n = 3$		-1.51
$n = 2$		-3.40
$n = 1$	Ground State	-13.60

Energy Levels for the Hydrogen Atom

Question: Base your answers on the diagram below, which shows some energy levels for an atom of an unknown substance.

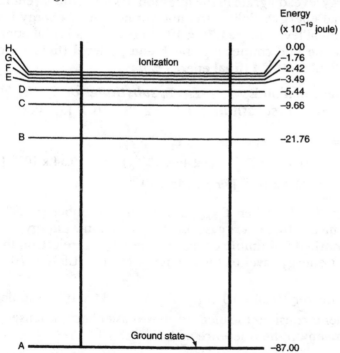

Energy
($\times 10^{-19}$ joule)

H	0.00
G	-1.76
F	-2.42
E	-3.49
D	-5.44
C	-9.66
B	-21.76
A (Ground state)	-87.00

Ionization

What is the **energy of** the **photon** absorbed (**minimum energy needed**) for an electron to change from the B energy level to the F energy level.

Solution:

Given: Diagram shows energy levels for an atom of an unknown substance. Electron goes from B energy level to F energy level.

Find: Energy of photon absorbed (minimum energy needed) for an electron to go from the B energy level to the F energy level.

Look for an equation on Reference Table: Modern Physics on page reference tables 20 that has energy and two different energy levels.

Use the equation:

$$E_{photon} \qquad = \qquad E_i \qquad - \qquad E_f$$

Energy of photon	Initial energy (beginning energy) of the electron	Final energy of the electron

The electron goes from B energy level (beginning or initial energy level) to F energy level (final energy level).

First find E_i (initial energy)and E_f(final energy) and then substitute E_i and E_f in the equation $E_{photon} = E_i - E_f$ to find energy of the photon (E_{photon}).

First find E_i (starting, **initial energy**) *and E_f* **(final energy)**. Look at the energy level diagram in the question to find E_i (initial energy) and E_f (final energy). Follow the line connecting B **energy level** (starting, initial level) to $-\textbf{21.76 x 10}^{-19}$ **J** (starting, **initial energy** E_i). Follow the line connecting the F **energy level** (final energy level) to $-\textbf{2.42 x 10}^{-19}$ **J (final energy E_f)**.

Then, in the equation $E_{photon} = E_i - E_f$ *substitute for E_i* -21.76 x 10^{-19} J (joules) and *substitute for E_f* -2.42 x 10^{-19} J (joules).

$$E_{photon} = \qquad E_i \qquad - \qquad E_f$$
$$E_{photon} = -21.76 \text{ x } 10^{-19} \text{ J} - (-2.42 \text{ x } 10^{-19}\text{J}) = -19.34 \text{ x } 10^{-19} \text{ J}$$
$$E_{photon} = -19.34 \text{ x } 10^{-19} \text{ J or } -1.934 \text{ x } 10^{-18} \text{ J}$$

In $E_{photon} = E_i - E_f$, when E_{photon} is a negative number (-1.934 x 10^{-18} J), it means that energy is absorbed (taken in). Energy of the photon absorbed (minimum energy needed) for the electron to go from the B energy level to the F energy level = 1.934 x 10^{-18} J (joules).

Answer 19.34 x 10^{-19} J(joules) or 1.934 x 10^{-18} J(joules).

Many students consider the method above easier because it uses the equation given on the reference table.

Alternate Method: (Equation used is not given on the reference table.) When an electron goes from a lower energy level to a higher energy level, you can use the equation final energy (E_f) minus initial energy (E_i) to get the amount of energy taken in (absorbed). This equation is not given on the reference table.

Follow the line connecting **B energy level** (starting, initial level) to **-21.76 x 10^{-19} J** (starting, **initial energy E$_i$**). Follow the line connecting the **F energy level**(final energy level) to **-2.42 x 10^{-19} J** (**final energy E$_f$**).

$$E_{photon} = E_f - E_i$$

$$E_{photon} = -2.42 \times 10^{-19}\,J - (-21.76 \times 10^{-19}\,J) = 19.34 \times 10^{-19}\,J$$

$$E_{photon} = 19.34 \times 10^{-19}\,J \text{ or } 1.934 \times 10^{-18}\,J$$

Energy of the photon absorbed (minimum energy needed) for the electron to go from the B energy level to the F energy level = 1.934 x 10^{-18} J (joules).

Answer 19.34 x 10^{-19} J(joules) or 1.934 x 10^{-18} J(joules).

Now Do Homework Questions #23-27, pages 46-47

Question: White light is passed through a cloud of cool hydrogen gas and then examined with a spectroscope. The dark lines observed on a bright background are caused by
  (1) the hydrogen emitting all frequencies in white light
  (2) the hydrogen absorbing certain frequencies of the white light
  (3) diffraction of the white light
  (4) constructive interference

Solution: Background: White light is made up of all colors (frequencies) of visible light (see the part of Reference Table: the Electromagnetic Spectrum which has visible light). When white light goes through a spectroscope, light separates into its colors (red, orange, yellow, etc. – called a bright background). In this experiment, white light goes through the hydrogen gas and then through a spectroscope.

When white light (energy) is shined on a hydrogen atom, the **hydrogen** atom **absorbs** photons of **energy** equal to the difference between two energy levels of hydrogen. By looking at the equation $E = hf$ (h is a constant), when a certain amount of energy from the white light is absorbed, a certain frequency (color) is also absorbed. The **hydrogen absorbed** certain **frequencies (colors),** which appear as **dark lines**. The **light** then goes through a spectroscope, which separates the light into different colors, **forming a bright background.** The **dark lines (on a bright background)** are called an **absorption spectrum** (the dark lines were **produced** when the **hydrogen absorbed certain frequencies** from the white light).

Answer 2

Question: Exposure to ultraviolet radiation can damage skin. Exposure to visible light does not damage skin. State *one* possible reason for this difference.

Solution: First, look on Reference Table: The Electromagnetic Spectrum below or on page reference tables 6-7, which has visible light, ultraviolet, and other electromagnetic waves. You can see visible light has a frequency of 3.84×10^{14} Hz to 7.69×10^{14} Hz; ultraviolet has a higher frequency, starting after visible light and going to almost 10^{18} Hz. **Ultraviolet** has a **higher frequency than visible light.**

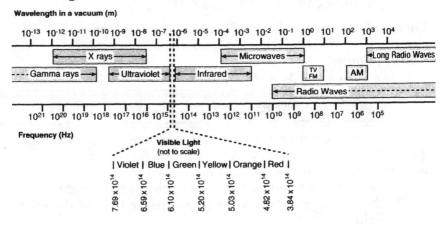

The **more energy** radiation (waves) has, the **more** it **damages** the **skin**.

Look for an equation on Reference Table: Modern Physics that has to do with f (frequency) and E (energy).

Use the equation

$$E_{photon} = hf$$

E = energy
f = frequency
h = Planck's constant

Look at the equation above. h is a constant (Planck's constant); therefore, the higher the frequency (f), the more energy (E) the electromagnetic wave has. Since ultraviolet has a higher frequency (f) than visible light, ultraviolet has more energy (E) than visible light and the extra energy damages the skin.

Now do Homework Question #53, page 49

Section 3:

THE ATOM

An atom is the **smallest part** of **an element** (example: oxygen) that has the characteristics of the element. The **nucleus** is in the center of the atom (see figure on next page). The nucleus is made up of **protons** (particles with a **positive charge**) and **neutrons** (particles with **no charge**). A proton or a neutron is called a nucleon. **Electrons** (particles with a **negative charge**) go around the nucleus.

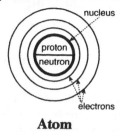

Atom

The protons (particles with a positive charge) repel each other (coulomb force of repulsion), which would cause the protons to move apart (even breaking up the nucleus).

Note: There is a very weak gravitational force of attraction between protons, which is not strong enough to hold the nucleus together.

But, there is a **strong nuclear force (attractive force)** which **holds the nucleons** (protons and neutrons) together (the strong force also holds protons and protons together) and prevents the nucleus from breaking apart. The **strong nuclear force** is effective (good) at **short range** (short distances) such as a length of 2 or 3 nucleons.

Question: The strong force is the force of

    (1) repulsion between protons
    (2) attraction between protons and electrons
    (3) repulsion between nucleons
    (4) attraction between nucleons

Solution: The strong force (also called strong nuclear force) is the attractive force which holds the nucleons (protons and neutrons) together.   Answer *4*

Question: What prevents the nucleus of a helium atom from flying apart?

Solution: The strong nuclear force (also called the strong force) prevents the nucleus of a helium atom from flying apart. The strong force holds the nucleus together.

Question: What type of nuclear force holds the protons and neutrons in an atom together?

    (1) a strong force that acts over a short range
    (2) a strong force that acts over a long range
    (3) a weak force that acts over a short range
    (4) a weak force that acts over a long range

Solution: A strong force (also called the strong nuclear force) holds protons and neutrons together in the atom over a short range (short distance).   Answer *1*

ANTIMATTER AND ANTIPARTICLES

Antimatter is matter (material) that is made of antiparticles. Examples of antiparticles are antiprotons, antineutrons, and positrons.

An **antiproton** has the same mass as a proton but the opposite charge; a proton is positive, an antiproton is negative.

A **positron** has the same mass as an electron but the opposite charge; an electron is negative, a positron is positive.

An **antineutron** has the same mass as a neutron; the neutron and antineutron have no charge. The neutron has its magnetic moment and spin in opposite directions; the antineutron has them in the same direction.

EINSTEIN'S THEORY: $E = mc^2$

Einstein's theory: $E = mc^2$. Energy (E) = mass (m) x the speed of light in a vacuum (c) squared. Mass changes into energy (explained below).

Look below or on Reference Table: Modern Physics on page reference tables 20.

$$E = m \qquad c^2$$

c = speed of light
in a vacuum

E = energy
m = mass

Energy = mass x speed of light in a vacuum squared

$E = mc^2$ is the equation you use when **mass changes into** (turns into or becomes) **energy**. The mass is no longer there, because it changed into energy. Mass was converted (changed) into energy.

To find the amount of energy produced, use the equation $E = mc^2$. Multiply mass (m) (mass that is changed into energy, mass that is no longer there) times the speed of light (c) squared and you get the amount of energy produced. *Note*: Mass does not move at the speed of light. Energy is in joules (J), mass is in kilograms (kg), and c is in meters/second (m/s).

Question: In the cartoon, Einstein is contemplating the equation for the principle that

(1) the fundamental source of all energy is the conversion of mass into energy
(2) energy is emitted or absorbed in discrete packets called photons
(3) mass always travels at the speed of light in a vacuum
(4) the energy of a photon is proportional to its frequency

Solution: Einstein is contemplating the equation $E = mc^2$, that mass can be converted (changed)into energy, and the source of all energy is the conversion of mass (changing mass) into energy. Answer *1*

Question: What is the energy equivalent of a mass of 0.026 kilogram?
(1) 2.34×10^{15} J   (2) 2.3×10^{15} J   (3) 2.34×10^{17} J   (4) 2.3×10^{17} J

Solution:
Given: Mass = 0.026 Kg
Find: Energy (E)
0.026 kg mass changes into or becomes energy; therefore, the mass is no longer there.

Look for an equation on Reference Table: Modern Physics that has mass (m) and energy (E) or mass (m) changing into energy (E).

Use the equation

$$E \quad = \quad m \qquad\qquad c^2$$

   c = speed of light
        in a vacuum
   E = energy
   m = mass

Energy = mass x speed of light in a vacuum squared

First find c (speed of light in a vacuum), then substitute c in the equation $E = mc^2$ to find E (energy).

First find c: Look at Reference Table: List of Physical Constants on page reference tables 2-3:

   Speed of light in a vacuum c 3.00×10^8 m/s

Then, in the equation $E = mc^2$, **substitute for m** (mass) 0.026 kg (given) . **Substitute for c** (speed of light in a vacuum) 3.00×10^8 m/s.

$$E \quad = \quad m \qquad\qquad c^2$$
$$E \quad = \quad (0.026 \text{ kg}) \ (3.00 \times 10^8 \text{ m/s})^2 \ = \ 2.3 \times 10^{15} \text{ J (joules)}$$

                                                      Answer *2*

On the calculator, to square any number, in this example c^2, you can use the X^2 key. To find energy (E), press .026 x 3.00 EE 8 X^2, then press equal, and you get 2.34×10^{15}. But, the answer (in a multiplication or division problem) must have the same number of significant figures as the one measurement with the smallest number of significant figures. Since .026 (mass m) only has two significant figures, the answer is 2.3×10^{15} J (two significant figures). See rules for significant figures on page 2:15.   Answer 2

Note: The prefix tera (**T**) means 10^{12}, given on Reference Table: Prefixes for Powers of 10. on page reference tables 4. If, in a different example, energy equals 3.4×10^{12} J, you can write energy = 3.4 TJ.

Question: The energy equivalent of the rest mass of an electron is approximately
(1) 5.1×10^{5} J (2) 8.2×10^{-14} J (3) 2.7×10^{-22} J (4) 8.5×10^{-28} J

Solution:
Given: An electron.
Find: Energy equivalent of the rest mass of an electron.

Look for an equation on Reference Table: Modern Physics on page reference tables 20 that has mass (m) and energy (E) or mass (m) changing into energy (E).

Use the equation

$E = mc^2$ c = speed of light in a vacuum
          E = energy
          m = mass

First find m (mass) and find c (speed of light in a vacuum), then substitute m and c in the equation $E = mc^2$ to find E (energy).

First find m (mass of an electron).
Look below or on Reference Table: List of Physical Constants on page reference tables 2-3 for mass of an electron.

Rest mass of the electron	m_e	9.11×10^{-31} kg
Rest mass of the proton	m_p	1.67×10^{-27} kg
Rest mass of the neutron	m_n	1.67×10^{-27} kg

m (**mass of electron**) = **9.11 x 10⁻³¹ kg**

Find *c*: Look below or on Reference Table: List of Physical Constants

Speed of light in a vacuum   c 3.00×10^8 m/s

Then, in the equation $E = mc^2$, *substitute* for m (mass of an electron) 9.11×10^{-31} kg. *Substitute* for c (speed of light in a vacuum) 3.00×10^8 m/s.

$E \quad = \quad m \quad\quad\quad c^2$

$E \quad = (9.11 \times 10^{-31}$ kg$) (3.00 \times 10^8$ m/s$)^2 = 8.2 \times 10^{-14}$ J (joules)
          Answer 2

Note: Mass (m) is in kg, speed of light (c) is in m/s, and energy (E) is in joules. (Energy can also be changed from joules to electronvolts.)

Now do Homework Questions #28-32, page 47, and #54-55, page 49.

Questions 1 and 2: When an electron and its antiparticle (positron) combine, they annihilate each other and become energy in the form of gamma rays.

Question 1: The positron has the same mass as the electron. Calculate how many joules of energy are released when they annihilate. [Show all work, including the equation and substitution with units.]

Question 2: What conservation law prevents this from happening with two electrons?

Solution 1:
Given: Positron has the same mass as the electron.

Find: How many joules of energy are released when a positron and electron annihilate. (This means the positron and electron are annihilated (destroyed) and change into energy. Find how much energy is produced.)

Look for an equation on Reference Table: Modern Physics on page Reference Tables 20 that has mass and energy or mass (m) changing into energy (E).

Use the equation

$$E = mc^2$$

c = speed of light in a vacuum
E = energy
m = mass

First find m (mass) and find c, then substitute m and c in the equation $E = mc^2$ to find E (energy).

First find m **(mass of a positron and electron).**

Mass of an electron: Look at Reference Table: List of Physical Constants on page Reference Tables 2-3.

Rest mass of the electron m_e 9.11×10^{-31} kg

Mass of positron is the same as mass of electron (given). Mass of an electron = 9.11×10^{-31} kg; therefore, mass of positron = 9.11×10^{-31} kg.

m (mass of electron plus positron) $= 2 \times (9.11 \times 10^{-31}$ kg)

Find c: Look below or at Reference Table: List of Physical Constants:

Speed of light in a vacuum   c 3.00×10^8 m/s

Then, in the equation $E = mc^2$, *substitute for m* (mass of electron

---

plus mass of positron), $2 \times (9.11 \times 10^{-31}$ kg). *Substitute for c,* 3.00 $\times 10^8$ m/s.

$$E \quad = \quad m \quad c^2$$

$$E \quad = 2(9.11 \times 10^{-31} \text{ kg})(3.00 \times 10^8 \text{ m/s})^2 = 1.64 \times 10^{-13} \text{ J (joules)}$$

Note: Mass (m) is in kg, speed of light (c) is in m/s, and energy (E) is in joules. (Energy can also be changed from joules to electronvolts.)

Solution 2: The law of conservation of charge: Charges must be the same on both sides of the equation.

In Question 1, it was possible for an electron and a positron to become energy (gamma rays). Charges on both sides of the equation (arrow) were equal:

electron	+	positron	$\longrightarrow$	energy (gamma ray)
-1 charge	+	$+1$ charge		0 charge
	0 charge		$\longrightarrow$	0 charge

In this question (Question 2), it is not possible for two electrons to become gamma rays, as explained below.

An electron is negative and has a -1 charge. Energy (gamma rays) has zero charge.

electron	+	electron	$\neq$	energy (gamma rays)
-1 charge	+	-1 charge	$\neq$	zero charge
	-2 charge		$\neq$	zero charge

The charges are **not the same** on the left and right sides of $\neq$ (the unequal sign).

The Law of Conservation of Charge prevents 1 electron + 1 electron from changing into energy (gamma rays) because the charges are NOT the same on both sides of the unequal sign (inequality). You learned the law of conservation of charge says that the charge must be the same on both sides of the equation.

Questions 1 and 2: During the process of beta (β^-) emission, a neutron in the nucleus of an atom is converted into a proton, an electron, an electron antineutrino, and energy.

neutron $\longrightarrow$ proton + electron + electron antineutrino + energy

Question 1: Based on conservation laws, how does the mass of the neutron compare to the mass of the proton.

Question 2: Since charge must be conserved in the reaction shown, what charge must an electron antineutrino carry?

Solution 1: The neutron breaks down into a proton, an electron, an electron antineutrino, and energy.

neutron ———▶ proton + electron + electron antineutrino + energy

The neutron must have the biggest mass because the neutron is broken up into three pieces (proton, electron and electron antineutrino), and a little mass changed into energy. Obviously, then, the neutron must have a bigger mass than the proton.

Solution 2:

Particles:

neutron —▶ proton + electron + electron antineutrino + energy

Charges:

no charge —▶ __+1____−1__   ? charge
0 charge —▶   0 charge   +   0 charge

Answer: Electron antineutrino must have zero charge. The charges on both sides of the equation (arrow) must be equal.

===

Question: If a deuterium nucleus has a mass of 1.53×10^{-3} universal mass units less than its components, this mass represents an energy of

(1) 1.38 MeV (2) 1.42 MeV (3) 1.53 MeV (4) 3.16 MeV

Solution:

Given: Mass of deuterium nucleus = 1.53×10^{-3} universal mass units (u) less than its components, which means this mass was converted into energy.

Note: A deuterium nucleus is made of one proton and one neutron. The mass of the deuterium nucleus is less than the mass of one proton and one neutron, because some mass was converted into energy.

Find: Energy.

The question asks to find energy. You need to convert (change) universal mass units into MeV (megaelectronvolts, which is energy).

Look for an equation below or on Reference Table: List of Physical Constants that changes (converts) universal mass units (u) into MeV.

Use the equation

1 universal mass unit (u) 9.31×10^2 MeV

This equation can be used to **change universal mass units** *(u)* **into MeV** (energy) **or MeV** (energy) **into universal mass units** *(u)*.

Mass of deuterium nucleus = $1.53 \times 10^{-3}\, u$ (universal mass units) less than its components. Mass was changed into energy.

Multiply 1.53×10^{-3} **u** x $\dfrac{9.31 \times 10^2\ MeV}{u}$ $= 14.2 \times 10^{-1}$ MeV $= 1.42$ MeV

Answer 2

Note: Since 1.53 x 10^{-3} u is on top, *u* must be on the bottom of the fraction, therefore *u* cancels out, and you get MeV.

Note: The prefix mega (**M**) means **10^6**, given on Reference Table: Prefixes for Powers of 10. on page reference tables 4. 1.42 **MeV** means 1.42 x **10^6** eV (electronvolts).

FORCES IN THE UNIVERSE

There are four (fundamental) forces in the universe: Strong (nuclear) force, electromagnetic (electric and magnetic) force, weak force, and gravitational force. These four forces are listed and described below, from strongest to weakest:

1. **Strong nuclear force** (strong force) holds the protons and neutrons together in the nucleus of an atom.

2. **Electromagnetic force** is a combination of electrostatic (electric) and magnetic forces. Electrostatic force is an attractive force or repulsive force between charged objects. (You learned about electrostatic force in the electricity chapter, beginning on page 3:4.)

   Opposite charges attract each other. Positively charged objects (example protons) attract negatively charged objects (example electrons).

   Like charges repel each other. Positively charged objects (example protons) repel (move away from) positively charged objects (example protons). Negatively charged objects (example electrons) repel (move away from) negatively charged objects (example electrons).

   The equation for electrostatic force is

$$F_e = \frac{kq_1q_2}{r^2}$$

3. **Weak force** has to do with the decay of some particles in the nucleus.

4. **Gravitational force** is an attractive force between objects. (You learned about the gravitational force in the mechanics chapter, beginning on page 1:93.) The equation for gravitational force is

$$F_g = \frac{Gm_1m_2}{r^2}.$$

Relative Strength of Four Forces

Strongest	Strong (nuclear)
↓	Electromagnetic, Electrostatic
	Weak
Weakest	Gravitational

Question: Two protons are located one meter apart. Compared to the gravitational force of attraction between the two protons, the electrostatic force between the protons is
    (1) stronger and repulsive   (2) weaker and repulsive
    (3) stronger and attractive   (4) weaker and attractive

Solution: The **electrostatic force** is **stronger than** the **gravitational force** (see table above). Electrostatic force is an attractive force or repulsive force between charged objects. Since two **protons** are **positive**, they **repel** each other (the **electrostatic force** is **repulsive**). The electrostatic force is stronger and repulsive.   Answer *1*

Now Do Homework Question #33, page 48, and #56-60, pages 49-50

STANDARD MODEL OF PARTICLE PHYSICS

Standard Model of Particle Physics explains the interaction and behavior of the strong (nuclear) force, electromagnetic force (electric and magnetic forces), and the weak force.

As you can see from Reference Table: Classification of Matter at right or on page reference tables 12, **matter** is **divided into** two parts, **hadrons and leptons**, (depending on which forces act on the matter).

Hadrons have all 4 forces (see previous page) acting on them. Leptons have only 3 forces acting on them (the strong force does not act on leptons).

Part of Table:
Classification of Matter

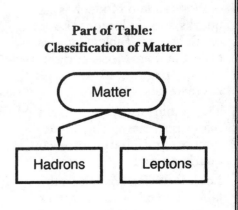

Table: Classification of Matter

To explain further:
Protons, neutrons, and many others **are hadrons**. **Electrons** (particles with a negative charge), **positrons** (particles with a positive charge) and **neutrinos** (particles with no charge) **are leptons**. Leptons have very little mass.

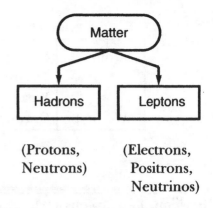

(Protons, Neutrons)

(Electrons, Positrons, Neutrinos)

Table: Classification of Matter

Look on Reference Table: Classification of Matter at right. The hadrons are divided into two groups, baryons and mesons. Protons and neutrons are baryons.

By looking at the reference table at right, you see a baryon (example a proton or neutron) is made up of three quarks; a meson is made up of one quark and one antiquark.

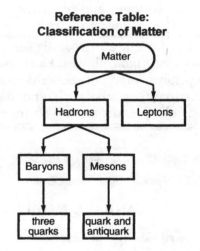

Reference Table: Classification of Matter

Table: Particles of the Standard Model

The Reference Table: Particles of the Standard Model has six quarks and six leptons. Look on Reference Table: Particles of the Standard Model at right, or on page 5:43 or page reference tables 13.

The table lists six quarks (basic particles). The name, symbol, and charge of each quark is given.

Look at the **first quark** on the table. The **name** of the quark is **up**, the **symbol** of the quark (particle) is **u**, and the

Part of table:
Particles of the Standard Model

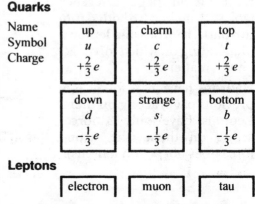

Quarks

Name	up	charm	top
Symbol	u	c	t
Charge	$+\frac{2}{3}e$	$+\frac{2}{3}e$	$+\frac{2}{3}e$
	down	strange	bottom
	d	s	b
	$-\frac{1}{3}e$	$-\frac{1}{3}e$	$-\frac{1}{3}e$

Leptons

| electron | muon | tau |

charge of the quark is $+\frac{2}{3}e$. e stands for one elementary charge (given on Reference Table: List of Physical Constants).

Look on the table at the quark below the up quark. The name of the quark is down, the symbol of the quark (particle) is d, and the charge of the quark is $-\frac{1}{3}e$. e stands for one elementary charge.

Similarly, for all quarks, the name of the quark is near the top of the box, the symbol below it, and the charge near the bottom of the box.

As you learned, **protons** and **neutrons** are **baryons** and are made of **three quarks** (see **Reference Table: Classification of Matter**).

The **proton** is **made** up **of three quarks having** the symbols **uud**. By looking at the charges of **uud**, on Reference Table: Particles of the Standard Model, you can find the charge of a proton. Look at the table at the right or the table on the bottom of the previous page. The charge of u quark = $+\frac{2}{3}e$. The charge of d quark is $-\frac{1}{3}e$. e stands for one elementary charge.

Add together the charges in a proton:

u   u   d

$+\frac{2}{3}e + (+\frac{2}{3}e) + (-\frac{1}{3}e) = 1e$

Charge of a proton = 1e (or you can say +1e) or +1.

As you can see, the proton is made of three quarks (particles), u (up), u (up), and d (down), having a total charge of 1e (or you can say +1e).

A **neutron** is also **made of three quarks**, **having** the symbols **udd**. By looking at the charges of **udd**, on Reference Table: Particles of the Standard Model, you can find the charge on a neutron. Look at the table at right or on the bottom of the previous page. The charge of the u quark $=+\frac{2}{3}e$. The charge of the d quark $= -\frac{1}{3}e$. e stands for one elementary charge.

Add together the charges in a neutron:

u   d   d

$+\frac{2}{3}e + (-\frac{1}{3}e) + (-\frac{1}{3}e) = 0e$

As you can see, the neutron is made of three quarks (particles) u (up), d (down), and d (down), having a total charge of 0e (zero charge, no charge).

Part of Table:
Particles of the
Standard Model
Quarks

Name	up
Symbol	u
Charge	$+\frac{2}{3}e$

	down
	d
	$-\frac{1}{3}e$

This part of the table shows quarks in a proton or neutron

Part of Table:
Particles of the
Standard Model
Quarks

Name	up
Symbol	u
Charge	$+\frac{2}{3}e$

	down
	d
	$-\frac{1}{3}e$

This part of the table shows quarks in a proton or neutron.

Table: Particles of the Standard Model

Note: The charges of baryons (ex.: protons, neutrons, etc.) must be a whole number, 0e, +1e, or ⁻1e.

ANTIQUARKS

Table: Classification of Matter

If the **charge** on a **quark** (example: u) is +⅔e, the **charge** of the **antiquark** (example: $\bar{u}$) is ⁻⅔e. The **antiquark** (example: $\bar{u}$) is the same type of particle with the same mass as the quark (example: u) but **opposite charge.** Example: Charge of d quark is ⁻⅓e, therefore charge of antiquark $\bar{d}$ is +⅓e (opposite charge).

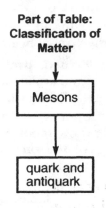

Part of Table: Classification of Matter

Mesons

quark and antiquark

The **anti**quark has a **bar or line** on top of the letter (examples, $\bar{u}\,\bar{d}\,\bar{c}\,\bar{s}$).

As you saw before on Reference Table: Classification of Matter on page 5:38 or to the right, a meson is made up of one quark and one antiquark (examples: quark u and antiquark $\bar{d}$ or quark u and antiquark $\bar{u}$).

Question: Protons and neutrons are examples of

    (1) positrons   (2) baryons   (3) mesons   (4) quarks

Solution: Protons and neutrons are examples of baryons.

                                                 Answer 2

Question: A baryon may have a charge of

    (1) $-\frac{1}{3}$e   (2) 0 e   (3) $+\frac{2}{3}$e   (4) $+\frac{4}{3}$e

Solution: The charge of a baryon must be a whole number, 0e, +1e, or ⁻1e.   Answer 2

Question: Which combination of quarks would produce a neutral baryon?

    (1) uud   (2) udd   (3) ūūd   (4) ūdd

Solution: A **baryon** is **made of three quarks** (see Reference Table: Classification of Matter). The charge of a baryon must be a whole number, 0e, +1e, or ⁻1e. The question asks for a neutral baryon; the **charge** of a **neutral baryon** must be **0e** (zero charge).

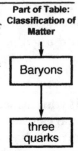

Part of Table: Classification of Matter

Baryons

three quarks

Choice 2 (udd): First look at the quarks udd on Reference Table: Particles of the Standard Model below or on page reference tables 13.

udd:
    charge of the u quark $= +\frac{2}{3}e$
    charge of the d quark $= -\frac{1}{3}e$
    e stands for one elementary charge.

Next, add the charges of udd together:

  u   d   d

$(+\frac{2}{3}e) + (-\frac{1}{3}e) + (-\frac{1}{3}e) = 0e$

udd is a neutral baryon, 0e (zero charge).

Answer 2

Part of Table:
Particles of the
Standard Model

Quarks

Name	up
Symbol	u
Charge	$+\frac{2}{3}e$

| down |
| d |
| $-\frac{1}{3}e$ |

Wrong choices:

Choice 1(uud): First look at the quarks uud on Reference Table: Particles of the Standard Model above or on page reference tables 13.

uud:
    charge of the u quark $= +\frac{2}{3}e$
    charge of the d quark $= -\frac{1}{3}e$

Next, add the charges of uud together:

     u   u   d

$(+\frac{2}{3}e) + (+\frac{2}{3}e) + (-\frac{1}{3}e) = +1e$

uud is not a neutral baryon.
A neutral baryon must have a charge of 0e (zero charge).

Choice 3 ($\bar{u}\bar{u}d$) : First look at the quarks uud on Reference Table: Particles of the Standard Model above or on page reference tables 13.

$\bar{u}\bar{u}d$:
    charge of u $= +\frac{2}{3}e$, therefore,
    charge of $\bar{u}$ (antiquark) $= -\frac{2}{3}e$
    charge of d $= -\frac{1}{3}e$
Next, add the charges of $\bar{u}\bar{u}d$ together:

    $\bar{u}$ $\bar{u}$ d

$(-\frac{2}{3}e) + (-\frac{2}{3}e) + (-\frac{1}{3}e) = -5/3e$

$\bar{u}\bar{u}d$ is not a baryon.
A baryon must have a charge that is a whole number, 0e, +1e, or −1e.
A neutral baryon must have a charge of 0e (zero charge).

Choice 4 ($\bar{u}$dd): First look at the quarks udd on Reference Table: Particles of the Standard Model on the previous page.

$\bar{u}$dd:

charge of u = $+\frac{2}{3}$e, therefore,

charge of $\bar{u}$ (antiquark) = $-\frac{2}{3}$e

charge of d = $-\frac{1}{3}$e

e stands for one elementary charge.

Next, add the charges of $\bar{u}$dd together:

$\bar{u}$	d	d	
$(-\frac{2}{3}$e)	$+(-\frac{1}{3}$e)	$+(-\frac{1}{3}$e)	= $-4/3$ e

$\bar{u}$dd is not a baryon.

A baryon must have a charge that is a whole number, 0e, +1e, or $-$1e.

A neutral baryon must have a charge of 0e (zero charge).

Question: A meson may *not* have a charge of

   (1) +1e   (2) +2e   (3) 0e   (4) $-$1e

Solution: Look at Reference Table: Classification of Matter on page 5:40 or on page reference tables 12; you see a meson is made of a quark and an antiquark.

There are six quarks on Reference Table: Particles of the Standard Model (see next page); the **charges** on a **quark** can be $+\frac{2}{3}$e or $-\frac{1}{3}$e.

Antiquarks have the same charge as quarks, but with the **opposite sign**, therefore, **charges** on an **antiquark** can be $-\frac{2}{3}$e or $+\frac{1}{3}$e.

Since a meson is made of a quark and an antiquark, combine the charges of one quark and one antiquark to find the charge of a meson. The table below shows the charges produced from all four different ways that one quark and one antiquark can combine to form a meson.

Quark		Antiquark		Charge of Meson
$+\frac{2}{3}$e	+	$-\frac{2}{3}$e	=	0e
$+\frac{2}{3}$e	+	$+\frac{1}{3}$e	=	+1e
$-\frac{1}{3}$e	+	$-\frac{2}{3}$e	=	$-$1e
$-\frac{1}{3}$e	+	$+\frac{1}{3}$e	=	0e

Adding the charges of one quark and one antiquark does not give a charge of +2e. Therefore, a meson cannot have a charge of +2e.

Answer 2

Question: According to the Standard Model, a proton is constructed of two up quarks and one down quark (*uud*) and a neutron is constructed of one up quark and two down quarks (*udd*).

During beta decay, a neutron decays into a proton, an electron, and an electron antineutrino. During the process there is a conversion of
(1) u quark to a d quark   (2) d quark to a meson
(3) baryon to another baryon   (4) lepton to another lepton

Solution:

Given: A proton is made of two up quarks and one down quark (*uud*). A neutron is made of one up quark and two down quarks (*udd*).

Part of Table: Classification of Matter

Find: What is the conversion during this process.

Baryons are made of three quarks (see Reference Table: Classification of Matter at right). Protons and neutrons are made of three quarks (given), and therefore are baryons (see table). During beta decay, a **neutron** (a **baryon**) decays (breaks down) into a **proton** (also a **baryon**), which means a **baryon** is **changed into** another **baryon**.

Baryons → three quarks

Answer 3

LEPTONS

You learned leptons have very little mass. Look at the bottom half of Reference Table: Particles of the Standard Model. The table lists six leptons. One electron is one lepton, one muon is one lepton, one tau is one lepton, one electron neutrino is one lepton, one muon neutrino is one lepton, and one tau neutrino is one lepton.

Since one electron is one lepton, two electrons are two leptons, and three electrons are three leptons, etc.

Particles of the Standard Model

Quarks

Name	up	charm	top
Symbol	u	c	t
Charge	$+\frac{2}{3}e$	$+\frac{2}{3}e$	$+\frac{2}{3}e$

	down	strange	bottom
	d	s	b
	$-\frac{1}{3}e$	$-\frac{1}{3}e$	$-\frac{1}{3}e$

Leptons

electron	muon	tau
e	μ	τ
$-1e$	$-1e$	$-1e$

electron neutrino	muon neutrino	tau neutrino
v_e	v_μ	v_τ
0	0	0

Note: For each particle, there is a corresponding antiparticle with a charge opposite that of its associated particle.

Now do Homework Questions #34-35, page 48, and #61-65, page 50.

When you answer Regents questions on **MODERN PHYSICS,** use Reference Table Modern Physics, Reference Table List of Physical Constants, Reference Table The Electromagnetic Spectrum, Reference Table Energy Level Diagrams, Reference Table Classification of Matter, and Reference Table Particles of the Standard Model.

1 An x-ray photon collides with an electron in an atom, ejecting the electron and emitting another photon. During the collision, there is a conservation of

(1) momentum, only

(2) energy, only

(3) both momentum and energy

(4) neither momentum nor energy

2 According to the quantum theory of light, the energy of light is carried in discrete units called

(1) alpha particles   (3) photons

(2) protons   (4) photoelectrons

3

Base your answer on the diagrams below, which show a photon and an electron before and after their collision.

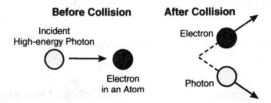

Compared to the total momentum of the photon-electron system before the collision, the total momentum of the photon-electron system after the collision is

(1) less   (2) greater   (3) the same

4 Which characteristic of electromagnetic radiation is directly proportional to the energy of a photon?

(1) wavelength   (3) frequency

(2) period   (4) path

5 What is the energy of a photon with a frequency of 5.0×10^{14} hertz?

(1) 3.3 eV   (3) 3.0×10^{48} J

(2) 3.2×10^{-6} eV   (4) 3.3×10^{-19} J

6 A photon of which electromagnetic radiation has the least energy?

(1) ultraviolet   (2) x ray   (3) infrared   (4) microwave

7 In Rutherford's model of the atom, the positive charge

(1) is distributed throughout the atom's volume

(2) revolves about the nucleus in specific orbits

(3) is concentrated at the center of the atom

(4) occupies most of the space in the atom

8 Rutherford performed "scattering" experiments by bombarding thin gold foil with alpha particles. Which conclusion is supported by the results of his experiments?

(1) Most of an atom's mass occupies a very small portion of its volume.

(2) The emission of light by electrons must be quantized.

(3) Alpha particles are deflected into parabolic paths.

(4) Electrons circling the nucleus of an atom cannot emit energy.

9 Which observation was made by Rutherford when he bombarded gold foil with alpha particles?

(1) Alpha particles were deflected toward a positive electrode.

(2) Some alpha particles were deflected by the gold foil.

(3) Most alpha particles were scattered 180º by the gold foil.

(4) Gold foil had no effect on the path of alpha particles.

10 In an experiment, Ernest Rutherford observed that some of the alpha particles directed at a thin gold foil bounced back or were scattered at large angles. This bouncing back or scattering occurred because the

(1) negatively charged alpha particles were attracted to the gold's positive atomic nuclei

(2) negatively charged alpha particles were repelled by the gold's negative atomic nuclei

(3) positively charged alpha particles were attracted to the gold's negative atomic nuclei

(4) positively charged alpha particles were repelled by the gold's positive atomic nuclei

11 The diagram at right represents the hyperbolic path of an alpha particle as it passes very near the nucleus of a gold atom. The shape of the path is caused by the force between the

(1) positively charged alpha particle and the neutral nucleus

(2) positively charged alpha particle and the positively charged nucleus

(3) negatively charged alpha particle and the neutral nucleus

(4) negatively charged alpha particle and the positively charged nucleus

12 Which diagram shows a possible path of an alpha particle as it passes very near the nucleus of a gold atom?

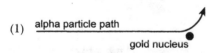
(1)

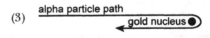
(3)

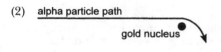
(2)

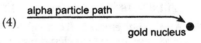
(4)

13 Alpha particles were directed at a thin metal foil. Some particles were deflected into hyperbolic paths due to

(1) gravitational attraction

(2) electrostatic repulsion

(3) electrostatic attraction

(4) magnetic repulsion

14 The term "electron cloud" refers to the

(1) electron plasma surrounding a hot wire

(2) cathode rays in a gas discharge tube

(3) high-probability region for an electron in an atom

(4) negatively charged cloud that can produce a lightening strike

15 In the currently accepted model of the atom, a fuzzy cloud around a hydrogen nucleus is used to represent the

(1) electron's actual path, which is not a circular orbit

(2) general region where the atom's proton is most probably located

(3) general region where the atom's electron is most probably located

(4) presence of water vapor in the atom

16 An electron in a hydrogen atom drops from the $n = 3$ energy level to the $n = 2$ energy level. The energy of the emitted photon is

(1) 1.51 eV   (3) 3.40 eV

(2) 1.89 eV   (4) 4.91 eV

17 An electron in a hydrogen atom drops from the $n = 4$ energy level to the $n = 2$ energy level. The energy of the emitted photon is

(1) 1.51 eV   (3) 2.55 eV

(2) 1.89 eV   (4) 4.91 eV

18 An electron in a hydrogen atom drops from the $n = 5$ energy level to the $n = 3$ energy level. The energy of the emitted photon is

(1) 0.97 eV   (3) 3.40 eV

(2) 1.89 eV   (4) 4.91 eV

19 Which electron transition in the hydrogen atom results in the emission of a photon of greatest energy?

(1) $n = 2$ to $n = 1$

(2) $n = 3$ to $n = 2$

(3) $n = 4$ to $n = 2$

(4) $n = 5$ to $n = 3$

20 The electron in a hydrogen atom drops from energy level $n = 2$ to energy level $n = 1$ by emitting a photon having an energy of approximately

(1) 5.4×10^{-19} J   (3) 2.2×10^{-18} J

(2) 1.6×10^{-18} J   (4) 7.4×10^{-18} J

21 A photon emitted from an excited hydrogen atom has an energy of 3.02 electronvolts. Which electron energy-level transition would produce this photon?

(1) $n = 1$ to $n = 6$ (3) $n = 6$ to $n = 1$

(2) $n = 2$ to $n = 6$ (4) $n = 6$ to $n = 2$

22 In returning to the ground state from the $n = 2$ state, the maximum number of photons a hydrogen atom can emit is:

(1) 1   (3) 3

(2) 2   (4) 4

23 What is the minimum energy required to ionize a hydrogen atom in the $n = 3$ state?

(1) 13.60 eV   (3) 5.52 eV

(2) 12.09 eV   (4) 1.51 eV

24 An hydrogen atom could have an electron energy-level transition from $n = 2$ to $n = 3$ by absorbing a photon having an energy of

(1) 1.51 eV   (3) 4.91 eV

(2) 1.89 eV   (4) 10.20 eV

25 An electron in a mercury atom that is changing from the a to the g level absorbs a photon with an energy of

(1) 12.86 eV   (3) 7.90 eV

(2) 10.38 eV   (4) 2.48 eV

26 What is the minimum energy required to excite a mercury atom initially in the ground state?

(1) 4.64 eV   (3) 10.20 eV

(2) 5.74 eV   (4) 10.38 eV

     Hint: To *excite* means (for an electron) to go to a higher energy level. A minimum level of energy is needed for an electron to go to a higher energy level.

27 What is the *minimum* amount of energy needed to ionize a mercury electron in the c energy level?

(1) 0.57 eV   (3) 5.52 eV

(2) 4.86 eV   (4) 10.38 eV

28 What is the force that holds the nucleons of an atom together?

(1) coulomb force

(2) magnetic force

(3) atomic force

(4) strong nuclear force

29 Which statement most accurately describes the interaction which binds a nucleus together?

(1) long-range and weak

(2) long-range and strong

(3) short-range and weak

(4) short-range and strong

30 The energy equivalent of 5.0×10^{-3} kilogram is

(1) 8.0×10^5 J   (3) 4.5×10^{14} J

(2) 1.5×10^5 J   (4) 3.0×10^{19} J

31 What is the energy equivalent of a mass of 0.052 kilogram?

(1) 4.68×10^{15} J   (2) 4.6×10^{15} J

(3) 4.68×10^{17} J   (4) 4.6×10^{17} J

32 The energy equivalent of the rest mass of an electron is approximately

(1) 5.1×10^5 J   (3) 2.7×10^{-22} J

(2) 8.2×10^{-14} J   (4) 8.5×10^{-28} J

     Hint: mass of electron is given on Reference Table List of Physical Constants

33 The force that holds protons and neutrons together is known as the

(1) gravitational force   (3) magnetic force

(2) strong force   (4) electrostatic force

34A Protons and neutrons are examples of

(1) positrons   (2) baryons   (3) mesons   (4) quarks

34B Which combination of quarks could produce a neutral baryon?

(1) cdt (2) cdb (3) cts (4) cdu

34C The charge of an antistrange quark is approximately

(1) -5.33×10^{-20} C   (2) $+5.33 \times 10^{-20}$ C   (3) -5.33×10^{20} C   (4) $+5.33 \times 10^{20}$ C

35 A lithium atom consists of 3 protons, 4 neutrons, and 3 electrons. This atom contains a total of

(1) 12 quarks and 6 leptons   (3) 21 quarks and 3 leptons

(2) 14 quarks and 3 leptons   (4) 9 quarks and 7 leptons

CONSTRUCTED RESPONSE QUESTIONS: Parts B-2 and C of NYS Regents Exam

36 A photon has a wavelength of 9.00×10^{-10} meter. Calculate the energy of this photon in joules. [Show all work, including the equation and substitution with units.]

37 Calculate the wavelength of the photon emitted when an electron in a hydrogen atom changes from $n=5$ energy level to the $n = 1$ energy level. Energy of the emitted photon = 13.06 eV or 2.09×10^{-18} J.

38 The electron in a hydrogen atom drops from energy level $n = 6$ to energy level $n = 3$. Find the energy of the emitted photon in joules.

Base your answers to questions 39-42 on the information below.

The light of the "alpha line" in the Balmer series of the hydrogen spectrum has a wavelength of 6.58×10^{-7} meter.

39 Review question. Calculate the energy of an "alpha line" photon in joules [Show all work, including the equation and substitution with units.]

40 Review question. What is the energy of an "alpha line" photon in electronvolts?

41 Using your answer to the last question, explain whether or not this result verifies that the "alpha line" corresponds to a transition from energy level $n = 3$ to energy level $n = 2$ in a hydrogen atom.

42 In the Balmer series, during which of the following energy state changes of the hydrogen atom is the photon with the most energy emitted?

(1) $n = 5$ directly to $n = 2$ (3) $n = 2$ directly to $n = 4$

(2) $n = 4$ directly to $n = 2$ (4) $n = 2$ directly to $n = 5$

43 Calculate the frequency of the photon emitted when an electron in a hydrogen atom changes from $n=4$ energy level to the $n = 1$ energy level. [Show all work, including the equation and substitution with units.]

Base your answers to questions 44-46 on the information below.

A hydrogen atom emits a 2.55-electronvolt photon as its electron changes from one level to another.

44 Using the Reference Tables for Physics, determine the energy level change for the electron.

45 Express the energy of the emitted photon in joules.

46 Determine the frequency of the emitted photon. [Show all calculations, including the equation and substitution with units.]

Base your answers to questions 47-49 on the information below.

When an electron in an excited hydrogen atom falls from a higher to a lower energy level, a photon having a wavelength of 6.58×10^{-7} meter is emitted.

47 Review question. Calculate the energy of a photon of this light wave in joules. [Show all calculations, including the equation and substitution with units.]

48 Review question. Convert the energy of the photon to electronvolts.

49 Determine which two energy levels the electron has fallen between to emit this photon.

50 An electron in a mercury atom drops from energy level g to the ground state by emitting a single photon. Find the energy of the photon in eV; find the energy of the photon in J (joules).

51 An electron in a mercury atom drops from energy level e to the ground state by emitting a single photon. Find the energy of the photon in eV; find the energy of the photon in J (joules).

52 Which choice produces the bright-line emission spectrum of an element; explain your answer.

(1) electrons transitioning between discrete energy levels in the atoms of that element

(2) protons acting as both particles and waves

(3) electrons being located in the nucleus

(4) protons being dispersed uniformly throughout the atoms of that element

53 Explain how the dark lines on a bright background are produced when white light is passed through a cool gas such as hydrogen or oxygen.

54 Find the energy equivalent of the rest mass of a proton (see reference table list of physical constants)

55 Find the energy equivalent of the rest mass of a neutron (see reference table list of physical constants)

56 What conservation law prevents two protons from annihilating each other?

57 If a nucleus has a mass of 2.2×10^{-3} universal mass units less than its components, how much energy in MeV does this mass represent?

Base your answers to questions 58-60 on the passage below and on your knowledge of physics.

Forces of Nature

Our understanding of the fundamental forces has evolved along with our growing knowledge of the particles of matter. Many everyday phenomena seemed to be governed by a long list of unique forces. Observations identified the gravitational, electric, and magnetic forces as distinct. A large step toward simplification came in the mid-19th century with Maxwell's unification of the electric and magnetic forces into a single electromagnetic force. Fifty years later came the recognition that the electromagnetic force also governed atoms. By the late 1800s, all commonly observed phenomena could be understood with only the electromagnetic and gravitational forces.

Particle Physics–Perspectives and Opportunities (adapted

A hydrogen atom, consisting of an electron in orbit about a proton, has an approximate radius of 10^{-10} meter.

58 Determine the order of magnitude of the electrostatic force between the electron and the proton. Use the equation for electrostatic force.

59 Determine the order of magnitude of the gravitational force between the electron and the proton. Use the equation for gravitational force

60 In the above passage there is an apparent contradiction. The author stated that "the electromagnetic force also governed atoms." He concluded with "all commonl observed phenomena could be understood with only the electromagnetic and gravitational forces."

Use your responses to the last two questions to explain why the gravitational interaction is negligible for the hydrogen atom.

61 A particle is made of three quarks, dbs. What is the charge of the particle? Is thi particle a baryon or a meson? Explain.

62 What is the charge of a particle made of $u\bar{s}$? Is this particle a baryon or a meson Explain.

63 What is the charge of $u\bar{c}$? What is the charge of $u\bar{t}$?

64 Write two examples of the particles in a baryon (for example dbs)

65 Write two examples of the particles in a meson (for example $d\bar{d}$)

REFERENCE TABLES

You will be given Reference Tables with the Regents Examination. Use the reference tables the way you learned in the book. If you don't understand how to use a reference table, go back to the page that explains the table.

The Reference Table booklet that is given with the Regents exam is arranged as follows:

The front page has the following tables:
List of Physical Constants
Prefixes for Powers of 10
Approximate Coefficients of Friction

When you open the booklet, you will have three pages facing you. They have the following tables:
Electromagnetic Spectrum
Absolute Indices of Refraction
Energy Level Diagrams
Classification of Matter
Particles of the Standard Model
Electricity
Circuit Symbols
Resistivities

When you close the right side of the booklet (electricity), the tables showing are:
Waves
Modern Physics
Geometry and Trigonometry

The back cover of the booklet has one table:
Mechanics

The reference tables in this book are in the same order as the reference tables given out with the Regents exams. The reference table section in this book explains how to use each table.

2002 Edition ♦ Reference Tables for Physical Setting/Physics

List of Physical Constants

Name	Symbol	Value
Universal gravitational constant	G	6.67×10^{-11} N•m^2/kg^2
Acceleration due to gravity	g	9.81 m/s^2
Speed of light in a vacuum	c	3.00×10^8 m/s
Speed of sound in air at STP		3.31×10^2 m/s
Mass of Earth		5.98×10^{24} kg
Mass of the Moon		7.35×10^{22} kg
Mean radius of Earth		6.37×10^6 m
Mean radius of the Moon		1.74×10^6 m
Mean distance—Earth to the Moon		3.84×10^8 m
Mean distance—Earth to the Sun		1.50×10^{11} m
Electrostatic constant	k	8.99×10^9 N•m^2/C^2
1 elementary charge	e	1.60×10^{-19} C
1 coulomb (C)		6.25×10^{18} elementary charges
1 electronvolt (eV)		1.60×10^{-19} J
Planck's constant	h	6.63×10^{-34} J•s
1 universal mass unit (u)		9.31×10^2 MeV
Rest mass of the electron	m_e	9.11×10^{-31} kg
Rest mass of the proton	m_p	1.67×10^{-27} kg
Rest mass of the neutron	m_n	1.67×10^{-27} kg

How to Use List of Physical Constants

This table has a list of constants, their symbol, and their value (amount) with the proper units. You substitute these numbers (values) in many equations in physics.

Example (in mechanics chapter):

In the equation $\quad g \quad = \quad \dfrac{F_g}{m}$

Acceleration due to gravity $= \dfrac{weight \ or \ force \ due \ to \ gravity}{mass}$

Substitute for g 9.81 m/s² given on Reference Table: List of Physical Constants.

Example (in electricity chapter):

In the equation $F_e = \dfrac{kq_1q_2}{r^2}$

Electrostatic force $= \dfrac{\underline{constant \ x \ charge \ of \ one \ object \ x \ charge \ of \ other \ object}}{distance \ between \ objects \ squared}$

Substitute for k 8.99 x 10⁹ N•m²/C², given on Reference Table: List of Physical Constants.

Example (in modern physics):

In the equation $E = \dfrac{hc}{\lambda}$

energy $= \dfrac{\underline{Planck's \ constant \ x \ speed \ of \ light}}{wavelength}$

Substitute for c 3.00 x 10⁸ m/s, given on this reference table. Substitute for h 6.63 x 10⁻³⁴ J•s, given on this reference table.

Review pages: **Universal** gravitational constant (G), Mass of Earth, Mass of Moon, Mean distance is used in $F_g = \dfrac{Gm_1m_2}{r^2}$: pages 1:93-1:98.

Acceleration due to gravity (g) is used in $g = \dfrac{F_g}{m}$: 1:18-1:21, 1:24-1:27, 1:31, 1:98-1:101. **Speed** of light in a vacuum (c) is used in $n = \dfrac{c}{v}$: 4:45-4:53, 4:56, used in $E_{photon} = \dfrac{hc}{\lambda}$: 5:3-5:7, used in $E = mc^2$: 5:30-5:34, used to substitute for v in $v = f\lambda$ to find frequency (f) or wavelength (λ) of electromagnetic waves: 4:76-4:79. **Electrostatic** constant (k) is used in $F_e = \dfrac{kq_1q_2}{r^2}$: 3:10-3:13, 3:17-3:20. **Planck's** constant (h) is used in $E_{photon} = hf = \dfrac{hc}{\lambda}$, 5:2-5:7. **One** elementary charge (e), pages 3:1-3:3. **One** coulomb (C), page 3:1. **One** electronvolt(eV), pages 5:5, 5:11. **One** universal mass unit (u), 5:35-5:36. **Mass** of electron, proton, neutron, 5:32-5:34.

Prefixes for Powers of 10

Prefix	Symbol	Notation
tera	T	10^{12}
giga	G	10^{9}
mega	M	10^{6}
kilo	k	10^{3}
deci	d	10^{-1}
centi	c	10^{-2}
milli	m	10^{-3}
micro	μ	10^{-6}
nano	n	10^{-9}
pico	p	10^{-12}

How to Use Prefixes for Powers of 10

The prefix is given in the first column of Reference Table: Prefixes for Powers of 10, the symbol in the second column, and the (scientific) notation in the third column.

You know the symbol for gram is g and for meter is m.

The symbol for milli (given in the second column of the table) is m, therefore, 10 **milli**grams is written as 10 **mg**; 10 **milli**meters is 10 **mm**. The symbol for kilo (given in the second column of the table) is k, therefore, 50 **kilo**grams is written as 50 **kg**; 50 **kilo**meters is 50 **km**.

On the table, the prefix milli is 10^{-3}. 1 millimeter is 10^{-3} meter (0.001 meter); 5 millimeters is 5×10^{-3} meter (0.005 meter). 1 milligram is 10^{-3} gram (0.001 gram); 8 milligrams is 8×10^{-3} gram (0.008 gram).

On the table, the prefix centi is 10^{-2}, therefore 1 centimeter is 10^{-2} meter (0.01 meter); 7 centimeters is 7×10^{-2} meter (0.07 meter).

On the table, the prefix kilo- is 10^{3}, therefore 1 kilometer is 10^{3} meter (1000 meters); 5 kilometers equals 5×10^{3} meters (5000 meters).

Example 1: 0.750 kilometers (km)= ____meters (m)

Conversion factor: 1 km = 10^{3} m (1000 m) from table above

Multiply 0.750 km x $\dfrac{10^{3}\ m\ or\ 1000\ m}{1\ km}$ = 750 m Answer 750 meters

Since 0.750 km is on top, km must be on the bottom of the fraction, so that km cancels out and you get m (meters).

OR Method 2 $\dfrac{1\ km}{1000\ m} = \dfrac{0.750\ km}{x}$;

(0.750 km)(1000 m) = x(1 km);   750 km(m) = x(1 km);   x = 750 m

Example 2: 15 centimeters (cm) = ____ meters (m).

1 cm = 10^{-2} m (from table above);   15 cm = 15×10^{-2} m or 0.15 m

Review pages 1:17,5:35-5:36.

Approximate Coefficients of Friction

	Kinetic	Static
Rubber on concrete (dry)	0.68	0.90
Rubber on concrete (wet)	0.58	
Rubber on asphalt (dry)	0.67	0.85
Rubber on asphalt (wet)	0.53	
Rubber on ice	0.15	
Waxed ski on snow	0.05	0.14
Wood on wood	0.30	0.42
Steel on steel	0.57	0.74
Copper on steel	0.36	0.53
Teflon on Teflon	0.04	

How to Use Approximate Coefficients of Friction

The table Approximate Coefficients of Friction lists the coefficients of kinetic friction and static friction of rubber on concrete (dry), rubber on concrete (wet), wood on wood, steel on steel, etc.

For example, there is a wooden block on a wooden surface. Look at Reference Table: Approximate Coefficients of Friction, for wood on wood. When the block is at rest, the static coefficient of friction (μ_s) = 0.42. When the block is moving, the kinetic coefficient of friction (μ_k) = 0.30.

When a question asks to find force of friction (F_f) when a wooden crate weighing 25 N (newtons) is moving on a horizontal wooden floor, we use the equation $F_f = \mu F_N$ (force of friction = coefficient of friction times normal force). (Note: On a horizontal surface, F_N = weight = 25 N (newtons)). You need to find μ (coefficient of friction). Look on Reference Table: Approximate Coefficients of Friction to find μ (coefficient of friction) of wood on wood. Since the crate is moving, look for kinetic friction of wood on wood, which equals 0.30. Now, in the equation $F_f = \mu F_N$, you can substitute 0.30 for μ (coefficient of friction).

Review pages 1:107-1:113.

The Electromagnetic Spectrum

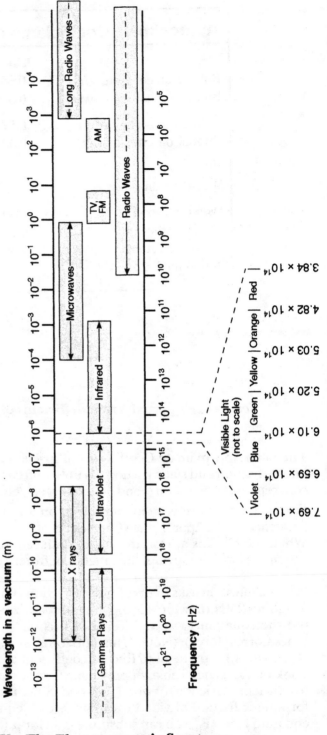

How to Use The Electromagnetic Spectrum

The electromagnetic spectrum is given on Reference Table: The Electromagnetic Spectrum.

Gamma rays, x rays, ultraviolet, visible light, infrared, microwave, radio waves, and long radio waves are all part of the electromagnetic spectrum. The speed of the waves in the electromagnetic spectrum (in a vacuum) is 3.00×10^8 m/s (just like the speed of light in a vacuum, 3.00×10^8 m/s, given on Reference Table: List of Physical Constants).

Look at Reference Table: The Electromagnetic Spectrum. The word wavelength (m) is written above the waves (gamma rays, x rays, etc.). The word frequency (Hz) is written below the waves (gamma rays, x rays, etc.). The top half shows the wavelength of gamma rays, x rays, ultraviolet, infrared, and the rest of the electromagnetic spectrum. The bottom half shows the frequency of gamma rays, x rays, ultraviolet, infrared, and the rest of the electromagnetic spectrum, and further below are the frequencies of the different colors of visible light (see Reference Table: the Electromagnetic Spectrum).

Look at wavelength, which is at the top of the reference table above. The length of the longest waves, biggest wavelength, is more than 10^4 m, which is long radio waves and radio waves. The shortest wavelength is less than 10^{-13} m, which is gamma rays.

The vertical line on the reference table between ultraviolet and infrared represents visible light. You can see that the wavelength of visible light is about 10^{-6} m.

Look at frequency, which is at the bottom half of Reference Table: The Electromagnetic Spectrum. The smallest frequency is less than 10^5 Hz, which is radio waves and long radio waves. The highest frequency is more than 10^{21} Hz, which is gamma rays.

Look at the frequency for visible light below.
The frequency of visible light goes from 3.84×10^{14} Hz, which is red light, to 7.69×10^{14} Hz, which is violet light.
If the frequency of the light wave is between 3.84×10^{14} Hz and 4.82×10^{14} Hz, the color of the light is red (see reference table). If the frequency is between 4.82×10^{14} Hz and 5.03×10^{14} Hz, the color is orange (see reference table). You know light with a frequency of 5.00×10^{14} Hz is orange, because 5.00×10^{14} Hz is between 4.82×10^{14} Hz and 5.03×10^{14} Hz.
If the frequency is between 6.59×10^{14} Hz and 7.69×10^{14} Hz, the color is violet.

If the question asks to find what kind of electromagnetic radiation has a wavelength of 4.90×10^{-14} m, look at Reference Table: The Electromagnetic Spectrum, at wavelength and you see gamma rays are the only ones on the table that have a wavelength of 10^{-13} m or less (10^{-13} m, 10^{-14} m, 10^{-15} m).

If the question asks what part of the electromagnetic spectrum has a frequency of 2.00×10^{13} Hz, look at frequency on the reference table. Infrared rays are the only rays shown on the table that have a frequency of 10^{13} Hz.

Review pages 4:72-4:80, 5:27-5:28.

Absolute Indices of Refraction

$(f = 5.09 \times 10^{14} \text{ Hz})$

Air	1.00
Corn oil	1.47
Diamond	2.42
Ethyl alcohol	1.36
Glass, crown	1.52
Glass, flint	1.66
Glycerol	1.47
Lucite	1.50
Quartz, fused	1.46
Sodium chloride	1.54
Water	1.33
Zircon	1.92

How to Use **Absolute Indices of Refraction**

Use Reference Table: Absolute Indices of Refraction **to find *n*, (absolute index of refraction)** (example: absolute index of refraction of air = 1.00).

This **reference table** is also **used** with the **following equations**:

In the equation $n = \dfrac{c}{v}$, to find v (speed of light in a medium, example lucite) look at Reference Table: Absolute Indices of Refraction to first find *n* (absolute index of refraction) (example: lucite, n = 1.50) and then substitute n (example 1.50) and c in the equation $n = \dfrac{c}{v}$ to find v. Note: c = 3.00 x 10^8 m/s, given on Reference Table: List of Physical Constants. Note: The equation $n = \dfrac{c}{v}$ is given on Reference Table: Waves.

In the equation $n_1 \sin \theta_1 = n_2 \sin \theta_2$, to find $\sin \theta_1$, θ_1, $\sin \theta_2$, θ_2, n_1 or n_2, look at Reference Table: Absolute Indices of Refraction to first find n_1 (absolute index of refraction of first medium, example: air, which is 1.00), see figure at right. Or, you can look at the reference table to first find n_2 (absolute index of refraction of second medium, example: lucite, which is 1.50), see figure,

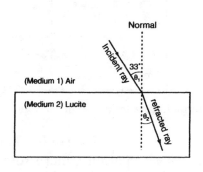

and then substitute n_1 or n_2 in the equation $n_1 \sin \theta_1 = n_2 \sin \theta_2$.

In the equation $\dfrac{n_2}{n_1} = \dfrac{v_1}{v_2} = \dfrac{\lambda_1}{\lambda_2}$, to find v_1, v_2, λ_1, λ_2, n_1 or n_2, look at Reference Table: Absolute Indices of Refraction to first find n_2 (absolute index of refraction of second medium, example: water which is 1.33), see figure at right. Or you can look at the reference table to first find n_1 (absolute index of refraction of first medium,

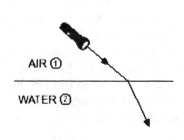

example: air which is 1.00) and then substitute n_1 or n_2 in the equation above or part of the equation above.

Review pages 4:45-4:72.

Energy Level Diagrams

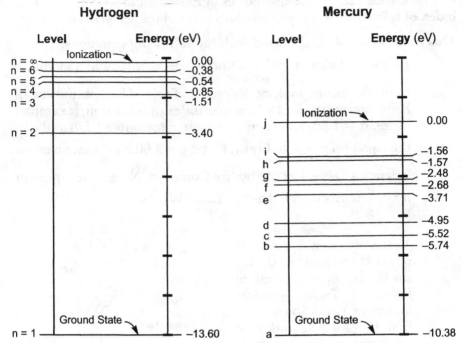

Hydrogen   **Mercury**

Energy Levels for the Hydrogen Atom   A Few Energy Levels for the Mercury Atom

How to Use Energy Level Diagrams

The horizontal line going across shows **how many eV** (electronvolts) are at each **energy level. For hydrogen**, when n = 1, first energy level, energy = -13.60 eV (electronvolts). When n = 3, third energy level, energy = -1.51 eV. When the electron goes away from the atom (at ionization), the energy = 0 eV.

Use this table when the question involves going from one energy level to the next.

1. Use the table to find the energy of the emitted photon.

Example 1: Electron of hydrogen atom drops from n = 3 to n = 2 energy level. Use the equation $E_{photon} = E_i - E_f$ (because it has two different energy levels).

Follow the line connecting **n = 3** (initial or starting level) to **-1.51 eV** (**initial energy E_i**). Follow the line connecting **n = 2** (final energy level) to -3.40 eV (**final energy E_f**).

Then, in the equation $E_{photon} = E_i - E_f$, *substitute for E_i*, -1.51 eV and *substitute for E_f*, -3.40 eV (see above).

$$E_{photon} = E_i - E_f$$

$$-1.51eV - -3.40eV = 1.89 \text{ eV}$$

Example 2: electron of mercury drops from energy level i to ground state by emitting a photon. Use the equation $E_{photon} = E_i - E_f$ (because it has two different energy levels). Follow the line connecting **level i**

(initial or starting level) to -1.56 eV (**initial energy E_i**) . Follow the line connecting **ground state** (final energy level) to -10.38 eV (**final energy E_f**). *Then, substitute for E_i* (initial energy of electron) -1.56 eV *and substitute for E_f* (final energy of electron) -10.38 eV in the equation $E_{photon} = E_i - E_f$. *Use a calculator to solve the equation below.*

Reference Table: Modern Physics

E_{photon}	=	E_i	−	E_f	
Energy of photon		Initial energy (beginning energy) of the electron		Final energy of the electron	
E_{photon}	=	-1.56 eV	−	$(-10.38$ eV$)$	$= 8.82$ eV

$$E_{photon} = 8.82 \text{ eV} \qquad \text{Answer 2}$$

2. Use the table to calculate the minimum energy needed to ionize a hydrogen or mercury atom.
Example: Hydrogen atom is in the n = 2 energy state. Follow the line connecting n = 2 to the number of eV, which is -3.40 eV. Follow the line connecting n = ∞ (ionization) to number of eV, which is 0.00 eV. When n = 2, energy is -3.40 eV. At ionization, energy is 0.00 eV. When the question asks how much energy is needed to ionize an atom, take the initial (starting) energy level (at n = 2, energy = -3.40 eV) and, obviously, you must add $+3.40$ eV (energy needed to ionize the atom) to make 0.00 eV (at ionization, eV must equal 0).
Note: For mercury, look at the energy level diagram for mercury and use the same method as above.

3. Use this table to explain why a hydrogen atom can absorb a certain amount of eV and not other amounts of eV. Example: hydrogen atom can absorb 10.20 eV and not 11.00 eV. The difference between energy level n = 1, -13.60 eV, and energy level n = 2, -3.40 eV, = 10.20 eV When an electron goes from a lower energy level to a higher energy level, it **absorbs** a **photon of energy** (which is **always equal** to the **difference between** the **two energy levels**). The **difference** between the two energy levels, $n = 1$, -13.60 eV and $n = 2$, -3.40 eV, is 10.20 eV, therefore, the atom **can absorb 10.20 eV.**
When you take the **difference** between (subtract) any **two energy levels** of hydrogen, you do **NOT get 11.00 eV**; therefore, an atom of hydrogen **cannot absorb 11.00 eV.**

4. Minimum energy needed for an electron to go from a lower energy level to a higher energy level (two different levels)
Example: In a hydrogen atom from n = 2 to n = 3, use the equation $E_{photon} = E_i - E_f$. Follow the line connecting n = 2 to -3.40 eV. Follow the line connecting n = 3 to -1.51 eV.
$E_{photon} = E_i - E_f$
$E_{photon} = -3.40 - (-1.51) = -1.89$ eV. Using $E_{photon} = E_i - E_f$, E_{photon} equals a negative number (-1.89 eV) means that energy is absorbed.
Review pages: Topic 1: 5:14-5:18   Topic 2: 5:23-5:24
          Topic 3: 5:24-5:25   Topic 4: 5:25-5:27

Classification of Matter

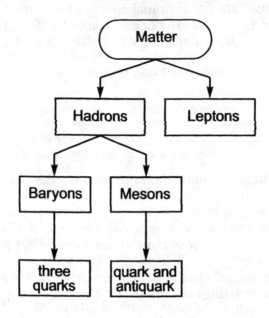

How to Use **Classification of Matter**

Matter is divided into two parts, hadrons and leptons, depending on which forces act on the matter.

The hadrons are divided into two groups, baryons and mesons.

By looking at the reference table, you can see, a baryon (which is a proton or neutron) is made up of three quarks; a meson is made up of one quark and one antiquark.

Review pages 5:37-5:40, 5:42-5:43.

Particles of the Standard Model

Quarks

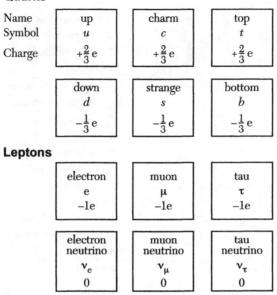

Name	up	charm	top
Symbol	u	c	t
Charge	$+\frac{2}{3}e$	$+\frac{2}{3}e$	$+\frac{2}{3}e$

down	strange	bottom
d	s	b
$-\frac{1}{3}e$	$-\frac{1}{3}e$	$-\frac{1}{3}e$

Leptons

electron	muon	tau
e	μ	τ
–1e	–1e	–1e

electron neutrino	muon neutrino	tau neutrino
ν_e	ν_μ	ν_τ
0	0	0

Note: For each particle there is a corresponding antiparticle with a charge opposite that of its associated particle.

How to Use Particles of the Standard Model

This reference table lists six quarks (basic particles). The name, symbol, and charge of each quark is given. This table also has six leptons.

Look at the **first quark** on the table. The **name** of the quark is **up,** the **symbol** of the quark (particle) is **u,** and the **charge** of the quark is $+\frac{2}{3}e$. e stands for one elementary charge (given on Reference Table: List of Physical Constants).

As you learned, **protons** and **neutrons** are **baryons** and baryons are made of **three quarks** (Reference Table: Classification of Matter).

The **proton** is **made up of three quarks having** the symbols **uud.** By looking at the charges of **uud,** on Reference Table: Particles of the Standard Model, you can find the charge of a proton. Look at the table at the right or the table above. The charge of u quark = $+\frac{2}{3}e$. The charge of d quark is $-\frac{1}{3}e$. Add together the charges of uud in a proton:

Part of Table:
Particles of the
Standard Model

Quarks

Name	up
Symbol	u
Charge	$+\frac{2}{3}e$

down
d
$-\frac{1}{3}e$

u	u	d
$\frac{2}{3}e$	$+\frac{2}{3}e$	$+(-\frac{1}{3}e) = 1e$

Charge of a proton = 1e

Antiquarks: If the **charge** on a **quark** (example: u) is $+\frac{2}{3}e$, the **charge** of the **antiquark** (example: ū) is the opposite charge, $-\frac{2}{3}e$. Example: Charge of d quark is $-\frac{1}{3}e$, therefore charge of antiquark d̄ is $+\frac{1}{3}e$ (opposite charge).

Review pages 5:38–5:43.

Electricity

$$F_e = \frac{kq_1q_2}{r^2}$$

$$E = \frac{F_e}{q}$$

$$V = \frac{W}{q}$$

$$I = \frac{\Delta q}{t}$$

$$R = \frac{V}{I}$$

$$R = \frac{\rho L}{A}$$

$$P = VI = I^2R = \frac{V^2}{R}$$

$$W = Pt = VIt = I^2Rt = \frac{V^2t}{R}$$

A = cross-sectional area
E = electric field strength
F_e = electrostatic force
I = current
k = electrostatic constant
L = length of conductor
P = electrical power
q = charge
R = resistance
R_{eq} = equivalent resistance
r = distance between centers
t = time
V = potential difference
W = work (electrical energy)
Δ = change
ρ = resistivity

Series Circuits

$$I = I_1 = I_2 = I_3 = \ldots$$

$$V = V_1 + V_2 + V_3 + \ldots$$

$$R_{eq} = R_1 + R_2 + R_3 + \ldots$$

Parallel Circuits

$$I = I_1 + I_2 + I_3 + \ldots$$

$$V = V_1 = V_2 = V_3 = \ldots$$

$$\frac{1}{R_{eq}} = \frac{1}{R_1} + \frac{1}{R_2} + \frac{1}{R_3} + \ldots$$

How to Use Electricity

Use these equations to solve electricity problems, such as F_e (electrostatic force), E (electric field strength), V (potential difference), I(current), R(resistance), P (power), W (work).

1. To find electrostatic force (F_e) use $F_e = \dfrac{kq_1q_2}{r^2}$. Substitute for k 8.99 x 10^9 N•m²/C², given on Reference Table: List of Physical Constants.

2. In the equations $F_e = \dfrac{kq_1q_2}{r^2}$, $V = \dfrac{w}{q}$, $E = \dfrac{F_e}{q}$, $I = \dfrac{\Delta q}{t}$,

q means the **charge** in **coulombs**.
Examples: If in the question you are given charge on a sphere is + 5.0 x 10^{-4} C (coulombs), it means q = +5.0 x 10^{-4} C. Substitute for q +5.0 x 10^{-4} C in the equations $F_e = \dfrac{kq_1q_2}{r^2}$, $V = \dfrac{w}{q}$, $E = \dfrac{F_e}{q}$, $I = \dfrac{\Delta q}{t}$, etc.

If in a question you are given one proton (which is one elementary charge), substitute for q 1.60 x 10^{-19} C (one elementary charge) given on Reference Table: List of Physical Constants, in the equations $F_e = \dfrac{kq_1q_2}{r^2}$, $E = \dfrac{F_e}{q}$, $V = \dfrac{w}{q}$, $I = \dfrac{\Delta q}{t}$.

3. To calculate the resistance (R) of a wire (example, nichrome), use the equation $R = \dfrac{\rho L}{A}$ (Resistance $= \dfrac{resistivity \; x \; length}{area}$), given on Reference Table: Electricity. You need to find ρ (resistivity) from Reference Table: Resistivities, then substitute ρ in the equation $R = \dfrac{\rho L}{A}$ to find resistance.

The ρ (resistivity) of aluminum $= 2.82 \times 10^{-8} \; \Omega \bullet m$, and the ρ (resistivity) of five other metals are given on the table of resistivities. If the metal is aluminum, substitute for ρ (resistivity) 2.82×10^{-8} in the equation $R = \dfrac{\rho L}{A}$ to find resistance (R).

Series Circuit:
A series circuit has only one path for the charges to flow. If the circuit drawn has only one path for the charges to flow, you know it is a series circuit.
•To find current (I), use the equation $I = I_1 = I_2 = I_3 = \ldots$ The current is the same in all parts of a series circuit. If the total current = 10A, then the current at any point of the circuit = 10A.
•To find potential difference (V), use the equation $V = V_1 + V_2 + V_3$ +... Total volts = sum of the volts.
•To find total resistance (also called equivalent resistance, R_{eq}), use the equation $R_{eq} = R_1 + R_2 + R_3 + \ldots$ Total resistance = sum of the resistances.

Parallel Circuit
A parallel circuit has **more** than one path (example: two paths, three paths) for the charges to flow. If the circuit has 2 paths or 3 paths for the charges to flow, you know it is a parallel circuit.
•To find current (I), use the equation $I = I_1 + I_2 + I_3 + \ldots$ Total current = sum of the currents.
•To find potential difference (V), use the equation $V = V_1 = V_2 = V_3$ =... The potential difference (voltage or volts) is equal in every part of the circuit. If the total number of volts = 10 V, then the number of volts in any part of the circuit = 10V.
•To find resistance (R), use the equation $\dfrac{1}{R_{ea}} = \dfrac{1}{R_1} + \dfrac{1}{R_2} + \dfrac{1}{R_3} + \ldots$

Review pages: $F_e = \dfrac{kq_1 q_2}{r^2}$ 3:10-3:13, 3:17-3:20 $E = \dfrac{F_e}{q}$ 3:21-3:24, 3:26, 3:27. $V = \dfrac{W}{q}$ 3:29-3:35, $I = \dfrac{\Delta q}{t}$ 3:35-3:39, 3:41-3:42 $R = \dfrac{V}{I}$ 3:40-3:46, 3:63-3:72, 3:83-3:93, 3:96-3:97 $R = \dfrac{\rho L}{A}$ 3:47-3:57 P (power) 3:104-3:110, W (work) 3:111-3:114.
Series Circuits 3:58-3:73, **Parallel Circuits** 3:73- 3:77, 3:80-3:83, 3:85-3:95, 3:97-3:100.

Circuit Symbols

$\perp$ cell

$\equiv$ battery

$\diagup$ switch

$-(V)-$ voltmeter

$-(A)-$ ammeter

$\wedge\!\wedge\!\wedge$ resistor

$\wedge\!\wedge\!\wedge$ variable resistor

$-(\text{lll})-$ lamp

How to Use Circuit Symbols

These are the symbols used in circuit diagrams.

Example of a circuit diagram:

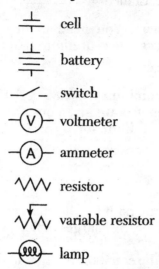

By looking at Reference Table: Circuit Symbols you know $\equiv$ means battery, $-(A)-$ means ammeter, $-(V)-$ means voltmeter, and $\wedge\!\wedge\!\wedge$ or turned around $\lessgtr$ means resistor.

Review pages 3:47, 3:49, 3:58-3:60, 3:62-3:65, 3:67, 3:69, 3:70, 3:72-3:73, 3:75- 3:80, 3:82, 3:84, 3:86-3:88, 3:92-3:94, 3:97-3:100.

Resistivities at 20°C	
Material	**Resistivity ($\Omega \cdot$m)**
Aluminum	2.82×10^{-8}
Copper	1.72×10^{-8}
Gold	2.44×10^{-8}
Nichrome	$150. \times 10^{-8}$
Silver	1.59×10^{-8}
Tungsten	5.60×10^{-8}

How to Use Resistivities

Resistivity (ρ) for various materials is given on Reference Table: Resistivities.

As you can see from the table:

resistivity (ρ) for Aluminum is 2.82×10^{-8} $\Omega \cdot$m.
resistivity (ρ) for Nichrome is $150. \times 10^{-8}$ $\Omega \cdot$m.

To calculate the resistance (R) of a wire (example, nichrome), use the equation $R = \dfrac{\rho L}{A}$ (Resistance = $\dfrac{resistivity \; x \; length}{area}$), given on Reference Table: Electricity. You need to find ρ (resistivity) from Reference Table: Resistivities above, then substitute ρ in the equation $R = \dfrac{\rho L}{A}$ to find resistance.

Example: to find the resistance (R) of a nichrome wire, substitute for ρ (resistivity) of nichrome $150. \times 10^{-8}$ $\Omega \cdot$m (from the table above) in the equation $R = \dfrac{\rho L}{A}$.

To find what material a wire is made of:

If you know the resistance (R), length (L) and area (A) of a wire, you can calculate the resistivity (ρ) by using the equation $R = \dfrac{\rho L}{A}$. Since you know ρ (resistivity), you can find out which metal or material has that resistivity (ρ). If the wire has a resistivity of 2.82×10^{-8} $\Omega \cdot$m, by looking at Reference Table: Resistivities, you see the material is aluminum. If the wire has a resistivity of 1.72×10^{-8} $\Omega \cdot$m, by looking at Reference Table: Resistivities, you see the material is copper.

Review pages 3:47-3:48, 3:52-3:57.

Waves

$v = f\lambda$

$T = \dfrac{1}{f}$

$\theta_i = \theta_r$

$n = \dfrac{c}{v}$

$n_1 \sin \theta_1 = n_2 \sin \theta_2$

$\dfrac{n_2}{n_1} = \dfrac{v_1}{v_2} = \dfrac{\lambda_1}{\lambda_2}$

c = speed of light in a vacuum

f = frequency

n = absolute index of refraction

T = period

v = velocity or speed

λ = wavelength

θ = angle

θ_i = angle of incidence

θ_r = angle of reflection

How to Use Waves

v = fλ is used to find velocity (v), frequency (f), or wavelength (λ).
Example: Wavelength = 3.0 meters, frequency = 12 Hz, find velocity.

$\quad$ V = f λ

$\quad$ V = (12 Hz or $12\dfrac{1}{s}$)(3.0 m) = 36 m/s $\qquad$ Note: Hz = $\dfrac{1}{s}$

T = $\dfrac{1}{f}$ (period = $\dfrac{1}{frequency}$). By using this equation, if period (T) is
given, you can find frequency (f), and if frequency (f) is given, you can
find period (T).

$\theta_i = \theta_r$. This equation tells you that the angle of incidence (θ_i) = angle
of reflection (θ_r). If the angle of incidence (θ_i) is 30°, then the angle of
reflection (θ_r) equals 30°.

n = $\dfrac{c}{v}$ is used to find n (index of refraction) and v (speed of light in a
medium, examples: in water, in lucite).
To find n or v, substitute for c (speed of light in a vacuum) 3.00×10^8
m/s, given on Reference Table: List of Physical Constants.

Also, use this equation $n = \dfrac{c}{v}$ to find in which material light has a given speed (v) (example: 2.25×10^8 m/s). Substitute for c 3.00×10^8 m/s and substitute for v (in this example) 2.25×10^8m/s to find n (absolute index of refraction), and then use Reference Table: Absolute Indices of Refraction to find which material has that n.

Look at the figure at right.
$n_1 \sin\theta_1 = n_2 \sin\theta_2$ is used to find n_1 (absolute index of refraction of first medium, example air) or n_2 (absolute index of refraction of second medium, example lucite), or θ_1 (angle of incidence) or θ_2 (angle of refraction).

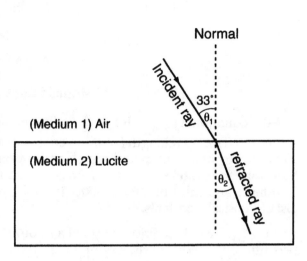

(Medium 1) Air

(Medium 2) Lucite

$\dfrac{n_2}{n_1} = \dfrac{v_1}{v_2} = \dfrac{\lambda_1}{\lambda_2}$ can be used to see what happens to v_2 when n_2 is bigger.

$\dfrac{n_2}{n_1} = \dfrac{v_1}{v_2} = \dfrac{\lambda_1}{\lambda_2}$ can also be used to find n_1 (absolute index of refraction of medium 1), n_2 (absolute index of refraction of medium 2), v_1 (velocity in medium 1), v_2 (velocity in medium 2), λ_1 (wavelength in medium 1) or λ_2 (wavelength in medium 2).

Review: $v = f\lambda$ pages 4:14-4:17, $T = \dfrac{1}{f}$ 4:7-4:9, $\theta_i = \theta_r$, 4:37-4:38,

$n = \dfrac{c}{v}$ 4:45-4:53, 4:56, $n_1 \sin\theta_1 = n_2 \sin\theta_2$ 4:59-4:64, 4:66-4:70 ,

$$\dfrac{n_2}{n_1} = \dfrac{v_1}{v_2} = \dfrac{\lambda_1}{\lambda_2} \quad \text{4:54-4:59.}$$

Modern Physics

$$E_{photon} = hf = \frac{hc}{\lambda}$$

$$E_{photon} = E_i - E_f$$

$$E = mc^2$$

c = speed of light in a vacuum

E = energy

f = frequency

h = Planck's constant

m = mass

λ = wavelength

How to Use Modern Physics

Use the equation $E_{photon} = hf = \frac{hc}{\lambda}$ to find energy of a photon (E_{photon}), frequency (f) or wavelength (λ) when energy of a photon and frequency (f) or energy of a photon and wavelength (λ) are in the question. Substitute for h 6.63×10^{-34} J•s, given on Reference Table: List of Physical Constants, and substitute for c 3.00×10^8 m/s, given on Reference Table: List of Physical Constants.

Use $E_{photon} = E_i - E_f$ to find energy of a photon (E_{photon}) when there are two different energy levels. Example: Electron of hydrogen atom drops from n = 3 to n = 2 energy level. Use the equation $E_{photon} = E_i - E_f$ (because it has two different energy levels).

On the energy level diagram for hydrogen on page reference tables 10, follow the line connecting **n = 3** (initial or starting level) to **- 1.51 eV** (**initial energy E_i**). Follow the line connecting **n = 2** (final energy level) to **- 3.40 eV** (**final energy E_f**).

Then, in this equation $E_{photon} = E_i - E_f$, *substitute for E_i*, - 1.51 eV and *substitute for E_f*, - 3.40 eV (see above).

$$E_{photon} = E_i - E_f$$
$$-1.51 eV - -3.40 eV = 1.89 eV$$

Note: Obviously, in a different example, if you know E_{photon} (energy of a photon), E_i and E_f, you do not need to use the equation $E_{photon} = E_i - E_f$, because there is no unknown.

Use $E = mc^2$ when the question has energy (E) and mass (m); use the equation when mass changes into energy. Substitute for c 3.00×10^8 m/s, given on Reference Table: List of Physical Constants.

Review $E_{photon} = hf = \frac{hc}{\lambda}$ pages 5:2-5:8, 5:11-5:14, 5:18-5:19.

Review $E_{photon} = E_i - E_f$ for hydrogen pages 5:14-5:17, for mercury pages 5:21-5:23, for unknown element 5:25-5:27.

Review $E = mc^2$ pages 5:30-5:34.

Geometry and Trigonometry

Rectangle

$A = bh$

Triangle

$A = \frac{1}{2}bh$

Circle

$A = \pi r^2$

$C = 2\pi r$

A = area

b = base

C = circumference

h = height

r = radius

Right Triangle

$c^2 = a^2 + b^2$

$\sin \theta = \dfrac{a}{c}$

$\cos \theta = \dfrac{b}{c}$

$\tan \theta = \dfrac{a}{b}$

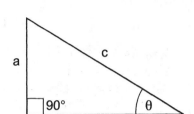

How to Use Geometry and Trigonometry

The table gives the area of a rectangle A = bh, area of a triangle, A = $\frac{1}{2}$bh, area of a circle A = πr^2, and circumference of a circle C = $2\pi r$.

Distance around a **circular path** = circumference = **$2\pi r$**. To find average velocity around a circular path, use the equation $\bar{v} = \dfrac{d}{t}$ and substitute for d (distance) $2\pi r$.

For a right triangle $c^2 = a^2 + b^2$. See figure above. c is the hypotenuse and a and b are two sides of the right triangle. Example: sides of triangle are 3 N and 4 N. Find hypotenuse (resultant) (c). Use the equation $c^2 = a^2 + b^2$.

For a right triangle (see figure above):

$\sin \theta = \dfrac{a}{c} = \dfrac{opposite}{hypotenuse}$ $\quad \cos \theta = \dfrac{b}{c} = \dfrac{adjacent}{hypotenuse}$ $\quad \tan \theta = \dfrac{a}{b} = \dfrac{opposite}{adjacent}$

Look at the figure at the right: cos θ can be used to find the horizontal vector:

Example: $\cos 30 = \dfrac{horizontal\ vector\ (adjacent)}{10\ N\ (hypotenuse)}$

sin θ can be used to find the vertical vector:

Example: $\sin 30 = \dfrac{vertical\ vector\ (opposite)}{10\ N\ (hypotenuse)}$

Review pages 1:9, 1:14-1:15, 1:42-1:44, 1:46-1:49, 1:51, 1:74, 1:89-1:90, 1:116, 2:15, 2:23.

Mechanics

$$\bar{v} = \frac{d}{t}$$

$$a = \frac{\Delta v}{t}$$

$$v_f = v_i + at$$

$$d = v_i t + \frac{1}{2}at^2$$

$$v_f^2 = v_i^2 + 2ad$$

$$A_y = A \sin \theta$$

$$A_x = A \cos \theta$$

$$a = \frac{F_{net}}{m}$$

$$F_f = \mu F_N$$

$$F_g = \frac{Gm_1 m_2}{r^2}$$

$$g = \frac{F_g}{m}$$

$$p = mv$$

$$p_{before} = p_{after}$$

$$J = F_{net}t = \Delta p$$

$$F_s = kx$$

$$PE_s = \frac{1}{2}kx^2$$

$$F_c = ma_c$$

$$a_c = \frac{v^2}{r}$$

$$\Delta PE = mg\Delta h$$

$$KE = \frac{1}{2}mv^2$$

$$W = Fd = \Delta E_T$$

$$E_T = PE + KE + Q$$

$$P = \frac{W}{t} = \frac{Fd}{t} = F\bar{v}$$

a = acceleration

a_c = centripetal acceleration

A = any vector quantity

d = displacement or distance

E_T = total energy

F = force

F_c = centripetal force

F_f = force of friction

F_g = weight or force due to gravity

F_N = normal force

F_{net} = net force

F_s = force on a spring

g = acceleration due to gravity or gravitational field strength

G = universal gravitational constant

h = height

J = impulse

k = spring constant

KE = kinetic energy

m = mass

p = momentum

P = power

PE = potential energy

PE_s = potential energy stored in a spring

Q = internal energy

r = radius or distance between centers

t = time interval

v = velocity or speed

$\bar{v}$ = average velocity or average speed

W = work

x = change in spring length from the equilibrium position

Δ = change

θ = angle

μ = coefficient of friction

How to Use **Mechanics**

1. The first 5 equations on Reference Table: Mechanics , $\bar{v} = \dfrac{d}{t}$, $a = \dfrac{\Delta v}{t}$, $v_f = v_i + at$, $d = v_i t + \dfrac{1}{2}at^2$, $v_f^2 = v_i^2 + 2ad$, deal with d (distance), t (time), v (velocity), a (acceleration), or a combination of distance, time, velocity, and acceleration. If a question asks for distance (d), time (t), velocity (v), or acceleration (a), look at these equations.

2. Use $A_y = A \sin \theta$ to find the vertical component (A_y) when the resultant (A) and θ are given and use $A_x = A \cos \theta$ to find the horizontal component (A_x) when the resultant (A) and θ are given.

3. The next 4 equations, $a = \dfrac{F_{net}}{m}$, $F_f = \mu F_N$, $F_g = \dfrac{Gm_1 m_2}{r^2}$, and $g = \dfrac{F_g}{m}$ deal with different forces (F_{net} net force, F_f force of friction, F_g weight/force due to gravity, and g acceleration due to gravity or gravitational field strength). If you need to find F_{net} (net force), F_f (force of friction), F_g (weight/force due to gravity), or g (acceleration due to gravity/gravitational field strength), look at these equations.

4. The next 3 equations deal with p (momentum): $p = mv$, $p_{before} = p_{after}$, $J = F_{net}t = \Delta p$. If a question asks about momentum (p), look at these equations.

5. The next 2 equations deal with springs: $F_s = kx$ (force on a spring) and $PE_s = \dfrac{1}{2}kx^2$ (potential energy of a spring). If a question deals with springs (force on a spring or potential energy stored in a spring), look at these equations.

6. The next 2 equations deal with objects moving in a circle: $F_c = ma_c$ (centripetal force) and $a_c = \dfrac{v^2}{r}$ (centripetal acceleration). If a question deals with centripetal force (F_c) or centripetal acceleration (a_c), look at these equations.

7. The last 5 equations on Reference Table: Mechanics deal with E (energy), W (work), or P (power): $\Delta PE = mg\Delta h$, $KE = \dfrac{1}{2}mv^2$, $W = Fd = \Delta E_T$, $E_T = PE + KE + Q$, $P = \dfrac{W}{t} = \dfrac{Fd}{t} = F\bar{v}$. If a question deals with energy, work, or power, look at these equations.

Review pages: (Numbers 1., 2., 3., 4., 5., 6., 7. below refer to 1., 2., 3., 4., 5., 6., 7. above on this page.) 1. **first 5 equations**: 1:1-1:8, 1:18, 1:22-1:31, 1:69-1:71, 1:78-1:79. **2.** 1:45-1:51, 1:72-1:73, 1:76-1:77, 1:117, 2:15; **3.** 1:57-1:63, 1:93-1:117, 2:14 **4.** 1:117-1:127 **5.** 2:18-2:21, 2:23-2:28 **6.** 1:82-1:88, 1:90-1:93; **7.** 2:1-2:12, 2:14-2:17, 2:28-2:33, 2:35-2:38, 2:41-2:43, 2:45-2:48

GLOSSARY

A

absolute index of refraction: ratio of the speed of light in a vacuum to the speed of light in a medium (material such as water, corn oil, flint glass, etc.).

acceleration:

$$\frac{change\ of\ velocity}{time}$$

acceleration: equals net force (F_{net}) divided by mass.

ammeter: an instrument that measures current.

ampere: an amount of current (I) equal to one coulomb of charge (6.25×10^{18} elementary charges) passing a point in one second.

amplitude: in a pendulum, angle between the string and the equilibrium position.

amplitude: height of a wave from the rest position or equilibrium position to the top (crest) of the wave or from the rest position to the bottom (trough) of the wave.

angle of incidence: angle between the incident ray (hitting the mirror) and the normal.

angle of reflection: angle between the reflected ray (bouncing off the mirror) and the normal.

angle of refraction: angle between the refracted ray (bent ray) and the normal.

antinode: points on a standing wave that vibrate with the largest amplitude (height) above and below the axis.

antiparticle: a subatomic particle that has the same mass as another particle but opposite charge (example: positron, + charge, is the antiparticle of the electron, − charge; both have the same mass).

antiquark: antiparticle that is identical to a quark, with the same mass, but it has the opposite charge. Example: quark has a $+\frac{2}{3}$ e charge; antiquark has a $-\frac{2}{3}$ e charge.

atom: smallest part of an element (example: oxygen) that has the characteristics of the element.

B

baryon: a particle (example proton or neutron) made of three quarks. A baryon must have a charge of 0, +1, or −1.

Bohr model: Electrons revolve (go) around the nucleus in concentric circular orbits. Each orbit is a specific distance away from the nucleus. Electrons can gain or lose only specific amounts of energy, called quanta of energy, when the electrons go from one orbit to another.

C

centripetal acceleration: acceleration toward the center of the circular path (circle) that the object is moving on. Centripetal acceleration equals speed^2 divided by radius.

centripetal force: force pulling objects toward the center of a circle. Centripetal force equals mass times centripetal acceleration.

charged object: object that lost or gained electrons.

circuit: a closed path where current (charges) flow.

circuit symbols: symbols (e x a m p l e —(A)— a m m e t e r, —(V)— voltmeter, etc.) used in circuits.

coefficient of friction: force of friction divided by normal force.

conductor: a material in which electric charges move easily. Metals are good conductors.

conservation of energy: energy cannot be created or destroyed. The total

amount of energy of an object or a system is constant (stays the same).

conservation of momentum: total amount of momentum before (example: before cars collide) equals total amount of momentum after (example: after cars collide).

constructive interference: when the displacements (heights) of both waves in the same place are above the axis or below the axis and the resultant displacement (height) is a bigger distance (further) away from the x axis than either wave.

coulomb: has 6.25×10^{18} (elementary) charges. (One elementary charge is the charge of one proton, which is positive, or the charge of one electron, which is negative).

Coulomb's Law: F_e (electrostatic force) between point charges is directly proportional to the product of the charges and inversely proportional to the square of the distance between them.

crest: in a transverse wave, point of maximum upward displacement, top of the wave.

current: amount of charge that goes past a point in one second.

D

destructive interference: when, in the same place, the displacement (height) of part of one wave is above the axis and the displacement (height) of part of the other wave is below the axis. The resultant displacement is less than the bigger wave.

diffraction: spreading of a wave into a region behind a barrier.

diffuse reflection: reflection from a rough (not smooth) surface; reflected rays are not parallel to each other and are scattered in all directions.

displacement: both distance (example, 100 meters) and direction (north, south, etc.).

distance: how far an object moves; total length of a path.

Doppler effect: frequency and wavelength appear to change (higher or lower frequency, longer or shorter wavelength) when the person and the object making the sound move closer or further from each other.

E

Einstein's theory: $E = mc^2$. energy = amount of mass used up (changed into energy) x (speed of light)^2.

electric field: any place where there is electrostatic force between two charged particles.

electric field strength: how strong the electric field is. Electric field strength equals electrostatic force (F_e) divided by the charge (q) in coulombs.

electromagnet: an iron core inside a coil of wire; the electromagnet has a magnetic field only when a current goes through the wire.

electromagnetic force: combination of electrostatic and magnetic forces. Electrostatic force is an attractive or repulsive force between charged objects.

electromagnetic induction: producing a potential difference, also called induced potential difference, by moving a wire across a magnetic field.

electromagnetic spectrum: includes gamma rays, ultraviolet, visible light, infrared, radio, long radio, microwave, x rays, etc. All these waves have a speed of 3.00×10^8 m/s.

electron: particles that go around the nucleus. An electron has a negative charge and very little mass (1/1836 atomic mass unit).

electrostatic force: force of attraction between opposite charges (+ and −) and force of repulsion between like charges (+ and + or − and −).

elementary charge: charge of one electron or charge of

one proton, which equals 1.60×10^{-19} C.

energy: ability to do work.

energy level: each energy level is a region around the nucleus where an electron can move; each level has a specific amount of energy.

equilibrium: at equilibrium, net force (all the forces) on an object must equal zero; there is no extra force in any direction. Object is at rest or moving at constant velocity.

equilibrium position of spring: where free end of spring has no force pushing up or pulling down on it.

equilibrium position of pendulum: position where the end of the string of a pendulum is closest to and perpendicular to the ground.

F

free fall: when a rock or other object falls on its own or is dropped, not thrown down; speed increases as it falls (due to gravity).

frequency: number of waves that pass a point (reach a point) in one second. Frequency is also the number of cycles a pendulum makes in one second. Frequency is given in hertz (Hz) or waves (cycles) per second.

G

gravitational field: area where an object is surrounded by

gravitational force.

gravitational field strength: acceleration due to gravity; how strong a gravitational field is.

gravitational force (force due to gravity)(F_g) : force of attraction between objects. F_g equals weight and force due to gravity.

gravitational potential energy: the energy an object has because of its height. The higher up the object (example, rock) is, the more potential energy the object has.

H

Hooke's Law: force on a spring equals spring constant times change in length of spring from equilibrium position.

I

impulse: force times time, equals change in momentum.

incident ray: a ray of light that hits a surface (example mirror).

interference: the result of superposition. Interference is a combined wave that is a different height than either wave which occupied the same place at the same time.

J

joule: unit of energy or work; equals one newton•meter.

K

kinematics: branch of mechanics dealing with motion (movement), without discussing force and mass.

kinetic energy: energy of motion (movement).

L

law of conservation of charge: charge cannot be created or destroyed; the total amount of charge (in the system) remains constant.

law of reflection: angle of incidence equals angle of reflection.

lepton: low mass subatomic particle (examples: electron, neutrino, muon).

longitudinal wave: a wave in which the particles vibrate parallel to the motion of the wave (the direction the wave is moving). (Example: wave is moving $\rightarrow$ and the particles move parallel $\leftrightarrow$.)Examples: sound waves, compression waves in a spring.

M

magnetic field lines: (magnetic lines of force or magnetic flux lines) imaginary lines that show the magnetic field.

magnetic field strength: how strong a magnetic field is (how close together are the magnetic field lines (lines of force or lines of flux)).

maximum constructive interference: the two waves in the same place are in phase (phase difference = 0°). The crests overlap and the resultant displacement has the largest possible value.

mechanical energy: the sum of the potential energy and kinetic energy of an object or a system.

mechanical wave: a wave that needs a medium (material, example air or water) to travel through, example: sound wave or water wave.

mechanics: study of the motion (movement) of an object.

meson: particle made of a quark and antiquark.

momentum: mass times velocity.

N

net force (F_{net}): equals mass times acceleration.

neutron: in the nucleus, has no charge and a mass of 1 atomic mass unit. A neutron is made of 3 quarks having the symbols udd.

Newton's First Law of Motion: an object at rest remains at rest. An object that moves will continue to move at constant velocity unless an unbalanced force acts on it.

Newton's Second Law of Motion: net force = mass times acceleration. F_{net} = ma.

Newton's Third Law of Motion: for every action, there is an equal and opposite reaction.

Newton's Universal Law of Gravitation: Two bodies attract each other with a force that is directly proportional to the product of the masses and inversely proportional to the square of the distance between them.

node: a point on a standing wave that does not move (zero displacement).

normal: a line perpendicular to a surface.

nucleus: the center of an atom, consisting of protons (positive particles) and neutrons (particles with no charge).

O

ohm: unit of electrical resistance, equals one volt per ampere.

Ohm's Law: resistance (in ohms) equals potential difference (in volts) divided by current (in amperes).

P

parallel circuit: has more than one path (2 or 3, etc.) for current (charges) to flow.

pendulum: a mass at the end of a string. The beginning of the string is attached to a pivot point that lets it move.

period: the time it takes for one wave (one complete vibration or one cycle). Period (T) is given in seconds.

periodic wave: the same pulse, which means one pulse, repeated many times, or several identical repeating pulses that are evenly spaced.

phase: position of a point on a wave compared to a point on the next wave. One point on one wave is in phase with a point on the next wave when both points are the same distance above or below the rest position (x axis) and moving in the same direction.

photon: a specific amount (quantum) of energy, considered a particle with no mass and no charge. Electromagnetic waves are both waves and particles; photons are the particles.

point charges: charged objects that are small in comparison with the distance between them.

potential difference: pushes charges and makes them flow (move). Potential difference (V) is the amount of work (electrical energy) (W) needed to move a positively charged particle toward a positively charged particle (or a negatively charged particle toward a negatively charged particle) divided by the charge in coulombs (q). $V = \dfrac{W}{q}$.

potential energy: the energy an object has due to its position (how high up the object is) or condition (example, stretched or compressed spring).

power:

$= \dfrac{work}{time} = \dfrac{force \ x \ distance}{time}$

$=$ force x average velocity (or average speed).

power (electrical): =potential difference x current

$=$ current^2 x resistance

$= \dfrac{(potential \ difference)^2}{resistance}$

proton: in the nucleus, has a positive charge and a mass of 1 atomic mass unit. A proton is made of 3 quarks having the symbols uud.

pulse: a single vibratory disturbance (one vibration) that moves from one point to another point. It moves horizontally (example, left to right) and vertically (up and down).

Q

quantum: a specific amount of energy.

quark: one of 6 particles (shown on Reference Table: Particles of the Standard Model) that have charges of $+\frac{2}{3}$e or $-\frac{1}{3}$e. Protons and neutrons, etc., are made up of quarks.

R

ray: a straight line that shows the direction that waves are traveling.

reflected ray: ray of light that bounces off a surface (example, mirror) when an incident ray hits the surface.

refraction: the bending of light waves when light goes from one medium (example, air) to a different medium (example, water).

regular reflection: reflection from a smooth surface (example, mirror); reflected rays are parallel to each other.

resistance: resists or hinders the flow of charge. Resistance (R) equals potential difference (V) divided by current (I).

resistivity (ρ): equals resistance times area divided by length. Resistivity is different for each metal.

resistor: an object used in a circuit that adds resistance and makes current smaller (less).

resonance: when one object vibrates and causes another object with the same natural frequency to vibrate (even without touching it).

Rutherford model: model of the atom with positive charges (protons) in a small nucleus, electrons on the outside, and most of the atom made of empty space.

S

scalar: a scalar quantity only has magnitude (a number) but no direction. Example: speed 40m/s.

series circuit: has only one path for the current (charges) to flow.

slope of a graph: change in y divided by change in x.
slope $= \frac{\Delta y}{\Delta x}$.

Snell's Law: index of refraction of first medium times sin of angle of incidence = index of refraction of second medium times sin of angle of refraction.
$n_1 \sin \theta_1 = n_2 \sin \theta_2$.

speed: the rate at which distance is covered.
speed $= \frac{distance}{time}$.

standing wave: made when two waves with the same amplitude and frequency travel in opposite directions in the same medium. A standing wave is a stationary wave pattern.

strong nuclear force (strong force): force which holds protons and neutrons together and prevents the nucleus from breaking apart.

superposition: when two or more waves travel through the same medium (material, example: air), in the same place at the same time.

switch: used to open or close a circuit.

T

Thomson model: model of the atom with evenly spread out positive charge and electrons embedded in the atom.

total energy: total energy of a nonideal mechanical system (example: where there is friction) is made up of potential, kinetic and internal energy.

transverse wave: wave in which the particles vibrate perpendicular to the motion of the wave (the direction the wave is moving). (Wave is moving → and the particles move perpendicular ↕.) Examples of transverse waves: electromagnetic waves (which include light waves), water waves, earthquake S-waves.

trough: in a transverse wave, point of maximum downward displacement, bottom of the wave.

U

uniform circular motion: motion (movement) of an object at constant speed in a circular path.

V

variable resistor: a resistor in which the resistance can be changed.

vector: a vector quantity has both magnitude (a

number) and direction. Example: 40 m/s west.

velocity: velocity (v) equals frequency (f) times wavelength (λ).

velocity: speed (example, 30 m/s) and direction (example, south); velocity equals 30 m/s south.

voltmeter: an instrument that measures potential difference in volts.

W

wave: A wave (example, sound wave, water wave) is produced by particles vibrating (shaking ~~or~~ moving back and forth), causing the particles' surroundings to vibrate. A wave is a ~~vibratory~~ disturbance.

wave front: all points on a wave that are in phase (example: all points on a crest of a wave).

wavelength: how long the wave is; the distance from a point on one wave (example: crest) to the same point on the next wave (example: crest). Wavelength ~~is~~ the horizontal length of a wave, which is 360°.

weak force: force involved in the decay of some particles in the nucleus.

weber: unit of magnetic flux

work: = force x distance = change in total energy.

work (electrical energy): = power x time = potential difference x current x time = current^2 x resistance x

time = (potential difference)^2 x time divided by resistance.

X

Y

Z

INDEX

A

absolute index of
    refraction 4:40-47, 4:50, 4:53-60
acceleration 1:6-8, 1:11-13, 1:18, 1:22-24, 1:26-33, 1:49, 1:53, 1:57-63,
    1:65-71, 1:73, 1:75, 1:77, 1:79-80, 1:83-86, 1:88, 1:91,
    1:95, 1:98-101, 1:104-116, 1:115, 1;125-127, 1:133; 2:8,
    2:10-12, 2:14, 2:16-17, 2:19, 2:33-34, 2:41-42, 2:46, 2:48;
    3:28, 3:29
ammeter 3:36, 3:58, 3:62, 3:64, 3:77-79, 3:82-84, 3:86-90,3:92,
    3:96-98, 3:100-102
ampere 1:17; 3:35-41, 3:64, 3:65
amplitude 1:110, 1:113; 4:4, 4:9-11, 4:13, 4:14, 4:20, 4:22, 4:26,
    4:28, 4:29
angle of incidence 4:33-35, 4:37, 4:51-55, 4:60, 4:62
angle of reflection 4:33-35
antinode 4:23, 4:32, 4:33
antiquark 5:31, 5:33-35
applied force 1:89-98, 1:101; 2:18
atom 3:1; 5:1, 5:5, 5:8-13, 5:15-21, 5:23-29, 5:34, 5:36

B

baryon 5:38-43
Bohr model 5:9

C

centripetal force 1:83-88, 1:90-92
charged object 3:2, 3:4, 3:5
circuit 3:37, 3:40, 3:47, 3:49, 3:57-103, 3:108-109, 3:113, 3:124,
    3:126
circuit symbols 3:47, 3:58, 3:62, 3:76, 3:78, 3:80, 3:93, 3:94, 3:96, 3:98,
    3:99, 4:126
conductor 4:42-45, 4:47, 4:50, 4:53-56, 4:123-125
conservation of charge . 3:101
conservation of energy .. 2:38, 2:39, 2:41
conservation of
    momentum 1:121, 1:122
constructive interference 4:23, 4:25-26, 4:29;
coulomb 1:16; 3:1, 3:8, 3:10, 3:21, 3:22, 3:26, 3:30, 3:31, 3:36,
    3:41; 5:24
Coulomb's Law 3:10
current 1:16; 3:35-49, 3:57-57, 3:62-78, 3:80, 3:82-90, 3:92-106,
    3:111-113, 3:125, 3:126

D

destructive interference . 4:23-27, 4:30-33.
diffraction .... 4:35-36; 5:1-2.
diffuse reflection 4:39

X

Y

Z

NYS REGENTS EXAMS

DESCRIPTION OF PHYSICS PHYSICAL SETTING REGENTS

The Regents consists of Parts A, B, and C.

Part A has 35 multiple choice questions: 35 points.

Part B-1 has multiple choice questions.

Part B-2 has mostly extended response questions.

Parts B-1 and B-2 together total 30 points.

Part C has extended constructed response questions-a series of questions based on topics and applications: 20 points.

Some of the questions in Parts B-2 and C may have multiple parts.

The 85 points for Parts A, B, and C are scaled up to 100 points.

All questions on the Physics: The Physical Setting Regents must be answered.

STRATEGIES FOR TEST TAKING

1 **Use the Reference Tables**. In the book, you learned which tables to use for mechanics, energy, waves, electricity, and modern physics. You can get a much higher mark on the Regents by using the Tables.

2 Read each question carefully.

3 For a **lengthy question**, pick out the **main words** of the question to make it easier to find the answer.

4 If you do not understand the choices (which choice is correct), look at the question, think of how you would answer it, then see which choice is closest to your answer.

5 You must answer all questions. If you do not know the answer, take a guess. You don't lose points for wrong answers.

6 When you guess **eliminate the wrong choices**. This increases the chance of getting the right answer.

---

7 Stay with your first guess if you don't have a better one.

8 For questions which have models, graphs, data tables, or pictures:

Read every word in the model, graph, data table, or picture very carefully.

  a. For graphs, look at the title and the labels on the x and y axes. See what the relationship is between the two variables.

  b. For data tables, see the title and the headings on the top and sides of the columns. Look for the relationships shown in the table. You can be asked to draw a graph based on the data table.

  c. For models, diagrams, and pictures, look carefully at all details in the model, picture, diagram, etc, and use **all** the information given to answer the question.

9 For longer constructed responses, each part of the question should be answered in a separate sentence or paragraph, so the one marking it knows where each answer is.

If a question has 3 or 4 parts, make sure you answer **all** the parts.

See what the question asks. Does the question ask for similarities, differences, or examples? Does the question ask why, explain why (give a reason) or how (by what means or what method)? Make sure you answer what the question asks for.

10 Go to the easy questions first. If there is a hard question, skip it and come back to it. Make a mark near the question to remember to come back for it.

11 Pace yourself. Make sure you have enough time to complete the exam. You will have three hours for the physics regents exam.

12 Review the test.

Make sure you are given the Reference Tables with the Physics Regents.

Wednesday, June 22, 2005

Part A   1:15 to 4:15 p.m., only

Answer all questions in this part.

Directions (1–35): For *each* statement or question, write on the separate answer sheet the *number* of the word or expression that, of those given, best completes the statement or answers the question.

1 A 2.0-kilogram body is initially traveling at a velocity of 40. meters per second east. If a constant force of 10. newtons due east is applied to the body for 5.0 seconds, the final speed of the body is

(1) 15 m/s
(2) 25 m/s
(3) 65 m/s
(4) 130 m/s

2 An object is dropped from rest and falls freely 20. meters to Earth. When is the speed of the object 9.8 meters per second?

(1) during the entire first second of its fall
(2) at the end of its first second of fall
(3) during its entire time of fall
(4) after it has fallen 9.8 meters

3 A 5.0-newton force and a 7.0-newton force act concurrently on a point. As the angle between the forces is increased from 0° to 180°, the magnitude of the resultant of the two forces changes from

(1) 0.0 N to 12.0 N
(2) 2.0 N to 12.0 N
(3) 12.0 N to 2.0 N
(4) 12.0 N to 0.0 N

4 A 5.0-newton force could have perpendicular components of

(1) 1.0 N and 4.0 N
(2) 2.0 N and 3.0 N
(3) 3.0 N and 4.0 N
(4) 5.0 N and 5.0 N

5 A golf ball is hit at an angle of 45° above the horizontal. What is the acceleration of the golf ball at the highest point in its trajectory? [Neglect friction.]

(1) 9.8 m/s^2 upward
(2) 9.8 m/s^2 downward
(3) 6.9 m/s^2 horizontal
(4) 0.0 m/s^2

6 At the circus, a 100.-kilogram clown is fired at 15 meters per second from a 500.-kilogram cannon. What is the recoil speed of the cannon?

(1) 75 m/s
(2) 15 m/s
(3) 3.0 m/s
(4) 5.0 m/s

7 A ball is thrown horizontally at a speed of 24 meters per second from the top of a cliff. If the ball hits the ground 4.0 seconds later, approximately how high is the cliff?

(1) 6.0 m
(2) 39 m
(3) 78 m
(4) 96 m

8 Which cart has the greatest inertia?

(1) a 1-kilogram cart traveling at a speed of 4 m/s
(2) a 2-kilogram cart traveling at a speed of 3 m/s
(3) a 3-kilogram cart traveling at a speed of 2 m/s
(4) a 4-kilogram cart traveling at a speed of 1 m/s

9 A container of rocks with a mass of 65.0 kilograms is brought back from the Moon's surface where the acceleration due to gravity is 1.62 meters per second^2. What is the weight of the container of rocks on Earth's surface?

(1) 638 N
(2) 394 N
(3) 105 N
(4) 65.0 N

10 An astronaut drops a hammer from 2.0 meters above the surface of the Moon. If the acceleration due to gravity on the Moon is 1.62 meters per second^2, how long will it take for the hammer to fall to the Moon's surface?

(1) 0.62 s
(2) 1.2 s
(3) 1.6 s
(4) 2.5 s

11 The spring in a scale in the produce department of a supermarket stretches 0.025 meter when a watermelon weighing 1.0×10^2 newtons is placed on the scale. The spring constant for this spring is

(1) 3.2×10^5 N/m
(2) 4.0×10^3 N/m
(3) 2.5 N/m
(4) 3.1×10^{-2} N/m

12 A satellite weighs 200 newtons on the surface of Earth. What is its weight at a distance of one Earth radius above the surface of Earth?

(1) 50 N
(2) 100 N
(3) 400 N
(4) 800 N

13 The diagram below shows a 5.00-kilogram block at rest on a horizontal, frictionless table.

Which diagram best represents the force exerted on the block by the table?

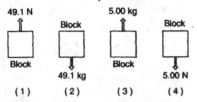

(1)   (2)   (3)   (4)

14 Two positively charged masses are separated by a distance, r. Which statement best describes the gravitational and electrostatic forces between the two masses?

(1) Both forces are attractive.
(2) Both forces are repulsive.
(3) The gravitational force is repulsive and the electrostatic force is attractive.
(4) The gravitational force is attractive and the electrostatic force is repulsive.

15 The diagram below shows the lines of magnetic force between two north magnetic poles.

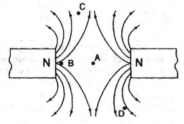

At which point is the magnetic field strength greatest?

(1) A   (3) C
(2) B   (4) D

16 As shown in the diagram below, a student exerts an average force of 600. newtons on a rope to lift a 50.0-kilogram crate a vertical distance of 3.00 meters.

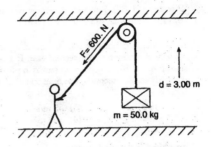

Compared to the work done by the student, the gravitational potential energy gained by the crate is

(1) exactly the same   (3) 330 J more
(2) 330 J less   (4) 150 J more

17 A 1.0-kilogram book resting on the ground is moved 1.0 meter at various angles relative to the horizontal. In which direction does the 1.0-meter displacement produce the greatest increase in the book's gravitational potential energy?

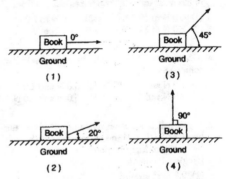

18 A 95-kilogram student climbs 4.0 meters up a rope in 3.0 seconds. What is the power output of the student?

(1) 1.3×10^2 W   (3) 1.2×10^3 W
(2) 3.8×10^2 W   (4) 3.7×10^3 W

19 What is the resistance at 20°C of a 1.50-meter-long aluminum conductor that has a cross-sectional area of 1.13×10^{-6} meter²?

(1) 1.87×10^{-3} Ω (3) 3.74×10^{-2} Ω
(2) 2.28×10^{-2} Ω (4) 1.33×10^{6} Ω

20 The resistance of a 60.-watt lightbulb operated at 120 volts is approximately

(1) 720 Ω (3) 120 Ω
(2) 240 Ω (4) 60. Ω

21 An immersion heater has a resistance of 5.0 ohms while drawing a current of 3.0 amperes. How much electrical energy is delivered to the heater during 200. seconds of operation?

(1) 3.0×10^{3} J (3) 9.0×10^{3} J
(2) 6.0×10^{3} J (4) 1.5×10^{4} J

22 The diagram below represents part of an electric circuit containing three resistors.

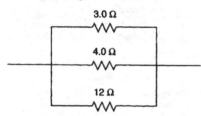

3.0 Ω

4.0 Ω

12 Ω

What is the equivalent resistance of this part of the circuit?

(1) 0.67 Ω (3) 6.3 Ω
(2) 1.5 Ω (4) 19 Ω

23 In the circuit represented by the diagram below, what is the reading of voltmeter V?

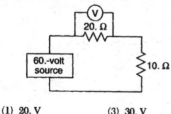

V

20. Ω

60.-volt source

10. Ω

(1) 20. V (3) 30. V
(2) 2.0 V (4) 40. V

24 A transverse wave passes through a uniform material medium from left to right, as shown in the diagram below.

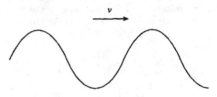

v

Which diagram best represents the direction of vibration of the particles of the medium?

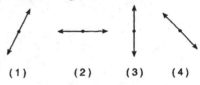

(1)   (2)   (3)   (4)

25 The diagram below shows a ray of light passing from air into glass at an angle of incidence of 0°.

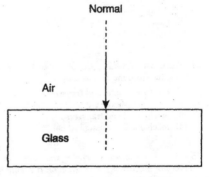

Normal

Air

Glass

Which statement best describes the speed and direction of the light ray as it passes into the glass?

(1) Only speed changes.
(2) Only direction changes.
(3) Both speed and direction change.
(4) Neither speed nor direction changes.

Note that question 26 has only three choices.

26 A ray of monochromatic light is incident on an air-sodium chloride boundary as shown in the diagram below. At the boundary, part of the ray is reflected back into the air and part is refracted as it enters the sodium chloride.

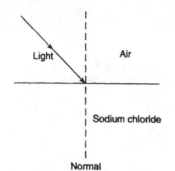

Normal

Compared to the ray's angle of refraction in the sodium chloride, the ray's angle of reflection in the air is

(1) smaller
(2) larger
(3) the same

27 Which pair of terms best describes light waves traveling from the Sun to Earth?

(1) electromagnetic and transverse
(2) electromagnetic and longitudinal
(3) mechanical and transverse
(4) mechanical and longitudinal

28 Which wave characteristic is the same for all types of electromagnetic radiation traveling in a vacuum?

(1) speed   (3) period
(2) wavelength   (4) frequency

29 If the speed of a wave doubles as it passes from shallow water into deeper water, its wavelength will be

(1) unchanged   (3) halved
(2) doubled   (4) quadrupled

30 Radio waves diffract around buildings more than light waves do because, compared to light waves, radio waves

(1) move faster
(2) move slower
(3) have a higher frequency
(4) have a longer wavelength

31 A metal sphere has a net negative charge of 1.1×10^{-6} coulomb. Approximately how many more electrons than protons are on the sphere?

(1) 1.8×10^{12} (3) 6.9×10^{12}
(2) 5.7×10^{12} (4) 9.9×10^{12}

32 Light of wavelength 5.0×10^{-7} meter consists of photons having an energy of

(1) 1.1×10^{-48} J   (3) 4.0×10^{-19} J
(2) 1.3×10^{-27} J   (4) 1.7×10^{-5} J

33 Wave-particle duality is most apparent in analyzing the motion of

(1) a baseball   (3) a galaxy
(2) a space shuttle   (4) an electron

34 The tau neutrino, the muon neutrino, and the electron neutrino are all

(1) leptons   (3) baryons
(2) hadrons   (4) mesons

35 Which statement is true of the strong nuclear force?

(1) It acts over very great distances.
(2) It holds protons and neutrons together.
(3) It is much weaker than gravitational forces.
(4) It repels neutral charges.

Part B–1
Answer all questions in this part.

Directions (36–47): For *each* statement or question, write on the separate answer sheet the *number* of the word or expression that, of those given, best completes the statement or answers the question.

36 The approximate height of a 12-ounce can of root beer is
  (1) 1.3×10^{-3} m
  (2) 1.3×10^{-1} m
  (3) 1.3×10^{0} m
  (4) 1.3×10^{1} m

37 Which physical quantity is correctly paired with its unit?
  (1) power and watt•seconds
  (2) energy and newton•seconds
  (3) electric current and amperes/coulomb
  (4) electric potential difference and joules/coulomb

38 In the diagram below, S is a point on a car tire rotating at a constant rate.

Which graph best represents the magnitude of the centripetal acceleration of point S as a function of time?

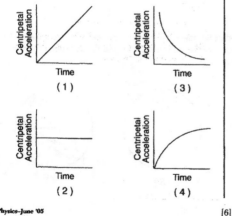

39 When a 1.53-kilogram mass is placed on a spring with a spring constant of 30.0 newtons per meter, the spring is compressed 0.500 meter. How much energy is stored in the spring?
  (1) 3.75 J
  (2) 7.50 J
  (3) 15.0 J
  (4) 30.0 J

40 The current through a lightbulb is 2.0 amperes. How many coulombs of electric charge pass through the lightbulb in one minute?
  (1) 60. C
  (2) 2.0 C
  (3) 120 C
  (4) 240 C

41 A 330.-ohm resistor is connected to a 5.00-volt battery. The current through the resistor is
  (1) 0.152 mA
  (2) 15.2 mA
  (3) 335 mA
  (4) 1650 mA

Note that question 42 has only three choices.

42 Compared to the period of a wave of red light the period of a wave of green light is
  (1) less
  (2) greater
  (3) the same

43 A hydrogen atom with an electron initially in the $n = 2$ level is excited further until the electron is in the $n = 4$ level. This energy level change occurs because the atom has
  (1) absorbed a 0.85-eV photon
  (2) emitted a 0.85-eV photon
  (3) absorbed a 2.55-eV photon
  (4) emitted a 2.55-eV photon

44 Which graph best represents the relationship between resistance and length of a copper wire of uniform cross-sectional area at constant temperature?

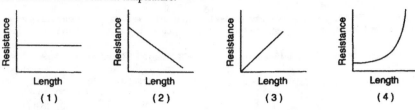

(1) (2) (3) (4)

45 The diagram below represents a block at rest on an incline.

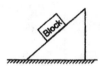

Which diagram best represents the forces acting on the block? (F_f = frictional force, F_N = normal force, and F_w = weight.)

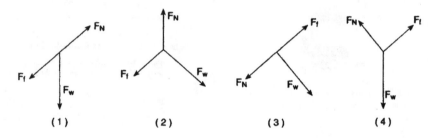

(1) (2) (3) (4)

46 A 1.0×10^3-kilogram car travels at a constant speed of 20. meters per second around a horizontal circular track. Which diagram correctly represents the direction of the car's velocity (v) and the direction of the centripetal force (F_c) acting on the car at one particular moment?

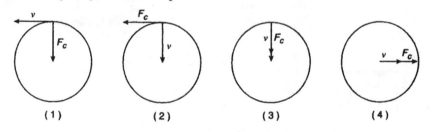

(1) (2) (3) (4)

47 Which graph best represents the relationship between the magnitude of the electrostatic force and the distance between two oppositely charged particles?

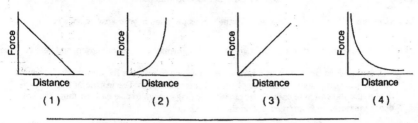

Part B–2
Answer all questions in this part.

Directions (48–61): Record your answers in the spaces provided in your answer booklet.

Base your answers to questions 48 through 51 on the information, circuit diagram, and data table below.

In a physics lab, a student used the circuit shown to measure the current through and the potential drop across a resistor of unknown resistance, R. The instructor told the student to use the switch to operate the circuit only long enough to take each reading. The student's measurements are recorded in the data table.

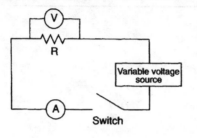

Data Table

Current (A)	Potential Drop (V)
0.80	21.4
1.20	35.8
1.90	56.0
2.30	72.4
3.20	98.4

Directions (48–50): Using the information in the data table, construct a graph on the grid *in your answer booklet*, following the directions below.

48 Mark an appropriate scale on the axis labeled "Potential Drop (V)." [1]

49 Plot the data points for potential drop versus current. [1]

50 Draw the line or curve of best fit. [1]

51 Calculate the slope of the line or curve of best fit. [Show all work, including the equation and substitution with units.] [2]

52 An electron is accelerated through a potential difference of 2.5×10^4 volts in the cathode ray tube of a computer monitor. Calculate the work, in joules, done on the electron. [Show all work, including the equation and substitution with units.] [2]

53 A ray of monochromatic light with a frequency of 5.09×10^{14} hertz is transmitted through four different media, listed below.

> A. corn oil
> B. ethyl alcohol
> C. flint glass
> D. water

Rank the four media from the one through which the light travels at the slowest speed to the one through which the light travels at the fastest speed. (Use the letters in front of each medium to indicate your answer.) [1]

54 The diagram below represents a transverse wave moving along a string.

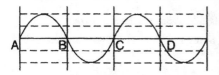

On the diagram *in your answer booklet*, draw a transverse wave that would produce complete destructive interference when superimposed with the original wave. [1]

55 How much energy, in megaelectronvolts, is produced when 0.250 universal mass unit of matter is completely converted into energy? [1]

Base your answers to questions 56 and 57 on the information below.

A car traveling at a speed of 13 meters per second accelerates uniformly to a speed of 25 meters per second in 5.0 seconds.

56 Calculate the magnitude of the acceleration of the car during this 5.0-second time interval. [Show all work, including the equation and substitution with units.] [2]

57 A truck traveling at a constant speed covers the same total distance as the car in the same 5.0-second time interval. Determine the speed of the truck. [1]

58 The gravitational force of attraction between Earth and the Sun is 3.52×10^{22} newtons. Calculate the mass of the Sun. [Show all work, including the equation and substitution with units.] [2]

59 What are the sign and charge, in coulombs, of an antiproton? [1]

Base your answers to questions 60 and 61 on the information below.

A lambda particle consists of an up, a down, and a strange quark.

60 A lambda particle can be classified as a
(1) baryon   (3) meson
(2) lepton   (4) photon

61 What is the charge of a lambda particle in elementary charges? [1]

Part C

Answer all questions in this part.

Directions (62–72): Record your answers in the spaces provided in your answer booklet.

Base your answers to questions 62 through 64 on the information and diagram below.

A 250.-kilogram car is initially at rest at point *A* on a roller coaster track. The car carries a 75-kilogram passenger and is 20. meters above the ground at point *A*. [Neglect friction.]

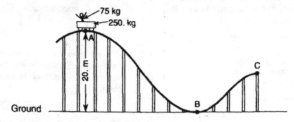

62 Calculate the total gravitational potential energy, relative to the ground, of the car and the passenger at point *A*. [Show all work, including the equation and substitution with units.] [2]

63 Calculate the speed of the car and passenger at point *B*. [Show all work, including the equation and substitution with units.] [2]

64 Compare the total mechanical energy of the car and passenger at points *A*, *B*, and *C*. [1]

Base your answers to questions 65 through 67 on the information and diagram below.

A 10.-kilogram box, sliding to the right across a rough horizontal floor, accelerates at –2.0 meters per second² due to the force of friction.

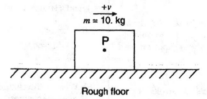

Rough floor

65 Calculate the magnitude of the net force acting on the box. [Show all work, including the equation and substitution with units.] [2]

66 On the diagram *in your answer booklet*, draw a vector representing the net force acting on the box. Begin the vector at point *P* and use a scale of 1.0 centimeter = 5.0 newtons. [2]

67 Calculate the coefficient of kinetic friction between the box and the floor. [Show all work, including the equation and substitution with units.] [2]

Base your answers to questions 68 through 70 on the information and diagram below.

A projectile is launched horizontally at a speed of 30. meters per second from a platform located a vertical distance h above the ground. The projectile strikes the ground after time t at horizontal distance d from the base of the platform. [Neglect friction.]

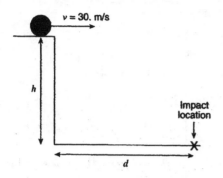

68 On the diagram *in your answer booklet,* sketch the theoretical path of the projectile. [1]

69 Calculate the horizontal distance, d, if the projectile's total time of flight is 2.5 seconds. [Show all work, including the equation and substitution with units.] [2]

70 Express the projectile's total time of flight, t, in terms of the vertical distance, h, and the acceleration due to gravity, g. [Write an appropriate equation and solve it for t.] [2]

Base your answers to questions 71 and 72 on the information and diagram below.

A ray of light of frequency 5.09×10^{14} hertz is incident on a water-air interface as shown in the diagram below.

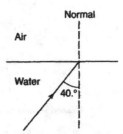

71 Calculate the angle of refraction of the light ray in air. [Show all work, including the equation and substitution with units.] [2]

72 Calculate the speed of the light while in the water. [Show all work, including the equation and substitution with units.] [2]

The University of the State of New York

REGENTS HIGH SCHOOL EXAMINATION

PHYSICAL SETTING
PHYSICS

Wednesday, June 22, 2005 — 1:15 to 4:15 p.m., only

ANSWER SHEET

Student .... Sex: ☐ Male ☐ Female Grade ....

Teacher .... School ....

Record your answers to Part A and Part B–1 on this answer sheet.

<table>
<tr><td colspan="3">Part A</td><td colspan="2">Part B–1</td></tr>
<tr><td>1............</td><td>13............</td><td>25............</td><td>36............</td><td>42............</td></tr>
<tr><td>2............</td><td>14............</td><td>26............</td><td>37............</td><td>43............</td></tr>
<tr><td>3............</td><td>15............</td><td>27............</td><td>38............</td><td>44............</td></tr>
<tr><td>4............</td><td>16............</td><td>28............</td><td>39............</td><td>45............</td></tr>
<tr><td>5............</td><td>17............</td><td>29............</td><td>40............</td><td>46............</td></tr>
<tr><td>6............</td><td>18............</td><td>30............</td><td>41............</td><td>47............</td></tr>
<tr><td>7............</td><td>19............</td><td>31............</td><td></td><td>Part B–1 Score</td></tr>
<tr><td>8............</td><td>20............</td><td>32............</td><td></td><td></td></tr>
<tr><td>9............</td><td>21............</td><td>33............</td><td></td><td></td></tr>
<tr><td>10............</td><td>22............</td><td>34............</td><td></td><td></td></tr>
<tr><td>11............</td><td>23............</td><td>35............</td><td></td><td></td></tr>
<tr><td>12............</td><td>24............</td><td>Part A Score</td><td></td><td></td></tr>
</table>

Write your answers to Part B–2 and Part C in your answer booklet.

The declaration below should be signed when you have completed the examination.

I do hereby affirm, at the close of this examination, that I had no unlawful knowledge of the questions or answers prior to the examination and that I have neither given nor received assistance in answering any of the questions during the examination.

_____
Signature

The University of the State of New York

REGENTS HIGH SCHOOL EXAMINATION

PHYSICAL SETTING
PHYSICS

Wednesday, June 22, 2005 — 1:15 to 4:15 p.m., only

ANSWER BOOKLET

Student .... Sex: ☐ Male ☐ Female

Teacher. ....

School. .... Grade ....

Answer all questions in Part B–2 and Part C. Record your answers in this booklet.

Part	Maximum Score	Student's Score
A	35	
B–1	12	
B–2	18	
C	20	

Total Written Test Score (Maximum Raw Score: 85)	
Final Score (From Conversion Chart)	

Raters' Initials:

Rater 1 .... Rater 2 ....

Part B–2

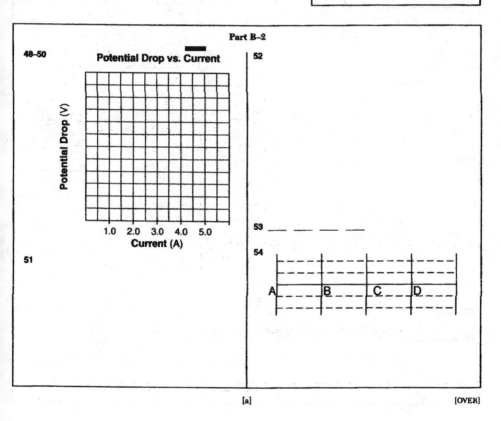

48–50

Potential Drop vs. Current

Potential Drop (V)

1.0 2.0 3.0 4.0 5.0

Current (A)

51

52

53

54

A   B   C   D

[a]

[OVER]

---

55 _____ MeV

56

57 _____ m/s

58

59 _____ C

60 _____

61 _____ e

62

63

64 _____

_____

_____

_____

65

[b]

66

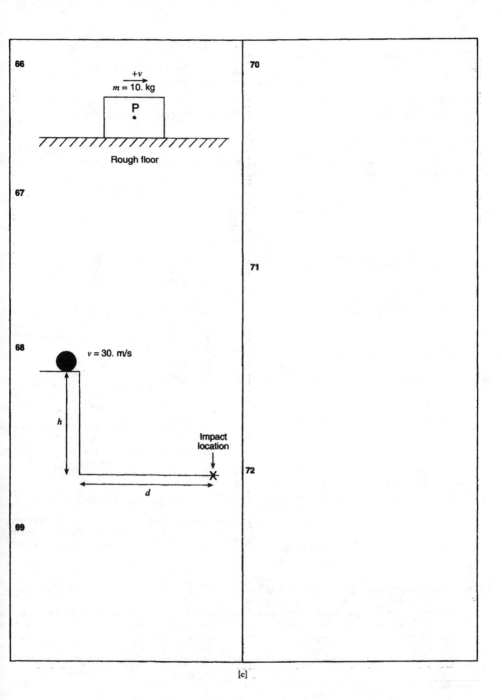

+v

m = 10. kg

P

Rough floor

67

68

v = 30. m/s

h

Impact
location

d

69

70

71

72

[c]

Directions (1–35): For *each* statement or question, write on the separate answer sheet the *number* of the word or expression that, of those given, best completes the statement or answers the question.

1 The speed of a wagon increases from 2.5 meters per second to 9.0 meters per second in 3.0 seconds as it accelerates uniformly down a hill. What is the magnitude of the acceleration of the wagon during this 3.0-second interval?

(1) 0.83 m/s^2 (3) 3.0 m/s^2
(2) 2.2 m/s^2 (4) 3.8 m/s^2

2 A 1.0-kilogram ball is dropped from the roof of a building 40. meters tall. What is the approximate time of fall? [Neglect air resistance.]

(1) 2.9 s   (3) 4.1 s
(2) 2.0 s   (4) 8.2 s

3 Which is a scalar quantity?

(1) acceleration   (3) speed
(2) momentum   (4) displacement

4 A projectile is fired with an initial velocity of 120. meters per second at an angle, θ, above the horizontal. If the projectile's initial horizontal speed is 55 meters per second, then angle θ measures approximately

(1) 13°   (3) 63°
(2) 27°   (4) 75°

5 A 2.0-kilogram laboratory cart is sliding across a horizontal frictionless surface at a constant velocity of 4.0 meters per second east. What will be the cart's velocity after a 6.0-newton westward force acts on it for 2.0 seconds?

(1) 2.0 m/s east   (3) 10. m/s east
(2) 2.0 m/s west   (4) 10. m/s west

6 A 25.0-kilogram space probe fell freely with an acceleration of 2.00 meters per second^2 just before it landed on a distant planet. What is the weight of the space probe on that planet?

(1) 12.5 N   (3) 50.0 N
(2) 25.0 N   (4) 250. N

Base your answers to questions 7 and 8 on the diagram below, which shows a 1.0-newton metal disk resting on an index card that is balanced on top of a glass.

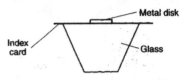

7 What is the net force acting on the disk?

(1) 1.0 N   (3) 0 N
(2) 2.0 N   (4) 9.8 N

8 When the index card is quickly pulled away from the glass in a horizontal direction, the disk falls straight down into the glass. This action is a result of the disk's

(1) inertia   (3) shape
(2) charge   (4) temperature

9 A vertical spring 0.100 meter long is elongated to a length of 0.119 meter when a 1.00-kilogram mass is attached to the bottom of the spring. The spring constant of this spring is

(1) 9.8 N/m   (3) 98 N/m
(2) 82 N/m   (4) 520 N/m

Note that question 10 has only three choices.

10 Compared to the force needed to start sliding a crate across a rough level floor, the force needed to keep it sliding once it is moving is

(1) less
(2) greater
(3) the same

11 A 400-newton girl standing on a dock exerts a force of 100 newtons on a 10 000-newton sailboat as she pushes it away from the dock. How much force does the sailboat exert on the girl?

(1) 25 N   (3) 400 N
(2) 100 N   (4) 10 000 N

Note that question 12 has only three choices.

12 A student on her way to school walks four blocks east, three blocks north, and another four blocks east, as shown in the diagram.

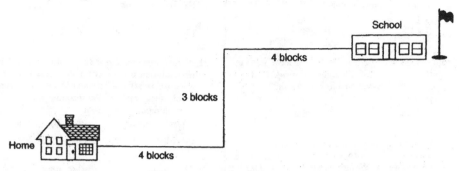

Compared to the distance she walks, the magnitude of her displacement from home to school is

(1) less
(2) greater
(3) the same

---

13 The diagram below represents two satellites of equal mass, A and B, in circular orbits around a planet.

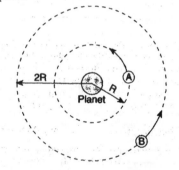

Compared to the magnitude of the gravitational force of attraction between satellite A and the planet, the magnitude of the gravitational force of attraction between satellite B and the planet is

(1) half as great
(2) twice as great
(3) one-fourth as great
(4) four times as great

14 The diagram below shows a 5.0-kilogram bucket of water being swung in a horizontal circle of 0.70-meter radius at a constant speed of 2.0 meters per second.

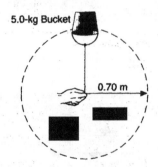

The magnitude of the centripetal force on the bucket of water is approximately

(1) 5.7 N (3) 29 N
(2) 14 N (4) 200 N

15 A 6.8-kilogram block is sliding down a horizontal, frictionless surface at a constant speed of 6.0 meters per second. The kinetic energy of the block is approximately

(1) 20. J   (3) 120 J
(2) 41 J   (4) 240 J

16 Through what vertical distance is a 50.-newton object moved if 250 joules of work is done against the gravitational field of Earth?

(1) 2.5 m   (3) 9.8 m
(2) 5.0 m   (4) 25 m

17 When a mass is placed on a spring with a spring constant of 15 newtons per meter, the spring is compressed 0.25 meter. How much elastic potential energy is stored in the spring?

(1) 0.47 J   (3) 1.9 J
(2) 0.94 J   (4) 3.8 J

Note that question 18 has only three choices.

18 Two students of equal weight go from the first floor to the second floor. The first student uses an elevator and the second student walks up a flight of stairs. Compared to the gravitational potential energy gained by the first student, the gravitational potential energy gained by the second student is

(1) less
(2) greater
(3) the same

19 A 55.0-kilogram diver falls freely from a diving platform that is 3.00 meters above the surface of the water in a pool. When she is 1.00 meter above the water, what are her gravitational potential energy and kinetic energy with respect to the water's surface?

(1) $PE = 1620$ J and $KE = 0$ J
(2) $PE = 1080$ J and $KE = 540$ J
(3) $PE = 810$ J and $KE = 810$ J
(4) $PE = 540$ J and $KE = 1080$ J

20 A 0.25-kilogram baseball is thrown upward with a speed of 30. meters per second. Neglecting friction, the maximum height reached by the baseball is approximately

(1) 15 m   (3) 74 m
(2) 46 m   (4) 92 m

21 A truck weighing 3.0×10^4 newtons was driven up a hill that is 1.6×10^3 meters long to a level area that is 8.0×10^2 meters above the starting point. If the trip took 480 seconds, what was the *minimum* power required?

(1) 5.0×10^4 W   (3) 1.2×10^{10} W
(2) 1.0×10^5 W   (4) 2.3×10^{10} W

22 The graph below represents the relationship between the potential difference (V) across a resistor and the current (I) through the resistor.

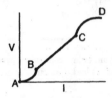

Through which entire interval does the resistor obey Ohm's law?

(1) AB   (3) CD
(2) BC   (4) AD

23 Aluminum, copper, gold, and nichrome wires of equal lengths of 1.0×10^{-1} meter and equal cross-sectional areas of 2.5×10^{-6} meter^2 are at 20.°C. Which wire has the greatest electrical resistance?

(1) aluminum   (3) gold
(2) copper   (4) nichrome

24 How much electrical energy is required to move a 4.00-microcoulomb charge through a potential difference of 36.0 volts?

(1) 9.00×10^6 J   (3) 1.44×10^{-4} J
(2) 144 J   (4) 1.11×10^{-7} J

25 What must be inserted between points A and B to establish a steady electric current in the incomplete circuit represented in the diagram below?

(1) switch
(2) voltmeter
(3) magnetic field source
(4) source of potential difference

26 In a series circuit containing two lamps, the battery supplies a potential difference of 1.5 volts. If the current in the circuit is 0.10 ampere, at what rate does the circuit use energy?

(1) 0.015 W   (3) 1.5 W
(2) 0.15 W   (4) 15 W

27 An electron placed between oppositely charged parallel plates A and B moves toward plate A, as represented in the diagram below.

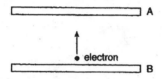

What is the direction of the electric field between the plates?

(1) toward plate A (3) into the page
(2) toward plate B (4) out of the page

28 A sonar wave is reflected from the ocean floor. For which angles of incidence do the wave's angle of reflection equal its angle of incidence?

(1) angles less than 45°, only
(2) an angle of 45°, only
(3) angles greater than 45°, only
(4) all angles of incidence

29 How are electromagnetic waves that are produced by oscillating charges and sound waves that are produced by oscillating tuning forks similar?

(1) Both have the same frequency as their respective sources.
(2) Both require a matter medium for propagation.
(3) Both are longitudinal waves.
(4) Both are transverse waves.

30 The diagram below represents a transverse wave traveling in a string.

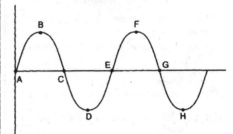

Which two labeled points are 180° out of phase?

(1) A and D (3) D and F
(2) B and F (4) D and H

31 When observed from Earth, the wavelengths of light emitted by a star are shifted toward the red end of the electromagnetic spectrum. This redshift occurs because the star is

(1) at rest relative to Earth
(2) moving away from Earth
(3) moving toward Earth at decreasing speed
(4) moving toward Earth at increasing speed

32 The diagram below represents shallow water waves of constant wavelength passing through two small openings, A and B, in a barrier.

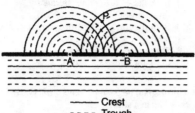

——— Crest
- - - - Trough

Which statement best describes the interference at point P?

(1) It is constructive, and causes a longer wavelength.
(2) It is constructive, and causes an increase in amplitude.
(3) It is destructive, and causes a shorter wavelength.
(4) It is destructive, and causes a decrease in amplitude.

33 Oil droplets may gain electrical charges as they are projected through a nozzle. Which quantity of charge is *not* possible on an oil droplet?

(1) 8.0×10^{-19} C   (3) 3.2×10^{-19} C
(2) 4.8×10^{-19} C   (4) 2.6×10^{-19} C

34 All photons in a vacuum have the same

(1) speed   (3) energy
(2) wavelength   (4) frequency

35 Which phenomenon best supports the theory that matter has a wave nature?

(1) electron momentum
(2) electron diffraction
(3) photon momentum
(4) photon diffraction

Part B–1

Answer all questions in this part.

Directions (36–47): For *each* statement or question, write on the separate answer sheet the *number* of the word or expression that, of those given, best completes the statement or answers the question.

36 What is the approximate mass of an automobile?

    (1) 10^1 kg   (3) 10^3 kg

    (2) 10^2 kg   (4) 10^6 kg

37 Which pair of quantities can be expressed using the same units?

    (1) work and kinetic energy

    (2) power and momentum

    (3) impulse and potential energy

    (4) acceleration and weight

38 The graph below represents the relationship between speed and time for an object moving along a straight line.

Speed vs. Time

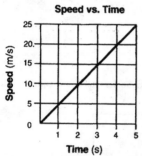

What is the total distance traveled by the object during the first 4 seconds?

    (1) 5 m   (3) 40 m

    (2) 20 m   (4) 80 m

39 An electrical generator in a science classroom makes a lightbulb glow when a student turns a hand crank on the generator. During its operation, this generator converts

    (1) chemical energy to electrical energy

    (2) mechanical energy to electrical energy

    (3) electrical energy to mechanical energy

    (4) electrical energy to chemical energy

40 In the diagram below, a cart travels clockwise at constant speed in a horizontal circle.

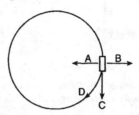

At the position shown in the diagram, which arrow indicates the direction of the centripetal acceleration of the cart?

    (1) *A*   (3) *C*

    (2) *B*   (4) *D*

41 Which changes would cause the greatest increase in the rate of flow of charge through a conducting wire?

    (1) increasing the applied potential difference and decreasing the length of wire

    (2) increasing the applied potential difference and increasing the length of wire

    (3) decreasing the applied potential difference and decreasing the length of wire

    (4) decreasing the applied potential difference and increasing the length of wire

42 According to the Standard Model of Particle Physics, a meson is composed of

    (1) a quark and a muon neutrino

    (2) a quark and an antiquark

    (3) three quarks

    (4) a lepton and an antilepton

43 Which vector diagram best represents a cart slowing down as it travels to the right on a horizontal surface?

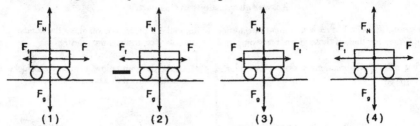

(1)   (2)   (3)   (4)

44 An object falls freely near Earth's surface. Which graph best represents the relationship between the object's kinetic energy and its time of fall?

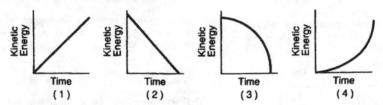

Time   Time   Time   Time
(1)   (2)   (3)   (4)

45 In the diagram below, a block of mass M initially at rest on a frictionless horizontal surface is struck by a bullet of mass m moving with horizontal velocity v.

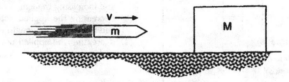

What is the velocity of the bullet-block system after the bullet embeds itself in the block?

(1) $\left(\dfrac{M+v}{M}\right)m$ (3) $\left(\dfrac{m+v}{M}\right)m$

(2) $\left(\dfrac{m+M}{m}\right)v$ (4) $\left(\dfrac{m}{m+M}\right)v$

46 Two 30.-newton forces act concurrently on an object. In which diagram would the forces produce a resultant with a magnitude of 30. newtons?

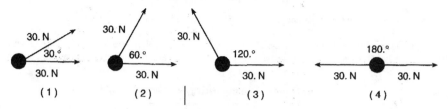

(1)   (2)   (3)   (4)

47 The diagram below represents the bright-line spectra of four elements, A, B, C, and D, and the spectrum of an unknown gaseous sample.

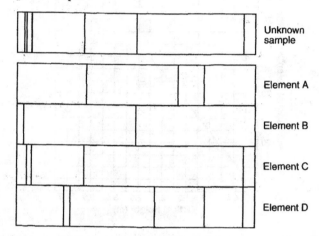

Unknown sample

Element A

Element B

Element C

Element D

Based on comparisons of these spectra, which two elements are found in the unknown sample?

(1) A and B

(2) A and D

(3) B and C

(4) C and D

Answer all questions in this part.

Directions (48–61): Record your answers in the spaces provided in your answer booklet.

Base your answers to questions 48 through 51 on the graph below, which represents the relationship between vertical height and gravitational potential energy for an object near Earth's surface. (The same graph appears in your answer booklet.)

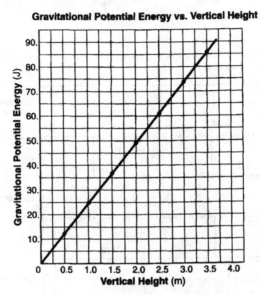

Gravitational Potential Energy vs. Vertical Height

48 Based on the graph, what is the gravitational potential energy of the object when it is 2.25 meters above the surface of Earth? [1]

49 Using the graph, calculate the mass of the object. [Show all work, including the equation and substitution with units.] [2]

50 What physical quantity does the slope of the graph represent? [1]

51 Using a straightedge, draw a line on the graph *in your answer booklet* to represent the relationship between gravitational potential energy and vertical height for an object having a greater mass. [1]

Base your answers to questions 52 through 55 on the diagram below, which represents a ray of monochromatic light (f = 5.09 × 10¹⁴ hertz) in air incident on flint glass. (The same diagram appears in your answer booklet.)

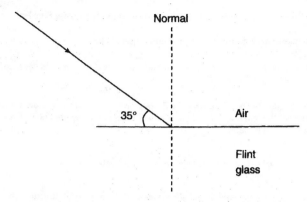

52 Determine the angle of incidence of the light ray in air. [1]

53 Calculate the angle of refraction of the light ray in the flint glass. [Show all work, including the equation and substitution with units.] [2]

54 Using a protractor and straightedge, draw the refracted ray on the diagram *in your answer booklet.* [1]

55 What happens to the light from the incident ray that is *not* refracted or absorbed? [1]

---

56 Objects in free fall near the surface of Earth accelerate downward at 9.81 meters per second². Explain why a feather does *not* accelerate at this rate when dropped near the surface of Earth. [1]

57 A skier on waxed skis is pulled at constant speed across level snow by a horizontal force of 39 newtons. Calculate the normal force exerted on the skier. [Show all work, including the equation and substitution with units.] [2]

58 A 1000-kilogram car traveling due east at 15 meters per second is hit from behind and receives a forward impulse of 6000 newton-seconds. Determine the magnitude of the car's change in momentum due to this impulse. [1]

59 On the diagram of a bar magnet *in your answer booklet,* draw a minimum of four field lines to show the magnitude and direction of the magnetic field in the region surrounding the bar magnet. [2]

60 After a uranium nucleus emits an alpha particle, the total mass of the new nucleus and the alpha particle is less than the mass of the original uranium nucleus. Explain what happens to the missing mass. [1]

61 An FM radio station broadcasts its signal at a frequency of 9.15 × 10⁷ hertz. Determine the wavelength of the signal in air. [1]

Part C

Answer all questions in this part.

Directions (62–74): Record your answers in the spaces provided in your answer booklet.

Base your answers to questions 62 through 64 on the information below.

A projectile is fired from the ground with an initial velocity of 250. meters per second at an angle of 60.° above the horizontal.

62 On the diagram *in your answer booklet*, use a protractor and ruler to draw a vector to represent the initial velocity of the projectile. Begin the vector at point *P*, and use a scale of 1.0 centimeter = 50. meters per second. [2]

63 Determine the horizontal component of the initial velocity. [1]

64 Explain why the projectile has *no* acceleration in the horizontal direction. [Neglect air friction.] [1]

Base your answers to questions 65 through 67 on the information below.

An 18-ohm resistor and a 36-ohm resistor are connected in parallel with a 24-volt battery. A single ammeter is placed in the circuit to read its total current.

65 In the space *in your answer booklet*, draw a diagram of this circuit using symbols from the *Reference Tables for Physical Setting/Physics*. [Assume the availability of any number of wires of negligible resistance.] [2]

66 Calculate the equivalent resistance of the circuit. [Show all work, including the equation and substitution with units.] [2]

67 Calculate the total power dissipated in the circuit. [Show all work, including the equation and substitution with units.] [2]

Base your answers to questions 68 through 70 on the information below.

A periodic wave traveling in a uniform medium has a wavelength of 0.080 meter, an amplitude of 0.040 meter, and a frequency of 5.0 hertz.

68 Determine the period of the wave. [1]

69 On the grid *in your answer booklet*, starting at point A, sketch a graph of *at least one* complete cycle of the wave showing its amplitude and period. [2]

70 Calculate the speed of the wave. [Show all work, including the equation and substitution with units.] [2]

Base your answers to questions 71 through 74 on the Energy Level Diagram for Hydrogen in the *Reference Tables for Physical Settings/Physics*.

71 Determine the energy, in electronvolts, of a photon emitted by an electron as it moves from the $n = 6$ to the $n = 2$ energy level in a hydrogen atom. [1]

72 Convert the energy of the photon to joules. [1]

73 Calculate the frequency of the emitted photon. [Show all work, including the equation and substitution with units.] [2]

74 Is this the only energy and/or frequency that an electron in the $n = 6$ energy level of a hydrogen atom could emit? Explain your answer. [1]

The University of the State of New York

REGENTS HIGH SCHOOL EXAMINATION

PHYSICAL SETTING
PHYSICS

Thursday, January 26, 2006 — 1:15 to 4:15 p.m., only

ANSWER SHEET

Student .... Sex: ☐ Male ☐ Female Grade ....

Teacher .... School ....

Record your answers to Part A and Part B–1 on this answer sheet.

Part A			Part B–1	
1	13	25	36	42 ....
2	14	26	37	43 ....
3	15	27	38	44 ....
4	16	28	39	45 ....
5	17	29	40	46 ....
6	18	30	41	47 ....
7	19	31		
8	20	32		
9	21	33		
10	22	34		
11	23	35		
12	24			

Part B–1 Score

Part A Score

Write your answers to Part B–2 and Part C in your answer booklet.

The declaration below should be signed when you have completed the examination.

I do hereby affirm, at the close of this examination, that I had no unlawful knowledge of the questions or answers prior to the examination and that I have neither given nor received assistance in answering any of the questions during the examination.

_____
Signature

PHYSICAL SETTING
PHYSICS

Thursday, January 26, 2006 — 1:15 to 4:15 p.m., only

ANSWER BOOKLET

Student .... Sex: ☐ Male ☐ Female

Teacher...

School... Grade ....

Answer all questions in Part B–2 and Part C. Record your answers in this booklet.

Part	Maximum Score	Student's Score
A	35	
B–1	12	
B–2	18	
C	20	

Total Written Test Score (Maximum Raw Score: 85)	
Final Score (From Conversion Chart)	

Raters' Initials:

Rater 1 .... Rater 2 ....

Part B–2

48 _____ J

49

50 _____

_____

51

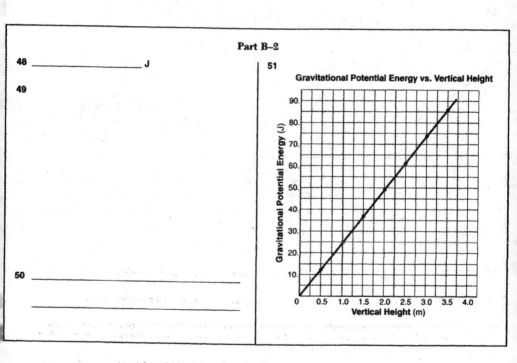

Gravitational Potential Energy vs. Vertical Height

[a]

[OVER]

---

52 _____ °

53

54

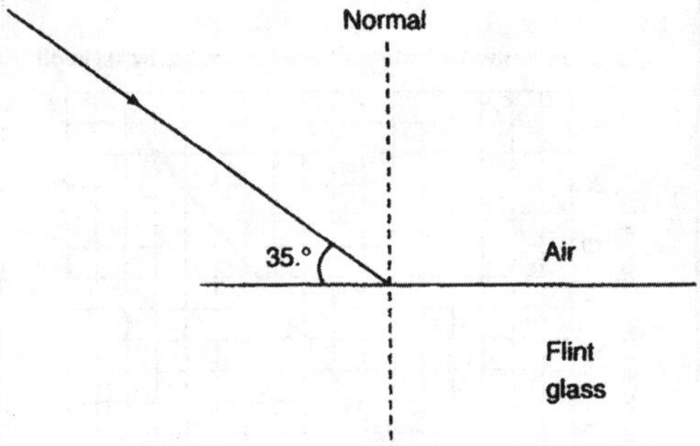

55 _____

_____

56 _____

_____

57

58 _____ $\dfrac{kg \cdot m}{s}$

59

| S | Magnet | N |

60 _____

_____

_____

61 _____ m

[b]

62

● P

Horizontal

63 _____ m/s

64 _____

_____

_____

_____

65

66

67

68 _____ s

69

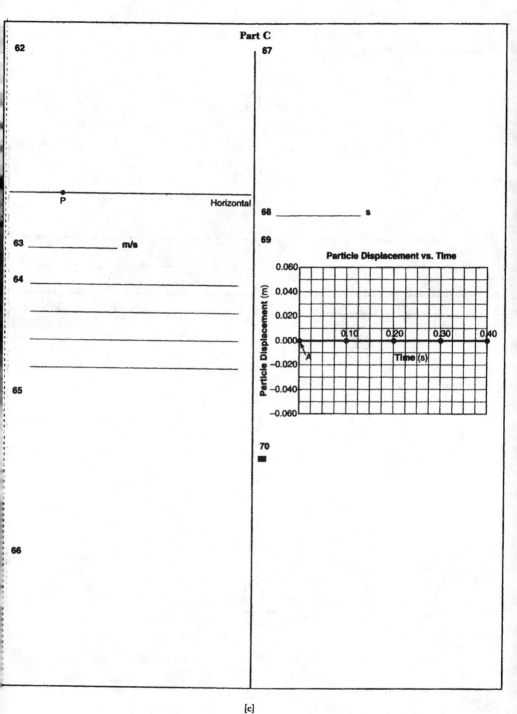

Particle Displacement vs. Time

70 ■

71 _____ eV

72 _____ J

73

74 _____

_____

_____

[d]

Answer all questions in this part.

Directions (1–35): For *each* statement or question, write on the separate answer sheet the *number* of the word or expression that, of those given, best completes the statement or answers the question.

1 A rock falls from rest off a high cliff. How far has the rock fallen when its speed is 39.2 meters per second? [Neglect friction.]

(1) 19.6 m   (3) 78.3 m
(2) 44.1 m   (4) 123 m

2 A rocket initially at rest on the ground lifts off vertically with a constant acceleration of 2.0×10^1 meters per second^2. How long will it take the rocket to reach an altitude of 9.0×10^3 meters?

(1) 3.0×10^1 s   (3) 4.5×10^2 s
(2) 4.3×10^1 s   (4) 9.0×10^2 s

3 The diagram below represents a force vector, A, and a resultant vector, R.

Which force vector B below could be added to force vector A to produce resultant vector R?

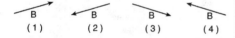

4 A golf ball is propelled with an initial velocity of 60. meters per second at 37° above the horizontal. The horizontal component of the golf ball's initial velocity is

(1) 30. m/s   (3) 40. m/s
(2) 36 m/s   (4) 48 m/s

5 Which object has the greatest inertia?

(1) a 1.0-kilogram object moving at 15 meters per second
(2) a 5.0-kilogram object at rest
(3) a 10.-kilogram object moving at 2.0 meters per second
(4) a 15-kilogram object at rest

6 A 3-newton force and a 4-newton force are acting concurrently on a point. Which force could *not* produce equilibrium with these two forces?

(1) 1 N   (3) 9 N
(2) 7 N   (4) 4 N

Base your answers to questions 7 and 8 on the information and diagram below.

The diagram shows the top view of a 65-kilogram student at point A on an amusement park ride. The ride spins the student in a horizontal circle of radius 2.5 meters, at a constant speed of 8.6 meters per second. The floor is lowered and the student remains against the wall without falling to the floor.

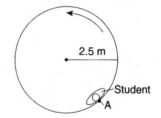

7 Which vector best represents the direction of the centripetal acceleration of the student at point A?

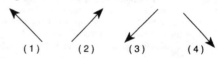

8 The magnitude of the centripetal force acting on the student at point A is approximately

(1) 1.2×10^4 N   (3) 2.2×10^2 N
(2) 1.9×10^3 N   (4) 3.0×10^1 N

9 A 60-kilogram student jumps down from a laboratory counter. At the instant he lands on the floor his speed is 3 meters per second. If the student stops in 0.2 second, what is the average force of the floor on the student?

(1) 1×10^{-2} N   (3) 9×10^2 N
(2) 1×10^2 N   (4) 4 N

10 A positively charged glass rod attracts object X. The net charge of object X

(1) may be zero or negative
(2) may be zero or positive
(3) must be negative
(4) must be positive

11 Which diagram best represents the gravitational field lines surrounding Earth?

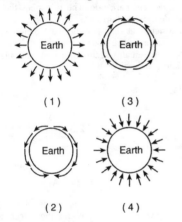

12 A 2.0-kilogram block sliding down a ramp from a height of 3.0 meters above the ground reaches the ground with a kinetic energy of 50. joules. The total work done by friction on the block as it slides down the ramp is approximately

(1) 6 J   (3) 18 J
(2) 9 J   (4) 44 J

13 A person weighing 6.0×10^2 newtons rides an elevator upward at an average speed of 3.0 meters per second for 5.0 seconds. How much does this person's gravitational potential energy increase as a result of this ride?

(1) 3.6×10^2 J   (3) 3.0×10^3 J
(2) 1.8×10^3 J   (4) 9.0×10^3 J

14 The potential energy stored in a compressed spring is to the change in the spring's length as the kinetic energy of a moving body is to the body's

(1) speed   (3) radius
(2) mass   (4) acceleration

Note that question 15 has only three choices.

15 The diagram below shows an ideal simple pendulum.

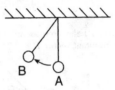

As the pendulum swings from position A to position B, what happens to its total mechanical energy? [Neglect friction.]

(1) It decreases.
(2) It increases.
(3) It remains the same.

16 During an emergency stop, a 1.5×10^3-kilogram car lost a total of 3.0×10^5 joules of kinetic energy. What was the speed of the car at the moment the brakes were applied?

(1) 10. m/s   (3) 20. m/s
(2) 14 m/s   (4) 25 m/s

17 Radio waves are propagated through the interaction of

(1) nuclear and electric fields
(2) electric and magnetic fields
(3) gravitational and magnetic fields
(4) gravitational and electric fields

18 What is the resistance at 20.°C of a 2.0-meter length of tungsten wire with a cross-sectional area of 7.9×10^{-7} meter^2?

(1) $5.7 \times 10^{-1}\ \Omega$ (3) $7.1 \times 10^{-2}\ \Omega$
(2) $1.4 \times 10^{-1}\ \Omega$ (4) $4.0 \times 10^{-2}\ \Omega$

19 A 6.0-ohm resistor that obeys Ohm's Law is connected to a source of variable potential difference. When the applied voltage is decreased from 12 V to 6.0 V, the current passing through the resistor

(1) remains the same   (3) is halved
(2) is doubled   (4) is quadrupled

20 In which circuit represented below are meters properly connected to measure the current through resistor R_1 and the potential difference across resistor R_2?

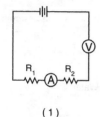

(1)

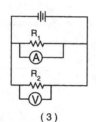

(3)

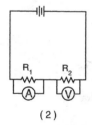

(2)

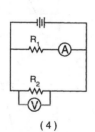

(4)

21 Two identical resistors connected in series have an equivalent resistance of 4 ohms. The same two resistors, when connected in parallel, have an equivalent resistance of

(1) $1\ \Omega$ (3) $8\ \Omega$
(2) $2\ \Omega$ (4) $4\ \Omega$

22 A 50-watt lightbulb and a 100-watt lighbulb are each operated at 110 volts. Compared to the resistance of the 50-watt bulb, the resistance of the 100-watt bulb is

(1) half as great   (3) one-fourth as great
(2) twice as great   (4) four times as great

23 A device operating at a potential difference of 1.5 volts draws a current of 0.20 ampere. How much energy is used by the device in 60. seconds?

(1) 4.5 J   (3) 12 J
(2) 8.0 J   (4) 18 J

24 As the number of resistors in a parallel circuit is increased, what happens to the equivalent resistance of the circuit and total current in the circuit?

(1) Both equivalent resistance and total current decrease.
(2) Both equivalent resistance and total current increase.
(3) Equivalent resistance decreases and total current increases.
(4) Equivalent resistance increases and total current decreases.

25 The energy of a sound wave is most closely related to its

(1) period   (3) frequency
(2) amplitude   (4) wavelength

26 A person observes a fireworks display from a safe distance of 0.750 kilometer. Assuming that sound travels at 340. meters per second in air, what is the time between the person seeing and hearing a fireworks explosion?

(1) 0.453 s   (3) 410. s
(2) 2.21 s   (4) 2.55×10^5 s

27 Electromagnetic radiation having a wavelength of 1.3×10^{-7} meter would be classified as

(1) infrared   (3) blue
(2) orange   (4) ultraviolet

28 The diagram below represents straight wave fronts passing from deep water into shallow water, with a change in speed and direction.

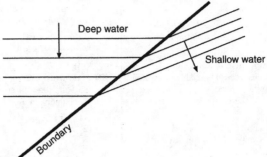

Which phenomenon is illustrated in the diagram?

(1) reflection   (3) diffraction
(2) refraction   (4) interference

29 Which diagram best represents the path taken by a ray of monochromatic light as it passes from air through the materials shown?

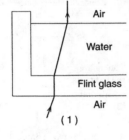

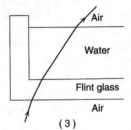

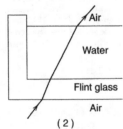

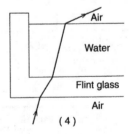

30 What is the speed of a ray of light ($f = 5.09 \times 10^{14}$ hertz) traveling through a block of sodium chloride?

(1) 1.54×10^8 m/s   (3) 3.00×10^8 m/s
(2) 1.95×10^8 m/s   (4) 4.62×10^8 m/s

31 A girl on a swing may increase the amplitude of the swing's oscillations if she moves her legs at the natural frequency of the swing. This is an example of

(1) the Doppler effect
(2) destructive interference
(3) wave transmission
(4) resonance

32 Two waves traveling in the same medium and having the same wavelength (λ) interfere to create a standing wave. What is the distance between two consecutive nodes on this standing wave?

(1) λ (3) $\frac{\lambda}{2}$
(2) $\frac{3\lambda}{4}$ (4) $\frac{\lambda}{4}$

33 An earthquake wave is traveling from west to east through rock. If the particles of the rock are vibrating in a north-south direction, the wave must be classified as

(1) transverse   (3) a microwave
(2) longitudinal   (4) a radio wave

34 A top quark has an approximate charge of

(1) -1.07×10^{-19} C   (3) $+1.07 \times 10^{-19}$ C
(2) -2.40×10^{-19} C   (4) $+2.40 \times 10^{-19}$ C

35 A tritium nucleus is formed by combining two neutrons and a proton. The mass of this nucleus is 9.106×10^{-3} universal mass unit less than the combined mass of the particles from which it is formed. Approximately how much energy is released when this nucleus is formed?

(1) 8.48×10^{-2} MeV   (3) 8.48 MeV
(2) 2.73 MeV   (4) 273 MeV

Part B–1

Answer all questions in this part.

Directions (36–51): For *each* statement or question, write on the separate answer sheet the *number* of the word or expression that, of those given, best completes the statement or answers the question.

36 The length of a dollar bill is approximately

(1) 1.5×10^{-2} m   (3) 1.5×10^1 m
(2) 1.5×10^{-1} m   (4) 1.5×10^2 m

37 A 2.0-kilogram object is falling freely near Earth's surface. What is the magnitude of the gravitational force that Earth exerts on the object?

(1) 20. N   (3) 0.20 N
(2) 2.0 N   (4) 0.0 N

38 A force of 6.0 newtons changes the momentum of a moving object by 3.0 kilogram•meters per second. How long did the force act on the mass?

(1) 1.0 s   (3) 0.25 s
(2) 2.0 s   (4) 0.50 s

39 The graph below represents the relationship between the force applied to a spring and spring elongation for four different springs.

Force vs. Elongation

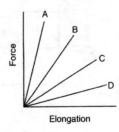

Elongation

Which spring has the greatest spring constant?

(1) A   (2) B   (3) C   (4) D

40 A 3.0-kilogram steel block is at rest on a friction-less horizontal surface. A 1.0-kilogram lump of clay is propelled horizontally at 6.0 meters per second toward the block as shown in the diagram below.

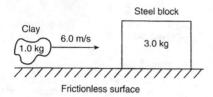

Frictionless surface

Upon collision, the clay and steel block stick together and move to the right with a speed of

(1) 1.5 m/s   (3) 3.0 m/s
(2) 2.0 m/s   (4) 6.0 m/s

41 Which two quantities can be expressed using the same units?

(1) energy and force
(2) impulse and force
(3) momentum and energy
(4) impulse and momentum

42 What is the magnitude of the electric field intensity at a point where a proton experiences an electrostatic force of magnitude 2.30×10^{-25} newton?

(1) 3.68×10^{-44} N/C   (3) 3.68×10^{6} N/C
(2) 1.44×10^{-6} N/C   (4) 1.44×10^{44} N/C

43 Pieces of aluminum, copper, gold, and silver wire each have the same length and the same cross-sectional area. Which wire has the *lowest* resistance at 20°C?

(1) aluminum   (3) gold
(2) copper   (4) silver

44 A volleyball hit into the air has an initial speed of 10. meters per second. Which vector best represents the angle above the horizontal that the ball should be hit to remain in the air for the greatest amount of time?

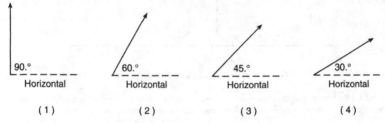

45 A box is pushed to the right with a varying horizontal force. The graph below represents the relationship between the applied force and the distance the box moves.

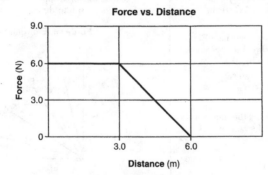

What is the total work done in moving the box 6.0 meters?

(1) 9.0 J   (3) 27 J
(2) 18 J   (4) 36 J

46 The diagram below represents two pulses approaching each other.

Which diagram best represents the resultant pulse at the instant the pulses are passing through each other?

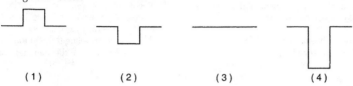

| (1) | (2) | (3) | (4) |

47 Which graph best represents the relationship between the strength of an electric field and distance from a point charge?

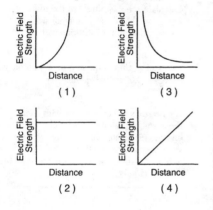

48 A 512-hertz sound wave travels 100. meters to an observer through air at STP. What is the wavelength of this sound wave?

(1) 0.195 m   (3) 1.55 m
(2) 0.646 m   (4) 5.12 m

Note that question 49 has only three choices.

49 Compared to the speed of microwaves in a vacuum, the speed of x rays in a vacuum is

(1) less
(2) greater
(3) the same

50 Which type of photon is emitted when an electron in a hydrogen atom drops from the $n = 2$ to the $n = 1$ energy level?

(1) ultraviolet   (3) infrared
(2) visible light   (4) radio wave

51 A lithium atom consists of 3 protons, 4 neutrons, and 3 electrons. This atom contains a total of

(1) 9 quarks and 7 leptons
(2) 12 quarks and 6 leptons
(3) 14 quarks and 3 leptons
(4) 21 quarks and 3 leptons

Part B-2

Answer all questions in this part.

Directions (52–60): Record your answers in the spaces provided in your answer booklet.

Base your answers to questions 52 and 53 on the information and diagram below.

A ray of monochromatic light of frequency 5.09×10^{14} hertz is traveling from water into medium X. The angle of incidence in water is 45° and the angle of refraction in medium X is 29°, as shown.

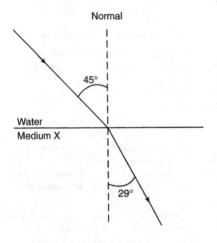

Normal

52 Calculate the absolute index of refraction of medium X. [Show all work, including the equation and substitution with units.] [2]

53 Medium X is most likely what material? [1]

54 The diagram in your answer booklet represents a transverse wave, A, traveling through a uniform medium. On the diagram *in your answer booklet*, draw a wave traveling through the same medium as wave A with twice the amplitude and twice the frequency of wave A. [2]

55 Explain the difference between a scalar and a vector quantity. [1]

56 A 10.-kilogram rubber block is pulled horizontally at constant velocity across a sheet of ice. Calculate the magnitude of the force of friction acting on the block. [Show all work, including the equation and substitution with units.] [2]

57 Determine the frequency of a photon whose energy is 3.00×10^{-19} joule. [1]

58 If a proton were to combine with an antiproton, they would annihilate each other and become energy. Calculate the amount of energy that would be released by this annihilation. [Show all work, including the equation and substitution with units.] [2]

Base your answers to questions 59 and 60 on the information and diagram below.

A 10.-kilogram block is pushed across a floor by a horizontal force of 50. newtons. The block moves from point A to point B in 3.0 seconds.

59 Using a scale of 1.0 centimeter = 1.0 meter, determine the magnitude of the displacement of the block as it moves from point A to point B. [1]

60 Calculate the power required to move the block from point A to point B in 3.0 seconds. [Show all work, including the equation and substitution with units.] [2]

Part C

Answer all questions in this part.

Directions (61–72): Record your answers in the spaces provided in your answer booklet.

Base your answers to questions 61 through 63 on the information and diagram below.

A 3.0-kilogram object is placed on a frictionless track at point *A* and released from rest. (Assume the gravitational potential energy of the system to be zero at point *C*.)

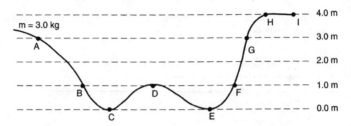

61 Calculate the gravitational potential energy of the object at point *A*. [Show all work, including the equation and substitution with units.] [2]

62 Calculate the kinetic energy of the object at point *B*. [Show all work, including the equation and substitution with units.] [2]

63 Which letter represents the farthest point on the track that the object will reach? [1]

Base your answers to questions 64 through 66 on the information below.

A car on a straight road starts from rest and accelerates at 1.0 meter per second^2 for 10. seconds. Then the car continues to travel at constant speed for an additional 20. seconds.

64 Determine the speed of the car at the end of the first 10. seconds. [1]

65 On the grid *in your answer booklet*, use a ruler or straightedge to construct a graph of the car's speed as a function of time for the entire 30.-second interval. [2]

66 Calculate the distance the car travels in the first 10. seconds. [Show all work, including the equation and substitution with units.] [2]

Base your answers to questions 67 through 69 on the passage and data table below.

The net force on a planet is due primarily to the other planets and the Sun. By taking into account all the forces acting on a planet, investigators calculated the orbit of each planet.

A small discrepancy between the calculated orbit and the observed orbit of the planet Uranus was noted. It appeared that the sum of the forces on Uranus did not equal its mass times its acceleration, unless there was another force on the planet that was not included in the calculation. Assuming that this force was exerted by an unobserved planet, two scientists working independently calculated where this unknown planet must be in order to account for the discrepancy. Astronomers pointed their telescopes in the predicted direction and found the planet we now call Neptune.

Data Table

Mass of the Sun	1.99×10^{30} kg
Mass of Uranus	8.73×10^{25} kg
Mass of Neptune	1.03×10^{26} kg
Mean distance of Uranus to the Sun	2.87×10^{12} m
Mean distance of Neptune to the Sun	4.50×10^{12} m

67 What fundamental force is the author referring to in this passage as a force between planets? [1]

68 The diagram below represents Neptune, Uranus, and the Sun in a straight line. Neptune is 1.63×10^{12} meters from Uranus.

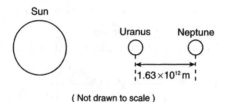

(Not drawn to scale)

Calculate the magnitude of the interplanetary force of attraction between Uranus and Neptune at this point. [Show all work, including the equation and substitution with units.] [2]

69 The magnitude of the force the Sun exerts on Uranus is 1.41×10^{21} newtons. Explain how it is possible for the Sun to exert a greater force on Uranus than Neptune exerts on Uranus. [1]

Base your answers to questions 70 and 71 on the information and diagram below.

A student standing on a dock observes a piece of wood floating on the water as shown below. As a water wave passes, the wood moves up and down, rising to the top of a wave crest every 5.0 seconds.

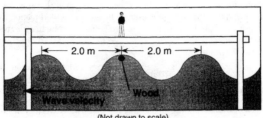

(Not drawn to scale)

70 Calculate the frequency of the passing water waves. [Show all work, including the equation and substitution with units.] [2]

71 Calculate the speed of the water waves. [Show all work, including the equation and substitution with units.] [2]

72 The diagram below shows two resistors, R_1 and R_2, connected in parallel in a circuit having a 120-volt power source. Resistor R_1 develops 150 watts and resistor R_2 develops an unknown power. Ammeter A in the circuit reads 0.50 ampere.

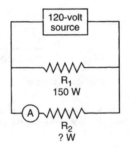

Calculate the amount of charge passing through resistor R_2 in 60. seconds. [Show all work, including the equation and substitution with units.] [2]

The University of the State of New York

REGENTS HIGH SCHOOL EXAMINATION

PHYSICAL SETTING
PHYSICS

Thursday, June 22, 2006 — 9:15 a.m. to 12:15 p.m., only

ANSWER SHEET

Student .... Sex: ☐ Male ☐ Female Grade ....

Teacher .... School ....

Record your answers to Part A and Part B–1 on this answer sheet.

Part A			Part B–1	
1	13	25	36	44 ....
2	14	26	37	45 ....
3	15	27	38	46 ....
4	16	28	39	47 ....
5	17	29	40	48 ....
6	18	30	41	49 ....
7	19	31	42	50 ....
8	20	32	43	51 ....
9	21	33		
10	22	34		
11	23	35		
12	24			

Part B–1 Score

Part A Score

Write your answers to Part B–2 and Part C in your answer booklet.

The declaration below should be signed when you have completed the examination.

I do hereby affirm, at the close of this examination, that I had no unlawful knowledge of the questions or answers prior to the examination and that I have neither given nor received assistance in answering any of the questions during the examination.

_____
Signature

The University of the State of New York

REGENTS HIGH SCHOOL EXAMINATION

PHYSICAL SETTING
PHYSICS

Thursday, June 22, 2006 — 9:15 a.m. to 12:15 p.m., only

ANSWER BOOKLET

Student .... Sex: ☐ Male ☐ Female

Teacher ....

School .... Grade ....

Answer all questions in Part B–2 and Part C. Record your answers in this booklet.

Part	Maximum Score	Student's Score
A	35	
B–1	16	
B–2	14	
C	20	

Total Written Test Score (Maximum Raw Score: 85)	
Final Score (From Conversion Chart)	

Raters' Initials:

Rater 1 .... Rater 2 ....

52

53 _____

54

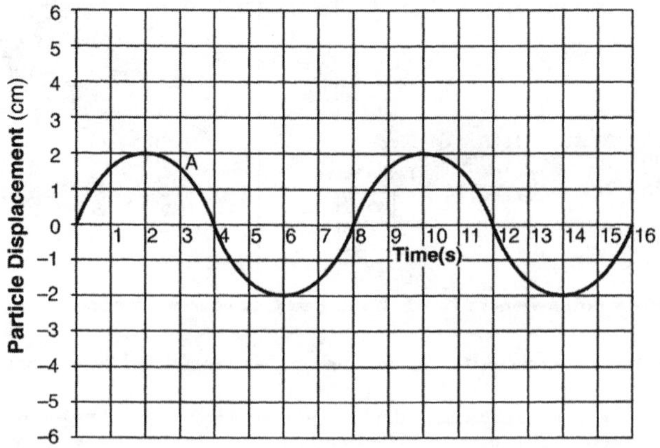

[a]

[OVER]

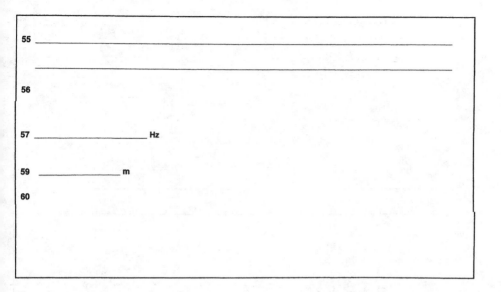

55 _____
_____

56

57 _____ Hz

59 _____ m

60

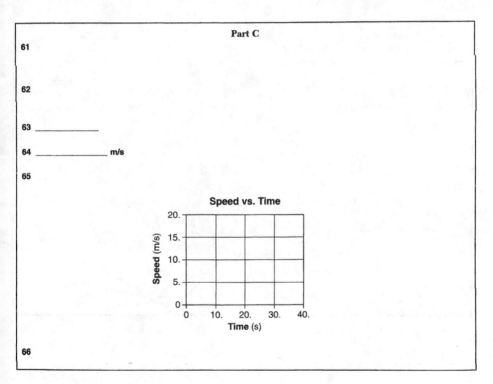

Part C

61

62

63 _____

64 _____ m/s

65

Speed vs. Time

67 _____

68

69 _____
_____

70

71

72

[d]

Directions (1–35): For *each* statement or question, write on the separate answer sheet the *number* of the word or expression that, of those given, best completes the statement or answers the question.

1 Which is a vector quantity?

  (1) electric charge
  (2) electric field strength
  (3) electric potential difference
  (4) electric resistance

Note that question 2 has only three choices.

2 A 6.0-newton force and an 8.0-newton force act concurrently on a point. As the angle between these forces increases from 0° to 90°, the magnitude of their resultant

  (1) decreases
  (2) increases
  (3) remains the same

3 A car increases its speed from 9.6 meters per second to 11.2 meters per second in 4.0 seconds. The average acceleration of the car during this 4.0-second interval is

  (1) 0.40 m/s²   (3) 2.8 m/s²
  (2) 2.4 m/s²   (4) 5.2 m/s²

4 What is the speed of a 2.5-kilogram mass after it has fallen freely from rest through a distance of 12 meters?

  (1) 4.8 m/s   (3) 30. m/s
  (2) 15 m/s   (4) 43 m/s

5 A machine launches a tennis ball at an angle of 25° above the horizontal at a speed of 14 meters per second. The ball returns to level ground. Which combination of changes *must* produce an increase in time of flight of a second launch?

  (1) decrease the launch angle and decrease the ball's initial speed
  (2) decrease the launch angle and increase the ball's initial speed
  (3) increase the launch angle and decrease the ball's initial speed
  (4) increase the launch angle and increase the ball's initial speed

6 A ball attached to a string is moved at constant speed in a horizontal circular path. A target is located near the path of the ball as shown in the diagram.

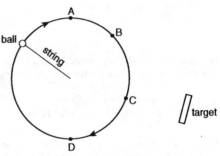

At which point along the ball's path should the string be released, if the ball is to hit the target?

  (1) A   (3) C
  (2) B   (4) D

7 A plane flying horizontally above Earth's surface at 100. meters per second drops a crate. The crate strikes the ground 30.0 seconds later. What is the magnitude of the horizontal component of the crate's velocity just before it strikes the ground? [Neglect friction.]

  (1) 0 m/s   (3) 294 m/s
  (2) 100. m/s   (4) 394 m/s

8 A woman with horizontal velocity v_1 jumps off a dock into a stationary boat. After landing in the boat, the woman and the boat move with velocity v_2. Compared to velocity v_1, velocity v_2 has

  (1) the same magnitude and the same direction
  (2) the same magnitude and opposite direction
  (3) smaller magnitude and the same direction
  (4) larger magnitude and the same direction

9 Which object has the greatest inertia?

(1) a 5.0-kg object moving at a speed of 5.0 m/s
(2) a 10.-kg object moving at a speed of 3.0 m/s
(3) a 15-kg object moving at a speed of 1.0 m/s
(4) a 20.-kg object at rest

10 As an astronaut travels from the surface of Earth to a position that is four times as far away from the center of Earth, the astronaut's

(1) mass decreases
(2) mass remains the same
(3) weight increases
(4) weight remains the same

11 A 0.15-kilogram baseball moving at 20. meters per second is stopped by a catcher in 0.010 second. The average force stopping the ball is

(1) 3.0×10^{-2} N   (3) 3.0×10^{1} N
(2) 3.0×10^{0} N   (4) 3.0×10^{2} N

12 A spring with a spring constant of 80. newtons per meter is displaced 0.30 meter from its equilibrium position. The potential energy stored in the spring is

(1) 3.6 J   (3) 12 J
(2) 7.2 J   (4) 24 J

13 The work done in accelerating an object along a frictionless horizontal surface is equal to the change in the object's

(1) momentum   (3) potential energy
(2) velocity   (4) kinetic energy

14 As a block slides across a table, its speed decreases while its temperature increases. Which two changes occur in the block's energy as it slides?

(1) a decrease in kinetic energy and an increase in internal energy
(2) an increase in kinetic energy and a decrease in internal energy
(3) a decrease in both kinetic energy and internal energy
(4) an increase in both kinetic energy and internal energy

15 If 60. joules of work is required to move 5.0 coulombs of charge between two points in an electric field, what is the potential difference between these points?

(1) 5.0 V   (3) 60. V
(2) 12 V   (4) 300 V

16 Which statement best describes a proton that is being accelerated?

(1) It produces electromagnetic radiation.
(2) The magnitude of its charge increases.
(3) It absorbs a neutron to become an electron.
(4) It is attracted to other protons.

17 The diagram below represents a simple circuit consisting of a variable resistor, a battery, an ammeter, and a voltmeter.

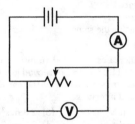

What is the effect of increasing the resistance of the variable resistor from 1000 Ω to 10000 Ω? [Assume constant temperature.]

(1) The ammeter reading decreases.
(2) The ammeter reading increases.
(3) The voltmeter reading decreases.
(4) The voltmeter reading increases.

18 If the distance separating an electron and a proton is halved, the magnitude of the electrostatic force between these charged particles will be

(1) unchanged   (3) quartered
(2) doubled   (4) quadrupled

19 Two similar metal spheres, A and B, have charges of $+2.0 \times 10^{-6}$ coulomb and $+1.0 \times 10^{-6}$ coulomb, respectively, as shown in the diagram below.

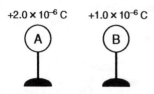

+2.0 × 10⁻⁶ C   +1.0 × 10⁻⁶ C

A   B

The magnitude of the electrostatic force on A due to B is 2.4 newtons. What is the magnitude of the electrostatic force on B due to A?

(1) 1.2 N   (3) 4.8 N
(2) 2.4 N   (4) 9.6 N

20 In the diagram below, P is a point near a negatively charged sphere.

⊖ •P

Which vector best represents the direction of the electric field at point P?

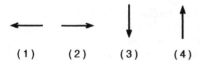

(1)   (2)   (3)   (4)

Note that question 21 has only three choices.

21 If the amplitude of a wave traveling in a rope is doubled, the speed of the wave in the rope will

(1) decrease
(2) increase
(3) remain the same

22 Two waves having the same amplitude and frequency are traveling in the same medium. Maximum destructive interference will occur when the phase difference between the waves is

(1) 0°   (3) 180°
(2) 90°   (4) 270°

23 What is the speed of a radio wave in a vacuum?

(1) 0 m/s   (3) 1.13×10^3 m/s
(2) 3.31×10^2 m/s   (4) 3.00×10^8 m/s

24 A ringing bell is located in a chamber. When the air is removed from the chamber, why can the bell be seen vibrating but *not* be heard?

(1) Light waves can travel through a vacuum, but sound waves cannot.
(2) Sound waves have greater amplitude than light waves.
(3) Light waves travel slower than sound waves.
(4) Sound waves have higher frequency than light waves.

25 As a transverse wave travels through a medium, the individual particles of the medium move

(1) perpendicular to the direction of wave travel
(2) parallel to the direction of wave travel
(3) in circles
(4) in ellipses

26 A straight glass rod appears to bend when placed in a beaker of water, as shown in the diagram below.

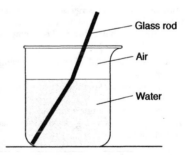

Glass rod

Air

Water

What is the best explanation for this phenomenon?

(1) The water is warmer than the air.
(2) Light travels faster in water than in air.
(3) Light is reflected at the air-water interface.
(4) Light is refracted as it crosses the air-water interface.

27 What happens to the speed and frequency of a light ray when it passes from air into water?

(1) The speed decreases and the frequency increases.
(2) The speed decreases and the frequency remains the same.
(3) The speed increases and the frequency increases.
(4) The speed increases and the frequency remains the same.

28 Parallel wave fronts incident on an opening in a barrier are diffracted. For which combination of wavelength and size of opening will diffraction effects be greatest?

(1) short wavelength and narrow opening
(2) short wavelength and wide opening
(3) long wavelength and narrow opening
(4) long wavelength and wide opening

29 Which wave phenomenon occurs when vibrations in one object cause vibrations in a second object?

(1) reflection   (3) intensity
(2) resonance   (4) tuning

30 A photon having an energy of 9.40 electronvolts strikes a hydrogen atom in the ground state. Why is the photon *not* absorbed by the hydrogen atom?

(1) The atom's orbital electron is moving too fast.
(2) The photon striking the atom is moving too fast.
(3) The photon's energy is too small.
(4) The photon is being repelled by electro-static force.

31 Metal sphere A has a charge of –2 units and an identical metal sphere, B, has a charge of –4 units. If the spheres are brought into contact with each other and then separated, the charge on sphere B will be

(1) 0 units   (3) –3 units
(2) –2 units   (4) +4 units

32 A photon of light traveling through space with a wavelength of 6.0×10^{-7} meter has an energy of

(1) 4.0×10^{-40} J   (3) 5.4×10^{10} J
(2) 3.3×10^{-19} J   (4) 5.0×10^{14} J

33 What is the net electrical charge on a magnesium ion that is formed when a neutral magnesium atom loses two electrons?

(1) -3.2×10^{-19} C   (3) $+1.6 \times 10^{-19}$ C
(2) -1.6×10^{-19} C   (4) $+3.2 \times 10^{-19}$ C

34 The charge of an antistrange quark is approximately

(1) $+5.33 \times 10^{-20}$ C   (3) $+5.33 \times 10^{20}$ C
(2) -5.33×10^{-20} C   (4) -5.33×10^{20} C

35 What fundamental force holds quarks together to form particles such as protons and neutrons?

(1) electromagnetic force
(2) gravitational force
(3) strong force
(4) weak force

Part B–1

Answer all questions in this part.

Directions (36–51): For *each* statement or question, write on the separate answer sheet the *number* of the word or expression that, of those given, best completes the statement or answers the question.

36 A cart travels with a constant nonzero acceleration along a straight line. Which graph best represents the relationship between the distance the cart travels and time of travel?

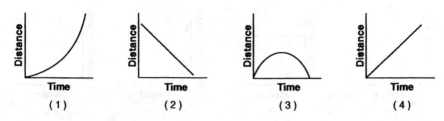

37 Which graph best represents the relationship between the acceleration of an object falling freely near the surface of Earth and the time that it falls?

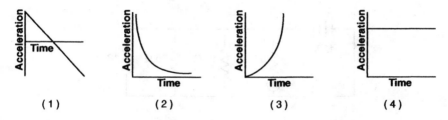

38 The diagram below shows a 4.0-kilogram object accelerating at 10. meters per second^2 on a rough horizontal surface.

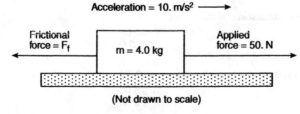

(Not drawn to scale)

What is the magnitude of the frictional force F_f acting on the object?

(1) 5.0 N   (3) 20. N
(2) 10. N   (4) 40. N

39 What is the magnitude of the force needed to keep a 60.-newton rubber block moving across level, dry asphalt in a straight line at a constant speed of 2.0 meters per second?

(1) 40. N   (3) 60. N
(2) 51 N   (4) 120 N

40 Which graph best represents the relationship between the gravitational potential energy of an object near the surface of Earth and its height above Earth's surface?

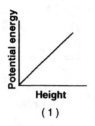   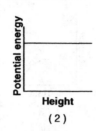   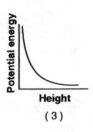   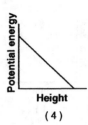

(1)   (2)   (3)   (4)

Base your answers to questions 41 through 43 on the diagram below, which represents an electric circuit consisting of four resistors and a 12-volt battery.

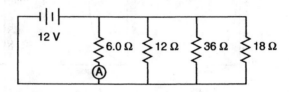

41 What is the current measured by ammeter A?

(1) 0.50 A   (3) 72 A
(2) 2.0 A   (4) 4.0 A

42 What is the equivalent resistance of this circuit?

(1) 72 Ω   (3) 3.0 Ω
(2) 18 Ω   (4) 0.33 Ω

43 How much power is dissipated in the 36-ohm resistor?

(1) 110 W   (3) 3.0 W
(2) 48 W   (4) 4.0 W

44 A 1.00-kilogram ball is dropped from the top of a building. Just before striking the ground, the ball's speed is 12.0 meters per second. What was the ball's gravitational potential energy, relative to the ground, at the instant it was dropped? [Neglect friction.]

(1) 6.00 J   (3) 72.0 J
(2) 24.0 J   (4) 144 J

45 As shown in the diagram below, a child applies a constant 20.-newton force along the handle of a wagon which makes a 25° angle with the horizontal.

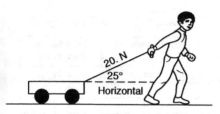

How much work does the child do in moving the wagon a horizontal distance of 4.0 meters?

(1) 5.0 J   (3) 73 J
(2) 34 J   (4) 80. J

46 A 110-kilogram bodybuilder and his 55-kilogram friend run up identical flights of stairs. The bodybuilder reaches the top in 4.0 seconds while his friend takes 2.0 seconds. Compared to the power developed by the bodybuilder while running up the stairs, the power developed by his friend is

(1) the same
(2) twice as much
(3) half as much
(4) four times as much

47 Which quantity and unit are correctly paired?

(1) resistivity and $\dfrac{\Omega}{m}$

(2) potential difference and eV

(3) current and C•s

(4) electric field strength and $\dfrac{N}{C}$

48 Which wavelength is in the infrared range of the electromagnetic spectrum?

(1) 100 nm   (3) 100 m
(2) 100 mm   (4) 100 μm

49 The diagram below represents a wave.

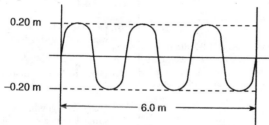

What is the speed of the wave if its frequency is 8.0 hertz?

(1) 48 m/s   (3) 3.2 m/s
(2) 16 m/s   (4) 1.6 m/s

50 What is the wavelength of a light ray with frequency 5.09×10^{14} hertz as it travels through Lucite?

(1) 3.93×10^{-7} m   (3) 3.39×10^{14} m
(2) 5.89×10^{-7} m   (4) 7.64×10^{14} m

51 What is the total number of quarks in a helium nucleus consisting of 2 protons and 2 neutrons?

(1) 16   (3) 8
(2) 12   (4) 4

Part B–2

Answer all questions in this part.

Directions (52–62): Record your answers in the spaces provided in your answer booklet.

Base your answers to questions 52 through 54 on the information and diagram below.

Force *A* with a magnitude of 5.6 newtons and force *B* with a magnitude of 9.4 newtons act concurrently on point *P*.

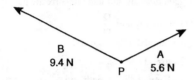

52 Determine the scale used in the diagram. [1]

53 On the diagram *in your answer booklet*, use a ruler and protractor to construct a vector representing the resultant of forces *A* and *B*. [1]

54 Determine the magnitude of the resultant force. [1]

_____

55 Calculate the resistance of a 1.00-kilometer length of nichrome wire with a cross-sectional area of 3.50×10^{-6} meter^2 at 20°C. [Show all work, including the equation and substitution with units.] [2]

56 A generator produces a 115-volt potential difference and a maximum of 20.0 amperes of current. Calculate the total electrical energy the generator produces operating at maximum capacity for 60. seconds. [Show all work, including the equation and substitution with units.] [2]

Base your answers to questions 57 through 59 on the information and data table below.

A student performed an experiment in which the weight attached to a suspended spring was varied and the resulting total length of the spring measured. The data for the experiment are in the table below.

Attached Weight vs. Total Spring Length

Attached Weight (N)	Total Spring Length (m)
0.98	0.37
1.96	0.42
2.94	0.51
3.92	0.59
4.91	0.64

Directions (57–58): Using the information in the data table, construct a graph on the grid in your answer booklet, following the directions below.

57 Plot the data points for the attached weight versus total spring length. [1]

58 Draw the line or curve of best fit. [1]

59 Using your graph, determine the length of the spring before any weight was attached. [1]

_____

High Marks: Regents Physics Made Easy

60 The graph below represents the relationship between wavelength and frequency of waves created by two students shaking the ends of a loose spring.

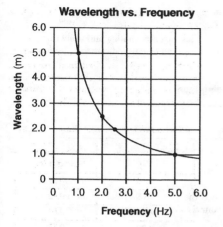

Wavelength vs. Frequency

Calculate the speed of the waves generated in the spring. [Show all work, including the equation and substitution with units.] [2]

Base your answers to questions 61 and 62 on the statement below.

The spectrum of visible light emitted during transitions in excited hydrogen atoms is composed of blue, green, red, and violet lines.

61 What characteristic of light determines the amount of energy carried by a photon of that light?

(1) amplitude   (3) phase
(2) frequency   (4) velocity

62 Which color of light in the visible hydrogen spectrum has photons of the shortest wavelength?

(1) blue   (3) red
(2) green   (4) violet

Part C

Answer all questions in this part.

Directions (63–77): Record your answers in the spaces provided in your answer booklet.

Base your answers to questions 63 through 66 on the information and diagram below.

A spark timer is used to record the position of a lab cart accelerating uniformly from rest. Each 0.10 second, the timer marks a dot on a recording tape to indicate the position of the cart at that instant, as shown.

Recording Tape   **End**

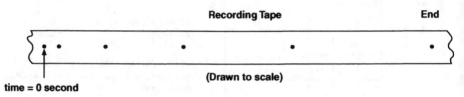

(Drawn to scale)

time = 0 second

63 Using a metric ruler, measure the distance the cart traveled during the interval $t = 0$ second to $t = 0.30$ second. Record your answer *in your answer booklet*, to the *nearest tenth of a centimeter.* [1]

64 Calculate the magnitude of the acceleration of the cart during the time interval $t = 0$ second to $t = 0.30$ second. [Show all work, including the equation and substitution with units.] [2]

65 Calculate the average speed of the cart during the time interval $t = 0$ second to $t = 0.30$ second. [Show all work, including the equation and substitution with units.] [2]

66 On the diagram *in your answer booklet*, mark *at least four* dots to indicate the position of a cart traveling at a constant velocity. [1]

Base your answers to questions 67 through 69 on the information and diagram below.

A 50.-ohm resistor, an unknown resistor R, a 120-volt source, and an ammeter are connected in a complete circuit. The ammeter reads 0.50 ampere.

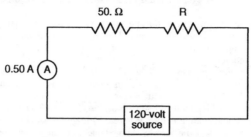

67 Calculate the equivalent resistance of the circuit. [Show all work, including the equation and substitution with units.] [2]

68 Determine the resistance of resistor R. [1]

69 Calculate the power dissipated by the 50.-ohm resistor. [Show all work, including the equation and substitution with units.] [2]

Base your answers to questions 70 through 73 on the information and diagram below.

A ray of light ($f = 5.09 \times 10^{14}$ Hz) is incident on the boundary between air and an unknown material X at an angle of incidence of 55°, as shown. The absolute index of refraction of material X is 1.66.

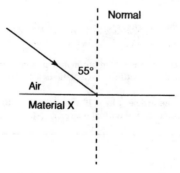

70 Identify a substance of which material X may be composed. [1]

71 Determine the speed of this ray of light in material X. [1]

72 Calculate the angle of refraction of the ray of light in material X. [Show all work, including the equation and substitution with units.] [2]

73 On the diagram in your answer booklet, use a straightedge and protractor to draw the refracted ray of light in material X. [1]

Base your answers to questions 74 through 77 on the passage below and on your knowledge of physics.

More Sci- Than Fi, Physicists Create Antimatter

Physicists working in Europe announced yesterday that they had passed through nature's looking glass and had created atoms made of antimatter, or antiatoms, opening up the possibility of experiments in a realm once reserved for science fiction writers. Such experiments, theorists say, could test some of the basic tenets of modern physics and light the way to a deeper understanding of nature.

By corralling [holding together in groups] clouds of antimatter particles in a cylindrical chamber laced with detectors and electric and magnetic fields, the physicists assembled antihydrogen atoms, the looking glass equivalent of hydrogen, the most simple atom in nature. Whereas hydrogen consists of a positively charged proton circled by a negatively charged electron, in antihydrogen the proton's counterpart, a positively charged antiproton, is circled by an antielectron, otherwise known as a positron.

According to the standard theories of physics, the antimatter universe should look identical to our own. Antihydrogen and hydrogen atoms should have the same properties, emitting the exact same frequencies of light, for example. . . .

Antimatter has been part of physics since 1927 when its existence was predicted by the British physicist Paul Dirac. The antielectron, or positron, was discovered in 1932. According to the theory, matter can only be created in particle-antiparticle pairs. It is still a mystery, cosmologists say, why the universe seems to be overwhelmingly composed of normal matter.

Dennis Overbye, "More Sci- Than Fi, Physicists Create Antimatter," *New York Times*, Sept. 19, 2002

74 The author of the passage concerning antimatter incorrectly reported the findings of the experiment on antimatter. Which particle mentioned in the article has the charge incorrectly identified? [1]

75 How should the emission spectrum of antihydrogen compare to the emission spectrum of hydrogen? [1]

76 Identify *one* characteristic that antimatter particles must possess if clouds of them can be corralled by electric and magnetic fields. [1]

77 According to the article, why is it a mystery that "the universe seems to be overwhelmingly composed of normal matter"? [1]

The University of the State of New York

REGENTS HIGH SCHOOL EXAMINATION

PHYSICAL SETTING
PHYSICS

Thursday, January 25, 2007 — 1:15 to 4:15 p.m., only

ANSWER SHEET

Student .... Sex: ☐ Male ☐ Female Grade ....

Teacher .... School ....

Record your answers to Part A and Part B–1 on this answer sheet.

Part A			Part B–1	
1	13	25	36	44 ....
2	14	26	37	45 ....
3	15	27	38	46 ....
4	16	28	39	47 ....
5	17	29	40	48 ....
6	18	30	41	49 ....
7	19	31	42	50 ....
8	20	32	43	51 ....
9	21	33		Part B–1 Score
10	22	34		
11	23	35		
12	24	Part A Score		

Write your answers to Part B–2 and Part C in your answer booklet.

The declaration below should be signed when you have completed the examination.

I do hereby affirm, at the close of this examination, that I had no unlawful knowledge of the questions or answers prior to the examination and that I have neither given nor received assistance in answering any of the questions during the examination.

_____

Signature

The University of the State of New York

REGENTS HIGH SCHOOL EXAMINATION

PHYSICAL SETTING
PHYSICS

Thursday, January 25, 2007 — 1:15 to 4:15 p.m., only

ANSWER BOOKLET

Student . . . . Sex: ☐ Male ☐ Female

Teacher. . . . .

School . . . . Grade . . . .

Answer all questions in Part B–2 and Part C. Record your answers in this booklet.

Part	Maximum Score	Student's Score
A	35	
B–1	16	
B–2	14	
C	20	

Total Written Test Score
(Maximum Raw Score: 85) ☐

Final Score
(From Conversion Chart) ☐

Raters' Initials:

Rater 1 . . . . Rater 2 . . . .

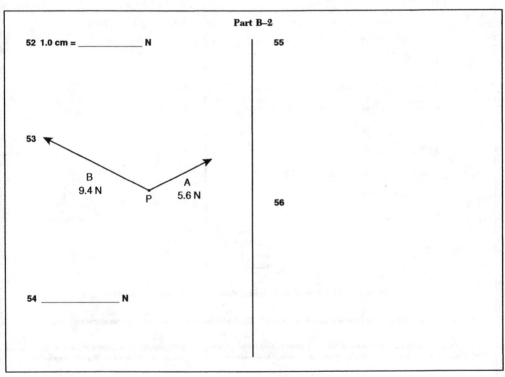

Part B–2

52 1.0 cm = _____ N

53

B
9.4 N   A
P   5.6 N

54 _____ N

55

56

[a]

57–58

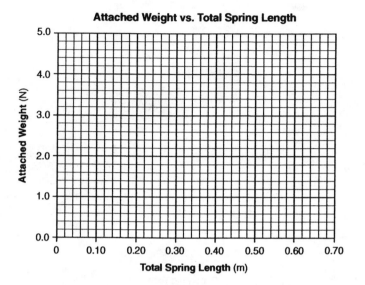

Attached Weight vs. Total Spring Length

(y-axis) Attached Weight (N): 0.0, 1.0, 2.0, 3.0, 4.0, 5.0

(x-axis) Total Spring Length (m): 0, 0.10, 0.20, 0.30, 0.40, 0.50, 0.60, 0.70

59 _____ m

60

61 _____

62 _____

[b]

Part C

63 _____ cm

64

65

66

Recording Tape

67

68 _____ Ω

69

[c]

70 _____

71 _____ m/s

72

73

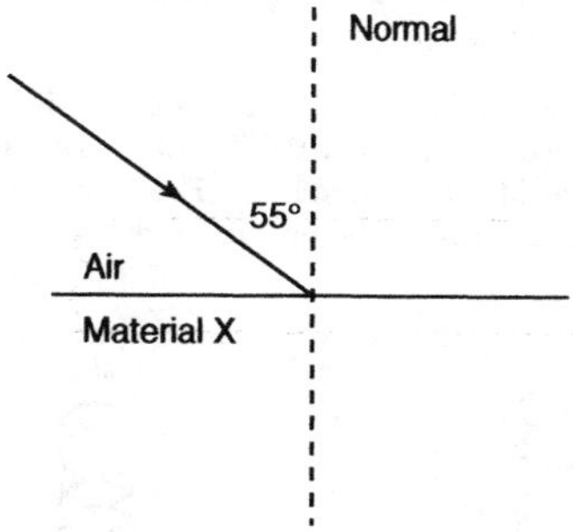

Normal

55°

Air

Material X

74 _____

75 _____

76 _____

77 _____

_____

[d]

Directions (1–35): For *each* statement or question, write on the separate answer sheet the *number* of the word or expression that, of those given, best completes the statement or answers the question.

1 Which is *not* a vector quantity?

(1) electric charge
(2) magnetic field strength
(3) velocity
(4) displacement

2 An astronaut standing on a platform on the Moon drops a hammer. If the hammer falls 6.0 meters vertically in 2.7 seconds, what is its acceleration?

(1) 1.6 m/s²   (3) 4.4 m/s²
(2) 2.2 m/s²   (4) 9.8 m/s²

3 A 2.00-kilogram object weighs 19.6 newtons on Earth. If the acceleration due to gravity on Mars is 3.71 meters per second², what is the object's mass on Mars?

(1) 2.64 kg   (3) 19.6 N
(2) 2.00 kg   (4) 7.42 N

4 A car moves with a constant speed in a clockwise direction around a circular path of radius *r*, as represented in the diagram below.

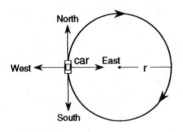

When the car is in the position shown, its acceleration is directed toward the

(1) north   (3) south
(2) west   (4) east

Note that question 5 has only three choices.

5 As the angle between two concurrent forces decreases, the magnitude of the force required to produce equilibrium

(1) decreases
(2) increases
(3) remains the same

6 A child walks 5.0 meters north, then 4.0 meters east, and finally 2.0 meters south. What is the magnitude of the resultant displacement of the child after the entire walk?

(1) 1.0 m   (3) 3.0 m
(2) 5.0 m   (4) 11.0 m

7 The diagram below represents a spring hanging vertically that stretches 0.075 meter when a 5.0-newton block is attached. The spring-block system is at rest in the position shown.

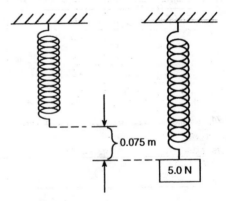

The value of the spring constant is

(1) 38 N/m   (3) 130 N/m
(2) 67 N/m   (4) 650 N/m

8 A 0.50-kilogram object moves in a horizontal circular path with a radius of 0.25 meter at a constant speed of 4.0 meters per second. What is the magnitude of the object's acceleration?

(1) 8.0 m/s²   (3) 32 m/s²
(2) 16 m/s²   (4) 64 m/s²

9 Which situation will produce the greatest change of momentum for a 1.0-kilogram cart?

(1) accelerating it from rest to 3.0 m/s
(2) accelerating it from 2.0 m/s to 4.0 m/s
(3) applying a net force of 5.0 N for 2.0 s
(4) applying a net force of 10.0 N for 0.5 s

10 Earth's mass is approximately 81 times the mass of the Moon. If Earth exerts a gravitational force of magnitude F on the Moon, the magnitude of the gravitational force of the Moon on Earth is

(1) F (3) $9F$
(2) $\dfrac{F}{81}$ (4) $81F$

11 The table below lists the mass and speed of each of four objects.

Data Table

Objects	Mass (kg)	Speed (m/s)
A	1.0	4.0
B	2.0	2.0
C	0.5	4.0
D	4.0	1.0

Which two objects have the same kinetic energy?

(1) A and D (3) A and C
(2) B and D (4) B and C

12 A horizontal force of 5.0 newtons acts on a 3.0-kilogram mass over a distance of 6.0 meters along a horizontal, frictionless surface. What is the change in kinetic energy of the mass during its movement over the 6.0-meter distance?

(1) 6.0 J   (3) 30. J
(2) 15 J   (4) 90. J

13 Which quantity is a measure of the rate at which work is done?

(1) energy   (3) momentum
(2) power   (4) velocity

14 The diagram shows two bowling balls, A and B, each having a mass of 7.00 kilograms, placed 2.00 meters apart.

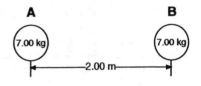

What is the magnitude of the gravitational force exerted by ball A on ball B?

(1) 8.17×10^{-9} N   (3) 8.17×10^{-10} N
(2) 1.63×10^{-9} N   (4) 1.17×10^{-10} N

15 If 1.0 joule of work is required to move 1.0 coulomb of charge between two points in an electric field, the potential difference between the two points is

(1) 1.0×10^{0} V   (3) 6.3×10^{18} V
(2) 9.0×10^{9} V   (4) 1.6×10^{-19} V

16 The current through a 10.-ohm resistor is 1.2 amperes. What is the potential difference across the resistor?

(1) 8.3 V   (3) 14 V
(2) 12 V   (4) 120 V

17 A copper wire of length L and cross-sectional area A has resistance R. A second copper wire at the same temperature has a length of $2L$ and a cross-sectional area of $\frac{1}{2}A$. What is the resistance of the second copper wire?

(1) R (3) $\frac{1}{2}R$

(2) $2R$ (4) $4R$

18 A 6.0-ohm lamp requires 0.25 ampere of current to operate. In which circuit below would the lamp operate correctly when switch S is closed?

(1)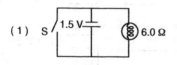

(2)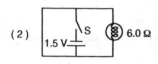

(3)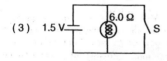

(4)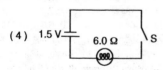

19 What is the total current in a circuit consisting of six operating 100-watt lamps connected in parallel to a 120-volt source?

(1) 5 A   (3) 600 A

(2) 20 A   (4) 12 000 A

20 A 4.50-volt personal stereo uses 1950 joules of electrical energy in one hour. What is the electrical resistance of the personal stereo?

(1) 433 Ω   (3) 37.4 Ω

(2) 96.3 Ω   (4) 0.623 Ω

Note that question 21 has only three choices.

21 As yellow light ($f = 5.09 \times 10^{14}$ Hz) travels from zircon into diamond, the speed of the light

(1) decreases

(2) increases

(3) remains the same

22 The diagram below represents a transverse wave.

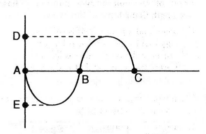

The distance between which two points identifies the amplitude of the wave?

(1) A and B (3) A and E

(2) A and C (4) D and E

23 The diagram below represents a periodic wave.

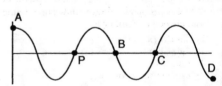

Which point on the wave is in phase with point P?

(1) A (3) C

(2) B (4) D

24 What is the period of a 60.-hertz electromagnetic wave traveling at 3.0×10^8 meters per second?

(1) 1.7×10^{-2} s   (3) 6.0×10^1 s

(2) 2.0×10^{-7} s   (4) 5.0×10^6 s

25 At an outdoor physics demonstration, a delay of 0.50 second was observed between the time sound waves left a loudspeaker and the time these sound waves reached a student through the air. If the air is at STP, how far was the student from the speaker?

(1) 1.5×10^{-3} m   (3) 6.6×10^2 m

(2) 1.7×10^2 m   (4) 1.5×10^8 m

26 A microwave and an x ray are traveling in a vacuum. Compared to the wavelength and period of the microwave, the x ray has a wavelength that is

(1) longer and a period that is shorter

(2) longer and a period that is longer

(3) shorter and a period that is longer

(4) shorter and a period that is shorter

27 Which type of wave requires a material medium through which to travel?

(1) electromagnetic   (3) sound

(2) infrared   (4) radio

28 A car traveling at 70 kilometers per hour accelerates to pass a truck. When the car reaches a speed of 90 kilometers per hour the driver hears the glove compartment door start to vibrate. By the time the speed of the car is 100 kilometers per hour, the glove compartment door has stopped vibrating. This vibrating phenomenon is an example of

(1) the Doppler effect

(2) diffraction

(3) resonance

(4) destructive interference

29 A beam of monochromatic light approaches a barrier having four openings, A, B, C, and D, of different sizes as shown below.

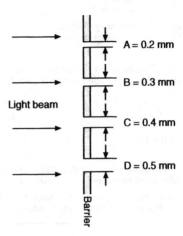

Which opening will cause the greatest diffraction?

(1) A   (3) C

(2) B   (4) D

30 Two waves having the same frequency and amplitude are traveling in the same medium. Maximum constructive interference occurs at points where the phase difference between the two superposed waves is

(1) 0°   (3) 180°

(2) 90°   (4) 270°

31 A student sees a train that is moving away from her and sounding its whistle at a constant frequency. Compared to the sound produced by the whistle, the sound observed by the student is

(1) greater in amplitude

(2) a transverse wave rather than a longitudinal wave

(3) higher in pitch

(4) lower in pitch

32 Which quantity of excess electric charge could be found on an object?

(1) 6.25×10^{-19} C
(2) 4.80×10^{-19} C
(3) 6.25 elementary charges
(4) 1.60 elementary charges

33 The diagram below represents two electrically charged identical-sized metal spheres, A and B.

$+2.0 \times 10^{-7}$ C $+1.0 \times 10^{-7}$ C

If the spheres are brought into contact, which sphere will have a net gain of electrons?

(1) A, only
(2) B, only
(3) both A and B
(4) neither A nor B

34 Light demonstrates the characteristics of

(1) particles, only
(2) waves, only
(3) both particles and waves
(4) neither particles nor waves

35 The energy produced by the complete conversion of 2.0×10^{-5} kilogram of mass into energy is

(1) 1.8 TJ
(2) 6.0 GJ
(3) 1.8 MJ
(4) 6.0 kJ

Part B–1

Answer all questions in this part.

Directions (36–46): For *each* statement or question, write on the separate answer sheet the *number* of the word or expression that, of those given, best completes the statement or answers the question.

36 What is the approximate length of a baseball bat?

(1) 10^{-1} m   (3) 10^{1} m

(2) 10^{0} m   (4) 10^{2} m

37 A force of 1 newton is equivalent to 1

(1) $\dfrac{kg \bullet m}{s^2}$ (3) $\dfrac{kg \bullet m^2}{s^2}$

(2) $\dfrac{kg \bullet m}{s}$ (4) $\dfrac{kg^2 \bullet m^2}{s^2}$

Base your answers to questions 38 and 39 on the information below.

A stream is 30. meters wide and its current flows southward at 1.5 meters per second. A toy boat is launched with a velocity of 2.0 meters per second eastward from the west bank of the stream.

38 What is the magnitude of the boat's resultant velocity as it crosses the stream?

(1) 0.5 m/s   (3) 3.0 m/s

(2) 2.5 m/s   (4) 3.5 m/s

39 How much time is required for the boat to reach the opposite bank of the stream?

(1) 8.6 s   (3) 15 s

(2) 12 s   (4) 60. s

40 An observer recorded the following data for the motion of a car undergoing constant acceleration.

Time (s)	Speed (m/s)
3.0	4.0
5.0	7.0
6.0	8.5

What was the magnitude of the acceleration of the car?

(1) 1.3 m/s^2 (3) 1.5 m/s^2

(2) 2.0 m/s^2 (4) 4.5 m/s^2

41 Which graph best represents the relationship between the velocity of an object thrown straight upward from Earth's surface and the time that elapses while it is in the air? [Neglect friction.]

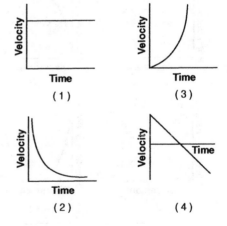

42 In the diagram below, scaled vectors represent the momentum of each of two masses, A and B, sliding toward each other on a frictionless, horizontal surface.

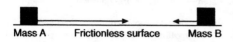

Mass A   Frictionless surface   Mass B

Which scaled vector best represents the momentum of the system after the masses collide?

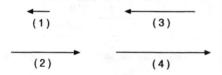

(1)

(3)

(2)

(4)

43 A pendulum is pulled to the side and released from rest. Which graph best represents the relationship between the gravitational potential energy of the pendulum and its displacement from its point of release?

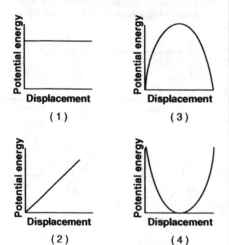

(1)

(3)

(2)

(4)

44 Which graph best represents the relationship between the power required to raise an elevator and the speed at which the elevator rises?

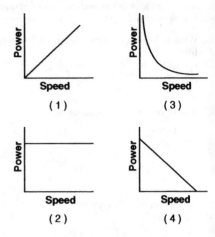

(1)

(3)

(2)

(4)

45 Baryons may have charges of

(1) $+1e$ and $+\frac{4}{3}e$ (3) $-1e$ and $+1e$

(2) $+2e$ and $+3e$ (4) $-2e$ and $-\frac{2}{3}e$

46 The slope of a graph of photon energy versus photon frequency represents

(1) Planck's constant
(2) the mass of a photon
(3) the speed of light
(4) the speed of light squared

Part B–2

Answer all questions in this part.

Directions (47–60): Record your answers in the spaces provided in your answer booklet.

Base your answers to questions 47 and 48 on the information below.

The magnitude of the electric field strength between two oppositely charged parallel metal plates is 2.0×10^3 newtons per coulomb. Point P is located midway between the plates.

47 On the diagram *in your answer booklet*, sketch *at least five* electric field lines to represent the field between the two oppositely charged plates. [Draw an arrowhead on each field line to show the proper direction.] [1]

48 An electron is located at point P between the plates. Calculate the magnitude of the force exerted on the electron by the electric field. [Show all work, including the equation and substitution with units.] [2]

Base your answers to questions 49 through 51 on the information below.

A student generates a series of transverse waves of varying frequency by shaking one end of a loose spring. All the waves move along the spring at a speed of 6.0 meters per second.

49 Complete the data table *in your answer booklet*, by determining the wavelengths for the frequencies given. [1]

50 On the grid *in your answer booklet*, plot the data points for wavelength versus frequency. [1]

51 Draw the best-fit line or curve. [1]

Base your answers to questions 52 and 53 on the information and diagram below.

A force of 60. newtons is applied to a rope to pull a sled across a horizontal surface at a constant velocity. The rope is at an angle of 30. degrees above the horizontal.

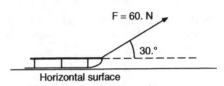

52 Calculate the magnitude of the component of the 60.-newton force that is parallel to the horizontal surface. [Show all work, including the equation and substitution with units.] [2]

53 Determine the magnitude of the frictional force acting on the sled. [1]

54 A book sliding across a horizontal tabletop slows until it comes to rest. Describe what change, if any, occurs in the book's kinetic energy and internal energy as it slows. [2]

Base your answers to questions 55 through 57 on the information and diagram below.

A projectile is launched into the air with an initial speed of v_i at a launch angle of 30.° above the horizontal. The projectile lands on the ground 2.0 seconds later.

55 On the diagram *in your answer booklet*, sketch the ideal path of the projectile. [1]

56 How does the maximum altitude of the projectile change as the launch angle is increased from 30.° to 45° above the horizontal? [Assume the same initial speed, v_i.] [1]

57 How does the total horizontal distance traveled by the projectile change as the launch angle is increased from 30.° to 45° above the horizontal? [Assume the same initial speed, v_i.] [1]

Base your answers to questions 58 through 60 on the information and diagram below.

A 3.0-ohm resistor, an unknown resistor, R, and two ammeters, A_1 and A_2, are connected as shown with a 12-volt source. Ammeter A_2 reads a current of 5.0 amperes.

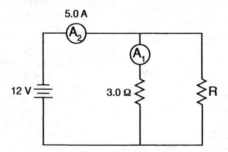

58 Determine the equivalent resistance of the circuit. [1]

59 Calculate the current measured by ammeter A_1. [Show all work, including the equation and substitution with units.] [2]

60 Calculate the resistance of the unknown resistor, R. [Show all work, including the equation and substitution with units.] [2]

Part C

Answer all questions in this part.

Directions (61–74): Record your answers in the spaces provided in your answer booklet.

Base your answers to question 61 through 65 on the information and diagram below.

A horizontal force of 8.0 newtons is used to pull a 20.-newton wooden box moving toward the right along a horizontal, wood surface, as shown.

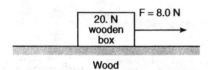

Wood

61 Starting at point *P* on the diagram *in your answer booklet*, use a metric ruler and a scale of 1.0 cm = 4.0 N to draw a vector representing the normal force acting on the box. Label the vector F_N. [1]

62 Calculate the magnitude of the frictional force acting on the box. [Show all work, including the equation and substitution with units.] [2]

63 Determine the magnitude of the net force acting on the box. [1]

64 Determine the mass of the box. [1]

65 Calculate the magnitude of the acceleration of the box. [Show all work, including the equation and substitution with units.] [2]

Base your answers to questions 66 and 67 on the information and diagram below.

A pop-up toy has a mass of 0.020 kilogram and a spring constant of 150 newtons per meter. A force is applied to the toy to compress the spring 0.050 meter.

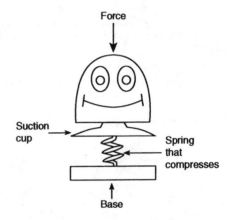

66 Calculate the potential energy stored in the compressed spring. [Show all work, including the equation and substitution with units.] [2]

67 The toy is activated and all the compressed spring's potential energy is converted to gravitational potential energy. Calculate the maximum vertical height to which the toy is propelled. [Show all work, including the equation and substitution with units.] [2]

Base your answers to questions 68 through 71 on the diagram below, which shows a light ray (f = 5.09 × 10^{14} Hz) in air, incident on a boundary with fused quartz. At the boundary, part of the light is refracted and part of the light is reflected.

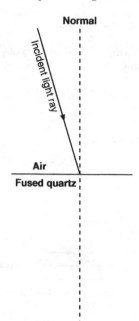

Normal

Incident light ray

Air

Fused quartz

68 Using a protractor, measure the angle of incidence of the light ray at the air-fused quartz boundary. [1]

69 Calculate the angle of refraction of the incident light ray. [Show all work, including the equation and substitution with units.] [2]

70 Using a protractor and straightedge, construct the refracted light ray in the fused quartz on the diagram *in your answer booklet*. [1]

71 Using a protractor and straightedge, construct the reflected light ray on the diagram *in your answer booklet*. [1]

Base your answers to questions 72 through 74 on the information below.

A photon with a frequency of 5.02 × 10^{14} hertz is absorbed by an excited hydrogen atom. This causes the electron to be ejected from the atom, forming an ion.

72 Calculate the energy of this photon in joules. [Show all work, including the equation and substitution with units.] [2]

73 Determine the energy of this photon in electronvolts. [1]

74 What is the number of the *lowest* energy level (closest to the ground state) of a hydrogen atom that contains an electron that would be ejected by the absorption of this photon? [1]

The University of the State of New York

REGENTS HIGH SCHOOL EXAMINATION

PHYSICAL SETTING
PHYSICS

Thursday, June 21, 2007 — 9:15 a.m. to 12:15 p.m., only

ANSWER SHEET

Student .... Sex: ☐ Male ☐ Female Grade ....

Teacher .... School ....

Record your answers to Part A and Part B–1 on this answer sheet.

Part A			Part B–1	
1	13	25	36	42 ....
2	14	26	37	43 ....
3	15	27	38	44 ....
4	16	28	39	45 ....
5	17	29	40	46 ....
6	18	30	41	

Part B–1 Score

Part A		
7	19	31 ....
8	20	32 ....
9	21	33 ....
10	22	34 ....
11	23	35 ....
12	24	

Part A Score

Write your answers to Part B–2 and Part C in your answer booklet.

The declaration below should be signed when you have completed the examination.

I do hereby affirm, at the close of this examination, that I had no unlawful knowledge of the questions or answers prior to the examination and that I have neither given nor received assistance in answering any of the questions during the examination.

_____

Signature

The University of the State of New York

REGENTS HIGH SCHOOL EXAMINATION

PHYSICAL SETTING
PHYSICS

Thursday, June 21, 2007 — 9:15 a.m. to 12:15 p.m., only

ANSWER BOOKLET

Student .... Sex: ☐ Male ☐ Female

Teacher...

School... Grade ....

Answer all questions in Part B–2 and Part C. Record your answers in this booklet.

Part	Maximum Score	Student's Score
A	35	
B–1	11	
B–2	19	
C	20	

Total Written Test Score (Maximum Raw Score: 85)	
Final Score (From Conversion Chart)	

Raters' Initials:

Rater 1 .... Rater 2...........

Part B–2

47

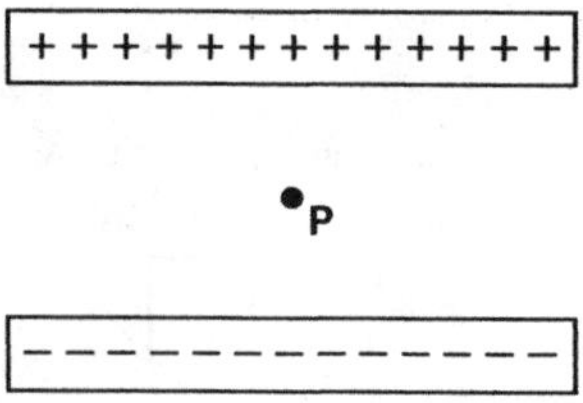

48

49

Data Table	
Frequency (Hz)	Wavelength (m)
1.0	
2.0	
3.0	
6.0	

50–51

Wavelength vs. Frequency

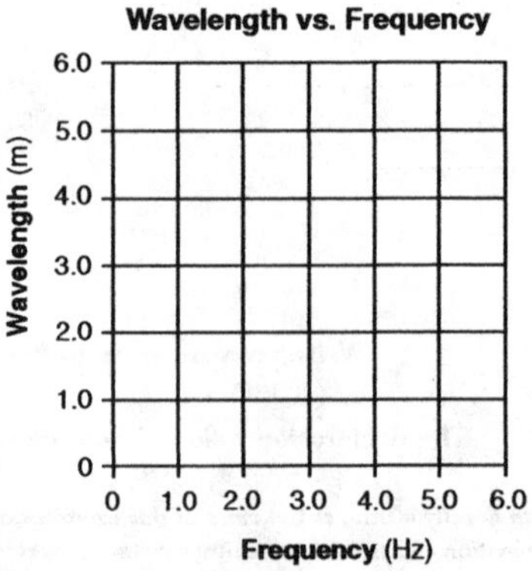

[a]

[OVER

52

53 _____ N

54 _____

_____

55

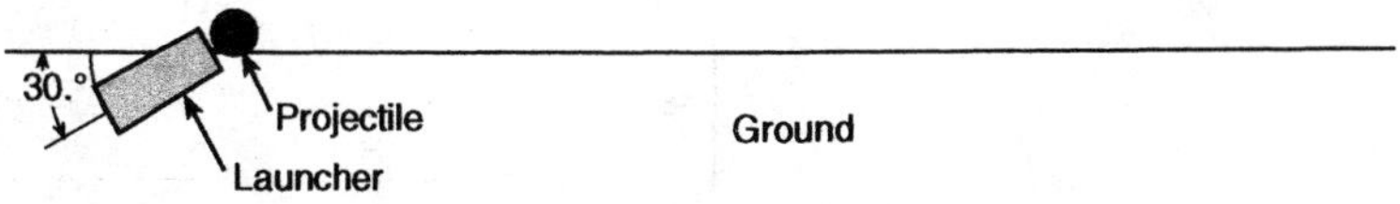

30.° Projectile
Launcher   Ground

56 _____

_____

57 _____

_____

58 _____ Ω

59

[b]

60

Part C

61

64 _____ kg

65

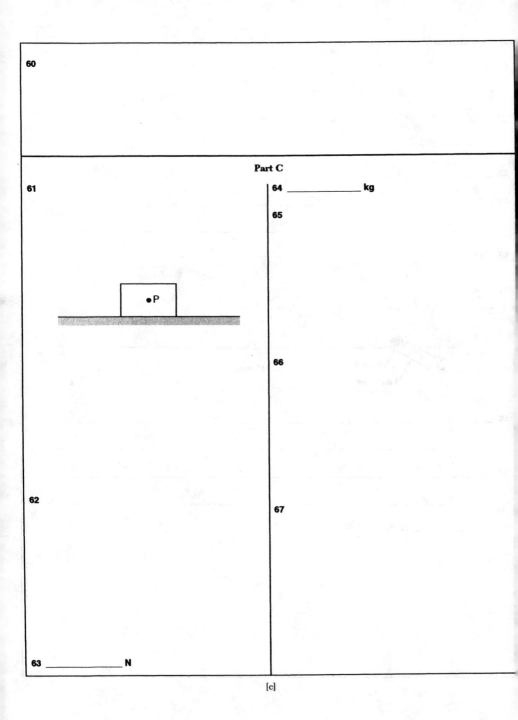

66

62

67

63 _____ N

[c]